Gertrude Himmelfarb

POVERTY AND COMPASSION

Gertrude Himmelfarb is Professor Emeritus of History at the Graduate School of the City University of New York. She is a fellow of the British Academy, the Royal Historical Society, the American Philosophical Society, and the American Academy of Arts and Sciences. Her previous books include *Lord Acton: A Study in Conscience and Politics; Darwin and the Darwinian Revolution; On Liberty and Liberalism: The Case of John Stuart Mill; Victorian Minds; The Idea of Poverty: England in the Early Industrial Age; Marriage and Morals Among the Victorians;* and *The New History and the Old.* Miss Himmelfarb has also edited works by Acton, Malthus, and Mill. In 1991 she gave the Jefferson Lecture in the Humanities, under the auspices of the National Endowment for the Humanities.

ALSO BY GERTRUDE HIMMELFARB

The New History and the Old (1987)

Marriage and Morals Among the Victorians (1986)

The Idea of Poverty: England in the Early Industrial Age (1984)

On Liberty and Liberalism: The Case of John Stuart Mill (1974)

Victorian Minds (1968)

Darwin and the Darwinian Revolution (1959)

Lord Acton: A Study in Conscience and Politics (1952)

EDITOR OF

John Stuart Mill, *On Liberty* (1974)

John Stuart Mill, *Essays on Politics and Culture* (1962)

T. R. Malthus, *On Population* (1960)

Lord Acton, *Essays on Freedom and Power* (1948)

Poverty and Compassion

Gertrude Himmelfarb

POVERTY AND COMPASSION

*The Moral Imagination of
the Late Victorians*

Vintage Books
A Division of Random House, Inc.
New York

FIRST VINTAGE BOOKS EDITION, NOVEMBER 1992

Library of Congress Cataloging-in-Publication Data
Himmelfarb, Gertrude.
Poverty and compassion: the moral imagination of the late
Victorians / Gertrude Himmelfarb— 1st Vintage Books ed.
p. cm.
Originally published: New York: Knopf, 1991.
ISBN 0-679-74173-9 (pbk.)
1. Poor—England—History—19th century.   2. Charities—England—
History—19th century.   3. Great Britain—Economic conditions—
19th century.   I. Title.
HV4086.A3H554   1992
362.5'0942'09034—dc20   92-50066
CIP

Manufactured in the United States of America
10 9 8 7 6 5 4 3 2

For the "rising generation"
(as a Victorian would say)
of Himmelfarbs and Kristols

Some paradox of our natures leads us, when once we have made our fellow men the objects of our enlightened interest, to go on to make them the objects of our pity, then of our wisdom, ultimately of our coercion. It is to prevent this corruption, the most ironic and tragic that man knows, that we stand in need of the moral realism which is the product of the free play of the moral imagination.

LIONEL TRILLING

Contents

Acknowledgments

THIS BOOK WAS originally meant to be part of a short monograph. That monograph has become two substantial volumes. The first was published in 1984 under the title *The Idea of Poverty: England in the Early Industrial Age*.

In the many years devoted to this subject, I have incurred numerous obligations. For this volume I am especially indebted to the staff of the Paleography Room of the University of London library, which made available to me the extensive collection of Booth manuscripts, including the letters of Charles and Mary Booth, the memoirs of their friends and relatives, and documents bearing upon the planning, composition, and reception of *Life and Labour of the People in London*. The Goldsmiths' Library of Economics and the library of the Royal Statistical Society (also in the University of London) contain other relevant sources: letters by Canon Barnett, the founder of Toynbee Hall; the diaries of Charles Loch, the secretary of the Charity Organisation Society; and material on the much debated standard-of-living controversy. The British Library of Political and Economic Science at the London School of Economics has the valuable archives of Sidney and Beatrice Webb (the Passfield Papers); because the published editions of the correspondence and diaries are incomplete, they need to be supplemented by the original manuscripts. Less well known but no less important are its Booth collection (notebooks of interviews, case histories, and early drafts of his work), a local Government Collection containing documents on the Poor Law, and the papers of William Beveridge and other reformers.

Other archival sources utilized in this study include the Barnett papers in the Greater London Record Office, materials on Robert Giffen's statistical surveys in the British Library (the British Museum), the newspaper collection in the Guildhall Library, and the John Burns papers held by the Trades Union Congress. For much of the contemporary published material as well as secondary sources, I am indebted to the New York Public Library, the Library of Congress, the library of the Graduate School of the City University of New York, and the research facilities of the Woodrow Wilson International Center for Scholars.

Mr. H. T. Turner, formerly of the firm of Alfred Booth and Co., took the trouble to seek out and make available to me manuscripts from the early history of the Booth Steamship Company, as well as a privately printed memoir by Booth's niece. Norman MacKenzie, editor of *The Letters of Sidney and Beatrice Webb,* permitted me to examine transcripts of some of those letters before they were published and graciously responded to my inquiries about some questionable sources. Myron Magnet, who is working on a similar subject in another period and another country, offered much appreciated advice and encouragement. And Senator Daniel Patrick Moynihan gave me the benefit of his practical experience in government and his ideas about social problems and policies when he commented on an essay that was a preliminary prospectus for this book at the Woodrow Wilson Center many years ago.

I am also grateful to the Lynde and Harry Bradley Foundation for providing me with so gifted a research assistant as Diana Schaub, who relieved the tedium of borrowing books, photocopying articles, and checking footnotes by bringing to this very modern subject the perspective of philosophy, ancient and modern. Anne Himmelfarb was also helpful in tracking down some elusive references and sharing with me her impressive knowledge of eighteenth-century literature and philosophy. Above all and as always, I am indebted to my husband, Irving Kristol, for reading, rereading, and criticizing the several versions of this book and for good-naturedly enduring my obsessive habits of research and revision.

G. H.

Poverty and Compassion

Compassion
"Properly Understood"

"TO COMPASSIONATE, i.e., to join with in passion. . . . To commiserate, i.e., to join with in misery. . . . This in one order of life is right and good; nothing more harmonious; and to be without this, or not to feel this, is unnatural, horrid, immane."[1] It was the Earl of Shaftesbury in the early eighteenth century who enunciated the principle that was to reappear in other guises throughout the century, as "sympathy," "benevolence," "moral sense," "moral sentiments," "social affections," and "social virtues." In one of the most notable works of this genre, *The Theory of Moral Sentiments,* Adam Smith introduced a crucial distinction: "Sympathy" was the "fellow-feeling" that all human beings had for each other; "compassion" was the "fellow-feeling" for the "sorrow" of others.[2]

For Smith, as for Shaftesbury, compassion was a moral sentiment, not a political principle, a sentiment evoked by "misery" or "sorrow," not by poverty as such. The kind of poverty that was the normal condition for the great majority of people—the "laboring poor," as they were known— was properly a subject of sympathy, a "fellow-feeling" for ordinary people enduring the ordinary hardships of life; that feeling required no intervention in the affairs of others but only a sense of humanity and goodwill. Compassion was a more active sentiment appropriate for a more extreme condition of adversity, a condition that called for some charitable or benevolent action. When the late-eighteenth-century moralist and philanthropist Hannah More characterized her age (not entirely in praise) as an "Age of Benevolence," she had in mind the proliferation of societies for the relief of the afflicted and unfortunate—abandoned infants, abused children, fallen women, maimed seamen, the deaf, dumb, blind, crippled, and insane.[3] In an excess of enthusiasm these benevolent efforts sometimes spilled over to a larger population of the poor; when they did, as in the case of the Speenhamland laws (parish relief for laborers), they were criticized for "pauperizing" the poor by reducing the "independent" poor to a state of dependency.

It took another century for compassion to be "democratized," as it were—extended to the ordinary laboring poor. Josephine Butler gave voice to a common sentiment of late-Victorian reformers when she spoke of "the awful abundance of compassion which makes me fierce."[4] Earlier in the century Evangelicals had displayed the same "fierce" compassion in the denunciation of the slave trade and the campaign to limit child labor, but they lacked that "abundance" of compassion that would have embraced the poor in general. Theirs was a religious zeal derived from a rigorous theological creed. A later generation of reformers, with a much attenuated commitment to religion, redoubled their social zeal as if to compensate for the loss of religious faith. It was then that the passion for religion was transmuted into the compassion for humanity. Humanitarianism became a surrogate religion, a "Religion of Humanity," the Positivists called it. "Social questions," Beatrice Webb wrote in her diary in 1884, "are the vital questions of today: they take the place of religion."[5]

The new "religion" had its critics, some deploring the subversion of the old religion, others, including some secularists, scorning the new. Fitzjames Stephen, himself a resolute skeptic, complained that those who once would have found a home in Puritanism, with its "stern conceptions of duty and of a divine order of the universe," were turning instead to "a kind of vapid philanthropic sentiment which calls itself undenominational; a creed of maudlin benevolence from which all the deeper and sterner elements of religious belief have been carefully purged away."[6] But Stephen, who was vigilant in exposing any suspicion of sentimentality, whether in law, literature, religion, or politics, was less than fair in describing the new philanthropy, which, in fact, made a strenuous effort to avoid being vapid and maudlin.

IN FACT, the moral imagination of the late Victorians, in public affairs as in private, was neither sentimental nor utopian. It was every bit as stern as the old religion—perhaps because it was a displacement of the old. It was stern not only in the personal demands it made upon its missionaries, the commitment in time, labor, and energy it exacted from philanthropists and reformers, but also in the nature of that commitment. Compassion had its reasons of mind as well as of the heart. A sharp, skeptical intelligence was required to ensure the proper exercise of that sentiment.

The God of Humanity turned out to be as strict a taskmaster as the God of Christianity.

Compassion, Kant said, has "no proportion in it"; a suffering child fills our heart with sorrow, while we are indifferent to the news of a terrible battle.[7] The driving mission of most of the late-Victorian reformers, philanthropists, and social critics was precisely to infuse a sense of proportion into the sentiment of compassion, to make compassion proportionate to and compatible with the proper ends of social policy. This is what Charles Booth most notably did in his survey of the London poor, when he insisted upon the importance of "proportion" in calculating the "arithmetic of woe"—the proportion of the "very poor" to the "poor" and the "comfortable," and the ratio of "misery" to "happiness" in the daily lives of the poor.[8] It is what the Charity Organisation Society meant by a "science" of charity that would provide sufficient and appropriate but not "indiscriminate" relief to specific groups of the poor. It is what the Settlement House movement hoped to achieve with its educational and cultural programs designed to help the "earnest" poor achieve the full potentialities of their humanity. It is what inspired the Philosophical Idealism of T. H. Green: the "best self" as the basis of individual morality and the "common good" as the basis of social morality. It is what moved Alfred Marshall to create a "new economics" that would reconcile "chivalry" with the free market and alleviate poverty without undermining the principles and practices of a sound political economy. It is even what most socialists tried to do in expanding the role of the state to cope with particular social problems and to further particular moral ends.

Compassion—"properly understood," as Tocqueville would have said—was the common denominator behind all these enterprises. Over and over again contemporaries testified to the extraordinary accession of social consciousness and social conscience in the last decades of the century, and most conspicuously in the 1880s.[9] "Books on the poor, poverty, social questions, slums and the like subjects, rush fast and furious from the press," the Charity Organisation Society journal reported in 1884. "The titles of some of them sound like sentimental novels."[10] What is remarkable is how few of them, apart from their titles, were in fact sentimental.

In its sentimental mode, compassion is an exercise in moral indignation, in feeling good rather than doing good; this mode recognizes no principle of proportion, because feeling, unlike reason, knows no proportion, no limit, no respect for the constraints of policy or prudence. In its unsentimental mode, compassion seeks above all to *do* good, and this requires a stern sense of proportion, of reason and self-control. The late Victorians, as this book abundantly demonstrates, differed greatly on the best way of doing good. But they were agreed that what was important was to do good to others rather than to feel good themselves. Indeed, they were painfully aware that it was sometimes necessary to feel bad in order to do good—to curb their own compassion and restrain their benevolent impulses in the best interests of those they were trying to serve.

"In democratic ages," Tocqueville wrote, "men rarely sacrifice themselves for one another, but they show a general compassion for all the human race."[11] This perfectly describes the ethos of most late-Victorian reformers and philanthropists. To be truly humane, genuinely compassionate, was not to be selfless; it was only to be true to one's "best self" and to the "common good" that included one's own good. This was not a heroic goal, not the aspiration of a saint or a martyr. But it was eminently moral and humane.

To be compassionate in this sense was also to be practical, even "scientific." It was to utilize means that were consonant with ends, and to define ends in terms that were realistic rather than utopian. Thus the Charity Organisation Society, while incessantly inveighing against "indiscriminate" charity, was no less committed to "discriminate" charity, a charity organized to dispense relief in such a manner and to such families as would best profit from it. It was in this cause that so many men and women gave so freely (literally, freely) of their time and energy to a "science of charity" that, as the secretary of the COS said, was the true "religion of charity."[12] If the Fabians rejected that science of charity, it was in order to replace it by a "science" of socialism—an empirically scientific socialism, they liked to think, in contrast to the Marxist idea of "scientific socialism." Beatrice Webb expressed the tension between the means and the ends of Fabianism in the form of a dialogue between the "Ego that Denies" and the "Ego that Affirms": the former denied that anything other than scientific method was required for social change; the latter affirmed the need for some more ultimate value, as ultimate as religion itself, to give purpose and power to the cause of reform.[13] She herself had no doubt that the Affirmative Ego had the better of that argument. Others saw no conflict, no tension between means and ends; for them the passion of public service was perfectly consistent with the dispassionate performance of that service. Compassion, properly understood, was at the same time passionate and dispassionate.

* * *

BEATRICE WEBB called her Affirmative Ego religion; others called it morality. If the new philanthropy was not as vapid and maudlin as Fitzjames Stephen thought it, it was because it had to meet the criterion of morality as well as practicality; indeed morality was a primary test of the efficacy of any activity. The social imagination of the late Victorians, the ideas and sentiments they brought to bear upon social affairs, was an eminently moral imagination. And morality, as the late and great Victorians knew it, was every bit as demanding as the old Puritanical religion.

The Victorian obsession with morality, as some may now think it, may be the most difficult thing for a later generation to understand. When people today object to the term "Victorian values," they do so for different reasons. They properly point out that "Victorian" covers a long and extremely varied span of time, distinguished by periods known as "early" Victorianism, "high" (or "mid-") Victorianism, and "late" Victorianism; if these periods differ markedly in economic, political, and social respects, the "values" of these periods may be presumed to be equally distinctive. It has also been argued that what are usually characterized as Victorian values—thrift, prudence, diligence, self-discipline, self-dependence—were the values of the middle class rather than of the working class, capitalistic values imposed on workers to make them more productive, profitable, and docile. Or these values are said to be neither Victorian nor capitalistic but Christian, or Jewish, or Puritan, or Methodist. Or they are assumed to have been more rhetorical than real, more often invoked than practiced. These and other objections are discussed in the course of this book in the context of particular movements and ideologies.* But on the central issue of morality itself, whether morality played a significant role in social affairs, the evidence is irrefutable.

Whatever the differences (and they were considerable) among those of all parties and classes who addressed themselves to the subject of poverty, there was a strong consensus that the primary objective of any enterprise or reform was that it contribute to the moral improvement of the poor—at the very least, that it not have a deleterious moral effect. It was on this ground that laissez-faireists argued against state intervention, and on the same ground that socialists argued for it. The key word in economics, one socialist at the time said, was "character": The reason why

---

* One objection that is rarely heard, although it has much validity, is to the word "values" itself, which prejudices the discussion by giving it a thoroughly relativistic cast. It is interesting that when Margaret Thatcher first raised the subject, she spoke not of "Victorian values" but of "Victorian virtues."[14]

"individualist economists fear socialism is that they believe it will deteriorate character, and the reason why socialist economists seek socialism is their belief that under individualism character is deteriorating."[15] Unless one discounts everything that contemporaries said, and the passion with which they said it, one must credit their abiding, overriding concern with the question of moral character. And the character of the poor was of special concern because their situation was so precarious and the consequences of moral failure so disastrous.

The ethic implicit (sometimes explicit) in matters of social policy and behavior was not a lofty or exalted one. It did not celebrate heroism, or genius, or nobility, or spiritual grace. Its virtues were more pedestrian: respectability, responsibility, decency, industriousness, prudence, temperance. These virtues depended on no special breeding, talent, sensibility, or even money. They were common, everyday virtues, within the capacity of ordinary people. They were the virtues of citizens, not of heroes or saints—and of citizens of democratic countries, not aristocratic ones. Even the "best self" that Green made so much of was a best self attainable by every citizen; indeed, it was the only true basis of equality and the only requisite for citizenship. So too the "economic chivalry" that Alfred Marshall advocated: this modern form of chivalry required no heroic exertion but only restraint and solicitude—restraint in the pursuit and consumption of wealth, and solicitude for those less fortunate than oneself.

Today the language of morality, applied to social problems and social policies, is often assumed to be the language of conservatism. In late-Victorian England it was the common language of radicals, liberals, conservatives, and those of no particular political disposition. The historian Stefan Collini has said that "character"—not in the neutral, sociological sense, but in the normative, moral sense—"enjoyed a prominence in the political thought of the Victorian period that it had certainly not known before and that it has, arguably, not experienced since."[16] Other historians are beginning to speak of "respectability" more respectfully, without the quotation marks that commonly distance them from that benighted Victorian word.[17] "Respectability studies," one reviewer has remarked, "have almost become a formal branch of Victorian historiography."[18] Another historian disputes the assumption that the idea of respectability was confined to an ambitious and conservative "labor aristocracy." Brian Harrison has pointed out that working-class autobiographers, however untypical of their class, articulated values that were widely diffused. Their works helped to "recruit respectability's ranks, and deserve more prominence in the discussion than they often receive; they spontaneously corroborate one another on details, and they evoke a common philosophy of life."[19]

If historians are beginning to take the idea of respectability seriously, it is because contemporaries quite plainly did. And if historians cannot define the idea precisely, this too reflects contemporary usage. Victorians were fully aware that respectability meant somewhat different things to different individuals and classes, but this did not make it less a fact of life or less important a fact. Poverty too (like health, housing, education, and most of the other facts of life) meant different things to different people, and was nonetheless real and urgent. Whether respectability was signified by the wearing of clean clothes, or providing for a proper funeral, or belonging to a friendly society, or attending a mechanics' institute, or reading edifying books, or not being on relief, or not getting drunk and rowdy, the line separating the respectable worker from the "rough" was as plain to the working classes as to the middle classes; it was, in fact, the main theme of many working-class memoirs.*

That line was all the more important precisely because the temptations to cross it were so plentiful. To take the pledge of temperance (even if not always to adhere to it) was itself a token of respectability. The historian who belittles the idea of respectability by relegating it to the realm of "middle-class values" does justice neither to the facts of history nor to the working classes who struggled so hard to attain what the middle-class historian finds it so easy to deride. Brian Harrison reminds us that it is all the more important to respect those facts about the past which are no longer respected in the present.

Respectability was never cramped within any clearly distinct statusgroup or occupation; it was an attitude of mind which deeply influ-

---

* In 1906, 45 of the 51 Labour Members of Parliament replied to a poll on the books that had influenced them most in their youth. The largest single group (12) had been miners, all were solidly working-class (with relatively few from the "labor aristocracy"), none had attended university. The Bible and *Pilgrim's Progress*, as one might expect, were most frequently cited, followed by Carlyle, Ruskin, Cobbett, Henry George, Dickens, Shakespeare, and Macaulay; there were also occasional references to Gibbon, Milton, Scott, Mill, Darwin, Byron, Shelley, and others.[20] Even allowing for some exaggeration and self-congratulation, one has to be impressed by the books they claimed to have read—books which, at the very least, they thought it appropriate for them to have read, which represented a level of aspiration, a measure of respectability.

enced those who rose, remained stationary, or fell. It impinged on groups of working men of every political opinion and religious denomination, in every region, and at every status-grade within their class, at whatever stage they had reached in their progress towards self-improvement. It was an anxious state of mind, rendered tolerable only by the companionship available in respectability's institutional framework. It is a structure that has now either vanished or decayed, and if only for that reason it deserves to be discussed.[21]

IT IS NOT ONLY the moral framework of late-Victorian England that has "vanished or decayed"; it is the entire framework in which poverty was conceived. And it is this distinctive framework that has to be reconstructed if we are to understand this period and this subject. We are constantly, and properly, being reminded of the Whig fallacy, the tendency to read the past in terms of the present. This is the fallacy that makes of late-Victorian England a halfway house, an uneasy resting place between the old and the new, an interregnum between the past and the present.[22] The same fallacy may tempt us to interpret as a failure of nerve or imagination what contemporaries saw as a matter of principle or conviction. Thus we may be impatient with reformers who stopped short of a welfare state, or philanthropists who professed to be individualists, or economists who were content with a "neoclassical" revision of economics, or philosophers who were essentially moralists, or socialists who persisted in being, above all, Victorians.

There is another fallacy that is equally tempting and equally delusive. This fallacy is inherent in the very term "Victorian," which suggests a specious unity for the period as a whole and thus obscures the differences between early- and late-Victorian England. The confusion is further compounded by the identification of early-Victorian England with the powerful but overly melodramatic image of Dickensian or Mayhewian England.

"It was forty years after 1849," E. P. Thompson has written, "before the middle-class consciousness of poverty was discovered again."[23] The reference is to the forty-year interval between the publication of Henry Mayhew's *London Labour and the London Poor* and Charles Booth's *Life and Labour of the People in London*. The two works are a fascinating study in contrast: Mayhew's personal, colorful, dramatic; Booth's sober, analytic, and, in intention at least, objective. No less striking is the contrast between the two periods. "When 'poverty' was rediscovered in the

1880s," Thompson observed, "few remembered that Mayhew had been there before."[24] If few remembered Mayhew, it was because he had not, in fact, been there before. The poverty that Booth "rediscovered" in the 1880s was very different from that which Mayhew had "discovered" in the 1840s.

Mayhew's "poverty" was primarily that of the "Street-Folk" and "Those That Will Not Work" (as the subtitles of his work put it). His subjects—street sellers, street performers, street laborers, paupers, beggars, prostitutes—were, by his own account, a relatively small part of the population of London (2.5 percent). Yet his portraits of them were so striking, his representation of them as a distinctive "race" with a distinctive "moral physiognomy" so memorable, that they overshadowed the much larger class of workers who did not appear in his pages, workers who lived and worked indoors rather than on the streets and who led mundane and unsensational lives. Many readers and reviewers (and occasionally Mayhew himself) were so impressed by his dramatic "revelations" that they assumed that the extreme and even exotic poverty he described was the condition of the working classes as a whole—that the "street-folk" of the subtitle were equivalent to the "London Labour and the London Poor" of the title.[25]

Booth tried to correct this mistaken identity by creating separate categories for the "very poor," the "poor," and the "comfortable" working classes. The statistic commonly cited from his work has 30 percent of the population in "poverty." But that figure, as Booth made clear, included two distinct groups, the "very poor" (7.5 percent) and the "poor" (22.3 percent). The "very poor" were in a state of "chronic want," largely because of their aversion to regular work or their incapacity for it (caused by drunkenness or other debilitating habits). The "poor," on the other hand, although not in "want" (not ill nourished or ill clad), were in "poverty," engaged in a constant struggle to make ends meet. His own "clients," Booth candidly admitted—the poor he himself cared most about and whom he thought most worthy of society's concern—were those whose poverty was caused mainly by irregular employment; they might be "shiftless and improvident," but they were also "hard-working, struggling people, not worse morally than any other class."[26]

Where Mayhew, however unwittingly, had "de-moralized" the laboring poor by confounding them with the lowest classes of the poor (the "residuum," as they were called), Booth "re-moralized" the poor by separating them from the "very poor" and freeing them from the stigma of pauperism and degradation. He thus redefined the idea of poverty and reinterpreted the social problem. The problem was no longer what it had been earlier in the century: the Malthusian poor (the "excess" population who lived in a state of "misery and vice"), or the pauperized poor (who were the subjects of the Poor Law Reform of 1834), or the Mayhewian poor (the "street-folk" and "those that will not work"). The heart of the problem, as Booth saw it, was the large group of laboring poor whose poverty, while not catastrophic, was nonetheless problematic. Even when he offered a radical proposal for the very poor, he did so less out of solicitude for them than for the poor.

The poor who now came to the center of the stage were not the old "deserving poor." That term became increasingly rare in the 1880s (it was officially discarded even by the Charity Organisation Society), both because it was thought condescending to the deserving poor and because of the invidious implication that other poor were undeserving. The "deserving poor" of earlier times were judged deserving precisely because they did not qualify as a social problem. They were simply the laboring poor, existing in the natural condition of poverty that had been the fate of humanity since time immemorial, the condition of all those who earned their daily bread by the sweat of their brow. By the late-Victorian period, that "condition" had become a "problem." It had become problematic not because it had become worse—on the contrary, the condition of most of the poor, as most contemporaries knew, was better than ever before—but because people had come to believe that it could and should be better than it was. The poor who now emerged as the social problem were deserving, not in the sense of being paragons of virtue, but in the sense of being deserving of society's attention and concern. And they were thought deserving because most of their difficulties (unemployment, sickness, old age) were recognized as not of their own making; because in spite of adversity and temptation most of them, most of the time, made a strenuous effort to provide for themselves and their families; and because for society's sake as much as their own they should be prevented from lapsing into the class of the very poor.

It was the poor, rather than the very poor, who were the beneficiaries of most of the reforms of the late-Victorian and Edwardian periods. Instead of yet another revision of the Poor Law dealing with paupers, Parliament enacted laws for the benefit of the laboring poor: housing, workmen's compensation, extended schooling, school meals, old age pensions, cheap trains, labor exchanges, unemployment and health insurance. And instead of new and improved workhouses for paupers, philanthropists concentrated on new and improved houses for workers:

"model dwellings" and renovated flats and houses, supervised by rent collectors who doubled as social workers.

The programs legislated and subsidized by the government supplemented the scores of philanthropies and institutions that were initiated, financed, and administered by private individuals and groups. And the intention of both was not to abolish poverty, not even to wage "war against poverty," but only (a very large "only") to ameliorate poverty. Nor were they inspired by any egalitarian agenda. Most reformers assumed that there would always be a residue (a "residuum") of the very poor. They hoped only to keep them from dragging down the rest of the poor. They also assumed that there would always be inequalities of wealth and status, just as there would always be inequalities of natural inclinations and endowments. Some people would be richer and others poorer, some more talented and others less, some better born, bred, and privileged than others. The "social problem," for the late Victorians, was not inequality but poverty, the kind of poverty that threatened to reduce the laboring poor to a state of dependency and degradation.

WHEN E. P. THOMPSON spoke of the "middle-class consciousness" that rediscovered poverty in the 1880s, he had in mind those philanthropists, reformers, philosophers, social critics, and socialists who gave this age its distinctive character—what Beatrice Webb called its "Time-Spirit," or what the eminent jurist A. V. Dicey called "public opinion." Toward the end of the century, Dicey delivered a series of lectures on the relation between law and public opinion in determining social policy. Critics have challenged the character and chronology of his three stages: the Tory "quiescence" of the late eighteenth and early nineteenth centuries, the Benthamite "individualism" of the mid-nineteenth century, and the "collectivism" of the last quarter. But there has been little discussion of the thesis implied in the title, *The Relation between Law and Public Opinion*. Dicey was perfectly aware of the role of interest in the creation of both law and social policy. He was also aware—and he quoted Hume to this effect—that interest was shaped by opinion. "Though men be much governed by interest, yet even interest itself, and all human affairs, are entirely governed by *opinion*."[27]

Dicey saw himself as standing against the tide of public opinion, as an individualist in an age of collectivism. The socialist Sidney Webb was pleased to think of himself as very much in the tide; Fabianism, he boasted, was the wave of the future because it was the wave of the present.

For all their differences, however, they were in agreement on two crucial propositions: the primacy of public opinion in social affairs and the primacy of the middle classes in the formation of that opinion. Public opinion, Dicey explained, was that held by "the people of England, or, to speak with more precision, by the majority of those citizens who have at a given moment taken an effective part in public life." In this collectivist age, public-minded citizens were inspired by "the desire to ease the sufferings, to increase the pleasures, and to satisfy the best aspirations of the mass of wage-earners."[28] Webb had the same people in mind when he spoke of that "small intellectual yet practical class" without whose consent nothing was ever done, and when he made it the mission of the Fabians to "permeate" that class and channel its energies and resources into the fulfillment of the Fabian program.[29]

Some historians have disputed the benevolent motives of this class. The rich were moved, it has been said, not by a desire to "ease the sufferings" and "increase the pleasures" of the poor, but to ease their own guilt and increase their profits, or to allay their fears of riots and revolution, or to exercise the "social control" that would ensure their economic power and social "hegemony." These arguments appear as a refrain throughout this book, not because contemporaries made much of them but because historians have.[30] Even those historians, however, who are most suspicious of "elitist" history would not deny the important, sometimes decisive, role played during this period by the "middle" or "intellectual" class—the "professional" class, as Harold Perkin has identified it.[31]

THE POOR DID NOT have to "rediscover" poverty; they had never forgotten it. Nor were they passive observers in the making of their history. There is ample history of their own making (and ample material for the social historian) in their private and public lives, the way they lived and worked, spent their time and money, expressed their ideas, beliefs, fears, and aspirations.[32] There were also the multitude of formal and informal institutions they created or dominated: trade unions, friendly societies, cooperatives, temperance groups, public houses, chapels, missions, music halls, sporting events. All of this testifies to a rich and varied working-class culture—or rather working-class cultures, since there was no single working class. It does not, however, testify to a distinctive working-class "consciousness," in the sense of a distinctive political ideology or social agenda.

Thomas Wright, a metalworker and occasional author, wrote in 1873 that the working classes were "not a single-acting, single-idea'd body." They were not, in fact, a single working class. "They are practically and plurally *classes,* distinct classes, classes between which there are as decisively marked differences as there are between any one of them and the upper or middle classes."[33] Wright's testimony stands in dramatic contrast to E. P. Thompson's famous thesis of the emergence, by 1832, of a unified, self-conscious, politically independent working class hostile to capitalism and receptive to alternative forms of economic and social organization.[34] If there ever was such a "single-acting, single idea'd" working class, it seems to have fragmented or dissolved by the latter part of the century. The historian Gareth Stedman Jones makes the point well. "If the 'making of the English working class' took place in the 1790–1830 period, something akin to a remaking of the working class took place in the years between 1870 and 1900." That "remaking," as he describes it, was more like an "unmaking." In place of Thompson's single, radical working class committed to the class struggle and the overthrow of capitalism, Jones finds a late-Victorian working class that was not at all radical, that gave a "de facto recognition" to capitalism and to the entire social order—monarchy, aristocracy, empire, even the religious establishment. And the agenda of this class was not to seize power but to achieve "welfare."[35]

It is at this point that "history from below" and "history from above" merge. For the ideal of "welfare" was one that the middle classes shared—indeed that they, as the articulators of "public opinion," often took the initiative in promoting—sometimes, as in the cases of workmen's compensation and old age pensions, over the objections of the trade unions.

If late-Victorian England witnessed a "remaking" of the working classes, it also witnessed a "remaking" of the middle classes. When Marxists speak of "reformism," it is the working classes they have in mind—the rejection of the class struggle in favor of social reforms within the capitalist system. But the term is as applicable to the middle classes, who underwent a similar reformist transformation when they renounced the doctrine of laissez-faire and recognized the legitimacy of some degree of state intervention on behalf of the poor. For the middle classes, as for the working classes, reformism was an accommodation to reality; laissez-faire, like the class struggle, had long since been abandoned in practice, if not in principle. What was new about this period was the deliberate repudiation of ideas and policies that had once been honored (even if, often, more in the breach than in the observance); the conscious articulation of alternative ideas and policies that would once have been anathema; and the rapidity with which these reformist, even heretical, ideas and policies were embraced by that large and varied body known as "public opinion."

This reformist tendency, on the part of both the middle and working classes, was obviously not as homogeneous as is implied in such monolithic terms as "public opinion," or "time-spirit," or even "reformism" itself. The whole of this book testifies to the diversity of ideas and policies, movements and institutions generated by the intellectual and social ferment of the time. Nor was it as universally or uniformly pervasive as might be thought; it penetrated different groups and classes in different ways and degrees, and it was strongly resisted not only by some eminent and uncompromising laissez-faireists but also by some militant socialists and trade unionists. It was not seen as a remedy for all social problems, and certainly not as a prescription for social equality; it was meant to alleviate, not solve, the most urgent problems, and to mitigate the most onerous class differences. In fact, some class differences were actually magnified— differences, as Wright testified, within the working classes as well as between the working and middle classes. But these were compensated by a greater mobility within and between the classes, from the lower to the upper ranks of the working classes and from the "labor aristocracy" to the middle classes. The ideal even of the most enthusiastic reformers (even of the most militant socialists) was not a classless society but a more open and humane society.

The ideal was a civil society in which the concept of citizenship would transcend that of class. Half a century earlier the Chartists had made this the centerpiece of their movement. They sought the franchise for the most classical of reasons: because only as "political animals," people "born for citizenship," would they enjoy the full measure of their humanity. A later generation of philosophers and reformers extended the idea of citizenship from the political to the social and moral realms. Citizenship in this broader sense did not eliminate poverty, but it did mitigate, as the Chartists had predicted, some of its indignity. Above all, it mitigated the "two nations" problem that had exacerbated the problem of poverty earlier in the century.

One of the most brilliant historians of modern England, Elie Halévy, coined a memorable phrase to describe that earlier period of English history. It was the "miracle of modern England," he said, to have been spared the agony of revolution at a time when much of Europe was convulsed by revolutions.[36] That "miracle" was the unique conjunction

of institutions and traditions—religious, political, social, and economic—
which promoted continuity and stability in a period of tumult abroad and
of rapid change at home. By the end of the nineteenth century, the threat
of revolution had receded, but the possibility of social strife and exacerbated class tensions remained. It was then that the reformist temper
helped meliorate those tensions and perpetuate that "miracle."

The late Victorians did not "solve" their social problems, still less
abolish poverty. But they did bring to their problems a moral imagination
that was remarkable in its intensity and "earnestness" (that very Victorian word)—and that was also remarkably free of the complacency and
hypocrisy so often attributed to them. If they failed to understand all the
causes and dimensions of their problems or to accomplish all they hoped
by way of improvement, a later generation, aware of its own failures (in
spite of its greater sophistication and experience), may be more forgiving
of the Victorians than they were of themselves.

I MYSELF CAME only belatedly to a recognition of the extent to which
the late Victorians were engaged in a "remaking" of their history. I had
appreciated the efforts of the early Victorians to meliorate the effects of
industrialism, urbanism, and all the social and psychological dislocations
of that very troubled period. But I had not anticipated the intellectual and
social ferment of the later period, the enormous surge of philanthropic
and reform enterprises, the intensity and diversity of ideas, the earnestness and pervasiveness of the spirit of compassion. No period (least of
all any period in English history, which is notoriously tradition-bound)
is *sui generis*. But late-Victorian England, I discovered, was more *sui
generis* than I had expected.

It is for this reason that what had been planned as a sequel to my
earlier book *The Idea of Poverty* has turned out to be a very different kind
of work. My original intention was to write a volume that would be
symmetrical with the first in theme and structure: Adam Smith would be
paralleled by Alfred Marshall, Malthusianism by Social Darwinism, the
New Poor Law of 1834 by the Poor Law Commission of 1909, Chartism
by socialism, Mayhew by Booth, Gaskell by Gissing. It was a neat and
plausible schema—belied only by the reality of history. The present book
took on a life of its own because the period had a vitality and actuality of
its own.

Smith and Malthus were decisive figures in the earlier volume because they set the terms of the debate that dominated that period, the

debate between the "optimists" and the "pessimists." The former, deriving from Smith, were confident that a free and expanding economy would benefit the entire nation, including the entire body of the poor. The latter, following Malthus, assumed that the growth of population would condemn the lowest class of the poor to a life of "misery and vice" and doom all of the poor to a perpetual struggle for survival. There was nothing equivalent to that debate in the later period, largely because Smith (as revised by Alfred Marshall) finally and decisively triumphed over Malthus. The laissez-faireists were too weak to mount a serious campaign even against socialism, let alone against the "neoclassical" economics of Marshall. The Social Darwinists were more interested in eugenics than in economics or social affairs. And many socialists (or those who loosely adopted that label) welcomed the new economics as the first step to socialism.

Booth and Mayhew are more nearly parallel, but Booth looms larger and appears earlier in this volume because he significantly defined and explicated the social problem, whereas Mayhew merely popularized and dramatized it. The poor-law commissions of 1834 and 1909, which seemed to promise a nice basis of comparison, proved to be not really comparable, the later one being far less consequential than the earlier one. Nor is there any "social" novelist among the late Victorians who can begin to compare with Dickens, Disraeli, or even Gaskell.

It was also originally my intention to carry this volume into the twentieth century. Just as early-Victorian England started well before the accession of the Queen, so, I had thought, late-Victorian England terminated not with the death of the Queen but with that of her son, or, perhaps, with the war that threatened to destroy not only "liberal England," as has been said, but traditional England. Again I underestimated the distinctiveness of the late Victorians. While there were important and obvious continuities between the Victorian and Edwardian periods (so that the chapter on the Fabians spans both), there were also, as the epilogue suggests, larger discontinuities than I had suspected. To do justice to the "time-spirit" of this later period would require yet another book by yet another historian. For this historian, one "remaking" must suffice.

Book One

"THE ARITHMETIC
OF WOE"

CHAPTER I

Social Statistics

TOWARD THE END of the first volume of *Life and Labour of the People in London,* published in 1889, Charles Booth warned his readers that his statistics could be read in very different ways. One might reasonably conclude that it was "not so very bad" that a tenth of the population of the most poverty-stricken area of London should be found to be "very poor." Alternatively, one might be aghast at the thought of 100,000 individuals, or 20,000 families, who made up that tenth of the population. In the divergence between these two points of view, the relative and the absolute, Booth saw the explanation for "the whole difference between pessimism and optimism." A balanced judgment required that both absolute numbers and percentages be kept in mind. But this was difficult for those whose experience or imagination made them vividly aware of the trials and sorrows of the poor as individuals. "They refuse to set off and balance the happy hours of the same class, or even of the same people, against those miseries; much less can they consent to bring the lot of other classes into the account, add up the opposing figures, and contentedly carry forward a credit balance. In the arithmetic of woe they can only add or multiply, they cannot subtract or divide."[1]

Booth was not unsympathetic to those well-intentioned people who could only add and multiply and could not bring themselves to subtract or divide, who felt it unseemly to take any account of happiness in calculating the "arithmetic of woe." Appalled by the evidence of misery, they could see nothing but misery. Horrified by the existence of the very poor, they could give no thought to the much larger class of the less poor. In such an "intensity of feeling," Booth acknowledged, "lies the power to move the world." But it was by statistics, he hastened to add—the ability to subtract and divide as well as add and multiply, to consider percentages as well as absolute figures—that "this power [must] be guided if it would move the world aright."[2]

This poignant appeal came from a man whose own experience and imagination made him acutely sensitive to both orders of reality: the existential lives of the poor and the statistical incidence of poverty, the tragic connotation of absolute numbers and the mitigating effect of relative numbers. Booth was speaking to the reformers of his own time, but his words are a timely reminder to historians who permit themselves too easily to be categorized as "pessimists" or "optimists" in the perennial debate over the condition of the working classes as a result of industrialism.[3] The dispute, as Booth observed, reflects not so much different facts as different perspectives from which the facts are viewed; percentages and averages lend themselves to an optimistic view of the condition of the poor, absolute numbers and individual case histories to a pessimistic one. If this is so, the two schools of thought are not entirely incompatible. Nor can the pessimists claim, as they sometimes do, a monopoly of moral righteousness, nor the optimists, as they sometimes do, a monopoly of hard reason. A true "arithmetic of woe," Booth reminds us, is no less compassionate because it can subtract and divide as well as add and multiply.

In addition to the relative dimension of numbers, there is the relative perspective of history. Was poverty better or worse than it had been a few decades, or half a century, or a century earlier? Were there more or fewer poor? Were more or fewer of them in worse or less worse (or perhaps simply different) conditions of poverty? And what were the prospects of their children and children's children? This historical perspective may unwittingly make an optimist of the most confirmed pessimist, for the more pessimistic one's view of an earlier period, the more optimistic may be the implications for a later period.

The historian John Foster, in his study of three English towns in the mid-nineteenth century, has had the ingenious idea of applying to them the standards of subsistence developed by social reformers of the early twentieth century. By those standards, he finds, 28 percent of the families of Northampton in 1849 had incomes below a minimum subsistence level, compared with 8 percent of the families of Northampton in 1913.[4] Foster interprets these statistics as irrefutable testimony of the utter destitution of over one-quarter of the population of that town in one of the more prosperous years of the early industrial age. Another historian might cite those same figures as evidence of the enormous improvement of conditions in the course of the following sixty-odd years and the relative well-being of the working class on the eve of the First World War. This conclusion would no doubt be as distressing to Foster as to the reformers of the early twentieth century who, ignoring the comparison with earlier times, took their statistics as evidence of the unparalleled state of misery in their own time.

SOME CONTEMPORARIES were remarkably adept not only in calculating the arithmetic of woe but in doing so while moving backward and forward in time—an achievement all the more impressive in view of the limited and imprecise materials available at the time. One of the most able practitioners of this craft was Robert Giffen, chief statistician of the Board of Trade and editor of the journal of the Royal Statistical Society. Giffen's presidential address to the society in 1883, "The Progress of the Working Classes in the Last Half-Century," echoed, in its title and theme, an influential book by his predecessor at the Board of Trade half a century earlier. G. R. Porter's *Progress of the Nation,* first published in 1838 and reissued in new editions in the following decades, was in its time a model of statistical analysis as well as a mine of valuable data. Drawing upon that book and upon the statistics of wages and prices that Porter had made a permanent feature of the work of the Board of Trade, Giffen charted the changes that had taken place since 1838.

By one measure after another, Giffen found a significant improvement in the condition of the working classes. Weekly wages for comparable work had risen by at least 20 percent and, in most industries, by 50 percent to 100 percent. Hours of work had decreased by almost 20 percent, so that the money return per hour had increased by as much as 70 percent to 120 percent. The cost of food was substantially lower, and, almost as important, fluctuations in the price of wheat were considerably diminished, thus eliminating the extreme distress caused by a rapid doubling or even tripling of the price. Although meat was more expensive, it had also become more common as a staple in the working-class diet; fifty years earlier, Giffen observed, the ordinary worker "had little more concern with its price than with the price of diamonds."[5] Other foods were also being consumed by workers in larger quantities: sugar, tea, cheese, butter, eggs, beer, and spirits. And essential commodities such as clothing and shoes were cheaper and more plentiful. By far the largest increase in the working-class budget was rent, but considerable as that was—often as much as 150 percent—it still left most workers with a substantial gain in real income.

These statistics, Giffen pointed out, did not take into account the benefits of government expenditures on education, sanitation, factory inspection, postal services, free libraries, and the like. At just this time, when workers were paying fewer taxes, they were receiving far more from the state in the form of public services. In 1851, for example, less than a quarter of a million children received government-assisted education; in 1881 there were over ten times that number. The improvement in the material and physical conditions of life was reflected in the vital statistics: a decline of about 30 percent in the death rate of adults, and an increase in longevity of two years for males and almost three and a half years for females. Other "social statistics" were equally encouraging. There was not only a relative but an absolute decline in the incidence of both crime and pauperism, and a considerable rise in the number of depositors in savings banks, especially among the working classes.

Returning to the subject three years later, Giffen was pleased to report that such criticisms as had been made of his earlier paper demonstrated that the improvement in the condition of the working classes was even more substantial than he had said. His estimates had been based on comparisons of wages in the same occupation. But there had also taken place a large shift from poorly-paid to better-paid occupations. Where fifty years earlier half the laboring population of Great Britain had been in agriculture, now only one-fourth were. The figures for the United Kingdom were even more dramatic. Earlier one-third had been British agricultural laborers and another third Irish laborers (agricultural and nonagricultural, who together earned half as much as British agricultural laborers). Now each of these groups was reduced to one-eighth, thus raising still further the proportion of the better-paid nonagricultural British workers. This occupational change alone, even without a rise in the wages of each occupation, would have resulted in a considerable rise in the income of the working classes as a whole. In fact the worst-paid occupations—in both agriculture and industry, and in Ireland as well as England—were better paid now than they had been. Within the artisan class there was a movement to better-paid work, and there was also a movement from the artisan class to the lower middle class.

What had happened in those fifty years, Giffen concluded, was nothing less than a "revolution of the most remarkable description." And it was a revolution that promised to continue into the future. "From being a dependent class without future and hope, the masses of working men have in fact got into a position from which they may effectually advance to almost any degree of civilisation." While every means, political and

private, should be exerted to continue that advance, the workers themselves, Giffen was confident, had "the game in their own hands." All that
were required were education and thrift, and these were now happily
within their capacity.[6]

This optimistic conclusion was confirmed by other statisticians and
economists at the time. In his first paper Giffen had referred to an earlier
work by Leone Levi, and in his second paper he cited Levi's more recent
and comprehensive *Wages and Earnings of the Working Classes,* published in 1885. On the basis of a detailed study of wages and the distribution of wealth between 1857 and 1884, Levi deduced that the
condition of the working classes had improved by 30 percent in little
more than a quarter of a century.[7] By focusing on this particular period,
Levi implicitly disposed of one of the objections brought against Giffen:
that the latter, taking as his starting point a year when the conditions of
the working classes were perhaps at their worst, created an overly dramatic impression of improvement. Since 1857 was a relatively good year
and 1884 a relatively bad one, the improvement between these dates was
all the more notable.

Utilizing still other dates and sources, other contemporary studies
came to much the same conclusion. Michael Mulhall's *Fifty Years of
National Progress,* published in 1887, showed the national wealth increasing three times faster than the population between 1837 and 1887,
with a corresponding diffusion of wealth among all classes, including the
lowest. Probate court returns in 1877, for example, had 31 percent of the
people who died that year leaving estates of at least £100 compared with
17 percent in 1840, suggesting that 14 percent of the population had
been "lifted out of a position of indigence to one of absolute or comparative affluence."[8]

The next generation of statisticians confirmed and refined the evidence of improvement. In 1904 A. L. Bowley found that real wages rose
by almost 50 percent between 1850 and 1885 and by another 40 percent
in the next fifteen years—more than a 100 percent increase over the last
half of the century.[9] Five years later George Wood amended these figures;
taking unemployment into account, real wages rose by almost 40 percent
between 1850 and 1885 and another 40 percent by 1900.[10] Much of this
increase was the result of falling prices rather than rising wages, and some
of it reflected the shift to better jobs; but even within the same occupation
real wages rose considerably during this period.

* * *

EVEN THOSE CONTEMPORARIES—radicals and socialists—who were inclined to be skeptical about the magnitude of improvement did not dispute the fact that there had been a significant rise in real wages for most workers during most of this period. The testimony of the Christian socialist J. M. Ludlow is especially telling. In 1850 he had formulated, independently of Marx and Engels, something very like the Marxist theory of "immiseration." The condition of the workers, Ludlow had predicted, would get progressively worse until the whole of the working class would be reduced to the status of paupers.[11] In 1867, perhaps inspired by the Reform Act of that year, Ludlow dramatically reversed himself. In a volume written in collaboration with Lloyd Jones (a leader of the cooperative movement) and fittingly titled *Progress of the Working Class,* Ludlow now argued that while the condition of the working class still left much to be desired, it had considerably improved since the passage of the first Reform Act thirty-five years earlier. Partly as a result of legislation, partly because workers had availed themselves of the opportunities presented by the growth of prosperity, "the progress of the working class in our country since 1832 has been general and continuous."[12]

By the time of the third Reform Act in 1884, the improvement was still more considerable and less disputable. In that year Thorold Rogers, a vigorous champion of trade unionism, published a *History of Work and Wages* that went so far as to suggest that the bulk of the working classes early in the century had been in worse condition than were the lowest and most disreputable class of the 1880s. "Evil as the condition is of destitute and criminal London, with its misery and recklessness, it is not, I am persuaded, so miserable and so hopeless as nearly all urban labour was sixty years ago."[13]

Other working-class advocates were conceding the same point. When Levi's findings were presented at the meeting of the National Association for the Promotion of Social Science, the secretary of a London Workman's Association protested that instead of being allowed to speak for themselves, the working classes were being discussed as if they were "some new-found race, or extinct animal." Statistics, he added, could be made to prove anything; the official poor-law figures, for example, underestimated the actual number of poor who were virtually paupers. Yet he conceded Levi's main point. "Everyone might take it for granted that the working classes were better off now than they were twenty-seven years ago, but ought they not to be? The question was, were they as much better off as they ought to be?"[14] The next speaker, the well-known radical George Holyoake, praised Levi's "very wise paper" and defended his use of statistics. "In fact, the condition of the workman had every-where improved considerably, and the facts brought forward by the Pro-fessor were very valuable."[15]

Giffen's second paper, two years later, elicited much the same re-sponse from working-class spokesmen. One of its severest critics was Benjamin Jones, secretary of the Working Men's Cooperative Society, who criticized Giffen for exaggerating the rarity of meat earlier in the century and for minimizing the adverse effects of the increase in rent and the deterioration of housing. Particular groups of workers, Jones pointed out, were worse off than before, and the artisan class, although better off, included not only those who had risen from the lower strata of the work-ing class but also those who had fallen from the ranks of the lower middle class (shopkeepers who could not compete with larger firms). Moreover, the working class itself had not shared in the increase of national wealth either in proportion to its numbers or in proportion to its contribution to that wealth. In spite of these objections, however, Jones agreed with most of the speakers that there had been a substantial improvement in the condition of a large majority of the working classes in the course of the preceding half century—not the 100 percent claimed by Giffen, but 20 percent or 25 percent.[16]

Historians and economists have not seriously quarreled with the find-ings of contemporaries; the latest figures, based upon the most sophisti-cated econometric techniques, are remarkably close to the earlier ones.[17] Some historians have tried to detract from the "optimistic" conclusions implicit in these statistics, while admitting the basic validity of the figures themselves. G. D. H. Cole and Raymond Postgate, in a book published just before the Second World War, said that while wages varied consid-erably from trade to trade, there was no doubt that in the last quarter of the nineteenth century "the *absolute* living standards of the working classes considerably improved."[18] Helen Lynd, a few years later, also accepted Wood's statistics, suggesting, however—but without offering any evidence for this supposition—that they were based largely on the earnings of skilled workers.[19]

More recently the Marxist historian E. J. Hobsbawm has cited the same figures, pointing out that the largest increase of real wages occurred between 1880 and 1895. These figures, he adds, do not give a "realistic picture" of the working class because they fail to take into account the findings of Charles Booth and Seebohm Rowntree that 40 percent of that class were below the poverty line.[20] This demurral, however, has little bearing on the issue of improvement since neither Booth nor Rowntree offered comparable statistics for the earlier part of the century. Indeed Booth himself was confident that there was a considerable improvement in the conditions of the working classes; had there been a comparable study earlier, he wrote, it would have shown "a greater proportion of depravity and misery than now exists, and a lower general standard of fare."[21]

Another radical historian, Gareth Stedman Jones, citing Bowley's statistics, observes that wages in London were higher than those in other parts of the country and that London "thrived on its surplus of unskilled labour." But his documentation unwittingly supports the "optimistic" position, because it shows a considerable increase of wages in each of four categories: London artisans and provincial artisans, town laborers and agricultural laborers.[22] Elsewhere Jones cites two surveys of wages and rents in one of the poorest sections of London, the first taken in 1848 and the other in 1887, to support his point about the considerable increase of rent in that period; but the statistics also confirm an increase of wages more than sufficient to absorb that rise of rent.[23]

WAGES ARE NOT the only index of improvement. Many contemporaries were more impressed by the evidence of increased consumption, especially of what then passed as "luxuries." In her diary Beatrice Webb recorded the discussion she had with Benjamin Jones after Giffen had delivered his second paper. Although she sympathized with Jones's criticisms and was suspicious of Giffen's "special pleading," she confessed that she found irrefutable the main point that told in favor of Giffen. "The one argument of Mr. Giffen's which seems difficult to touch is the increased consumption of luxuries, tea, sugar, etc."[24]

Historians have made much of the increased consumption of these and other "luxuries." One study refers to the 1880s as "a crucial decade in the improvement of English diet."[25] Others take issue with Walt Rostow, who assigned the label "the age of high mass-consumption" to the early twentieth century; that label, they say, more properly belongs to the late nineteenth century.[26] The increase of consumption in this late-Victorian period was the result not only of the rise of wages and decline of prices but also of an international economy that encouraged the import of cheap foreign goods and of a domestic economy that witnessed significant innovations in both mass production and mass distribution. The rise of multiple shops and chain stores, as much as new manufacturing techniques, had the effect of making more goods, and more varieties of goods, available at lower cost to a larger market. This was true of durable goods as well as food and clothing. By 1890 bicycles, selling for £4, had come within the means of a large part of the working class, while sewing machines could be bought on the hire-purchase (or installment) plan. A more affluent and aspiring working-class family could even afford to own a piano. In 1873 a Yorkshire miners' leader boasted, "We have got more pianos and perambulators, but a piano is a cut above a perambulator."[27]

"Pessimistic" historians, hard pressed to substantiate their "arithmetic of woe" on the basis of quantitative evidence, sometimes retreat to the "quality of life" argument—the "total life-experience" of an exploited, alienated class.[28] Even here the weight of the evidence, although not precisely measurable, is far from supporting that image of exploitation and alienation. One may not be able to calculate the exact effect of public services, for example, on the quality of life of the poor, but there can be little doubt that they enlarged and enriched their lives. Some of these services were the result of parliamentary legislation: free education, limitations on hours of work, protection against accidents in factories and mines and compensation for such accidents, sanitary and health reforms, laws against the adulteration of food and spirits, official bank holidays (four paid holidays a year in most industrial and commercial establishments). Others were provided by local authorities: sewage systems, gasworks and waterworks, street-lighting and street-cleaning, baths, libraries, parks. Joseph Chamberlain, mayor of Birmingham from 1873 to 1876, proudly described his city as "parked, paved, assized, marketed, Gas-and-Watered and *improved*."[29] Other municipalities had less to boast of, but all were, to one degree or another, "improved." And all of this was happening at a time when the working classes were bearing less of the burden of taxation as indirect taxes gave way to direct taxes. (In 1894 inheritance taxes were introduced in the form of "death duties.")

The cumulative effect of these improvements was reflected in the vital statistics, especially in the decline of mortality rates both in large towns and in the countryside—a decline due more to improvements in sanitation and public health than to medical discoveries.[30] But no amount of statistics can convey the decline of anxiety that came with the virtual elimination of cholera and typhus, which had been the scourges of the earlier part of the century.

Nor can statistics convey the impact upon the quality of life of other amenities which derived not from legislation or administration but from industrialism and urbanism. Trams costing a penny or so a trip made it possible for workers to live more comfortably some distance from their work and to visit friends and relatives in other neighborhoods. Cheap railway fares facilitated day-trips to the seaside for those who, in another generation, might never have seen the sea or, indeed, enjoyed any respite from work. Holidays became, as one historian puts it, "community events"; by 1900 most Lancashire cotton towns went en masse to the seaside for the annual holiday.[31] Music halls, freed of the restrictions earlier imposed on them, became even more popular than they had been. Workingmen's clubs were to be found in every good-sized town. And new spectator sports such as cricket and association football became major social events for mass audiences; by the 1880s football games were being played at night under electric lights. If there were surely many "disamenities," as is now said, associated with industrial and urban life, there were many amenities which cannot be easily quantified but which have to be factored into the "arithmetic of woe."

CHAPTER 2

Rising Expectations and Relative Deprivations

WHY, THEN, if conditions were better than they had been before, did they seem worse? Why was there so much social unrest and ideological ferment at precisely the time when the conditions of the working classes, measured by the usual standard-of-living and quality-of-life indices, were visibly improving? Why was poverty dramatically "rediscovered" at just the time when the poor were becoming less poor, when more of them were moving from unskilled to skilled occupations and from worse-paid to better-paid ones, when women and children were working fewer hours and many more children were being educated, when the working classes were reaping the benefits of social reforms, public services, and, above all, industrial progress?

Half a century earlier, when Thomas Carlyle first raised the "condition-of-England question," he had explained that it was a question not only of the material "condition" of the people but also of their "disposition"—their "thoughts, beliefs, and feelings," their "bitter discontent."[1] At that time, faced with all the hardships of the early stages of industrialism, before there had been any notable social reforms to mitigate those hardships and before the economy had expanded sufficiently to relieve them, contemporaries had good reason to believe (although even then not everyone, and certainly not Carlyle himself, shared this belief) that the "condition" of the people was the direct cause of their "disposition," that there was a clear correlation between their condition and their disposition. Toward the end of the century the situation was quite different. However unsatisfactory the condition of the working classes, it had visibly improved, for most workers in most respects. Yet the disposition of the people had not improved commensurately.

This phenomenon, the disjunction between "condition" and "disposition," is by now all too familiar. As Tocqueville so memorably observed, a rising standard of living (like an accession of political power) creates rising expectations that are never entirely satisfied and that inevitably generate frustration and discontent. Tocqueville was actually quoted to this effect in 1891 by the radical economist J. A. Hobson. Just as the French before the Revolution, Tocqueville had said, "found their condition all the more intolerable according as it became better," so, Hobson remarked, the English became more conscious of poverty and more distressed by it precisely as the material, political, and educational conditions of the poor improved.

> If by poverty is meant the difference between felt wants and the power to satisfy them, there is more poverty than ever. The income of the poor has grown, but their desires and needs have grown more rapidly. Hence the growth of a conscious class hatred, the "growing animosity of the poor against the rich," as Mr. Barnett notes in the slums of Whitechapel. The poor were once too stupid and too sodden for vigorous discontent, now though their poverty may be less intense, it is more alive, and more militant. The rate of improvement in the condition of the poor is not quick enough to stem the current of popular discontent.[2]*

The "relativization" of the problem of poverty—poverty seen as a function of "felt wants" rather than of basic needs—had still another relative dimension. For poverty was measured not only against the rising expectations of the working class but also against the rising affluence of the upper class. When contemporaries complained that the rich were getting richer while the poor were getting poorer, what they really meant was that the rich were getting richer at a faster rate than the poor were getting less poor. No one, not even Henry George, who made so much of the disparity between "Progress and Poverty," seriously claimed that the poor were actually getting poorer.[4] The old article of faith, that the poor

---

* A modern historian confirms this Tocquevillian view. Disputing Eric Hobsbawm's assertion about the earlier period—"On a gloomy interpretation, the popular discontent of the early nineteenth century makes sense; and on an optimistic interpretation it is almost inexplicable"—J. A. Banks makes exactly the opposite point, that the discontent was more in keeping with the optimistic interpretation. "The discontent of women with their traditional lot of childbearing and child-rearing . . . arose not because they had now become worse off than their mothers and grandmothers had been, but because they saw themselves worse off than they *might* be."[3]

were being pauperized, had long since been abandoned by most radicals. The contention now was that the poor were being deprived not so much of the means of subsistence as of the means of acquiring a higher standard of living and a larger share of the national wealth. This was the real grievance and source of *ressentiment*.

Thus the "condition-of-England question" was triply relativized, as it were. The issue was not only the condition of the working class compared with its previous condition, not only its condition compared with its expectations, but also its condition compared with that of other classes. Were the workers, individually and collectively, keeping pace with the general increase in wealth? Was income being distributed more or less equitably among the classes? And if not, should measures be taken to redistribute income and wealth so as to reduce, if not eliminate, the gap between rich and poor? The final turn of the argument was crucial, for it transformed the problem of poverty—the problem of destitution or indigence—into a problem of equity, and equity, in turn, into equality.

Contemporaries were sensitive to these distinctions and well aware of the implications of these issues. In his first paper Giffen addressed them at some length, although only after registering a demurral. If everyone's condition was improving, he protested, why should anyone begrudge the more rapid improvement of another? In fact, he went on, wage earners, both as a class and as individuals, had received more than a "fair share" of the increase of wealth during the preceding fifty years. While the total return from capital increased by 100 percent and the per capita return by 15 percent, the total income of the working class had increased by 160 percent and average individual wages by 100 percent. Indeed, the share accruing to capital was even less favorable than these figures suggest because capital itself had increased by 150 percent at a time when the total return had increased by only 100 percent. Moreover, it was not the very rich who were getting richer, but the moderately rich (salaried employees as well as small capitalists) who were becoming more plentiful. "Thus the rich have become more numerous, but not richer individually; the 'poor' are, to some smaller extent, fewer; and those who remain 'poor' are, individually, twice as well off on the average as they were fifty years ago. The 'poor' have thus had almost all the benefit of the great material advance of the last fifty years."[5]

Levi presented an even more dramatic picture of the relative improvement of the working classes vis-à-vis other classes. Between 1851 and 1881, he calculated, the average income of workers rose by 59 percent, that of the lower middle class by 37 percent, while that of the "income taxpayers" actually declined by 30 percent.[6] Bowley took issue with both Giffen and Levi, offering evidence of a more modest but still substantial gain on the part of the working classes. In the 1880s, according to his statistics, the workers' share of the national income more than made up for the slight decline in the preceding decades. That share continued to rise throughout the 1890s and started to decline only after the turn of the century.[7]

In the face of these facts, the arguments of the pessimists became increasingly refined and complicated. Thus Hobson maintained that even if it could be proved that the wages of the working class had increased faster than the income of the propertied class, it did not follow that the "standard of comfort" of the former increased as much as that of the latter. Moreover, if the term "poor" was confined to the lower level of wage earner, it would probably be true that the rich were getting richer more rapidly than the very poor were getting less poor. Finally, even if the relative number of very poor had decreased, their absolute number had increased, and this, Hobson concluded, was an unprecedented evil of the greatest magnitude.[8]

A less subtle strategy was adopted by the socialist Chiozza Money in his widely quoted *Riches and Poverty*. Published in 1905, the book was a passionate indictment of capitalism and a plea for the nationalization of the means of production. It became celebrated, however, not for its ideology but for its statistics, which seemed to prove that a minute portion of the rich was monopolizing a large part of the wealth of the country. Half of the national income, Money wrote—and it was this statistic that was most often cited—went to 12 percent of the population and over a third to little more than 3 percent. Less often quoted were his other figures proving that the situation had been worse forty years earlier, when half of the national income had gone to 10 percent of the population and one-fourth of the income to one-half percent of the population. Moreover, while the proportion going to the entire class of manual workers remained the same (40 percent), that class had become a smaller part of the population as a whole, so that the real wages of the individuals in that class had risen significantly. Money himself reluctantly concluded that "there can be no question that the actual position of the wage earner has considerably improved in the last forty years"—hastening to add, however, that "these facts are only relatively satisfactory, and serve but to fill us with horror of the past."[9]*

Most historians now agree—as most serious contemporaries did—that during the last quarter of the century the position of the working class as a whole, and of most individuals within that class, improved relative to that of the propertied class. One sophisticated statistical analysis arrives at estimates somewhat lower than Bowley's but of the "same order of magnitude."[10] Another sees a decided shift in favor of wage earners between 1873 and 1896, with a reversal in the following years, so that by 1912 the relative position of the classes was similar to that in 1873.[11] Even this later reversal has been disputed by economists who point out that the evidence for it is based on income figures for the classes as a whole and does not take into account the decline in the number of wage earners relative to property owners; this study concludes that the income of the average wage earner increased more than that of property owners from 1880 to 1913 (although at the extremes there may have been little change).[12] Scholars continue to differ on dates and details but not on the general proposition that during the last quarter of the century there was "a marked increase in the share of the national income going to wages at the expense of profits."[13] Or, as another put it: "The national income was being redistributed away from the capitalists toward the workers."[14]

IF, AS MOST SCHOLARS now believe, there was no gross inequity (at least no grosser inequity) in the condition of the working class relative to other classes in this last quarter of the century—if both real wages and labor's share of the national product had increased—perhaps the inequity lay within the working class itself. Averages and percentages may well conceal a considerable disparity within the class, with some workers benefiting disproportionately (thus driving up the aggregate figures) and others, possibly even the majority, suffering disproportionately.

This was the argument advanced by Friedrich Engels in 1885 in an

---

* At this point, to convey the horror of the present, Money retreated to absolute numbers. More bread was consumed in 1903 than in 1867, but in 1903 forty people perished on the streets of London from exposure and starvation; the death rate declined between 1867 and 1903 from 20.8 to 15.7, but in 1903, 137,490 infants died within their first year. (One recalls Booth's dictum that the difference between pessimism and optimism is the difference between absolute and relative figures.)

article entitled "England in 1845 and 1885." As it happened, 1845 was the date of publication of his own book *The Condition of the Working Class in England,* which was about to be translated into English and which, no doubt, provoked this comparison. (The article was later incorporated in the American edition of 1887 and the English edition of 1892.) Having earlier predicted the inevitable pauperization of the working class and the imminent outbreak of revolution, Engels had to confront the fact that forty years later neither of these prophecies had come to pass. Not only had there been no revolution, none was even on the horizon. So far from being in a state of total pauperization ("immiseration," in Marxist terminology), a great many workers had experienced a marked improvement in their condition. That improvement, Engels now explained, was limited to two "protected" groups: factory workers whose gains were secured by legislation, such as laws limiting the hours of work, which "restored their physical constitution and endowed them with a moral superiority"; and workers belonging to trade unions, who succeeded in "enforcing for themselves a relatively comfortable position" and who now constituted an "aristocracy among the working class."[15]

For this working-class "aristocracy" Engels had nothing but contempt. "They are the model working men of Messrs. Leone Levi & Giffen, and they are very nice people indeed nowadays to deal with, for any sensible capitalist in particular and for the whole capitalist class in general." While their conditions had "remarkably improved" as a result of their privileged position, the conditions of most of the working class had deteriorated. "As to the great mass of the working people, the state of misery and insecurity in which they live now is as low as ever, if not lower." This was inevitable, for the laws of capitalism, which reduced the value of their labor to the barest minimum necessary for their subsistence, had the effect of "the irresistible force of an automatic engine which crushes them between its wheels."[16]

Engels did not explain how the state of that "great mass" of workers could have deteriorated so much in view of the fact that a good many of them were factory workers "protected" by social legislation. At one point he did concede a "temporary improvement even for the great mass."[17] But he went on to predict that the improvement would be reversed with the introduction of new machinery and the arrival of new immigrants. Moreover, it was only so long as England maintained its "industrial monopoly" that the great mass shared in the benefits of that monopoly. Once the monopoly was lost, the whole of the working class—"the privileged and leading minority not excepted"—would be reduced to the level of the proletariat abroad. "And that," Engels concluded, "is the reason why there will be Socialism again in England."[18]*

A later generation of Marxists and Leninists, confronted with the discouraging fact of the absence of any mass revolutionary movement in Victorian England (neither the socialist groups nor the Labour Party qualified as revolutionary), invoked the idea of the labor aristocracy to account for the "reformism" and "class collaborationism" of the working class. This theory, revived by Eric Hobsbawm in 1954, has since become a staple of historical controversy.[20] Like Engels and Lenin, Hobsbawm identified the labor aristocracy largely with the old craft trade unions; like them, he regarded it as a politically conservative influence; and like them, he saw it as evidence of a large and growing gap within the working class between 1840 and 1890 (and possibly for the quarter of a century after that).[21] In effect the concept has served as a modified version of the theory of immiseration. If the working class as a whole was not being pauperized, a large part of the working class was getting relatively (although not absolutely) poorer.

More recently Hobsbawm has reaffirmed the validity and utility of the concept of the labor aristocracy, while diminishing the significance he and other Marxists had attached to it. He no longer insists upon the regressive political character of the labor aristocracy, nor does he mention the widening gap between the labor aristocracy and the rest of the working class. (He explains that he had not been entirely candid in his original essay because he had not wanted to "stress views which were then heterodox among Marxists" and because he preferred to "engage in polemics against those who, on anti-Marxist grounds, denied the existence or analytical value of the concept of a labor aristocracy."[22]) Another radical historian, Gareth Stedman Jones, has gone further in abandoning the concept, which he now finds "ambiguous and unsatisfactory"—not so much an explanation as evidence of "a vacant area where an explanation should be."[23] Long before this retreat by Marxists, Henry Pelling had argued that the idea of the labor aristocracy was so problematic and unuseful that it was time to retire it. It could not, for example, accommodate the

---

* Reprinting parts of this article in 1892, in the preface to the English edition, Engels took credit for predicting the rise of socialism that had taken place in the preceding decade. But he did not repeat his prediction of immiseration. Instead he took satisfaction in the fact that the East End of London was no longer the "immense haunt of misery" it had once been, a "stagnant pool" of "torpid despair," and had become instead the home of the unskilled but now organized working class.[19]

familiar case of a family in which several members worked at unskilled or
semiskilled jobs and thus enjoyed a higher standard of living than a
skilled worker in a unionized trade.[24]

THE TERM "labor aristocracy" did not originate with Engels. First used
in the 1830s and '40s as a synonym for "artisans," it became less common
in the following decades and was revived in the 1880s.[25] Even then,
however, it had neither the pejorative nor the ideological connotations
given it by the Marxists. Nor was it generally assumed that the disparity
between the labor aristocracy and the rest of the working classes was
growing. On the contrary, Alfred Marshall expressed the consensus of
informed opinion when he wrote that "the wages of unskilled labour have
risen faster than those of any other class, faster even than those of skilled
labour."[26] Taken in conjunction with his other finding—that the numbers of the skilled and semiskilled had increased relative to the unskilled—
the conclusion was inescapable: the gap within the working class had
significantly diminished. Bowley's statistics bore out this view: while the
wages of the London artisan rose by 11 percent between 1867 and 1897
and those of the provincial artisan by 26 percent, the town laborer's rose
by as much as 25 percent. The wages of the agricultural laborer rose by
a more modest 14 percent, but since this was a period of decline in the
agricultural population, large numbers of agricultural laborers were now
to be found in the ranks of the better-paid town laborers.[27]

Changing occupation patterns reinforced these findings, for there was
a movement not only from the country to the town but also within the
town, largely as a result of the expansion of service occupations. Bowley
estimated that even if there had been no change in occupations in the last
two decades of the century, there would have been an average increase of
money wages of 15 percent; as it was, because of the "very considerable
flow from low-paid to better-paid trade," the increase was 30 percent.[28]
The flow extended into the "lower middle class"—a term becoming increasingly common to accommodate the large numbers of superior clerks,
foremen, and managers who fitted uneasily into the category of "working
class" or even "labor aristocracy."[29]

To criticize the concept of the labor aristocracy on the ground that it
has become ambiguous and tendentious is not to deny the fact that there
were significant differences within the working classes. These differences
were clearly implied in the plurality of the term "working classes"—a
term that remained, even at the end of the century, more common than

the singular "working class." The issue is whether these differences, especially as measured by wage differentials, were increasing or decreasing. On this point recent scholarship seems to be confirming the view of Marshall and other contemporaries that during most of the last quarter of the century the gap between the skilled and the unskilled was narrowing.[30]

The larger issue is how to explain the "rediscovery" of poverty—the emergence of poverty as a new and urgent social problem—at a time when, as most contemporaries conceded and most studies confirmed, poverty was diminishing. If the problem seemed more grievous than ever, one explanation surely lies in the heightening of "relative expectations" that went beyond the actual degree of improvement, and in a sense of "relative deprivation" that was aggravated rather than abated by that improvement. In this respect, the problem was bound to get worse the more it got better.

The problem was also complicated by the fact that poverty as such was only part of it. There was no single social problem but a multiplicity of social problems, some of which were not reflected in statistics about wages or consumption but were felt to be so grievous as to outweigh all the other evidence of improvement. The most distressing of these problems were housing and unemployment, each of which impinged on particular groups of the poor in different ways and affected the quality of their lives in different fashions.

CHAPTER 3

Unemployment and the
Casual Laborer

JUST AS ONE historian speaks of poverty as having been "rediscovered" in the 1880s, so another speaks of the "discovery" of unemployment.[1] This is not to say that there was no unemployment before its "discovery," and no poverty before its "rediscovery." What was discovered, or rediscovered, was a concept that made that problem more abstract and impersonal than it had been, and at the same time more problematic and urgent.

It has often been pointed out that the word "unemployment" made its appearance only in the late 1880s.* Until then the familiar terms were "want of employment" and "unemployed" (the latter used both as an adjective and a noun, as in "the unemployed"), and, of course, such older expressions as "idle" and "out of work."[3] There were isolated instances of "unemployment" before then. Jeremy Bentham, noted for his neologisms and his penchant for abstractions, actually used "unemployment" in the late 1790s, in a manuscript of his plan for a National Charity Company; the word did not, however, find its way into the published version.[4] Another example dates from 1840 in a little-known book on utopia.[5]

The first entry for "unemployment" in the *Oxford English Dictionary* cites an article in *Science* in 1888. A more memorable example that year came in the testimony of Alfred Marshall before the Gold and Silver

---

* E. P. Thompson disputes the "legend" about the late arrival of "unemployment." "Cuckoos," he observes derisively, "generally arrive in these islands some weeks before they are announced in *The Times*." In refutation of that "legend," he asserts that " 'unemployed,' 'the unemployed,' and (less frequently) 'unemployment' are all to be found in trade union and Radical or Owenite writing of the 1820s and 1830s."[2] But it is only "unemployment" that is at issue, and for that usage he gives no specific examples.

Commission, when he complained of the inadequacy of the "official returns of unemployment." But he apparently attached no great significance to the word, for the rest of his testimony spoke of "want of employment," "irregularity of employment," "out of employment," and "unsteadiness of employment."[6] His great work, *Principles of Economics,* published two years later, devoted only two pages to the subject and did not refer to "unemployment"; that word was first introduced in the 5th edition of 1907.[7]

J. A. Hobson's *Problems of Poverty,* appearing in 1891, made no mention of "unemployment." Four years later the word was featured in the titles of two of his essays, "The Meaning and Measure of 'Unemployment' " and "The Economic Cause of Unemployment," and the following year in the text, although not the title, of *The Problem of the Unemployed.*[8] The word appeared in the proceedings—again not in the title— of the Select Committee on Distress from Want of Employment, which issued its report in 1895.[9] By then, the term was becoming part of the social vocabulary, but only tentatively and intermittently; one writer spoke of it at the time as "practically a word new to the English language."[10]

Only after the turn of the century did the significance of the term begin to be appreciated. William Beveridge's *Unemployment,* published in 1909, had as its subtitle *A Problem of Industry.* Later the Webbs were to describe unemployment as "a disease of the modern industrial system."[11] Unlike "the unemployed," which conjured up the image of particular persons who, for one reason or another, suffered from a "want of employment," the term "unemployment" suggested an impersonal condition resulting from impersonal causes. In the new usage it was the condition that was problematic, not the individuals afflicted by it.

As the problem became impersonalized, so did responsibility for it. The older terms implied that the sources and causes of unemployment could be found in the individual—his character, capacity, will, situation, chance, or misfortune. The new term directed attention to the larger forces affecting the economy and the nature of the "industrial system." (Although "capitalism" had entered the social vocabulary, "industrial system" was far the more common term.)[12] And as responsibility for the problem became impersonalized, so did the solution. Neither alms dispensed by individuals, nor the assistance offered by philanthropic associations, nor the benefits provided by trade unions or friendly societies were adequate or appropriate to the new problem. A problem beyond the control of individuals could only be remedied by forces and agencies beyond the reach of individuals. For social reformers this meant the intervention of the state; for Marxists it meant a radical reconstitution of the economy.

These implications, however, emerged gradually and erratically. In 1911 the *Encyclopaedia Britannica* introduced for the first time an entry for "unemployment"—"a modern term for the state of being unemployed among the working classes." The problem of unemployment, it explained, was "specially insistent" in the twentieth century, not because of its "greater intensity"—indeed, there had probably been more unemployment in the Middle Ages—but rather because of such other developments as the expanded facilities for publicity, the growth of industrial democracy, the application of scientific methods to the solution of economic questions, and the enhanced spirit of humanitarianism. It was these circumstances that gave rise to the demand for new solutions to the problem. The old remedies were "temporary expedients," whether by voluntary agencies or public authorities, which "more properly fall under the description of charity" (hence, for the earlier history of the subject, the reader was referred to the article "Charity and Charities"); the new were "permanent" remedies such as labor exchanges and unemployment insurance.[13] For the *Encyclopaedia* at least, the new problem, as signified by the new word, was defined by its solutions rather than by its intrinsic nature.

By the time of the First World War, "unemployment" had come into general circulation. But even then it was not consistently used; nor, when it was used, did it always have this special connotation. Well into the twentieth century "the unemployed" alternated with "unemployment" in public discourse. And "unemployment" itself was not as impersonal or abstract as might be thought. Personal characteristics—indolence, improvidence, intemperance, incompetence—continued to be regarded as factors, although usually not the main one, contributing to unemployment.

By the same token, the older terms used in the late nineteenth century, while they did put great emphasis on the individual, did not always do so in an invidious sense. "Broadly speaking," one historian has said, "the Victorian ethos ascribed such evils as poverty, destitute old age, and even much of the suffering from unemployment to individual inadequacies rather than to any more general failure of the social mechanism."[14] But this may overstate the case. Even earlier in the century, as José Harris has pointed out, commentators were by no means uniformly convinced of the "personal delinquency" of the unemployed.[15] They offered a range of intermediate explanations between "individual inadequacies" and the "social mechanism" to account for unemployment. That many of "the unemployed" were unemployed for reasons beyond their control, that their "want of employment" was often occasioned by sickness, "hard times," or the seasonal, "irregular," or "casual" nature of the trade—these facts were understood and were reflected in social policies long before "unemployment" became common. The New Poor Law of 1834, both in the rationale supporting it and in its actual operation, revealed a high degree of differentiation among the various categories of the unemployed. Some of these distinctions were coarsely expressed in the subtitle of Henry Mayhew's *London Labour and the London Poor: Those That Will Work, Those That Cannot Work, and Those That Will Not Work*. Mayhew and his contemporaries were fully aware that "those that cannot work" were in that condition for reasons of infirmity or old age, and that many of those who "will work" could not always find work.

EVEN QUANTITATIVELY, "unemployment" did not signify a radically new condition. This too was appreciated by contemporaries as much as by later historians. The *Encyclopaedia* made the point almost in passing when it said that the problem of unemployment did not become "insistent" in the twentieth century because of any greater "intensity"; indeed, it suspected that there was probably more unemployment in the early Middle Ages. Modern historians do not go quite that far back in time by way of comparison, but they do agree with T. S. Ashton that the emergence of the term in the late nineteenth century was not the result of any greater incidence of unemployment at that time.[16] Others have pointed out that not only was unemployment toward the end of the century no worse, in terms of intensity or incidence, than it had been in the "bad times" earlier in the century; it was no worse than it had been in the supposedly "good times." "Average unemployment levels," one study demonstrates, "may not have differed substantially in the mid-Victorian boom and the late-Victorian 'depression.' " In 1858, for example, almost 12 percent of union members in two trades were unemployed, which was a larger percentage than in the worst years of 1879 and 1886.[17] Other studies conclude that although the rate of unemployment was as high as 10 percent to 20 percent in the most afflicted industries in the worst of those later years, the overall rate of unemployment increased only slightly from 4.5 percent during most of the third quarter of the century to 5.4 percent in the last quarter.[18] For workers in unions, the figures varied enormously from year to year, reaching a high of 11.4 percent in 1879, declining to 2.3 percent in 1882, rising again to 10.2 percent in 1886, and falling again to 2.1 percent in 1889.[19] The Board of Trade estimated that over 13 percent of the skilled work force was unemployed in 1886 at the height of the depression, and little more than 1 percent in the boom period early in 1890.[20]

For contemporaries, as for historians, the great problem was to distinguish between the "irregularly" unemployed and the "regularly," so to speak, unemployed. Charles Booth, who would dearly have liked to provide statistics on this subject, was chary of doing so, because, he explained, he found it difficult to separate the "irregularly" unemployed from the "*definitely* unemployed"—the former being a normal condition in certain trades at certain times and the latter resulting from the decline of an industry or a depression of trade. In his first volume, published in 1889, he gave only one figure for unemployment, 43 percent, which applied not to the London working class as a whole but only to those in East London whose poverty resulted from "irregular" or "definite" unemployment, with far the larger number falling in the first category.[21] Seebohm Rowntree's figures for York in 1899 were even less satisfactory although they looked more precise. For 2.83 percent of those in "primary poverty," the principal cause was irregularity of work, and for 2.31 percent it was the unemployment (presumably long-term unemployment) of the chief wage earner. Since Rowntree made no attempt to provide comparable figures for the much larger class in "secondary poverty," these figures were virtually meaningless.[22] They do, however, suggest that contemporaries were well aware that "unemployment" was not a simple or monolithic condition attributable to a single factor or reducible to a single number, but a varied and complicated one—indeed different conditions that had to be distinguished (disaggregated, we would say today), even if they could not be precisely quantified.

THERE WERE WORSE years of unemployment than 1886, but it was then that public awareness of the problem was at its height. The previous spring the Lord Mayor of London had appointed a Mansion House Committee "to inquire into the causes of permanent distress in London, and the best means of remedying the same." The report issued the following January gave as the first and principal cause of distress "the want, irregularity, and low remuneration of employment." Other causes included the removal from London of some trades and the decline of others, the general depression in the country, indiscriminate charity and relief, high rents, immigration and the increase of population, and the "character of the people," especially of the "Residuum" which was "recruited from the incapable or immoral" and which had a "contagious" and "degrading" effect on the other classes.[23] If this analysis of the causes of distress was not novel, neither were its proposed remedies: emigration, industrial schools, better organization at the docks, greater control of charity and relief, the encouragement of thrift and self-reliance, more education and recreation, and a further investigation into the conditions of employment of the large class of the unskilled and the underpaid.

Although there was nothing very dramatic in the report, its release in January 1886, in one of the worst months of the decade, was itself newsworthy, and the "permanent distress" of the title had the effect of making the situation seem more grave and less transitory than the usual reports of a "bad winter" or "bad time." A trade union deputation to the Lord Mayor shortly afterward requested the establishment of a fund for the relief of the unemployed, whose numbers, he was assured, "were very few in excess of the average."[24] Two days later Lord Salisbury was visited at his home by a group of the unemployed urging the creation of public works. Three days after that, on February 8, a demonstration at Trafalgar Square, ostensibly of the unemployed but dominated by the Social Democratic Federation, turned into a riot that was soon dubbed "Black Monday." No one was killed or even badly hurt, but there were enough broken windows, overturned carriages, petty pilfering, shop looting, and general tumult to cause much alarm in the newspapers and rumors of worse riots to come.[25]

It may be thought, plausibly enough, that the Mansion House Fund for the relief of the unemployed was a direct consequence of "Black Monday." In fact the relief fund was decided upon before then, although the considerable amount of money raised was no doubt partly the result of public attention generated by the riot. It has also been claimed that the public responded so generously out of "panic," a "spasm of terror" that seized the propertied classes who tried to avert revolution by buying off the poor.[26] But these motives could as well have inspired punitive and repressive measures. The fact is that at this time, as later in the dock strike, there was a surge of sympathy for the poor, a sympathy strong enough to withstand the warnings of the Mansion House Committee Report, issued only a few weeks earlier, against just such "indiscriminate charity." Within a few weeks something like £100,000 had been raised by the Mansion House Fund and separate appeals conducted by other organizations and newspapers. A reaction set in only when it was discovered that relief tickets were being bought and sold and that much of the money was being diverted from the neediest. By that time attention had turned to another relief device, public works.

PUBLIC WORKS had always been a last resort in times of acute distress, and so it was now. Two days before the Trafalgar Square affair, Joseph Chamberlain, president of the Local Government Board, argued against a proposal to establish a public works program on the ground that the situation was not serious enough to warrant government intervention; two days after the riot, he repeated that denial. This rejection of public works was all the more telling because only the previous year Chamberlain had fought and won election on the basis of his (and Charles Dilke's) "Unauthorized Programme," a manifesto calling for higher taxes for the rich, free education and more public housing and services for the poor, better conditions for laborers and tenants, and other "socialistic" measures. By the end of February, responding to pressure from members of both parties as well as trade unions and socialist groups, Chamberlain had become privately convinced of the need for some kind of public works program. In a candid letter to Beatrice Potter, he took issue with a piece she had just published on the subject in the *Pall Mall Gazette*. (It was also a rather awkward letter, since she had recently rejected his offer of marriage.) He agreed with her that the Mansion House Fund did more harm than good, but he thought her suggestion for a labor registry to inform workers where jobs were available would be little more than a "trifling convenience." The problem, he said, was not an insufficiency of knowledge but an "insufficiency of employment." "Something *must* be done to make work. The rich must pay to keep the poor alive."[27]*

What Chamberlain now proposed was a public works program to be administered by local governments under clearly specified conditions. The work should be "poorly remunerated," at wages lower than that for

---

* The remark about the rich paying to keep the poor alive has been described as Chamberlain's "well-known doctrine of 'Ransom.' "[28] The implication, that his public works proposal was a strategy to forestall revolution, is not supported by the rest of the letter, which expressed genuine concern for the "suffering of the industrious non-pauper class," those workers who were unemployed and on the verge of starvation, yet too proud and independent to seek poor relief.

comparable work in private employment; it should be such as would not tempt the worker to remain at it longer than necessary; it should not be degrading; it should not compete with privately employed workers; and it should be within the capacity of any worker, whatever his regular trade. Only one kind of work met these specifications: "spade labour." In rural districts this meant the cultivation of land; in the metropolis the closest approximation to it would be work on sewage disposal, street cleaning, the clearing of recreation grounds, and the like.

It is curious to read the reply of Beatrice Potter, who only a few years later, as Beatrice Webb, was to become a prominent socialist of the Fabian variety. At this time she firmly rejected the very idea of a public works project. Such a program, she argued, even on the terms specified by Chamberlain, would perpetuate a class of dependent poor, demoralize and degrade the worker, and incapacitate him for "true productive service" once the crisis had passed. She also took exception to the idea that "something must be done"—that is, by the state. All that was called for, she insisted, was a policy of "sternness from the state, and love and self-devotion from individuals, a very old and self-evident remedy."[29]

Although Chamberlain was by then privately committed to a public works program, he delayed acting on it. Two weeks later he conceded that the government had some responsibility for the relief of distress but doubted that public works was the answer, since most of the "unemployed," he suspected, were of the class that shunned any kind of work.[30] Three days later, however, on March 15, he issued the famous "Circular" authorizing local authorities to establish public works where necessary and in such a manner as to avoid the stigma of pauperism. The Circular, one historian has pointed out, was neither novel nor practicable. Local authorities had long had recourse to public works in times of emergency, and the kinds of works specified in the Circular, such as painting and road-mending, were not suitable for winter months when unemployment was at its worst and had proved to be expensive for the government and demoralizing for the worker.[31] Another historian has described public works in this period as a "policy of charity relief by local authorities, without economic significance."[32] Yet if it had no economic significance, no theoretical originality, no practical efficacy, it did have, as contemporaries recognized, considerable social significance, for it testified to a widespread public concern with the problem of the unemployed—not yet the problem of "unemployment"—and with the willingness of the government to intervene to ameliorate that problem, if only by the old familiar means.

* * *

THE IMPORTANCE of unemployment, in the sense of "irregular" or "casual" employment, is suggested by one of the most dramatic events of the period, the dock strike. The dockers were the largest, most conspicuous, and perhaps most hard-pressed group of casual laborers. Their conditions toward the end of the century were not very different from those described by Henry Mayhew forty years earlier, when he depicted the selection process on the docks as a primitive, brutal struggle for existence.[33] If the account of the dockers in Charles Booth's work was less sensationalistic, it was not because conditions had gotten much better but because Beatrice Potter (who wrote this chapter) took a more analytic approach to the subject. After relating the history of the docks and their recent decline, she distinguished the various classes of workers according to the degree of the irregularity of their employment, explained their improvident habits and demoralized lives in terms of the irregularity of their work and earnings, and made it clear that her own sympathies lay not with those who preferred this irregular mode of life but only with those who were its innocent victims.[34] This account of the dockers appeared as a journal article in October 1887, was reprinted as a chapter in Booth's first volume in April 1889, and was widely and liberally quoted from in the press (often without acknowledgment) when the strike broke out four months later. Yet the article, perceptive as it was, gave no intimation of the strike that was to put the dockers in the forefront of public attention. Indeed the nature of dock labor and of the dockers themselves made any organized action seem most unlikely.

The strike itself came unexpectedly on August 14, 1889, as the result of a minor dispute over the "plus" (the bonus over the regular 5d. an hour) on a particular cargo at one of the docks. In retrospect, one can see it as the sequel to the strike of the match girls the previous year (which was also unexpected) and the successful demand for a reduction of hours (achieved without a strike) by the gas workers earlier in 1889. Both of these had led to the formation of unions—the match girls' union being especially notable because it was a union not only of unskilled workers but of women to boot. It was the prospect of organizing the larger and potentially more powerful group of dockers that seized the imagination of the strike leaders, Ben Tillett, Tom Mann, and Will Thorne. (The most prominent leader, John Burns, had originally been skeptical of the possibility of unionizing the dockers, and with good reason, in view of earlier failures to organize them.) The grievance over the "plus" quickly escalated into a series of other demands: a minimum engagement of four hours, the abolition of contract work and piecework, a penny increase of the hourly wage, and an additional twopence for overtime. Although the formation of the union itself was not one of the demands, it was the first and most momentous consequence of the strike—and, as it later turned out, not only for dockers but for other unskilled workers.

The other unanticipated development, which proved to be a crucial factor in the strike, was the sympathetic response of the press and the public. This was all the more remarkable because the dockers, unlike the match girls, were not the most likely objects of sympathy. Beatrice Potter found some of them to be rough and tough, prone to violence and drink, and others so abject as to seem indifferent to their own misery. Moreover, the very size of the striking force might have been expected to arouse fear and hostility. At its height the strike involved 40,000 to 50,000 men directly and almost twice that number indirectly by way of sympathy strikes; at one point there was even the threat of a general strike. Nor were the 15,000 pickets at the docks and the huge open-air demonstrations and processions (80,000 men were said to have taken part in one march early in the strike) calculated to allay those fears.[35] The pickets and demonstrators, however, were peaceful, the call for a general strike was withdrawn, and both the workers and the leaders of the strike behaved with great restraint and prudence. While the Social Democratic Federation supported the strike and some of the strike leaders were known to be socialists (they were later prominent in the socialist faction in the Trades Union Congress), during the course of the strike Burns and the others were careful to stay aloof from the SDF. And the strikers themselves were resistant and even hostile to the socialist rhetoric and banners.[36]

The strike even acquired a kind of religious imprimatur, first from Cardinal Manning, who intervened ostensibly on behalf of the many Catholics among the dockers but in effect on behalf of the strike itself, and then from the Salvation Army, which set up food depots for the strikers. "What with the Cardinal on one side and General Booth on the other," a reporter from the *Pall Mall Gazette* told John Burns, "you are quite in the odour of sanctity"—to which Burns modestly replied that he was not sure of the sanctity but he was confident that with "the moral support of all the best people going," victory was assured.[37] This was early in September, when the moral support of the "best people" had begun to be reflected in substantial material support. Banks remitted money to the strike fund without charge, the Post Office dispatched free cables, football clubs donated their gate receipts, the Salvation Army turned over the profits from its journal, and even the directors of the dock companies made substantial personal contributions.[38] By the time the strike was settled in mid-September, the English public had contributed almost £18,000 to the strike fund, and the Australians the extraordinary sum of over £30,000.* There was even a hint of divine intervention in the unusually fine weather throughout the five weeks of the strike. "A bitter east wind," one writer pointed out at the time, "or a drenching downpour, will take the courage out of a crowd in a way that the most fervid oratory can do little to counteract."[41]

The conventional interpretation of the strike sees it as a victory for the dockers, a decisive gain for what had been one of the most impoverished and demoralized groups of workers. Most of the dockers' demands were met and their union was firmly established; within two months the union claimed a membership of 30,000 and soon acquired branches throughout England and Scotland. More important was the stimulation given to the "new unionism" movement. Earlier efforts to organize unskilled and semi-skilled workers—the agricultural laborers' union, for example, led by Joseph Arch in the early 1870s—had been short-lived and ineffectual. The success of the dockers resulted in the revival of some of these older unions and the establishment of new ones. Within a year, over 200,000 workers, most of them unskilled or semiskilled, were added to the ranks of the trade unions.[42]

More important still was the fact that these unions were widely accepted as a legitimate, even necessary, part of the industrial system. If the *Times* and *Economist* were sometimes suspicious of the new unionism, other papers and commentators felt reassured that the growth of unionism, accompanied by occasional strikes, would have the salutary effect of correcting some of the abuses of industrialism without undermining the industrial system itself. Charles Booth, himself one of the largest employers of dock labor, took the occasion of his presidential address to the Royal Statistical Society to review recent developments on the docks. He re-

---

* It has been said that public sympathy for the strike began to "waste away" during the last weeks of the strike and turned to "outright opposition" in the following months.[39] The main evidence for this comes from the *Times,* which warned the union not to engage in "intimidation," by which was meant violence against the scabs. In spite of this the *Times*'s reports remained remarkably sympathetic. Even toward the end of the strike, when the union appeared to be rejecting a settlement proposed by the Mansion House Committee, the *Times* praised Burns for his judicious leadership and predicted a "hopeful" conclusion to the strike.[40]

called that when he had first addressed himself to the issue in 1887, he had found the employers content with a mode of hiring that gave them an ample supply of labor at low wages, while the laborers were unorganized and demoralized by what seemed to be a hopeless situation. In only five years, all that had changed. The unions had a "wonderful career," and if mistakes had been made and hopes disappointed, there remained a solid foundation to build on and an "inspiring record."[43] Booth's favorable opinion was shared by most employers, and not only on the docks. Surveys by the Board of Trade showed that in 1889 only 20 percent of the employers were hostile to the unions—their hostility measured by demands to restrict "agitators," prevent picketing, and the like. That figure rose to 24.6 percent in 1890 and 27.6 percent in 1894, when there were several bitter strikes, but by 1895 it had gone down to 18 percent.[44]

ANOTHER READING of the strike sees it not as a victory for the working classes as a whole but as a defeat for the lowest stratum of the working classes. Its effect, Stedman Jones maintains, was to reduce the casual laborers to the status of an "outcast" class. In a sophisticated version of the Leninist critique of "reformism"—according to which social reforms and trade unions are seen as strategies to forestall socialism and revolution—Jones interprets the unionization of the dockers in particular, and of the unskilled in general, as "a means towards the socialization of the poor." Where the middle classes had once thought of unions as a threat to the economic and social order, an instrument of class conflict and an intrusion upon the free market, they now saw them as "agents of self-help and moral improvement," thus of a pacified and "socialized" working class. The dock strike itself was "a cathartic release from the social tension of the mid-1880s."[45] Unlike the riots of 1886 and 1887, which generated fears of revolution, the dock strike was peaceful, orderly, law-abiding— and nonsocialistic. Feelings of apprehension on the part of the middle class gave way to relief, and relief to enthusiastic support. Hence the novel phenomenon of a strike subsidized by the City and "cheered on by stockbrokers."[46]

The strike served the interests of the middle class, this theory has it, not only by "socializing" the poor but also by separating "the 'respectable' working class from the residuum, the fit from the unfit." The "decasualization" of one class of workers, the more regularly employed dockers, had the effect of "weeding out" the truly casual poor, stigmatizing them as unfit, reducing their opportunities for employment, and (in the labor camp schemes of Charles Booth and others) physically removing them from the labor market.[47] For the casual poor who contributed so much to the success of the strike, the result was a "pyrrhic victory."[48]

It is an intriguing thesis, if only because it so completely reverses the conventional, commonsense view of the strike. Like all "social control" theses, however, it is (as a Freudian might say) "overdetermined"; it makes suspect any reform, any improvement of condition, any action with or on behalf of the poor. The "decasualization" of dock labor, the regularization of work, the improvement of wages and hours, the prospect of some longer-term security by means of a trade union—surely these were the aims of the dockers themselves, at least as much as of the middle class intent upon "socializing" them. If the casual laborers at the docks were for the first time seen by the middle classes as "respectable," if their strike was subsidized and "cheered on" by philanthropists and stockbrokers, and if as a result of that strike at least part of that casual labor force was "decasualized" and incorporated into the working class proper—surely a partisan of these laborers might be moved to commend these developments rather than deplore them as yet another plot on the part of the rich to divide and conquer the poor.

Contemporaries did, to be sure, distinguish between the respectable and the unrespectable poor. But this was hardly a new phenomenon. What was new was the expansion of the respectable class to include a large number of casual workers who had formerly been relegated to the class of the unrespectable. Jones quotes a contemporary who made just this point. The strike, he said, "proved that the average docker himself was by no means the 'failure,' the ne'er-do-well, the hopeless wreck of humanity, of popular fancy."[49] So far from creating a new "outcast" class, the strike had the effect of rehabilitating, as it were, a large part (although not all) of the old outcast class, bringing them into the working class proper and thus into the mainstream of society. To Jones, who takes a dim view of the "respectable" working class (hence his quotation marks around "respectable"), this was a mixed blessing, for such a class was obviously more inclined to conformity and quiescence than to socialism and revolution.

Jones's interpretation of the strike bears an interesting contrast to that of one contemporary observer with impeccable socialist credentials, who hailed the strike not only as a great victory for the outcast class but as a prelude to the socialist revolution. In the second week of the strike Friedrich Engels wrote a glowing account of it to his German comrade Eduard Bernstein. It was waged, he explained, by "the lowest of the outcasts, . . . a mass of broken-down humanity who are drifting toward total ruination, for whom one might inscribe on the gates of the docks the words of Dante: *Lasciate ogni speranza voi che entrate*." And it promised to change the fate of those "outcasts" and of the working class as a whole. "How glad I am to have lived to see this day!" Engels rejoiced. If "*this* stratum, . . . the lowest stratum of East End workers," could be organized, the rest of the workers would follow their lead, and not only in London but in the provinces as well. Moreover, the organization of this class, the least skilled section of the proletariat, would separate them from the "gutter proletariat" (the "lumpenproletariat," as he elsewhere called them), with whom they had unfortunately been identified.

> For lack of organisation and because of the passive vegetative existence of the real workers in the East End, the gutter proletariat has had the main say there so far. It has behaved like *and has been considered* [emphasis by Engels] the typical representative of the million of starving East Enders. That will now cease. The huckster and those like him will be forced into the background, the East End worker will be able to develop his own type and make it count by means of organisation. This is of enormous value for the movement. Scenes like those which occurred during Hyndman's procession through Pall Mall and Piccadilly will then become impossible and the rowdy who want to provoke a riot will simply be knocked dead.[50]

Some months after the strike, Engels remained confident that the "immediate" and "provisional" demands of the strike would be transformed into the "final aim" of socialism, even if the workers themselves were unsure about the nature of that aim. And having earlier predicted that the unskilled workers would be separated from the "gutter proletariat," he now predicted that they would resist the "bourgeois 'respectability' bred into the bones of the workers"[51]—that is, the reformist respectability that shunned socialism and revolution.

It is an interesting commentary on both Engels and Jones that half a century after the strike, the dockworkers were among the highest-paid and most privileged workers, forming, as one historian says, "an exclusive, almost hereditary caste like a labouring House of Lords, with riparian rights."[52]

CHAPTER 4

The Housing of
"Outcast London"

"THE PROBLEM of the distribution of wealth," Arnold Toynbee concluded a lecture in 1881, "is sure, in the near future, to take the form of the question, how to house the labourers of our towns."[1] It was a prophetic statement, for two years later that question did indeed become the paramount social question.

It is difficult to imagine how housing could not have been a major problem at that time, given the sheer force of numbers.[2] The population of England, having doubled in the first half of the century, fell just short of doubling again in the second, thus rising overall from 9 million to 32½ million. At the same time the country was evolving from a predominantly rural economy to a predominantly urban one, the turning point coming at mid-century. In 1800 there was only one city (London) with a population of over 100,000; by 1850 there were eight, and by 1900 thirty. London, of course, was *sui generis*, not only in Britain but in the world. From a population of a million in 1800 it tripled in the first half of the century and doubled again in the second; by the end of the century Greater London had 6½ million people, one-fifth of the entire population of England and Wales. (Paris, by comparison, doubled in the first half of the century, from half a million to a million, and increased by another 150 percent in the second half; by 1900 it had 2½ million of a total population of 38½ million, about one-fifteenth of the population of France.) Although the rate of increase in metropolitan London slowed down after 1850, the absolute increase continued for another three decades, and in some districts to the end of the century.

In London the physical density of population was reinforced by what the French sociologist Emile Durkheim called the "moral or dynamic density."[3] In fact, the physical density was actually greater in a few other cities. In 1868, there were 39.5 people per acre in London, 39.8 in Edinburgh, 87.1 in Glasgow, and 96.4 in Liverpool—far more, of course, in the central areas of those cities and still more in the slums of those central areas. But London was a natural focus of attention, not only because it was *the* metropolis—the premier city, the heart of the empire, and, as was often said at the time, the apex of civilization—but also because it was so overwhelming by virtue of numbers. If the density of population was greater elsewhere, the number of people affected by that density—the "moral" as well as physical density—was far greater in London.

London was as preeminent as it was—numerically, geographically, socially, "morally"—because it was a magnet for the rest of the country. It was to London that masses of people came in the constant tide of migration that was so conspicuous a part of the "demographic revolution." The rate of migration to London peaked in the 1840s and again in the 1870s, accounting in part for the huge population growth in those decades—and accounting, too, for the density of population in the already overdense areas. The movement away from central London started in the 1860s but did not make itself felt for at least two decades because it was more than compensated for by the new immigrants who settled in the older, cheaper, and more crowded districts of the metropolis. In the 1870s, when London had its largest gain in absolute numbers, almost five-sixths of that increase came from immigration. During the entire second half of the century, 35 percent or more of the population of London had been born elsewhere, the overwhelming number (about 30 percent) coming from other counties of England, with smaller infusions from Ireland in the middle of the century and from other countries toward the end. A late-nineteenth-century edition of Baedeker noted that there were more Scotsmen in London than in Aberdeen, more Irishmen than in Dublin, more Jews than in Palestine, more Roman Catholics than in Rome.[4]

THIS "CONCENTRATION" of population (the word "urbanization" had not yet been coined) obviously created an acute problem of overcrowding, with too many families living in the poorest areas and too many individuals in the same house or room. The problem was aggravated by the massive demolition of old houses resulting from the laying of railroad lines (which was itself a policy of slum clearance, the lines having been deliberately planned to run through the worst of the slums), the widening of thoroughfares, the expansion of the docks, and the building of new commercial facilities. The effect of clearing some streets was to make the adjoining streets still more crowded. Moreover, all these enterprises led to an increase of employment and thus to the immigration of additional workers to these areas. It has been said that the congestion resulting from the extension of the Great Eastern Railway from Shoreditch to Liverpool Street was the effect not so much of the displacement of population by the construction itself as of the new jobs created by the installation and operation of the line.[5]

The situation was not significantly relieved by the building of new houses. Between 1851 and 1881, 182,000 houses were built in London—this at a time when the population increased by almost a million and a half. And most of the new houses were for the middle classes. To be sure, the houses they vacated were taken over by the working classes, but there were not enough to accommodate the growing numbers. The ratio of persons to houses reached a peak in the early 1880s, when the movement to the suburbs finally began to ease the situation in central London.

The scarcity of housing naturally resulted in a rise of rents. Between 1844 and 1884—the dates of the two Royal Commissions on housing—rents rose as much as 150 percent. This increase was most grievous for the lowest class of the poor living in the densest neighborhoods. According to one witness appearing before the Royal Commission in 1884, almost half of those living in the "lowest parts" of London had to spend between a quarter and a half of their meager earnings on rent.[6] Two years later a Mansion House Committee reported that rents in London for a single room took one-sixth to one-third of earnings.[7] Whether measured by density per acre, house, or room (the official measure of overcrowding was two or more people per room), or by the proportion of income that had to be spent on rent, there is no doubt that the housing conditions of the poor deteriorated severely in the period between the two housing commissions.

The commission reports, as well as other contemporary evidence, point to another striking fact about housing—the redefinition of the problem itself. In the 1840s the housing problem had been perceived as essentially a "sanitary problem": the lack of drainage and clean water in the slums, shacks built alongside foul ditches (open sewers, in effect), common lodging houses that were the breeding grounds, as was often said, of crime as well as disease, and, of course, disease itself, appallingly dramatized in the periodic outbreaks of cholera and typhus. The last cholera epidemic in England was in 1866, and typhus deaths in London decreased from 716 in 1869 to 28 in 1885, this in spite of the rising population. (There were no typhus deaths at all in 1906, although the causes of the disease were not discovered for another three years—additional proof that the decline of the death rate was more a consequence of improved sanitation than of advanced medical knowledge.)[8]

If overcrowding was a more serious problem in the 1880s than it had been earlier in the century, the sanitary problem was very much better. Lord Shaftesbury, who had been agitating for sanitary reforms for almost half a century, recalled how much worse the situation had been, not only in the 1840s, when public concern was at its height, but as recently as the 1860s. Testifying before the Royal Housing Commission in 1884, he described the once notorious London slum known as Bermondsey Island as he had seen it only twenty years earlier.

> It was a large swamp; a number of people lived there, as they do in Holland, in houses built upon piles. Only two days ago I met a gentleman with whom I had inspected that place twenty years before. He put me in mind of it, and he said it was now completely drained and houses built upon it. So bad was the supply of water there that I have positively seen the women drop their buckets into the water over which they were living, and in which was deposited all the filth of the place, that being the only water that they had for every purpose—washing, drinking and so on.[9]

It would have been no comfort to the residents of the slums, although it is of some interest to historians, to know that housing conditions, even at their worst, were better in London than in Paris (which had not experienced so rapid a growth in population), and far better than in another eminently civilized city, Vienna.[10] Yet it was in London, not Paris or Vienna, that public concern was most aroused—which is also a fact of considerable historical interest.

IN THE AUTUMN of 1883, one of the most sensational documents of the decade appeared, an anonymous penny pamphlet called *The Bitter Cry of Outcast London,* which riveted public attention upon the problem of housing. This was twenty years after the first "model buildings" were erected, after a generation of social workers had been trained by Octavia Hill to manage those houses, and after the passage of three major housing acts.[11] Yet the pamphlet exposed and dramatized the problem as if no one had ever been aware of it.

The reception of *The Bitter Cry* recalls that of Henry Mayhew's *London Labour and the London Poor* in 1850. Then too, after repeated exposés of the appalling conditions in the rookeries of London—Royal Commission and Select Committee reports, investigations by half a dozen associations for sanitary reform, and an extensive debate in Parliament followed by the passage of a major Public Health Act—Mayhew's "revelations" came as a bombshell. They were revelations, commentators agreed, of an "unknown country," a "poor man's country," so wondrous and horrendous that, as one reviewer put it, "few histories can equal, and no fiction surpass them."[12] Reviewers of *The Bitter Cry* echoed those very words. Yet only a few months earlier similar revelations had appeared in a series of articles in the *Pictorial World* under the title "How the Poor Live."[13] Written by the well-known journalist George Sims, and illustrated by the popular artist Frederick Barnard, the articles created such a stir that they inspired similar series in other papers. The *Daily News* started two regular columns, "Homes of the London Poor" and "Evenings with the Poor," and set aside an entire correspondence page for a discussion of housing. The *Daily Telegraph* inaugurated a column on housing under the banner "Why Should London Wait?" Later that year *How the Poor Live* was published as a book, and Sims was commissioned by the *News* to write another series of articles to be entitled "Horrible London."[14]

Sims's "poor," like Mayhew's, were foreigners, denizens of "Outcasts' Land"; they were "natural curiosities" akin to such other savages as "the Zenanas, the Aborigenes, and the South Sea Islanders."[15] The "aristocrats" among them—thieves, cheats, and their female companions—inhabited luxurious houses complete with "blinds and doors," while the honest laboring poor lived in such wretched conditions that they could only drown their miseries in drink. "The gin-palace is heaven to them compared to the hell of their pestilent homes."[16] Worse yet were those who had no homes at all, who slept in lodging houses which were breeding places for crime, disease, and filth. Had he been writing in a medical journal, Sims hinted, he might have been able to describe other "nameless abominations" that took place in these miserable quarters.[17] In a household publication he could only warn his readers that "this mighty mob of famished, diseased, and filthy helots is getting dangerous, physically, morally, politically dangerous."[18]

Sims's description of the problem was more arresting than his solution. "Careless almsgiving," he was certain, was no remedy. Those who were really interested in helping the poor had to give their time as well as money personally investigating the cases they wanted to relieve and determining the individual causes of distress.[19] These private efforts had to be supplemented by "State help and State protection," designed to raise the "social status" of the laboring classes and ensure that they have all the "rights of citizenship" enjoyed by the upper class.[20]

IT IS NOT CLEAR why Sims's articles, which were provocative enough at the time, were overshadowed four months later by *The Bitter Cry of Outcast London.* Perhaps Sims laid the groundwork, preparing the public for yet another set of revelations that were all the more scandalous because they were not totally unfamiliar. The shock of recognition may be more potent, because more credible, than the shock of novelty. Or perhaps it was the title of the later pamphlet that captured the attention of the public. Or perhaps it was the naming of the "nameless abominations" that Sims had only hinted at.

In any event, "Bitter Cry" and "Outcast London" immediately entered the social vocabulary. If they did not quite become household words, they did become journalistic clichés expressing the moral degradation of the poor and the moral indignation of the rich. The auspices under which the pamphlet appeared also gave it an authority that made it instantly compelling. Although ostensibly anonymous, it seemed to bear the imprimatur of the London Congregational Union in the note suggesting that communications be addressed to the Reverend Andrew Mearns of that denomination. (Mearns is generally taken to be the author of the pamphlet, although some historians believe that it was actually written by another Congregational minister, William Preston, on the basis of information supplied by Mearns.[21]) A reverend, it may have been supposed, unlike a mere journalist, would not willfully indulge in sensationalism.

The Bitter Cry of Outcast London, the title page announced, was "An Inquiry into the Condition of THE ABJECT POOR." The contents amply bore out that subtitle, for they portrayed a condition of abject, unrelieved poverty, misery, and immorality. Anticipating the obvious objections, the author assured his readers that he did not draw upon "selected cases" but on typical conditions in "house after house, court after court, street after street." And in describing those conditions he insisted that he told the literal truth. "There *has been absolutely no exaggeration.* It is a plain recital of plain facts." Indeed, it was something less than the plain facts, for no respectable printer would publish all the facts. *"So far from making the worst of our facts for the purpose of appealing to emotion, we have been compelled to tone down everything, and wholly to omit what most needs to be known, or the ears and eyes of our readers would have been insufferably outraged.*"[22]

This assurance (italicized for better effect) made the revelations that followed even more sensational, for they appeared to be only the tip of the iceberg, with far worse evils lurking beneath the surface. As one shocking detail followed another, the reader was repeatedly reminded that still more shocking ones remained to be told—or not told, because the details were too shocking to be related. What was told was grim enough. The courts enclosing the houses, unpenetrated by sun or air, reeked with the "poisonous and malodorous gases" of sewage, swarmed with vermin, and stank from the putrefying carcasses of dead cats or birds "or viler abominations still." The houses, approached by staircases that were a menace to life and limb, were so decrepit that if the wind ever reached them they would collapse on the heads of their occupants; their only furnishings were a broken-down chair or bedstead or more often boards and boxes. In slums such as these tens of thousands of human beings were crowded together, a family or two in each room, sometimes with a few pigs for good measure.[23]

Even these houses were beyond the means of those who wandered the streets all day and took refuge at night in the common lodging houses. Here sixty or eighty people, of both sexes, might be found sleeping in a single room, with no means of observing even the "commonest decency." At a "lower depth" still were hundreds of people who lacked even the twopence for a bed in a lodging house and had to spend the night huddled on the stairs and landings; the "lair of a wild beast" would seem a "comfortable and healthy spot" by comparison.[24] The homeless living on the streets were better off than those condemned to these lodging houses. "Have you pitied the poor creatures who sleep under railway arches, in carts or casks, or under any shelter which they can find in the open air? You will see that they are to be envied in comparison with those whose lot is to seek refuge here."[25]

It was no wonder that in such conditions "the vilest practices are looked upon with the most matter-of-fact indifference."[26] The wonder was that the people were not even more depraved than they were. Thrown together with criminals, the most honest man became habituated to crime. Seeking to escape that grim reality a man readily took to drink, a woman to prostitution. In one street of thirty-five houses, thirty-two were brothels. In a small area around the Congregational chapel there were one hundred gin palaces. For children the public house was a second home;

there toddlers who could barely walk were taught to steal, and mothers could be seen forcing the fiery liquid down the throats of crying infants.

Yet even in the midst of all the misery and immorality, the honest poor far outnumbered the dishonest. Here lived the sewing woman who worked seventeen hours a day to earn sixpence or a shilling, and the seven-year-old child who received twopence for a gross of matchboxes. Out of such pittances and for such accommodations the poor had to pay rents amounting to as much as half their earnings. And even the social reforms meant to benefit them contributed to their penury; the Education Act, for example, obliged them to spend a penny or two for school fees for each child, pennies sorely needed for bread.

In gory detail the pamphlet depicted some typical "scenes of misery": a consumptive mother living in a single room with a drunken husband and five starving children; another mother nursing an infant, seated on the only chair in front of a fireless grate in a room at the top of an abandoned house, surrounded by six barefoot children; a hungry, ragged four-year-old girl left in charge of a crawling infant for six or eight hours until her drunken mother came home; a room occupied by a man, his wife, and three children, one of whom had died as a result of the "foul atmosphere" and, because the parish had no mortuary, was cut open in the very room where the family lived; another room with eight children whose father had recently died and where the mother was found lying in her coffin.[27]

Each of these scenes and many others like them, the pamphlet said, was based upon a newspaper account or was personally attested to by a responsible visitor or missionary. And each was typical, representing "the general condition of thousands upon thousands in this metropolis."[28] One missionary, reporting on one such scene, declared it to be a "fair specimen" of untold others. Beyond the misery actually witnessed by these observers was a good deal more that "no human eye discovers."[29] And the misery was spreading, the degradation of the "abject poor" overtaking all the poor. "The poor have been growing poorer, the wretched more miserable, and the immoral more corrupt; the gulf has been daily widening which separates the lowest classes of the community from our churches and chapels, and from all decency and civilization. . . . THIS TERRIBLE FLOOD OF SIN AND MISERY IS GAINING UPON US."[30]

After all of this, it must have come as something of a relief to the reader, but also as an anticlimax, to be confronted with the practical issue, "What it is proposed to do," and to find only the vaguest and most modest proposals. The author agreed with those who insisted (Sims was not mentioned but was clearly in mind) that some state intervention was required, although he pointed out that one such act of intervention, the housing act of 1875, had only made matters worse by raising rents in the cleared districts and increasing the crowding in the remaining slums. In spite of this, he called upon the state to "make short work of this iniquitous traffic," and (again echoing Sims) "secure for the poorest the rights of citizenship, the right to live as something better than the uncleanest of brute beasts."[31] He did not specify how the state would do this, only that it had to be done if his own proposal was to be effective. This called for the erection by the London Congregational Union, in the three worst districts of London, of mission halls where services and meetings would be held, visitations organized, and relief distributed in some "wise and practical, though very limited" form. Eventually other districts would establish similar halls and facilities.

If this proposal attracted little attention, it was because it was so trivial and mundane compared with the evils it was meant to correct—especially the one evil that stood out from all the rest. In a single phrase in the middle of a paragraph appeared the three startling words: "Incest is common."[32] The unmentionable had finally been mentioned, and it sent a shock wave through the community. Promiscuity, prostitution, "precociousness" (juvenile sexuality), illegitimacy—these were familiar enough and openly discussed. Incest, however ("consanguinity," as it was sometimes delicately called), was rarely referred to, and then only in the medical literature.[33] Three years after *The Bitter Cry,* the Poet Laureate, Lord Tennyson, was emboldened to utter the word in "Locksley Hall Sixty Years After."

Is it well that while we range with Science, glorifying in the Time,
City children soak and blacken soul and sense in city slime?

There among the looming alleys Progress halts on palsied feet,
Crime and hunger cast our maidens by the thousand on the street.

There the Master scrimps his haggard sempstress of her daily bread,
There a single sordid attic holds the living and the dead.

There the smouldering fire of fever creeps across the rotted floor,
And the crowded couch of incest in the warrens of the poor.[34*]

---

* A Poet Laureate, even so proper a one as Tennyson, might speak the unspeakable, but a woman writer might not. In 1888 Beatrice Webb (then Potter) published "The

*　*　*

INCEST WAS unquestionably the most shocking, certainly the most titillating, of the revelations that gave *The Bitter Cry* its special éclat. But even without that fillip, the pamphlet was sensational enough. It was also well timed for reasons its author could not have anticipated. Only two months earlier W. T. Stead had taken over the editorship of the *Pall Mall Gazette,* and he was looking for a cause suitable for his mode of "new journalism" (a term coined shortly afterward by Matthew Arnold).[36] *The Bitter Cry* perfectly served that purpose. On October 16 the *Gazette* published the first of a series of articles, editorials, and letters quoting extensively from the pamphlet, especially the more lurid passages, thus publicizing the issue while promoting itself. Other papers quickly followed suit. *Reynolds Newspaper* (which needed no lessons in the new journalism) published extracts from the pamphlet, which was sending, it explained, "a tremendous sensation and thrill of horror through the land."[37] Less sensationalist papers, including the *Times,* also quoted liberally from it, urging that something be done about this horrendous situation.

The one demand the papers agreed on was the appointment of a Royal Commission to investigate the housing of the poor. This, as it turned out, was the most significant practical result of the pamphlet. The *Times* called for a Royal Commission to determine just how representative this "outcast" class was. That the living conditions of the "abject poor" were miserable it did not doubt. The question was whether those were the conditions of the "working classes" and the bulk of the "poor"—whether, as *The Bitter Cry* insisted, they were typical of "house after house, court after court, street after street," whether the "honest poor" were forced to live in the same pestilential dens as thieves and prostitutes, and whether all the poor were being reduced to the status of the most "abject poor."

The *Times* was not alone in suspecting that the pamphlet may have been exaggerating the situation, not of the "abject poor"—no one questioned that—but of the bulk of the working classes. The Reverend Barnett deplored the "sensationalism" that he took to be as much an

---

Pages of a Workgirl's Diary," which was reproduced, she later explained, almost verbatim from her diary, with the facts disguised only sufficiently to avoid libel and the experiences "expurgated to be 'suited to a female pen.' " One of the expurgated sentences referred to the prevalence of incest in one-room flats.[35]

expression of self-indulgence and "self-love" as of genuine compassion, but he did not doubt the gravity of the conditions depicted in the pamphlet.[38] What is surprising is that there were not more skeptics, that so many journalists and commentators accepted at face value the account of "tens of thousands" of Londoners living in such bestial conditions.[39] Even patently dubious "facts" were rarely challenged—the assertion, for example, that the "abject poor" had to spend precious pennies on school fees. In fact, the law provided for "free tickets" for parents who could not afford the fees, and stipulated that no stigma of pauperism be attached to them. (Sims had earlier raised the question of school fees but had gone on to say that "the remission of fees is one of the principal items of business at a 'B' [School Board] meeting."[40]) The scientific journal *Lancet,* which had long been concerned with housing reform, so far forgot its own involvement with this issue—to say nothing of that of some notable philanthropists and social workers—as to claim that until the appearance of *The Bitter Cry* everyone else had "preached almost to deaf ears" and had "scarcely ruffled the conscience of political men."[41]

Among those political men whose consciences had long been ruffled by this issue was Lord Salisbury. He had raised it in his first electoral address as far back as 1853, had written about it in the *Saturday Review* in the 1850s and '60s, and had referred to it in his speeches since becoming leader of the Conservative Party in 1881, most recently in a speech at Birmingham in March 1883. In November, perhaps inspired by *The Bitter Cry,* he published an article on the same subject that was far less dramatic (it was simply entitled "Labourers' and Artisans' Dwellings"), but perhaps for that reason all the more influential among serious reformers. It confirmed the fact of serious overcrowding and called for specific measures of reform: government loans at low rates of interest, stricter supervision of speculative builders, housing to be made available by factories for their employees, and in general a larger degree of public as well as private action to remedy conditions in the slums.[42]

In one respect Salisbury's article proved to be more sensational than *The Bitter Cry.* No one accused the latter of being "socialistic" or "collectivist." But this charge was leveled repeatedly against Salisbury. The *Times* said that his article "stated with new force the chief argument in favour of State intervention"; the *Manchester Guardian* condemned it as "State Socialism pure and simple"; and the *Pall Mall Gazette* pronounced it a "final and decisive repudiation" of laissez-faire and the beginning of a "new epoch" in social affairs. "Liberal doctrinaires and conservatives of the old school," the *Gazette* gloated, "will gnash their teeth over the sudden plunge of the leader of a great party into the turbid waters of State socialism."[43]

In the course of his article, Salisbury had alluded to the urgent need for more precise information. After Parliament reassembled early the next year he moved the appointment of a Royal Commission to inquire into the extent of overcrowding and the best means of correcting it. At the risk, he said, of being charged with socialism, he threw down the gauntlet to his laissez-faire critics by declaring that "there are no absolute truths or principles in politics"[44]—thus preparing the way for the legislation that might result from such a commission.

THE ROYAL COMMISSION concluded that overcrowding affected the "honest poor" as well as the dishonest, but qualified that finding by pointing out that while the housing conditions of the poor had become worse, there had been great improvement in other conditions of their life and work.[45] The commission report, however, was almost as impressionistic as *The Bitter Cry* in the way it collected and presented its evidence. Witnesses reported on the prevalence of the "one-room system" and even the "one-bed system," and gave examples of six or eight people sharing a single room or bed, but there was no attempt to determine how many or what proportion of the poor lived under such conditions. One of the few bits of statistical information (much quoted by later historians) was the proportion of income that went for the payment of rent. But the report did not explain how this one witness, a school inspector, arrived at such remarkably precise figures: 88 percent of the poor paid more than one-fifth of their income in rent, 46 percent one-fourth to one-half, 42 percent one-fourth to one-fifth, and 12 percent less than one-fifth.[46]

While witnesses made much of the immorality caused by overcrowding, some attributed the "worst phases of immorality" to other causes, such as drunkenness.[47] The "worst phase," of course, was incest. Citing the notorious statement in *The Bitter Cry,* "Incest is common," the report quoted one observer who testified that the one-room system was responsible for "every case of incest" he had come across (without specifying how many such cases there were). Other witnesses, however, denied knowledge of any such cases. The vicar of St. Paul's said that inquiries on just this point had been made of missionaries, visitors, doctors, and other people intimately acquainted with the poorest neighborhoods. "The testimony of all these, without exception, is that they have never known a single case of it. They have heard of cases but have never known a case."[48]

Royal Commissions are often suspected, and with good reason, of being devices to defuse public sentiment and delay or forestall action. In Victorian England they were more often the opposite. They were initiated and often dominated by reformers who not only wanted to call attention to a social problem but who had a fairly good idea of what legislative measures should be taken to solve that problem. In some cases Royal Commissions actually created the social agenda. This was true of the Housing Commission. It defined the problem as overcrowding rather than sanitation (noting that earlier attempts to improve sanitation had led to greater overcrowding); it claimed that the problem was so widespread and serious as to require public action; and it proposed the means of ameliorating it. The *Pall Mall Gazette* hailed the report as "epoch-making": "There is nothing which the most advanced school of state socialists have ever dreamed of which is not found advocated in principle if not pushed to its extremist [sic] application within the corners of the report."[49]

The Housing Act passed in 1885 was based largely on the commission's recommendations. If it did not go as far as some would have liked (it did not apply to rural housing, nor did it alter the leasehold system that was said to contribute to the deterioration of houses), it went far enough to cause considerable debate in and outside Parliament and to raise the familiar specter of "socialism." On the surface the act looked deceptively modest, for it seemed only to be revising existing laws. It extended the Lodging Houses Act of 1851, which had applied only to common lodging houses, to all working-class dwellings; it moved responsibility for the enforcement of the act from the local vestries (where a majority vote was required) to the Metropolitan Board of Works and the Commissioners of Sewers (which had no such restrictions); and it amended other laws to strengthen the administrative agencies in their dealings both with landlords and with local authorities.

To some contemporaries the cumulative effect of these changes was momentous—nothing less than an invitation to socialism. This judgment has been echoed by one historian who sees the act as the beginning of a "new awareness, a new era." By sanctioning house building and ownership by the London government, Anthony Wohl says, Parliament gave its "stamp of approval to municipal socialism in housing."[50] Such a policy was actually initiated four years later when the London County Council started to build large blocks of flats to rehouse those evicted by its slum-clearance projects. Ten years after that, that authority of the LCC was extended to permit it to build houses for all workers, including those who had not been evicted.[51]

Whatever the practical effects of the Royal Commission in bringing about "municipal socialism in housing," it did not discharge one of its primary missions: to provide reliable, objective information about "the housing of the working classes." Its report was, in fact, less informative and far less systematic or analytic than comparable reports earlier in the century—most notably, the Poor Law Report of 1834 that had made the kinds of distinctions (between "pauper" and "poor," for example) which not only determined social policy on this particular issue but defined social problems and policies in general.[52] That contemporaries were well aware of these distinctions was implied in the announcement by the *Pall Mall Gazette,* shortly before the appointment of the Royal Commission, that in conducting its own investigation of working-class housing, it deliberately chose to focus on a district of London that was not a slum area. The four-part series, entitled "The Housing of London Workmen—Not in the Slums," turned out to be no more systematic or factual than most such journalistic enterprises. But it did point to the need to inquire into "typical" conditions rather than "fearful examples," and to put the slum population in the context of the working classes as a whole. "What is wanted now," the *Gazette* declared, "is not more sensation but more light. It is for this reason that we have always advocated a Royal Commission."[53]

The Royal Commission did not fulfill that charge. Although it purported to be an inquiry into "the housing of the working classes," both the witnesses and the report itself spoke more often of the "poor" than of the "working classes," and did not distinguish between the "poor" and the "abject poor." Nor did it confront the question of whether those "fearful examples," were typical or exceptional. What it did do, however, was to focus attention once more upon the housing of the poor, giving it the official status, so to speak, of a "social problem," thus making it a legitimate subject for state intervention.

CHAPTER 5

The "Great Depression" and
the "Great Decline"

APART FROM THE serious problem of housing, the "condition-of-England question," as Carlyle earlier baptized it, had demonstrably improved in the latter part of the century. In his book of that title, C. F. G. Masterman, a radical then known as a "New Liberal," admitted as much. "Certainly by all material and tangible tests—income, prices, security, comfort, addition to leisure and wages—the bulk of the people of this country have advanced so incredibly since the 'Hungry Forties' that the reality of those days would appear to the present generation but as bad dreams." Yet in spite of that enormous increase of "life's comforts and material satisfactions," Masterman observed, the "proletariat" was in a state of discontent that one could "neither appease nor forget."[1]

One of the many paradoxes in this situation was the fact that this "material and tangible" improvement in the condition of the working classes should be taking place in the period now known as the "Great Depression." To a generation familiar with another Great Depression, the term suggests a time of severe distress, prolonged unemployment, and a poverty so acute as to be tantamount to pauperism.

The word "depression" was common throughout the century and contemporaries had all too much occasion to use it—in 1816, 1819, 1826–27, 1830–31, 1842–43, 1848–49, 1857, and 1866. But never before did it have the kind of official recognition and status that it acquired from the Royal Commissions appointed to inquire into the state of the economy following the agricultural depression of 1873 and the trade and industrial depressions of 1879 and 1886. It remained for historians, however, to conflate these depressions into the "Great Depression," and to apply that term to almost the whole of the last quarter of the century. (While the label is sometimes used more sparingly to describe the period of 1873 to 1886, it is often extended to 1896.)[2]

For most of this time the great majority of workers, as has been shown, fared better than ever before. Prices fell sharply and continuously in the last quarter of the century, with the result that real wages, taking unemployment into account, rose 1.85 percent a year; only between 1877 and 1879 was there a relatively small decline in real wages. Even in agriculture, where the depression was most serious and most prolonged, the laborers were in a relatively good condition. Those who left the farm enjoyed the increase of wages that came with industrial employment, while those who remained enjoyed the increase of wages that came with the scarcity of labor. One historian has described the improvement in the condition of the agricultural laborer achieved in this "unspectacular" way—not by trade union action or government legislation but by the undirected effects of the economy—as "one of the most impressive events of its time."[3] In this judgment he was echoing the Royal Commission *Report on the Agricultural Labourer,* which declared that "a quiet economic revolution, accomplished with little aid from legislation, has transferred to the labourers from one-fourth to one-third of the profit which the landowners and farmers then received from cultivation of the land."[4]

In speaking of the transfer of profits from landowners to laborers, the Royal Commission was echoing the opinion common at the time, and since confirmed by historians, that the agricultural depression affected landlords more than laborers (and some landlords more than others).[5] Similarly the industrial depression, as Alfred Marshall pointed out in his testimony before the Precious Metals Commission in 1887, affected businessmen more than workers. The country, Marshall said, was experiencing "a depression of prices, a depression of interest, and a depression of profits"—but not, he added, "any considerable depression in any other respect."[6] Later economists and historians may differ with Marshall on the causes of the depression, but they agree that it had a more adverse effect on prices, interest, and profits than on wages.[7] The recent demythologizing of the "Myth of the Great Depression" has been concerned more with questions of productivity and investment than with wages and unemployment. The quarrel between "pessimists" and "optimists" has been not over the condition of the working classes but over the condition of the economy and industry.

This does not mean that there were no depressed groups among the working classes—"slop" workers, "sweated" workers, "casual" laborers, the "residuum," the aged. Even among regularly employed workers, there were depressed seasons and years when unemployment rose and wages fell. And there was always, at least until the situation began to improve toward the end of the century, the wretched housing situation. But these conditions, however grievous, did not add up, for the working classes as a whole, to a "Great Depression."*

One of the least remarked upon but most intriguing aspects of Victorian England is the contrast between the "Great Depression" and the "Golden Age" that had preceded it. The theme of a "Golden Age" was first inspired by the Crystal Palace Exhibition of 1851 and was sustained through that decade and much of the next by the mood of exhilaration generated by that event.[9] For the working classes, however, that "Golden Age"—measured by the usual standards of wages, employment, and living conditions—was in fact less golden than the period of the "Great Depression." And the bad years of that "Golden Age," 1858 and 1862–63, were as depressed as the worst years of the "Great Depression." Yet in that mid-Victorian period poverty seemed so unobtrusive, so unproblematic, as hardly to qualify as a "social problem," while in late-Victorian England poverty emerged as *the* social problem, a problem commanding the attention and calling upon all the resources of reformers and philanthropists, social workers and socialists.

The "Golden Age" has also been called "The Age of Equipoise," attesting to the political and social harmony that distinguished it from the tumultuous decades preceding and following it—the 1840s and the 1880s.[10] Yet this "Age of Equipoise" was not notably an Age of Reform. It is interesting that 1867 should be taken as the terminal date of this irenic period, for that year marked not the end but the beginning of a process of reform that led to the incorporation of the working classes into the political life of the nation. The Reform Acts of 1867 and 1884 enfranchised the bulk of the working classes, rural as well as urban (with the exception of women); the Redistribution Act of 1885 virtually implemented the old Chartist principle of equal electoral districts; local government was turned over to elected county councils; labor leaders became Members of Parliament and even, in one instance, a member of the cabinet; and workers were invited to serve on local government committees and Royal Commissions.[11]

Yet it was just then, in the last decades of the century, when the

---

* It has been pointed out that those workers who enjoyed regular employment and a rise in real wages might be unaware of their good fortune. At a time when real wages reflected falling prices more than rising money wages, it was the housewife who appreciated the benefits of lower prices while the wage earner knew only that his pay packet had not increased and might even have decreased.[8]

working classes were becoming not only the beneficiaries of a more benevolent political system but also the possessors of political power, and
when their conditions were improving by relative as well as absolute
standards (relative both to the middle classes and to the "labor aristocracy"), that the age lost whatever equanimity it had had and took on a
frenetic quality. In a massive surge of social consciousness, respectable
middle-class people pronounced themselves socialists, and socialist organizations vied for membership and recognition with each other and with
a multitude of other causes and societies—land reform leagues, charitable
associations, settlement houses, model building projects, children's
homes, "missions" to the poor. And all of these, in turn, produced a
massive number of tracts, reports, exposés, newspaper and journal articles, casual surveys and ambitious research studies focused on one or
another aspect of the "social problem." Whatever the effects of the "Great
Depression" upon the economy of England, there was evidently no depression in the intellectual, political, or social life of the country.

THE "GREAT DEPRESSION" was accompanied or followed by what
might be called the "Great Decline." This too has been a subject of much
historical controversy. For contemporaries, the decline meant not only
the loss of England's industrial and imperial preeminence but also the
physical and mental deterioration of the "race," especially among the
urban population.[12] For economists it refers to the period of the "climacteric," when England experienced a lag in technological development, a
decline in capital investment and industrial productivity, and a less favorable balance of trade.[13] For historians (and journalists) it is the "English disease" that sapped the entrepreneurial spirit, debilitated industry,
commerce, and finance, and induced an unwholesome retreat from the
bustling city to the bucolic countryside.

   The chronology, causes, symptoms, and effects of the disease are all
in dispute. Correlli Barnett traces it back to the evangelicalism of the
eighteenth century, transmuted in the following century into various
forms of romanticism, sentimentalism, humanitarianism, and idealism; by
1870 these distempers, "like a clove of spiritual garlic, had permeated
British life."[14] Martin Wiener provides a less remote etiology of the
disease, dating it from the middle of the nineteenth century with the
emergence of a culture inimical to the "Puritan ethic," contemptuous of
materialism, acquisitiveness, competitiveness, and the other vulgarities
associated with industrialism, and anxious to cultivate a genteel and "gen-

trified" mode of life.[15] E. J. Hobsbawm has the decline starting in 1860 and (preferring, as he says, economic to sociological explanations) attributes it not to any lapse of entrepreneurial spirit but to "deficiencies of the private-enterprise mechanism."[16] Paul Kennedy agrees with Bernard Porter that a "steady and almost unbroken decline" began in 1870 and exhibited itself in political and military as well as economic affairs.[17] Aaron Friedberg puts off the "experience" of decline until 1895, and even then makes it only a "relative decline."[18]

The divergencies and inconsistencies of diagnosis may call in question the disease itself. Barnett has the failure of will setting in even before the industrial revolution got under way, making it difficult to understand how that revolution could have occurred at all, still less how it could have taken place precisely in those areas where evangelicalism, and with it the Puritan ethic, throve. Wiener does not take into account the animus against industrialism earlier in the century, nor the entrepreneurial vitality later in the century; the late-Victorian generation of Lipton and Boot, Beecham and Lever, Cadbury and Fry, Guinness and Bass can hardly be said to have been lacking in industrial or commercial spirit. Kennedy and Porter are obliged to qualify the thesis to accommodate statistics which do not quite conform to it, suggesting that the decline was relative rather than absolute, that it characterized some industries but not others, and that it was offset to some extent by considerable economic strengths and imperial assets. Friedberg's work is less disputable, if only because it is less extensive in time (it deals with the single decade of 1895 to 1905) and more modest in its claims—the subtitle emphasizes the relative nature of the decline. Other historians are more dismissive of the evidence of decline, whether in absolute or in relative terms.[19]

It is interesting that none of these historians ascribes the beginning of the decline to the 1880s, when poverty emerged as the major social problem, and none of them suggests that the decline manifested itself in the greater impoverishment or even the greater discontent of the working classes.* Yet there was something in that decade that lends itself to the sense of a decline—a decline reflected not so much in statistics of invest-

---

* Engels did make this point at just this time. In 1884 he explained to the German socialist August Bebel that since 1870 England had been losing its monopoly in the world market. "That is the secret of the present sudden emergence of a socialist movement here, sudden—though it has been slowly preparing for three years." The movement, he continued, sprang not from the organized workers in the trade unions but from "eddicated" elements among the bourgeoisie.[20]

ment and production, imports and exports, military and imperial power, as in public spirit and morale. It was in this context that poverty—again, not statistically measurable—came to the center of public consciousness.

THERE HAS ALWAYS been a tension between commerce and culture, between economic activity and the good life. In the early period of industrialism that tension had been mitigated by what seemed to be the ineluctable force of technological development and the immutable laws of political economy. As industrialism became more "mature," however, it lost its original, dynamic impetus and its natural, moral authority. This happened, paradoxically, just when industrialism started to pay visible dividends to the working classes in the form of higher standards of living, and to society at large in the form of civic and public amenities. Impatient with the rate of social progress, frustrated by problems that seemed to defy solution, eager to translate their good will into good works, some of the most thoughtful and articulate members of that generation began to lose faith in the "industrial system" ("capitalism," as it was less commonly referred to) and entertained novel ideas that went under the capacious label of "socialism." (If by later standards most of these alternatives were only minimally socialistic, the label itself was symptomatic of a lapse of faith.) Other contemporaries, equally thoughtful and articulate, resisted the call of socialism and sought to bolster the existing system by varieties of social reforms and voluntary institutions—unions, cooperatives, friendly societies, settlement houses, charities, and philanthropic missions.

Modern historians are in the habit of thinking of social reforms and private philanthropies as instruments of the status quo—as "safety valves" to deflect popular discontent, or mechanisms of "social control" to keep the lower classes passive and submissive, or devices to perpetuate the "Puritan ethic" and thus the capitalist spirit, or institutions to ensure the "hegemony" of the bourgeoisie. Yet there is a sense in which reform and philanthropy were profoundly, if unwittingly, subversive of the existing order. This was especially, and most ironically, true of philanthropy. Professedly committed to the industrial system, philanthropy actually operated outside of it; intended as a corrective for the system, it was implicitly a critique of it. In effect philanthropy announced to the world that it had to do for the poor what the system could not do for them. Thus the solution became part of the problem. Moreover, by enlisting in its ranks some of the most energetic and intelligent people—by creating a "class" of philanthropists—philanthropy diverted talents and passions that might otherwise have gone into industry and commerce. In this sense the philanthropic spirit, so conspicuous in the last quarter of the century, can be seen as yet another symptom of the decline of the industrial spirit.

Even the spirit of social inquiry, of disinterested research and analysis, may be said to have had the same equivocal effect. Seeking to explicate social problems, the inquiries unwittingly exacerbated them, giving them a greater urgency and gravity than they might otherwise have had. *The Bitter Cry of Outcast London* might be dismissed as a journalistic screed, but the seventeen volumes of *Life and Labour of the People in London* could not be ignored. However sober and careful Booth's analysis, however cautious and qualified his conclusions, the effect of his work was to legitimize, publicize, and aggrandize the problem itself, often in ways he himself deplored.

This thesis too—reform, philanthropy, and social inquiry as symptoms of "decline"—can be overstated. Many reformers, philanthropists, and researchers were, in fact, vigorous and successful entrepreneurs at the very time that they were engaged in other activities. They were also staunch and unambiguous defenders of the "industrial system," so that by their example as well as teaching they testified to its moral legitimacy. Regarding philanthropy as a necessary and logical appendage to a free economy, they pursued their philanthropic enterprises in the same rational, scientific spirit that they brought to their industrial enterprises. Instead of fleeing the city and taking refuge in the country, they deliberately immersed themselves in the urban scene. They were not lady bountifuls distributing their largesse from the manor house or country squires erecting maypoles on the village green. Some of them (the residents of Toynbee Hall and the other settlement houses) actually lived in the East End; others (Octavia Hill and her "rent collectors," the "visitors" of the Charity Organisation Society, the "soldiers" of the Salvation Army) spent their days working among the poor in the city slums; still others (Charles Booth in London, Rowntree in York) conducted their research by going from house to house, street to street, trying to take the measure of urban poverty.

The "Great Decline" carries with it a connotation of despair, of a condition that is beyond consolation because it is beyond repair. If there was something of that spirit in the Edwardian period, there was nothing of it in the 1880s. That generation exhibited an acute, an almost exacerbated, consciousness of social problems. But its social consciousness was accompanied by a firm belief in social amelioration, the conviction that evils were amenable to correction by good will and good sense. *The Bitter Cry* was not a cry of desperation; it was a cry of outrage. The appeal of Henry George's *Progress and Poverty* came not from its economic analysis intended to demonstrate the increasing poverty of the working classes (this was the most difficult and dubious part of the book), but from its promise of a simple reform that would solve the problem of poverty. Similarly, the dominant philosophical tendencies of the time—Idealism, Positivism, and what might be called Ethical Utilitarianism—were profoundly, perhaps incorrigibly, optimistic.

Even the proliferation of socialist movements was predicated on the assumption that social problems had, if not solutions, at least remedies, and remedies requiring no violent overthrow of the social order. The very ease with which so many middle-class people proclaimed themselves socialists—"We are all socialists now," in the memorable words of Sir William Harcourt—was comforting; if Sir William was a socialist, socialism could not be very subversive. To the extent to which the socialist movements attracted more middle-class than working-class members, this too was reassuring. Moreover, the heightened social consciousness did not result in an intensified or embittered class conflict. With so many middle-class socialists proudly parading their socialism, even the most militant socialists (themselves, more often than not, middle-class) found it difficult to maintain a posture of intransigent class struggle.

Late-Victorian England was a time less of social malaise than of social ferment, of an extraordinary plenitude of ideas, theories, and activities. At the center of this ferment was Charles Booth, one of the most interesting and admirable individuals of the time, as well as the author of one of its most enduring memorials. Booth did not so much "rediscover" poverty as "discover" the poverty unique to that time. And he communicated that discovery in a work that is still the single best source for the social history of late-Victorian England—and not only its social history but its moral history as well.

Book Two

LIFE AND LABOUR OF THE PEOPLE IN LONDON

CHAPTER 6

Charles Booth:
A Man of Property
and Conscience

BEATRICE WEBB described her cousin by marriage, Charles Booth, as the perfect embodiment of the "Time-Spirit" of her generation: "the union of faith in the scientific method with the transference of the emotion and self-sacrificing service from God to man." He was the epitome of those "men of intellect and men of property" who had a highly developed "collective or class consciousness," an acute awareness of those less favored than themselves and a sense of responsibility to them.

Booth was not only a man of intellect and property; he was an active and successful businessman. One cannot make too much of this fact (although one can distort it by suggesting that his study was prejudiced or faulty on that account). He was a businessman before he embarked on his great work, the seventeen-volume *Life and Labour of the People in London,* and during all the seventeen years of research and writing.[1] He was neither ashamed nor proud of being a businessman; he thought it perfectly natural and enjoyed the daily, active participation in the family firm, the Booth Steamship Company. Nor did he find the dual roles he took upon himself at all anomalous. It suited him to come home after a full day at the office or docks and spend the evening and well into the night working on the survey—this in spite of a lifelong frailty and illnesses that would have incapacitated an ordinary man for an ordinary day's work. (It is typical of him that he did not fuss about his ill health, nor, like so many of his contemporaries, did he enjoy it.) Beatrice Webb recalled his appearance when she first met him in the late 1870s. "Nearing forty years of age, tall, abnormally thin, garments hanging as if on pegs, the complexion of a consumptive girl, and the slight stoop of the sedentary worker, a prominent aquiline nose, with moustache and pointed beard barely hiding a noticeable Adam's apple, the whole countenance dominated · by a finely-moulded brow and large, observant grey eyes, Charles Booth was an attractive but distinctly queer figure of a man."[2]

Rather than the schizophrenic that some commentators have made of him—a man torn between the conflicting roles of businessman and humanitarian, or of businessman and social scientist—Booth was all of a piece, complicated but not contradictory.[3] The same beliefs and principles that were evident in his research and philanthropic activities governed his business affairs. What is even more interesting is how conscious he was of those principles, in his personal and public life as in his business.

BORN IN 1840, Charles Booth was the third generation of a Liverpool family of merchants and traders. He left school at the age of sixteen (like his older brothers and like most young men of his class in that community) to be apprenticed into the Liverpool shipping firm of a distant relative. After finishing his four-year apprenticeship (and after coming into an inheritance, on the death of his father, of £20,000), he set out for a grand tour of Palestine and Europe. The trip was tragically cut short by the death of the young woman whom he had hoped to marry, and he returned to Liverpool, where he and his brother Alfred started a business as commission agents in the leather trade. The firm later expanded into shipping and became the well-known Booth Steamship Company.[4] Charles was the more active member of the firm, with special responsibility for the foreign side; this involved month-long (on one occasion a seven-month-long) trips to the United States and Brazil as well as shorter trips to the Continent. He was also the more enterprising of the partners, seeking to expand the firm in new directions, while his brother favored a more modest, less venturesome business.[5]

Booth's business credo, which he consciously articulated and conscientiously acted upon, reflected the Unitarian traditions of his family and social circle. It was an amalgam of the time-honored ethic of honesty, fairness, and dependability, and of the modern, rationalist canon of knowledge, efficiency, and ingenuity. After visiting the grand mansion in Bourges built by the fifteenth-century magnate Jacques Coeur, he speculated about the character of that "merchant prince." "I wonder what was the secret—what the combination of opportunity and character that gave such wealth in some cases in those days. Honesty was one element I have no doubt—and I think a large mind another."[6] The comment tells us more about Booth than about Coeur; not many people would have assumed that that lavish mansion testified to a devotion to honesty. Booth himself was scrupulously honest and conspicuously modest and unostentatious in his way of life. Complaining to his brother of one of their partners, he took the occasion to reflect upon the combination of integrity and enterprise that made for a proper business ethic.

> Tom's idea, and the practice also, adopted in America and perhaps always hitherto in our business, seems based on the idea that it is our object to get the better of the men we sell to. To let them in for buying what if they knew what we knew they would not buy. I doubt if it succeeds even then; but it injures our business to act on this idea, whether it succeeds or not. It is not our interest to get the better of either the men we buy from or those we sell to—but to do the best we can for each, subject to a moderate remuneration for ourselves—and to give our chief attention to getting the utmost value out of the goods we deal in 1) by proper preparation and 2) by bringing the skins into use for the purposes they best fulfill.[7]

This was the credo not of a merchant prince or robber baron but of Carlyle's "captain of industry," who combined a zest for enterprise with an enlightened rationality—"self-interest properly understood." In the metaphor of a later generation, Booth believed not in competing for a larger share of the pie but in enlarging the pie itself, seeking profits in the exploitation of new markets, new technologies, and the more efficient organization and utilization of resources. He applied the same principle to his relations with his workers. His son-in-law recalled his saying, "It always pays to give the highest price you can afford in business"[8]—the highest price to workers as well as to suppliers. "We go on the plan of high pay," he once reminded his partners.[9] At a time when such practices were rare, he instituted not only a pension plan for employees but also a profit-sharing plan; annual bonuses, given in good years as well as bad (on the ground, he argued, that workers should be encouraged to exert themselves more in periods of depression than of prosperity), remained with the firm earning a high rate of interest until the worker's retirement.[10]

Unlike some philanthropists, Booth did not wait until he had acquired his fortune before embarking upon his philanthropic career. His social consciousness was not an afterthought, a diversion in retirement or a bid for recognition once he had satisfied his private ambitions. His interest in public affairs started in the 1860s when he was a young businessman hard pressed for time and money. He was active in Radical local politics, supported the extension of the franchise, helped establish a trades hall for union members, and, inspired by Joseph Chamberlain's Birmingham Education League, devised a similar pilot scheme for Liverpool, based on the principles of free, secular, universal education. When Herbert Spencer opposed the Education Act of 1870, Booth wrote a long, unpublished article criticizing him and defending a national, state-supported system of education as a "humanizing influence" in the lives of the poor.[11]

FOR BOOTH, popular education was the means not only to a more humane society but to a more scientific society, a society that would use science for the promotion of social welfare. In 1870, in a privately printed family journal, Booth wrote an essay in praise of Positivism, a system that "recognizes the existing evils in our social condition and offers a remedy." The evils derived from an unrestrained "race for wealth," which was productive insofar as it developed the physical resources of the world and gave value and dignity to work, but at the same time tended to sacrifice everything to blind competition and the creation of wealth. The remedy was to subordinate wealth to the public welfare, and this required an "organized religious influence"—not, however, the old organized religions, which were too divorced from modern thought and science to be effective as agencies of moral change. Only Positivism would suffice because only it embraced "all things human and divine so far as knowledge goes or can go." To be a Positivist, Booth said, one need not accept the whole of Comte's utopia. One need only adhere to the objective of Positivism, "the true welfare and right progress of the human race," and to its method, "the scientific study of all the phenomena of mental and social life." In this combination lay "the true solution of the problem of government."[12]

Booth's Positivism was a domesticated, tempered, peculiarly English version of that creed, with none of the theological and theocratic extravagances that Comte had imposed upon it.[13] He probably came to it by way of his cousins, the Cromptons, but unlike them he never formally joined the Positivist "Church" (or rather churches, after a schism in the sect).* In 1879 and 1880, reporting to his wife about Positivist meetings

---

* Charles and Henry Crompton belonged to the faction led by Henry Congreve, which dissociated itself from the parent body in France, while their sister Emily and

he attended in Liverpool, he spoke mockingly of the cult of the *Etre Suprême* and of Comte's concept of "ideal womanhood," but was otherwise respectful and sympathetic.[14] Three years later, he wrote a favorable analysis of Comte's *Positive Philosophy,* criticizing it in minor respects (he found in his own children no evidence of the fetishistic stage that Comte had ascribed to the mental development both of the individual and of the race) and suggesting that some of Comte's failings came from his being insufficiently Comtean.[15] For all his reservations, however, and his reluctance to join the sect, Booth reaffirmed his belief in the "Religion of Humanity"—to the distress of his immediate family, who were good Unitarians.[16] Among his manuscripts is a "Positivist Prayer" that opens with an invocation to the "Great Being": "Great Being, of whom I am a part, teach me to respect myself, and forgetting my separate insignificance in your greatness, strive to be your worthy child." The prayer goes on to acclaim the Great Being as an exalted embodiment of the human virtues of patience, humility, sympathy, and love.[17]

A personal testament of faith, written by Booth in August 1883, deserves to be quoted in full.

> I am a Positivist—by which as to religion, I mean that I worship Humanity.
>
> By humanity I mean the human race conceived as a great Being— and by worship I mean that I feel for this Being love, gratitude and reverence.
>
> By Religion I mean the double bond to the object of my worship and to others similarly bound. And to this bond and this worship I look for hopefulness, strength, and constancy in seeking and holding fast to the higher life.
>
> By higher life I mean that individual life which is in harmony with the collective life.
>
> I abandon inquiry into the origin of Humanity which I believe to be impenetrable, and also into the origin of the laws of its life and development; as I abandon also all inquiry into the origin of the rest of creation and of its laws. I hold as certain the fixed character of these laws. They seem to me as that "necessity" which the Greeks placed above their Gods.

---

her husband Spencer Beesly (translator of Comte and a prominent figure in the international socialist movement) remained with the group led by Laffitte. In their London years the Booths were good friends with the Beeslys and kept abreast of Positivist affairs.

Of the author of these laws, if they have an author, I know nothing beyond the laws themselves which I accept as the atmosphere in which I have to live. They seem to be consistent as well as constant but I find in them no trace of any active will.

The Great Being, which I worship and of which I am myself a part, has led, and now leads, its life amongst these laws, taking shape from them and from its own forces and forming between the two new laws.

It is these secondary laws which, if discovered and rightly understood, would enable us to explain the past and even foresee the future. And their study is for me "Theology."

I resolve to do that which I believe to be right, guided by the Great Being of which I am part, and trusting in that Greater Order in which Humanity lives and grows and will doubtless one day perish.

Standing between past and future and looking back, I thankfully recognise my great debt to Humanity, to my ancestors, to the crowd of the living and the dead whose influence presses upon me, and to those dear ones in whose lives I have made my home.

I also recognise the responsibility that is mine to live a pure, honest, and open life so as to transmit undimmed to others the best that I have received.

May my knowledge and love of that Great Being whose child and servant I am, help and strengthen me throughout my life.

Amen.[18]

That this creed was not an idle or academic exercise is evident from another manuscript written about the same time in which Booth translated this testament into personal, practical, even monetary terms. He reckoned that he had a "surplus income" well in excess of his needs, his income being £2,000 and his expenditures £1,000. Of the sum spent on food, £150, perhaps half represented the cost of "ill remunerated labour"; if the wages were doubled, his food costs would increase by 50 percent. That difference, of £75, he acknowledged as "a debt owed and to be paid if any way can be found to do it." Similarly his other expenditures would amount to 50 percent, or £500, more "if the world was as I would have it," and this sum too he would be pleased to pay if it could go toward "equalizing the lots of poor and rich" without hurting those it was meant to help.[19]

These manuscripts, written only a few years before embarking on his great work on poverty, show how intensely serious Booth's commitment to Positivism was, not only as a philosophy and "religion" but as a personal way of life. This in itself is not surprising. While some Victorian philanthropists, like their latter-day counterparts, simply lent their names to worthy causes, many of the most notable ones gave of themselves, in time, energy, money, and passion, to a degree that is uncommon today. What may give a modern reader pause is the way Booth translated his "debt" into monetary terms, carefully calculating a sum that would be just and affordable, discharging his responsibility to society and to his family alike. This too was typically Victorian, typical at least of a Victorian businessman unashamed of his calling, knowing and respecting the value of money and not shy about speaking of pounds, shillings, and pence. (In our own time, it has been said, money has replaced sex as the "dirty word," the unmentionable.)

IT IS INTERESTING to speculate about Booth's life and career had he remained in Liverpool.[20] He might well have produced a "Life and Labour of the People in Liverpool," just as Seebohm Rowntree was later to produce his study of poverty in York. But Liverpool would not have caught the imagination of the country as did London, the capital not only of Britain but, as the British thought, of the world—and now, as many came to believe, the capital of poverty. If London provided the dramatic focus of such a study, it also provided the stimulus required to undertake it. For in London, Booth found the kind of community and intellectual climate that encouraged him to embark upon so ambitious an enterprise.

Booth might not have found his way to London had it not been for his wife. Mary Macaulay came from a distinguished London family. Her father was Charles Z. Macaulay, a high-ranking civil servant; one uncle was the eminent historian Thomas Babington Macaulay; another uncle was the civil service reformer Sir Charles E. Trevelyan; and her grandfather was the famous Evangelical reformer and founder of the Clapham Sect, Zachary Macaulay.[21] The world of the Macaulays was very different from that of the Booths—cosmopolitan rather than provincial, church rather than chapel, a world dominated by literature and politics rather than industry and commerce. Yet there were bridges between the worlds, and it was one of these that brought Mary Macaulay to Liverpool in 1868. She was visiting her cousin Laurencina Potter Holt, recently married to the Liverpool shipowner Robert Holt, when she met another local shipowner, Charles Booth. In marrying Charles three years later, she was, in a sense, repeating the experience of her parents, except that in the previous generation it was the husband, Charles Macaulay, who was seen, at least by his family, as losing status by marrying Mary Potter of

Manchester, whereas now it was the wife who was marrying the provincial. The London Macaulays tended to look down on the Liverpool Booths as they had looked down on the Manchester Potters—this in spite of the fact that the Booths and Potters were eminently respectable. (Mary Macaulay's maternal grandfather, Richard Potter, was a Member of Parliament and a founder of the *Manchester Guardian,* and her brother, another Richard, was a prosperous railway director and company promoter who had moved to Gloucestershire with his large family, including his daughter Beatrice, later Beatrice Webb).*

When Mary Macaulay and Charles Booth were married in 1871, they settled in Liverpool, where the lively, sophisticated, strong-minded young Londoner found herself bored and unhappy. But her personal feelings were soon overshadowed by the more serious problem of her husband's health. Perhaps because of the habits developed before his marriage, of working from early morning to ten or eleven at night and eating erratically and inadequately, he developed a severe form of indigestion accompanied by a loss of weight, pain, and fatigue. He was finally prevailed upon, late in 1873, to withdraw from the business and go abroad for a complete rest. After two peaceful years in Switzerland, with no visible improvement in his health, the family returned to England. (There were two children then; eventually there were to be six, three girls and three boys.)

They returned, however, not to Liverpool but to London, perhaps to avoid the pressure of the Liverpool business, perhaps out of deference to Mary. After a year or so Charles resumed his business activities (a London branch of the firm was founded) and later took on the awesome burden of his social inquiries as well. He was periodically assailed by his old ailments and he always looked gaunt and sickly. But until 1905, when he suffered another severe attack and retired from business at the respectable age of sixty-five, he led a life that would have taxed a far younger, healthier man.

It was a happy marriage, for all their temperamental differences. Mary was more of an intellectual than Charles. She had literary ambitions in her

---

* A psychohistorian might find significance in the plethora of Charleses and Marys in this genealogy, especially in the fact that Mary Booth's father and husband were both Charleses. (In the following generation the youngest Booth child, another Charles, married yet another Mary.) The conventional historian will simply note the fact that Charles and Mary were among the most common names at the time, that children were frequently named after their parents, and that Charles Booth married a Mary rather than an Emily (his mother's name).

youth and after her marriage wrote a good part of a novel, some essays, and several Platonic-type dialogues. She later gave up writing, she explained, because she enjoyed her children more and because she disliked the idea of "publicity, success, criticism"[22]—an allusion, perhaps, to the inevitable, invidious comparisons with her uncle, the historian. But she never lost her interest in books. She was also more passionate than her husband about politics. Unlike most Macaulays, and the Booths as well, she was a staunch Tory, a great admirer of Disraeli and an implacable critic of Gladstone; when she wanted to express her contempt for someone, she could think of no worse abuse than calling him "as plausible as Gladstone, and almost as unscrupulous."[23] Her husband was more moderate and less partisan, generally favoring the Liberals on domestic issues and the Conservatives in foreign policy. (Toward the end of his life he became more consistently Conservative.)

They also had religious differences. For a time Mary Booth tried to accommodate herself to her husband's Positivist faith, but she soon reverted to Anglicanism. Although she was not especially orthodox or pious, she took comfort in prayer and declared herself "thrilled and moved" by the figure of Christ in the Gospels.[24] At one point their disagreements became so acute that he promised to "tread ever so carefully" on the subject of religion, while she said she would stop "argufying" and suggested that they "hold their tongues" before the world, for whatever their "intellectual" differences, they were "united in heart."[25]

That they were, in fact, "united in heart" is testified to by their children and grandchildren, who describe a harmonious counterpoint of "partisan eloquence" on her part and "cooler comment" on his.[26] During his frequent absences they exchanged almost daily letters. He consulted her about business as well as domestic affairs, she related the witticisms of the children and the choicest bits of her latest reading, and they expressed their love more warmly and openly than was customary among proper Victorian husbands and wives.

With his health on the mend and his spirits restored, the Booths began to take the measure of their prospects. In her usual self-deprecating fashion, Mary described their aspirations and limitations:

> I do think that the achieved success of a home and a future for yourself is something considerable; not enough to give you a place as a shining light, but quite enough to entitle you to respect and consideration. As for me, my impression is that I should still be the better for a good dose of bitter physic in the shape of taking down. I am very

conceited; I think more so than my abilities will warrant; yet I do
think that you and I may both of us not unfairly cherish the hope that
in spite of many drawbacks and weaknesses in our characters, we
have that amount of stuff and determination about us which will out;
and will eventually make its mark not in the world, but among those
who know us.[27]

Three months later Mary returned to the subject of "our joint purposes
and our joint action." Again, her tone was modest but firm. "At present
there are only beginnings, a fair and promising opening of such a serious
life of effort as we may hope to carry on to some perhaps not wholly
satisfying but still worthy and intelligible conclusion."[28]

"A SERIOUS life of effort"—Liverpool was serious enough but London
provided an intellectual ferment that gave public service an extra dimension, making it an exercise in mind as well as good works. Liverpool's
great philanthropist, William Rathbone, complained that his city's charities and relief agencies exhibited more "muddle" than "method."[29] There
was enough muddle in London as well, but there was also a conscious,
concerted effort to bring method into the muddle, to think about social
problems as well as act upon them. If London was, as the historian Asa
Briggs has said, not only the nation's capital but also a "centre of home-
produced discontents,"[30] it was also a center of home-produced remedies.
The Charity Organisation Society, the model dwellings projects, the
settlement houses, the varieties of philanthropic societies and socialist
organizations, each had theories about the nature of the social problem
and proposals for solving it.[31]

The theories, like the groups themselves, overlapped and interlocked.
Describing the "intellectual aristocracy" of the early part of the century,
Noel Annan found that "philanthropy was the magnet which drew them
together."[32] This was even more true in the later part of the century.
When Booth arrived in London he was drawn to the "philanthropic
aristocracy" as by a magnet—drawn to them not only by common interests but by family connections. Mary Booth's uncle, Sir Charles Trevelyan, was one of the founders and leading lights of the Charity
Organisation Society. Her cousins were the Potter girls, one of whom,
Kate, worked with Octavia Hill as a rent collector (*qua* social worker) in
the "model" houses. When Kate was married, her job was taken over by
her younger sister, Beatrice, who had earlier been a visitor for the COS

and was later to become a researcher, writer, and collaborator of Charles Booth (and, later still, the wife and collaborator of the Fabian leader Sidney Webb).

A prominent figure in this interlocking directorate was the Reverend Samuel Barnett, rector of St. Jude's in the East End and, later, founder of Toynbee Hall. (Kate's marriage was performed by Barnett in his unfashionable church.) It is not clear whether the Booths came to know the Barnetts through Kate (by way of Octavia Hill) or met them independently, but by 1878 they had become good friends and the Booths were frequent visitors to Whitechapel.[33] On one occasion during her husband's absence, Mrs. Booth had a long talk with Barnett about "work and waiting and enthusiasm." The question, she told her husband, was: "Whether it was better to mould an organization that did some harm but gave the world an example of heroic self devotion, or to deny oneself the satisfaction of definite achievement, hold one's hand, be true to oneself and one's convictions, and never move except when one is quite, quite sure, listening to every doubt, silencing no question of other people or one's own inner self."[34] Barnett, paradoxically, himself an organizer and activist, recommended a policy of waiting and thinking, while Mrs. Booth, "to draw him out," as she said, took the other position.[35] After another visit to the Barnetts, Mrs. Booth reported, "I have been all the afternoon at Whitechapel, seeing and hearing horrible things. Ach! what a world this is!"[36] It was a few days later that she wrote the letter raising the subject of "our joint purposes and our joint actions" and expressing the hope that their "serious life of effort" would be brought to a "worthy and intelligible conclusion."[37]

CHAPTER 7

The Science of Social Research

THE "WORTHY and intelligible conclusion" of Booth's life, the means by which he discharged his "debt to humanity," was *Life and Labour of the People in London*.[1] The immediate genesis of that work is not entirely clear. According to the standard version, it was the response to a survey conducted by the Social Democratic Federation which found that 25 percent of the workers of London earned so little that they were doomed to "slow but sure physical deterioration."[2] Booth is said to have been suspicious of this figure and to have undertaken his own inquiry in order to refute it.[3]

This account originates in a memoir written many years later by H. M. Hyndman, the leader of the SDF, who claimed that the survey had been "published in various ways" and had been greeted with shock and disbelief. One of the skeptics, Hyndman said, was Charles Booth, who had come to him with an introduction from the editor of the *St. James's Gazette*. Booth admitted that there was undoubtedly great poverty in the metropolis, but thought the figure of 25 percent exaggerated and "incendiary." Hyndman defended the figure: "I think I may claim for myself that I have never yet been shown to be wrong in my statistics, even when handling them alone, while here I had the help of capable friends." He added that he welcomed any further examination of the situation, whereupon Booth informed him that he intended to do just that, "to make, at his own expense, an elaborate inquiry into the condition of the workers of London." Hyndman congratulated him on his public spirit. The account concludes less graciously, with Hyndman complaining that Booth failed to give the socialists credit for calling attention to the facts that inspired Booth's investigation, and for not withdrawing the "imputations" he had cast upon Hyndman personally and upon his party.[4]

It is only recently that historians have thought to question this account, although Hyndman's memoir has long been known to be untrustworthy.[5] There is, in fact, no record of any serious survey by the SDF—only some random reports of unemployment (not poverty) published in its journal, *Justice*. Hyndman may have been confusing these reports with a series of articles published in the *Pall Mall Gazette* in February and March 1886. Introducing those articles, the *Gazette* explained that Hyndman had been challenged to produce evidence of the "terrible distress" that his party claimed to exist throughout London, and had suggested that the paper "test his statements by an independent inquiry."[6] It was this inquiry, conducted by the *Gazette,* not the SDF, which concluded that "a quarter at least of the population was always on the verge of distress."[7] The *Gazette* did not refer to any earlier survey by the SDF; nor did Hyndman refer to any such survey. Nor is there any evidence that Booth was inspired by the *Gazette* inquiry. He never referred to it; nor did anyone else when *Life and Labour* was published.[8]

Nor is there any evidence that Booth was inspired, as some historians have suggested, by a desire to refute the sensationalist revelations of *The Bitter Cry*.[9] Nor that he "committed himself" to the inquiry "in response to the crisis of February 1886"—the demonstration in Trafalgar Square known as "Black Monday."[10] Nor that he was provoked by the riots later that year; Mary Booth, reporting on one of them to her absent husband, accurately described it as a "farce."[11] Nor that "the first impulse of this labour" had come from Canon Barnett.[12]

More plausible is the suggestion, implied by Beatrice Potter in her diary, that Booth's interest was first aroused by the Mansion House Committee appointed in March 1885 to inquire into the "causes of permanent distress" in London. In her diary a few months later, Potter spoke of Booth "working away with clerk on the Mansion House Inquiry into unemployed."[13] While Booth was not a member of the committee and his name did not appear on the report issued the following January, he may well have been an unofficial consultant. It is entirely probable that he was the "experienced witness" cited in the report who suggested that "great advantage might arise from a careful and exhaustive inquiry into the nature of the employments" of the people of London.[14] For Booth was then engaged in just such an inquiry. In that same entry Beatrice Potter referred to his "other work of statistical sort"—an allusion to a paper he was preparing for the Statistical Society on the occupations of the English people.[15]

Booth became a fellow of the Statistical Society in 1885, his election coinciding with the society's celebration of its jubilee year and the award of the royal charter. Some of the statements made on that occasion were particularly relevant to Booth, for they elevated statistics to the status of a "science" dealing with the "structure of human society" and concerned with "moral truths" as well as "social agencies." One speaker noted that if this conception of statistics had not been sufficiently appreciated until now, it was because history had been thought of as an affair of rulers and administrators. Only when "the life of the people has entered into the domain of history" could "social statistics" come into its own.[16] The next speaker announced that this was already happening, that in the "social revolution" that England was experiencing, statistics was becoming the "indispensable ally of state-craft and legislation."[17]

It was in this milieu, inspired by the Positivist's ideal of a "science of society" and the statistician's ideal of a science of "social statistics" applied to the "life of the people," that Booth undertook his inquiry into the "life and labour of the people in London." More relevant than sensationalistic tracts like *The Bitter Cry* or impressionistic accounts in the *Pall Mall Gazette* was the sober, professional research of men like Robert Giffen. At just the time that Booth was working on his paper on occupations, Giffen was preparing another paper for the Statistical Society on "the progress of the working classes."[18] The meeting of the society when Giffen presented that paper was reported in the press on January 20, 1886— alongside an account of a meeting of the Committee on Metropolitan Distress. Booth was out of town at the time but his wife brought the notice of the Statistical Society meeting to his attention, and he subsequently read Giffen's essay with great care.[19] The conjunction of that essay and the Mansion House report, the one testifying to the "progress" of the working classes, the other to their "permanent distress," was a more provocative challenge to Booth than the figures bandied about by the SDF or the *Pall Mall Gazette*.

IN HER MEMOIR of her husband, Mrs. Booth described him as "ever more earnestly" seeking answers to the questions: "Who are the people of England? How do they really live? What do they really want? Do they want what is good, and if so, how is it to be given to them?"[20] Today the historian or sociologist is likely to ask a different set of questions: How did Booth pursue his investigations? How scientific were his methods and how objective and accurate were his findings? Did he impose upon his study his own moral or political prejudices, and if so did they distort his work?

Booth gave a good deal of thought to questions of methodology, in part on the insistence of Beatrice Potter, who had a more abstract turn of mind than he. Well before the inception of *Life and Labour,* she had decided to pursue the "craft" of "social investigator."[21] When she entered the philanthropic world, first as a visitor for the Charity Organisation Society and then as a rent collector for Octavia Hill, it was not so much to help the poor as to observe and understand them. She was candid and unapologetic about her intentions. "Unlike my sister Kate, who had toiled for six years as a volunteer rent-collector, I was not led into the homes of the poor by the spirit of charity." She was interested in the "condition of the people" primarily as a subject of "investigation."[22] This was also why she left the COS for the model dwellings project. The COS dealt with "cases of extreme destitution," whereas she wanted the "opportunity of watching, day by day, in their homes and in their workshops, a sufficient number of normal manual-working families to enable me to visualize the class as a whole."[23] "Mere philanthropists," she complained, "are apt to overlook the existence of an independent working class, and when they talk sentimentally of the 'people' they mean really the 'ne'er-do-wells.' "[24] On the one occasion when she met Octavia Hill, she argued with her about the need to keep better records and get more accurate information about the tenants, to which Hill replied that there was already too much "windy talk," that what was needed was "action"—men and women working every day to help the less fortunate.[25]

Beatrice Potter did not have to argue this point with Booth. But she did try to persuade him to formulate his ideas about the "methodology of social science" more consciously than he might otherwise have done.[26] When she asked him to describe "the right relation of personal observation to statistical inquiry,"[27] he replied that "the statistical method was needed to give bearings to the results of personal observation and personal observation to give life to statistics."[28] He gave a similar answer to her question about the proper roles of the "deductive" and "inductive" methods: "I seem to need both eternally and never could separate them in my own mind nor decide which moved first."[29] He admitted that he was less interested in such matters than in the task of determining "the relative character, or the proportion of facts to each other." Single facts and sets of statistics might be true, "yet entirely misleading in the way they are used."[30] Years later, delivering the presidential address to the Royal Statistical Society, he eschewed the kinds of reflections on the methods or state of the discipline that might have been expected on such an occasion and chose rather to present the results of his latest study of the dock-workers. He was not a general, he told the society, only a divisional leader. "Instead of a plan of campaign, all I have to offer is a faithful report of a skirmish."[31]

If Booth was impatient with such methodological questions as the "right relation" of induction and deduction, he had infinite patience with the right relation and proper proportion of facts. This was what Beatrice Potter recalled as the main lesson she learned from him in the "art" of social investigation.

> However accurate and comprehensive might be the description of technical detail, however vivid the picture of what was happening at the dock gates or in the sweated workshops, I was always confronted by Charles Booth's sceptical glance and critical questions: "How many individuals are affected by the conditions you describe; are they increasing or diminishing in number?" "What proportion do they bear to those working and living under worse or better conditions?" "Does this so-called sweating system play any considerable part in the industrial organization of the four million inhabitants of London?"[32]

Relations and proportions: these were so paramount in Booth's mind that they defined his very subject. He proposed to study not this or that class—paupers, or poor, or working class—and not this or that condition or problem—unemployment, or pauperism, or even poverty—but the entire population in the totality of its existence: "the life and labour of the people in London." It was a breathtakingly ambitious subject for a very modest man, but nothing less would have served his purpose, for nothing else would have shown the relation of paupers to the poor, the poor to the working class, and the working class to the whole of society.

This was one of the many respects in which Booth differed from the man who is generally regarded as his predecessor, Henry Mayhew. Forty years earlier, Mayhew had begun what seemed to be a comparable study, *London Labour and the London Poor.* Commentators have remarked upon the striking methodological and stylistic differences between the two works: Mayhew's, impressionistic, haphazard, disorganized, melodramatic; Booth's, factual, systematic, comprehensive, objective. But no less important were the substantive differences between the two. Mayhew's subject was narrower than his title suggested, for a good part of his work, and certainly the part that attracted most attention, was on the "street-folk." His preoccupation with that small but very colorful class—a distinctive "race" or "tribe," as he described them—and with the most bizarre details of their lives, so overwhelmed the rest of his work that the unwitting reader was left with a distorted picture of the ostensible subject, "London labour and the London poor."[33]

Perhaps because he was a businessman rather than a journalist, Booth was drawn to the larger and more conventional body of "London labour and the London poor," the kinds of workers who were employed in his own leather and shipping firm. These were the people whose conditions and problems he understood; it was, after all, his business to know about his workers' (and other workers') wages and earnings, their hours of work and periods of unemployment, even their living conditions and personal habits. His daily walks from his home to his office at the docks took him through working-class quarters, so that he was more familiar than most employers with the "life and labour" of his employees. In this respect he differed not only from journalists like Mayhew but also from charity visitors and poor-law guardians, whose only experience was with "cases of extreme destitution," as Beatrice Webb said, rather than the working classes as a whole.[34]

Booth also carried over to his research the habits of inquiry he had cultivated in his business. One of his partners complained of his frequent requests for "statistics and statements and tabular figures"; these were all very well, his partner objected, but they tended to distract from the real business of the firm.[35] In the same fashion some philanthropists protested that the facts and figures Booth was amassing for his social survey were irrelevant to the real business of philanthropy. Even Barnett, Beatrice Webb reported, upon first hearing of Booth's plan, "threw cold water" on it. "It was impossible to get the information required," he protested. But she suspected that he was "evidently sceptical of the value of facts when there."[36] (Barnett was helpful when the survey was actually under way, and Toynbee Hall became an important source of information for Booth.)

THE AMBITIOUS SCOPE of Booth's project, the "life and labour of the people in London," makes even more remarkable the modest way it was organized. Most notable (and most conspicuous in contrast with our own time) was the fact that the project was financed entirely by Booth himself, without benefit of government agencies, foundations, universities, or even tax deductions. In the beginning Booth made a feeble effort to formalize its structure by creating a Board of Statistical Research consisting of half a dozen people who had expressed interest in the work. At the first meeting of the board, in March 1886, literally no one appeared but himself. A second meeting was better attended, and Booth presented a plan of the project which was dutifully approved; this was the last that was heard of the board. The survey was initially housed in the offices of the Booth shipping firm, then moved to premises of its own, and later still to the offices of the Statistical Society.

The principal project director, as we would now say, was Booth, the rest of the staff consisting of several assistants (sometimes called secretaries), most of whom worked part-time. His chief assistant was Jesse Argyle, a junior clerk in his firm with no formal higher education (and a pronounced cockney accent); in addition to doing research, he wrote several chapters of the work, among them "Literature and Education." Others, like Ernest Aves and Hubert Llewellyn Smith, were university graduates (Llewellyn Smith having worked his way through Oxford), whose principal qualifications for this work came from their residency at Toynbee Hall. Arthur Baxter and George Duckworth joined the project in its early years and stayed until the end, while Beatrice Potter and Clara Collet were associated with it for a shorter time and for specific subjects. Mrs. Booth had a more active role in it than was generally realized, editing the sections written by her husband and preparing abstracts of reports, articles, and books; it was she who insisted that her contribution be kept secret even from the other workers on the project.[37]

Booth himself was as much an amateur as the others. During the seventeen years he was engaged in the project, he worked full-time with the shipping firm; for much of that period he spent four days a week in Liverpool and about a month each year in America. Yet he managed not only to direct and organize the survey but to be actively involved in the research and to write about half of the seventeen volumes. All of that work was done in the evenings and weekends, on trains and ships, and in spare moments stolen from hasty meals (which could not have helped his chronic indigestion). Yet he never prided himself on this extraordinary regimen or tried to impose it on anyone else; indeed, he seemed oblivious of the fact that his activities were in any way remarkable or commendable.

The first abortive meeting of the "board" took place in March 1886; the actual work of research started in September; and in May 1887 Booth delivered a fifty-page paper to the Statistical Society on Tower Hamlets, a district of East London. A second paper delivered the following year included some of the material from the earlier one, in addition to research on the rest of East London. The first volume, published in 1889 under the title *Life and Labour of the People,* was entirely on East London; the section entitled "Classes" included much of the material in the journal articles, while the other two sections, "Trades" and "Special Subjects," were largely new. (More than half the chapters were written and signed by Booth's associates, which is why the title page listed him as editor rather than author.) A second volume in 1891, entitled *Labour and Life of the People,* extended the inquiry to the rest of London. (The title was changed so as not to conflict with an earlier book by Samuel Smiles, *Life and Labour, or Characterisations of Men of Industry, Culture and Genius.*) These two volumes were reissued (and somewhat revised) in 1892–93 in a four-volume edition under the new (and permanent) title, *Life and Labour of the People in London.*[38] These four volumes constituted the "Poverty" series.

At the start of the project, Booth had predicted, without much confidence, that it *might* (he underlined the word) be completed in three years.[39] In 1892, having finished the four volumes of the "Poverty" series, he estimated that another two volumes would be required for the "Industry" series.[40] Five volumes and as many years later, the last of that second series appeared, and both series were published in a nine-volume edition. In the final volume Booth announced a third series of three volumes, to take three years, on "the forces for good or evil that are acting upon the condition of the population of London."[41] Seven volumes and five years later that series, called "Religious Influences," was completed.[42] A final volume, "Notes on Social Influences and Conclusions," concluded the seventeen-volume work published in 1902.

Each of the series was meant to complement the others. Yet together they added up to something less than a whole. Booth's initial expectation was that the Poverty and Industry series would fit into a single framework, that the data about households and streets would somehow correlate with the data about trades and industries—that the "Life and Labour" of the title would fit together tidily. Instead the two series ran along separate lines, sometimes parallel, sometimes crossing or at an angle with each other. Booth himself, like commentators after him, regretted the asymmetry of this schema, but made no effort to make it appear more symmetrical than it was. Indeed he complicated it further by introducing, in the final volume of the Industry series, yet another criterion of classification: "crowding," the number of occupants in each room. The crowding index turned out to have a close correlation to the poverty index, but this was almost fortuitous or tautological, the result of arbitrary definitions.[43]

IF THE WORK was not as rigorous and "scientific" as modern sociologists might like, this is because Booth never intended it to be that. He meant it to be qualitative as well as quantitative, based upon "personal

observation" as well as statistics. The observations he relied upon, especially in the early volumes, were principally those of school board visitors
(some two or three hundred in the whole of London), "whose life is spent
amongst the people they describe."[44] It did not occur to him to take his
observations from the people themselves.

This is not the "history from below" that so many historians today
favor. Only occasionally were the people themselves directly interviewed
by Booth and his associates; women workers, for example, were asked
about their wages, and the information they gave conformed to a large
extent with that provided by their employers.[45] For the most part, whatever information came from the people was filtered through the school
visitors. Perhaps Booth chose this method for reasons of expediency,
school board records being readily available, or perhaps because he
thought that these records were more objective than interviews with
householders, or perhaps because he wanted to avoid the sensationalistic
effect of Mayhew's interviews. In any case, he never seriously considered
using the people as a primary source; nor did Beatrice Potter ever make
that suggestion in the course of her many discussions of "personal observations"; nor was the absence of that source a cause for criticism or even
comment when the work appeared.*

What made the school visitors so important for Booth's purposes was,
once again, the question of relations and proportions. Unlike the COS
visitors, who dealt only with applicants for relief and charity, the school
visitors had "continual and natural relations with all classes of the
people."[47] They were charged with making annual (and sometimes more
frequent) "house to house visitations" of every family with school-age
children; these records normally started two or three years before the
children came of school age and continued after they left school. They also
recorded data about employment and earnings because one of their jobs
was to determine which families were eligible for the remission of school
fees. The visitors actually knew more about the residents than their books

---

* At one point Booth seemed to address the issue of "first-hand" and "second-hand"
sources. In 1891 Herbert Samuel asked his advice about an investigation he was
planning of the area around Oxford. After cautioning Samuel that the classes and
conditions in those villages would be very different from those in London, Booth went
on to suggest that preference be given to "second hand over direct information": "I
think it safest to consult existing local authorities such as schoolmasters, rate collectors, postmasters, relieving officers, the clergy (Church and Dissent), and the doctors,
and only to supplement and enliven the information from such sources with what the
inquirer himself sees and hears from the people themselves."[46]

conveyed, and it was to extract this additional information from them that Booth conducted extensive interviews with them. In the Tower Hamlets district each visitor was interviewed for a total of twenty hours, in the Hackney district for almost twenty-four hours.

About half to two-thirds of the population, Booth estimated, came under the purview of the school visitors. For the rest he relied upon other informants and sources—poor-law officials, rent collectors, sanitary inspectors, factory inspectors, clergymen, the police, residents in the settlement houses. He also utilized the census returns (he himself helped revise the questionnaire of 1891 so that it would be more informative), and he was given access, by the Registrar General, to the unpublished householders' schedules.

As Booth became more familiar with his subject, he extended the principle of observation to include observations by the investigators themselves.

> At the outset we shut our eyes, fearing lest any prejudice of our own should colour the information we received. It was not till the books were finished that I or my secretaries ourselves visited the streets amongst which we had been living in imagination. But later we gained confidence, and made it a rule to see each street ourselves at the time we received the visitors' account of it.[48]

Booth and his staff not only visited each street, they lived in the community for varying periods. Aves and Llewellyn Smith were residents at Toynbee Hall in Whitechapel. For a time Beatrice Potter made her "London home," as she called it, in a small residential hotel in Bishopsgate within walking distance of the docks (which was the first subject she wrote about for Booth); later, when she was gathering material on the tailoring trade, she carried "personal observation" a step forward by taking a job as a "trouser-hand."[49] Booth himself always made it a practice to visit and, when possible, take lodgings in working-class quarters. For the first series he spent several weeks at a time with three families representing different classes (with the exception of the "very poor"). For the final series he and his associates "moved camp" from one district to another, living in each for a few weeks or months; he likened it to a "voyage of discovery."[50] He had no illusions about sharing, in those brief periods and under those special circumstances, the conditions and experiences of the poor. Nor did he make any attempt to disguise himself. "He used to say," his granddaughter recalled, "that the only possible disguise was to be himself, and he never made the smallest alteration in his clothes or conversation."[51] But since his clothes were at best nondescript, his bearing unassuming, and his conversation unpretentious (he still had something of a Liverpool accent), that natural "disguise" worked reasonably well. He did not pass as poor, but neither was he recognized for what he was—a prosperous businessman and professional researcher.

This mass of material, statistical and impressionistic, was collated by Booth and his staff in a series of notebooks. For the volume on East London, every family was itemized individually, specifying the composition of the household, the size and condition of the lodgings, the occupations and, where the information was available, the earnings of the inhabitants. These entries were occasionally enlivened by more personal comments: one man was a "cadging loafer," another was "industrious, struggling," a wife was "brutally ill-treated."[52] For the rest of London, the street rather than the household was taken as the main unit. This schematic presentation was supplemented, in both the Poverty and the Industry series, by long case studies of individual families.

Booth also prepared a detailed street map to assist him in gathering as well as recording information. Each street was colored to represent the predominant class; two classes would be designated by running black lines, for example, across a blue background. The original of the map—16 by 13 feet, drawn to a scale of 25 inches to the mile—was displayed at Toynbee Hall and Oxford House, where residents and visitors were invited to correct and add to it. (The map, or a version of it, was displayed on a screen when Booth delivered his second paper to the Statistical Society.) Much reduced in size, cut up into sections, and separately bound, the maps were included as an appendix to the second volume of the first edition and to all later editions.

ALL OF THIS added up to a formidable job of research and a massive quantity of information. Yet a modern sociologist, impressed by the will and energy that went into Booth's work and grateful for the results, may be more than a little dismayed by his methods. Compared with the elegancies of modern social research, in which the smallness of the sample is a measure of the sophistication of the technique, Booth's procedure of "wholesale interviewing," as Beatrice Potter called it,[53] seems naïve and crude—"empirical," one might say derogatorily. It was, of course, preferable to the kind of impressionistic evidence found in *The Bitter Cry* or even the typical Royal Commission report. But judged in purely technical terms, Booth's "methodology" (again, Potter's term) was not as refined as that of some of his colleagues in the Statistical Society, who were writing articles with titles such as "The History of Pauperism Treated by Frequency Curves."[54] Booth never mentioned frequency curves, margins of error, or the other tools of the trade. Yet he must have known about them; he was, after all, a distinguished member of the Statistical Society, elected to the council after only two years and president five years later. He was also a friend and admirer of Alfred Marshall, whose own work was highly mathematical (although the mathematics was deliberately relegated to appendices).

If Booth chose not to avail himself of more sophisticated statistical techniques, it was because they were irrelevant to his purpose. "Wholesale interviewing," as comprehensive and as detailed as possible, was the only method that could produce the results he wanted, precisely because it elicited facts that were qualitative as well as quantitative. When he announced, early in the first volume, his "resolution to make use of no fact to which I cannot give a quantitative value," it was to emphasize once again the importance of relation and proportion. For the same reason he chose not to print all the "sensational stories" that appeared in the notebooks, because his object was "to show the numerical relation which poverty, misery, and depravity bear to regular earnings and comparative comfort, and to describe the general conditions under which each class lives."[55] Statistics were a corrective to sensationalism; they put the extreme in the context of the average, the extraordinary in the context of the ordinary. Statistics alone, however, were inadequate. And highly sophisticated statistical techniques were even more deceptive because they gave the impression of greater precision and reliability than was warranted by the evidence. Only a combination of observation and statistics, of qualitative and quantitative evidence, could do justice to the "life and labour of the people in London."

CHAPTER 8

Poverty and the Poor

TO HIS CONTEMPORARIES Booth was memorable as the man who discovered that almost one-third of the population of London was poor. To sociologists and historians he is commemorated as the man who focused attention upon "poverty" rather than "the poor" and who invented the "Poverty Line." William Beveridge, known as the father of the welfare state, explained the significance of the shift from "the poor" to "poverty": "The difference is not simply that to speak of 'The Poor' assumed a strictly classified society; the phrase had also the implication that 'The Poor' would always be with us; when Charles Booth got to work, after a hundred years of industrialization and rising productivity, the question that presented itself was why with so much wealth should there be so much poverty."[1]

Booth did not, of course, "invent" the concept of poverty. Nor was he the first to give it prominence. Nor, for that matter, did he make of it as much as Beveridge suggested. Beveridge's comment might more appropriately be applied to Henry George's *Progress and Poverty,* published ten years earlier, the thesis of which was precisely the "paradox" of the coexistence of wealth and poverty. George's work was more ideological and less "scientific" than Booth's, so that the latter's concept of "poverty," even if not consistent or rigorous, may well have been more influential.

"Poverty," like "unemployment," had the effect of moving the discussion from the subjective realm of persons to the objective condition that defined them. The emphasis thus shifted from the personal characteristics of the poor—their particular circumstances, characters, habits—to the impersonal causes of poverty: the state of the economy, the structure of society, the action (or inaction) of government, the institutions and forces affecting social conditions and relations. Booth, as will be seen, interwove the concepts of poverty and the poor, so that his analysis of the causes of poverty included personal as well as impersonal factors. From a later perspective he may appear as an ambivalent or transitional figure, pointing the way to the modern "structural" mode of thought but all too often regressing to an older "moralistic" tradition. A more instructive approach would be to locate him in his own time, to try to see the situation as he saw it and as he represented it, and thus to appreciate his influence upon the thinking and policies of his contemporaries.

It is because so much importance has been attached to the concept of poverty that so much has been made of the "Poverty Line." "Booth invented the Poverty Line," his biographers write, "perhaps his most striking single contribution to the social sciences."[2] There is hardly a reference to Booth that does not repeat this claim.[3] The editors of a volume of selections from *Life and Labour* take it as axiomatic that "Charles Booth's invention of the term 'poverty line' should be familiar to all those aware of current bureaucratic rhetoric about poverty."[4] A reviewer of that volume wonders whether "Poverty Line" was suggested to Booth, the shipowner, by the law passed only a few years earlier on the "Plimsoll Line," the line on the hull of ships showing the level of submergence.[5] Booth's granddaughter also alluded to his shipping interests, claiming that his "expressive phrase," Poverty Line, came to be known as "the Booth Line."[6]

In fact, Booth did not use, let alone invent, "Poverty Line." The closest he came to it was "line of poverty."[7] The difference is not trivial. "Poverty Line," capitalized and in that syntactical construction, is more abstract and more striking than "line of poverty"; it is a hypostatized concept rather than an empirical generalization. But even "line of poverty" was less prominent in Booth's work than might be thought. The phrase was used infrequently and casually, with no intimation either of its novelty or of its importance. It appeared three times in Booth's first paper to the Statistical Society, each time in the middle or end of a sentence and never as the subject.[8] Of the nine commentators on that paper, only one referred to the term, professing himself pleased that a large proportion of the population fell above the "line of poverty" and wondering about the difference between "on" and "below" the line.[9] In his reply Booth addressed himself to other points raised by this commentator but not to this one. In his paper the following year, the term appeared once in a table and twice in the text.[10] This time it was entirely ignored in the discussion.

In *Life and Labour,* "line of poverty" was mentioned half a dozen times in the first volume of the Poverty series, once in the second, and once in the fourth.[11] In the Industry series, it appeared only in the final volume, once in a footnote, and three times in the text, once with the qualification "our supposed line of poverty."[12] It was absent from the whole of the third series and from the concluding volume. Nor did it figure in the indices to any of the volumes (although "Poverty" and "Poor" were indexed, with numerous subheads), nor in the detailed abstracts of the volumes appended to the end of the Industry series and the final volume. Nor did contemporary reviewers make much of it; "line of poverty" was mentioned occasionally in the reviews of Booth's first *Journal* paper, but rarely thereafter. (One reviewer spoke of a "line of plenty" but not of a "line of poverty.")[13]

The most significant omission occurred in the final volume of Booth's work in his discussion of the recently published book by Seebohm Rowntree on poverty in York. Rowntree conspicuously and repeatedly used the expression "Poverty Line," as the title of a chapter of his book and (sometimes in lowercase) throughout the text; moreover, he made a large point of giving that "line" a precise, quantitative definition.[14] Even then Booth apparently did not think it worthy of comment. Others, however, did fasten upon the term, and it was only then, following the publication of Rowntree's book in 1901, that the term gained currency and was retroactively attributed to Booth—a misattribution that was unjust to both men, for it obscured precisely that which was unique to each.[15]

IT MAY BE SAID that even if Booth did not invent the Poverty Line, he did invent the quantitative measure that signified that line—the frequently cited 18 to 21 shillings. "By the word 'poor' I mean to describe those who have a sufficiently regular though bare income, such as 18s. to 21s. per week for a moderate family, and by 'very poor' those who from any cause fall much below this standard."[16] Perhaps the most notable aspect of this definition is how vague it was; "such as" and "much below" hardly connote a precise figure or line. Moreover, the range of income, 18–21 shillings, is notably inexact. At that income level, a single shilling can be momentous, as Mr. Micawber testified when he made that single shilling the crucial difference between happiness and misery. Booth himself had a healthy respect for a single shilling: "Just as, starting from about 24s. for a moderate family, each shilling a week less is a direct step into poverty, so each shilling a week more tells no less quickly in the opposite direction."[17]

Even these income figures were cited less frequently and less consistently, by Booth himself and by contemporary commentators, than might be thought. In the first paper the line of poverty was given first as "18s. to 21s." and then as "not exceeding 21s." When Leone Levi, who was the only commentator to mention the figures, gave them as "18s. to 20s.," Booth did not bother to correct him.[18] In response to Levi's suggestion that he provide typical budgets of income and expenditure, he included in the first volume a table of thirty budgets. Of the six families in class B (defined earlier in the book as "very poor" and "much below" the 18–21s. income), three had "supposed" incomes of 21s. or 22s.[19] Elsewhere, in a classification of streets, a family of two adults and five children with an income of 20s. was placed in class B, while another of the same size with an income of 16–18s. was in class C.[20] Only once, in the rest of the Poverty series, were the 18–21s. figures cited, and then tentatively and parenthetically: "standard poverty" was defined as those whose "earnings are small (say 18s. to 21s. a week for a moderate family)."[21] In the last volume of the Industry series, after using the 21s. figure, Booth allowed, on the same page, that a family might have earnings of 25–30s. and "still fall within the lines of our measure of poverty."[22] Several pages later, the line of poverty was "below 22s. or 23s."[23] By the end of this volume, Booth concluded that "one-third of the population are on or about the line of poverty or are below it, having at most an income which one time with another averages 21s. or 22s. for a small family (or up to 25s. to 26s. for one of larger size), and in many cases falling much below this level."[24]

This last quotation directs attention to another variable in the definition of poverty: the size of the family. In the initial and most often quoted definition, 18–21s. was the weekly income of a "moderate"-sized family;[25] elsewhere in the first volume "moderate" was defined as "father, mother, and three children of, say, 11, 8, and 6."[26] By the last volume of the Industry series, 21s. was the income of a "small" family in poverty, "small" defined as "about four members"; a "larger" family (presumably including the earlier "moderate" family of five) was poor if its earnings were 25–26s.[27] To compound the confusion (or perhaps to justify it), midway in this volume Booth observed that in some occupations as few as 60 to 65 percent of the adult males were heads of families; in one instance it was only 30 percent, and the highest it reached for any industry was 85 percent.[28]

It is not necessarily a criticism of Booth to point to the vagaries and inconsistencies of the income figures. He never pretended to any greater precision than his sources permitted. And his sources, as he well knew, were inadequate and unreliable. "We can get from the visitors," he told

Beatrice Potter early in the research, "an *opinion* on the earnings of each man and I should like to find some way of noting this down for averages; but I feel that at the end it is only an opinion and I hesitate to make it the basis of our classification."[29] In his first paper he was optimistic about the visitors' ability to get "exceptionally good information on questions of employment and earnings, especially as regards the poorer classes."[30] By the time he came to publish the first volume, he evidently had second thoughts about their reliability, because he omitted that sentence, introducing instead such expressions as "supposed income" and "apparent status as to means."[31]

One might have thought that the Industry series would have produced more satisfactory income figures, for Booth drew upon information from employers as well as the Board of Trade. Unfortunately, the former gave "average earnings for an average number," and the latter made no allowance for over-time or short-time.[32] And neither of these sources was useful for the poorer classes who were less likely to be regularly employed by a single employer. At a time when earnings were notoriously "irregular," and when there were no compelling reasons to keep accurate records (for purposes of taxation, pensions, social security), one can well understand Booth's settling for "supposed" income and "apparent" means.

In contrast to the income figures, Booth's figures of expenditures were remarkably, and suspiciously, precise. Like earnings, expenditures varied widely from week to week, the consumption of meat, for example, being high in a good week and reduced to nothing in a bad one. And the poorer classes were no more likely to keep accurate records of their expenditures than of their earnings. Yet Booth's table of thirty budgets specified the expenses of each family down to the last farthing for each of thirty items, with suet itemized separately from butter and dripping, bread from flour, and flour from oatmeal. This was in marked contrast to the single entry of "supposed income." Booth commented on one anomaly in these budgets: the "admitted expenditure" generally exceeded the "supposed income."[33] The discrepancy, he explained, could be accounted for by the understatement of income or by the use of credit which was either not repaid or met by a windfall outside of regular earnings—all of which cast additional doubt on the "supposed" income.

In laboring this problem of income, one runs the risk of inflating its importance in Booth's work. However vague his definition of the "line of poverty" or imprecise his income figures, these were not fatal flaws because they were not central to his work. He would no doubt have preferred more exact and accurate figures, but the fact that he did not have them did not vitiate his work. His concept of poverty was not, and was not meant to be, reducible to shillings and pence. A modern researcher may be impatient with his typically vague locutions: "supposed," "say," "such as," "on or about," "much below," "moderate." For his purposes these were sufficient. Indeed anything more precise would have been a case of misplaced precision—would not only have been inaccurate but would have distorted his meaning and distracted from his main point.*

THE REAL SIGNIFICANCE of Booth's "quantitative" method was not as a monetary measure of poverty—the 18–21s. that supposedly demarcated the line of poverty—but as a quantitative measure of the several classes of the poor. The definitions and distinctions of these classes were essentially qualitative. But it was their quantification, the number and percentage belonging to each class, that seemed to give Booth's schema a hard, objective, "scientific" reality. The percentages also had the effect of establishing the "relations" and "proportions" that were so important to him—the relations and proportions of the "poor" to the "very poor," and of both to the working classes who were not poor.

Of Booth's eight classes, four were below and four above the "line of poverty."

    A. The lowest class of occasional labourers, loafers, and
       semi-criminals.
    B. Casual earnings—"very poor."
    C. Intermittent earnings ⎫
                     ⎬ together the "poor."
    D. Small regular earnings ⎭
    E. Regular standard earnings—above the line of poverty.
    F. Higher class labour.
    G. Lower middle class.
    H. Upper middle class.[35]

The four classes, A to D, comprising the "very poor" and the "poor," added up to the commonly cited figure of 30.7 percent of the population

* Reviewers were not troubled by Booth's vagueness. Nor did they quarrel with his figures. One historian has pointed out that while his standard of poverty might be considered low by present-day standards, it could not have been very far from the standard of his own time, else his book would have been more widely and severely criticized than it was.[34]

of London that was "in poverty." Sometimes Booth excluded A (0.9 percent) from this group on the ground that its problem was not so much poverty as "disorder." "The true problem of poverty" was to be found in B, C, and D.[36] Of these, B, the "very poor," constituted 7.5 percent; and C and D, the "poor," 22.3 percent. Above the line of poverty were E and F, the "comfortable" working classes (51.5 percent); and G and H, the middle and upper classes (17.8 percent).

In the initial analysis of East London the eight classes were kept distinct. When the inquiry was extended to the whole of London, A and B remained separate, but the other classes were grouped together: C and D, E and F, G and H. It was this latter classification, with their numbers and percentages, that was most often quoted at the time.

A (lowest)	37,610	or	.9%	In poverty,
B (very poor)	316,834	"	7.5%	30.7%
C and D (poor)	938,293	"	22.3%	
E and F (working class, comfortable)	2,166,503	"	51.5%	In comfort,
G and H (middle class and above)	749,930	"	17.8%	69.3%
	4,209,170		100%	
Inmates of Institutions	99,830			
	4,309,000			

Graphically, the proportions may be shown thus:

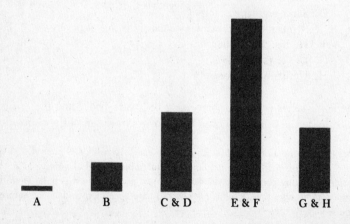

The definitions of "poor" and "very poor" were notably vague: "The 'poor' are those whose means may be sufficient, but are barely sufficient, for decent independent life; the 'very poor' those whose means are insufficient for this according to the usual standard of life in this country." Nor did the sentence that followed help matters: "My 'poor' may be described as living under a struggle to obtain the necessaries of life and make both ends meet; while the 'very poor' live in a state of chronic want."[37] And these terms were only slightly clarified by his distinction of the different degrees of poverty: "poverty," which was the least onerous condition; "want," which was an aggravated form of poverty; and "distress," which was an aggravated form of want.[38]

More memorable were the descriptions of the individual classes. The lowest class, A, was a largely "hereditary" class, except for those who drifted down from other classes. It contained many criminals but also others who were better described as "barbarians" (a term Booth attributed to Henry George).[39] These were not, however, the "hordes of barbarians" that some writers made of them; they were "a handful, a small and decreasing percentage: a disgrace but not a danger." They lived the life of savages, but it was not easy to say how they lived or how they picked up whatever small means they had. They ate the coarsest food and drank whenever they could. They slept in common lodging houses if they could scrape together threepence, and in the streets if they could not. They were the beggars and bullies who "foul the record of the unemployed," hanging around the public houses, being disorderly, or cadging the odd copper. "They render no useful service, they create no wealth: more often they destroy it. They degrade whatever they touch, and as individuals are perhaps incapable of improvement." While they seemed to be a necessary evil in every large city, their numbers and conditions depended upon the state of the classes above them, the discretion of charities, and the pressure of the police.[40]

Class B was much more numerous than A and far more serious a threat to society. It consisted mainly of casual laborers, the largest group being dockworkers. Most worked three days a week and would not have worked full-time if they had that opportunity. Unlike A, B was not a class "in which men are born and live and die, so much as a deposit of those who from mental, moral, and physical reasons are incapable of better work." As A could not be equated with a criminal class, so B was not a pauper class, although it contained many paupers and was the "material from which paupers are made."[41] It was the "leisure class" of the poor, whose leisure was "habitual to the extent of second nature," limited only by the pressure of want. Individuals in this class were often drunk, but drink was neither their "special luxury," as it was for those in the lowest class, nor their "passion," as for some in the class above them. Booth's description of them was strikingly reminiscent of Mayhew's street folk: "They cannot stand the regularity and dulness of civilized existence, and find the excitement they need in the life of the streets, or at home as spectators of or participators in some highly coloured domestic scene."[42] Only a small part of this class was "in distress," the larger part being "in want"—that is, "ill-nourished and poorly clad."[43]

Class C consisted of those who were "irregularly employed" and had "intermittent earnings": dockworkers, building laborers, wharf and warehouse hands, handlers of coal, grain, and timber. When they were employed they might earn 15s. or 20s. in a short time in exhausting work, after which they might spend it as quickly and freely. Or they might receive even higher wages, as high as those of the artisans in class F. Because of the nature of their work—which was seasonal, by the job, or especially vulnerable to trade depressions—they were often unemployed. But whether employed or not, they were inclined to "take things as they come," to work in their own trade when they could or, if hard up, to try for casual work. Except in special circumstances, they were not "in want," "neither ill-nourished nor ill-clad, according to any standard that can reasonably be used." They were, however, "in poverty," involved in an endless struggle to make ends meet.[44] The more enterprising of them rose into class E, the less enterprising fell into B. Although they tended to have a "very bad character for improvidence," most of them were "hard-working, struggling people, not worse morally than any other class, though shiftless and improvident."[45]

If irregularity of work was the distinctive characteristic of class C, regularity of work was that of class D. The workers in D had "small regular earnings" not exceeding 21s. a week. They worked on a fairly regular basis (although they were occasionally unemployed), and their earnings were fairly (although not entirely) constant. Their work required little skill or intelligence; they were factory laborers, carmen, messengers, porters, and the "better end" of the dockworkers who were more regularly employed. Except in case of sickness or a drunken wife, they were, like those in class C, poor without being in "actual want." For the most part they were "decent steady men, paying their way and bringing up their children respectably." They were also thrifty, for without that "make-the-most-of-everything" trait they would not have been able to keep up so respectable an appearance on so small an income.[46]

Above the line of poverty was class E, with "regular standard earnings" of 22s. to 30s. a week. The largest single class, it included most of the artisans, the "best class" of street sellers and dealers, many small shopkeepers and small employers, and the regularly employed and better-paid carmen, porters, messengers, warehousemen, and dockworkers. With such varied occupations and wide divergencies of "character, interests, and ways of life," its members did not, in a sense, make up a single class. What they had in common were comfortable homes and, above all, the determination to lead "independent lives." While they gave and received friendly help "without sense of patronage or degradation," against anything that resembled charity "their pride rises stiffly."[47]

Class F comprised the best-paid artisans and foremen earning between 30s. and 50s. a week and notable for their "very good character and much intelligence." While the artisans saw themselves as part of the working classes, the foremen more often identified with their employers. The latter were the "non-commissioned officers of the industrial army," a small group but a "distinct and very honourable one." Although they did not share in the profits of the firm, they were loyal and devoted, led comfortable lives, and provided for their old age.[48] (One can hear the voice of Booth the employer in this tribute to his employees.)

Classes G and H were only briefly described. G consisted of shopkeepers, clerks, small employers, and lesser professionals; they were "hard-working, sober, energetic." H was the upper middle class, or "servant-keeping class." (The servants themselves generally belonged to class E.)[49]

Having named and defined these classes, Booth added the cautionary note that the dividing lines between them were "indistinct." Each had a "fringe" that overlapped with the class above or below it; and each contained so many "grades of social rank" that no class was "homogeneous."[50] He might also have noted what was obvious from his account: that the classes were neither homogeneous nor exclusive in terms of occupation; there were, for example, both dockworkers and artisans in B, C, D, and E. Nor was the distinction between skilled and unskilled labor as important as might be thought. Skill helped separate the "comfortable" working classes (E and F) from the poor (C and D), but not the poor from the very poor (B), both of whom were unskilled or little skilled. D, for example, did work requiring "little skill or intelligence."[51] (Just how heterogeneous these classes were may be seen in the table on the following pages, one of twenty such tables collating occupations and classes in East London.[52])

TABLE OF SECTIONS AND CLASSES. SHOREDITCH.

NOTE: The figures in these tables must only be taken as approximately correct.

DIVIDED INTO SECTIONS ACCORDING TO CHARACTER OF EMPLOYMENT OF HEADS OF FAMILIES

Class		Description	Heads of Families	More or less Dependent			Unmarried Males over 20 and Widowers	Total	Percentage
				Wives	Children —15	Young Persons 15—20			
MALES									
Labour	1	Lowest class, loafers, &c.	300	300	41	148	118	907	0·75
	2	Casual day-to-day labour	681	681	1,347	338	267	3,314	2·73
	3	Irregular labour	538	538	1,029	258	211	2,574	2·15
	4	Regular work, low pay	1,093	1,093	1,895	475	430	4,986	4·10
	5	,, ,, ordinary pay	1,709	1,709	3,088	774	672	7,952	6·55
	6	Foremen and responsible work	145	145	271	68	57	686	0·57
Artisans	7	Building trades	1,788	1,788	3,268	822	703	8,369	6·90
	8	Furniture, woodwork, &c.	3,365	3,365	6,392	1,604	1,320	16,046	13·25
	9	Machinery and metals	1,095	1,095	2,033	507	431	5,161	4·25
	10 A.	Printing	977	977	1,845	462	385	4,646	3·86 ⎫
	B.	Watches, instruments, &c.	323	323	600	150	127	1,523	1·26 ⎪
	C.	Furs and leather	497	497	920	230	195	2,339	1·92 ⎬ 10·95
	D.	Silk weaving	34	34	72	18	13	171	0·14 ⎪
	E.	Sundry artisans	962	962	1,819	457	377	4,577	3·77 ⎭
	11	Dress	2,012	2,012	3,815	956	789	9,584	7·91
Locomotion	12	Food preparation	414	414	748	187	162	1,925	1·56
	13	Railway servants	147	147	274	68	58	694	0·57
	14	Road service	289	289	586	146	114	1,424	1·17
Assistants	15	Shops and Refreshment Houses	731	731	1,301	327	287	3,377	2·78
Other Wages	16	Police, soldiers, and sub-officials	304	304	584	146	119	1,457	1·20

			Males				Total	%
Manufacturers, &c.	17 Seamen	17	17	26	6	7	73	0·06
	18 Other wage earners	1,159	1,159	1,482	371	454	4,625	3·83
	19 Home industries (not employing)	722	722	1,388	348	283	3,463	2·86
	20 Small employers	634	634	1,308	329	249	3,154	2·60
	21 Large „	34	34	65	16	13	162	0·13
Dealers	22 Street sellers, &c.	376	376	685	171	147	1,755	1·46
	23 General dealers	178	178	304	76	70	806	0·66
	24 Small shops	550	550	966	242	215	2,523	2·07
	25 Large „ (with assistants)	434	434	857	214	170	2,109	1·74
Refreshments	26 Coffee and boarding houses	82	82	156	39	32	391	0·32
	27 Licensed houses	140	140	244	61	55	640	0·53
Salaried, &c.	28 Clerks and agents	719	719	1,239	311	282	3,270	2·70
	29 Subordinate professional	111	111	161	41	43	467	0·39
	30 Professional	85	85	140	35	32	377	0·32
No work	31 Ill and no occupation	65	65	115	29	26	300	0·25
	32 Independent	36	36	56	14	14	156	0·13
	Total of male heads of families		22,746					
FEMALES	33 Semi-domestic employment	741	—	1,180	296	—	2,217	1·84
	34 Dress	410	—	601	150	—	1,161	0·96
	35 Small trades	414	—	640	160	—	1,214	1·02
	36 Employing and professional	52	—	72	18	—	142	0·12
	37 Supported	141	—	198	49	—	388	0·32
	38 Independent	22	—	31	8	—	61	0·05
	Total of female heads of families	(1,780)						
	39 Other adult women	—	—	—	—	—	9,995	8·25
	Total	24,526	22,746	43,842	11,125	8,927	121,161	100·00
	Inmates of Institutions	—	—	—	—	—	2,839	—
	Total population	—	—	—	—	—	124,000	

TABLE OF SECTIONS AND CLASSES. SHOREDITCH.

NOTE: The figures in these tables must only be taken as approximately correct.

DIVIDED INTO CLASSES ACCORDING TO MEANS AND POSITION OF HEADS OF FAMILIES

Section	Very Poor			Poor		Comfortable	Well-to-do		Total
	A Lowest Class	B Casual Earnings	C Irregular Earnings	D Regular Minimum	E Ordinary Standard Earnings	F Highly Paid Work	G Lower Middle	H Upper Middle	
1	907	—	—	—	—	—	—	—	907
2	—	3,182	132	—	—	—	—	—	3,314
3	—	504	2,061	—	9	—	—	—	2,574
4	—	70	—	4,881	35	—	—	—	4,986
5	—	—	—	954	6,936	62	—	—	7,952
6	—	—	—	9	9	668	—	—	686
7	27	528	1,350	1,350	4,320	794	—	—	8,369
8	27	1,168	2,040	3,263	8,495	1,053	—	—	16,046
9	9	188	387	798	3,125	654	—	—	5,161
10 A	—	127	218	566	3,001	734	—	—	4,646
10 B	—	55	126	198	813	331	—	—	1,523
10 C	—	135	233	476	1,386	109	—	—	2,339
10 D	—	19	29	10	103	10	—	—	171
10 E	9	254	536	1,102	2,438	238	—	—	4,577
11	—	872	1,583	2,282	4,496	348	—	—	9,584
12	—	74	160	483	1,134	74	—	—	1,925
13	—	9	—	99	468	118	—	—	694
14	18	38	103	272	973	38	—	—	1,424
15	—	160	169	815	2,002	213	—	—	3,377
16	—	—	—	111	1,126	220	—	—	1,457

									Total
17	—	—	8	33	32	—	—	—	73
18	—	145	237	842	3,119	282	—	—	4,625
19	—	258	430	660	1,381	734	—	—	3,463
20	—	—	9	29	343	1,997	767	9	3,154
21	—	—	—	—	—	—	135	27	162
22	36	286	573	340	493	27	—	—	1,755
23	26	35	95	95	346	209	—	—	806
24	—	—	35	238	1,242	982	26	—	2,523
25	—	—	—	18	47	650	595	817	2,109
26	—	—	—	27	210	145	18	175	391
27	—	9	87	208	27	149	253	9	640
28	—	26	8	32	1,357	1,247	336	8	3,270
29	—	8	—	—	162	184	65	325	467
30	—	—	62	9	—	26	26	—	377
31	—	211	—	—	9	9	—	8	300
32	—	—	—	—	74	33	41	—	156
33	—	1,301	500	267	149	—	—	—	2,217
34	—	364	270	344	178	5	5	—	1,161
35	5	398	274	369	158	5	5	—	1,214
36	—	—	—	24	54	30	34	—	142
37	—	49	49	138	152	—	—	—	388
38	—	—	—	5	26	15	15	—	61
39	96	940	1,054	1,918	4,544	1,109	210	124	9,995
Total	1,160	11,413	12,821	23,265	54,972	13,502	2,526	1,502	121,161
Per cent	0·96	9·42	10·55	19·21	45·39	11·14	2·09	1·24	100·00

More important than income, occupation, or skill in defining class was the regularity or irregularity of work and earnings, for these determined the "style of life."[53] Thus, the poverty of C and D was "similar in degree but different in kind." While C's earnings might be larger than D's (might even be as large as E's), the irregularity of C's earnings made for a more unsettled life and a more onerous kind of poverty than D's.[54] Similarly, B and C—divided not only by class but by the critical distinction of "very poor" and "poor"—both had irregular earnings; but B's came from casual work engaged by the hour and paid by the hour, whereas C, also paid hourly, was engaged by the week, month, or season.[55] Moreover, B was inclined to that mode of employment by an aversion to the "regularity and dulness of civilized existence"; whereas C, however improvident and shiftless, worked when work was available.

To the modern reader, Booth's vocabulary—"barbarians" and "savages," "evil" and "degraded," "shiftless" and "improvident," "decent" and "respectable," "honourable" and of "good character"—belie any claim to objectivity. Indeed the terms of approbation may be deemed as objectionable as the terms of obloquy. For Booth himself, however, as for most of his contemporaries, these terms were necessary and appropriate—not for purposes of judgment (although that was implicit as well) but for objective analysis. Attitudes and habits, as much as income and occupation, were the facts of life; they described the poor "as they actually exist."[56] In this respect Booth was less moralistic than those who denied the poverty of those whose distress was said to be "self-inflicted"—the result of bad habits or character.

As if he were anticipating his critics, Booth distinguished between two alternative ways of defining poverty:

> On the one hand we may argue that the poor are often really better off than they appear to be, on the ground that when extravagances which keep them in poverty are constant and immediate in their action, the state of things resulting cannot reasonably be called poverty at all. For instance, a man who spends ten or fifteen shillings in drink one week, cannot be called poor because he lacks the money for some necessity a few days later.[57]

Booth did not identify those who argued in this fashion, although it is obvious that he had the COS in mind. But he did make it clear that he himself took the opposite view, that poverty was poverty regardless of how it was caused, whether by lack of income or failure of character.

On the other hand we may as logically, or perhaps more logically, disregard the follies past or present which bring poverty in their train. For how distinguish between degrees of folly more or less recent or remote? In this temper we prefer to view and consider these unfortunates only as they actually exist; constantly put to shifts to keep a home together; always struggling and always poor.[58]

Booth proposed to "disregard the follies" in determining whether people were poor or not. But he did not disregard them in describing these people or in assigning them to one or another category of poor, for this was to describe and categorize them "as they actually exist." He made this point again and again.

I do not here introduce any moral question: whatever the cause, those whose means prove to be barely sufficient, or quite insufficient, for decent independent life, are counted as "poor" or "very poor" respectively.[59]

My first business is simply with the numbers who, from whatever cause, do live under conditions of poverty or destitution.[60]

Poverty is not incompatible with there being "lots of money going."[61]

It must be remembered moreover that we can only deal with *apparent* poverty. A man who earns good wages may spend but little of them on his home.[62]

"Apparent" poverty, the poor "as they actually exist"—it was this existential poverty that Booth tried to categorize and quantify. And it was for this reason that he regarded income as only one factor in the "style" or "standard" of life.[63] If most of his income figures were estimates made by school visitors on the basis of their observations of living standards, this was partly for want of better sources, but also partly because living standards were more crucial in Booth's schema than actual income.*

* * *

---

* This was also the reason for introducing in the second series, as another measure of poverty, the index of "crowding"—the number of occupants of each room. This too was a measure of "standards" rather than income, but a more objective measure, he came to think, than the observations of the school visitors which were based "on *opinion* only."[64]

POVERTY WAS POVERTY, "whatever the cause."[65] This did not mean that Booth ignored the question of cause. On the contrary, he distinguished three main causes of poverty and tried to quantify each:

> Questions of employment—Lack of work or low pay
> Questions of habit, idleness, drunkenness or thriftlessness
> Questions of circumstance, sickness, or large families.[66]

From a sample of 4,000 in East London, he estimated the principal causes of poverty for the "very poor" and the "poor":

	A and B	C and D
Employment	55%	68%
Habit	18	13
Circumstance	27	19[67]

It may have come as a surprise to Booth's readers (and it may give pause to those today who criticize him for being obsessively moralistic) to find "questions of employment" emerge as the principal cause of poverty for over half of the very poor and two-thirds of the poor. In the case of the very poor, he could not separate low pay from irregular employment; but among the poor, of the 68 percent for whom employment was the principal cause of poverty, 43 percent was attributed to irregular work and 25 percent to low pay. He was troubled by his inability to determine how many of that 43 percent were experiencing the normal kind of irregular employment, as distinct from those who were "*definitely* unemployed," in trades so depressed that there was no work available. The latter, the victims of the ebb and tide of industry, were the "saddest form of poverty, the gradual impoverishment of respectability, silently sinking into want."[68]

A modern economist would find much to quarrel with in Booth's discussion of unemployment (a word he rarely used, since it was only then coming into circulation).[69] But it cannot be said that he ignored or belittled the problem (he found it the largest single cause of poverty), or that he failed to distinguish various kinds of unemployment and underemployment, or that he regarded the unemployed as an undifferentiated mass of shiftless, incompetent people who were unemployed simply because of their personal inadequacies. Although he was not a professional economist, he was knowledgeable enough to identify some of the principal elements in unemployment: the state of the currency and the machinery of exchange; the factors determining "aggregate demand" on the one hand and credit and investment on the other; the "cycles of inflation and contraction" affecting industry in general and particular trades; seasonal variations in consumption and production; the interdependence of local, national, and international markets; the relationship of imports and exports; the effects of fiscal policies and legislative actions; population increase and internal and external migration; new modes of production and new products; fluctuations of fashion; the transferability of skills from one trade to another; trade union practices and contractual obligations in regard to hiring and firing; the "hand of nature" affecting not only agriculture but industry as well (especially the building and shipping trades).[70]

One may take issue with Booth's analysis of trade cycles, for example, but it is hardly just to accuse him, as one critic does, of neglecting that factor.[71] Nor were the Webbs justified in criticizing him for suggesting that "the modern system of industry will not work without some unemployed margin—some reserve of labour."[72] That quotation was only the first part of Booth's sentence, which continued: "but the margin in London to-day seems to be exaggerated in every department, and enormously so in the lowest class of labour." Booth himself went on to criticize those employers who were shortsighted enough to think that a large margin of unemployed was in their interest. "Labour deteriorates under casual employment more than its price falls." The true interest of employers, as well as of the community, was to have as many regularly employed workers as possible. "To divide a little work amongst a number of men—giving all a share—may seem kind and even just, and I have known such a course to be taken with this idea. It is only justifiable as a temporary expedient, serving otherwise but to prolong a bad state of things."[73]

If Booth's analysis of unemployment was more sophisticated than some critics have supposed, it was not so sophisticated as to deny the personal element.[74] Unemployment, he said, was the product of a complicated "intermixture" and "conjunction" of the personal and the economic.[75] Personal deficiencies counted for less in good times than in bad and in some industries than in others. Moreover, they were as much the effect as the cause of unemployment, "irregular work" being inevitably coupled with "irregular lives."[76] The "threads of causation" were often too "tangled" to be separated and identified, but were unmistakable.

> The individual for the most part pursues his task unconscious of the interacting forces which play around him. At times, when some powerful influence causes unusual dislocation, his attention may be ar-

rested. But as a rule the threads of causation are never traced. The woof is too tangled. The majority are, however, saved and sustained by a more or less persistent and reasonable self-regard, and by this self-regard mainly is order preserved and progress made amid the apparent chaos.

But, meanwhile, the uncertainty and irregularity of their industrial position lead to the personal degradation of large numbers. For them change and uncertainty have no stimulating force. They tend to fall alike in the industrial and the social scale, and although several of the influences that have been considered are signs, and even conditions, of a general progress, they make also for greater industrial stress and in many cases seem but to stereotype poverty.[77]

THAT BOOTH WAS a moralist of a special kind was evident in his discussion of one of the other causes of poverty, drink. It was axiomatic among most Victorians, professional philanthropists as well as casual observers, that drink was a major cause of poverty. To them Booth's statistics came as a revelation.[78] As a "principal" cause of poverty, he discovered, drink and thriftlessness combined (he found it impossible to separate the two) accounted for 14 percent of the poverty in classes A and B and 13 percent in C and D. As a "contributory" cause, to be sure, that figure would have been much higher. But it was only principal causes he could measure, and as such drink played a much smaller part than had generally been thought.

Booth neither exaggerated the problem of drink nor trivialized it. In his case studies of individual families it commonly appeared together with dirt, disorderliness, thriftlessness, the neglect of children, and the incapacity for work. But like these other evils, he saw it as more often the consequence of poverty than its cause. For the most part the poor drank because they were poor. And different groups of the poor drank for different reasons, some as a "luxury," others as an occasional "passion" to be indulged after an exhausting bout of work.[79] Among all classes there was more drinking than formerly, but also less drunkenness. There was also more drinking among women—one of the ironic results, Booth observed, of the social emancipation of women. "On the one hand she has become more independent of man, industrially and financially, and on the other more of a comrade than before, and in neither capacity does she feel any shame at entering a public house."[80]

For the temperance movement, Booth had no sympathy at all, regarding it as excessive and repressive. Public houses were the most important social institutions in the lives of the people, places for friends to meet and chat, where drunkenness was the exception rather than the rule.

> Go into any of these houses—the ordinary public-house at the corner of any ordinary East End street—there, standing at the counter, or seated on the benches against wall or partition, will be perhaps half-a-dozen people, men and women, chatting together over their beer—more often beer than spirits—or you may see a few men come in with no time to lose, briskly drink their glass and go. Behind the bar will be a decent middle-aged woman, something above her customers in class, very neatly dressed, respecting herself and respected by them. The whole seems comfortable, quiet, and orderly.[81]

He opposed not only the temperance movement but licensing laws designed to prohibit or limit the sale of liquor or make it inaccessible to the working classes. He even thought it unwise to bar children from public houses, for then the women would have had to fetch the beer, and they were more likely than the children to be tempted to drink. The only licensing laws that were justified were those designed to encourage the "decent and respectable" houses and discourage the "disreputable," so that women and children could enter them without jeopardy.[82]

There were not many reformers at the time who were so tolerant of public houses.* Booth was no less "moralistic" than they, no less concerned with decency and respectability, but he took a larger view of what was decent and respectable. Liquor was evil in excess but not in moderation; in moderation, for the poor as for the rich, it was a means of relaxation and sociability. It was, to be sure, sometimes abused, but that was no reason to outlaw it entirely, just as it was no reason to condemn those who occasionally drank to excess. The occasional bouts of drunkenness characteristic of class C did not make that class "worse morally" than any other class.[83] The classes that were worse morally were A and B, who were not habitually drunk but who were degraded and who threatened to degrade the other classes of the poor.

* * *

---

* John Stuart Mill had earlier opposed licensing laws which restricted the number of public houses or made them inaccessible, simply on the grounds of liberty. Booth opposed such laws because he regarded public houses as salutary social institutions.

THIS WAS Booth's innovation: not the concept of "poverty," or the invention of the "Poverty Line," or the quantitative measure of poverty, but the delineation of classes of the poor—the creation of a new typology, as it were, of poverty.

For most of recorded history, "the poor" had been virtually synonymous with "the lower classes," "the laboring classes," "the working classes." In the early nineteenth century a distinction emerged that was to dominate social discourse for much of the century: the distinction between the "dependent" and the "independent" poor, between "paupers" and the "laboring poor," between the "undeserving" and the "deserving" or "respectable" poor. The distinction had obvious moral implications, but also important social and political ones. The focus of public concern— of Royal Commission reports and journalistic exposés, of legislative reforms and private charities—was the dependent or potentially dependent poor. These were the poor who came within the province of the poor law, a law that was in fact a pauper law. They were the Malthusian poor who lived in a state of "misery and vice," on the verge of starvation and death. They were the Mayhewian poor, the "nomadic tribes" who wandered the streets of London, scrounging and scavenging for a bare existence. They were the "ragged" and "dangerous" classes for whom special schools were created and a metropolitan police force instituted. These poor were not, it should be said, always or even generally held in contempt or subjected to repressive measures. On the contrary, they were often the object of compassion and solicitude, of reforms intended to alleviate their conditions, improve their prospects, and bring them and their children into the mainstream of the working classes.

It was only in the last decades of the century that this dependent or pauper class ceased to dominate the public imagination. The social consciousness that Beatrice Webb identified with the "time-spirit" concerned precisely the "deserving" poor, the "laboring" poor who sought to be independent and who succeeded in being so, for the most part and most of the time—but who were nonetheless poor. It was for these poor that the "model dwellings" were intended. It was to them that the settlement houses catered. It was in their cause that so many people professed to embrace "socialism." And it was for their sake that Booth created the classes he did, differentiating the "poor" from the "very poor" and making the "poor" the worthy objects of attention and concern.

CHAPTER 9

"The Crux of the Problem"

THE MOST PROVOCATIVE part of *Life and Labour*—for the modern reader, although perhaps not for Booth's contemporaries—was his proposal regarding class B, a class that comprised 317,000 people in London, or 7.5 percent of the population.[1] This was the class of the "very poor," a class that was a "deposit of those who from mental, moral, and physical reasons are incapable of better work," not a "pauper class" (although it contained many paupers) but the "material from which paupers are made."[2]

Class B was the "crux of the social problem" because it was *"de trop."* Not only did it contribute nothing to industry (what little work it did could be done by C and D in their spare time); it was actually counterproductive, having a deleterious effect upon the other working classes. "The competition of B drags down C and D, and that of C and D hangs heavily upon E."[3] Were it not for class B, the other classes could take care of themselves. "These unfortunate people [in B] form a sort of quagmire underlying the social structure, and to dry up this quagmire must be our principal aim."[4]

For the sake of this class, and even more for the sake of those upon whom it impinged, Booth proposed to remove it, literally and physically, from the society of the rest of the poor. "Put practically, but shortly, my suggestion is that these people should be given the opportunity to live as families in industrial groups, planted wherever land and building materials were cheap; being well housed, well fed, and well warmed; and taught, trained, and employed from morning to night on work, indoors or out, for themselves or on Government account."[5] The residents of these "industrial groups" would build their own houses, cultivate their land, and make their clothes and furniture, with the government supplying the materials. For accounting purposes the goods they produced would be valued at the market rate and wages would be credited to their accounts. Although the enterprise would operate at a loss (the labor of this class being inferior), the state would set a limit to that loss by transferring to the workhouse any family whose account fell below that limit. Conversely, any family with a surplus in its account could leave the community and return to ordinary society by finding employment in private industry.

Booth did not mince words in characterizing his plan. It was nothing less than a proposal to place an entire class "under State tutelage—say at once under State slavery," with all the individuals in that class becoming "servants of the State."[6] The state could not physically force people into these groups, but it could do so legally by enforcing a "standard of life which would oblige everyone of us to accept the relief of the State in the manner prescribed by the State, unless we were able and willing to conform to this standard."[7] At a meeting with the COS, Booth was asked how the state would determine whether that standard was met—whether, in fact, an individual belonged to class B.

> "My notion is that it would be self-acting. The man would fail to satisfy the new standard in some particular; the law, rigidly enforced, would convict him of failure to maintain himself at the accepted level of decent independent life, and he would be offered maintenance in the State industrial homes."
>
> "But suppose that he declined with thanks?"
>
> "Well, then you would have the unmitigated workhouse behind. If he would not go into the Home or the House I take it that he would very soon find himself again falling below the standard, and, in time, he would learn to recognise his inability to remain independent. I trust to the pressure of the new standard to convince him in the long run. I reject any other form of compulsion."[8]

He was also pressed to consider the question of whether these families would have the right to beget children, and if so whether society would have the responsibility to support them. His answer to both questions was "yes." Public sentiment would not consent to the "severance of man and wife," and he himself shared that view; he could only hope that the children would be trained to be self-supporting. The commentator concluded amiably by remarking that he had never met "a more reasonable social reformer."[9]

In his book Booth explained that since his plan was meant to "control the springs of pauperism," it was really an extension of the poor law, which was itself a "limited form of Socialism."[10] There was already a "dual system" at work. The industrial groups would only extend that system by creating "a Socialistic community (aided from outside) living in the midst of an Individualist nation."[11] By enlarging the socialist sphere to comprehend the whole of class B (rather than merely the pauper class) and by demarcating it more sharply from the individualist sphere, individualism would be strengthened. "Our Individualism fails because our Socialism is incomplete. In taking charge of the lives of the incapable, State Socialism finds its proper work, and by doing it completely, would relieve us of a serious danger." At present individualism was constantly being invaded by socialistic schemes designed to take care of those who could not care for themselves. But if society were "purged" of such people, individualism would have a better chance of surviving. "Thorough interference on the part of the State with the lives of a small fraction of the population would tend to make it possible, ultimately, to dispense with any Socialistic interference in the lives of all the rest."[12]

Here, as in his remarks about "State slavery," Booth was putting the matter as harshly as he could in order to face up to the gravity of the problem. "Socialism" was hardly an honorific term in his vocabulary, and it was not lightly that he proposed to subject an entire class to an avowedly socialistic experiment. But he did so for the sake of the larger and more worthy classes of the poor so that they could lead better lives, and for the whole of society so that it might be spared any further socialistic interference. One suspects that he intended it less as a practical proposal than as a way of defining and focusing attention upon the problem. Although it did capture the attention of readers, it occupied only a few pages in the first volume and was mentioned briefly in the final volume. And in marked contrast to his proposal for old age pensions, he never wrote about it in any detail, lectured upon it, or in any way promoted it.[13]

UNLIKE MODERN commentators who find the proposal "retrograde," "doctrinaire," "Draconian," and "social imperialistic," most of Booth's contemporaries, including socialists, were well disposed to it, some welcoming it as a "heroic" remedy for an unfortunate problem.[14] It was, in fact, a familiar and respectable idea. Under the names of "industrial groups," "training camps," "labour colonies," "labour farms," and "la-

bour villages," such plans had been circulating throughout the 1880s.*
And they were being advanced by individuals and groups of varied dis-
positions: Samuel Barnett, Alfred Marshall, Robert Giffen, Herbert Mills
(a minister and founder of the Home Colonisation Society), Henry Solly
(organizer of the Society for Promoting Industrial Villages, but better
known as the sponsor of working men's clubs), the London Congregational Union (under whose auspices *The Bitter Cry* was published), the
Whitechapel Guardians of the Poor, and the Mansion House Committee
of 1888.[16]

After the appearance of Booth's plan (perhaps inspired by it), a number of others were proposed, again by a wide variety of people: Geoffrey
Drage (secretary of the Royal Commission on Labour in 1892–94), the
economist Arthur Pigou, the socialist and Labour Party leader George
Lansbury, Fabians (Annie Besant and the Webbs), new and old Liberals
(J. A. Hobson and William Beveridge), and both the Majority and Minority of the Poor Law Commission of 1909.[17] The principle of some
kind of compulsory labor was included in two unsuccessful Unemployed
Workmen's Bills proposed by the Labour Party in 1907 and 1908. The
best known of these schemes, and one that was actually carried out, was
the farm colony established by the Salvation Army.

The bitter enemies of labor colonies were not the socialists but laissez-
faireists who believed that any such plan was indeed, as Booth said,
"socialistic." The *Manchester Guardian* criticized Booth for proposing to
"extend the existing Socialism of our Poor Law scheme."[18] The *Saturday
Review* said it was unnecessary because all that was needed was a "hardheaded determination to drive the weak into the workhouse and leave the
idle to starve."[19] The secretary of the COS, C. S. Loch, derided the idea
that "one would wish to move the class, as if it were living on a floating
island, and could be towed into a new social state."[20] And the journal of
the COS protested that if a class had to be "harried" out of existence,
nature, operating through the medium of economic laws, was better at
that task than the state. "Nature performs her office without vindictive-

---

* As early as 1862 John Ruskin devised a plan that was harsher than most. He
proposed that the state be empowered to place any unemployed person into an institution and set him to work at a fixed wage. If he objected, he "should be set, under
compulsion of the strictest nature, to the more painful and degrading forms of necessary toil, especially to that in mines and other places of danger," where his wages
would be withheld until he came to "sounder mind respecting the laws of
employment."[15]

ness, without injustice. There is no appeal against her verdict. She visits the sins of the fathers on the children."[21]

The socialists, on the other hand, generally looked favorably upon the idea of labor colonies. The socialist journal *Today* was pleased to contemplate the adoption of Booth's plan, which would "send the old world spinning down the grooves of collectivist change with considerable impetus."[22] Sidney Webb, in the Fabian tract *Facts for Londoners,* was pleased that even "individualistic reformers" like Booth were seeking to eliminate from society the "chronic cases of sturdy vagrancy, idle mendicity, and incorrigible laziness."[23] J. A. Hobson (at that time a Fabian sympathizer) agreed with Booth that a labor colony would benefit both class B and the classes above it. For the former it would provide "humane care and a decent standard of material comfort"; for the latter, "relief from the glut of low-skilled inefficient labour."[24]

BOOTH HIMSELF had no doubt about the classes he wanted to benefit. "It is chiefly for the sake of these two classes [C and D] that my proposals for dealing with Class B are made. They are my clients, and to their service I dedicate my work."[25] It was B that put an intolerable pressure upon C and D, taking away resources that could be better used by them and thus dragging them down. If B were "swept out of existence," or at least removed from competition, all the work they did could be done by C and D and all the money they earned and spent could be earned and spent by C and D.[26] The irregularly employed in C would have more work, the badly paid in D would have better wages, and both would enjoy higher standards of living.

It was because C and D were Booth's "clients" that B, rather than A, was the "crux" of the problem. A was small in numbers, a largely "hereditary" class whose problem was not poverty but "disorder," and which should be dealt with as such.[27] Heavily concentrated in particular streets, it should be dispersed and "harried" so as to make the streets habitable for others. Here too the main objective was to separate this class from that contiguous to it: to "heighten the distinction between them [A] and the lowest industrial class [B], and put an end to the interchange and give and take which now makes it difficult to draw the line between Classes A and B."[28] Only by sharpening that distinction could B, the "lowest industrial class," be identified and removed from competition with the other industrial classes, C and D.

This was the true novelty and significance of Booth's proposal—not the labor colony itself, which was all too familiar at the time and which, in fact, never came to anything, but the conception of the social problem that inspired that scheme. It was Booth's work, more than any other, that shifted the focus from the "very poor" to the "poor." The COS had made it its mission to encourage the "respectable" element among the very poor, the dependent class. But it was still the very poor that were its "clients," the proper objects, as they saw it, of solicitude and assistance. At the very time that Booth's first volume appeared, the secretary of the COS delivered a lecture in France explaining what he took to be the basic tenets of social policy. "Self-sustaining poverty," he declared, should be "left to look after itself." Society should see to the enforcement of measures, such as sanitary laws, that were for the well-being of all citizens, and should see to it that no hindrances be put in the way of thrift. But beyond that, the less it "meddled with" poverty, the better. Pauperism was another matter. "Our business should not be with the poor as such, but with those who are in distress or destitution or who have in them the seeds of pauperism."[29]

Booth would have agreed that the proper beneficiaries of relief, and of charity as well, were those in "distress or destitution"—paupers and potential paupers. But his own concern, his "clients," were the "poor," who, by his definition, were not in "distress," not even in "want," but in "poverty," engaged in an endless struggle to lead a "decent, independent life."[30] It was this poverty that had to be ameliorated—not by relief in the conventional sense, but by creating the conditions in which the poor could be independent. And this meant relieving the poor of the intolerable burden of the very poor. "To the rich the very poor are a sentimental interest; to the poor they are a crushing load. The poverty of the poor is mainly the result of the competition of the very poor."[31] Booth's solution to this problem may have been ill conceived and in any case was never implemented. But his identification of the problem, "the poverty of the poor" rather than the distress of the destitute, had momentous implications.

It is also notable that Booth did not feel obliged to make of the poor paragons of virtue. His poor—"my poor," as he said[32]—were sometimes drunk and often shiftless and improvident. This was especially true of class C, because of the irregular nature of their employment and earnings. But even the improvident members of this class were "deserving" and "respectable"—deserving of society's concern and essentially, if not invariably, respectable. The moral standard Booth set for them, he once explained to the COS, was not a standard of perfect virtue but an "acceptable level of decent independent life."[33] He may have had the COS in mind when he wrote that class C, with its irregular employment and improvident habits, was "most hardly judged, and perhaps, also, most hardly used." Toward the unfortunates of that class "modern sentiment turns its hard side of moral condemnation"; the more it knows of them, the harder it finds it to draw the line between the "deserving" and the "undeserving," and the fewer it ranks with the deserving. The industrious and thrifty usually needed no help; it was those who fell below "the ideal standard of energy, prudence, or sobriety" who were a problem. The problem, moreover, was with the entire class. "To select the few picked cases or even that larger number who are comparatively deserving, and simply to admonish the rest, is not enough. To raise this class we need some larger plan."[34]

HERE AGAIN "relations" and "proportions" were decisive. The plan for class B was feasible (if not politic) because that class was relatively small compared with the classes that would benefit by it. It was appalling, Booth said, to think of 100,000 individuals who were "very poor," but less appalling when one considered that they constituted only one-tenth of the population in the poorest districts of the East End.[35] By the same token, it was distressing to think of class B consigned to "state slavery," but less distressing if one kept in mind the relative numbers in the classes: 7.5 percent in B compared with 22.3 percent in C and D.

That 22.3 percent consisted not of one but of two classes. Booth said little of this pairing of classes, but it was crucial to his scheme, if only because it made the proportions more favorable. To sacrifice the 7.5 percent of the very poor for the sake of the 22.3 percent of the poor made for a better "cost-benefit ratio," as we would now say, than if C alone were compared with B. Indeed in the study of East London, where C and D were calculated separately, B was larger than C—11.2 percent compared with 8.3 percent. Only by adding to C the 14.5 percent of D could the sacrifice of B be justified.[36]

The pairing of classes had another important effect. A and B were kept separate for good practical reasons, not only because they had distinctive characters but because Booth proposed to treat them in distinctive ways. C and D, on the other hand, were paired in spite of the fact that they had distinctive characters; the difference between irregular and regular employment, as Booth frequently pointed out, was more crucial than any difference of income. Theoretically they could have been kept distinct (and were, in fact, in the original study of East London). The effect of pairing them was to strengthen the case for them as Booth's "clients." It was C who was in the most precarious position—who was most easily confused with B, most likely to be tainted by B, and most in need of protection from the competition of B. By associating C with D, Booth made C seem more worthy and deserving than it might otherwise have appeared to be. And by uniting them in the common category of the "poor," Booth created a common alliance against the common enemy, as it were, B.

This is not to suggest that Booth was being Machiavellian in juggling figures and classes so as to produce a predetermined effect. His classes, and the figures associated with them, corresponded to his sense of the existential situation. If he tried to distinguish between the casual laborers in B, who would have preferred not to work and did so only when it was absolutely necessary, and the irregularly employed laborers in C (the dockworkers, most notably), who were often unemployed because of the nature of their trade, it was because he saw this distinction as essential not only in defining the classes but in defining the social problem. B was "very poor" generally for reasons of its own making; C was "poor" generally for reasons beyond its control. Thus the claim of C to consideration was greater than that of B and could be satisfied even at the expense of B. B was the "crux" of the social problem only because C was the true focus of the social problem.

BY THE SAME TOKEN, the working classes as such did not constitute a "social problem." Contemporaries (and historians) fastened upon the 30.7 percent of the population who were "in poverty"—the "poor" and "very poor" combined. Less often cited, but no less important, were the 69.3 percent of the population who were "in comfort," this figure including 51.5 percent of the working classes.[37] As was dramatically evident in the graph accompanying these figures (see p. 109), the "comfortable" working classes, E and F, constituted the largest group by far, even in East London, the poorest part of the city.

Classes E and F were important not only quantitatively, in absolute and relative numbers, but qualitatively. Theirs was the "standard of life in England," the "accepted level of decent independent life," against which poverty was measured and the poor were found wanting.[38] Just as B was a "crushing load" on C and D, so C and D were a "heavy weight" on E and F.[39] And just as C and D would be the beneficiaries of any plan to remove B, so E and F would benefit from whatever policies would relieve the poverty of C and D. Moreover, the improvement of C and D would be reflected not only in the material conditions of the working classes as a whole but in their institutions. If the poor were lifted out of poverty, they would come to share an interest in trade unions, cooperatives, and friendly societies, which would be immeasurably strengthened if they could "build from the bottom, instead of floating, as now, on the top of their world."[40]

At one point Booth suggested another reason for attending to the well-being of the "comfortable" working class: the potential for discontent in class E especially.

Class E contains those whose lot today is most aggravated by a raised ideal. It is in some ways a hopeful sign, but it is also a danger. Here, rather than in the ruffianism of Class A, or the starvation of Class B, or the wasted energy of Class C, or the bitter anxieties of Class D, do we find the springs of Socialism and Revolution. The stream that flows from these springs must not be dammed up, and therefore it is to this class and its leaders in Class F that I particularly appeal in favor of what I have called "limited Socialism"—a socialism which shall leave untouched the forces of individualism and the sources of wealth.[41]

This anxiety about social discontent and revolution was a rare note in Booth's work. He did not overestimate the "comforts" enjoyed by the "comfortable" working classes; indeed he made much of the precariousness of their lives, the fact that sickness, trade depression, or personal problems could quickly impoverish them, and that no amount of prudence on their part could protect them against such misfortunes. But he was also impressed by their decency and devotion to their families. After living among them, he came away convinced that "the simple natural lives of working-class people tend to their own and their children's happiness more than the artificial complicated existence of the rich." Lest this sound too complacent, he hastened to add that their condition could be much improved without jeopardizing that simple happiness and that "it would be well if their lot included the expenditure of a larger proportion of our surplus wealth than is now the case."[42] Even in the passage in which he spoke of the "springs of Socialism and Revolution," he made it clear that he did not want to dam up "the stream that flows from these springs"—the desire for more comfort and a greater share of wealth.

Another cause for confidence was the overlapping and interacting of the working and middle classes. In the clubs of East London, Booth pointed out, E, F, and G "consort together in a free and friendly way," and in some cases even mingle with some in C and D.[43] That mingling was reflected in his definitions of the classes. E was primarily a class of regularly employed workers with "standard earnings," but it also included small shopkeepers and small employers, while G, the lower middle class, consisted of clerks as well as small employers. The middle classes, moreover, were more numerous than might be thought. Even in East London they were only slightly smaller than the very poor, and in the whole of London they were closer in size to the poor.

The classes impinged upon each other and at their borders merged with each other. But the essential distinctions remained and were of the essence, because they defined not only the social classes but also the problem of poverty. To the casual reader the problem was expressed as a precise fact empirically derived from the data: 30.7 percent of the population were poor. But this fact was itself a logical construct inherent in the organization of the data—in the classes, categories, and definitions that were the foundation stones of the survey.

IF BOOTH'S WORK seemed to differ so dramatically from Giffen's or Levi's—if his seemed to focus on poverty and theirs on progress—it was partly because theirs were historical surveys and his, as Beatrice Webb put it, was "static."[44] By comparison with conditions earlier in the century, Giffen and Levi had no difficulty demonstrating a considerable improvement in the conditions of the working classes, as much as 100 percent in half a century according to Giffen, or 30 percent in a quarter of a century according to Levi.[45] Booth was concerned only with "how things are," not "how they came to be as they are, or whither they are tending."[46] He was in fact confident that had there been a comparable study for earlier times, it would have shown a "greater proportion of depravity and misery than now exists, and a lower general standard of fare." But he could not assign specific figures to that proportion or standard.[47] His figures—or rather the one figure that attracted most attention—was the 30.7 percent in poverty.

That figure was the product not only of a "static," unhistorical study but also of a highly differentiated one. In this respect too Booth's work was in sharp contrast to that of Giffen or Levi. Their statistics dealt with the working classes as a whole, and from that undifferentiated category and those undifferentiated statistics, they came to the conclusions they did. Booth's great achievement was the disaggregation, as we would now say, of that category and those statistics. By distinguishing subclasses within the working classes, Booth was able to demonstrate the considerable degree of poverty that coexisted with the larger degree of comfort among those classes.

It was this differentiation of classes that radically altered the terms of social discourse. Booth was not the first to define the "social problem" as the problem of poverty rather than pauperism. That idea had, in fact, become prevalent by the early 1880s and was the tacit assumption of the philanthropic and reform movements of that time. In this sense Booth was reflecting rather than creating the climate of opinion. What he so notably did, however, was to take a vague and diffuse idea and give it precision and substance: precision by means of statistics, and substance by the distinction and definition of classes. Others had tried to distinguish between paupers and the poor, between the idle and the laboring poor, between the undeserving and the deserving poor. But Booth identified and quantified that distinction in such a manner as to make it seem eminently objective and scientific. Just as Malthus's theory, a century earlier, seemed to have all the authority and certainty of the multiplication tables, so Booth's schema—the classes of A, B, C, etc.—appeared to be as natural and indisputable as the alphabet itself. And his findings seemed as precise and unequivocal as numbers and decimals could make them.

If Booth's classifications were meant to identify the poor and define the problem of poverty, they were also meant to identify those workers who were not poor and who did not constitute a social problem. He made the point sharply, almost polemically.

> The question of those who actually suffer from poverty should be considered separately from that of the true working classes, whose desire for a larger share of wealth is of a different character. It is the plan of agitators and the way of sensational writers to confound the two in one, to talk of "starving millions," and to tack on the thousands of the working classes to the tens or hundreds of distress. Against this method I protest. To confound these essentially distinct problems is to make the solution of both impossible; it is not by welding distress and aspirations that any good can be done.[48]

It is ironic, but not surprising, that Booth's contemporaries confounded his distinctions in just this way. In 1907 Alfred Marshall, the great economist and Booth's friend, rebuked those who cited Booth's statistics as if they demonstrated that "a third of the people of this country are on the verge of hunger." This, he said, was one of the few things that every German knew for a certainty about England. What Booth actually wrote, a German would be astonished to learn, was that a third were poor in the sense that they belonged to families with an income of 21 shillings a week or less. By that standard 70 percent or more of the German working classes would be deemed poor.[49]

It is rather more surprising to find reputable historians misreading Booth in the same way. Booth had made a large point of distinguishing the "poor" from the "very poor" and "poverty" from "want" and "distress." Yet one historian has him discovering that "about 30% of the people of London were indeed living in poverty so abject that they were deprived not only of luxury but of the basic necessities of life."[50] And another suggests that he "demonstrated conclusively that the old 'submerged tenth,' generally admitted in the 1870s to be the 'submerged fifth,' now constituted one-third of the population of London."[51]

Booth concluded his first volume by describing what he took to be the proper function of statistics: "In intensity of feeling . . . and not in statistics, lies the power to move the world. But by statistics must this power be guided if it would move the world aright."[52] It may be that he underestimated the emotive and dramatic effect of statistics themselves. The figure "30.7 percent" was as expressive of an "intensity of feeling" as the most sensational passage in *The Bitter Cry*. In the face of that statistic, all other statistics and distinctions tended to fade into obscurity.

CHAPTER 10

"Special Subjects":
Women, Children, Jews,
the Aged

SOME OF THE MOST memorable chapters of *Life and Labour* have nothing to do with the schema of classes or the statistical analyses that qualify Booth as the premier "social scientist" of his time, perhaps as the first true social scientist.[1] But if they make Booth less of a social scientist, they make him more of a social observer. Although he did not write most of the chapters under the heading "Special Subjects," he did decide that they should be written and he gave them a prominent place in his work.[2]

Women appeared throughout *Life and Labour* as wives and mothers as well as workers. A drunken wife was a grave misfortune, a sober and provident one a great boon; either could determine the class of the worker. One long chapter was devoted to women workers, but even here their domestic roles featured prominently, for most women workers were either married, shortly to be married, or widowed, and these facts impinged on their working conditions and prospects.[3]

Women workers in East London were concentrated in various branches of the garment trades (trousers, vests, children's clothes, ties, trimmings, corsets, furs, caps), in the production of umbrellas, boxes, matches, brushes, confectionery, artificial flowers, and ostrich feathers, and in such service trades as laundering.[4] Wages, working conditions, and the regularity of employment varied enormously within and among the trades. Fur sewing, for example, in the better branch of the trade, paid reasonably well, whereas in the lowest branch it was the worst-paid of all trades. (The fur sewers were also the most immoral of the women workers, but whether this was a cause or effect of their being in that trade, the author could not determine.) In those industries which employed both men and women, the women had the least skilled and lowest-paid jobs. On the other hand, some women had workrooms of their own with a few assistants or subcontracted the work to other women who preferred to work at home. The best-organized and most cooperative group of women workers were the match makers, mainly because they all did the same kind of work under the same conditions in factories. They also had good relations with their employers, in spite of occasional strikes, because the union provided a mechanism for the adjudication of minor disputes as well as for the organization of strikes.

Homeworking was obviously more prevalent among women than among men, but, contrary to the general impression, homeworkers were not worse paid than shop workers. The more skilled garment workers earned 20 shillings a week at home during the season and were never entirely without work; this reflected the fact that women homeworkers were to be found in the better branches of the trade as well as in the worst. In those trades where the work was done either in the shop or at home, unmarried women tended to work in the shop and married and widowed women at home. Lower-middle-class girls and single women, however, often preferred the privacy of homework rather than having to mingle with their social inferiors. (Another class difference was the fact that every girl in the lowest classes got married, whereas those in the lower middle classes sometimes did not.) Women worked at home for a variety of reasons: to earn enough for the barest necessities of life, to provide for small luxuries, to pay for the education of their children, or to put aside money for the future. It was a common complaint of widowed homeworkers that married women worked for lower wages because they were working for pocket money. But this was generally not the case; those women who worked for the lowest wages were usually supporting their families because their husbands were unemployed or disabled. The wages of women homeworkers were determined by the nature and state of the trade, the competition of employers for contracts and the number of subcontracts, the skill of the individual worker, and her particular circumstances, such as the position of her husband or the "mental and moral defects" of either husband or wife.[5]

"Factory girls" had the worst reputation among the public. Yet they themselves were acutely aware of the differences among them. "The manner in which one set of girls in a factory keep themselves aloof from another, and in which one factory regards itself as superior or inferior to another, laughable as it seems at first, is not nearly as ridiculous as much of the class prejudice satirized by Thackeray and Du Maurier."[6] Although there were thousands of "quiet, respectable, hard-working" factory girls, the common image was of a young woman promenading on

Bow Road on a Saturday evening or Sunday afternoon, arm in arm with two or three girls and sometimes a young man, flashily dressed, talking and laughing loudly. While some factory girls earned over 11 shillings a week, others earned well below that, being frequently absent from work and wanting only enough money for fancy clothes and drink. They generally lived with their families in a dirty and crowded couple of rooms; their fathers, often the lowest kind of dockworker, were frequently out of work and more often drunk.[7]

WOMEN WORKERS were not classified according to Booth's schema, but the schoolchildren were. The lowest type of elementary school in the poorest districts catered to children largely from classes A and B (there were twenty or more "Special Difficulty" schools for children who were habitually truant); the middle type of school to classes C and D; and the upper to E and F, with much overlapping among them. But even the children in schools of the lower type, who were often ill fed and ill clothed, were remarkably orderly and obedient, not out of fear—the atmosphere was usually friendly and relaxed—but out of respect and even pride.

Until the virtual abolition of school fees in 1891, parents paid a penny to sixpence a week for each child. But these fees were waived for the poorest classes and were not always paid by the others. It was good value for the money; for a penny, a working mother could send her three-year-old to "school" for the entire school day. Compulsory schooling started at the age of five and normally concluded at the age of thirteen. Before the revision of the curriculum in 1890, the main subject taught, after the three R's, was grammar, with an emphasis on the parsing of sentences and the ability to explain, for example, why the subjects of a sentence were "he and I" rather than "him and me." After the revision of the curriculum, the requirements for completion of the last grade of compulsory schooling included:

> Reading with fluency and expression from any book chosen by the Inspector.
> Writing any passage of prose or poetry from dictation, with Spelling. More than three mistakes "fail" a child.
> Arithmetic, Compound Rules with principles, Reduction, Tables of Weight, Length, Area, Capacity, etc.
> Needlework for Girls, Drawing for Boys. Singing.

Recitation of eighty lines of poetry, the meanings and allusions being properly understood.

Class subjects, Grammar, Geography, Elementary Science, History. Two of these are usually taken.[8]

Having earlier commended the public school system as "the high-water-mark of the public conscience,"[9] the author of this chapter went on to criticize this mode of education as ill suited to the children for whom it was intended. The poor and the very poor required different curricula, the very poor needing above all training in "habits of decency, cleanliness, and common self-respect, and . . . the rudiments of civilized, social, and domestic life."[10] Children who received no encouragement at home had to have school made attractive to them, and it was pointless to impose on them useless and difficult subjects while ignoring the cultivation of habits that would be of greatest service to them.

This account by one of Booth's associates is interesting in light of Booth's own discussion, in a later volume, of education as one of the "preventive remedies" for poverty. Education, he said, was not only a matter of conventional schooling. What was required was the "education of the citizen," an education that would encourage every person to "act more freely and more intelligently for himself," thus promoting the "individualism" that was the best remedy for poverty.[11] In commenting on this section many years later, Beatrice Webb, by then an ardent socialist, raised no objection to this concept of education, an education in habits and attitudes as much as in subjects and skills. What she did find anomalous, and commendable, was the fact that this man, so committed to individualism, should have favored a measure that was "the very reverse of individualist." For what he enthusiastically supported, she said, was the "essentially collectivist organization of compulsory education by the London Education Authority at the public expense—an organization that was, in these very years, being hotly denounced as a form of Socialism."[12] (She might have added that he approved of another measure that was at the time hotly denounced as socialistic: free school meals for poor children.[13])

THE CHAPTER on "sweating" was written by Booth himself and had his distinctive tone. At a time when the subject was being debated in Parliament and the press, when sensationalist accounts were being published and harsh remedies proposed, Booth managed to be both analytic and sensible. He traced the extension of the term "sweating" from home-workers in the tailoring trade to other industries (boot-making, for example) where work was contracted out to workers in their homes or to small workshops. It finally came to mean almost any kind of contracting, subcontracting, or middleman operation, or any trade where the competition for jobs was acute, especially among immigrants—"greeners," as they were called. (On the docks, it was sometimes applied to the practice of systematically deducting sums from the workers' earnings, a form of bribery in return for jobs.[14]) Sweated industries were characterized by long hours, irregular employment, low pay, and crowded and unsanitary conditions of work.

Without belittling these "evils"—indeed, he used the word repeatedly—Booth corrected the common impression that they were the result of exploitation by rich, ruthless, unscrupulous masters. More often, he pointed out, they were typical of the small workshop where the master was himself a worker, laboring as hard and as long as his employees and making little more, sometimes even less, than his skilled hands. In these shops master and men belonged to the same class, talked freely with each other, and were generally on good terms, a relationship in which there was "nothing that is monstrous, much that is very human."[15] But the evils of sweating were none the less real, and the worst of them could be remedied, Booth said, by a more rigorous application of existing laws (limiting the hours of women and children, for example) and by the licensing and more systematic inspection of workshops.

The sweated industries generally had the largest contingent of immigrants, and, most conspicuously, of Jews. Equating sweating with immigrants, immigrants with Jews, and both with the worst forms of exploitation and degradation, some journalists and politicians concluded that the only solution was a cessation of immigration or even the expulsion of recent immigrants.* Booth disputed these assumptions and con-

---

* It is interesting that the official reports in 1889, of the House of Lords committee on sweating and the House of Commons committee on immigration, were far less hostile to the immigrants than most journalistic accounts. The Lords report quoted some witnesses who described the Jews as "uncleanly," but went on to say that everyone agreed that they were "thrifty and industrious, and they seldom or never come on the rates." The Commons report contrasted them to the Italians, who were said to be "immoral, illiterate, vicious, and low," and to the Hungarians, who were even worse in all these respects.[16] Both came out against any restrictions on immigration—unlike the Trades Union Congress, which repeatedly called for a halt to immigration. In 1903 the Royal Commission on Alien Immigration again rejected the idea of restrictions.

clusions. Jewish employers often earned little more by way of profits than their workers did in the form of wages. The Jewish residents in the East End were no worse than their native-born neighbors; indeed, in many respects they were superior. And the Jewish immigrants were not paupers, as Arnold White, the chief crusader against immigration, claimed; they were hard workers who, if they fell on bad times, were supported by their own charities rather than public relief. Those who wanted to limit immigration could do so only on the ground of "England for the English," not on the cry of "no admittance to paupers."[17]

THE CHAPTER on the Jewish community, by Beatrice Potter, was sympathetic almost to the point of being philo-Semitic.* Her own highly developed religious sensibility made her appreciative of the piety of the Jews, the tenacity with which they clung to their "majestic religion" in the face of all their difficulties, their stubborn resistance to Christian missionary efforts, and the refusal of the more established of them to succumb to the temptation to assimilate. She was also taken with the moral and communal nature of their faith, the fact that it was non-ascetic and this-worldly, concerned as much with social duties as with ceremonial observances. Paramount among those duties was charity, which the Jews practiced, she said, in a distinctive and eminently satisfactory way. If so few Jews received public relief, it was because the Jewish Board of Guardians assumed responsibility for their coreligionists; and if so few Jewish recipients of charity remained that for long, it was because help was given them, whenever feasible, in the form of business capital rather than the dole.

This portrait of the typical Jewish immigrant was prefaced by an historical account of the persecution and oppression to which he had always been subject and which had become especially violent in recent years in Eastern Europe. Fleeing from the pogroms, the Jew arrived in London pathetic and penniless, slaved away for the barest subsistence until he acquired some skills, worked and scrimped to take care of his

---

* Some historians have accused Beatrice Webb of being anti-Semitic.[18] There is no persuasive evidence of this, although she was certainly, later in life, anti-Zionist, as her husband was. It has also been said that she was, or thought herself to be, one-quarter Jewish. But this is highly speculative, derived from the fantasies of her grandmother, who, when she was released from a lunatic asylum, took upon herself the mission of leading the Jews back to Jerusalem, and got as far as Paris before she was rescued by her family.

family and better himself. If he managed to resist the main vice to which he was subject, the "Jewish passion for gambling," he would end up as a small master living in a model dwelling, a devoted family man ("he treats his wife with courtesy and tenderness, and they discuss constantly the future of the children"), and a respectable member of his congregation and community. "In short, he has become a law-abiding and self-respecting citizen of our great metropolis, and he feels himself the equal of a Montefiore or a Rothschild."[19]

It was their intellectual superiority, Beatrice Potter claimed, that made Jewish laborers in the East End so much more successful than the English. The poorest Jew had "inherited through the medium of his religion a trained intellect." Unlike Christian societies with their sharp class divisions, the Jews were a "nation of priests." Every male child, rich or poor, was versed in the literature and language of his race and was able to interpret "the subtle reasoning and strange fantasies of that great classic of the Hebrews, the Talmud." Thus the Jews were intellectually equal among themselves and superior to other groups. In the struggle for existence in the East End, they were "a race of brain-workers competing with a class of manual labourers." If they had to perform manual work they did so as "the first rung of the social ladder," and unless they were distracted by the "vice of the intellect," gambling, they would rise to the status of small trader or master. This did not mean that they were more "cultured" than others; on the contrary, their vision was restricted to their own history, traditions, and people. But they did have the advantage of highly developed faculties of reason, memory, and calculation.[20]

Another ingredient in their success was the "moral and physical regime" that protected them against abuse and disease and fortified their stamina and self-control. The religious Jew was "a being at once moral and sensual; a creature endowed with the power of physical endurance, but gifted with a highly-trained and well-regulated appetite for sensuous enjoyment." This non-ascetic, religious morality was reflected in the "perfection" of Jewish family life, which prescribed obedience to parents, devotion to children, respect for women, and a high regard for chastity. With three thousand years of training behind them, the "chosen people" realized the nineteenth-century ideals of "physical health, intellectual acquisition, and material prosperity," thus fulfilling the promise of Moses: "Thou shalt drive out nations mightier than thyself, and thou shalt take their land as an inheritance."[21]

Just as the Jews were intelligent although not notably cultured, so they had a highly developed personal and communal morality without that "highest and latest development of human sentiment—social morality." This did not mean, Beatrice Potter hastened to say, that they failed to respect the law or their contractual obligations. On the contrary, they were scrupulously law-abiding, paid their debts, and honored their contracts. They understood that these laws and contracts were the *sine qua non* of a free and open society, and that their own success depended upon such a society. But they did not have a sense of personal dignity that prescribed a "definite standard of life," or feelings of "class loyalty" or "trade integrity." They drove themselves as hard as they could, competed as ruthlessly as they could, and recognized no social obligations except those exacted by law and contract and by their familial and communal duties. They were the very model of the "economic man" of the political economists: "an Always Enlightened Selfishness, seeking employment or profit with an absolute mobility of body and mind, without pride, without preference, without interests outside the struggle for existence and welfare of the individual and the family."[22]

It is curious to find so glowing a portrait of the Jewish community in an otherwise dispassionate book. It is, in fact, not so much a collective portrait as the representation of an "ideal type" ("ideal" in the sociological rather than moral sense), a composite of abstract qualities. The reality obviously included Jews who were drunkards as well as gamblers, who abandoned their wives and children (and even their faith), who were not notably intelligent, or moral, or successful. It is especially curious to find Beatrice Potter not only depicting this ideal type but clearly approving of it. At this time she was an incipient though not yet a full-fledged socialist. Yet she paid tribute to the Jews for embodying the virtues of "economic man": hard work, thrift, sobriety, rationality, respectability, self-reliance, self-discipline, a spirit of competitiveness, a desire for improvement and advancement. If she was something of a socialist, she was evidently more of a Victorian, and it was the Victorian in her that approved of virtues that were conducive not only to economic well-being but to a decent, moral life. Later these "values" were to be denigrated, by socialists and others, as the "Puritan ethic" or "capitalist ethic."[23] And the Jews themselves were to be vilified for embodying this ethic in its most acute form.* But

---

* Half a century earlier, Karl Marx portrayed the Jew as "economic man," indeed "capitalist man," but in a quite different spirit from Beatrice Potter. "Money is the jealous god of Israel before whom no other god may exist. . . . The god of the Jews has been secularized and has become the god of the world. The bill of exchange is the

here, as in other parts of Booth's work, the ethic was a subject of admiration and emulation.

This chapter attracted more attention than almost any other. A few commentators, including some radicals and socialists, argued that since the Jews were willing to work at any wages and forgo present satisfactions for future expectations, they were undesirable competitors in the labor market and their immigration should be limited. "Just as a base currency," Hobson wrote, "drives out of circulation a pure currency, so does a lower standard of comfort drive out a higher one."[25] But many more reviewers were impressed by this account of the Jews, often against their initial inclinations. After quoting the passage about the Jews' lack of "social morality," the *Times* was reassured by their habits of independence and hard work and cited them as a lesson to the English in the "folly and mischief of indiscriminate charitable relief."[26] The *Newcastle Daily Chronicle* devoted almost its entire review to this chapter, concluding that "even the lowest type of Jew possesses many first-class virtues which render him in a way superior to the English and Irish casual labourers among whom he dwells." "Social morality," it concluded, would no doubt come in time, as it already had for his "Ashkenazite brethren."[27]

Few reviewers went so far in praise of the Jews as the *Charity Organisation Review,* which acclaimed the "great and indelible nationality" that had made a virtue out of misfortune by acquiring "an individualistic training in a socialist world." Prohibited from owning land and thus spared the "demoralising influence of customary cultivation," Jews were obliged to enter trades that were "full of peril, but free for the development of private enterprise and the training of character." Persecuted instead of being protected by society, they acquired "a character for industry, thrift, and patience which is altogether wanting in a population cradled among the enervating influences of Socialism." Forced to live within "the limits of economical necessity," they were an example to the Gentiles of "how to live well."[28] It was a remarkable tribute—to the ethic, perhaps, rather than to the people.

BEATRICE POTTER also wrote the chapter on the dockworkers, again exposing some popular and contradictory misconceptions: that the work-

---

Jew's actual god. . . . What is the worldly cult of the Jew? Bargaining. What is his worldly god? Money."[24]

ers were either ne'er-do-wells or fallen angels; that the employers were at
fault in attracting a surplus of cheap labor, or in failing to make that labor
more attractive (hence creating an even larger surplus); that the system
was inevitable and had to be accepted whatever its evils, or that the evils
were so heinous that the system had to be condemned unequivocally.
Echoing Booth, she warned against the philanthropist whose "mental
vision is focussed on one huge spot of misery, and in his solicitude to
lessen it, he forgets, and would sometimes sacrifice, the surrounding area
of happiness."[29] There were no villains in the system, only objective
conditions with undesirable consequences. The introduction of steam
vessels, for example, meant that the old relaxed pattern of employment
had to give way to a more frenetic, spasmodic pattern, because the economics of the industry required that loading and unloading be completed
within a single day. The unintended effect was to exacerbate the irregularity and casualness of dock labor.

Again, like Booth (perhaps inspired by him), Beatrice Potter took
care to distinguish the several classes of workers on the docks. The
permanent workers, including the foremen, earned 20–25 shillings a
week, which placed them above the "line of poverty."[30] (She was perhaps
the only contributor to use this expression.) Regarding themselves as
superior to the other dockworkers, they set themselves physically apart
by residing in model dwelling flats or in small houses far from the docks.
The "preference" laborers ("ticketmen" with priority over the rest) were
honest and hardworking, earned 15–20 shillings, were irregularly employed, and tended to live among the lower classes of casual labor. The
casual laborers consisted of two classes which were often unfortunately
confused. The "professional" casual laborers earned 12–15 shillings a
week and lived with their families in single rooms or, if they were unmarried, in the more respectable common lodging houses. At the mercy
of the daily fluctuations of demand, they never knew whether their work
would last two or twenty hours, or when and what they would be paid;
thus their steady companions were the publican and the pawnbroker.
One of their grievances was the fact that they were often mistaken for the
lowest class of casuals, who were that not by "profession" but by "inclination" or "misfortune," having drifted into the trade as a result of drink
or "bad character." Many of these were not so much dockworkers as
professional cadgers or semiprofessional criminals who hung around the
docks for the odd hour of work or the free breakfast or handout. They
were the "leisure class" of the lower orders, superior to their counterparts
among the upper classes only because the imminence of starvation made

"communism," the sharing of what little they had, a "necessity of their life." Apart from that "quixotic" virtue, there was little to commend them. "Economically they are worthless, and morally worse than worthless, for they drag others who live among them down to their own level. They are parasites eating the life out of the working class, demoralizing and discrediting it."[31]

Although these "classes" were not explicitly identified with Booth's, the connections were obvious. The foremen and permanent laborers belonged to E and F, the preference laborers to C and D, the professional casuals to B and C, and the lower order of casuals to A and B.[32] Beatrice Potter's sympathies were also those of Booth's. It was the preference laborers and the "more constant of the casuals" who were the "real victims of the irregular trade."[33] And her fear, like his, was that these classes would be confused with the lower class of casuals, both in public opinion and in the reality of their lives. Living in the same area and under the same conditions and competing for the same jobs, the more able and willing workers found it hard to retain their identity and their precarious hold on respectability. Their situation was aggravated by employers whose hiring practices favored the most casual class of laborers, and by philanthropists who demoralized them by making it easier to receive relief than to work. They were thus caught up in the dilemma of "the difficulty of living by regular work, and the ease of living without it."[34] The second part of that dilemma, Potter suggested, could be resolved if the educated classes learned to curb their generous but misguided impulse for indiscriminate charity; and the first part by adopting a scheme that might be called "municipal socialism"—a "Public Trust" to improve the organization of the trade, reduce the dependence on casual labor, and create a more stable and permanent labor force.[35]

ONE SUBJECT conspicuously missing from the section "Special Subjects," indeed from *Life and Labour* as a whole, was the problem of old age. This is all the more conspicuous, and curious, because Booth made so much of it elsewhere, writing and lecturing about the problem and his remedy for it.

The neglect of this subject was most striking in the discussion of the causes of poverty, where old age did not figure as a cause at all. One might suppose that it was subsumed under the category of "illness or infirmity," but the figures for the latter—10 percent in the case of the very poor, 5 percent for the poor—were too low to include old age.[36] In an analysis sufficiently detailed to have "drunken or thriftless wife" appear as a separate item, it is odd to find no mention of old age. Nor did it appear as a category in other contexts where one might expect it: in a survey of the population enumerating married men, unmarried men, wives, widows, unmarried women, young persons, and children—but not the aged;[37] or in the list of forty "sections," including female heads of families and inmates of institutions—but again not the aged.[38]

One obvious explanation for this omission was the nature of Booth's data. To the extent to which he relied upon school visitors, his attention was necessarily drawn to the younger part of the population. Yet elsewhere he tried to supplement their findings, using other sources to obtain, for example, information about casual laborers and others who did not ordinarily come within the province of the visitors. The visitors did record all the members of the household including, presumably, grandparents living with their families. Yet there were few references to such households. When the elderly appeared at all, they seemed to be living on their own. (An examination of these records might throw doubt upon the conventional view of the "extended family" among the working classes.) Even in the districts with a heavy concentration of the very poor, there were entire streets which apparently had no elderly residents. Some of the aged were included in the category of paupers, either as recipients of outdoor relief or as "inmates of institutions." But even here Booth made no attempt to determine the numbers and proportions who were aged.

Yet at this very time, Booth was doing more than perhaps any other single person to call attention to old age as a cause of poverty—or, more precisely, as a cause of pauperism. Just before the last of the Poverty series appeared in 1891, he delivered a paper to the Statistical Society entitled "Enumeration and Classification of Paupers, and State Pensions for the Aged." The first part of the paper was an analysis of three poor-law unions where the aged turned out to be the largest single group of paupers; 30 percent of the population over the age of 65 (40 to 45 percent of the working-class population over that age) were on relief. The second part was Booth's proposal for a state system of old age pensions: a non-contributory plan to be administered outside the poor-law machinery, providing for a pension of 5 shillings a week for every person over the age of 65.[39] The discussion of this proposal became so heated that it had to be carried over to the next meeting of the society. Provoked by this response, Booth issued an expanded version of the paper in both book and pamphlet form, again with a double-barreled title, *Pauperism, a Picture; and Endowment of Old Age, an Argument.* Three years later he published

The Aged Poor in England and Wales, an extensive study of all the 648 poor-law unions. The results were identical with his original sample: 30 percent of those over the age of 65 received relief. (In London the figure was 38 percent.)[40]

While he was working on this larger study, Booth was appointed to the Royal Commission on the Aged Poor, where he testified about the extent of pauperism among the aged and presented his pension plan. His plan was not accepted by the majority of the commission, and he had to content himself with signing a minority report. (He found himself in the odd company of two people who were politically and personally uncongenial to him: Sidney Webb, who wrote the minority report, and Joseph Chamberlain, who endorsed it.) After writing yet another pamphlet on the subject in 1899, he was moved to engage in the kind of public activity he generally avoided; he went on a lecture tour of seven cities to explain and defend his proposal. He was also one of the founders and principal subsidizers of the National Committee of Organized Labour on Old Age Pensions, which tried to stimulate support for the plan—without much assistance, in spite of the title, from organized labor, which looked upon it with suspicion, and with much opposition from the Charity Organisation Society, which denounced it as a form of socialism.[41] It took almost a decade before Booth had the satisfaction of seeing his work bear fruit in the form of the Old Age Pensions Act (which differed from his in some respects, principally in setting the age at 70 instead of 65).*

Life and Labour, however, reflected little of this issue or of Booth's personal involvement with it. Even the revised volumes of the Poverty series, published after he had finished the first of his papers on the aged, gave little intimation of the problem itself, still less of his proposed solution. The subject was not raised until the fourth volume of the Industry series, published in 1896, a volume devoted to miscellaneous groups which had not been dealt with earlier in the series—public and professional workers, domestic servants, and the "unoccupied" classes (people of leisure, pensioners, the retired). It was there that parts of his 1892 pamphlet were printed, omitting the pension scheme itself. The inappro-

---

* Booth was not the first to propose a system of old age pensions. After developing his own plan, he discovered that R. P. Hookham had written a pamphlet on the subject in 1879, and he then dedicated his book to him. Similar plans had been proposed by Canon Blackley and Canon Barnett; according to Beatrice Webb, it was Barnett who converted Booth.[42] But there is no doubt that Booth's empirical findings, as well as his reputation, were influential in preparing the way for this major piece of social legislation.

priateness of this context—the aged appearing in the Industry rather than the Poverty series—and the equally inappropriate half dozen pages on the pension plan in the chapter on "charity" (in the third volume of the third series) are so obvious that they suggest some deliberate strategy on his part.[43]

It may be that Booth wanted to shield *Life and Labour* from the kind of controversy provoked by his pension plan. The controversy was a response to the plan rather than to an analysis of the problem of the aged, but he may have felt that the subject itself would stimulate a debate that would distract from the rest of the work. (This is probably the reason he omitted the pension plan when he did finally deal with the aged in the Industry series.) The subject would also have been distracting for another reason. While the aged loomed large in the class of paupers, the paupers themselves were a relatively small part of the population as a whole: at one point Booth estimated them as 2.7 percent in both the country and London, at another as 5 percent.[44] To have singled out the aged as a separate problem would have been to focus attention on the problem of pauperism rather than poverty, which would have been at odds with his main purpose.[45]

Whatever Booth's reasons for avoiding this subject in *Life and Labour,* the omission is regrettable. If old age was a prominent cause of pauperism, it was also a cause (although a lesser one) of poverty. By the same token, old age pensions would surely have a significant effect upon the poor as well as upon paupers. Some of these issues were addressed by Booth in his other writings. But it was here that they would have illuminated such crucial questions as the relationship between pauperism and poverty and between the "very poor" and the "poor."

CHAPTER 11

Religion, Morality, Ideology

"CHARLES BOOTH: Moralist or Social Scientist?"—that is the issue posed by historians debating whether Booth's work was so dominated by "value judgments" as to belie his professions of objectivity.[1] Booth would have been bewildered by this controversy. He would have readily conceded the flaws in his work: the failure to provide the correlations he had hoped for between classes and income and between trades and classes, or the unreliability of his quantitative evidence and the insufficiency of his qualitative evidence. But he would have rejected the antithesis between morality and science implied in this debate. He would not have understood why it was scientific to regard low wages as a cause of poverty but not intemperance or improvidence. And he would not have appreciated the dubious defense of him on the ground that he completely disregarded "moral categories or individual worth" and treated people solely on the basis of their "income level."[2] He would hardly have recognized his own work in the description of it as "too coldly scientific."[3] Nor would he have thought it scientific to ignore the objective, empirical, demonstrable facts about the poor—moral and religious facts as well as economic and social ones.[4]

This Positivist image of the "social scientist" is belied by the whole of *Life and Labour,* and most patently by the final series, "Religious Influences." The seven volumes of this series were written entirely by Booth himself (with the exception only of some of the "illustrations") and were a serious attempt to elucidate what he regarded as an essential part of the "life and labour" of the people, the spiritual and moral fabric of their life. He made a conspicuous point of not trying to quantify the evidence. "Spiritual influences," he noted, "do not lend themselves readily to statistical treatment. . . . The subject is one in which figures may easily be pressed too far, and if trusted too much are likely to be more than usually dangerous." Nor did he approach religion from an institutional point of view, except insofar as the institutional structure of the church affected its spiritual influence upon its parishioners. The question of influence, he believed, could best be ascertained from "truthful and trustworthy impressions"—an enterprise that sounded more modest than it actually was, those "impressions" having been derived from almost 1,800 personal interviews covering every area of London and dealing with every religious denomination and sect.[5]

The seven volumes echo the same refrain: the apathy, indifference, and essential irreligiosity of the great bulk of the working classes. Having disclaimed any attempt at statistical analysis, Booth cited the impressions of three ministers, two of whom estimated that "not 5% of the working classes ever go to church," and the third that "certainly not 10%" go.[6] The apathy was so pronounced that it rarely rose to the level of active hostility; doctrinaire secularism was less prevalent than in earlier decades, and overt atheism was rarer still. It was also striking because it corresponded so closely to social class. Although the middle classes were less religious than they had been previously, they were more religious than the working classes, and the poorer of the working classes were conspicuously the least religious. Booth noted (not once but twice) that his street map, colored to represent the different classes residing on each street (with red representing the "well-to-do" or middle classes, pink the "fairly comfortable" working class, blue the poor, and black the lowest class), corresponded almost exactly with the degree of religious commitment.

> Where the streets are red, we find a vigorous middle-class religious development combined with active social life. Where the streets are pink, there is, as regards religion, a comparative blank. Where the colour is blue we have the missions, and step by step, as it deepens to black, the more hopeless becomes the task. From these broad conclusions there is no escape.[7]

The religious indifference of the working classes was all the more conspicuous because it contrasted so dramatically with the vigorous attempts by the churches to engage them. This too is a refrain throughout the series: the great disproportion between efforts and results. All the churches made heroic endeavors to attract the working classes, not only with religious services and sermons that were appropriate and often surprisingly eloquent, but with a variety of social programs—schools (in the larger churches, day schools as well as Sunday schools), clubs, guilds, mothers' meetings, benefit societies, excursions, concerts, dances, plays, even outright charities. For the most part they were notably unsuccessful. Those churches that had some small success were the more orthodox ones. The Roman Catholic Church had the largest number of working-class and poor parishioners; the Nonconformists had more of the "chosen few" than the Church of England; and the most "liberalized" churches had the fewest.[8]

Apart from the Roman Catholic Church, which did have a substantial body of devout congregants among the poor, the small working-class constituency in the other churches tended to be of the "respectable" sort. This did not mean that the church had inspired them to become respectable. Booth made a point of dispelling the common illusion that when a working-class family joined a church, it tended to rise in the "social scale." This may have been true in a few cases, but not in general. "It is respectability that causes people to come to church far more than it is church-going that makes them respectable." Moreover, the nonchurchgoer was apt to be as "decent and respectable" as the churchgoer.[9]

Where the churches, and even the missions, failed most dismally was in the case of the very poor. "Women will go where they are helped, and in some of these a rather debased form of piety is aroused. Men seldom attend at all."[10] Of most of the missions Booth spoke respectfully: they were earnest, energetic, well-intentioned, if ineffectual. Of the Salvation Army, he was more critical, especially of its social work. In providing free food and shelter, it harmed the very people it professed to help. "For the great bulk of the homeless poor who frequent the shelters, the cheap food and cheap lodgings are merely conveniences, which tend to confirm them in the manner of life to which they have fallen. Not only are their lives unaltered, they become more unalterable."[11] Booth did not doubt the religious convictions of the missionaries themselves, and he judged the Salvation Army, as a "religious body," to be one of the most vital and flourishing of the missions. But he suspected that the Army was less interested in spreading the gospel than in attracting missionaries "who may find their own salvation while seeking vainly to bring salvation to others."[12] He quoted one minister from another mission who complained that the Army was making it difficult for the other missions to attract the class they were intended for, the very poor. "They [the very poor] are Gospel-hardened and sick of religion: the Salvation Army has made it too cheap. You can buy a congregation, but it melts away as soon as the payments cease."[13]

It is interesting that when Booth spoke of the "influence" of the churches, he did not mean merely their moral influence. As for that, he was convinced that the considerable moral improvement that had already taken place among the working classes was the result of "structural" changes—better housing, sanitation, and policing—rather than of religion or even education.[14] What he looked for in the churches was a distinctive spiritual influence, a sense of reverence and awe. (For Booth, a lax Positivist and lapsed Unitarian, reverence and awe were as close as he could get to a belief in God.) And here the churches were ineffectual. He cited the experience of those who had fought for the Saturday half-holiday, in the expectation that Sunday would then be reserved for religion, and who sadly discovered that Sunday then became a day for recreation rather than worship. "The maw of pleasure," he observed, "is not easy to fill. The appetite grows."[15] The churches were not puritanical; they tried to satisfy the appetite for pleasure by providing a variety of pleasurable activities. But they could not compete with the public house, music hall, or racecourse. And to the extent that they did, they succeeded at the expense of their spiritual mission. Booth regretted the absence of religiosity—in the undoctrinal sense in which he understood that word—because he thought it an impoverishment of life and mind. But he was sympathetic with the workers who lacked that religious experience. He even went so far as to credit them with a more exacting conception of religion than some churchmen had.

> They expect a religious man to make his life square with his opinions. They like their club with its pot of beer, its entertainments, its game of cards or billiards, or the "pub" and its associates and a bet on tomorrow's race, but they look on these things as inconsistent with all religious profession, and every form of religious association thus becomes (if they think seriously about the matter at all) something from which, in honesty, they must hold themselves aloof.[16]

BOOTH BROUGHT to the discussion of morality the same attitude of sympathy and tolerance. That subject pervaded the whole of his work, and the final volume most explicitly under the rubric "Social Influences." Here too he was dispassionate without making any pretense of being "scientific" or "value-free."

Legal marriage, he found, was the general rule even among the lowest class, at least early in life. In later years, cohabitation, without benefit of law or clergy, was common, and such extralegal relationships were often more peaceable than legal ones. Children, whether legitimate or illegitimate, were generally treated with "careless kindness and ill-regulated affection." The problem was more often the neglect of parents than of children; working children took lodgings outside the home and did not contribute to the support of their elderly parents.[17] The independence of the young also expressed itself in freer sexual relationships, which were generally conducted with a fair degree of "virtuous restraint." Premarital relations were usually a prelude to marriage, the more respectable marrying several months before the birth of the child, others immediately before the birth. In general the poor married earlier than the middle classes and had more children, although even among the poor the average age of marriage was rising.[18]

Whatever loose conduct or immorality there was among the poor, it was entirely different, Booth insisted, from prostitution. Toward the latter he was uncompromising, regarding both parties as equally immoral: the man who wanted to satisfy his sexual passions without the responsibility of marriage or even any extramarital commitment, and the woman who wanted to make a living in the easiest way available to her. Believing the evil in some form to be inevitable, Booth preferred that it be carried on in "houses of accommodation" (hotels or lodgings occasionally used for that purpose), rather than brothels where prostitutes lived and plied their trade and which were the "worst forms of organized and associated vice." By illegalizing brothels and enforcing rules of decency and order in hotels and lodgings, he hoped to bring the trade under control without sanctioning or encouraging it.[19]

Booth's moral pronouncements in such matters were firm and unapologetic, without being hectoring or dogmatic. While adhering to the principle of "individual responsibility," he recognized the need for judicious legislation to counteract the prevailing "moral laxity." Legislation should not be far in advance of public opinion, but it should lead the way in awakening the individual conscience, impressing an "undeniable seal of condemnation" on wrongdoing, and contributing to a "rising standard of public judgment and expectation."[20]

IF SOME HISTORIANS find Booth excessively moralistic, others find him excessively ideological, his "value judgments" reflecting his commitment to laissez-faire. Thus his editors contrast Booth the "investigator," who was "radical" in pursuit of the truth and exposed poverty with a "fresh and unbiased eye," to Booth the "man of affairs," who was an "implacable conservative" in policy and a "staunch defender of laissez-faire liberalism." It was the latter Booth who was willing to sacrifice the liberty of class B in order to strengthen "individualism" and who, while admitting the evils of the existing order, "sang paeans of praise to the capitalist system and condemned interference with the prerogatives of entrepreneurs."[21] The implication of this critique is that he would have been less biased and more consistent had he been more "radical" in ideology as well as methodology—had he been a socialist, in short, rather than an individualist.

To some critics, Booth's ideological bias derived from his incorrigibly "middle-class" bias, his habit of looking at the working class through the "filters of middle-class perception," "middle-class eyes," the "dominant middle-class view."[22] One historian complains that this middle-class proponent of "letting the facts speak for themselves" did not let the facts speak for themselves when they led to conclusions "adverse to the capitalist system" or conducive to "socialistic" remedies. While Booth professed to criticize the a priori theories of orthodox political economy, he was at the mercy of his own "unexamined beliefs and popular dogma," which were essentially those of the classical economists.[23]

Others have charged Booth with being at best "conservative," at worst "reactionary." One historian maintains that even his seemingly "progressive" proposals, like old age pensions, had something "reactionary" in them, the pensions being limited to the aged rather than the poor as a whole, and excluding among the aged those who had previously been on relief.[24] Another historian denies that there was anything "progressive" or "benevolent" in this proposal, any more than in his labor camp scheme, both being "strategic interventions that made other intervention unnecessary"—that is, made socialism unnecessary. Instead of a dualistic Booth, who was "progressive" in some respects and "authoritarian" in others, this historian sees in him only a "tired philosophical conservatism that doubted the possibility of collective action."[25]

Yet another critic finds evidence of Booth's pervasive ideological bias in the very terms and categories of his analysis, particularly in the sharp distinction between class B and classes C and D. The effect of this distinction was to create and perpetuate the image of a "residuum of casual labor" too degraded to cohabit with the "respectable working class" and too dangerous to be controlled by any means except segregation and coercion. This image was reinforced by Booth's "crowding index," which confirmed the "theory of urban degeneration" and consigned the residuum to a class of "outcasts."[26]

* * *

IT IS QUITE TRUE that Booth was firmly committed to a system of individualism (as capitalism was commonly referred to) and as firmly opposed to socialism (or collectivism). Early in life he had declared himself a Positivist but not a socialist. The "but" is significant, for most Positivists, including Saint-Simon, the founder of the movement, were socialists—not Marxists, to be sure, but socialists of a different mode.[27]

By Marxist standards, Henry George was not a socialist either; indeed he himself rejected the label.[28] But his *Progress and Poverty,* advocating a "single tax" on land, was generally regarded as a socialist scheme, so that Booth's critique of it was, at least in part, a critique of socialism. That critique was delivered in January 1883 to a meeting of the Democratic Federation (the Social Democratic Federation, as it was soon to be renamed). Booth's basic objection to the single tax was that it would not eliminate the monopoly of land; it would only transfer that monopoly from the landed classes to the state. The question was how the state would use that monopoly and what it would do with the wealth it would then control. Without some form of "artificial" government action, Booth predicted, the struggle would continue to be what it had always been, between "those who have wealth already, and those who have not"—that is, between capital and labor. Indeed, that struggle would be exacerbated, for the impoverishment of the landed classes would worsen the conditions of the agricultural laborers and sap the power of labor in general by pitting those who had work against those who did not.[29]

Mary Booth later recalled that while Booth was listened to most courteously, "a certain amazement showed itself and grew as his quiet voice advanced points of view so widely different from those usually taken before that audience."[30] What is remarkable is that Booth, the least contentious of men, should have chosen to criticize socialism before a socialist audience—and that he continued to do so, attending meetings of the Social Democratic Federation and engaging them in respectful but firm controversy.[31] He took other opportunities to debate the issue of socialism with socialists. Among his manuscripts is a long paper reporting on three meetings held in his home, probably in the fall of 1884, between two socialist working men (a tailor and a window cleaner, whom Booth addressed as Mr. Williams and Mr. Macdonald) and Booth and Alfred Cripps (Beatrice Potter's brother-in-law and Mary Booth's cousin by marriage).[32]

The socialists advanced the familiar theory that labor alone created value and that the profits of capital represented "unpaid wages" and therefore "robbery." This system was not only unjust, they argued, it was unnecessary, because man's command over nature was so great that all the requirements of life could be provided without competition or struggle. At a time when two hours of labor a day would suffice to provide for everyone's needs, the mass of workers were "without freedom and without leisure and without a future." Conceding that workers were better dressed and had comforts and even luxuries lacking to their grandparents, the socialists protested that the working class as a whole had not gained relative to other classes. Pressed to explain how the system should be changed, they proposed the establishment of a "central board of trade" which would determine who worked at each trade, what the hours and wages would be, and how much would be produced. They also predicted that by a process of "historical evolution" the state would acquire one after another of the "means of production," until eventually a new set of motives and incentives would emerge. "The spirit that animated a Newton, a Faraday, or a Livingstone, would be gradually developed in all, . . . thus supplanting the energy and pressure of greed and want, which is the motive power of society today."[33]

The counter-arguments of Booth and Cripps were no less familiar. Against the idea that property was robbery, they cited the productive nature of capital, the value created by the entrepreneur, the need for capital investment and skillful management, and the greater efficiency of the free market compared with a state bureaucracy. The interests of the workers would be better served by reforming rather than abolishing the system—by expanding the cooperative movement (not to replace but to compete with private industry), revising the land laws, giving workers a voice in the selection of managers, and making education more available. In the course of the discussion, Cripps observed that many of the socialists' demands were not specifically socialistic and should not be characterized as such. Booth took the opposite view, that it was more accurate to describe all "combined action" as more or less socialistic, thus seeing it clearly in its proper relation to individualism.

Collective action could only take up what individual action had commenced and created; and from this it would follow that the individual principle could not be universally superseded by collectivism without universal stagnation, and that individual action must not only continue in order to create, but must also stand by to resume and recreate any portion of the collective work which might go wrong.[34]

The socialism Booth was talking about was "collectivism," not Marxism. Booth was by then familiar with Marxism, although he had probably not read Marx. Half a dozen years earlier, during a visit to the United States, he had had long talks with one of his employees, a German socialist refugee—but not, Booth assured his wife, one of the "Karl Marks (—is that the name?—) and the ultra set."[35] By 1883 and 1884, when Booth was debating the question of socialism, he would not have misspelled Marx's name. He knew about Marx from his acquaintances among the SDF and from his relative and friend Spencer Beesly, who managed to be both a Positivist and a Marxist.[36] In 1887 he read a long essay on Marxist economic theory by another cousin-by-marriage, Beatrice Potter.* The essay was never published, but Beatrice was pleased to report that the Booths were "delighted" with it and that Charles was "enthusiastic."[38] (They sent it on to Beesly, who was less than enthusiastic since it was critical of Marx.)

It was perhaps this essay that prompted Mary Booth to read *Capital,* which had recently appeared in an English translation. In 1888, while her husband was lodging with a poor family in Liverpool, she wrote to him in her usual breezy fashion: "[I] enjoyed an hour and a half over a good fire yesterday night with Karl Marx in our own bedroom. . . . Marx is decidedly amusing. His style is simple and lively, and he has got ideas, but is steeped in the German craze for abstractions, as Comte is in the French craze for systems."[39] Two days later, still deep in the book, she reported on it more soberly, although she still professed to find it "very amusing." "I am reading him carefully, the first part twice over to be sure I do justice to his ideas—as far as any intellect is capable."[40]

Booth apparently did not find the prospect of reading *Capital* amusing; there is no evidence that he ever did read it. But he did continue to give thought to socialism and collectivism. In an address to the Political Economy Club in April 1888, he defended free trade and private enterprise, declaring it "inconceivable" that the state could be an effective entrepreneur. He then went on to make a point that was more novel and especially pertinent to his work on *Life and Labour.* Socialism, he said,

---

* In May 1883, two months after Marx's death, Beatrice Potter met his daughter Eleanor in the refreshment room of the British Museum. They talked mainly about religion, Eleanor describing Christianity as an "immoral illusion." When Beatrice asked her what the socialist program was, Eleanor replied that the question was too complicated for any brief answer, that it was "a deduction from social science which was the most complicated of all sciences."[37]

confused the conflict between "labour and capital" with that between "poverty and wealth." Although many workers were poor, poverty and labor were distinct concepts and represented distinct classes.

> The force of labour considered as a class consists in the amount of its earnings, the regularity and value of its work. The force of the poor considered as a class consists in their poverty, in the irregularity of their work or the smallness of their earnings. . . . There is no uniformity of interest and can be no uniformity of aim, any more than there is uniformity of social position, amongst the millions who fill up the ranks of poverty and labour.

Those socialist proposals which benefited the *poor* at the expense of taxpayers (relief works or public education) did not represent a conflict between labor and capital. The conflict arose only when socialists proposed to benefit *labor* at the expense of capital. So far this was not a real threat, but if the system of free trade should fail to produce "national well-being," there might well be a serious struggle between labor and capital.[41]

Two years later, the Booths had a long talk about socialism with Beatrice Potter, who had recently joined the Fabian Society. (This was their last serious conversation with her, her engagement and subsequent marriage to Sidney Webb leading to a cooling of relations.) Booth proposed a new definition of socialism: "The prevention by a paternal state of the consequences of a man's action: *the substitution of a new set of consequences for the natural set of consequences* following upon a man's action." Potter objected that it was precisely under socialism that people would suffer the exact consequences of their actions because they would no longer be protected by private property; the only exception would be paupers or "incapables" who would be dealt with, as at present, by a poor law. Mary Booth retorted that this was not the view of Marx or of such English Marxists as William Morris and Belfort Bax, to whom socialism meant "the giving according to the needs, the equalizing of conditions, the levelling of all classes to one standard of comfort." Charles Booth then expanded his definition of socialism to include "the substitution of the will of the State for the wishes of the individual"; since the state would assign each man a trade in return for his food and lodging, it would also assure him of his food and lodging regardless of his performance. This was why a socialist or "paternal" government would impose "artificial consequences" for a man's action in place of the "natural consequences" that obtained in a competitive system.[42]

* * *

Life and Labour did not explicitly address the issue of socialism, but it did defend, although not uncritically, "individualism" and the "industrial system" (a common synonym for capitalism). The passages frequently cited to support the image of Booth as an unreconstructed laissez-faireist appear in a discussion of trade cycles in the final volume of the Industry series.

> Looked at from near by, these cycles of depression have a distinctly harmful and even a cruel aspect; but from a more distant point of view, "afar from the sphere of our sorrow," they seem less malignant. They might then perhaps, with a little effort of the imagination, be considered as the orderly beating of a heart causing the blood to circulate—each throb a cycle. . . .
>
> There are some victims, but those who are able and willing to provide in times of prosperity for the lean years which inevitably follow, do not suffer at all; and, if the alternations of good and bad times be not too sudden or too great, the community gains not only by the strengthening of character under stress, but also by a direct effect on enterprise. As to character the effect is very similar to that of the recurrence of winter as compared to the enervation of continual summer. As to enterprise, it is not difficult to understand the invigorating influence. In bad times men's wits are exercised to escape loss, and only the more capable managers, or those who command some special advantages, can stand the strain. There result a constant seeking after improvement, a weeding-out of the incapable, and a survival of the fittest. . . .
>
> On its good side the system is extraordinarily efficient. Every power of man is stimulated, guided, and brought to bear on the desired object, and the forces of nature are more and more subdued to his service. No other system has been found equally productive. Some of the workers suffer from pressure, but every worker is also a consumer, and as consumers all gain; while the standard of life rises in every, or almost every, class. . . . [43]

These passages appear in the midst of a volume devoted largely to the "evils," as Booth repeatedly called them, of irregular work, low pay, long hours, and trade depressions. It was to present the economic system in a larger perspective, to balance its evils against its virtues, that he reminded his readers of the "good side" of a system that, for all its faults, benefited workers as it did almost everyone else.

Even in this context, Booth devoted as much space to a defense of trade unionism as to the defense of capitalism. Unions were desirable, he said, even when they were most aggressive in pursuing their demands. If those demands conflicted with the interests of the community to the extent of inviting public arbitration, that would be beneficial in developing "traditions of diplomacy." And if they conflicted with the interests of employers, that too would be salutary, for employers might be obliged to offer their workers better wages, more regular employment, profit-sharing, cheap insurance, or old age pensions. "It may, perhaps, be said that it is not till masters have experienced the rough side of union action that they learn to value free relations, and hence that either way it is to the unions that improvement is due."[44]

For those industries that were not unionized, such as the sweated industries, Booth proposed other remedies: strengthening the inspection and supervisory provisions of the factory acts and supplementing regular inspectors by "peripatetic staffs" that would engage in a form of "guerilla warfare," descending on the shops without notice to inspect them;[45] registering and licensing all workshops, however small; and making landlords as well as employers responsible for safety and sanitary conditions, on the theory that landlords were in a better position than the small master to enforce these regulations. He confessed that he would have liked to make employers responsible for conditions of their homeworkers as well, but could see no way of enforcing this measure. His principle was simple: "The net must be large and its meshes small."[46] Contemplating his elaborate and detailed proposals for regulation, Sidney Webb observed that they would have "delighted the heart of Jeremy Bentham."[47]

In general, however, Booth looked to the expansion of trade and education, rather than government regulation, for the material and moral progress of the working classes. Apart from being inherently desirable, education had the advantages of improving the skills and opportunities of the poor and, more important, of enabling the individual "to act more freely and more intelligently for himself."[48] But even for this individualistic purpose, Booth recognized that some government regulation was required—in this case, a raising of the legal age of employment.

IF CONTEMPORARY reviewers of Booth's work did not find in it the moral and ideological deformations that some historians have, it was perhaps because most of them shared his "value judgments," "middle-class" bias, and "individualism." The work was reviewed widely and at length, in papers and journals of every description. In the dailies and weeklies alone there were a hundred or so reviews of the first volume and almost that number of the second, and the later editions continued to attract considerable attention. Even Booth's papers to the Statistical Society (the first of which was also issued as a pamphlet) received long and serious notices.[49]

In some respects the reviewers were more faithful to the work than were later commentators. They did not, for example, make much of the "line of poverty," or even of the income figures supposedly demarcating that line. Like Booth himself, they were more concerned with the descriptions and proportions of the various classes than with monetary sums. Nor did they regard the lack of precision as detracting from the scientific character of the work. On the contrary, one after another paid tribute to Booth's "scientific" method, all the more because it was accessible to the ordinary reader. The *Daily News* was pleased to have the "statistical method made readable," while the *Manchester Guardian* liked the way Booth combined statistics with case studies, which were "types and standards of the whole."[50] The *St. James's Gazette* predicted, only half facetiously, that aspiring philanthropists would have to pass a competitive examination in order to practice their profession and that *Life and Labour* would become the textbook of the new "science of philanthropy."[51] The *Spectator* declared it the equal of any work produced by any European government, and at the same time readable enough to become a best-seller in the lending libraries.[52] In this chorus of praise, the *Athenaeum* was one of the few dissenting voices, judging the first volume informative but so "entirely without literary merit" that only a professional philanthropist would be likely to read it.[53*]

So far from interpreting it as a conservative document, most reviewers commended it for providing a statistical verification of evils that had previously been described emotionally and sensationalistically. The *Daily News* saw it as "another version of 'The Bitter Cry' . . . with chapter and verse for each note of anguish."[55] The radical press was enthusiastic.

---

* In fact not all professional philanthropists felt obliged to read it. Octavia Hill privately confessed that she had no intention of doing so. "I know in my heart of hearts what I think, and *that* is that it all depends on the spiritual and personal power; and *that* we must measure, if at all, in the courts [the slum houses], rather than in the book."[54]

Sidney Webb, in the *Star,* said that Booth had presented the socialist case more accurately and vividly than Marx, Engels, or any other socialist. (He also took the occasion to compliment Beatrice Potter as "the only contributor with any literary talent.")[56] Some radical journals, while deploring Booth's "a priori individualism," praised him for pricking "many a complacent fallacy about poverty" and revealing the "injustice of our social and industrial system."[57] The *Pall Mall Gazette,* which had described Booth's first paper as a "complacent and comforting bourgeois statement," reversed itself when the volumes were published, finding the first volume confirmation of the worst evils of unrestricted competition, and the second "perhaps the grimmest book brought out in our generation." It praised Booth for exposing "all the foul sores of the body politic," and for doing so with "no object to serve but that of truth: no master but science, . . . no sensationalism, no class hatred, no partisanship, no sentimentality." Booth was nothing less than a "Social Copernicus" revolutionizing the study of poverty and rendering the work of a Mayhew or a Sims obsolete.[58]

While professing to be delighted with the absence of sensationalism, some journals could not resist the opportunity to indulge in it. The article in the *Pall Mall Gazette* acclaiming the lack of sensationalism bore the headline "A City Very Much Like Hell"—an allusion to Shelley's famous line, "Hell is a city much like London." The San Francisco *Sunday Chronicle* reported on Booth's first paper under the title "The Great Homeless," with the subtitle "London City's Suffering Millions";[59] this article, with the same titles, was widely reprinted, appearing as far abroad as New Zealand. It was all the more ironic because Booth himself, in that very paper, had warned against those "sensational writers" who confounded the suffering poor with the working classes by glibly speaking of "starving millions."[60] In his second paper Booth again protested against the inflation of figures that resulted from the amalgamation and confusion of classes.[61] When another journal, reviewing the second volume, spoke of 34 percent of the population of London as being in "chronic want," Bernard Bosanquet wrote a letter to the editor pointing out that this figure included classes C and D, which Booth had explicitly said were *not* in "chronic want."[62]

What is surprising is not that there were instances of sensationalism but that they were relatively rare. Most of the reviewers, heeding Booth's injunction to keep the subject in its proper proportions, managed to convey a sense of urgency without lapsing into melodrama. While some in the radical press read his work as confirming their worst fears, others concluded that the extent of "irremediable poverty" was less than had been imagined, that the "darkest tints of the popular picture" were relieved by lighter tones.[63] The *Saturday Review* went so far as to imply that the work belied the "twaddle" about *The Bitter Cry* voiced by "sentimentalists and warm-hearted ladies."[64] But most were temperate even in their optimism. The *Manchester Guardian,* once an uncompromising advocate of laissez-faire, suggested that some of Booth's statistics had been outdated by recent improvements in the economic situation, but noted that Booth himself refrained from either "optimistic or pessimistic conclusions."[65] One reviewer pointed out that Booth's statistics could be turned around to read not that one person in five in East London was in a condition of poverty, but that four in five had incomes "at least sufficient for decent maintenance."[66] Others were reassured by his statement that class A did not represent "hordes of barbarians" about to overwhelm civilization, but rather "a handful, a small and decreasing percentage: a disgrace but not a danger."[67] The most serious dissent came from the Charity Organisation Society, which criticized Booth for failing to make more of the fact that the poor were not always poor by "necessity," that many were poor because of the way they spent their money rather than because of the lack of money. By focusing on "apparent" poverty rather than "unavoidable" poverty, the COS argued, Booth inflated the amount of poverty and obscured its causes.[68]

While the SDF criticized Booth for trotting out "the old saws about laziness, drink and extravagance producing want of employment, poverty, and pauperism,"[69] most reviewers, radical and conservative, were persuaded by his statistics showing the relatively small role of drink, idleness, and improvidence as the main causes of poverty. George Bernard Shaw told a meeting of Fabians that Booth had refuted the received opinion. "When the smug apostles of competitive scoundrelism declare that the poor are made poor by their vices, the poor themselves half believe it, even though when Mr. Charles Booth goes down among them to count heads he finds in every five hundred East Enders only four scamps to every hundred of the miserably poor."[70] J. A. Hobson cited Booth to dispute the widely quoted statement by Arnold White: "It is a fact apparent to every thoughtful man that the larger portion of the misery that constitutes our Social Question arises from idleness, gluttony, drink, waste, indulgence, profligacy, betting, and dissipation."[71] Hobson himself did not deny the importance of the "moral aspects of poverty"; on the contrary, he devoted an entire chapter of *Problems of Poverty* to just this question, and elsewhere he insisted that "moral import" was part of the very nature of social facts.[72] Like Booth, however, he wanted to place these moral facts in the larger context of poverty, and to see them as the effects as well as the causes of poverty.

Contemporaries appreciated what some later historians have not: that Booth's "scientific method" did not preclude moral characterizations. His schema of classes and analysis of poverty were all the more credible because they took account of "values" that most people recognized as an essential part of reality—the reality of social problems as well as of social policies.

IT WAS BECAUSE Booth's "science" was of a piece with the moral sensibilities of his generation that he was so highly regarded. He received the formal tokens of public esteem: a Privy Councillorship (which he chose in preference to a knighthood), the presidency of the Royal Statistical Society, a fellowship in the Royal Society, honorary degrees from the universities of Oxford, Cambridge, and Liverpool, appointments to parliamentary committees and Royal Commissions (on the aged poor, the tariff, the poor law), and numerous other invitations for public service which he declined.[73] He had the satisfaction of seeing his associates (Hubert Llewellyn Smith and Ernest Aves, among others) appointed to important administrative positions.[74] And he was frequently consulted about surveys inspired by his, not only the well-known study of York by Seebohm Rowntree but less ambitious ones (a survey of two working-class districts in Manchester and Salford and another of Oxford).

More significant were the frequent references to his work in books and articles, parliamentary debates and committee hearings. These are all the more revealing because they are so casual; his classes and statistics were referred to as if they were obvious, well-established facts. In 1903 the Liberal Party leader Henry Campbell-Bannerman cited Booth and Rowntree as evidence that many working-class families could not afford additional taxes.[75] Two years later a relief works project in London used Booth's survey as the basis for the allotment of jobs to the various boroughs.[76] When Gerald Balfour, president of the Local Government Board (and brother of the Prime Minister), introduced the Unemployed Workmen Bill to the House of Commons in 1905, he explained that it was intended not for all the unemployed but for the "respectable workmen" who were normally employed and were temporarily out of work because of circumstances beyond their control—Booth's classes D and E, he specified.[77] The following year, during the debate on the Old Age

Pensions Bill, G. P. Gooch (the historian and Member of Parliament) urged the House to pay attention to "the facts and opinions published by Mr. Charles Booth on this subject."[78] John Burns, president of the Local Government Board, went on to praise Booth's proposal as "the best, the simplest, and the fairest scheme."[79]

While Booth's pension scheme was the most obvious example of his influence, *Life and Labour* may have been more important in focusing attention upon particular classes of the poor and making them the objects of public concern. It is significant that two measures aimed specifically at classes A and B—the reform of the poor law and the labor colony plan— were not implemented, whereas those directly affecting Booth's "clients," C and D, were.[80] The Unemployed Workmen Act was one such case. Although Balfour described it as directed at D and E primarily, it proved to be of far greater benefit to C. Testifying before the Commission on the Poor Laws in 1907, Beveridge said that the workers who availed themselves of the act in the greatest numbers were not the regularly employed but the "underemployed."[81] Two years later Beveridge had the satisfaction of seeing the passage of the Labour Exchanges Act, which he had devised for the express purpose of helping casual laborers (dockworkers, for example) find employment. Skilled and unionized workers, he explained, were less in need of exchanges because their wages, supplemented by unemployment benefits, were normally sufficient to tide them over temporary periods of unemployment. For casual workers, on the other hand—Booth's class C—the national organization of the labor market would mean better access to more regular employment and thus promote "de-casualisation."[82] The Trade Boards Act the previous year authorized minimum wages for workers in "sweated" industries—an important segment of class D.

The "class character" of much of the legislation of this period may be seen in the conscious decision to create institutions entirely separate from the poor law and to enact reforms free of any stigma of pauperism. The Education (Provision of Meals) Act of 1906 and another education act the following year (providing for vacation schools, medical inspection, and the like) were deliberately kept distinct from the poor law, and both explicitly denied any franchise disqualification such as that attendant upon poor relief. One of the defects of the Unemployed Workmen Act, it had become apparent, was that the local committees—"Distress Committees," as they were unfortunately named—included representatives of the Boards of Guardians. As a result the "respectable workmen" for whom the act was designed would have little to do with it. That experience persuaded Beveridge that the labor exchanges should not be concerned with the "direct relief of distress" and should be entirely controlled by the Board of Trade. The dissociation from the poor law was all the more necessary because it was especially important to protect the casual laborers, who were the primary beneficiaries of the exchanges, from any taint of pauperism.

The same rationale lay behind the Old Age Pensions Act. To dispel any suspicion of relief, Booth had proposed that pensions be given to everyone regardless of means or need. The 1908 act did not adopt that proposal, largely because the cost would have been prohibitive, but also because some kind of "discrimination" and "qualifying conditions" were thought desirable. Thus the law specified that paupers, criminals, lunatics, and those who "habitually failed to work" (equivalent to Booth's class A and much of B) would not be eligible for pensions and would continue to fall within the province of the poor law.[83] Pensions would be given to those with incomes below £31 a year (12s. a week), with the maximum pension of 5s. a week reserved for incomes of £21 a year (8s. a week) or less. The age qualification—70 rather than 65 as in Booth's plan—was obviously meant to keep the cost down, but it was defended by Lloyd George on the ground that a good many workers, including the healthier and more skilled ones, were capable of working beyond the age of 65. The net effect of these conditions was to make the act especially beneficial to classes C and D and somewhat less so to E and F.* To obviate any taint of pauperism or moral stigma, the pensions were paid by the Post Office. For the same reason the act specified that the pensioner would not be deprived of "any franchise, right, or privilege" or subjected to any "disability."[84]

Even the National Insurance Act of 1911, which was a universal measure, had as its primary beneficiaries classes C and D. The contributory aspect of the bill effectively excluded paupers and those of the "very poor" who rarely worked and thus did not contribute, but included those

---

* This interpretation is borne out by the fact that the friendly societies and trade unions, who represented, as Chamberlain put it, the "thriftily-minded section of the working class" (the "comfortable" working classes, as Booth described E and F), were initially opposed to any old age pensions plan, whether universal or limited, contributory or noncontributory. While a good part of their opposition derived from their own institutional interests—a state system of pensions would obviously diminish the importance of the unions and societies—some of it reflected the indifference of the better-paid and better-organized working classes, who had less need for pensions and had more confidence in their own institutions than in the state.

who were irregularly employed. And the unemployment provision, as Winston Churchill informed the House, applied (at least initially) to those trades where unemployment was "not only high and chronic, but marked by seasonal and cyclical fluctuations."[85] Similarly the health provision (also contributory) was of "greatest benefit," Lloyd George noted, to the "very class who generally fail to keep in insurance"—that is, the irregularly employed and underpaid.[86]

This is not to say that there was any precise correspondence between these laws and Booth's classes. As Booth himself allowed for an overlapping of classes, so the laws did, if only for reasons of political expediency, fiscal exigency, and all the other contingencies that enter into the parliamentary process. Yet the nature of the reforms, the declared intentions of their proponents, and their practical consequences do suggest some interesting parallels and some rough equivalence.

HERE LIES the essential ideological import of Booth's work—not so much in the individualism or laissez-faireism of his policies, as in his definition of the social problem. His statistics, it was pointed out at the time, could be read in two ways: if one-third of the population was in a condition of poverty, two-thirds (a majority of the working classes) were in a condition of relative comfort. In the climate of the time (perhaps in the climate of all times), problems, not mere facts, dominated public attention. And the critical problem was the one-third in poverty rather than the two-thirds in comfort. This definition of the problem defined the parameters of the solution. A problem affecting two-thirds of the population might have required a radical, structural change in society and the economy, whereas a problem involving one-third could be accommodated by reforms within the system. And not only within the social and economic framework of the system but within its moral framework, for that one-third was as "respectable" and "deserving" as the two-thirds.

This definition of the problem distinguished Booth and most of the reformers of the time (including many socialists) from the Marxists. The latter, identifying the problem with the whole of the working class—a singular "working class" whose common characteristic was not poverty but propertylessness ("alienation" from the means of production)—found the solution to that problem in the nationalization of property or the radical redistribution of wealth. Booth, like most of his contemporaries, persisted in thinking and speaking of the working classes in the plural; this was, indeed, the main point of his work. The differentiation of classes implied a differentiation of problems and thus of remedies—specific measures designed to alleviate specific forms of poverty rather than a "generic" condition of propertylessness.

If Booth's definition of the problem was incompatible with Marxism, it was no less incompatible with the welfare state. Some of Booth's biographers have made of him an unwitting proponent of the welfare state.

> Had he been able to grasp it, a whole system of welfare was embodied in the results of the work he had done. By his application of the principle of "limited socialism" to the problems of poverty he had, in fact, arrived at the concept of the "minimum accepted standard" below which society could not, for its own sake, allow any of its members to sink, which was to become the corner stone of the Welfare State.[87]

But this is to miss the point Booth himself made so carefully and repeatedly. His "limited socialism" was deliberately limited to the "very poor," in order to strengthen the system of "individualism" that he thought to be in the best interest of the "poor." Similarly his concept of the "minimum accepted standard" had a specific purpose; government action was required only "to raise permanently the lowest levels of human life," those levels "at which life falls below a minimum accepted standard."[88]

The welfare state extended and universalized that concept, applying it to all of society in the form of a universal system of welfare embracing poor and nonpoor alike, indeed the rich as well. In universalizing it, the welfare state (in theory at least) also raised it from a "minimum" to an "optimum" standard.[89] Nothing could have been further from Booth's intention—not only because it violated his principle of "individualism" but because it violated his distinctions of classes and social problems.

In 1920 a young member of the Labour Party, Clement Attlee (who was to preside over the establishment of the welfare state twenty-five years later), wrote that Booth had "dispelled for ever the complacent assumption that the bulk of the people were able to keep themselves in tolerable comfort."[90] It was, of course, precisely Booth's finding that the bulk of the people, even the bulk of the working classes, were in a condition of "comfort"—and thus not in need of anything like a welfare state.

CHAPTER 12

Booth and Rowntree

BOOTH AND ROWNTREE—the two names are so often linked that they appear to be collaborators in the thriving enterprise of social research. For contemporaries, the significance of Rowntree's work was its confirmation of Booth's. The similarity of their findings—the much quoted figures of 30.7 percent poverty in London and 27.84 percent in York—suggested that London was not, as many suspected, a "special case." In a letter to Rowntree, Booth commented on the closeness of their figures, adding that he had suspected that studies of other cities would produce poverty statistics not unlike those of London.[1] Quoting Booth's letter in his book, Rowntree went on to say that since York was a "typical provincial town," it was likely that 25 to 30 percent of the town population of the United Kingdom was living in poverty; and since 77 percent of the population of the United Kingdom was urban, something like the same percentage of the entire country was probably in poverty.[2] Historians have since disputed the claim that either London or York was typical. One has argued that conditions elsewhere were better because London and York were short of the factories and large workshops which provided steady work and rising wages for much of the working classes.[3] Another comes to the opposite conclusion from a survey of three other provincial towns, which showed a larger proportion of poor among the working classes than in York.[4] Most of Rowntree's reviewers, however, seemed to accept his assurances that York at least was representative of a good part of the country—an impression supported by the title of his book, *Poverty: A Study of Town Life*, which gave no indication that it was confined to York.

As striking as the similarity of their conclusions was the dissimilarity of their methods. Rowntree, it is now generally agreed, was the more scientific of the two. Unlike Booth, he did not vitiate his study by "value judgments," and he developed a more objective standard and measure of poverty than Booth had done.[5] Even those who concede that he was not entirely successful in applying that standard or in abstaining from subjective judgments find him superior to Booth in intention and method—more scientific and, because he was less moralistic, more "progressive."[6]

Although only a dozen years separated Booth's first volume from Rowntree's, the two men were more than a generation apart. Booth's work was the climax of his career, Rowntree's the beginning of his. Born in 1871, thirty-one years after Booth, Seebohm Rowntree lived through the Second World War (Booth died in the midst of the First) and well into the formative period of the welfare state; a sequel to his first book appeared in 1941 and two others in 1951, three years before his death. Yet in some respects the two men were very much alike. Both were active and prosperous businessmen (Rowntree chocolates were as well known as the Booth shipping line); both were Nonconformists (the Rowntrees, like others who made their fortune in chocolate, were Quakers); both were provincials (unlike Booth, Rowntree remained in his hometown of York); both were inspired in their research by philanthropic motives; and both resisted the appeal of socialism (Booth began as a moderate Liberal and ended as a moderate Conservative, Rowntree began as a New Liberal and ended as an old Liberal).[7]

It was no accident that they both undertook research projects on the same subject. Rowntree was directly inspired by Booth. He wanted to do for York what Booth had done for London. Unlike Booth, who started with the suspicion that the prevailing estimates of poverty were too high, Rowntree had no such doubts. He wanted only to see how the situation in London compared with that in York. Yet he chose to pursue his study on quite different premises, using different definitions of poverty and different classifications of the poor.

The most obvious difference was in the definition of classes. Where Booth's classes were defined in terms of regularity of work and mode of life as well as income, Rowntree's were ostensibly based entirely upon income. This distinction was somewhat obscured by the fact that Rowntree's classes bore labels that looked deceptively like Booth's. In fact, the two sets of classes were very different, in income as in other respects. Booth's class A was an institutional rather than wage-earning class, so it had no income figure attached to it; B to D were not differentiated by income except that they all fell at or below the "line of poverty," which was 18–21s. (with B closer to the 18s. mark); E and F, the "comfortable" working classes, earned 22–30s. and 30–50s., respectively. In Rowntree's schema, A (2.6 percent of the population) had a family income of under 18s.; B (5.9 percent), 18–21s.; C (20.7 percent), 21–30s.; and D (32.4 percent), over 30s. His other classes were not defined in terms of income: E (5.7 percent) consisted of female domestic servants; F (28.8 percent) was the servant-keeping class; and G (3.9 percent) included all those who were in public institutions.*

It is strange that Rowntree should have chosen the same labels to signify different classes. But odder still is the fact that his classes did not correspond to his poverty statistics. No combination of them added up, either in absolute figures or in percentages, to the 20,302 people, or 27.84 percent of the population, in poverty. If few readers seem to have noticed this, it was perhaps because the two charts, on classes and poverty, were separated by 86 pages, so that it would have taken an especially attentive reader or carping critic to see the discrepancy.[9] If they also failed to see the discrepancy between his classes and Booth's, it was because Booth's continued to dominate public discussion; when contemporaries referred to class B, it was Booth's B they had in mind. What did catch the public eye, however, was Rowntree's definition of poverty—or rather his two definitions of poverty.

ROWNTREE'S GREAT contribution to social discourse was the distinction between "primary" and "secondary" poverty. Primary poverty was the poverty of families "whose total earnings are insufficient to obtain the minimum necessaries for the maintenance of merely physical efficiency." Secondary poverty was that of families "whose total earnings would be sufficient for the maintenance of merely physical efficiency were it not that some portion of it is absorbed by other expenditure, either useful or wasteful."[10] That distinction depended upon the correlation of three sets of facts: the actual earnings of families; the minimum "standard of life" (food, housing, clothing, etc.) required for "merely physical efficiency" (or "physical health," as he sometimes put it); and the income needed to provide that level of efficiency.[11] The latter was the basis of "The Poverty Line."

The poverty line—or "the 'primary' poverty line," Rowntree some-

---

* In effect, Rowntree's class A was equivalent to Booth's B; Rowntree's B to Booth's C and D; Rowntree's C to Booth's E; Rowntree's D to Booth's F; Rowntree's F to Booth's G and H; and Rowntree's G to Booth's A. Compounding this confusion was the introduction later in the book of yet another set of classes: class 1, working-class families under 26s.; class 2, working-class families 26s. and over; class 3, the "servant-keeping" class.[8]

times specified—for a family of two parents and two children was 18s. 1od.; for three children, 21s.8d.; and four children, 26s.[12] Based upon this standard, 9.91 percent of the population of York (15.46 percent of the working classes) were in a condition of "primary poverty," lacking the income sufficient for bare physical efficiency. This income level, Rowntree emphasized, was based on the assumption that every penny of income went toward absolute necessities, with no allowance for such "useful" expenditures as travel, recreation, or sickness or funeral clubs, to say nothing of such "wasteful" expenditures as drink or gambling.

"Secondary poverty" was based on the opposite assumption: that some part of the family income was used for nonessentials. In a sense there was no "secondary poverty line," because income was not the determining factor in the concept of secondary poverty. Indeed, income alone would have placed these families above the poverty line. If they were below it—if they were "poor"—it was because they gave the "appearance" of poverty, of "obvious want and squalor."[13] It was this appearance of poverty, based upon the "observations" of the investigator, that consigned 17.93 percent of the population to the category of secondary poverty, almost twice as many as those in primary poverty.[14] And it was the combination of primary and secondary poverty that produced a total of 27.84 percent in poverty.

It was also this combination of primary and secondary poverty that made for the close correspondence between Booth's figure and Rowntree's. Inspired by Booth's study and with the avowed intention of comparing York with London, Rowntree could hardly rest content with a poverty figure of 9.91 percent, which was so far below that of London— less than one-third of the latter. If primary poverty in York fell drastically short of the "appearance" of poverty, it had to be supplemented by another kind of poverty that would bring the total up to par.

Thus Rowntree's much publicized figure of 27.84 percent was not derived from a poverty line determined by income alone or by the conjunction of income and a minimum standard of life. Nor did that poverty line correspond to the class divisions, which were based on actual income. Nor did the distinction between primary and secondary poverty correspond to those classes. Unlike Booth's categories of "very poor" and "poor," which did coincide with specific classes, Rowntree's "primary" and "secondary" poverty did not.* Moreover, "secondary poverty" was

---

* Nor did Booth's "very poor" and "poor" correspond to Rowntree's "primary" and "secondary" poverty. The "very poor" were visibly in a worse condition than the

not only based on appearance rather than income; it was based on the appearance of "want and squalor" as well as physical "inefficiency" and ill health.

The disparity between the definition of poverty and the delineation of class was most conspicuous in the case of class C, which included families on both sides of the poverty line. One of the anomalies in Rowntree's work was the inclusiveness of C, which ranged from 21s. to 30s. for a family of moderate size. Rowntree himself commented on this wide "margin of income," which meant that those at the lower end of the spectrum approximated the condition of B while those at the upper end were "little inferior" to D.[15] Most of C must have been among the 27.84 percent of the population in poverty, since there was no other class or combination of classes large enough to account for that number. Yet the average income of C was 26s.7d., with an average family size of 4.11, which would place the average family in that class well above the poverty line. If so many of them were nevertheless poor, it was obviously secondary poverty that was their affliction.[16]

Class C would seem to be at the heart of the social problem, the problem of a serious and pervasive poverty that did not derive from an inadequacy of income. Yet Rowntree deliberately shied away from any serious analysis or even description of it. "It is not proposed," he said dismissively and without explanation, "to describe this class in great detail."[17] And indeed he did not, devoting only five pages to class C (which comprised 20.7 percent of the population), compared with fifteen to A (2.6 percent), thirteen to B (5.9 percent), and fifteen to D (who were not poor). And these few pages on C were almost entirely extracts from the investigators' notebooks, with none of the comments or generalizations that enlivened his accounts of the other classes. One can only assume a reluctance on his part to confront the nature and the extent of secondary poverty, which was clearly the dominant problem of this class—and of the poor in general.

THE SAME RELUCTANCE appears in Rowntree's discussion of the "immediate causes" of secondary poverty. Although secondary poverty was more considerable than primary poverty and its causes more varied, this subject too was dealt with only cursorily; the causes of primary

---

"poor," whereas those in secondary poverty might be, to judge by appearances and living conditions, in a worse state than those in primary poverty.

poverty occupied twenty-two pages compared with five pages for secondary poverty.[18] The main causes of primary poverty were low wages (51.96 percent), the largeness of the family (22.16 percent), the death of the chief wage earner (15.63 percent), illness or old age (5.11 percent), irregularity of work (2.83 percent), and the unemployment of the chief wage earner (2.31 percent). The precision of these findings, the detail of the analysis, the charts, tables, bar graphs, lists, and illustrations were in conspicuous contrast to the section on secondary poverty. In the case of secondary poverty, the causes were not itemized, let alone quantified or tabulated. Instead they were briefly and haphazardly summed up: "Drink, betting, and gambling. Ignorant or careless housekeeping, and other improvident expenditure, the latter often induced by irregularity of income."[19] As if by way of apology, Rowntree explained that it was not possible to ascertain the proportion of each of these causes, but he assumed that they were probably all present in most households and that the predominant one was drink. The only evidence he offered for this last assumption was a study, conducted by his father some years earlier, of the consumption of liquor in England. On the supposition that York was not very different from the rest of the country, Rowntree estimated that the average working-class family in York spent no less than 6s. a week on drink, which was more than one-sixth of its income.

If drink did represent so substantial an expenditure, it is difficult to see why Rowntree did not try to discover the actual amount spent by the workers of York—and more important, the amount spent by those who were poor—instead of deducing that sum from the country as a whole. At the very least he might have listed drink as a separate item in his extremely detailed sample budgets of eighteen families. If he was able to determine the exact expenditure, down to the halfpenny, for soap, candles, matches, coke, coal, and dozens of other items, or to calculate the amount and the form of protein consumed by each worker each day, surely similar information about the cost and consumption of liquor would not have been beyond his capacity. (One item in the budgets was "food, including beverages," which presumably included liquor.) The figures about drink might not have been entirely reliable (although the information provided by the families could have been checked against that obtained from publicans, temperance reformers, and others), but they would probably have been as accurate as much of the other data that were recorded so meticulously and with such dubious precision.

Rowntree's biographer suggests that he chose to say little about secondary poverty in order to avoid the temptation to dwell on "moral" topics, such as drink and gambling.[20] This is undoubtedly true; the only question is whether he had any strong temptation to overcome. On the contrary, his inclination was clearly to explain away such "moral" factors—indeed, not to use the word "moral" in connection with them. He concluded his very brief account of the causes of secondary poverty— drink, gambling, improvidence—by explaining that they were the product of overcrowded and unhealthy housing, monotonous and laborious work, limited education and physical exhaustion. "What wonder that many of these people fall a ready prey to the publican and the bookmaker?"[21] The immediate causes of secondary poverty should be acted upon, he granted (although he did not say how this might be done), but he hastened to add that they should be looked at in the larger context of land tenure, the relative duties and powers of the state and the individual, and legislation affecting "the aggregation or the distribution of wealth." The ultimate elimination of poverty, he concluded, would come only when these immediate causes were dealt with as part of the "wider social problem."[22]

IF THE LOGIC of Rowntree's analysis was less than compelling—if his classes bore little relation to his concept of poverty, if the poverty line had little bearing upon the large proportion of those in poverty, if the causes of secondary poverty were inadequately probed—his work nevertheless had one great attraction that obscured these failings. This was the idea of a minimum standard of "physical efficiency" which was presumed to be at the heart of his definition of poverty. It was this concept that made his work seem eminently scientific, both because it was measurable and because it was grounded in the biological, physiological nature of man.

A large part of his book was devoted to an analysis of nutrition: the constituents of food (proteins, fats, carbohydrates, calories); the functions of each; the minimum requirements of each according to sex, age, and work; the different standards prevailing in different countries and institutions (workhouses, prisons). Tables of typical diets, for men, women, and children of different ages, specified the precise foods consumed for breakfast, dinner, and supper in each day of the week, the amounts of each item, and the cost of each. It was an impressive feat—all the more so because it came at a time when people were much exercised by just this issue.

Rowntree's book was published in 1901, at the height of the agitation over "physical efficiency" precipitated by the Boer War. The revelation of physical incapacity on the part of volunteers for military service, young men in the prime of life, set off a clamor about the "deterioration of the race" and a campaign for "national efficiency."[23] It was in this atmosphere that Rowntree's book appeared, proposing a standard of "physical efficiency" based upon minimum nutritional requirements, and deriving a "poverty line" from that standard of efficiency and the minimum income required to meet it.

It took a determined critic to resist the scientific appeal of this thesis. Such a critic was Helen Bosanquet of the Charity Organisation Society. In a long article in the journal of the COS, Mrs. Bosanquet analyzed some of the weaknesses of Rowntree's work. The poverty line, she pointed out, was based upon income only in the case of the 9.91 percent in primary poverty, and even that figure was derived from inadequate and contradictory evidence. The rest of the 27.84 percent were placed in the category of the poor on the basis of "appearances" deduced from very hasty visits by a single investigator. And the nutritional standards were arbitrary and unscientific, exaggerating the number of people who were "underfed."[24]

In his reply Rowntree granted one of Mrs. Bosanquet's points, that the income figures applied only to primary poverty, and defended himself on the other counts. It was not one investigator, he said, but several, and over a longer period of time, who personally investigated every household. The estimates of wages (he conceded that they were often that) were based on more information than was suggested by the published versions of the notebooks, which omitted some details to preserve the anonymity of the families. And "underfed," as he used the term, referred to a standard of "physical efficiency" rather than a "sense of hunger." The real difference between them, Rowntree concluded, was that Mrs. Bosanquet belonged to that "extreme wing of the Individualistic school" which held that social improvement could come about only through the personal efforts of the individual rather than the influence of law, while he believed in the efficacy of "wise laws" in the formation of character and the amelioration of poverty.[25]

Mrs. Bosanquet, in turn, protested that she was not, in his sense of the term, an individualist; so far from denying the influence of laws, she attributed a good deal of the poverty in York to the unfortunate influence of the poor law. Nor was she persuaded by his defense of his methods. Repeating her objections to his statistics, she went on to make a more fundamental criticism of statistics itself as a measure of poverty. Rowntree's basic fallacy lay not in the data or methods by which he arrived at this or that poverty line, but in the very idea of a "Poverty Line."

> Notwithstanding all pious reservations about the importance of char-
> acter, once the "Poverty Line" has been erected, the classification of
> human beings becomes for the world at large a question of money
> income, and the remedy for poverty represents itself as the distribu-
> tion of money. And for most people this means the worst of all forms
> of distribution of money—distribution by the State.[26]

THIS, INDEED, was at the heart of Rowntree's "Poverty Line." It was also the crucial difference between him and Booth. When Booth used the term "line of poverty," he did so casually, infrequently, almost indiffer-ently, because he did not believe that poverty was only a "question of money income," still less that the remedy of poverty was a redistribution of income by the state. It was Rowntree who made the poverty line, and thus the question of money, a prominent part of his thesis and who brought the concept into popular discourse. Although he himself may not have intended any radical redistribution of income, a reader might infer just that from his comment that the remedy for poverty lay in legislation affecting "the aggregation or the distribution of wealth."[27]

The poverty line, however, was more than a question of money; it was also a question of "physical efficiency"—a level of income insufficient for the maintenance of "merely physical efficiency." Here too Booth differed signally from Rowntree. A decade earlier, responding to the "social prob-lem" of poverty, Booth addressed that problem in "social" terms, which for him, as for most of his generation, meant an inextricable mixture of the economic and the moral. For Rowntree, the crucial mixture was the economic and the physical (or physiological). Responding to the revela-tions of the unfitness of the military recruits and reflecting the increas-ingly scientific and materialistic temper of the times, he was inclined to put more credence in economic and physical facts than in moral or psy-chological ones, to think the former more basic, more primary, than the latter. It is interesting that he chose the term "primary" poverty to de-scribe a poverty that was entirely defined in economic and physical terms, and "secondary" poverty to describe that in which moral and psycholog-ical factors intruded. And it is not surprising that he chose to pay more attention to primary poverty than to secondary poverty, in spite of the far greater incidence and importance of the latter. How could one not be more interested in what is primary than in what is secondary, especially when the primary is the hard, irrefutable evidence of economic, material, physical, bodily facts?

Rowntree's work had obvious advantages over Booth's. It seemed to provide a more objective, scientific measure of poverty based not only on income but on nutrition as well. The inquiry itself was more detailed, involving an examination of every single working-class household in York. The results were more precisely quantified, down to the second decimal point (a refinement on Booth, who was content with only one decimal point). And all this was presented in a single, ordinary-sized readable volume. At the time that Booth was publishing the last of his seventeen volumes, Rowntree issued a slightly expanded version of his book in a cheap edition (2s.6d). (A shilling edition was published in 1914.)

Yet Rowntree's work never superseded Booth's. On the contrary, it remained something of a footnote to Booth's. Even those differences that loom large in retrospect were less evident and less important at the time. Rowntree's book was certainly more accessible than Booth's seventeen volumes, but by the same token it lacked the authority of that massive work. If Rowntree's statistics about poverty in York confirmed Booth's about poverty in London, the reverse was equally true. And while Rowntree's standards of nutrition and physical efficiency gave an additional scientific dimension to the study of poverty, the moral dimension continued to be seen as intractable and indisputable. Indeed, that moral dimension was assumed to be the chief factor in the concept of secondary poverty.

It was this combination of morality and science that defined what Beatrice Webb called the "time-spirit," the spirit that imbued not only social scientists but also social philosophers, economists, philanthropists, reformers, even socialists.

Book Three

THE "TIME-SPIRIT": CHARITY AND PHILANTHROPY

The "Time-Spirit"

THE "TIME-SPIRIT," commemorated by Beatrice Webb and epitomized by Charles Booth, consisted of two elements: a trust in science and a commitment to mankind.[1] The first, scientific method, was the means; the second, social service, the end. If the first was the more original and "salient" element, the second was no less vital, for it was "the warp before the woof," the emotion that gave strength to the intellect and purpose to life. The "impulse of self-subordinating service," which had once been inspired by a belief in God, now came from a belief in man. "It used to be devotion to God, under one form or another," Webb confided in her diary; "now this God is dead it must be devotion to other human beings."[2]

In fact, the devotion to science, as much as the devotion to humanity, had something of a religious quality, a faith that transcended reason. Looking back at this period half a century later, after the First World War had shown the equivocal uses to which science could be put, Beatrice Webb wondered at "the naive belief of the most original and vigorous minds of the seventies and eighties that it was by science, and by science alone, that all human misery would be ultimately swept away."[3] At the time, however, that belief seemed so plausible, so self-evident, as hardly to require justification. What was notable was the conjunction of the two faiths, the fact that the "most original and vigorous minds" chose to apply all the resources of reason and science to the alleviation of human misery, and that they did so with all the zeal and passion that would once have gone into the service of God.

The cult of humanity was not itself new. Beatrice Webb traced it back to the American and French revolutions which declared men to be free and equal, to Benthamism which affirmed the greatest happiness of the greatest number, to Owenism which exalted "the supremely good principle in human nature," and to Positivism which united religion and science in the service of mankind, a "Religion of Humanity."[4] Like Booth, Beatrice Webb (Potter as she then was) did not officially join the "Church of Humanity," but she did commit herself to the principle of "altruism," the duty to "live for others." In her diary she transcribed the credo of Comte that she found so compelling: "Towards Humanity, who is the only true Great Being, we, the conscious elements of whom she is the compound, shall henceforth direct every aspect of our life, individual and collective. Our thoughts will be devoted to the knowledge of Humanity, our affections to the Love, our actions to her service."[5]

One of the curious aspects of this time-spirit was the fact that the cult of science, which might be expected to be the peculiar faith of intellectuals, was shared by the working classes. "Halls of Science" were established in working-class districts, and Charles Bradlaugh, the militant secularist—"Iconoclast," he called himself—became one of the most popular speakers of the time. "Indeed," Beatrice Webb observed, "in the seventies and eighties it looked as if whole sections of the British proletariat—and these the élite—would be swept, like the corresponding class on the Continent, into a secularist movement."[6] On the other hand, the cult of humanity (at least as a conscious, explicit creed) was largely confined to the middle and upper classes. This is not to underestimate the extent of working-class charity, not only of the informal, spontaneous kind—the helping of neighbors and friends in times of need—but of a more institutionalized kind. According to one survey in the 1890s, half of the "respectable" working-class families made regular contributions to charities.[7] But even the most affluent of the working classes could hardly make a career of philanthropy, as could the "men of intellect and men of property," like Booth, and the "governing and guiding women," like Octavia Hill.[8]

The social consciousness of these men and women, Beatrice Webb explained, was aroused by a "new consciousness of sin." This was not, she hastened to add, a "consciousness of personal sin." It was "a collective or class consciousness; a growing uneasiness, amounting to conviction, that the industrial organization, which had yielded rent, interest and profits on a stupendous scale, had failed to provide a decent livelihood and tolerable conditions for a majority of the inhabitants of Great Britain."[9] This account was somewhat colored by her later socialist views. In the 1880s the "consciousness of sin" that preoccupied most of these men and women of intellect and property (apart from the socialists among them) was not the sin of the "industrial organization," or capitalism, but the misery of poverty. It was a "collective or class consciousness" in the sense that it recognized the collective responsibility of society, and of the privileged class in particular, for the mitigation of poverty. But it did not necessarily involve a collectivist solution to that problem; it did not assume that the problem could only be solved by the state or government. On the contrary, the most eminent of these men and women insisted upon meeting that responsibility personally and individually, by becoming actively involved in one or another (or several) philanthropic enterprises. It was the essence of their faith that while the government might do something to alleviate misery—just how much it should do was a matter of disagreement among them—the immediate responsibility and the primary moral obligation belonged to individuals and private associations.

This was a crucial element in the time-spirit. Not all philanthropists shared Webb's esteem for science. But they did share her conviction that the social consciousness was essentially a moral consciousness, requiring of each individual a personal, voluntary, sustained commitment to public service. From one point of view this may appear to be the least "progressive" aspect of the time-spirit. To the radical historian it is nothing less than reactionary, a regression to individualism and voluntarism precisely at a time when these modes (according to this view) were becoming most inappropriate, when the massive, impersonal nature of the social problem required nothing less than a massive, collective, governmental, "structural" solution. To the "Whig" historian, expecting history to progress in an orderly fashion, this late-Victorian mode of philanthropy was equally anomalous; it was regressive even by comparison with the early-Victorian period, when reformers, whatever the religious and moral impulses that personally inspired them, devoted most of their efforts to the passage of social legislation and the establishment of government agencies. There were, to be sure, important legislative and administrative reforms in the late-Victorian period as well. But these were not the most memorable aspects of this time; certainly they did not generate anything like the passion aroused by the Poor Law of 1834 or the Ten Hours Bill of 1847.

The late Victorians, however, had their own passions—in a sense more compelling precisely because they required so personal a commitment. There were, no doubt, Mrs. Jellybys among them, women more concerned with the natives of Borrioboola-Gha than with their own children, and men "whose charity increases directly as the square of the distance."[10] But the kind of "telescopic philanthropy" satirized by Dickens and George Eliot was not typical of this later generation; certainly it was not encouraged or even condoned by them. For the most part, the philanthropists, social workers, social missionaries, and researchers pursued their activities not on the shores of the Nile or even in the halls of Westminster and Whitehall but in the streets of the East End. And they did so not as paid professionals or functionaries of the state, but as private citizens, men and women who took it upon themselves to serve humanity in their own ways, from the promptings of their own consciences, out of their own resources, devoting their considerable talents, energies, fortunes, and, often, their entire lives to the service of others. These were the bearers of the "time-spirit," the agents of the new social consciousness, who gave new meanings to the old words "philanthropy" and "charity"—and, in the process, sometimes unwittingly, to the idea of "poverty."[11]

CHAPTER 13

The Science of Charity

IN JANUARY 1879, when the weather conspired with the economy to produce one of the worst winters of the depression, Henry James reflected on the social temper of his newly adopted country. He was impressed by the gigantic poor relief system which was "so characteristic a feature of English civilisation" and which was now being supplemented by equally huge sums from private charity. He was also impressed by the scientific way that charity was distributed.

> There is nothing more striking in England than the success with which an "appeal" is always made. Whatever the season or whatever the cause, there always appears to be enough money and enough benevolence in the country to respond to it in sufficient measure—a remarkable fact when one remembers that there is never a moment of the year when the custom of "appealing" intermits. Equally striking perhaps is the perfection to which the science of distributing charity has been raised—the way it has been analysed and organised and made one of the exact sciences.[1]

It was ten years earlier that "benevolence" had been raised to an "exact science." If anything as amorphous as a "time-spirit" can be said to have a birth date, 1869 would be it. For it was then that the Charity Organisation Society was founded, originally, and very briefly, under the ungainly name of the London Society for Organizing Charitable Relief and Repressing Mendicity.* This was not another charitable society of

---

* The earlier name makes for a nice contrast with another change of name in 1910: Society for Organizing Charity and Improving the Condition of the Poor. (The final

the kind so prevalent in England at the time. Almost half a century earlier the young Macaulay had sarcastically observed: "This is the age of societies. There is scarcely one Englishman in ten who has not belonged to some association for distributing books, or for prosecuting them; for sending invalids to the hospital, or beggars to the treadmill; for giving plate to the rich, or blankets to the poor."[3] A generation later Sir James Stephen was moved to the same observation: "Ours is the age of societies. For the redress of every oppression that is done under the sun, there is a public meeting. For the cure of every sorrow by which our land or our race can be visited, there are patrons, vice-presidents and secretaries. For the diffusion of every blessing of which mankind can partake in common, there is a committee."[4] By the time the Charity Organisation Society appeared on the scene there were about seven hundred philanthropic societies in London alone. And the combined cost of relief and charity in the metropolis, according to one contemporary estimate, came to £7,000,000 annually—a sum sufficient, it was calculated, to keep one in eight inhabitants of the city in idleness.[5]

It was because of this proliferation of societies that the COS (as it soon became known) was founded—not to add to their numbers but to subtract from them, to coordinate and rationalize their efforts so that they did not aggravate the problem of poverty by the evil of "indiscriminate charity." This was not the first such attempt. At the end of the eighteenth century, responding to a similar situation, Sir Thomas Bernard had formed the Society for Bettering the Condition and Increasing the Comforts of the Poor. Much more recently, only half a dozen years before the founding of the COS, William Rathbone had established in Liverpool a Central Relief Society, whose purpose, he explained, was to bring "method" out of "muddle" in charitable affairs.[6] The COS, then, was not especially original in its purpose; nor was it entirely effective in its operation. But it did succeed, as no other group had done, in publicizing both its principles and its activities. Within a year there were a dozen COS district committees and by 1872 three dozen. By the end of the decade it had established itself as the premier charitable organization in London and had become the model for similar societies throughout England and America.

---

name adopted in 1946, Family Welfare Association, suggests how infinitely adaptable any well-endowed organization is to the prevailing time-spirit.) Other versions of the original name, such as the London Association for the Prevention of Pauperism and Crime, and other founding dates, such as 1868 and 1870, are among the many disputed facts about the origins of the society.[2]

The longtime secretary of the COS, Charles Stewart Loch (who held that office from 1875 to 1914), commented on the apparent paradox in its title.

> At first sight the words Charity and Organisation seem to be a con-
> tradiction in terms. Charity is free, fervent, impulsive. Organisation
> implies order and method, sacrifice for a common end, self-restraint.
> There is a kind of wildness in the enthusiasm of charity. But organ-
> isation and its kindred words suggest the quietness of gradual growth,
> the social results of a circumspect sobriety, a balanced and temperate
> progress.[7]

If Loch's rhetoric suggested a partiality for "organisation" over "charity," for "order" over "wildness," his intention was to integrate both, to pre-serve "the quickness and discretion and even the secretness of personal charity" and at the same time "by union and cooperation to improve the condition of the poor."[8] So far from being contradictory, he insisted, charity and organization were logically and practically complementary. Charity was the end or "motive" of the society; organization its means or "force," "our armour and our weapons."[9]

The COS did not, in fact, have the power to organize other charitable societies or even to serve as a clearinghouse for them; it was only another voluntary body with the same legal status as the others. It did, however, aspire to be *primus inter pares*. Thus it undertook to keep a register of local charities and their beneficiaries, to inspect other institutions (soup kitchens, model houses, the Barnardo Homes) and issue reports on them, and above all to investigate applications for relief and make recommen-dations for assistance. But it could not oblige the other societies to accept its recommendations, or prevent the establishment of new ones such as the Salvation Army, or deter the Lord Mayor from sponsoring yet an-other Mansion House Fund.[10] Indeed, in spite of its frequent protesta-tions that its mission was not to give relief, still less to raise money for relief, many of its district committees did both (which is why it was obliged to repeat these protestations so often).

The COS was more effective in those instances where its members were active in other philanthropic organizations and in the Boards of Guardians administering the poor law. By means of this network they were able to influence the activities of private charities and coordinate them with public relief. The latter task had been a major purpose of the COS from its inception. In 1869, in a minute issued to the Boards of

Guardians, G. J. Goschen, president of the Poor Law Board, strongly urged the coordination of private and public relief, and the COS took that as an official endorsement of its own mission. COS members who were also Poor Law Guardians were in a position to eliminate any duplication with charity and at the same time to apply the poor law in accord with the principles of the society. But there were many Boards of Guardians that they did not control and that persisted in dispensing more outdoor relief than the COS would have sanctioned. And their own members were often recalcitrant. The society was far from being a monolithic organization; even the members of the council differed among themselves, still more the members of the district committees.

The importance of the COS, however, cannot be measured by its immediate, practical influence. Its achievement was of a different order, in setting the terms of social discourse for an entire generation and shaping both the idea of poverty and the conception of the problem of poverty. In this sense it was successful even when its principles were violated in practice, as they so often were. The experience of the COS recalls that of the poor-law reformers of the 1830s, whose practical success was similarly limited but whose ideological influence was felt far beyond the actual operations of the New Poor Law. Unlike those earlier reformers, the COS did not have the satisfaction of seeing its principles incorporated into law. But it functioned within a larger social framework that comprehended both the private and the public sphere, charity as well as relief. And it was by refining the relationship between the two that the COS redefined the concepts of poverty and pauperism.

IN ONE SENSE, the COS may be seen as carrying out the agenda of 1834, the effort to prevent the "pauperization of the poor" by discouraging the independent laborer from seeking relief. It endorsed the principles of the New Poor Law: "less-eligibility," which required that the condition of the pauper (the recipient of relief) be less "eligible," less desirable, than that of the independent laborer; and the "workhouse test" providing relief to the able-bodied only within the workhouse. If the COS rarely mentioned these principles by name, it was because they had become the object of intense hostility in the decades following the passage of the New Poor Law, and the COS was loath to rekindle those old passions and controversies. But the ideas were reflected in the distinction the COS insisted upon between poor relief and charity. Poor relief should be given only to the indigent and, in the case of the able-bodied, only in the workhouse, while charity should be reserved for the "deserving poor" who were not indigent, who were employed and might even have some resources such as savings or possessions. (Indeed, the latter might be taken as evidence of their being deserving.)

In another respect, however, the COS significantly departed from the principles of earlier reformers. The New Poor Law tried to solve the problem of the pauperization of the poor by drawing "a broad line of distinction between the class of independent labourers and the class of paupers."[11] The principle of less-eligibility and the workhouse test were intended to enforce that distinction by separating (literally as well as conceptually) paupers from the independent, laboring poor. The COS, concerned not only with the proper limits of relief but also with the proper role of charity, had to devise a further distinction and create an additional category. Between the independent laboring poor who required no assistance and the paupers who were eligible for relief, the COS recognized an intermediate class of poor. Neither entirely self-sufficient nor indigent, these were the poor who were the proper beneficiaries of charity. They were needy, although not actually destitute. But they might become destitute unless they were given timely and adequate help. And they could be helped by charity that was carefully adapted to their needs and given in such a way and in sufficient quantity as to help them become truly independent. If it was the task of the poor law to relieve destitution, it was the task of private charity to prevent destitution by relieving the kind of poverty that might lead to destitution.

This intermediate class of poor, which came within the purview of charity rather than the poor law, was often characterized as the "deserving poor." "Deserving" and "undeserving" were terms used freely by the COS in its early years, both in its statements of principle and in its accounts of individual cases and the reports of the district committees. The terms, however, were not unambiguous; nor did they define very precisely the respective provinces of charity and relief. The "deserving poor" who were the proper recipients of charity were not paragons of virtue; if they were they might not need any assistance (although there were occasions, the COS recognized, when even the most virtuous fell upon bad times). "They do not save, or join clubs, or in any way look forward to the future; they simply spend their earnings as they come; but they are on the whole industrious and sober and possessed of tidy homes."[12]* And while the "undeserving"—the improvident and intem-

---

* The COS sometimes exhibited a surprising degree of sympathy and tolerance toward what might have been regarded as moral failings. Helen Bosanquet wrote an

perate, the shiftless and thriftless—were the responsibility of the poor law, not all of those who received relief were undeserving; there were also those who were destitute because of illness or old age rather than any fault of character.

By the mid-1880s the term "undeserving," used to characterize those who were deemed ineligible for charity, began to seem invidious. In 1886 it was altered (in the reports although not in the case studies) to read "not likely to benefit," and two years later to the still more neutral "not assisted."[14] By 1905 the revised edition of the COS's *Principles of Decision* officially abandoned the criterion of "deserving": "The test is not whether the applicant is deserving but whether he is helpable."[15] These changes were intended to remove any aspersion upon the sickly and elderly who were not the proper beneficiaries of charity but who were worthy recipients of relief under the terms of the poor law. So far from signifying any change in policy, however, they represented a reaffirmation of principle. Character remained an important criterion for charitable assistance because only those of good character were "helpable." "We have to use Charity to create the power of self-help"; "charity takes account of character, and selects those cases in which assistance will lead to self-support."[16] The applicants themselves were given to understand this. The first item in the form distributed to them read: "The Society desires to help those persons who are doing all they can to help themselves, and to whom temporary assistance is likely to prove a lasting benefit."[17]

The COS's "poor," its special clients, were thus the deserving poor who were needy although not destitute. And their need was of a particular nature: "temporary," "exceptional," "causeless"—these were the recurrent words in the society's reports and case studies. The need had to be temporary rather than chronic if it was to be effectively relieved by the

---

entire essay on debts among the poor, in which she barely stopped short of commending the poor for resorting to the pawnbroker rather than saving for future contingencies. "Of course," she conceded, "the old-fashioned morality goes in favour of thrift as opposed to credit," but there was much to be said for the familiar adage that the pawnbroker was the "poor man's friend," his salvation in times of need. Pawnbroking was to the poor what credit was to the rich. "Thus the prestige which attaches to credit in the commercial world is fast being transferred to the region of private indebtedness, and as we turn to the poorer classes we find ourselves regarding it as tinged with a curious kind of semi-professional, semi-sentimental benevolence." It was unfortunate, however, that the money obtained from the pawnbroker too often went on "boozing," gambling, and wasteful luxuries.[13]

temporary assistance charity could provide. It had to be exceptional rather than ordinary—not the predictable contingencies of life, the brief spells of sickness or slack employment or the incapacity of old age, which should be anticipated and provided for out of the individual and collective resources of the poor (friendly societies, for example). And it had to be "causeless"—not caused, that is, by the poor themselves, by drunkenness, slothfulness, or other self-inflicted ills.

In defining the mission of charity, the COS also distinguished the several kinds of unemployment to which the poor were subject. Chronic unemployment should not be relieved by charity, partly because it would be too costly but also because it would discourage the economic and industrial adjustments that were the only solutions to this problem. Nor should periodic (seasonal) unemployment, which was predictable and which the poor should provide for themselves. The unemployment that charity was properly and uniquely qualified to relieve was "exceptional unemployment," the result of trade depressions which could not be anticipated or insured against even by the most provident workers. These distinctions belie the simplistic, moralistic view of unemployment that has been attributed to the COS.[18] A book review in its journal in 1885 sharply criticized the idea that unemployment was principally caused by the mental or moral incapacity of the worker. More often, the reviewer argued, it was the result of "fluctuations in the market of the world, the displacement of labour by machinery, the dissociation of labour from the land, . . . [and other] social and economic causes which seriously affect the well-being of the working classes, and often render their members powerless in the struggle for existence."[19]

In practice, of course, these distinctions were not easily or consistently applied. The district committees often approved loans or outright grants to the seasonally unemployed and pensions to the aged. Even so staunch a believer as Sir Charles Trevelyan could be found introducing a resolution in 1878 to give pensions to "deserving chronic" cases; it was not passed because many district committees could not raise the necessary funds, but some did and small pensions were regularly provided by many committees. By 1890 almost seven hundred pensions were being granted, and they absorbed an increasing part of the COS's resources until 1908, when the Old Age Pensions Act made them redundant.[20]

The principle, however, was clear, and if it was sometimes violated, it was more often observed. Only those who were needy through no fault of their own and whose unfortunate condition was both temporary and unpredictable were the proper beneficiaries of charity. In these cases charity of an "appropriate and adequate" kind (again, a recurrent phrase in the COS vocabulary) should be given, tailored to specific needs and sufficient for those needs, designed to prevent that lapse into pauperism from which there might be no return. Only such charity—not the poor law or any other means of public relief or public works—could avail in these cases, and only the COS was trained to give this discriminating kind of charity.

THE COS CLAIMED to be able to make the proper distinctions and discriminations because it alone acted in accord with the principles of "social science"—"the science," as one of the founders of the COS put it, "of doing good and preventing evil."[21] It was in this scientific spirit that the COS set up an "Enquiry Department" to conduct investigations and collect information which it published in its journals and in reports modeled on the official "Blue Books." In the same spirit it founded the "School of Sociology" for the training of social workers. The principal technique taught in that school, and the COS's claim to inaugurating the "science" of social work, was the system of "casework." The COS did not originate that system, but it did publicize and use it more systematically than had been done before. (The term itself first appeared in the literature of the COS in the early 1880s; by 1913 it was recognized as the distinctive contribution of the society.[22])

Just as an earlier generation of poor-law reformers relied upon the principle of less-eligibility and the workhouse test to determine those paupers who qualified for parish relief, so the COS sought, by means of casework, to identify those poor for whom it assumed responsibility: the deserving poor who were not indigent but who were in need of temporary assistance. The contrast between the two procedures could not have been more dramatic. The pride of the earlier reformers was that the New Poor Law made it possible to decide who should get relief without having to inquire into the applicant's conditions or needs. The workhouse was a "self-acting test": "If the claimant does not comply with the terms on which relief is given to the destitute, he gets nothing; and if he does comply, the compliance proves the truth of his claim, namely his destitution."[23] And since the workhouse was the least "eligible," most onerous mode of life, none but the most destitute would accept relief under those terms. Thus the instrument of relief was itself the test of relief—and a more certain test, the reformers were persuaded, than any "merit test" the Poor Law Guardians or justices of the peace might devise.[24]

The COS did not quarrel with this as the basis of poor relief; on the contrary, it insisted upon it and deplored the continued prevalence of outdoor relief. But such a "self-acting test," while appropriate for relief, was not appropriate for charity. To reach the kind of people worthy of charity and to give them the kind of charity suitable to them required, the COS believed, the closest and most careful inquiry, not only into the neediness of applicants but also their ability to profit from assistance. This was precisely the "merit test" that the poor-law reformers had abjured—a merit test that went beyond what was later to be called a "means test" because it included a test of the moral as well as the financial status of the applicant.

Casework was not the original emphasis of the COS. In its early years the main function of the district committees (which were coterminous with the poor-law unions) was to keep registers of applicants for charity and relief so as to avoid duplication. Very soon, however, this task became subordinate to the social work conducted by the COS itself, and the registers were then supplemented by detailed case records of the applicants and their families. Special forms and books were devised to record information about each family, its condition and needs, the disposition of the case, and follow-up investigations. Much of the information was obtained from "visitors"—volunteer workers or, later, paid employees— who visited the applicant at home before a grant was made to determine his eligibility and afterward to monitor his progress and give him counsel; they also made inquiries among neighbors, relatives, parish ministers, and school officials.

A later critic of the COS, looking back at it from the vantage point of the welfare state, described its "essential duality": it was "professionally pioneering" in developing the casework techniques that were to become the staples of social work, but "ideologically reactionary" in the individualistic, moralistic ethic that guided it.[25] That duality, however, was in the mind of the historian. For contemporaries the striking fact about the COS was its essential unity of purpose and method. Casework and visiting were the necessary means to achieve its ends: to select those families who qualified for charity (the family being the unit of the "case"), to determine their needs, and to give the charity in the most suitable forms—a grant or loan for the purchase of clothing or coal, tools or merchandise, a sewing machine or mangle, a surgical appliance or stay in a convalescent home. The COS also prided itself on being "rehabilitative" rather than merely "palliative"; here too the casework method was useful since the visitors maintained contact with each family and exerted the kind of personal influence that helped it become and remain self-supporting.

The family was the unit of casework and the principal concern of the COS. This too has been criticized as inconsistent with the political economy professed by the COS, which made the individual the primary unit.[26] But the principle of individualism was never intended to belittle or undermine the family; the individual was seen as standing in opposition to the state and possibly the class, but not the family. There was no contradiction between an economic doctrine based on the individual and a social doctrine based on the family, perhaps because it was assumed that the wage-earning individual was the natural head of the family. It might also be said that the very purpose of the COS, the "organization" of charity, was a violation of laissez-faire—or even that charity itself was. By this time, however, political economy had been so considerably modified, in theory as well as practice, that only the most dogmatic laissez-faireist would have objected to the kind of charity that was intended to restore the economic independence of the family.

ANOTHER ASPECT of casework, "visiting," was hardly original to the COS, having its roots in the venerable practice of the parish clergyman visiting his flock or the squire's wife making her rounds with baskets of food and clothing. There were even institutions that made visiting their specific mission. The Benevolent or Strangers' Friend Society was founded by the Methodists as early as 1785. In 1828 the Evangelicals established the General Society for Promoting District Visiting; within three years it had twenty-five district societies, a roster of 573 visitors, and 163,695 visits to its credit. Fifteen years later the Bishop of London organized the Metropolitan Visiting and Relief Association, for the purpose, as its full title put it, of "Promoting the Relief of Destitution, and for Improving the Condition of the Poor, by means of Parochial and District Visiting, under the superintendance and direction of the Bishops and Clergy, through the Agency of Unpaid Visitors, and without reference to religious persuasion."[27] (The last two clauses in this title were allusions to the London Mission, which employed paid visitors and had a purely religious function.) A notable visitor was Dickens's Mrs. Pardiggle, who proudly described herself: "I am a School lady, I am a Visiting lady, I am a Reading lady, I am a Distributing lady; I am on the local Linen Box Committee, and many general Committees."[28] (Mrs. Pardiggle may be better remembered as an associate of Mrs. Jellyby, the practitioner of "telescopic philanthropy" who was so devoted to the natives of Borrioboola-Gha.)

It remained for the COS to secularize and systematize the practice of visiting—to make it a "scientific" instrument of charity. As the technique of visiting became part of the professional apparatus, the visitors themselves acquired the status of professionals. And they did so even when they were unpaid volunteers. It is generally assumed that the mark of professionalization was the payment of visitors—"social workers," as they began to be known in the 1890s. But while the secretary of the COS was paid almost from the beginning, and by the end of the century half the district committees had paid secretaries and in some cases paid supervisors and trainers of the visitors, the visitors themselves remained, for the most part, unpaid volunteers. There was a lively debate on the issue of payment. "Paid officers," some argued, "tend to kill voluntary work."[29] As late as 1912, Violet Butler, an eminent social investigator as well as social worker, explained the psychological rationale for unpaid voluntary work. She and her friends, she said, engaged in social work as a way of "paying your rent, do you see. . . . We *knew* we were comfortably off and we felt quite guilty. . . . We felt that one ought to be working like other people, like the poorer people, but nobody wanted us, so we preferred to do it *unpaid,* if we could afford to do it unpaid."[30]

Whether paid or not, the visitors were expected to abide by professional standards. These standards determined not only the way they collected information and made recommendations, but also the way they conducted themselves in relation to the poor. From the beginning the COS was sensitive to the charges of condescension and intrusion, of letting loose among the poor a gaggle of Mrs. Pardiggles. In 1870 in its second annual report, it adjured its visitors to behave toward the poor as they would toward their own kind. "Well-to-do strangers should no more knock at the door of a working man without some distinct object or introduction than they should at the door of one in their own rank of life."[31]* Helen Bosanquet, who was a district secretary and then a mem-

---

* In 1905 a manual on visiting nurses elaborated on the etiquette of knocking: "The first thing to be remembered in knockerless, bell-less regions is that a never-to-be-departed-from etiquette demands that only the hand should be used; and it is desirable that the neighbours should be able to testify that the first two or three taps, at any rate, have been soft and low." The manual then went on to the etiquette of names: "To call a person 'out of her name' is unpardonable, not to call her by it early and often is scarcely less wounding to her feelings." And of voice: "In all the preliminary conver-

ber of the council of the COS (and a sister-in-law of Charles Bosanquet, its first secretary), warned that "inquisitiveness into another person's affairs, and especially intrusion into their home unbidden, is a great offence against social etiquette."[33] Shortly before the First World War, Violet Butler prefaced her survey of Oxford with an epigraph from Dante's *Purgatorio*: *"Ma tu, chi sei, che nostre condizioni via domandando?"* By chance, she explained, she had come upon that timely passage in which the inhabitants of purgatory reply to the interrogations of the visitors: "Who are you, who come asking about our conditions?"[34]

The cultivation of a professional attitude, however, did not imply the kind of "objectivity" that is now identified with professionalism—an impersonality and neutrality that profess to be above moral judgments. Nor did the warnings against inquisitiveness and intrusiveness mean that the visitor was to refrain from inquiring into the habits and character of the applicant or from exerting any influence upon him; on the contrary, these were precisely the missions of the visitor. "The gift," Loch wrote, "avails little; the influence may avail much." Properly exercised, that influence could affect "the thousand and one relations of life."[35]

WHEN JOHN WESLEY, a century earlier, had enjoined his flock to visit the sick and aid the poor, he had described it as a religious duty that would serve benefactor and beneficiary alike; the gift of sustenance was the gift of grace. In the case of the COS that mutuality of purpose was all the more striking because the religious duty itself had been transmuted. The salvation that was now sought carried with it all the passion and authority of religion without the creedal and institutional constraints of a church. It was a religion that was secular rather than sectarian and scientific rather than dogmatic.

The religious metaphor was pervasive. Reflecting upon his long association with the COS, Charles Loch explained that he had originally been drawn to it by the hope of creating an association of people from different churches and classes who would find in charity "a common purpose and a new unity." That would be "worth anything," for without the interference of the state, "it could renew and discipline the life of the

---

sation the voice should be carefully lowered. Although the poor commonly speak to one another with what might be considered unnecessary loudness, they resent this tone in their social superiors, not only because it enables inquisitive neighbours to hear too much, but because they know that is not how a lady speaks to a friend."[32]

people by a nobler, more devoted, more scientific religious charity. . . . It could help us to realise in society the religion of charity without the sectarianism of religion.[36]*

Loch's grandson described him as a "natural Christian" rather than an "orthodox churchman."[38] And while many of his associates in the COS were orthodox churchmen, it was as "natural Christians" that they too functioned in what Loch called the "church of charity."[39] Like all such religious missions, this was intended to have a redeeming effect on giver and receiver alike. In this case the "giver" was not so much the donor of money as the visitor, who gave a gift—of time, energy, and spirit—that was greater than any mere contribution of money and more satisfying both to the giver and to the receiver. It relieved the giver's "consciousness of sin" more effectively than any impersonal monetary transaction might have done. And it more effectively relieved the poverty of the recipient, who obtained the kind of personal help that would enable him to help himself, morally as well as economically.

This was not the gift prescribed by the evangelist: "Give unto everyone that asketh thee." That gift was an end in itself, not so much a means of relieving the needy as a manifestation of the divine spirit, the infinite love of God expressing itself in infinite compassion for man. Infinite—not measured by need or means, not organized or supervised, but given freely and received freely, without conditions or limits. "When thou doest alms," the Gospel reads, "let not thy left hand know what thy right hand doeth." The COS operated under precisely the opposite dictate. Theirs was a "religion of charity" presided over by a "church of charity" and governed by a "science of charity." And their science required the left hand to know precisely what the right hand was doing, and made it a solemn obligation *not* to give to everyone who asketh.

The COS could appreciate the spiritual intention, if not the practical effects, of the gift in its original religious sense. What it could not appreciate was either the intention or the effects of the corrupt version of the gift as practiced by a lady bountiful. This was not a self-sacrificing but a self-serving gift, an act of self-indulgence that was more concerned with feeling good than with doing good, and that, in fact, did more harm than

---

* Earlier in the century, the Owenites, who were militantly opposed to orthodox religion, described their form of socialism as a "religion of charity." Their "Credo" of 1837 called for a "well devised, equitable and natural system of united property" that would bring about "an entire change in the character and condition of mankind" and establish throughout the world "the principle and practice of the religion of charity."[37]

good. It was mischievous not only because it was "indiscriminate" but because it was "benevolent" in the paternalistic (or, more literally, maternalistic) sense, designed to keep the poor in a state of dependency. Helen Bosanquet quoted one lady bountiful who was upset at the thought that poverty might be "cured," for if it were, "the rich would have no one upon whom to exercise their faculty of benevolence"; and another who objected to giving the poor the means of becoming self-sufficient because that would make them too independent. "I like them to come to me when they are in difficulties and ask for what they want," this lady explained. Without this "glow of benevolent patronage," Mrs. Bosanquet sarcastically commented, the ladies bountiful of this world would soon lose their interest in the poor.[40]

Shortly after she started work as a visitor in Soho, Beatrice Potter reflected on some of the anomalies of the new charity. Did it not favor the weak and helpless to the detriment of the stronger and more resourceful? And if this were so, should such considerations have any weight in the face of individual misery? Were "economic facts" as important as the "moral facts" with which charity was properly concerned? And was not the chief of these moral facts "the relationship of giver and receiver," above all "the moral effect on the person who receives"? About one thing she was clear: the personal relationship was as important for the giver as for the receiver. "It is distinctly *advantageous to us* to go amongst the poor." And not only because the knowledge and experience of the lives of others would contribute to a better understanding of their problems, but also for one's own character, because "contact with them develops on the whole our finer qualities, disgusting us with our false and worldly application of men and things and educating in us a thoughtful benevolence." This benevolence, to be sure, could take the form of "pharasaical self congratulation." But the real philanthropist was not likely to be guilty of this because he was "far too perplexed at the very '*mixed result*' (even if he can recognize any permanent result) of his work, to feel much pride over it."[41]

The importance of "the relationship of giver and receiver" went beyond the individuals involved in it. In 1870 Charles Trevelyan explained that one of the purposes of the "systematic visitation of the poor" was to narrow the gulf between the classes: "to bring back the rich into such close relation with the poor as cannot fail to have a civilising and healing influence, and to knit all classes together in the bonds of mutual help and goodwill."[42] In the mid-eighties, at a time when others, even within the COS, were urging some form of government action to cope with the problem of unemployment, Loch reaffirmed the role of the COS as "a Great Companionship of Charity, West with East, rich with poor, the elder with the younger generation."[43] Later still, in an appeal for volunteers, the COS suggested that the "social" aspect of visiting, even more than the "charitable," was the means by which "class distinctions may be partly effaced."[44] It also saw its network of visitors and committees as a corrective to the unfortunate effects of urbanism, restoring those links that had been broken in the anonymous, impersonal city and forging new bonds of community. It was for this reason among others that the COS urged its visitors to be friendly and "neighbourly," to give charity not as "from strangers to strangers" but as a transaction between people personally known to each other.[45] Only in such a personal relationship would the rich appreciate "the responsibility attaching to wealth and leisure" and the poor have "the comfortable assurance that if the day of exceptional adversity should come, they will not be left to encounter it without a friend."[46]

FROM THE PERSPECTIVE of the welfare state, and even more of a socialist society, the theories and practices of the COS seem at best jejune, woefully inadequate to the problems of poverty and unemployment, more effective in alleviating the guilt of the rich than the misery of the poor. A less generous judgment sees the COS as a systematic and ruthless attempt to curtail both relief and charity, to impose a new and more strenuous form of social control on the poor, to revive an outdated ideology of laissez-faire, and to thwart any serious movement of economic and social reform.

The COS would have conceded some of these charges. It did not deny that it wanted to restrict charity and relief, on the ground that indiscriminate charity and relief were more damaging to the poor than to the rich; the rich could survive the poor rates and alms, but the poor were degraded and pauperized by that misguided largesse. Nor would the COS have denied a commitment to laissez-faire, modified, as it had been by this time, by a considerable body of social legislation; indeed it prided itself on making charity an instrument of individualism. "Charity is a social regenerator," Loch wrote. "We have to use Charity to create the power of self-help."[47] His grandson, who was also the historian of the COS, said that the society "implied a sternly individualist philosophy, and paid the poor the compliment of assuming they shared it."[48] He might have added that it also paid them the compliment of assuming that they shared the capacity of acting on that individualist philosophy—of being prudent, temperate, and independent.

Some historians, finding it difficult to credit or respect this rationale, offer a psychological explanation of the COS (and of Victorian philanthropy in general). One account starts by granting to these philanthropists a measure of humanitarian concern, but dwells, at greater length and with greater conviction, on the more powerful motives that inspired them. Charity is represented as "conscience money" to atone for "self-conscious guilt-complexes about the possession of wealth"; philanthropy as compensation for some "emotional deficiency" resulting from bereavement, childless marriage, or "internal tension" (presumably sexual); "slumming" as a recreational activity for bored wives and idle spinsters; and philanthropic societies as an outlet for snobbery, social advancement, and professional ambition. This psychological explanation is supplemented by the familiar "social control" thesis, in which charity is seen as a means of pacifying the lower classes and forestalling revolution, visiting as "a cultural assault upon the working-class way of life," and "moral reformation" as the imposition upon the poor of those "middle-class values" and "self-help mentality" that would keep them in bondage to the established order.[49]

In another version of this thesis, casework appears as the primary instrument of social control. The "personalized welfare relationship" transmitted to the poor the middle-class ideal of "deferred gratification"; and the continued visiting perpetuated the relationship by continually reminding the applicant of his dependency and obligations.[50] Casework is seen as the enduring legacy of the COS. Whatever defeats the COS experienced during the rise of the welfare state, the retention of casework as the primary method of social work is its final triumph, for it is thus that social control continues to be exercised. A novel turn of this argument has the COS imposing social control upon its own members. As the organizing agency for all charities, it assumed control not only over the recipients of charity but over the donors as well. They too were being regimented, their spontaneous impulses curbed, their contributions used as others saw fit, and their personalities subordinated to a powerful "solidary" system (in Emile Durkheim's sense) that was as much beyond their control as it was beyond the control of the poor.[51]

Yet another theory sees the COS as a response to the profound social dislocation arising from the increasing separation of the classes, a gulf that had resulted in "a breakdown of social relationships and traditional methods of social control." Charity had always had a "status-maintaining" as well as a social control function, the act of giving being an assertion of superiority on the part of the giver and of subordination on the part of the receiver. But in late-Victorian England, the acute separation of classes and breakdown of social relationships resulted in "the deformation of the gift," with indiscriminate alms-giving and impersonal public relief replacing the personal exchange between giver and receiver which had been the original meaning of the gift. The COS represented one of several attempts to reestablish that relationship, to "remoralize" the poor and restore the "traditional fabric of social control."[52]

THE COROLLARY of the social control thesis is the "socialization" and "moralization" thesis—the idea that the COS (again, like other philanthropies) tried to impose upon the poor middle-class values which violated their indigenous working-class values. The implications of this thesis are disquieting. If thrift, prudence, sobriety, industry, cleanliness, and independence were middle-class values, is it to be assumed that profligacy, imprudence, drunkenness, idleness, dirtiness, and dependency were indigenous working-class values? The COS may well have been guilty of imposing their values upon the poor. But later historians may be doing so as well, attributing to the poor a contempt for "bourgeois" culture more congenial to intellectuals than to workers aspiring to that culture and to the material and social benefits associated with it.

The fact is that these values, summed up in the contemporary idea of "respectability," were hardly the exclusive prerogative of the middle class or even of the "labor aristocracy." If most of the poor could not hope to attain the status of the "respectable artisan" or the "better class of working men" (these were contemporary terms), the ideal of respectability was no less important to them. It may even have been more important, for it was they who were most vulnerable, in that precarious condition where the least misstep, the slightest misfortune or imprudence, might cast them into the company of the "residuum." In equating respectability with independence, the COS was reflecting contemporary values—and the values of the working classes as much as of the middle classes.[53]

Nor were these values called into question when the COS became controversial in the late 1880s. It was not its ethos that was then at issue but the way that ethos could best be implemented; the Barnetts, for example, believed that self-help was consistent with such forms of state aid as old-age pensions. (Even after the Barnetts withdrew from the central organization of the COS in 1895, they retained membership in their district committee.) Nor did the criticism of the COS necessarily imply a disparagement of charity itself. The Mansion House Fund in the winter of 1885–86 raised more money than ever before, and philanthropic societies of all kinds continued to be founded, in spite of the efforts of the COS. (London had one thousand charitable societies in the 1880s; in 1905 the COS register listed 1,700.)[54] Nor was the practice of visiting discredited. On the contrary, it was at the heart of other philanthropic enterprises, such as Octavia Hill's model houses. Toynbee Hall might be regarded as an extreme version of it, with the social worker not only visiting but actually residing among the poor.

Nor did the COS become redundant after the turn of the century, when a series of reforms culminating in the National Insurance Act of 1911 brought into being the "social service state," as it has been called. On the eve of the First World War, the COS raised almost twice as much money for charity as it had a quarter of a century earlier. And in this period of supposed decline and disfavor, it continued to attract converts among promising young men and women. In 1903 R. H. Tawney, then a resident in Toynbee Hall and contemplating a career in social work, considered two alternatives: the COS and the Children's Country Holiday Fund. He decided against the COS, not because he found its methods "inquisitorial," as one biographer claims, but because, as he himself said at the time, the Children's Fund paid twice as much and he would have had to remain at the COS twice as long to learn from the experience.[55] William Beveridge, on the other hand, chose to associate himself with the COS, and the report he wrote for it in 1908 became the basis of his classic work, *Unemployment*. A measure of the society's influence was the appointment in 1905 of six members of its council to the nineteen-member Royal Commission on the Poor Laws. In spite of the vigorous opposition of Beatrice Webb, it was their views that prevailed in the Majority Report issued four years later. And even the Minority Report, written by the Webbs and differing from the Majority Report in so many important ways, did not differ from it in one crucial respect: the idea that the aim of social policy was to encourage the poor to become respectable, responsible, and moral.

Later, to be sure, Beatrice Webb, among others, came to regard the COS as "reactionary," not only in its policies but in its moral principles.[56] To identify the poor in moral terms implied that poverty was a function of character rather than of economic and social conditions. And this, in turn, suggested that it could be alleviated only by the moral reformation of individuals rather than, as these critics would have liked, a fundamental reform of the economy and society.

IN FACT, the COS did not make of poverty entirely a function of character. On the contrary, it recognized the "causeless," "exceptional," and "temporary" nature of a good deal of poverty; indeed it took that poverty as its special domain. And it took as its special clients those who were suffering from that kind of poverty—the "deserving poor," as they had been called. This was, to be sure, a moral category. But its effect was quite different from that generally attributed to it. In "moralizing" these poor, the COS explicitly absolved them from the charge that they were poor because of a failure of character. They were poor and in need of assistance *in spite of* the fact that they were generally (although not always) hardworking, sober, and thrifty. In undertaking to assist them, the COS gave them a character reference, as it were, an official seal of approval. The applicant was subjected to a moral test, and certified as having passed it when he received aid. In some respects this moral test contrasts favorably not only with the workhouse test imposed by the poor law but with the means test that is the basis of relief today. A means test, judging only the need and not the character of the applicant, leaves open the suspicion that the need is a result of a failure of character; a moral test certifies that it is not.

The "moralization" of the poor had equivocal effects, which the COS did not anticipate and would have strenuously deplored. In making so much of the "deserving poor" (even while ceasing to call them that), in making them so deserving as to qualify for assistance, the COS implicitly made of them a "social problem" requiring a social solution. Thus "respectable" poverty, not indigence, became part of the social agenda. The COS thought it had prescribed the only logical solution to this kind of poverty: private charity given under carefully prescribed conditions so as not to "demoralize" or "pauperize" the poor. But by identifying these poor in this fashion—by making them both deserving and problematic— the COS prepared the way for very different solutions to that problem. If they were deserving of private charity, why not of public relief? And if they were a social problem, should not the state take it upon itself to solve that problem? And should not that state assistance be given as a matter of right rather than compassion, as a legal obligation of the state rather than the voluntary beneficence of individuals?

By "moralizing" the poor, the COS unwittingly legitimized them as the potential "clients" of the state. It may even be argued that a purely economic conception of poverty could not have done this as effectively as the moral conception the COS insisted upon, for the moral poor had a greater moral claim upon the public resources than the merely needy poor. Similarly, by legitimizing—that is, making "scientific"—the philanthropic movement, the COS unwittingly legitimized other movements (socialism, most notably) inspired by the same humanitarian zeal and scientific pretensions but committed to collectivist and statist ideologies.

The emphasis upon charity had a similarly paradoxical effect. To latter-day critics of the COS, this is yet another proof of the benighted nature of the enterprise. The decision to accommodate the deserving poor by "reorganizing" charity rather than by reforming and liberalizing the poor law seems regressive, a reversion to the private sphere at a time when the public sphere was emerging as the obvious and efficient arena for the solution of social problems. But it was precisely by distancing itself from the poor law that the COS was able to "create," so to speak, a class of the poor that could receive aid without being tainted by the poor law—without being "stigmatized" or "pauperized."

To the modern reader, the moral value ascribed to charity in contrast to relief may seem perverse as well as regressive. This is the way it appears to the historian David Owen: "That the giving and accepting of charity (under proper conditions) should be considered an ennobling transaction while state aid was inevitably pauperizing stands in retrospect as one of the more curious articles of faith."[57] But it may be no more curious than the opinion prevalent today that charity is ignoble while state aid is honorable, reflected in the common view that it is demeaning for elderly parents to be dependent on their families but not demeaning to have them dependent on the state. Today "charity" has an invidious ring; in Victorian England it was far less invidious than "relief," which retained the aroma of the workhouse even when relief was given (as it frequently was) outside the workhouse.* The COS's view of charity was shared by

---

* And not only in Victorian England. The repugnance against poor relief was a powerful sentiment in America during the depression, and in some circles well beyond it. There is still a generation alive that remembers when relief was regarded as shameful, while the assistance of family or friends, church or *Landsmannschaft,* was assumed to be natural and proper. The stigma of relief even affected social security for a while. It took years of education and habituation for the principle of social insurance to become sufficiently differentiated from relief so that those suspicious of public

some contemporaries—T. H. Green and Arnold Toynbee, for example—who had no principled objection to state aid, but who belonged to the COS because they believed charity to be more fitting, less degrading, for the deserving poor than relief. For Green and Toynbee, as for Loch, charity under the proper conditions was salutary, not only for the receiver and the giver but for society as a whole, for it united rich and poor in a common bond of citizenship.

IT IS NOT SURPRISING that the word "citizenship" should be so prominent in the vocabulary of the COS; both Loch and Bernard Bosanquet were students of Green, who made that concept central to his philosophy.[58] Even before the working classes as a whole had received the franchise, the COS endowed them with something like the status of social citizenship. And after they were enfranchised in 1884, the COS thought it all the more important that they acquire the independence that was the true mark of the citizen. (It is significant that one group not enfranchised at this time were paupers; anyone receiving parish relief during the year was not eligible to vote.) In a "world grown democratic," Loch explained, the idea of citizenship took on a new meaning. In the past the state could tolerate a class of dependents. It could no longer do so, for citizenship was inconsistent with dependency.

> The State wants citizens. It cannot afford to have any outcasts or excluded classes, citizens that are not citizens. All are citizens in name; it must see that they are so in reality. It must do its utmost to change the dependent sections of the community into independent. . . . Accordingly it becomes a duty of the State by some means to prevent pauperism, and of citizens to give their service to the State for that purpose.[59]

"It becomes a duty of the State by some means to prevent pauperism"—the COS thought it understood how the state could best fulfill that duty: by not intervening directly in the economic life of its citizens, by encouraging individuals to do all they could for themselves, and by leaving it to voluntary institutions such as the COS to relieve the deserving poor without making paupers of them. Others, however, interpreted that

---

largesse could accept, in good conscience, old age or disability benefits to which they themselves had contributed.

duty differently. In a "world grown democratic," it was tempting to assign the state a more direct role in carrying out that duty, using the agency and authority of the state itself to ensure the economic well-being of its citizens. This implied a new conception of citizenship—"social citizenship," as one contemporary put it.[60] If political citizenship entailed a full complement of political rights, "social citizenship" was thought to require a new set of "social rights."

The anomalous effects of the COS recall the famous dictum of Lord Acton: "Ideas have a radiation and development, an ancestry and posterity of their own, in which men play the part of godfathers and godmothers more than that of legitimate parents."[61] The COS was to find itself in just this situation, of being the godparent to ideas it would have heartily disowned. Having made so much of the deserving poor as the proper recipients of charity, it had to witness those poor being made the recipients of state aid. Having made so much of the social citizenship that united rich and poor in a bond of mutual obligations, it had to observe that citizenship being converted (perverted, as it thought) into a claim on the state for assistance and sustenance.* Having made of poverty—not indigence or destitution, but "respectable" poverty—a social problem, it had to watch others propose solutions to that problem which, in its judgment, only exacerbated it. Finally, and perhaps most distressingly, having made a science of philanthropy, it had to confront its archenemies, the socialists, who declared theirs to be the only truly scientific approach to a truly humane society.

---

* The COS had only one principle, Bernard Bosanquet wrote. "This principle is the support or restoration of the citizen (or social) mind. All methods are good, that are conducive to this end."[62] That last sentence was an invitation to the utilization of "methods" that, for Bosanquet as for the COS, were nothing less than disastrous.

CHAPTER 14

Model Dwellings and
Model Homes

"It seems to me that pauperism is not an affair so much of wages as of dwellings. If the working classes were properly lodged, at their present rate of wages, they would be richer. They would be healthier and happier at the same cost."[1] Thus spake Lothair, the hero of Disraeli's novel published in 1870. Lothair (or Lord Bute, upon whom the character was modeled) correctly appraised the problem but mistakenly characterized it. Bad housing was a problem not of pauperism but of poverty. The problem of pauperism was epitomized by the workhouse; the problem of poverty—the poverty of the working classes, especially the urban working classes—by the slum house.

It was about the middle of the century that the word "slum" ceased to mean a slumbering, unfrequented back alley and came to mean almost its opposite: an overcrowded street of bad houses. Even then, however, it had less disagreeable connotations than the older word "rookery," which had criminal overtones (a "rook" was a thief or swindler).[2] Philanthropic-minded ladies would not have ventured into rookeries to ply their trade, but they could go "slumming"—a word, and a practice, that became common in the 1880s. The socialist Henry Hyndman spoke sarcastically of the "boom in slumming."[3] But there was no sarcasm, no intentional irony, in Lady Violet Greville's comment after one such expedition when she had the satisfaction of comforting a poor old man on his deathbed: "These little incidents make 'slumming' a real pleasure. One can give so much happiness with so little trouble."[4]

Those ladies (and gentlemen as well) who went "slumming" as a matter of duty rather than pleasure—indeed, who made a profession of it—did so because, like Lothair, they regarded slum housing as the most serious of the problems afflicting the poor and the source of most of the others. Men who lived in pig sties, a popular saying had it, would live like pigs. It did not take a temperance preacher to see the connection between drinking and slum living. So long as homes were hovels, Dickens wrote, "gin palaces" would make up for them in number and splendor.[5] Shaftesbury declared that "nine-tenths of our poverty, misery, and crime are produced by habits of intoxication," and these evils, in turn, by the "pestilential and ruinous domiciliary condition" of the urban masses.[6] Unemployment itself seemed to many a lesser problem than housing. Arnold Toynbee, who did as much as anyone to focus attention on the economic problems arising from the industrial revolution, said that the crucial issue of the near future was not those economic problems but housing; this was to be the form that the question of the "distribution of wealth" would take.[7]

Even the COS, loath as it was to resort to the government for the alleviation of social problems, did so in the case of slum housing. In 1874 it formally presented a memorial to the Disraeli government complaining of the ineffectuality of existing legislation (the Torrens Act of 1868 in particular) and recommending that the London authorities be empowered to demolish slums on a large scale and, if private enterprise were not forthcoming, to undertake the construction of houses. The proposal was all the more persuasive because it came from that source, and it played a large part in persuading Parliament to pass the Artisans' and Labourers' Dwellings Improvement Act (the Cross Act) the following year and the still stronger Artisans' Dwellings Act in 1882. The COS also encouraged municipalities to adopt similar local measures.[8] In taking a position so at variance with its general principles, the COS was attesting to the special nature of the housing problem. Unlike unemployment, which was often temporary or "exceptional," bad housing was a permanent and pervasive condition for a large part of the working classes. Even more than employment, it was crucial to the development of character because the home was the heart and hearth of the family.

For the COS, as for most Victorian philanthropists, government intervention was a measure of last resort—and even then, an ancillary measure, intended to supplement rather than supplant private efforts. Private associations for the improvement of working-class housing had a long history. Much earlier in the century, Lord Shaftesbury (Anthony Ashley Cooper, as he then was) founded the Society for Improving the Condition of the Labouring Classes, one of whose functions was to provide capital for the building and renovating of houses. (The society, still in existence today, had Queen Victoria as patron and Prince Albert as president.)[9] In the following decades Angela Burdett-Coutts, George Peabody, and Edward Cecil Guinness followed suit, establishing building societies for the purpose of constructing "model dwellings" on the principle of "five per cent philanthropy." (Both of these terms were current at the time.)[10]

A five percent return on capital was considered respectable although not munificent. It signified a humanitarian enterprise based on sound commercial principles but not designed for speculation or maximum profit. In fact, five percent proved to be more a metaphor than a reality, most of the building societies realizing no more than half that amount. If more societies were not forced into bankruptcy, it was because they enjoyed indirect government subsidies. The housing acts of 1866 and 1867 enabled them to borrow money at four percent and repay the loan over forty years, and some of the slum-clearance projects provided for the purchase of land below its commercial value.

Contemporaries had few illusions about the ability of the model dwellings to "solve" the housing problem. One witness testifying before the Royal Commission on the Housing of the Working Classes in 1884 reported that "the labouring classes are increasing in London at the rate of some 30,000 or 40,000 a year; all the building societies do not provide for 10,000 a year."[11] But 10,000 a year was not a paltry number. Nor was the total of 160,000 residents accommodated in these houses at this time. (In half a dozen years that number was to come to 190,000, and it rose substantially by the end of the century.)[12] Nor was the sum of £2,000,000 that had been invested in these building societies as early as 1881. In fact the impact of these enterprises could not be measured entirely in quantifiable terms. One result was to familiarize the working classes in particular, and the metropolis in general, with a form of urban housing that was perhaps inevitable if not always agreeable. As the London County Council was later to discover, blocks of flats (tenement houses, as they were known in America) were not the most aesthetically pleasing form of architecture, but in the densely populated areas of central London they seemed to be the only practical means of increasing the stock of cheap housing. They enabled tens of thousands of workers to live near their place of work, and to do so in conditions that were a vast improvement over the old slum houses. The Lord Mayor of London, who was the chairman of one of the building societies, described them as "an oasis of wholesomeness in some dirty desert of dingy and rickety buildings."[13] Others, however, including some who might have been expected to welcome such oases, disliked them intensely. Workers accustomed to small houses were often repelled by the large, impersonal blocks of flats and resented the regulations imposed by the societies. Socialists denounced them as "bastilles" erected by capitalism for the incarceration of the proletariat. And some reformers regarded them as a blight upon the city as well as an affront to the workers condemned to living in them.

OCTAVIA HILL was among those reformers who saw these model buildings as part of the problem rather than the solution. A block building, she insisted, even a "model" block, was not a model home for the poor, any more than for anyone else; indeed it was the very negation of a home. Her own plan was in one sense more modest, in another more ambitious. By taking over the management of small houses, renovating them, and letting them out to tenants at low rentals and under strict supervision, she hoped to provide the conditions in which they could lead good, clean, moral, happy lives.

She came to this enterprise with good credentials. Her maternal grandfather was Dr. Southwood Smith, a leading "sanitary reformer" earlier in the century and an associate of Edwin Chadwick, that most indefatigable of Benthamite reformers. Her own initiation into the world of social work began at the age of fourteen as an assistant in the Ladies' Guild, a cooperative managed by her mother under the tutelage of the Christian Socialist Frederick Denison Maurice. (Maurice's son was to become Octavia Hill's brother-in-law as well as her biographer.) After supervising a Ragged School for children run by the Guild, she and her sisters established their own school. A few years later she became secretary to the women's classes at the Working Men's College founded by Maurice. Most of these were paid positions; unlike many of the philanthropists of the time, she had no independent income. (Her father, a corn and wool merchant, had died after a long, financially debilitating illness.)[14]

In 1865, at the age of twenty-seven, Octavia Hill persuaded another family friend, John Ruskin (who had earlier given her painting lessons), to finance her first housing experiment by purchasing three houses, which she undertook to renovate and manage.* Three years later she was one of

---

* Ruskin's crucial role in launching her upon her career made her later quarrel with him all the more painful. In 1877, offended by her remark (expressed privately) that he was incapable of carrying out any great practical work because he held to an "ideal standard of perfection," Ruskin publicly broke off relations with her.[15]

the small group of founders of what was to become the Charity Organisation Society. By the early seventies, her work in the housing movement and her association with the COS had made her a leading figure in the world of philanthropy, social work, and social reform. She was active in the campaign for the housing acts of 1875 and 1882; she appeared as an expert witness before parliamentary committees and commissions; she was a member of the Royal Commission on the Poor Law and contributed to the Majority Report; she belonged to the Commons Preservation Society and helped found the National Trust. She was, in short, one of those "governing and guiding women" who dominated the philanthropic world and gave the "time-spirit" its peculiar character.[16]

Even more important than Hill's personal activities was her role in inspiring and involving others. As a young girl Mary Macaulay (later Charles Booth's wife) worked as a volunteer in a playground organized by Hill. Booth himself became acquainted with Hill sometime before he embarked upon his great work.[17] Charles Loch's wife had been Hill's secretary before her marriage. Beatrice Potter's sister Kate served her apprenticeship under Hill and then applied her principles as rent collector in a model building project, a job Beatrice took over when her sister was married. The Reverend Barnett, the founder of Toynbee Hall, met Hill when he became vicar of St. Jude; he later said that Hill had "opened the whole world to him."[18]*

In describing her apprenticeship in this craft, Beatrice Webb explained that she herself was moved less by the "spirit of charity" than by the spirit of science. Even as a rent collector, she was more interested in the opportunity it gave her for social investigation than for social work. In this respect she was very different from her sister and her colleagues, who were definitely social workers, not social investigators. It was with some

---

* It was this world that rallied around Octavia Hill to console her in 1877 when she had a nervous breakdown after the breakup of her engagement to be married. "Poor Octavia," Mary Booth told her husband, was so ill that "they have now great fears for her brain."[19] After two years abroad Hill returned to London and resumed her work. According to Beatrice Webb, she came back a "changed woman," harder and more "despotic." In fact Webb did not know Hill at this time and was perhaps projecting upon her some of her own experiences in a similarly unrequited affair. (Webb also suggested that Hill's fiancé, Edward Bond, was the model for George Eliot's *Daniel Deronda*—a novel written before the scandal of the broken engagement.)[20] Lest it be thought that Hill turned to social work in compensation for unrequited love, it should be made clear that her work and fame long antedated this event and there is no evidence of any change in either her principles or her practices.

irritation, but also admiration, that she described the manager of a model building, who devoted her entire life to her work (she actually lived on the premises). This woman was no "lover of fact or theory," barely knew how many rooms she had to let, and had not the slightest desire to "solve the general questions of the hour." But she was full of love and sympathy for her charges, and without any "self-consciousness" (Webb's own besetting sin) she devoted herself to the practical work of keeping the building in repair, seeing to the needs of the tenants, giving advice and instruction, even providing entertainment and amusement. She too was one of the tribe of "governing and guiding women," although not quite of the type of Octavia Hill—or of Beatrice Webb herself. There was much admiration, and a good deal of self-criticism, in Webb's reflections upon this type.

> Unlike the learned woman, the emotional part of their nature is fully developed, their sympathy kept almost painfully active. Their eyes are clear of self-consciousness and bright with love and the pity from which it springs. They have the dignity of habitual authority. Often they have the narrow-mindedness and social gaucherie of complete absorption, physical and mental, in one set of feelings and ideas. The *pure organizer* belongs to a different class. She is represented by the active secretary to a growing society or the matron of a big hospital—to a certain extent unsexed by the justice, push, and severity required. Not that I despise these qualities; the former is indispensable in any work but with the manager it is more moral; with the organizer more technical justice. Push and severity are not *prominent* qualities of the governing and guiding woman. For the *guidance* of men by personal influence, *feeling* more than thought is required.[21]

> I think these strong women have a great future before them—in the solution of social questions. They *are not* just inferior men. They may have masculine faculty but they have the *woman's temperament*—and the stronger they are the more distinctively *feminine* they are in this.[22]

OCTAVIA HILL was not moved by the spirit of "science" in Webb's sense; she was not interested in her "tenants" (as she insisted upon calling them) as objects of social investigation. But she was scientific in the COS sense of that term: the belief that the well-being of the tenants depended upon the application of conscious, rational, systematic principles. One of these principles, essential to the welfare of the tenants as much as of the investors, was the operation of the houses on a "thoroughly sound commercial principle."[23] This required both a return on capital (not necessarily five percent but some percent) and the payment of rent (not necessarily the full commercial rent but some rent). Like a latter-day psychoanalyst justifying fees as a token of the patient's commitment to the psychoanalytic treatment, so Hill regarded rent as an earnest of good faith and good conduct on the part of the tenant. Rent was not only the means of ensuring the financial viability of the house. It was the means of promoting those virtues that were conducive to a good life: punctuality, regularity, economy, thrift, prudence. Recognizing that the irregularity of work was the main obstacle to the regular payment of rent, Hill encouraged her tenants to save (she offered to hold their savings if they did not want to entrust them to a friendly society), and during slack seasons she employed as many as she could in making repairs and improvements in the buildings. But she would brook no arrears in the payment of rent because that would be to undermine their independence and self-respect—their status as rent-paying tenants rather than charitable cases.

If the residents in Hill's buildings were tenants rather than clients, her rent collectors were "landladies" rather than "visitors." This is how Hill herself generally spoke of them and how the tenants themselves did. They were landladies, however, with a difference. Indeed, one of their functions was to free the poor from "the tyranny and influence of a low class of landlords and landladies." The typical slum landlords and landladies were either "struggling, cheated, much-worried, long-suffering," or, worse, "bullying, violent, passionate, revengeful, and cowardly."[24] Hill's landladies, by contrast, were professional social workers as well as house managers and rent collectors. Their job was not only to collect rents, supervise repairs and maintenance, recommend suitable tenants for vacancies, decide when a family required an additional room, and provide whatever amenities they could (a playground or drying area for clothes), but also to advise, cajole, rebuke, encourage, and otherwise induce the tenants to take pride in their homes and in themselves.* Only a professional—a professional volunteer, that is—

---

* In New York City in the early years of public housing, the rent collectors also doubled as social workers, inquiring into the welfare of the tenants and offering advice and help.

could "unite the fresh, loving, spontaneous, individual sympathy with the quiet, grave, sustained and instructed spirit of the trained worker."[25]

"Benevolent Despotism" is the title of the chapter on Octavia Hill in a scholarly work on Victorian housing.[26] The epithet is not without justice, although it may be misinterpreted. It derives from an obituary notice in which Hill's workers were said to refer to her as "general" and her volunteers and tenants were described as disciplined armies.[27] A few years after taking over the first of her houses, Hill said that she felt "somewhat like an officer at the head of a well-controlled little regiment, or, more accurately, like a country proprietor with a moderate number of well-ordered tenants." The image of the squire softened that of the officer, and the rest of the passage suggested that both metaphors were meant to convey the smallness of the enterprise and the intimacy of the relationship: "My people are numbered; not merely counted, but known, man, woman, and child."[28] On another occasion, contemplating some especially decrepit property she was about to acquire, she mused, "Truly a wild, lawless, desolate little kingdom to come to rule over." She promised to exercise her authority in accord with two principles: she would require of her tenants "a strict fulfilment of their duties to me," the chief of which was the punctual payment of rent; and she would "endeavour to be so unfailingly just and patient, that they should learn to trust the rule that was over them."[29]

If hers was a "benevolent despotism," she herself was as wary of such a regime as any of her critics. An excess of either benevolence or despotism would fatally undermine the independence that was the chief purpose of her enterprise. Her aim was not only to provide the decent housing that was a precondition of independence but to promote the habits, abilities, and sensibilities that would sustain that independence. This meant treating the tenants as equals rather than dependents, and helping them in the same spirit that one might help one's friends.

> I knew that I should learn to feel these people as my friends, and so should instinctively feel the same respect for their privacy and their independence, and should treat them with the same courtesy that I should show towards any other personal friends. There would be no interference, no entering their room uninvited, no offer of money or the necessaries of life. But when occasion presented itself, I should give them any help I could, such as I might offer without insult to other friends. . . . I am convinced that one of the evils of much that is

done for the poor springs from the want of delicacy felt, and courtesy shown, towards them, and that we cannot beneficially help them in any spirit different to that in which we help those who are better off. The help may differ in amount, because their needs are greater. It should not differ in kind.[30]

This was surely a counsel of perfection, an ideal that could rarely be achieved. But it was an ideal to aspire to, and it testified to an acute consciousness of the difficulty and delicacy of her task.

Hill valued independence as the means for the development of good character. But she also valued it for its own sake, as an attribute of individuality. To know a person's character, she said, was not merely to know whether he was a drunkard or a liar; it was to know something of his "passions, hopes and history," the temptations he was prone to, the plans he had for his life, the memories and hopes that sustained him.[31] Temperance, cleanliness, prudence, regularity, thrift were the desiderata of a good life but not the whole of it; the rest of it was the private preserve of the individual. "It is essential to remember that each man has his own view of his life, and must be free to fulfil it; that in many ways he is a far better judge of it than we, as he has lived through and felt what we have only seen."[32]

The good life was not entirely a function of good character; it had an aesthetic component as well. This was Hill's quarrel with the model dwelling advocates, who valued cleanliness and orderliness over beauty and spontaneity—indeed, who distrusted adornment and decoration, light and bright colors, trees and flowers, games and amusements, suspecting them of undermining rationality, utility, even morality. "The poor of London need joy and beauty in their lives," Hill declared, quoting approvingly the circus master in Dickens's *Hard Times,* who reminded Mr. Gradgrind, "People mutht be amoothed, Thquire."[33] In an article entitled "Space for the People," she argued that what was needed was not only living space within the home but free space outside: "Places to sit in, places to play in, places to stroll in, and places to spend a day in."[34] In her own projects she attended as much to the landscaping as to the interiors of the flats. And she tirelessly promoted plans for playgrounds and parks, art exhibits and musical performances, which would provide, as the title of another article put it, "Colour, Space and Music for the People."[35]

* * *

PLEADING FOR such amenities as "colour, space and music for the people," Octavia Hill had also to explain which "people" should be given the opportunity to enjoy them. She found that too many would-be bene-factors had a "depraved hunger for rags, sharp need, and slums," and had no desire to help the "industrious, thrifty working people, who show no evidence of want." One lady cheerily told her, "I should like to go where there is condensed misery." Others, shown a dark and cheerless court, asked to see one that was still darker and viler. Hill refused to pander to such low tastes. Those who could recognize only "extreme want," who could derive no satisfaction in "rendering a little fuller and gayer the somewhat same life of worthy working people," were not entitled to "lift the veil of greater want, or enter the haunts of sin."[36]

Hill's own projects were intended for the "industrious, thrifty work-ing people," the "worthy working people." If she did not speak of them as the "deserving poor," it was perhaps because that term had been preempted by the COS, and she wanted to distinguish her poor from theirs. The COS's deserving poor were, at least temporarily, in want, in need of charity. Hers were not. The pressing need of her poor was for houses which would be proper homes, enhancing their sense of indepen-dence and making their lives "a little fuller and gayer."

However industrious and worthy her tenants were, Hill insisted, they did not represent the "artisan class"—the "labour aristocracy," as it is now called. On this point she was very explicit. The model build-ings, she said, catered to the class of artisans who could afford the higher rents charged for the new flats. But the people displaced by these projects, and all the others crowded into the already overcrowded parts of town, could not afford these rents, and it was for them that her houses were intended. In renovating her houses, she was careful to do so in such a way as not to remove the occupants, or if they had to be removed, to relocate them in her other houses. Most of her tenants, she said, were "unskilled labourers" belonging to the "lower class," a class "far below that of mechanics." Some of them were costermongers and hawkers who were "almost the poorest class," the only class below them being the vagrants who had no settled habitation and spent the night in one or another common lodging house.[37] Distinguishing her tenants from the class of "mechanics" or artisans, she once characterized them as "the very poor."[38] If this term is now misleading, it is because it was later used by Charles Booth to describe the lowest classes of the poor, classes A and B. In fact, her tenants, the "industrious, thrifty, working people," corresponded to Booth's classes C and D, the "poor," who were neither "very poor" (like A and B) nor "comfortable" (like E and F).[39]

Most historians have confirmed Hill's description of her tenants as distinguished from those in the model buildings.[40] David Owen, in his study of English philanthropy, agrees that Hill did not confine her efforts to the "respectable" class of tenants but consciously chose to accommodate, as she said, "as low a class as have a settled abode."[41] Another describes her as deliberately operating at the "chaotic end of the housing market."[42] Gareth Stedman Jones, on the other hand, suspecting all philanthropists of looking at the working class "through the distorting lens of middle-class aspirations to gentility," finds Hill to be no better than the others. Like them, she had no concern for the truly poor, the "casual poor" of "outcast London"; indeed she pursued her philanthropic activities "at the expense of, rather than on behalf of, the casual poor." Her housing "scheme" worked (if it worked at all) only for that "hand-picked stratum" that could be molded in accord with her middle-class ideals. In passing, Jones admits that Hill put "pressure" on the Peabody Trust to change its policy against single-room tenements, a policy designed to keep out the casual poor.[43] He neglects to say, however, that many of Hill's own houses were single-room flats, precisely in order to cater to that poorer class, and that she persisted in this practice in spite of much criticism on the part of other reformers.

A more serious charge brought against Hill, by some contemporaries as well as historians, was that her efforts were ineffectual because they could not possibly reach the large class for which they were intended. In the 1880s she was managing some £70,000 worth of property (including a parcel of buildings entrusted to her by the Ecclesiastical Commission). By the end of her career her houses accommodated three to four thousand people by one account, well over six thousand by another.[44] In either case, it was a small number compared with the model building trusts, let alone with the considerable body of poor in need of better housing. By any quantitative measure her impact on housing was marginal. By other standards, however, her influence was considerable, for her principles about the proper conduct of the rent collectors were adopted not only by those who worked in the model buildings but by an entire generation of social workers and administrators.

In 1884 the Royal Commission asked one witness whether Hill's methods could solve London's slum problem. He replied, "I never thought of it with reference to very wide action. It requires very great personal attention. It is not everyone who is a Miss Octavia Hill."[45] Hill herself had anticipated this objection long before. "This is very well," she had fancied an interlocutor saying, "as far as you and your small knot of tenants are concerned, but how does it help us to deal with the vast masses of poor in our great towns?" Her answer may not have satisfied her critics; the fact that her reply took the form of a series of questions suggests that it may not have entirely satisfied her. But it does illuminate the state of mind of the patient reformer who does what good she can, hoping that others will do their part, and suspecting that any other remedy might be more productive of evil than good.

> Are not the great masses made up of many small knots? Are not the great towns divisible into small districts? Are there not people who would gladly come forward to undertake the systematic supervision of some house or houses, if they could get authority from the owner? And why should there not be some way of registering such supervision, so that, bit by bit, as more volunteers should come forward, the whole metropolis might be mapped out, all the blocks fitting in like little bits of mosaic to form one connected whole?[46]

CHAPTER 15

The Salvation Army and
the Barnardo Homes

IF THERE WAS a distinctive "time-spirit" in Victorian England, there was also a determined resistance to that spirit, a deliberate resolve to practice an older kind of philanthropy that derived from religion rather than science—not the modern, sophisticated Positivist religion but an old-fashioned, fundamentalist religion. The Salvation Army was the most successful example of this counter-spirit, defying the "scientific" precepts of the COS by engaging in precisely the kind of "indiscriminate" charity that that organization so bitterly condemned.

The Salvation Army was an offshoot of the Christian Mission, earlier known as the East London Revival Society, founded by William Booth (no relation to Charles Booth). A minister in the Methodist New Connexion sect in Cornwall, Booth moved to London in 1865, bringing with him some of the missionary habits of that sect. In the crowded slums of London, "open-air" services were conducted on street corners, and revivalist meetings in theaters, tents, and other unchurchly locations. In 1878 the Mission solemnly convened a "War Congress" and issued a declaration of war: "The Christian Mission has met in Congress to make War. It has glorified God for the conquests of 1877–8. It has organised a salvation army to carry the blood of Christ and the fire of the Holy Ghost into every corner of the world."[1] The military rhetoric was deliberate. The "salvation army" was to be a "church militant" in the almost literal sense of that term. The "army" was presided over by a "general" (Booth was addressed as "General Booth" or "the General"), local societies were "corps," shelters were "forts" or "barracks," members were "soldiers," and missionaries were "officers." The soldiers and officers wore uniforms, paraded to the tune of martial music, and were subject to a military-like discipline. Their banner was emblazoned with the official motto, "Blood and Fire."

This anomalous institution—anomalous by comparison both with the secular, rationalist reform movements of the time and with the "progressive" religious movements that were only somewhat less secular and rationalist—grew at an impressive rate. Starting in 1878 with 5,000 members, 127 officers, and 81 corps, by 1906 it boasted over 100,000 members, 2,868 officers, and 1,431 corps in the United Kingdom, and about as many more abroad. The number of people it ministered to in that period is almost incalculable; one estimate has four million people in England alone.[2] William Booth's *In Darkest England* (actually written, on the basis of Booth's notes, by W. T. Stead, the editor of the *Pall Mall Gazette*) was published in 1890, and soon rivaled in circulation and fame Henry George's *Progress and Poverty*. It sold 115,000 copies in the first year of publication and another 100,000 the following year; within months of its appearance £100,000 was raised to support the program proposed in the book.

While others were promoting the idea of science in the service of humanity, the Salvation Army was devoting itself to religion in the service of humanity. Its religion was nondoctrinal and nonritualistic, requiring nothing more than faith in the atoning power of Christ. The testimonial of faith, the "closing with Christ," was expressed in public prayer and confession. And the spiritual conversion was confirmed by a moral reformation. Because moral reform was regarded as the necessary condition of salvation, the Army assiduously attacked the citadels of corruption and depravity: public houses, music halls, dance halls, theaters, boxing rings, seaside resorts. In place of these dens of iniquity, it offered its followers a variety of edifying activities: revivalist meetings, gospel singing, band music, processions, and rallies. More important, it provided those without families or other social ties membership in a community where they were accepted and respected—and where they had the additional satisfaction of participating in the salvation of others.

EVEN THE SALVATION ARMY, however, was not immune to the time-spirit. If it did not share the zeal for science, it did share the zeal for humanitarianism. In its early years the Army adhered to the classic pattern of Christian revivalism, but by the mid-1880s it began to assume a different character. As immorality was an impediment to salvation, so, it now discovered, was poverty. The ultimate end, Booth explained, was the saving of the soul, but to save the soul, one had first to save the body. There was no point in giving a tract to a sinking man; he had to be put on firm ground and given the means of life. He might then be saved, for he will know "that it was you who pulled him out of the horrible pit and the miry clay in which he was sinking to perdition."[3]

The Army even invoked the fashionable language of socialism; in 1888 its official journal, *The War Cry,* featured an article entitled "Socialism of Salvation."[4] By this time the Army was committed to a social gospel as fundamental—and fundamentalist—as its spiritual and moral gospel. Instead of advocating legislative reform, economic change, or "scientific" philanthropy, it engaged in "good works" in the oldest sense of that term. It operated night shelters for the homeless, a home for "fallen women," a prison-gate "brigade" to assist discharged convicts, a corps of nurses to care for the sick and the very young, and a food depot to distribute food (free or at wholesale prices) to the needy (and, during the dock strike, to the strikers).

With the publication of *In Darkest England* in 1890, this social agenda was enormously expanded. Stead once described the book as "a bigger and a better *Bitter Cry*"[5]—bigger and better because it had all the passion of the early tract plus an elaborate program, complete with a budget and an appeal for funds. It called for the establishment by the Army of three kinds of "colonies"—city colonies, farm colonies, and overseas colonies— each to be a "self-helping and self-sustaining" community and each serving as a transition to the next. An unemployed man might enter a city colony where he would receive food and shelter in return for work until he was able to return to private employment; if he could not or would not find employment, he would be transferred to a farm colony, where he would have a second opportunity for rehabilitation; and if that failed, he would be helped to emigrate to an overseas colony. In addition to the colony scheme, the book proposed a variety of other programs: Labour Bureaus for job-seekers, Rescue Homes for Lost Women, Retreats for Inebriates, Homes for Discharged Prisoners, Enquiry Offices for the Discovery of Lost Friends and Relatives, Advice Bureaus (a kind of "poor man's Tribune"), Matrimonial Bureaus, Household Suffrage Brigades (a "civil force" to patrol the town and collect old clothes, toys, and other "waste commodities"), Poor Man's Banks, Poor Man's Lawyers, a Salvation Ship for emigrants, and a Whitechapel-by-the-Sea for slum dwellers.[6]

It was a formidable agenda, realized only in small part. But even that part was not insignificant. In the next decades the Army succeeded in establishing city colonies in London and other towns, a farm colony in Essex, overseas settlements (three in America, one for farm workers, another for the unemployed, and a third for drunkards), several work-shops, labor bureaus, and food depots. It also operated an extensive emigration program, assisting tens of thousands of emigrants to leave England and helping settle them in new jobs in their new countries. The bulk of its work, however, remained what it had always been: providing the occasional meal and lodging to the homeless, the unemployed, the destitute, and the transient; exhorting them to lead more temperate, moral lives; and welcoming them into the ranks of the Army, where they might spread the good word and perform good works.

BOOTH HAD NO TROUBLE integrating the good word with good works, the gospel of salvation with the gospel of sustenance. But others found an uneasy tension between the two. In this respect *In Darkest England* may have misrepresented Booth's views. Perhaps because it was written by Stead, it read more like a social tract than a religious one. At one point the religious mission was given priority: "I must assert in the most unqualified way that it is primarily and mainly for the sake of saving the soul that I seek the salvation of the body." But this statement was overshadowed by the main thesis of the book, which was that the soul could not be saved without saving the body and that both soul and body required for their salvation a new "moral life."[7] Most of the references to God were casual and commonplace: a passing remark about the "co-working power of God" or the "will" of God that had called Booth to his vocation—but even then it was not so much the voice of God that had moved him as the "agonising cries of suffering men and women and children."[8]

Contemporaries were of two minds about the relation between the religious and the social mission of the Salvation Army. One of Booth's most bitter critics, T. H. Huxley, quoting his statement that he was "primarily and mainly" interested in saving the soul, accused him of using social work as a mask for his proselytizing mission. "Men are to be made sober and industrious, mainly, that, as washed, shorn, and docile sheep, they may be driven into the narrow theological fold which Mr. Booth patronises."[9] Others had the opposite objection, complaining that the Army was essentially a "philanthropic and humanitarian agency in which religion is entirely subservient to social organization."[10]

After a visit to the Army's farm colony, Beatrice Webb drew a portrait of it that was sympathetic although not uncritical. She was much impressed by the dedication of the men and women engaged in social work—a "*Samurai* caste," she called them (alluding to the elite class in H. G. Wells's *A Modern Utopia*).[11] But she was taken aback by a religious atmosphere that seemed to her intrusive and oppressive: religious services throughout the week (some compulsory, others voluntary) and insistent appeals for conversion. She was not unmoved by the faith and rituals— "all this wonderful revivalist business"—and she was full of admiration for the Salvationists, "real living saints, who feel intensely all they are saying and acting." She demurred only at the religious pressure exerted upon men in a weakened condition by those in a position of authority.[12]

Other critics objected to the authoritarian and militaristic character of the Salvation Army. Booth boasted that his was the only religious institution founded in his time based on the principle of "voluntary subjection to an absolute authority," and that a telegram from him could send an officer to the "uttermost parts of the earth."[13] In a letter to the *Times,* Huxley quoted this remark, appalled at the proud assertion of "absolute authority" and at the manifestation of it in the hierarchical structure and militaristic trappings of the Salvation Army.[14] Yet there was a sense in which the Army was remarkably democratic, not only in its social mission but in its recruitment policies and organizational spirit.

UNLIKE THOSE who worked for other philanthropic institutions—the visitors for the COS, the rent collectors for the model dwellings, or the residents of Toynbee Hall—almost all of whom were middle-class, the soldiers and officers of the Salvation Army were largely working-class.* Those who had been succored and saved, the theory went, were best equipped to give material and spiritual sustenance to others. "Set a rogue to catch a rogue," Booth quoted, hastening to add that it was of course a "reformed rogue" who would do the catching.[15]

The "rogue" was not only a sinner; he—or, as often as not, she—was the poorest and least "deserving" of the poor. This was a very different

---

* This is not, of course, true of the most famous fictional Salvationist—Major Barbara in George Bernard Shaw's play, who is the daughter of Andrew Undershaft, a millionaire munitions manufacturer, and of Lady Britomart, daughter of the Earl of Stevenage. But she is also, according to Shaw, totally democratic in temper and demeanor, at ease with the poorest of the poor and the roughest of the "roughs."

In the real Salvation Army, the first "gentleman" to join was Judge Frederick Tucker, who gave up a position in the Indian Civil Service in 1881 to head the Salvation Army in India. He later scandalized some of his colleagues when, shortly after the death of his wife, he announced his engagement to the General's daughter.

class from that catered to by the COS, the model dwellings, or the settlement houses. "We are moral scavengers," Booth announced, "netting the very sewers."[16] The chapter titles of *In Darkest England* are a catalogue of that netherworld: the "Homeless," the "Out-of-Works," the "Vicious," the "Criminals," the "Children of the Lost," those on the "Verge of the Abyss." Reviewers were fond of citing the "Cab Horse" metaphor: the cab horse stumbling and falling in the street from overwork or underfeeding had first to be helped to his feet and then provided with his three basic needs—shelter, food, and work to earn his keep. The cab horse, Booth explained, was "poor broken-down humanity," and the program of the Salvation Army was nothing more than a "Cab Horse's Charter."[17]

The Salvation Army harked back not only to an older religious tradition and an older mode of philanthropy but also to an older image of poverty and class of the poor—the Mayhewian poor. Mayhew had equated the street-folk of London with the most barbarous tribes in the most backward countries: the Bushmen and Sonquas among the Hottentots, the Fingoes among the Kafirs, the Bedouin among the Arabs. Like them, the street-folk were immoral, irreligious, disinclined to regular work; they worked intermittently at odd and bestial trades, lived in rookeries that were dens of crime and vice, spoke a distinctive dialect and argot. But even as he drew this unsavory picture of them as a "race" apart, Mayhew invited his readers' sympathy and compassion. The effect was thoroughly paradoxical, for the more indignant he was at the society that tolerated such vice and degradation, the more vicious and degraded he made his subjects appear.[18]

Wittingly or not, Booth took exactly the same tactic. If he did not refer to Mayhew, it was because he had a more recent model at hand— Henry Stanley's *In Darkest Africa,* which suggested the title and the theme of Booth's book. Was the lot of a Negress in the Equatorial Forest, Booth asked, worse than that of a "pretty orphan girl in our Christian capital"? Or were the slave-traders raiding a village, capturing or killing the men and violating the women, more brutal than the "beasts of prey" who brought a "ghastly devastation" upon the streets of London? In England as in Africa, the victims of that devastation conspired in their own degradation. "Just as in Darkest Africa it is only a part of the evil and misery that comes from the superior race who invade the forest to enslave and massacre its miserable inhabitants, so with us, much of the misery of those whose lot we are considering arises from their own habits." Like African streams crisscrossing the forests, so gin-shops stood at every corner in the slums, pouring out the "Water of Death." And drunkenness produced all the other evils. "A population sodden with drink, steeped in vice, eaten up by every social and physical malady, these are the denizens of Darkest England amidst whom my life has been spent, and to whose rescue I would now summon all that is best in the manhood and womanhood of our land." The other philanthropists, Booth said, were engaged in rescuing those who least needed rescuing: "the thrifty, the industrious, the sober, the thoughtful." The Salvation Army alone offered salvation to "the improvident, the lazy, the vicious, and the criminal."[19]*

To redeem these lost souls, the Salvation Army had to convert the least deserving into the most deserving—deserving of the most strenuous efforts at redemption. As one of the converts in Shaw's play put it: "The better you are, the worse they likes to think you were before they rescued you."[21] In fact most of those who were actually drawn into the ranks of the Army came not from the "abyss" but from all levels of the working classes; the strongest and most reliable "corps" were not in Whitechapel but in the more stable working-class areas of London.[22] But if the reach of the Army was not quite as wide and deep as it would have liked, its message was clear: no one was beyond salvation.

By portraying his clients in the worst light, Booth, like Mayhew, may have hoped to attract attention to their plight. For the same reason (again, like Mayhew), he tended to exaggerate their numbers. As it happened, statistics on this subject had just been released. General Booth could hardly have failed to know of the other Booth, Charles Booth, whose widely reviewed and highly acclaimed first volume of *Life and Labour of*

---

* Jack London's *The People of the Abyss,* published in 1903, portrayed the poor in exactly the same light. Before he went down into the "underworld" of London, in the summer of 1902, London visited the American consul general so that someone would "identify" and "keep track" of him, as if he were truly embarking on a trip to the wilds of Africa. When his taxi driver asked him where in the East End he wanted to be driven, he replied "anywhere," on the assumption that the entire area was inhabited by a barbarous and dangerous "race." Momentarily discomfited to find that some poor families actually had "slaveys" (and annoyed that he could not rent a house for himself with a bathtub), he went on to depict the "people of the abyss" who lived in a state of utter misery and degradation, were totally "immoral and materialistic" and given to the most primitive "hedonism," whose sole interest was "booze," and whose occasional happiness was the "dull, animal happiness" that came from a "full belly."[20] This was a socialist describing not a "lumpenproletariat" in Marx's sense (a degraded class that was the enemy of the proletariat and the lackey of the bourgeoisie), but the proletariat itself, reduced to a state of utter "immiseration," which could be redeemed only by a total revolution—the socialist equivalent of Booth's "salvation."

the People in London appeared the year before *In Darkest England*. Nor
could he have failed to cite Charles Booth's statistics. But he used them
so selectively and extrapolated from them so freely that he did exactly
what Charles Booth had cautioned against: he sensationalized the problem by confounding the various classes of the poor and declaiming about
the "starving millions."[23] The starving millions—three million, by the
General's count—were what he called "the submerged tenth." These
were the people whose poverty was only one, and not the worst, of their
misfortunes. More than half of the men were in a constant state of drunkenness, an untold number of the women were at least occasional prostitutes, and some of the children used language so obscene that it could
"hardly be outdone even in Sodom and Gomorrah."[24]

IT IS NO WONDER that most social reformers at the time took a dim
view of the Salvation Army. Even if they had not been committed to a
"scientific" approach to poverty and opposed to "indiscriminate" charity,
they would have been wary of expending so much effort and money upon
a class that seemed to be least worthy of their concern and least likely to
profit by it. The COS was especially hostile. It conceded the first principle laid down by Booth: "Change the man when it is his character and
conduct which constitute the reasons for his failure."[25] But it found the
rest of his scheme hopelessly misguided; the food depots, for example,
aggravated the problem, for they encouraged workers to rely upon charity instead of their own labor, and employers to reduce wages since their
workers were receiving cheap food and shelter.[26] Huxley said that the
Salvationists threatened to become "a more dangerous nuisance than the
mendicant friars of the middle ages."[27]

Radicals were divided. While some labor leaders welcomed the money
and food dispensed by the Salvation Army, especially at the time of the
dock strike, the committed socialists (like H. M. Hyndman and William
Morris) protested that this kind of charity was nothing but "Workhouse
Socialism," designed to feed the workers at less expense to the
capitalists.[28] Engels, oddly enough, was well disposed to the Salvation
Army, in part because it helped keep alive the right of public speeches
and demonstrations, which socialists could use to their own advantage,
but also because he regarded it as subversive and potentially revolutionary. The British bourgeoisie, he said, did not understand that they were
supporting an institution which "revives the propaganda of early Christianity, appeals to the poor as the elect, fights capitalism in a religious

way, and thus fosters an element of early Christian class antagonism."[29]

George Bernard Shaw was more cynical, believing that the bourgeoisie knew exactly what they were doing in supporting the Salvation Army. In *Major Barbara,* Adolphus Cusins, Barbara's naïve fiancé, argues the point with Andrew Undershaft, her munitions-manufacturer father.

CUSINS: "I don't think you quite know what the Army does for the poor."

UNDERSHAFT: "Oh yes I do. It draws their teeth; this is enough for me as a man of business."

CUSINS: "Nonsense! It makes them sober—"

UNDERSHAFT: "I prefer sober workmen. The profits are larger."

CUSINS: "—honest—"

UNDERSHAFT: "Honest workmen are the most economical."

CUSINS: "—attached to their homes—"

UNDERSHAFT: "So much the better: they will put up with anything sooner than change their shop."

CUSINS: "—happy—"

UNDERSHAFT: "An invaluable safeguard against revolution."

CUSINS: "—unselfish—"

UNDERSHAFT: "Indifferent to their own interests, which suits me exactly."

CUSINS: "—with their thoughts on heavenly things—"

UNDERSHAFT: "And not on Trade Unionism nor Socialism. Excellent."[30]

More embarrassing to the Salvation Army than the opposition either of reformers or of socialists was the antagonism of many of the people it was trying to help. The Army was no sooner established than it found itself confronted, in one town after another, by hostile mobs—"Skeleton Armies," they were sometimes called.[31] These mobs, sometimes several hundred strong, were made up of laborers, semiskilled workers, shop assistants, and local "roughs." They were motivated in part by the kind of religious animus often displayed against Methodists, Catholics, and Jews, and in part by a resentment of the "foreigners" descending among them, preaching, moralizing, and proselytizing. In many cases the Skeletons were encouraged, even recruited, by publicans whose business was threatened by the temperance preachers, and by local authorities who resented the intrusion of the Army, passed laws against it, and tacitly or overtly sanctioned the demonstrations and riots. After a series of episodes in the winter of 1880–81, John Morley, then editor of the *Pall Mall*

Gazette, publicly protested against the behavior of the London police, and the *Daily Telegraph* complained when the police of Stoke Newington looked on benignly as some five hundred "roughs" knocked down and abused a group of Salvationists.[32]

In the first dozen years of the existence of the Salvation Army, it has been calculated, there were demonstrations and riots against it in at least sixty towns, including a fair number in London. They were not always violent; the intention was more often to intimidate, humiliate, and drive away the Salvationists than to do them physical harm. In some cases the Skeleton Army, as the name suggests, parodied the Salvation Army, with elaborate costumes, processions, music, and mock prayer sessions. That these were not the spontaneous activities of local hooligans is evident from the sophisticated nature of some of these parodies and from the frequent cooperation and collusion of groups in neighboring towns and villages.

Toward the end of the 1880s, when the Skeleton riots began to subside, another grievance arose among some of the working classes. The House of Lords Committee on Sweating reported the rumor that the Salvation Army was becoming a "sweating" employer, making matchboxes at a cheaper cost than the prevailing one. This was vigorously denied by the Army. But the charge was revived, with more substance, a few years later when the Army established a workshop for the manufacture of matchboxes, and again after the turn of the century when one of its carpentry shops was accused of hiring "unemployables" and paying them less than the going rate.[33]

THE RELATIONSHIP between the Salvation Army and the working classes has raised once more the much debated issue of "social control" and "socialization," this time in the intriguing form of two essays by the same historian arguing both sides of the case. In his first essay Victor Bailey represented the Army as engaged in a form of "moral imperialism" and "religious colonisation." Its attack on public houses and music halls demonstrated its contempt for "working-class mores and behaviour patterns," "popular leisure habits and life-styles." And its campaign to reform the poor was yet another attempt to impose upon them a "self help" ethic. The Skeleton riots were the workers' response to this "self-righteous cult of respectability" and assault on their "indigenous" mores.[34] If the local authorities supported the rioters, rather than, as one might expect, the Salvation Army in its attempt to control the workers, they did so in the interests of local businessmen and brewers as well as in their own interests. The Army, by presuming to deal directly with the poor, went over the heads of the local authorities, thus challenging their "social and legal influence" and depreciating the law itself. In supporting the rioters and regulating their "disorder," the authorities were thus exercising their own form of "social control."[35]

In his second essay Bailey has abandoned this thesis, emphasizing not the antagonism between the Salvation Army and the working classes but their essential compatibility. There were, he now finds, so many "ideological and social affinities" between the Army and the labor movement in the 1880s and 1890s that in effect they "ploughed parallel furrows toward the same end of the field."[36] Some of his examples of parallelism are so general as to be almost meaningless: their common interest in social reform, the welfare of the poor, temperance, and the improvement of character. In these respects most reformers and philanthropists, including the COS, would find themselves bedfellows. And his parallels between the Salvationists and the socialists are even less compelling: the fact that both took to the street for rallies and demonstrations, were engaged in proselytizing and converting, and were subject to attack by other workers.

Yet the basic point of this second essay, and evidently the cause for Bailey's change of heart, is itself interesting. This is the argument that the Salvation Army, like the labor and socialist movements, was a "moralizing" agency appealing to working-class "self-respect and self-discipline" and drawing its strength from "an emerging sense of self- and class-awareness."[37] This, in turn, has prompted a reevaluation of the social control thesis. That thesis is now seen as demeaning to the workers, in the presumption that they could be so readily dominated by the middle class and so easily alienated from their own indigenous culture and consciousness. In making the Salvation Army not an enemy but an ally of the working class, Bailey concedes that the moral "values" promoted by the Army—temperance, respectability, self-help—were those of the working class itself. Workers joined the Army because their own movements were in an "early stage of development" and because their "proletarian aspiration" could be expressed through the religious structure of the Army. Women workers found the Army especially attractive because it offered them a degree of equality and sense of accomplishment that they did not enjoy in the labor movement and, indeed, that few middle-class women enjoyed at the time. As for those socialists who opposed the Army, they were motivated by their own selfish interests. "The socialist bodies," Bailey wryly observes, "doubtless recognized that a sturdy competitor was setting up shop in the same street to sell some of the same wares."[38]

This revisionist interpretation of the Salvation Army, while a salutary corrective to the distortions of the social control thesis, has problems of its own. If it is erroneous to see the Army as an inveterate enemy of the working class, it is equally erroneous to see it as a staunch ally. In fact, its constituency, as its founder repeatedly insisted, was not the organized or politically sophisticated workers but the poor and very poor. And its mission was not to restore class consciousness to the working classes but to restore humanity to the "residuum," the "submerged tenth" mired in misery and vice. So far from being a competitor of labor or socialist movements—"setting up shop in the same street to sell some of the same wares"—the Army was engaged in quite a different enterprise, operating a different kind of shop, on a different street, selling entirely different wares.

THERE WERE OTHER shops on the same street as the Salvation Army—humanitarian enterprises of an old-fashioned kind. In 1884 Baroness Burdett-Coutts and Lord Shaftesbury, both prominent members of an earlier generation of philanthropists, established the London Society for Prevention of Cruelty to Children. (For Shaftesbury, who died the following year, this was the last public act in a long life of good works.) Three years later the London Methodist Mission was founded, a less publicized and less dramatic version of the Salvation Army, which within two decades had set up almost five hundred missions, or community houses, to serve as centers for preaching and social work.

Shaftesbury and his friends helped promote another philanthropic institution that attracted much public attention, not all of it favorable— Dr. Barnardo's Homes for Children. This was not the only facility for children; the National Children's Home had been established by the Methodists, and the Children's Society (the "Waifs and Strays," as it was called) by the Anglicans. But Barnardo's was the most ambitious, the most highly publicized, and the most enduring of these organizations.

One of the many charges brought against Barnardo was that he misrepresented his personal history, making his ancestry seem more illustrious, his family more affluent, and his religious background more conventional than they were. Thomas Barnardo was born in Dublin in 1845; his father, a once-successful investor and fur trader, was a Lutheran probably of Jewish descent, his mother a Catholic who passed herself off as a Quaker (concealing her real maiden name, O'Brien, and adopting the more Protestant-sounding name of her grandmother).[39] At the age of seventeen Thomas was converted to the Plymouth Brethren, and a few years later he came to London (in 1866, a year after William Booth arrived from Cornwall). Intending to become a medical missionary in China, he enrolled as a student at London Hospital. He also took up evangelist preaching in the East End, taught in a "ragged school," and became associated with the East End Juvenile Mission, all of which occupied him far more than the study of medicine. In 1870, after the mission had repeatedly delayed sending him to China, he gave up that plan, abandoned his studies, and made the daring and much publicized move of purchasing "Edinburgh Palace," a large and well-known "gin palace," which he converted into a mission house and community center.

In 1871 "Dr." Barnardo, as he called himself, opened the first of his homes for destitute and homeless boys in the East End. Five years later he founded a "village" for homeless girls in Ilford; by 1888 the village contained twenty cottages. His mission operated a variety of other establishments and services: a residence-cum-workhouse for older boys, work brigades for younger boys, "ragged schools" for poor children, a "Babies' Castle" and boarding-out system for illegitimate infants, an emigration service for boys going to Canada and Australia, a "rescue" mission to save young girls from prostitution, a medical mission for adults—all this in addition to the religious and social activities centered in the Palace itself. One of its most successful enterprises was a photography studio, which proved to be not only an effective fund-raising technique but an important means of publicizing (sensationalizing, some said) the condition of the homeless children.[40]

Almost from the beginning Barnardo was plagued by highly publicized controversies about his private and public life. He was accused of lying about his family, having an affair with his landlady, using the facilities and funds of the mission for his private benefit, failing to issue financial reports, doctoring the photographs of the children, staging rescue operations, mismanaging the homes, and even mistreating the children. One of these accusations, the affair with the landlady, was apparently false and malicious; others, involving financial irregularities and photographic distortions, were better founded, although perhaps not as serious as they were made out to be; another, the use of the title "Dr.," was more damaging, not only because the practice itself was illegal but because his attempts to cover it up resulted in one patent forgery (a letter ostensibly awarding him the degree from Giessen University) and a request written by himself for a medical degree in absentia.

The COS, which opposed Barnardo's enterprise for the same reason that it opposed the Salvation Army, took every opportunity to publicize the charges against him. Rather than expose himself to an investigation by the COS, Barnardo took the case to an arbitration court. In the fall of 1877, after several months of hearings and the testimony of over a hundred witnesses (Barnardo himself did not testify), the court absolved Barnardo of the most serious charges regarding the mistreatment of the children, mildly rebuked him for his use of "Dr." (by this time he had acquired a degree from the University of Edinburgh, which was not, however, recognized by the Royal College of Physicians), and cautioned him against deceptive photographs.

Chastened but not repressed, Barnardo went on devising new activities and expanding his operations. He continued to be dogged by controversy and disagreeable publicity, some of his own making. He quarreled not only with the COS but with philanthropies with which he had been associated and might have made common cause; in 1890 he publicly attacked the Society for the Prevention of Cruelty to Children on the grounds that it had come under the influence of Rome. His virulent anti-Catholic prejudice resulted in three lawsuits brought by Catholic parents who had committed their children to his homes and had asked for their return. Instead of honoring their requests, Barnardo arranged to have two of the children sent abroad and the third hidden in one of the homes. When the judgments went against him, he unsuccessfully appealed, in two instances to the House of Lords. It did not help his case, or his personal reputation, when he testified that one of the children had come to him half starved, covered with vermin, and clothed in rags, only to have his own admission record and photograph produced in evidence, showing a clean, well-dressed, and alert child. Because of these costly trials and the unfavorable effect on fund-raising, the organization began to experience serious financial difficulties in the early 1890s. By the time of Barnardo's death in 1905, it showed liabilities of £120,000. The contrast with his personal finances was unfortunate; he left an estate of £10,000, very little of which had been acquired by inheritance.

IN SOME RESPECTS Barnardo stands in sharp contrast to the other philanthropists of the time—to the traditional humanitarians as well as the "scientific" reformers. General Booth could be criticized for his authoritarian behavior and military posture but not for financial irregularities or personal dishonesty. Dr. Barnardo's offenses were more disreputable and self-serving.* His organization was also more vulnerable than Booth's, for it was so conspicuously ill managed and overexpanded as to invite criticism even by those who would otherwise have been well disposed to it.

The homes themselves were not above rebuke. The COS objected that they aggravated the problem of homelessness by encouraging parents to abdicate responsibility for their children; Barnardo claimed that the parents had already abdicated that responsibility, that his children came from homes where they had been physically abused, forced to beg, steal, or prostitute themselves, or that they had been roaming the streets, half starved, scrounging and pilfering to survive. There is no doubt that there were many such children for whom the Barnardo Homes provided refuge and a means of survival, even an opportunity for a good life. But he was not, contrary to his claims, the first to recognize the problem or to try to remedy it. London alone had some fifty orphanages, in addition to the facilities provided by the Waifs and Strays societies and the homes and schools operated by the Catholics. All three of the children involved in his lawsuits had been destined for Catholic institutions, and it was to save them from that fate that Barnardo "abducted" them.

The lawsuits also revealed serious abuses in some of the Barnardo Homes. The most graphic part of the earlier case involved charges of ill treatment of the children by the staff, some of which were dismissed but others were not. The court rebuked Barnardo for punishing children by putting them in solitary confinement for long periods in a small cell in the coal cellar. (Later reports show that this mode of punishment continued to be used.) A humanitarian might also be disturbed by the regimen in the "labour house" for older boys, where, Barnardo boasted, the rule was "plenty of hard work." Awakened at half past five, the boys worked from six in the morning to half past six at night, with half-hour intervals for breakfast, prayers, dinner, and military drill; a half hour of recreation was followed by supper at seven, classes until nine-fifteen, prayers, and bed at ten.[41]

Barnardo's emigration service was less open to criticism, although, again, he was not the first to undertake that function. The Salvation Army was engaged in similar efforts, and both had to concede priority to Annie Macpherson and Maria Rye, who in 1869 had established an

---

* Barnardo was one of the many prominent figures suspected of being Jack the Ripper in 1888, perhaps because of his medical background as much as his character. It was at this time that he was accused of abducting the three children.

agency to accompany groups of boys and girls to Canada. (Macpherson had also anticipated Barnardo in establishing a boys' home in Hackney and a "home of industry" in Spitalfields.) But the operation run by Macpherson and Rye was much smaller, and the Salvation Army dealt primarily with adults and families. By the turn of the century Barnardo's organization was responsible for the emigration of over 8,000 boys to Canada alone; it has been estimated that one in 300 of the Canadian male population at that time came from a Barnardo Home.[42]

It is remarkable that the Barnardo mission survived and even flourished in his own time, in spite of lawsuits and scandals, and for the most part by means of a considerable number of small contributions. Even more remarkable is the fact that it continues to prosper today. The Barnardo Homes are said to be the largest voluntary child-care organization in England—this in spite of the growth of the welfare state and the assumption by the state of responsibility for the care of abused and abandoned children. Like the Salvation Army and other charitable institutions which have endured since Victorian times (and some from long before), as well as the many which have sprung up since, the Barnardo Homes are a testimonial to a philanthropic impulse that survives in defiance of all predictions, and to social needs that are not adequately satisfied by the state. While the self-conscious and self-designated bearers of the "time-spirit" were redefining the "social problem," making it a problem of poverty rather than destitution and proposing "scientific" solutions to that problem, "Dr." Barnardo, like "General" Booth, addressed himself to an older problem and an older solution.

CHAPTER 16

Toynbee Hall

TOWARD THE END of his last lecture in 1883, Arnold Toynbee delivered a passionate *mea culpa*.

> We—the middle classes, I mean, not merely the very rich—we have neglected you; instead of justice we have offered you charity, and instead of sympathy, we have offered you hard and unreal advice; but I think we are changing. If you would only believe it and trust us, I think that many of us would spend our lives in your service. You have—I say it clearly and advisedly—you have to forgive us, for we have wronged you; we have sinned against you grievously—not knowing always; but still we have sinned, and let us confess it; but if you will forgive us—nay, whether you will forgive us or not—we will serve you, we will devote our lives to your service, and we cannot do more.[1]

This was not the culmination of the lecture, although it is sometimes quoted as such.[2] For Toynbee went on to demand a quid pro quo from the working classes.

> We will ask you to remember this—that we work for you in the hope and trust that if you get material civilisation, if you get a better life, you will really lead a better life. If, that is, you get material civilisation, remember that it is not an end in itself. Remember that man, like trees and plants, has his roots in the earth; but like the trees and plants, he must grow upwards towards the heavens. If you will only keep to the love of your fellow men and to great ideals, then we shall find our happiness in helping you, but if you do not, then our reparation will be in vain.[3]

This proved to be Toynbee's final testament. He left the hall in a state of "nervous collapse," lingered in that condition for almost two months, and died on March 8, 1883. Before his death Mrs. Toynbee informed Lord Milner, who was preparing the lectures for publication, that her husband said he would not have included this "sentimental passage" (as she called it) had he not been in so enfeebled a state.[4] It may be that this reflected Mrs. Toynbee's view of it rather than her husband's; she was notably less sentimental than he. In any event, the passage makes a fitting epigraph for the institution named in his honor, Toynbee Hall.

Toynbee did not originate or even endorse the idea of a settlement house; nor did he inspire it by his example. Although he often visited his friends the Barnetts in Whitechapel, he actually lived in the East End only briefly in 1875; as a student at Oxford, he spent a fortnight's vacation doing volunteer work for the Charity Organisation Society. The real inspiration for Toynbee Hall came from Samuel Barnett, the vicar of St. Jude's, who had long been encouraging the philanthropically minded young men from the universities to visit and work in his parish and who devised the plan of a residential hall to accommodate them on a more permanent basis. (What was novel about the proposal was not the idea that those ministering to the poor should live among them but the establishment of a communal residence for this purpose.) It was also his idea to name it in honor of Toynbee, who had recently died and was much revered by his colleagues and students. He prevailed over the objections of Mrs. Toynbee and others, who pointed out that Toynbee himself had no part in it and would have preferred a lecture series in his name.[5]

Toynbee Hall was nevertheless a fitting memorial to Toynbee, for it epitomized the idea of "citizenship" that he (like his mentor T. H. Green) valued so highly, a citizenship that was as much a moral as a political condition.[6] There is a nice coincidence in the founding of Toynbee Hall in 1884 and the passage of the Reform Act enfranchising most of the working classes. For the Hall was meant to bridge the gap between the "two nations" by making better citizens of both—by giving the rich the opportunity to fulfill their civic responsibilities and the poor the opportunity to realize their civic potentialities. Today the settlement house evokes the image of a charitable institution. Toynbee Hall, like the other establishments modeled upon it (by the end of the century there were thirty such houses, over half of them in London), more closely resembled a civic and educational institution. It did not dispense relief, as the poor law did, or supervise private charity, as the COS did, or house families and give them domestic counsel, as Octavia Hill's organization did, or dispense alms and moral exhortation, as the Salvation Army did. What it did do was to provide a place where workers in the area and the residents of the house could come together for meetings, discussions, classes, lectures, concerts, exhibits, outings, and whatever else might be edifying and serviceable.

SAMUEL BARNETT was a central figure in the London world of philanthropy. He came from a prosperous family of merchants in Bristol, studied at Oxford, taught for two years at Winchester, and seemed destined for a conventional career in the church when a trip to America "knocked all the Toryism out of me," as he later reported.[7] Returning to England, he sought a parish in London where he could minister to the social as well as the religious needs of his congregation. It was not a very impoverished parish, but it did bring him the acquaintance of Octavia Hill, who pressed him into service as an adviser on charitable cases and introduced him to one of her most dedicated rent collectors, his future wife, Henrietta Rowland. After his marriage in 1873, he became vicar of St Jude's in Whitechapel, a neighborhood distinguished not only by its extreme poverty but by its large immigrant (especially Jewish) population and by its notorious criminal element; it was there that Jack the Ripper later plied his trade. And it was there, next to the parish church, that Toynbee Hall was established in 1884.

Although Barnett was very much a clergyman (he remained vicar of St. Jude's while also serving as warden of Toynbee Hall and became a canon in 1895), Toynbee Hall was not only nondenominational but secular, having nothing of the character of a religious mission. There was no ambiguity (as there was in the case of the Salvation Army) about the relation between the religious function and the social; its purpose was entirely social. But it was not social in the Salvation Army mode. If the residents were not missionaries bringing the faith to the heathen, neither were they almoners bringing them money, food, or clothes. They were rather "settlers" who came to live among the poor—"to learn," Barnett said, "as much as to teach, to receive as much as to give."[8]

From the beginning, Toynbee Hall was known as a "University Settlement." The "settlers," or residents, were university men mainly from Oxford, partly because of Barnett's connections with that university and partly because of the influence of Green and Toynbee. (The largest contingent was from Balliol, home of Green and Toynbee.)[9] And the building itself (except for its red brick façade) was deliberately created in the image of a university, with the familiar quadrangle structure, "ecclesiastical" doors, and mullioned windows. It had suites and bed-sitters for the residents much like those in an Oxford college, a class-room that could accommodate three hundred, a "conversation" room, a drawing room, and a large dining-room-cum-library decorated with the crests of Oxford and Cambridge colleges.*

In this collegial setting—"civilised" but without "undue luxury or display," the architect described it[10]—fifteen to twenty residents lived for periods ranging from a minimum of three months to several years; the average was one and a half to two years. They paid for their room and board and for the privilege of serving the community. And it was regarded as a privilege—not everyone could purchase a residency. Applicants had to be approved by a committee of residents and reconfirmed for tenure, so to speak, after a three-month probationary period. The house rules were more reminiscent of a boarding school than a university: meals at fixed hours, "lights out" at a prescribed time, and specifically assigned duties. Some residents did social work in the East End while others pursued their careers elsewhere in the city, as teachers, civil servants, or lawyers. But all of them spent all their spare time, in the evenings and weekends, in communal activities.

THE UNIVERSITY MOTIF was also borne out in the ambitious educational program of Toynbee Hall. In retrospect this may appear as the dominant and most successful aspect of its work. It was not, to be sure, the first institution to offer "university extension" courses; thirty years earlier the Christian Socialist Frederick Maurice had established a Working Men's College in London, and in 1877 Barnett, Leonard Montefiore, and others started a series of university extension classes in Whitechapel. But Toynbee Hall was the most comprehensive of these and the most university-like, providing courses that were not vocational but humanistic in the traditional sense. The schedule for a typical month included courses on the sciences (geology, physiology, botany, chemistry), classical languages (Hebrew, Greek, Latin), European history, English

---

* The two settlements founded soon afterward were named Balliol House and Wadham House—Wadham being Barnett's college. And the settlement house in Mrs. Humphry Ward's novel *Robert Elsmere,* dedicated to Green, was called University Hall. (The settlement house Mrs. Ward actually helped found, in 1897, was the Passmore Edwards Settlement.)

history, French literature (Diderot, Molière, and *Hamlet* in French translation), Italian literature (Dante), German literature (Goethe), and, of course, English literature—Shakespeare (*Hamlet* and *The Taming of the Shrew*), other Elizabethan dramatists (Dekker and Lyly), *The Pilgrim's Progress,* Scott, and Browning.[11]

No less impressive were the classes, lectures, and discussion groups intended for younger people and adults which were not part of the university extension program. Some of the subjects were elementary and utilitarian, others more broadly educational and cultural. Again, a typical month's calendar included evening classes on arithmetic, writing, drawing, citizenship, chemistry, nursing, and music (one class was on "18th Century Music—works by Handel, Bach, Scarlatti, etc."); afternoon classes for girls on dressmaking, writing and composition, geography, bookkeeping, needlework, hygiene, reading and recitation, French, singing, cooking, and swimming; and evening sessions on the principles of law and current social questions.

It is extraordinary that all of this should have been taking place in the poorest section of the East End, but not surprising that most of the students, especially in the university extension program, were what one teacher called the "best sort" of workers—"steady, thrifty, interested in the improvement of their order"—or that the Latin and Greek students were mainly of the lower middle class (one was a foreman at the docks).[12] Nor is it surprising that there should have been a large contingent of Jewish students in a neighborhood heavily populated by Jews; within twenty years, one-quarter of the university extension students were Jewish. The "Popular Lectures" on Saturday evening attracted a larger audience from a wider range of the working classes. They also drew upon an impressive body of speakers. Among the "popular" lecturers were Charles Booth, who used Toynbee Hall as a source of information for his *Life and Labour of the People in London;* Leslie Stephen, the prolific writer and editor of the *Dictionary of National Biography* (now more famous as the father of Virginia Woolf); Arthur Sidgwick, the Greek scholar; his brother Henry Sidgwick, the philosopher; Mrs. Humphry Ward, the novelist; A. V. Dicey, the jurist; the Liberal Party leaders Herbert Asquith and Richard Haldane; the socialist Tom Mann; and, before notoriety overcame him, Oscar Wilde.

This educational agenda was so formidable it may distract attention from all the other activities sponsored by Toynbee Hall: cultural clubs (a Shakespeare Society and an Elizabethan Society), social clubs (a Smoker's club where political passions were supposed to be tempered by tobacco), youth clubs, sports clubs, a travellers' club that arranged trips abroad (mainly for local schoolteachers), flower shops, concerts, a library open to the public (and utilized by over 13,000 people each year), and art exhibits.* (The latter were so successful that when the paintings and photographs outgrew Toynbee Hall, a special building was erected called the Whitechapel Art Palace.) Barnett's favorite philanthropy, which antedated Toynbee Hall, was the Children's Country Holiday Fund; in 1888 more than 17,000 children from the East End were sent to the country for a holiday. The Hall also served as a civic center, a meeting place for trade unions and strike committees, county council and school board officials, social workers and investigators, tenant representatives and other local groups. The residents were especially active on behalf of the striking match girls and dockers in 1888 and 1889.

TO A LATER GENERATION it may seem that Toynbee Hall served the interests of the residents better than those of the community, thus perverting its essential purpose. Yet from the beginning the residential function was given at least as much weight as the communal function; indeed the two were seen as integrally related. It was Barnett's intention that the young men living among the poor would become better acquainted with them, move more easily among them, understand and sympathize with them, and serve them in whatever way they could—but not that they would live the life of the poor or lose themselves in the service of the poor. They were not to be latter-day St. Francises. On the contrary, they were to show the poor the possibility of a more elevated, more gracious, more fulfilling life, a life that the poor could not hope to emulate but that could, by its example, enrich and enlarge them.

Barnett described the residents, not ironically, as "clubmen," but membership in that "club" carried more obligations than privileges. "Toynbee Hall," he once wrote, "seems to its visitors to be a centre of education, a mission, a centre of social effort. It may be so; but the visitors miss the truth that the place is a club-house in Whitechapel, occupied by

---

*Before the establishment of Toynbee Hall, Barnett held annual painting exhibits at his church. On one of these occasions, a month before the formal opening of the Hall, Matthew Arnold presided at the unveiling of a mosaic at St. Jude's. In his address (printed in the *Times* under the heading "Mr. Matthew Arnold in Whitechapel"), he referred to those "idolatrous" classes who knew only how to "possess and enjoy," and to the young men from those classes who, dissatisfied with that idolatrous life, came to the East End and were among the "true saviours of society."[13]

men who do citizens' duty in the neighborhood."[14] When William Beveridge was subwarden of Toynbee Hall in 1904, he delivered a paper entitled "The Influence of University Settlements," which was devoted entirely to their influence upon the residents. The paper, he confessed, was a "foolish leg-pull," but "not wholly without point." While Toynbee Hall was a center of educational and social activities, "these were a consequence rather than the essence of the settlement." The essence lay in the "individual lives of the residents, as they are affected by the special experience of living in that particular place."[15]*

Other residents testified to the same experience, the sense that Toynbee Hall had a dramatic and enduring effect upon their personal lives long after they left the house. But that personal effect had public consequences. It was no mere exercise, as we would now say, in "consciousness-raising." For that consciousness was focused not on the self but on others. And not on others in the abstract—on the poor as the subject of legislation and administration or as members of a class or institution—but as individuals. "One by one," Barnett wrote, "is the phrase which best expresses our method, and the 'raising of the buried life' is that which best expresses our end."[17] Many of the former residents went on to assume legislative and administrative positions that took them far from that method and that end. But they did so with a difference, conscious not only of their social mission but also of the limitations of political and institutional reforms in fulfilling that mission.

George Lansbury, the socialist and, for a time, leader of the Labour Party, took a dim view of Toynbee Hall and the settlement movement in general, claiming that he had never seen any evidence of their influence on the "life and labour of the people." Their only achievement was "the filling up of the bureaucracy of government and administration with men and women who went to East London full of enthusiasm and zeal for the welfare of the masses, and discovered the advancement of their own interests and the interests of the poor were best served by leaving East London to stew in its own juice while they became members of Parliament, cabinet ministers, civil servants."[18] This is an odd criticism from

---

* The founders of Hull House (the American version of Toynbee Hall) had the same priorities. Jane Addams was unapologetic about her reasons for establishing the settlement: her first was to give purpose and meaning to her own life; her second was the desire to help the poor. Her friend and colleague Ellen Starr said of her: "Jane's idea, which she puts very much to the front and on no account will give up, is that [the settlement] is more for the people who do it than for the other class."[16]

one who was himself not only a Member of Parliament but a socialist as well, who might have been expected to welcome the civil servants and bureaucrats essential to the administration of a socialist economy. It is also odd coming from a leader of the Labour Party, which had in its ranks former residents of Toynbee Hall, including the future Prime Minister who was to usher in the welfare state. Clement Attlee was a resident and secretary of Toynbee Hall in 1910, resident again in 1919, and president (an honorary position) in 1945. As Prime Minister and the head of a socialist party, he paid tribute to an institution that was neither political nor socialistic.

> Alongside everything done by the local authority and by the state there are people who want to do a bit more. . . . I believe that we shall always have alongside the great range of public services, the voluntary services which humanise our national life and bring it down from the general to the particular. . . . The idea of our democracy does not mean that we sit down and have things done for us, but that we do things for ourselves. Toynbee [Hall] in its time has been a great nurse of democracy.[19]

"A GREAT NURSE of democracy"—this is a far cry from the recent account by a distinguished historian who represents Toynbee Hall as being governed by three main principles: "community, authority, and hierarchy." Standish Meacham grants Barnett's desire to establish a community of residents and workers, but finds that community flawed by his "authoritarian" habits, his commitment to a "hierarchy of values," and his assumption that only an "elite" could convey those values to the working class. "An instinctive fear lay behind the inability of Barnett and his co-workers to abandon authority and hierarchy in their search for community: fear of a town-bred proletariat; fear of the antagonisms of class-consciousness."[20]

"Fear," perhaps—although there is little evidence of the kind of fear that supposedly motivated men to make concessions or reforms they would not otherwise have made. "Distress" might be more appropriate— distress at the prospect of an urban proletariat deprived of the moral, cultural, and aesthetic experiences that Barnett (like most reformers of the time, including socialists of all stripes) believed to be the necessary, although not sufficient, conditions for a good life. It is true that Toynbee Hall represented an attempt to transmit a "hierarchy of values" by means of an "elite" of university men, although contemporaries would have put it less pejoratively, as an attempt to make available to the poor some of the privileges that had long been reserved for the rich. "One of the finest things," Beatrice Webb wrote to Sidney, "S. Barnett has ever said is that he would give the poor luxuries and not necessaries—a good program for your 'collective philanthropy.' "[21]

Toynbee Hall was, as Attlee insisted, a profoundly democratic enterprise. For it assumed that the poor who lived in the worst slums were capable of appreciating and imbibing that "hierarchy of values" and had the desire and capacity for a higher education—not a utilitarian or vocational one but precisely a university kind of education. It was also democratic in assuming that the university men who already enjoyed those values and that education had an obligation to impart them to those less privileged than themselves, and to do so personally, "one by one," not merely by lecturing to them but living among them, talking with them, and trying to create a bond of citizenship with them.

If the mission of the Charity Organisation Society was to organize and professionalize philanthropy, that of Toynbee Hall was to humanize and "civilize" it.* The "community" it established was not meant to be communal in any egalitarian sense. It implied no denial or even denigration of the distinctions of wealth, occupation, class, or talent. It was meant rather to be a civic community, based upon a common denominator of citizenship in the largest sense of that word, a citizenship that made tolerable all those other social distinctions which were natural and inevitable, but which should not be exacerbated and should not be permitted to obscure the common humanity of individuals. The settlement house was not an experiment in socialism; it was an experiment in democracy—which was no mean feat at that time and place.

As Evangelicalism was a formative influence for an earlier generation of reformers, so Idealism was for a later generation. Toynbee Hall was, in effect, the existential realization of Green's philosophy.[23] It was the place where the educators and the uneducated alike were to be educated to cultivate their "best self" and to pursue the "common good." This is what Beveridge meant when he described Toynbee Hall as "a school of humanity in Whitechapel for those who have done *Literae Humaniores* in Oxford."[24]

---

* It was probably the American COS Ellen Starr had in mind when she wrote of Hull House: "There is to be no 'organization' and no 'institution' about it."[22]

Book Four

SOCIAL PHILOSOPHY
AND SOCIAL REFORM

CHAPTER 17

"Positive" Liberalism

The Bitter Cry appeared in 1883. The same year saw the posthumous publication of the works of T. H. Green. *Prolegomena to Ethics* and *Lectures on the Principles of Political Obligation* were hardly the "household words" of the season. They did not come trippingly off the tongues of preachers, politicians, or pamphleteers; they did not inspire Royal Commissions or parliamentary acts. But they did provide the groundwork for an intellectual revolution that had profound effects on social thought and policy for almost half a century.

Green's influence was felt well before the publication of his work. He had died the year before at the age of forty-six, having spent the whole of his adult life at Balliol College, as student, tutor, fellow, and finally Professor of Moral Philosophy. Although his collected works comprise only four volumes (the bulk of it consisting of posthumously published lectures), he had established himself during his brief lifetime as mentor to scores of students and colleagues and as an inspiration to hundreds of others who attended his "lay sermons."[1] His philosophy spoke to politicians of both parties as well as to philosophers and writers. The roster of public figures acknowledging his influence included two Prime Ministers (Herbert Asquith, Henry Campbell-Bannerman) and Members of Parliament (Richard Haldane, Arthur Acland), prominent civil servants (Robert Morant, William Beveridge), and a host of government officials, administrators, philanthropists, reformers, and social workers.

Philosophical Idealism, the label given to Green's philosophy, did not, of course, originate with Green. But its peculiarly English form did. (Technically, F. H. Bradley could claim priority over Green, his *Ethical Studies* having been published seven years before Green's *Prolegomena*. When Bradley's sister proposed to make that claim after his death, Bradley's brother objected on the ground that it was Green who had influenced Bradley.)[2] Earlier attempts to import Kantianism and, even more, Hegelianism had met with little success. Coleridge, who is credited with bringing German philosophy to England, quoted Kant and Schelling although not Hegel. But even Kant was terra incognita for most cultivated Englishmen. Presented with a translation of Kant, Macaulay said that he could not understand a word of it "any more than if it had been written in Sanscrit."[3] If Green succeeded in making German philosophy intelligible as well as respectable, it was because in Anglicizing it he also liberalized it. And in that more palatable form, he placed it at the heart of the most compelling social concerns of his generation.*

Conceived in the academy, disseminated in the academy, bearing the stamp of approval of the academy, Philosophical Idealism was anything but "academic" in its implications and effects. Its critics accused it (some still accuse it) of being excessively abstract. But its abstractions were rooted in "praxis," as a Marxist would say, in the concrete, practical realities of private and public life. Green's metaphysics provided the rationale for his ethics; it was a secular metaphysics in aid of a social ethics—a secularized Evangelicalism, as it were. It is perhaps no accident that the three dominant figures among the Philosophical Idealists— Green, F. H. Bradley, and Bernard Bosanquet—were all sons of Evangelical clergymen; and, to one degree or another, they all transmuted that religious tradition. Bradley, whose father was the most orthodox of the three, was the most hostile to organized religion. Green, on the other hand, as Mrs. Humphry Ward once explained to Gladstone, did not believe in the miracles of Christianity but clung to "all the forms and associations of the old belief with a wonderful affection."[5] In her best-selling novel *Robert Elsmere,* published several years after Green's death and dedicated to his memory, Mrs. Ward praised him (in the guise of the fictional don Mr. Grey) for "that dissociation of the moral judgment from a special series of religious formulae which is the crucial, the epoch-making fact of our day."[6] But if Green discarded the burden (as Mrs. Ward saw it) of religious dogma, he retained, in both his metaphysics and his ethics, the spirit of religiosity. He spoke for many of his contemporaries when he said, "God has died and been buried, and risen again, and realised himself in all the particularities of a moral life."[7]

---

* In his autobiography, Haldane recalled a meeting with the Army Council when he became Secretary of War. Asked what kind of army he had in mind, he replied, "A Hegelian Army," which promptly terminated the conversation.[4]

* * *

BEATRICE WEBB prided herself on capturing the "time-spirit" of her age—the social consciousness and social conscience of a generation dedicated to the service of mankind, the "Religion of Humanity." But it could be argued that Green more effectively embodied that spirit. Her time-spirit was avowedly, irredeemably dualistic: it was ethical (or "religious," as she called it) in respect to the end or purpose of social action and rational (or "scientific") in respect to the means of action. She herself admitted that many of those who were committed to the end were not equally committed to the means. And no one knew better than she how unsatisfactory that dualism was, how painful the conflict between the religious "Ego that affirms" and the scientific "Ego that denies."[8]

Philosophical Idealism transcended that dualism. It was "idealistic" in respect to means as well as ends. It posited an Idea immanent in the universe which informed all aspects of reality. And it made people the repository of the Idea, their "ideals" being the means of realizing that immanent and evolving Idea. There was no discord between ends and means because both were purposive and moral. People were idealistic in the common sense of that word: they cherished the ideal of a "best self" which was something other than self-interest and which directed them to ends and purposes in harmony with the common good. That ideal inspired them even if, in its full measure, it evaded them. But they could realistically aspire to it, and be inspired by it, because it was congruent with reality. Their "idealism" was sanctioned by the metaphysics of "Idealism," by the Idea that permeated objective reality as well as their subjective beliefs and behavior.

For the Idealist, there was no debilitating conflict between an "Ego that denies" and an "Ego that affirms," between a scientific method devoid of moral purpose and a social end devoid of rational authority. There was no dichotomy between "facts and values," because facts, as much as values, were the product of the consciousness that knew and experienced them, that saw them in relation to other facts and values. People pursued their ends in the same spirit that they conceived them. And they could realize those ends—the "Religion of Humanity" in Webb's terms, the "common good" in Green's—because they were capable of behaving morally.

If Philosophical Idealism was idealistic in the comprehensive sense of that word, it was also philosophical in a comprehensive sense. It evoked the grand philosophical traditions of both the Ancients and the Moderns, at the same time that it appealed to the philosophical yearnings of ordinary people seeking the meaning and justification of their ordinary, mundane lives. Again, the comparison with Beatrice Webb is instructive. For her, the bearers of the time-spirit, the actors in history, were "men of intellect and men of property"; it was they who were caught up in the conflict between ends and means, between morality and science. The ordinary person—the "average sensual man," as she put it—was a creature of interests and appetites.[9] He had no bifurcated consciousness because he had no consciousness of anything beyond his immediate experiences and material wants; he had no better self to rebuke his worse self.

Green's philosophy, by contrast, was democratic and egalitarian. It applied to all people equally, as it applied to all modes of experience. The "average" man was no more or less "sensual" than the superior man. Consciousness, spirituality, morality defined human nature as such and suffused all aspects of human life—not totally and immediately, to be sure, but partially and progressively. Everyone, not just the reformer or intellectual, had the consciousness of a rational, moral being with the capacity for virtue as well as vice, for purposive behavior in a meaningful universe. And the universe itself was not hostile to the better self but congenial to it. If individuals failed of their purposes, if they succumbed to vice rather than virtue, it was their doing, their failure of will.

AS THERE WAS no duality of ends and means, no radical distinction between values and facts, so there was no conflict between morality and freedom. Real freedom, "positive freedom," was the freedom to will the best. Green himself did not use the term "negative freedom" to describe John Stuart Mill's idea of freedom. But it was clearly Mill's negative sense of "liberty" that Green contrasted to his own idea of freedom.

> We do not mean merely freedom from restraint or compulsion. We do not mean merely freedom to do as we like irrespectively of what it is that we like. We do not mean a freedom that can be enjoyed by one man or one set of men at the cost of a loss of freedom to others. When we speak of freedom as something to be so highly prized, we mean a positive power or capacity of doing or enjoying something worth doing or enjoying, and that, too, something that we do or enjoy in common with others. We mean by it a power which each man exercises through the help or security given him by his fellow-men, and

which he in turn helps to secure for them. When we measure the progress of a society by its growth in freedom, we measure it by the increasing development and exercise on the whole of those powers of contributing to social good with which we believe the members of the society to be endowed; in short, by the greater power on the part of the citizens as a body to make the most and best of themselves.[10]

There is no doubt, as Green's critics have argued, that "positive freedom" is semantically confusing.[11] And it has been made more confusing by the Marxist who interprets positive freedom as the freedom from want, in contrast to the negative freedom from restraint. This usage disparages such freedoms as speech, press, and religion as "negative," "formal," without real substance or value, thus inviting new and more insidious varieties of tyranny. And it lends itself to precisely the materialistic philosophy that Green (and Mill as well) deplored, by assuming that material and economic goods have a greater reality and a higher priority than other goods—intellectual, spiritual, and moral.

Green was well aware of these perils. "If it were ever reasonable to wish that the usage of words had been other than it has been (any more than that the processes of nature were other than they are), one might be inclined to wish that the term 'freedom' had been confined to the juristic sense of the power to 'do what one wills': for the extension of its meaning seems to have caused much controversy and confusion."[12] The extension of that meaning, however, was itself the product of an evolving consciousness and of continuing reflection upon the idea of freedom. A captive enjoying his newfound liberty or a child delighting in the power of his limbs could be satisfied for a time with the freedom that was simply the absence of restraint. But the "grown man" in civil society desired more by way of freedom than the ability to "will anything and everything," to "do as he likes so long as he does not prevent another from doing so." He saw no value in a conception of freedom that regarded getting drunk as an act of free will like any other act. And he appreciated the kind of freedom that incorporated within it the idea of self-improvement and self-fulfillment.

The freedom enjoyed by a citizen in a civilized society was similar to that experienced by a man who was "inwardly 'master of himself.' "[13] By the same token, the freedom of each person was related to the freedom of all. "We rightly refuse to recognise the highest development on the part of an exceptional individual or exceptional class, as an advance towards the true freedom of man, if it is founded on a refusal of the same opportunity to other men." Freedom was social as well as individual because its moral, positive purpose was at the same time the promotion of the "best self" and the pursuit of the "common good."[14]

It was at this point that Green parted company from Matthew Arnold. Arnold also made much of the best self and also related it to the state. But Arnold's best self was intellectual and aesthetic; it aspired to know and appreciate "the best which has been thought and said in the world."[15] Green's best self was moral and social; it aspired to be and do the best—the best for the individual and for society. There was no disjunction between the individual good and the common good, because the individual was an integral part of society and morality was inherently other-directed. The individual pursued the common good as he pursued his best self, often unwittingly and unconsciously. "He apprehends it only in some of its bearings; but it is as a common good that he apprehends it, i.e., not as a good for himself or for this man or that more than another, but for all members equally in virtue of their relation to each other and their common nature."[16]

THE COMMON GOOD was embodied in the idea of "citizenship," and citizenship was embodied in the idea of the "state." Ordinary citizens might have a limited conception of the common good or their relationship to the state. They might, in fact, have "no reverence for the 'state' under that name." But they intuitively appreciated the rights they shared with their neighbors and the claims they legitimately made upon each other. This elementary sense of a common good maintained by law was what differentiated citizens from the "dangerous classes." It was also what differentiated society from the state and gave the state its special importance. The state was "the society of societies, the society in which all their claims upon each other are mutually adjusted."[17]

Only in the state were citizens equal. In society ("civil society," in Hegel's terms) people were necessarily unequal: they were richer or poorer, more or less learned, belonging to different classes, with different talents and interests, occupations and lives. In the state (the democratic state, at any rate) they were essentially equal: they were members of one nation, equally protected and bound by the law. This political equality, the equality that derived from a common citizenship, was the only meaningful kind of equality, for it overrode all the natural differences and inequalities abounding in the social realm.

The Philosophical Idealists, it has been said, were "political democrats because they were first of all spiritual democrats"[18]—"spiritual" in the Idealist sense of "moral." The reform of the suffrage, Green insisted, was an end in itself because it was a moral end. "We said, and we were much derided for saying so, that citizenship only makes the moral man; that citizenship only gives that self-respect, which is the true basis of respect for others, and without which there is no lasting social order or real morality."[19] The fatal flaw of the Roman Empire was the lack of a real sense of citizenship. It created a body of "loyal subjects" rather than "intelligent patriots," subjects who enjoyed the rights given them by their government but did so passively, taking them for granted and becoming conscious of them when they had cause for resentment. Only when citizens participated, directly or indirectly, in the work of the state could they identify themselves with the state as a whole, rather than with that part of it which represented their immediate interests and rights.[20]

In Green's "citizen" one hears echoes of the ancient dictum "Man is a political animal." The classical formula testifies to the rationality and morality of man, his capacity to live not only in society (animals do that as well) but in the *polis,* which is a rational ordering of society for the achievement of the good life. If the modern state was unable to reproduce the quality or conditions of the *polis,* it could credit its citizens with something of the same rational capacity and moral will. Green's citizens found their best selves in subsuming their personal interests in the common good, and they recognized, if only instinctively, that their own moral development was dependent upon the ability of "the citizens as a body to make the most and best of themselves."[21]

It was his idea of citizenship, as much as his idea of freedom, that signified Green's radical break with modern liberalism, the liberalism that reached its apogee in Mill's *On Liberty.*[22] Mill too required that all members of the state be citizens, in the sense that they all have the vote. But citizenship was not at the heart of his philosophy because the state was not central to it. The primary reality for Mill was the individual, who was a citizen fortuitously, as it were, only to the extent that the state had the function of protecting its members from harm by others and providing those needs they could not provide for themselves, in return for which they assumed certain minimal obligations to the state. Such individuals, Green said, necessarily had an "inveterate irreverence" toward the state.[23] A less delicate way of putting it would be to say that they were in an adversarial relationship with the state, eternally vigilant against the encroachments of the state and determined to preserve their own individuality at all cost—even at the cost of their better selves, if that better self derived not from their own will but from the authority of the state.

Green's citizens, by contrast, had an essential and moral, not an instrumental or utilitarian, relationship to the state. Their individuality was enhanced rather than diminished by their membership in the state. The state not only protected but elevated them, giving them a special moral status by making them a part (and an equal part) of a larger moral enterprise, the common good. And the state itself acquired a moral character by virtue of the citizens who respected its moral as well as legal authority, and who freely, not coercively, accepted the moral and political obligations inherent in the idea of citizenship.

If the citizen had moral obligations to the state, the state had moral obligations to its citizens. Throwing down the gauntlet to Mill, Green entitled one of the chapters of his *Principles of Political Obligation* "The Right of the State to Promote Morality."[24] The state had the duty as well as the right to promote morality, but it had to do so in such a way as to strengthen the "moral disposition" of the individual rather than subject him to a new form of "moral tutelage."[25]* It had, therefore, to proceed with prudence, for while it could legitimately pass a law to encourage the moral disposition of its citizens, it had to be careful not to be too far in advance of the "social sentiment" necessary to sustain such a law.[27] The delusion of conventional liberalism was to think it an infringement of liberty for the state to promote morality; but it was as much a delusion to think that morality could be promoted by paternalistic means.

> The true ground of objection to "paternal government" is not that it violates the "laissez faire" principle and conceives that its office is to make people good, to promote morality, but that it rests on a misconception of morality. The real function of government being to maintain conditions of life in which morality shall be possible, and morality consisting in the disinterested performance of self-imposed duties, "paternal government" does its best to make it impossible by narrowing the room for the self-imposition of duties and for the play of disinterested motives.[28]

This was the great advantage of the modern state over earlier forms of organization: it was large and varied enough to provide the opportunity

---

* This expression recalls Kant's famous definition of enlightenment as "man's release from his self-incurred tutelage."[26] It also reminds us that if Green's theory of the state sometimes echoed Hegel's, his theory of morality was far more reminiscent of Kant. Even on the subject of the state Green was in many respects more Kantian than Hegelian. He abhorred war, was suspicious of nationalism, opposed imperialism, and was very much a "little Englander."

for moral choice and thus the development of moral character. In the clan individuals were so circumscribed, their relations to others so predetermined, that the restraint they experienced never took the form of self-restraint. In the state, however, individuals were presented with moral alternatives which enabled them to exercise that "free obedience" which was the mark of a "free morality," a morality they freely submitted to because they believed it to be the "true good."[29]

To the conventional liberal any attempt to "moralize" both the individual and the state—and of each in relation to the other—smacks of conservatism or worse, a kind of moral and social despotism. Yet Green himself was associated with the Radical wing of the Liberal Party, which sought social and economic as well as political reforms. In controverting the individualism of classical liberalism, he also subverted the individualistic, laissez-faire principles of classical political economy. And in legitimizing (or relegitimizing) the state, he gave warrant for the greater intervention of the state in social and economic affairs. If the state had the right to promote the moral welfare of its citizens, it had, a fortiori, the right to promote their social and economic welfare.

In the debate between "individualism" and "collectivism" (as it was characterized at the time), Idealism threw the weight of philosophy behind collectivism.[30] It did so not by arguing the case for collectivism as such, but rather by fostering a "moral disposition" that lent itself to collectivist theories and policies. The idea of the individual as citizen, the idea of the better self that can be realized only in community with others, the idea of the state as the vehicle for the common good, the idea of ethical standards transcending utilitarian or economic ones—these became powerful weapons in the arsenal of the collectivists.

In fact, Green himself was not a "collectivist" in the common meaning of that term. His theory of the proper role and limits of the state was developed in a lecture delivered in 1881 and printed as a pamphlet. "Liberal Legislation and Freedom of Contract" may well be regarded as the manifesto of what can be called "Positive Liberalism." Historically, Green explained, liberalism had gone through three stages: the first focusing upon Parliament and municipal government, the second upon freedom of trade, and the third upon social reforms. The first two periods had the effect of liberating the individual; the third, the present period, of constraining him. There were social reforms in the earlier periods as well, but these (the early factory acts, for example) were deliberately limited to children and women and to specific industries. Recent acts were more sweeping in scope and more restrictive in nature. Instead of enforcing the freedom of contract that had been the capstone of individual liberty, they suspended it.

What was now being limited was liberty in the conventional sense, the freedom to "do as we like irrespective of what it is that we like." What was being affirmed was positive freedom, the freedom to do that which was "worth doing or enjoying," and, moreover, worth doing and enjoying "in common with others." The test of progress was the degree to which the state helped its citizens "make the most and best of themselves."[31] By this test, the freedom of contract was only a means to an end, and as such could be properly limited. Just as slavery, even if voluntarily entered into, was a void contract, so contracts involving labor and housing could be deemed invalid if they were injurious to health. So too parents were not free to deny their children an education, because that would deprive them of the opportunity for the best development of their faculties. In such cases the state had the right to interfere with the freedom of contract, although it might choose not to do so if that would jeopardize other social goods; thus "over-centralization" might be a legitimate objection to a law, while "over-legislation" was not. It was preferable, to be sure, to have public health and education provided by the voluntary action of individuals rather than the compulsion of law. "But we must take men as we find them." And this meant that the state might be obliged to do that which individuals did not do of their own accord.[32]

ONE OF THE THINGS individuals might not do of their own accord was to refrain from excessive drinking. For Green this issue dramatized the crucial principle of positive freedom.* The problem was urgent, he believed, and the remedies obvious: more stringent rules of licensing and the exercise by localities of the right to prohibit the sale of liquor entirely. Such laws were justified on the same grounds as factory or education acts: "the recognised right on the part of society to prevent men from doing as

---

* It does not detract from Green's commitment to this principle to point out that he had good personal reasons to be aware of this problem, and not only to write about it but to be active in several temperance societies. His elder brother was a habitual drunkard, and Green made repeated and unsuccessful attempts to reform him. Returning to Oxford after one such futile attempt, he wrote, "As I have failed in the object that lay nearest me, I must be the more zealous about such general good as is to be done here."[33]

they like, if, in the exercise of their peculiar tastes in doing as they like, they create a social nuisance." And the concept of "social nuisance" meant more than physical harm to others, because the effects of drink were such that no limits could be placed on the idea of harm.[34] To the objection that liquor laws would undermine the self-reliance of those whose welfare was at stake, Green replied that as in the case of factory and education acts, legislation would reinforce the better nature of man. Although some people found it possible to rise above the temptation to which they were exposed, all too many succumbed to it. In any event, it was not the duty of the state to subject its citizens to temptation.

> It is a poor sophistry to tell us that it is moral cowardice to seek to remove by law a temptation which every one ought to be able to resist for himself. It is not the part of a considerate self-reliance to remain in presence of a temptation merely for the sake of being tempted. When all temptations are removed which law can remove, there will still be room enough, nay, much more room, for the play of our moral energies.[35]

The issue of liquor laws may seem trivial today, but at the time it was anything but that. Green was hardly alone in thinking that drunkenness was a vice in itself as well as a serious obstacle to freedom.[36] The subject is also important because it highlights the contrast between Green's idea of freedom and Mill's idea of liberty.

In *On Liberty*, Mill addressed the same problem to quite different effect. Taxes on alcohol, he argued, were legitimate only as revenue-raising measures, not as efforts to discourage drinking; and licensing laws only for the purpose of ensuring peace, not for limiting the number of drink-shops or making them less accessible. To try to prevent drunkenness by such means would be an intolerable infringement on liberty. Even to punish drunkenness was severely circumscribed by this principle. Drunkenness might be a legitimate cause for moral disapprobation, but not for social sanctions, still less for legal sanctions, unless the drunkenness resulted in "definite," "perceptible" harm to others. Thus a person convicted of an act of violence while drunk could be placed under some special restriction—but only after the event and after the legal conviction. Or a drunkard violating a "distinct and assignable obligation" to another (the failure to pay his debts or support his family) could be reproved and even punished—but only for the breach of obligation, not for the drunkenness as such. Or a soldier or policeman could be punished for being drunk on duty—but not an ordinary drunkard simply for being drunk. In any case, harm to others did not include the morally harmful effect of drunkenness, for it was only "definite damage, or a definite risk of damage" that warranted sanctions, not a merely "contingent" or "constructive" injury to others. And it was only a harm to others, not harm to the drunkard, "the agent himself."[37] All of this followed from the "one very simple principle" at the heart of *On Liberty:* "That the only purpose for which power can be rightfully exercised over any member of a civilized community, against his will, is to prevent harm to others. His own good, either physical or moral, is not a sufficient warrant."[38]

It was this principle, as much as this particular application of it, that Green challenged when he urged the passage of laws designed not for the punishment of drunkenness but for its prevention—and in the interests not only of others but of "the agent himself," his "best self." "It is the business of the law," he said, "to make virtue easy, and to make vice difficult."[39]

ANOTHER DRAMATIC BREAK with conventional liberalism (although not with Mill) was implicit in Green's attack on the land laws, for this threatened not only the freedom of the individual but the freedom of property. His lecture "Liberal Legislation" was delivered at the height of the controversy over the land question in Ireland and was published soon after the passage of the Irish Land Act of 1881 authorizing the famous "three F's": fixed rents, fixity of tenure, and the free sale of land. According to the jurist A. V. Dicey, the effect of that act was to make the rights of landlords and tenants "dependent upon status, not upon contract."[40] Green proposed a reform of the English land laws that would have the same effect, by curtailing the right of landlords to dispose of their land as they saw fit. The existing laws of entail, he argued, were socially harmful because they prevented the heir from selling his land or distributing it among his children, thus keeping large quantities of land in the possession of men too saddled by debt to improve it and preventing the formation of a class of small proprietors that would be the "mainstay of social order and contentment."[41]

This infringement upon the right of property, Green claimed, was justified by the same principle that established that right. Individuals had a right to property only by virtue of the guarantee given them by society; and society had the duty to protect the common interest by promoting the "free exercise of the social capabilities of all."[42] This principle was especially pertinent in the case of landed property because land was not a commodity like any other. It was the basis of all wealth and of our very existence, the ground upon which everyone lives and moves. Entrusted with the protection of the public interest, the state had a special obligation in respect to land. The individual could not exercise the same freedom over his land as over other goods because of "the simple and recognised principle that no man's land is his own for purposes incompatible with the public convenience."[43]

It is interesting that Green chose to make his case on this principle rather than another that was obviously available to him and that he mentioned in passing: the principle of freedom itself, the freedom of one generation not to be restrained by settlements imposed by an earlier generation. This argument would have appealed to all liberals, including laissez-faireists. Instead Green deliberately challenged one of the most sacred tenets of liberalism, the right of private property in land.

Yet in all these cases—factory and education acts, liquor and land laws—where Green justified a limitation on freedom, he did not do so by invoking any principle of social or economic equality. Nor did he display any animus against private property as such. On the contrary, he defended private property on the highest grounds, not simply as the product of labor or the means for the provision of future wants, but as an ethical principle in itself and the expression of an ethical consciousness. Property, he said, represented a "spiritual principle," the "rational will" of the individual. It was "the individual's effort to give reality to a conception of his own good . . . his consciousness of a possible self-satisfaction as an object to be attained . . . the constant apparatus through which he gives reality to his ideas and wishes."[44]

The obverse of property was poverty. While society provided the conditions for the appropriation of property, it did not provide everyone with the means of exploiting those conditions. "A man who possesses nothing but his powers of labour and who has to sell these to a capitalist for bare daily maintenance, might as well, in respect of the ethical purposes which the possession of property should serve, be denied rights of property altogether."[45] This did not mean, however, that poverty, or any considerable inequality, belied the moral rationale of property and therefore justified the abolition of the freedom of trade and inheritance that made for inequality and poverty. On the contrary, except in the case of land, Green argued, the freedom of trade and inheritance was grounded in the same principle as private property. And inequality was entirely consistent with the moral purposes of property, because it was the inevitable result of the conquest of nature by free individuals and the means by which those individuals fulfilled their natural and varied functions. If these functions were not left to individual efforts, society would have to provide for them; and this would entail "a complete regulation of life incompatible with that highest object of human attainment, a free morality."[46]

Free trade, moreover, so far from promoting and perpetuating poverty in the form of a permanent class of "proletariate," actually had the effect of redistributing wealth to labor in the form of wages. If the accumulation of capital did create masses of hired laborers, there was nothing to prevent individual laborers from improving their conditions, acquiring property in homes, furniture, and savings, and possibly eventually becoming small capitalists. The problem came with those laborers who were ill fed and badly reared, who had to sell their labor at a price barely sufficient for subsistence, who had not the resources to save, and whose living standards and expectations were so low that they would not save even if they could do so. Their condition had nothing to do with private property as such, although in some cases it was the result of landed property originally acquired and secured by force (as in countries with a tradition of serfdom) or of a legal system that gave landlords rights incompatible with the true principles on which private property rested.

It was landed property, then, not private property in general, that was at issue. "When we consider all this, we shall see the unfairness of laying on capitalism or the free development of individual wealth the blame which is really due to the arbitrary and violent manner in which rights over land have been acquired and exercised." A reform of the land laws was justified not to subvert private property but to restore its essential purpose, "to fulfil those functions which under a system of unlimited private ownership are necessary to maintain the conditions of a free life."[47]

ONE CAN SEE why the words "ambiguous" and "ambivalent" appear so often in discussions of Green—by later commentators, however, more often than contemporaries.[48] Those who think that any critique of specific economic arrangements (the land laws, for example) is incomplete without a radical critique of capitalism and private property, or that no reform is adequate that falls short of equality, obviously find Green's analysis deficient. For them Green resided in a halfway house between individualism and collectivism, unwilling to draw the logical conclusions from any serious social criticism—that is, to reject capitalism and espouse, if not socialism, at least some advanced form of welfare state.[49]

There are legitimate questions that may be raised about Green's philosophy: about positive and negative freedom, about a Hegelian (or neo-Hegelian) view of the state and a Kantian (or neo-Kantian) view of morality, about a spirit of religiosity that is averse to any institutional religion, or about the proper limits of government intervention. But such questions may be put to other philosophies as well (liberalism and socialism, for example) without imputations of ambivalence and ambiguity. Most contemporaries saw Philosophical Idealism not as a way-station from or to another system of thought but as an independent, coherent system, flawed, perhaps, but serious and sufficient unto itself. They may have disagreed with it, but they found nothing inherently equivocal or contradictory in the attempt to transcend the dichotomy of individualism and collectivism, or to reconcile the moral equality of man with the inequality of material possessions, or to respect the ordinary man while seeking to promote his best self, or to see the best self as an integral part of the common good.

It is impressive to find so many tributes to Green, not in pious obituaries but in the memoirs of eminent contemporaries not given to flattery or adulation. The literary critic A. C. Bradley confided to a friend that Green had "saved his soul."[50] The philosopher J. H. Muirhead recalled a reading by Green (from the work later to appear as the *Prolegomena*) which affected him in a manner "nearer to what in the language of the time was called 'conversion' than anything else I have ever experienced."[51] The jurist and historian James Bryce judged Green to be "the most powerful ethical influence, and perhaps also the most stimulative intellectual influence, that in those years played upon the minds of the ablest youth of the University." What especially impressed Bryce was "his hold upon practical life"; he was "a singular instance of a metaphysician with a bent towards politics and practical life."[52]

Even those contemporaries who differed with him acknowledged his authority. When Henry Sidgwick wanted to write a critique of Philosophical Idealism, he focused it not upon F. H. Bradley, who had written a pamphlet attacking him, but upon Green, whom he saw as the more formidable challenge to his own utilitarian ethics.[53] The "New Liberals" of the following generation—L. T. Hobhouse, J. A. Hobson, C. F. G. Masterman—who went much further than Green in advocating government intervention, continued to draw upon his moral philosophy. Hobhouse often cited Green in his quarrel with Bernard Bosanquet, a Philosophical Idealist who was more Hegelian than Green and at the same time more laissez-faireist. Indeed, the fact that they chose to describe themselves as New Liberals rather than as socialists was a tribute to him.[54] And those socialists who resisted Marxism found Idealism congenial as the basis for a socialist credo that was ethical rather than materialistic and that appealed to the common good rather than to class interests.[55] Even a Conservative Member of Parliament like G. J. Goschen, who deplored the collectivist tendency of the time, attested to the moral power that lay behind it, the "awakening of public conscience," the "assertion of claims of other than material interests," the "public imagination" that was touched by appeals to its higher nature.[56] Whatever other ideas and impulses entered into this accession of social consciousness, there is little doubt that Green's philosophy gave it a moral authority and intellectual substance it would not otherwise have had.

God spoke, Green once told a friend, not through the priest but through the "educated conscience."[57] For Evangelicals the guiding principle of conscience was religion; for Positivists it was science; for socialists it was equality; for many reformers and philanthropists it was simple humanitarianism. For the Philosophical Idealists it was moral philosophy, a philosophy that dignified man, even the poorest man, as a citizen capable of realizing his best self in a state devoted to the common good. Shortly after Green's death, the philosopher Edward Caird paid tribute to him as "in the best sense, a democrat of the democrats."

> I use this word for want for a better, but what I mean is, that from a somewhat exclusive interest in the essentials of humanity—in the spiritual experiences in which all men are alike—and from a natural disregard for the outward differences of rank and position and even of culture, by which these essentials are invested and concealed, his sympathies were always with the many rather than with the few. He was strongly inclined to the idea that there is an "instinct of reason" in the movement of popular sentiment, which is often wiser than the opinion of the so-called educated classes. The belief in the essential equality of men might, indeed, be said to be one of the things most deeply rooted in his character, though it showed itself not in any readiness to echo the commonplaces of Radicalism, but rather in a habitual direction of thought and interest to practical schemes for "levelling up" the inequalities of human lot, and giving to the many the opportunities of the few.[58]

Mill: Old Liberal or
New Socialist?

FOR GREEN, as for most Englishmen of his generation, Mill was the author of *On Liberty,* the bible of the old liberalism, the liberalism that exalted individuality and made a near-absolute principle of liberty. It was in protest against this liberalism that Green formulated the concept of "positive liberty" and developed a philosophy that helped turn the tide against laissez-faireism.

Apart from the extreme solicitude for liberty and individuality expressed in *On Liberty,* which would be difficult to reconcile with any collectivist scheme, there were passages toward the end of the book that were explicitly directed against government intervention of the kind that socialists were advocating.

> The third and most cogent reason for restricting the interference of government is the great evil of adding unnecessarily to its power. Every function superadded to those already exercised by the government causes its influence over hopes and fears to be more widely diffused, and converts, more and more, the active and ambitious part of the public into hangers-on of the government, or of some party which aims at becoming the government. If the roads, the railways, the banks, the insurance offices, the great joint-stock companies, the universities, and the public charities were all of them branches of the government; if, in addition, the municipal corporations and local boards, with all that now devolves on them, became departments of the central administration; if the employees of all these different enterprises were appointed and paid by the government and looked to the government for every rise in life, not all the freedom of the press and popular constitution of the legislature would make this or any other country free otherwise than in name.[59]

This was also one of Mill's main objections to the philosophy of Comte. Six years after the publication of *On Liberty* and four years before the writing of his *Chapters on Socialism,* Mill explained that he agreed with Comte that the laissez-faire doctrine, in its unqualified form, was "both unpractical and unscientific." But it did not follow, he added, "that those who assert it are not, nineteen times out of twenty, practically nearer the truth than those who deny it."[60]

Socialists, however, eager to claim Mill as one of their own, ignored *On Liberty* and his book on Comte, preferring to cite other texts that might be interpreted in their favor. To Sidney Webb, Mill was the author of *The Principles of Political Economy,* each edition of which, Webb claimed, was "more and more Socialistic," and of the *Autobiography,* which traced his development "from a mere political democrat to a convinced Socialist."[61] To William Morris, Mill was the author of the posthumously published *Chapters on Socialism,* where he "clearly gave the verdict against the evidence"—the evidence, according to Morris, favoring socialism, while the verdict was ostensibly against it; it was these essays, Morris told Shaw, that converted him to socialism.[62] The disciples of Henry George remembered Mill as the founding member of the Land Tenure Reform Association and the author of its manifesto calling for the abolition of primogeniture and entail, the public administration of waste lands, and a tax on the unearned increase of the value of land—not quite George's program, but, they liked to think, a prelude to it.[63] A more telling contemporary witness was the economist Alfred Marshall, who said that his early "tendency" to socialism was "fortified" by his reading of Mill's posthumous essays in 1879.[64] Some later historians have made similar claims, presenting Mill as a socialist, an incipient socialist, an evolutionary socialist, or a precursor of the socialists.[65]

If socialism is defined broadly enough, and if some of Mill's pronouncements are emphasized at the expense of others, he can be given the title of socialist. In his *Autobiography,* Mill actually described himself as such. In the "third period" of his "mental progress," he explained, the period of his marriage, "our ideal of ultimate improvement went far beyond Democracy, and would class us decidedly under the general designation of Socialists." That ideal was a society no longer divided between "the idle and the industrious," where the produce of labor was distributed according to an "acknowledged principle of justice," and where the "greatest individual liberty of action" was combined with "a common ownership in the raw material of the globe, and an equal participation of all in the benefits of combined labour." At the same time Mill cautioned against the danger in this ideal: "the tyranny of society over the individual which most Socialistic systems are supposed to involve." He also made it clear that socialism was very much an "ultimate" ideal; he could not foresee the "precise form of institutions" that might carry it out, or "how near or how distant" the time when it might be achieved. That time was evidently more distant than near, because any social transformation, he insisted, required a transformation of the character of both the laboring masses and their employers, so that they would both value the common good more than their private interests; and this could come about only by "slow degrees" and "successive generations." In the meantime, he warned his readers against "the folly of premature attempts" to dispense with the motive of private interest, and recommended only such "socialistic experiments by select individuals" as cooperative societies.[66]

It is difficult to quarrel with Mill's "general designation" of himself as a socialist. If he chose that term, who are we to deny it? One may, however, point out how vague and "general" it was as defined in the *Autobiography*. Nor was the evidence from *The Principles of Political Economy* more compelling. In the first edition, Mill explained, written before the revolutions of 1848, "the difficulties of socialism were stated so strongly, that the tone was on the whole that of opposition to it." But by the third edition of 1852, he had "cancelled" most of his arguments against socialism and replaced them by others which represented a "more advanced opinion."[67]*

These changes were indeed considerable. In the first edition Mill had said that the decisive objection to communism (a term he often used synonymously with socialism) was that it "abrogates this freedom [of individuality and action] entirely, and places every action of every member of the community under command."[69] In the third edition, this objection was reduced to: "It remains to be discovered how far the preservation of this characteristic [liberty] would be found compatible with the Communistic organization of society. No doubt this, like all the other objections to the Socialist schemes, is vastly exaggerated."[70] One after another of Mill's original criticisms was similarly qualified or dismissed. Either another form of socialism would obviate the difficulty; or

---

* Mill also explained, in the *Autobiography,* that the revised editions of the *Political Economy* owed much to the influence of Harriet Taylor (later his wife)—just how much is dramatically demonstrated in his letters, which show that all the crucial changes were made on her suggestion and, in some cases, he admitted, against his own better judgment.[68]

the same objection, to an even greater degree, could be raised against the present system; or the present system was so bad that any alternative would be preferable.

> The restraints of Communism would be freedom in comparison with the present condition of the majority of the human race.[71]

> If, therefore, the choice were to be made between Communism with all its chances, and the present state of society with all its sufferings and injustices . . . all the difficulties, great or small, of Communism would be but as dust in the balance.[72]

Interspersed with these favorable judgments, however, were other statements couched in so many negatives, conjectures, and imponderables that they amounted to considerably less than a rousing endorsement of socialism.

> The impossibility of foreseeing and prescribing the exact mode in which its [communism's] difficulties should be dealt with, does not prove that it may not be the best and the ultimate form of human society.[73]

> It would be extremely rash to pronounce it incapable of success, or unfitted to realize a great part of the hopes founded on it by its partisans.[74]

> We are too ignorant either of what individual agency in its best form, or Socialism in its best form, can accomplish to be qualified to decide which of the two will be the ultimate form of human society.[75]

IF *Political Economy,* even in its revised form, was not the unambiguous commitment to socialism that Webb thought it, *Chapters on Socialism* hardly provided the "evidence" in favor of socialism that Morris claimed. The *Chapters* were written in 1869 and never completed, although Mill continued to write on other subjects during the remaining four years of his life. In 1879, his stepdaughter Helen Taylor, who was active in various radical and socialist movements (she was a member of the First International and one of the founders of what later became the Social Democratic Federation), was prevailed upon to edit and publish the

incomplete manuscript in *Fortnightly Review.** Had there been any ideological bias in the editing, it would have been in favor of socialism. Yet
even in the published form, *Chapters on Socialism,* Mill's last and most
considered reflections on this subject, was more critical of socialism than
anything he had written previously.

Mill's critique was all the more telling because it was directed not
only against the "revolutionary Socialists" who wanted to transform all of
society (this was not an allusion to the Marxists—Mill never read Marx
and only barely knew his name), but also against the more moderate
"philosophic Socialists," Louis Blanc, Victor Considérant, and, to a lesser
extent, François Fourier. Although Mill professed great sympathy with
the aims of the second group—the relief of poverty and a more equitable
reward for labor—he was critical both of their analysis of the present
system and of their proposals for change. Contrary to their claims, he said,
wages had increased, and at an increasingly rapid rate; living conditions,
so far from having deteriorated, had improved; and any appearance to the
contrary was the result of some temporary calamity or bad law that could
be corrected, "while the permanent causes all operate in the direction of
improvement."[77] Socialists also had an "imperfect and one-sided" notion
of competition, seeing it only as an agency for grinding down wages, not
as a cause of high wages; indeed a state of perfect competition would have
the effect of reducing inequalities. To be sure, competition, while ensuring the cheapness of goods, did not also ensure quality, but the remedies
for this, Mill said, could easily be effected within the framework of the
existing system, through the passage of laws against commercial frauds
and the organization of additional cooperatives.

---

* It is not known how much editing Helen Taylor did on *Chapters on Socialism,* for
the original manuscript has been lost. But something of her editing techniques are
revealed in a letter written to her good friend Kate Amberley (now better known as
Bertrand Russell's mother). In 1869, at just the time Mill was writing the *Chapters,*
Helen Taylor offered to edit an article by Mrs. Amberley and explained why she was
well qualified to do so.

> I have a great deal of practice in doing this, beginning with Mr. Mill's writings
> which I go over five or six times, putting in words here, stops there; scratching
> through whole paragraphs; asking him to write whole new pages in particular
> places where I think the meaning is not clear; condensing, enlarging, polish-
> ing, etc. In short I take very much greater liberties with his things than with
> anyone else's, because there is no *amour propre* to be hurt in his case or mine,
> and I have confidence in him to reject my alterations if he does not really think
> them improvements.[76]

The more serious charge, that a greater proportion of the produce of the country was being diverted from those who produced it to those who did not, was based on the "illusion" that capital was unproductive and undeserving of any return. Land, Mill conceded, was another matter, which he promised to deal with separately; at this point he said only that the tenure of land might be considerably modified (even to the extent of making it the property of the state) "without interfering with the right of property in anything which is the product of human labour and abstinence."[78] He denied that the present system was in such a state of "general indigence and slavery" that only socialism could save humanity, and repeated his conviction that the evils and injustices, however great, were diminishing. He also pointed out that the inequalities in the distribution of wealth between capital and labor, which might "shock the feeling of natural justice," would not be alleviated by their "mere equalisation," since that would not provide "so large a fund for raising the lower levels of remuneration as Socialists, and many besides Socialists, are apt to suppose."[79]

Having corrected these "Socialist exaggerations" about the evils of capitalism, Mill proceeded to analyze the "difficulties of socialism." He was especially vehement toward the "revolutionary Socialists" (more common, he said, on the Continent than in Britain), who sought to bring the entire resources of the country under the one central authority of the government, and to do so with a "single stroke." On the strength of their "private opinion" alone, without any "experimental verification," they would forcibly deprive an entire class of the means of maintaining themselves, and would risk the frightful bloodshed and misery that would ensue if they were resisted. Such people, Mill judged, "must have a serene confidence in their own wisdom on the one hand and a recklessness of other people's sufferings on the other, which Robespierre and Saint-Just, hitherto the typical instances of those united attributes, scarcely came up to."[80]

Even the more modest varieties of "philosophic Socialism," such as those of Owen and Fourier, were practicable only so long as they confined themselves to the abolition of private property in small, local, "self-acting" units.* Any attempt to extend this system to the nation as a whole would

---

* The distinction between "revolutionary" and "philosophic" socialists does not correspond to a distinction between socialism and communism. Mill sometimes identified "simple Communism" as that "form of Socialism" which called for an equal division of the produce of labor, or, like Louis Blanc's scheme, proposed to divide the

be beset by grave difficulties, for it would require the collective ownership of all the means of production (although not consumption) and the
public division of the produce "according to rules laid down by the
community."[82] Unfortunately the "motive powers" and "directing minds"
necessary for such a system were lacking. For most people, the only
effective inducement to overcome their natural "indolence and love of
ease" was the prospect of bettering their family's economic condition, and
the closer the correspondence between their exertions and their rewards,
the more powerful was that motive. Except for a "select proportion of the
population," Mill predicted, "personal interest will for a long time be a
more effective stimulus to the most vigorous and careful conduct of the
industrial business of society than motives of a higher character."[83] Nor
did he expect socialism to bring about a greater degree of social harmony
than existed at present, for there were large potentialities for discord in a
system where the community, and still more the state, had to determine
the distribution of work and rewards and make all the other decisions
now made by individuals. Whatever the defects of private property and
competition, they could best be remedied within the present system by
such devices as profit sharing and land reform.

The most serious difficulty of communism, however, Mill said (re-
verting to the argument of On Liberty and the first edition of the Political
Economy), was the enlarged scope of the public authority and hence the
reduced scope for liberty and individuality. This was already a "great and
growing evil" in all societies governed by the majority; it would be an
immeasurably greater evil under communism, where so much more
power was vested in the collectivity.[84] In any case, the very idea of
conducting the whole industry of a country from a single center was "so
obviously chimerical" that no one had yet proposed any practical means
by which this might be done. Any attempt to do this would result in a
state of chaos resembling nothing so much as Hobbes's "state of nature."[85]

Chapters on Socialism, however inconclusive and incomplete—the
manuscript stops in the middle of a chapter—was conclusive enough in
regard to the "difficulties" of any but the most modest scheme of socialism.
In this respect it confirms what his other writings suggest: that if Mill was
often less of a liberal than he appeared to be in On Liberty, he was considerably less of a socialist than some socialists have made him out to be.

---

produce according to need rather than work or merit, in contrast to Fourier's system,
which was more spontaneous and flexible.[81] But he did not maintain this distinction
consistently.

CHAPTER 18

The New Radicalism

TWO DAYS AFTER Green's death, in March 1882, his pupil Arnold Toynbee was obliged to fulfill a long-standing commitment to address the Leicester Liberal Association. As it happened, only a year earlier Green himself had delivered his memorable lecture "Liberal Legislation and Freedom of Contract" before that same group. The chairman introduced Toynbee by thanking him for "following so well in the steps of his revered teacher."[1] The words were uncomfortably prophetic, for a year later, just short of the anniversary of the master's death, the disciple died.

Like Green, Toynbee was a Balliol man. If his career was less distinguished than Green's, it was partly because it was so brief; he was only thirty when he died. A sickly child with an erratic schooling, he had failed the examination for Balliol and was admitted only through the personal intervention of Jowett. He took a Pass degree and was appointed (again thanks to the good offices of Jowett) tutor to the probationers of the Indian Civil Service. What is remarkable is not that he wrote so little—his corpus amounted to a single posthumous volume of collected lectures— but that he managed to do as much as he did in spite of his recurrent ailments.* More impressive still is the personal effect he had on his own

---

* To the suggestion of one of Toynbee's admirers, that "he committed nothing to paper until he had fully elaborated it in his own mind," his wife tartly commented, "He never wrote if he could possibly help it or if there was any chance of talking instead."[2] (His wife was evidently not one of his excessive admirers; her acerbic comments provide a counterpoint to the extravagant compliments of his friends. Their marriage was itself a study in counterpoint: she was eleven years his senior, domineering in temperament, aristocratic in prejudice, sharing none of his intellectual, social, or political interests.)

generation during his short lifetime, and the influence of his not very scholarly lectures on the industrial revolution on later historians. Alfred Milner, a member of Toynbee's circle at Oxford and later a prominent figure in imperial affairs, recalled the impression Toynbee made upon him: "No man has ever had for me the same fascination, or made me realize as he did the secret of prophetic power—the kind of influence exercised in all ages by the men of religion and moral inspiration."[3]

It does not diminish Toynbee's stature to suggest that he was the poor man's Green, less abstract than the master but no less idealistic—in the philosophical as well as the mundane sense of that word. Where Green translated his philosophy into the language of practical morality and social reform, Toynbee made it even more concrete by applying it to the history and theory of economics.

"For the sake of religion," Milner said of Toynbee, "he had become a social reformer; for the sake of social reform he became an economist."[4] These were not successive stages of development but simultaneous ones. Toynbee did not grow out of religion; he grew into it. His religion was not a vestige of youth, an attenuated creed transmuted into a social gospel. He became religious only after he entered Oxford, and he remained as energetic in the cause of religious reform as in social reform. Moreover, his religion was neither pantheistic nor positivistic. Like Green, he associated true religion with positive freedom. "The beginning of religion is the cry of man for a law of life to restrain his freedom. The consciousness of an ideal self which includes the good of all, the consciousness of the ideal enshrined within the temple of the mind gives the answer to that cry."[5] But he went beyond Green in enshrining that "ideal self" not only in the "temple of the mind" but in the church as well—indeed, in an established church. If the state, he reasoned, had a positive role in promoting the social and moral welfare of the people, it also had a positive role in promoting their religious and spiritual welfare. There could be no separation between church and state because they shared the same essential qualities. "As the nation is a spiritual and secular community, so is the State a spiritual and secular power."[6] Where most of his contemporaries took the reform of the church to mean its disestablishment, Toynbee took it as an invitation to its reestablishment, its reorganization as a truly national church which would include Dissenters as well as Anglicans and which would encourage the active participation of the laity. Only such a church could resist passing fashions and satisfy the ideal self, for it would unite the spiritual and secular and bring together "free but isolated beings into a loving interdependent whole."[7]

* * *

IT WAS IN THIS religious spirit that Toynbee embarked upon the most secular of studies, economics. Just before he received his degree, he told a friend that his life as "a political economist and social agitator and philanthropist" was about to begin and that he hoped to become "a good soldier of Christ."[8] Four years later, he assured an audience at the Bradford Mechanics' Institute: "The thing assumed by political economy was identical with the thing assumed by morality and religion. The thing assumed by political economy was the development of man's life in all its aspects."[9] At Balliol he founded a society for the discussion of economic, political, and social issues, which Milner dubbed, only slightly facetiously, the society for the "Regeneration of Humanity."[10] Political economy properly understood—as Toynbee understood it—was to be an instrument for that regeneration.

> Because the laws of Political Economy express the action of self-interest, men have said that Political Economy enjoins men to value their self-interest to the disregard of their humanity, their morality, and their religion. That is not true. Political Economy as a practical science bids men follow their own self-interest only when it promotes the good of the community. Political Economy never said that there was no room for humanity or morality or religion in the world.[11]

Ricardian economics was fatally flawed because it did not realize that "morality must be united with economics as a practical science."[12] Its conception of political economy logically implied a world that Ricardo himself, a benevolent and humane man, never intended: a world inhabited by "gold-seeking animals, stripped of every human affection, for ever digging, weaving, spinning, watching with keen undeceived eyes each other's movements, passing incessantly and easily from place to place in search of gain, all alert, crafty, mobile."[13] That world was as unreal as the abstractions and laws of nature supposedly derived from it. Yet it was not until the "labour question" became pressing, and solutions had to be devised for problems once deemed insoluble, that those abstractions and laws were finally seriously challenged. Only then did economists discover that individual liberty was not of supreme value, that the self-interest of individuals did not invariably promote the general interest, that the wage-fund theory was not a law of nature, and that competition was not an "all-sufficient" principle for society.

The socialists were no wiser than the orthodox economists, for they merely substituted one absolute for another, proposing to abolish competition entirely and replace it with another all-sufficient principle, equality. Competition, however, not equality, was the essential feature of a free economy— "a great physical force which cannot be destroyed, but may be controlled and modified," by laws and institutions, customs and opinion, religion and morality.[14] Inequality too was necessary, again in a modified form, the inequality of wealth being mitigated by the equality of opportunity. In a proper economy employers could feel secure in the knowledge that trade unions, cooperatives, and social reforms would moderate competition without undermining an efficient industrial organization. And workers would understand that the faults of the old political economy did not vitiate the essential principles of any sound political economy: free trade, private property, the division of labor, and the operation of supply and demand.

IN HIS ADDRESS to the Leicester Liberal Association delivered just after Green's death, Toynbee started, in a sense, where Green had left off.[15] Green's quarrel had been with Mill, with a philosophy of liberalism that was, as he saw it, profoundly illiberal, demeaning to the individual and to the idea of freedom itself. As if to suggest that that philosophical battle had been won, Toynbee reformulated the terms of the debate so that the issue was no longer liberalism but radicalism and socialism.

Under the provocative title "Are Radicals Socialists?" Toynbee distinguished the several varieties of radicalism that had emerged since the 1840s: the middle-class, laissez-faire radicalism of Cobden and Bright (Mill was included in this group in passing), symbolized by the campaign against the Corn Laws; the working-class radicalism of the Chartists, concerned mainly with the extension of the suffrage; the Tory radicalism of Disraeli, a form of paternalistic socialism that proposed to solve the "condition of the people question" by factory laws and similar reforms; and Owenite socialism, which sought to replace the strife of competition with brotherhood and "association." The recent, more radical form of socialism, "German" or "continental" socialism committed to the abolition of private property, was a fantasy in England, Toynbee said, if only because so much of the "Socialist programme" had already been achieved there. And this had been done by time-honored Radical means: a combination of self-help, individualism, voluntary organizations, and legislative and administrative measures by the state. The latest phase of this program was the Irish Land Act of 1881. This act marked an epoch in the history of democracy, for "it means—I say it advisedly—that the Radical party has committed itself to a Socialist programme."[16]

It was at this point that Toynbee and Green converged—but with a difference. For Green the Irish Land Act epitomized the positive freedom that reconciled the best self with the common good, in contrast to the old negative liberty that made a fetish of the freedom of contract. For Toynbee it epitomized the new radicalism that reconciled positive freedom with the essential, minimal, principles of socialism, a socialism based upon the fundamental fact that "between men who are unequal in material wealth there can be no freedom of contract." This crucial fact justified the interference of the state—but only under certain conditions: where individual rights conflicted with the interests of the community; where the people were unable to provide something for themselves; and where that thing was of *"primary social importance."*[17] Land reform met these criteria, as did the urgent need for state-supported working-class housing. (Toynbee raised the housing issue more than a year before *The Bitter Cry* appeared.) In both cases state action was consistent with the principle of self-help. What it was not consistent with was either the old form of Tory socialism which relied upon a paternalistic government, or the new form of continental socialism which sought to abolish private property, by violence if necessary, and compounded the evil by recognizing only material interests rather than moral ones.

Toynbee concluded his lecture by calling upon the workers, in return for the material improvement that was the aim of social reforms, to see to their own moral improvement. High wages and good material conditions were not ends in themselves. Indeed high wages were often a cause of crime, and material prosperity without religious faith and moral ideals was "as little use to man as earth to the plants without the sun." Only by moral reformation could the workers enjoy the fruits of their material progress, and only then would they be able to exercise the full rights of citizenship.

> I repeat, we demand increased material welfare for those who labour with their hands, not that they may seize upon a few more coarse enjoyments, but that they may enter upon a purer and a higher life. We demand it also that the English workman may take his part worthily in the government of this country. We demand it in order that he may have the intelligence and the will to administer the great trust which fate has committed to his charge; for it is not only his own

home and his own country that he has to govern, but a vast empire—a duty unparalleled in the annals of democracy.[18]

This was a familiar refrain in Toynbee's lectures. In "Wages and Natural Law," he told his working-class audience that higher wages were not an end in themselves but a means to a higher end, that an increase of wages had all too often been accompanied by an increase of crime, and that if they expected their employers to behave more equitably, their employers had every right to expect them to reform themselves. "No one wants higher wages in order that working men may indulge in mere sensual gratification. We want higher wages in order that an improved material condition, with less of anxiety and less uncertainty as to the future, may enable the working man to enter on a purer and more worthy life."[19] His final lecture, on Henry George, concluding with the famous *mea culpa,* made the same point. "We work for you," he assured the workers, "in the hope and trust that if you get material civilisation, if you get a better life, you will really lead a better life."[20]

TOYNBEE NOT ONLY "moralized" economics; he "historicized" it. To make his case for a "new" political economy, he had to show that the dogmas of the old political economy were the products of a particular time and place, rather than the immutable laws of nature. Thus he took as his métier economic history rather than economic theory. Alfred Marshall, who knew him slightly, succeeded him at Balliol, and sympathized with his moral purposes, had no great regard for him as an economist and did not recognize him as a contributor to his own discipline of the "new" political economy. Instead he paid ambiguous tribute to him as a latter-day St. Francis, "brilliant in thought, eager in speculation," but governed more by his emotions than his intellect.[21] The economic historians, on the other hand—W. J. Ashley, for example, whose undergraduate notes on Toynbee's lectures were one of the sources for the published version—were pleased to claim him as their mentor.

Toynbee's most famous work, his *Lectures on the Industrial Revolution of the Eighteenth Century in England,* opens with a defense of the historical method as a means of understanding not only the past but, more important, the present. It is, in fact, an unabashedly "present-minded" history. "It would be well," Toynbee announced, "if, in studying the past, we could always bear in mind the problems of the present, and go to that past to seek large views of what is of lasting importance to the human race."[22] Because he himself believed the chief problem of the present to be the condition of the working classes, and because he saw this as a product of the industrial revolution, he selected this subject as the theme of his most ambitious series of lectures.*

Parts of the *Industrial Revolution* seem to confirm the most apocalyptic view of that event.

> There were dark patches even in his [Smith's] age, but we now approach a darker period,—a period as disastrous and as terrible as any through which a nation ever passed; disastrous and terrible, because, side by side with a great increase of wealth was seen an enormous increase of pauperism; and production on a vast scale, the result of free competition, led to a rapid alienation of classes and to the degradation of a large body of producers.[24]

This was the most dramatic and familiar part of Toynbee's story. But it was only part of it, for he confined that dark period to the early stage of industrialism, from the late eighteenth to the middle of the nineteenth century. By the 1840s, he found, the condition of the working classes had begun to take a turn for the better, and by his own time the improvement was so considerable that it more than made up for the miseries of the earlier period. The real wages of both industrial and agricultural workers had risen, their hours of work had decreased, their standard of living had improved, their savings had increased, employment had become more regular, and relations with employers were more satisfactory. Moreover, the condition of the working classes had improved relatively more than that of the middle classes, so that there was actually less inequality than before. These beneficent effects, Toynbee explained, were the results of free trade and a competitive economy, tempered by social legislation and such meliorative institutions as trade unions and cooperatives.[25] If his account of early industrialism places Toynbee among the "pessimistic" school of historians, his view of the later period clearly consigns him to the school of "optimists."

---

* Neither the subject nor the phrase "industrial revolution" originated with Toynbee. A little-known French economist used the term in 1838. Engels made much of it in his *Condition of the Working Class in England,* in 1844 (but that book appeared in German and was not translated into English until after Toynbee's). And John Stuart Mill referred to it in his *Principles of Political Economy* in 1848. By the eighties it had become familiar. But it was Toynbee who popularized it and made it a subject of heated debate that has persisted until this very day.[23]

* * *

TOYNBEE SOMETIMES described the kinds of reforms he advocated—the public control of railways, for example, or the supply of gas and water—as "socialist."[26] But he was careful to distinguish his variety of socialism from others that went by the same name—the socialist or communist communities in America which voluntarily adopted the principle of common property, and the European form which required the state to appropriate all the instruments of production and assume control over the whole of a nation's industry. His own socialism, he insisted, was more efficacious than the first and more prudent and practical than the second. It was, in fact, not socialism but a new form of radicalism—not the laissez-faire radicalism of an earlier generation, of Richard Cobden or John Bright, but a "positive," reformist, interventionist radicalism. The Fabians later assimilated this kind of radicalism with socialism, on the theory that small measures of reform would inevitably lead to large ones and that once the principle of state intervention was admitted, there would be no limit to the application of that principle. It was in this spirit that George Bernard Shaw started to write an essay, "The New Radicalism," with an opening sentence announcing that "the new Radicalism is Socialism."[27] But that was Shaw's notion of the new radicalism, not Toynbee's.

Toynbee's radicalism was also distinctive in being firmly rooted in the Puritan ethic. While he favored factory laws, subsidized housing, and measures now known as "municipal socialism," he firmly opposed any form of "indiscriminate charity" or even outdoor relief. Like the Charity Organisation Society, of which he was a member, he wanted to "make benevolence scientific," and this meant resisting any measure, like the dole, that inevitably "lowers wages, degrades the recipient, and diminishes self-reliance."[28] In the *Industrial Revolution,* he opened the discussion of pauperism by condemning the old political economy for failing to make any provision for the poor outside of the free economy, and ended by condemning the old poor law for debasing the poor by implying that "they had a right to relief independent of work"—or, worse yet, a right to "an indefinite share in the national wealth."[29] For most of history, he reflected, there had been an inverse relation between freedom and security. "It is a great law of social development that the movement from slavery to freedom is also a movement from security to insecurity of maintenance." Freedom had grown concomitantly with pauperism; indeed "the latter is the price we pay for the former." The great problem of modern times was how to combine freedom and sustenance—which is to say, "political and material freedom."[30]

One response to the problem of reconciling freedom and sustenance which Toynbee heartily approved of was the Irish Land Act. Another of which he as heartily disapproved was land nationalization. It was before an audience consisting largely of workers sympathetic to Henry George that he chose to deliver a forceful critique of *Progress and Poverty*. He dismissed the proposal for a single tax as a "delusive panacea" and criticized both the theory of rent and the supposed facts upon which it was based. The working classes, he said, so far from experiencing the "progressive degradation" George attributed to them, were much better off than they had been forty years earlier.[31] To be sure, they could and should be much better off, materially and morally, than they were. It was to this end, toward the conclusion of his lecture, that Toynbee dramatically pledged the efforts of middle-class people like himself and called upon the workers to cooperate in their own salvation.[32]

IT HAS BEEN SAID of Toynbee, as of Green, that his ideas were ambiguous and ambivalent, vague and illogical.[33] He professed to be a socialist, but he meant by socialism social reforms rather than the abolition of private property; and even these reforms were meant to supplement rather than replace individual efforts and voluntary associations. He deplored unrestricted competition, while seeking to retain a legitimate and necessary degree of economic competition. He criticized the old political economists who made no provision for the relief of the poor, and the old poor law which provided for it all too well. He enthusiastically favored land reform and as vigorously opposed land nationalization. He was an economist and economic historian who believed that both economics and economic history were essentially moral disciplines. He was an Idealist who made the state an active participant in the welfare of the community and made the individual an active agent in his own moral and material well-being. He was a social reformer who insisted upon applying moral criteria to social policies and believed that the aim of reform was the improvement of individual character.

One American commentator writing in the 1960s, perhaps reflecting the confidence of a generation newly launched on the "war against poverty," described Toynbee as suffering from the "disabilities" of a "middle-class intellectual" unable to liberate himself from the "persistent moralism" of his class and time.[34] A quarter of a century later, chastened by the failure of that "war," one may look back upon Toynbee's ideas with greater sympathy; one may even find in his "persistent moralism" a clue to some of the problems that continue to plague us. But whatever the present status of his ideas, there is no doubt that some of his most thoughtful contemporaries were enormously impressed by them—and by Toynbee himself. Milner's tribute to him as a "prophet" and "apostle" was echoed by others who testified to his inspiring presence and example.[35]

Toynbee's influence was all the more notable because he achieved it in so short a lifetime. This itself may have enhanced it, his premature death giving rise to the myth of martyrdom. It was said at the time that the cause of his death was the travail of those final lectures, his agonizing over the "miseries and misfortunes of the poor and wretched." Even so sober and unsentimental a journal as the *Economist* reported that he gave his life "for the masses"—and then rebuked him for not realizing that the masses would have been better served by a long lifetime of work than by "spurts of feeling, however noble, which practically end in an early grave."[36]* Without sanctifying him as a martyr, one can appreciate a sensibility that was more than sentimentality, and a high-mindedness that was also strong-minded and hardheaded.

---

* This was another myth that his wife tried to dispel. "I am always a little annoyed to have it stated," she wrote to Jowett's biographer, "that Arnold died as it were after those lectures on Progress and Poverty which of course is exaggeration—I believe his breakdown would have come just as surely without them."[37]

CHAPTER 19

The New Economics:
An "Economics of Chivalry"

HALF A CENTURY after Toynbee's death, the leading economist of a
later generation made a pronouncement that Toynbee would have heartily endorsed. John Maynard Keynes described the power of economic
ideas—wrong ideas as often as right ones—on "practical men."

> The ideas of economists and political philosophers, both when they
> are right and when they are wrong, are more powerful than is com-
> monly understood. Indeed the world is ruled by little else. Practical
> men, who believe themselves to be quite exempt from any intellectual
> influences, are usually the slaves of some defunct economist. . . . I am
> sure that the power of vested interests is vastly exaggerated compared
> with the gradual encroachment of ideas."[1]

What was remarkable about late-Victorian England and what Toynbee
died too soon to appreciate was not only the potency and primacy of ideas
but the rapidity with which new ideas were assimilated into the culture.
So far from being the slaves of "some defunct economist," practical Victorians were quick to respond to new theories and almost as quick to act
upon them.

In economics as in social affairs the 1880s were a period of intense
intellectual ferment. A few years earlier, in 1876, the Political Economy
Club commemorated the centenary of the *Wealth of Nations*—this was the
only memorial to Smith in all of Britain—and was assured that nothing
new was to be expected, either in economic theory or in economic policy.
"The great work has been done," Robert Lowe, former Chancellor of the
Exchequer, informed the distinguished assemblage, and unless sociology
(he apologized for the barbarous neologism) took a sudden leap forward,

he anticipated no significant development in political economy.* Glad-stone agreed; something might be done about the reform of the currency, but little else was required by way of theoretical or legislative innovation. Some members looked forward to some small reduction in the role of the government, others to some small expansion. W. S. Jevons went so far as to suggest that the deviations from laissez-faire, in matters of housing, sanitation, and public facilities (promenades, libraries, museums, a me-teorological office), might constitute a new branch of economics.[4]

The spokesmen on that occasion were pleased that political economy had come to so happy a fruition. Others, however, especially those of a more rigorously laissez-faire disposition, took a gloomier view of the state of the discipline. One year after that commemorative dinner, George Goschen, a prominent Liberal, gave the House of Commons the unhappy tidings that "Political Economy has been dethroned in that House and Philanthropy had been allowed to take its place."[5] Three years later Walter Bagehot deplored the lack of interest and loss of confidence in political economy. "Younger men either do not study it, or do not feel that it comes home to them, and that it matches with their most living ideas."[6] Lord Milner recalled that when he went up to Oxford in 1872, laissez-faire held the field, but within ten years the few men who continued to adhere to that doctrine with any rigidity were regarded as "curiosities."[7]

According to Milner, it was Toynbee who "restored freedom of thought to economic speculation and gave a new impulse to philan-thropy."[8] Until his premature death in 1883, Toynbee had spread the gospel of a political economy dedicated to the welfare of men as much as to the production of wealth. But in spite of his lectureship in economics at Balliol, Toynbee was not regarded as a serious economist by other professional economists. Jevons, at University College London, did have that distinction, his theory of marginal utility being recognized as an original contribution to economics. Yet he himself, as his diffident re-

---

* Intellectual history is full of such "finality" statements, usually uttered on the eve of a momentous change. The normally cautious Mill delivered himself of one such gem in his *Principles of Political Economy:* "Happily, there is nothing in the laws of Value which remains for the present or any future writer to clear up; the theory of the subject is complete."[2] That sentence survived all the editions of the *Principles,* in-cluding the last to appear in his lifetime in 1871, the very year that Jevons published his *Theory of Political Economy,* which significantly revised the laws of value.

In his memoir of Marshall, Keynes made another such assertion: "After Marshall's analysis [of value] there was nothing more to be said."[3] That was written in 1924 and republished in 1933, a few years before Keynes's *General Theory.*

marks at the Political Economy Club suggested, did not lay claim to any radical revision of political economy. In any event, he too died prematurely, a year before Toynbee (not, however, as prematurely as Toynbee—Jevons was forty-seven, Toynbee thirty at his death).

By this time it was evident that the leading member of the profession was Alfred Marshall, who succeeded Toynbee at Balliol and two years later was appointed to the coveted chair of political economy at Cambridge. Joseph Schumpeter dated this event as the beginning of the "Marshallian Age."[9] Yet Marshall's major work, *Principles of Economics,* was not to appear for another five years. At this time his only published work was *Economics of Industry,* written in collaboration with his wife and intended for use in university extension courses (he was later so displeased with it that he tried to have it withdrawn from circulation), and a privately printed pamphlet on foreign trade put together by his colleague Henry Sidgwick from several chapters of an unfinished work.[10] Like Toynbee, whose influence derived from his lectures and personal appeal rather than his writings, Marshall acquired his reputation on the basis of lectures, courses, and the acclaim of students and colleagues. Unlike Toynbee, however, who was an economic historian rather than a theorist, and a popularizer rather than an original or systematic thinker, Marshall was recognized, even before the publication of his *Principles,* as an eminent economist. Within two years of his accession to the chair at Cambridge, one of his colleagues (a former student) observed that "half the economic chairs in the United Kingdom are occupied by his pupils, and the share taken by them in general economic instruction in England is even larger than this."[11]

Just as Toynbee's influence was felt outside of academia, so was Marshall's. Another economist, F. Y. Edgeworth, said that he could readily believe what the Principal of Ruskin College told him, "that work-people studying the *Principles of Economics* recognized in the author a sympathetic friend."[12]* Marshall was in the habit of inviting working-class leaders—Thomas Burt, Ben Tillett, Tom Mann, and others—to Cambridge to address the undergraduate Discussion Society and to dine and talk with him; thus he came to know most of the leaders of the trade union and cooperative movements. He was also acquainted with the men and

---

* To a present-day reader, what is remarkable is not that the workers should have found Marshall a sympathetic friend, but that they should be studying and understanding his *Principles*—and, apparently, John Stuart Mill's *Principles* as well, for Edgeworth went on to say that the only other economist about whom they had the same feeling was Mill.

women who made up the world of philanthropy, social work, and social research. In 1886 Charles Booth sent him the prospectus for his grand inquiry, asking for his "criticism in advance." Marshall's enthusiastic response was the beginning of a long and warm friendship.[13] After Booth delivered his first paper to the Statistical Society in 1887, Marshall opened the discussion by praising him for providing economists with the "real facts of life."[14] Their roles were reversed six years later when Booth, sitting on the Royal Commission for the Aged Poor, put questions to Marshall, who was testifying before the commission, and elicited from him acute observations on changes in the conception of poverty.

MARSHALL'S UNIQUE contribution to economics reflects the curious intellectual route by which he came to that discipline. As an undergraduate at St. John's College, Cambridge, he read mathematics, and when he was elected a fellow of the college in 1865 he supplemented his stipend by coaching students in mathematics. He planned to become a molecular physicist, but his interest soon shifted from physics and mathematics to theology and then metaphysics, Mansel's *Limits of Religious Thought* and discussions with his friend Henry Sidgwick having persuaded him that metaphysics, not theology, was the critical subject. He then came under the spell of Kant—"my guide, the only man I ever worshipped"[15]—and went to Germany to learn the language properly. (During a later visit to Germany, at the time of the Franco-Prussian War, he read and was much impressed by Hegel's *Philosophy of History*.[16])

Marshall was well on his way to becoming a metaphysician in the German mode when his English heritage asserted itself. The important issues, he decided, were psychological rather than metaphysical—the possibility, for example, of "the higher and more rapid development of human faculties." This, in turn, raised the ethical problem of the "justification of the existing condition of society" and the practical problem of how far "the conditions of life of the British (and other) working classes generally suffice for fullness of life." Older and wiser friends assured him that if he knew anything about political economy he would not ask such questions, that the resources of production were insufficient to give the great body of the English people the opportunity to enjoy the "fullness of life."[17] It was at this point, in 1868, that Marshall, then a lecturer in "Moral Science" at Cambridge, took up the study of economics.

This intellectual saga took all of three years, and every phase of it (except perhaps his initial interest in physics) is reflected in his subsequent work. Marshall is generally credited with introducing the mathematical mode of analysis into economics. Yet he deliberately relegated most of the mathematical analysis in his *Principles* to an appendix, insisting that economics could be perfectly understood without it, indeed could be better understood without it. Since every fact, whether quantifiable or not, was intimately related as cause and effect to many other facts which were not quantifiable, mathematical analysis was either useless or misleading, and the world would have been better off "if the work had never been done at all."[18] Economics, he warned the reader of the *Principles,* was not a "simple science," and a man would be a better economist by trusting to his "common sense and practical instincts." The economist had "less need of elaborate scientific methods, than of a shrewd motherwit, of a sound sense of proportion, and of a large experience of life."[19]

Marshall's suspicion of mathematics in isolation from other facts recalls Booth's suspicion of quantitative evidence divorced from qualitative, facts from values, absolute figures from proportions. "The longer I live," Marshall wrote to one of England's leading statisticians, "the more convinced I am that, except in purely abstract problems, the statistical side must never be separated even for an instant from the non-statistical." Although he himself lectured extensively on the statistical aspects of economics, his purpose was "to help people to read *through* figures, and reach the real values, the true relative proportions represented by them."[20]

When Marshall's interests shifted from metaphysics to ethics, it was because he thought of ethics as a form of applied or practical metaphysics—Practical Reason rather than Pure Reason, as his favorite philosopher would have put it. And when he made the final move to economics, it was because he came to believe that economics was the practical application of ethics in the mundane, workaday world. He disliked the idea, held by many economists, that "economics proper" was "pure" or "abstract" theory; theory, he maintained, was an essential but relatively small part of "real" economics.[21]

This conception of "real" economics was reflected in Marshall's definition of political economy. Only a few years earlier Henry Sidgwick had repeated the familiar definition of political economy as an "inquiry concerned with the Production, Distribution, and Exchange of Wealth in a society."[22] Marshall opened his *Principles of Economics* with a very different definition:

> Political Economy or Economics is a study of mankind in the ordinary business of life; it examines that part of individual and social

action which is most closely connected with the attainment and with the use of the material requisites of well-being.

Thus it is on the one side a study of wealth; and on the other, and more important side, a part of the study of man.[23]*

IN BECOMING an economist, Marshall did not cease to be a moral philosopher; his economics was a species of moral philosophy. As much as anything else it was his rejection of an amoral ("value-free") utilitarianism that distinguished him from the classical economists.[25] Keynes pointed out that for Marshall, unlike his predecessors, the solution of economic problems involved "not an application of the hedonistic calculus, but a prior condition of the exercise of man's higher faculties, irrespective, almost, of what we mean by 'higher.' "[26] This is not to say that Marshall denigrated or ignored the "lower" aspects of man's nature: self-interest and material wants. The job of the economist, he said, was concerned largely with such matters, if only because they were translatable into monetary units and therefore measurable. Moreover, men were not and would never be "perfectly virtuous," so that self-interest and material gratification would continue to govern a good deal of economic behavior.[27] But these were not the only or necessarily dominant motives of most people most of the time, even in economic matters. Economists were beginning to realize that "the desire of men for the approval of their own conscience and for the esteem of others is an economic force of the first order of importance."[28]

When Schumpeter criticized Marshall for "the preaching of mid-Victorian morality, seasoned by Benthamism . . . a schema of middle-class values that knows no glamour and no passion," he did an injustice to Marshall, and to "mid-Victorian morality" in general.[29] His description surely does not apply to the great mid-Victorian moralists—Thomas Carlyle, George Eliot, Matthew Arnold, even John Stuart Mill—who

---

* This definition seems to have no bearing on the distinctive title of Marshall's book—"Economics" rather than "Political Economy." The definition suggests that he used these terms interchangeably. According to one interpretation, the elimination of "Political" in the title reflects the fact that by this time "political economy was formally divorced from moral sciences," leaving "simply economics—a subject far more statistical, than ethical, in approach."[24] If this were so, Marshall would surely have made a point of it and would certainly not have used "political economy" as the opening words of his book. In any event, he opposed the idea that political economy, or economics, could or should be divorced from "moral sciences."

had a passionate sense of morality; indeed who made of it something of a religion. Nor does it apply to such late-Victorian moralists as Green, Toynbee, or Sidgwick, who placed morality, a demanding and strenuous morality, at the heart of both private and public life. Nor to those less eminent Victorians who experienced a *crise de conscience* that left them not with an enervated but with an exacerbated sense of morality—a conscience that was called upon to do what religion no longer had the authority to prescribe and what utilitarianism refused in principle to prescribe.

Marshall was a moralist in the tradition of Kant or Green rather than Bentham. When he used the words "happiness," "pleasure," or "interest," he meant them to be understood in a "higher," more "permanent" sense— rather like Tocqueville's "self-interest properly understood." In the *Principles* he explained that he preferred "satisfaction" to "pleasure" because the latter had a hedonistic or utilitarian connotation, whereas the former (he quoted Green to this effect) suggested "the satisfaction of the permanent self." To pass from "individualistic Hedonism" to a "complete ethical creed," it was necessary to introduce an independent "premiss." For some that "premiss" was known as the "Categorical Imperative"; for others it was the "self-respect" implicit in any attempt "so to live as to promote the progress of the human race."[30] For Marshall himself it went under the name of "Duty." Not duty in the Tory sense in which the upper class had a duty to care for the lower, but in the Kantian sense of a moral instinct inherent in each person by virtue of his reason, an instinct that bids each of us to "do unto others what you would that they should do unto you."[31]

Unlike moralists and economists of an earlier generation, Marshall had an evolutionary conception of moral character. This was another of his objections to classical political economy: it had not only too low a view of human nature; it had too static a view. In Marshall's evolutionary schema, the struggle for existence among human beings led to the survival not so much of individuals as of those races where the individual was "most willing to sacrifice himself for the benefit of those around him," those races being best adapted "collectively" to their environment.[32] Thus social evolution ensured the moral as well as physical progress of mankind. The growth of wealth, since at least the seventeenth century, had been accompanied by the strengthening and diffusion of such virtues as prudence, self-control, and farsightedness. Modern man, far more than his ancestors, was capable of sacrificing his present ease to his future satisfaction and his private interests to the public good.[33]

If economists had to take this evolutionary process into account—to realize, for example, that one of the characteristics of modern man was "deliberateness, not selfishness"—they also had to heed the lesson of practical life: "that ordinary men are seldom capable of pure ideal altruism for any considerable time together." If all men were "perfectly virtuous," competition could be dispensed with and industry could be governed by some ideal form of cooperation. But since they were not, competition must continue to be the dominant form of the economy. It would be the height of irresponsibility to ignore the "imperfections which still cling to human nature." So long as those imperfections persisted, it would be irresponsible to decry competition in principle or to depreciate it in practice. Given the current state of human nature, the question had to be asked whether, in any particular situation, "the restraint of competition would not be more anti-social in its working than the competition itself."[34]

ETHICS LED Marshall to economics, and economics to the study of poverty. "I have devoted myself for the last twenty-five years," he informed the Royal Commission on the Aged Poor in 1893, "to the problem of poverty, and very little of my work has been devoted to any inquiry which does not bear upon that."[35] The remark seems suspiciously tailored to the occasion. Yet similar statements appear throughout his work and cannot be easily discounted. Early in his career, before he finally settled upon economics, he took to roaming the streets of the poorest quarters of whatever city he happened to be in, "looking at the faces of the poorest people."[36]* It was then that he resolved to dedicate himself to the

---

* Jevons recalled the same experience as the inspiration for his study of economics. He was a student of chemistry and botany in the early 1850s when he started to walk through the poorest sections of London. To guide him through those unfamiliar streets he purchased Henry Mayhew's *London Labour and the London Poor* (which had just appeared in a two-volume edition)—"the only book I know of," he wrote in his journal, "to learn a little about the real condition of the poor in London."[37] His first book, written after he moved to Australia, was a comparison of London and Sydney; one of the chapters, "Social Cesspools of Sydney," echoed Mayhew's account of the slums of London.

One wonders whether A. C. Pigou, Marshall's successor at Cambridge, had Marshall or Jevons in mind when he said, in his inaugural lecture: "I shall be glad if a man comes to Economics because he has been interested by Professor Edgeworth's Mathematical Physics or Dr. Fisher's Appreciation and Interest: just as I shall be glad if he comes to it because he is looking forward to business and wishes to learn something of the broader aspects of his future career; but I shall be far more glad if he comes

study of political economy in the hope of answering two questions "which we cannot think too much about":

> The first is, Is it necessary that, while there is so much wealth, there should be so much want? The second is, Is there not a great fund of conscientiousness and unselfishness latent in the breasts of men, both rich and poor, which could be called out if the problems of life were set before them in the right way, and which would cause misery and poverty rapidly to diminish?[39]

Unlike the other *Principles of Political Economy* written by his predecessors (and unlike Marx's *Das Kapital* as well), Marshall's *Principles* opens with the subject of poverty. After defining economics as principally concerned with the "material requisites of wellbeing," it goes on to define poverty as a state of "physical, mental, and moral ill-health." "Ill-health," Marshall conceded, was no doubt due to other causes than poverty; "but this is the chief cause." Thus "the study of the causes of poverty is the study of the causes of the degradation of a large part of mankind."[40] If the bulk of the *Principles* is not explicitly devoted to the subject of poverty, it is so implicitly, in the sense that for Marshall, as for Smith, the study of wealth is crucial to the study of poverty, the state of the economy being the most important determinant of the extent of poverty, and economic growth the most important remedy for poverty.

It is not surprising that Marshall's views of the poor should have been remarkably similar to Booth's, but it is interesting that Marshall should have arrived at those views independently of Booth. The *Principles* was published in 1890, the year after the first volume of *Life and Labour of the People in London* (and three years after Booth's first paper, which Marshall had commented on).[41] But most of it had been thought out long before, and the actual writing was well under way by 1885, before Booth had started his research. By that time too Marshall had delivered the lectures and published the articles upon which his reputation was based. Among these was an essay written in 1884 and a talk delivered the following year in which Marshall anticipated the hue and cry about "urban degeneration" that was to be provoked by the Boer War fifteen years later. He also anticipated not only Booth's account of class B but his proposal regarding that class.

---

because he has walked through the slums of London and is stirred to make some effort to help his fellow men. Wonder, Carlyle said, is the beginning of philosophy: social enthusiasm, one might add, is the beginning of economic science."[38]

Marshall's "residuum" or "surplus population" corresponded to Booth's class B. It consisted of those with "a poor physique and a feeble will, with no enterprise, no courage, no hope, and scarcely any self-respect." Like Booth, Marshall suspected that this class had a "hereditary taint," a "taint of vice" that was passed down from generation to generation. The "descendants of the dissolute" were naturally weak, and were weakened further by the corrupting atmosphere of the large towns where they tended to congregate. To remove them from that environment and to break that hereditary pattern, Marshall proposed establishing a colony "well beyond the range of London smoke," where they could be adequately housed and gainfully employed. The poor might resist this move; having always lived in the shadows of a London court they might shrink from the sunshine and greenery of the country. But with gentle persuasion and in the company of neighbors and friends, they could be prevailed upon to settle in the colony and create new lives for themselves and their children. Marshall (again like Booth) was convinced that this plan would benefit not only the lowest class of the poor who would be removed to a more salutary environment but also the "industrious" poor who would remain in London. Indeed the latter would be the main beneficiaries, for they would be relieved of the pressure of a class that depressed their wages, drove up their rents, took up jobs and space that they could better occupy, and had a deleterious effect upon the "average physique and the average morality of the coming English generation."[42]

One historian interprets Marshall's account of the residuum as evidence of his belief that "the evil to be combated was not poverty but pauperism."[43] In fact, Marshall went out of his way to demonstrate exactly the opposite proposition: that it was no longer pauperism but poverty that was the main problem. "The problem of poverty," he opened his statement to the Royal Commission in 1893, "is changing its character." Toward the end he summed up that change: "While the problem of 1834 was the problem of pauperism, the problem of 1893 is the problem of poverty."[44] Before 1834 the old poor law had aggravated the problem of pauperism by depressing wages, encouraging the growth of population, promoting political instability and administrative folly, and in general contributing to the "degradation of the labourers." The New Poor Law of 1834 corrected some of these faults by instituting one important principle that was still valid: the principle of "less-eligibility" requiring that the recipient of relief be no better off than the independent laborer. Other features of that law were only of temporary expediency: the provision that relief be given only to the destitute and that the test of destitution be the

willingness to enter the workhouse. At a time when the independent
laborer often had not enough food for bare subsistence, destitution had
been a proper qualification for relief. By 1893, however, when the purchasing power of the ordinary laborer had increased three- to fivefold, the
old kind of destitution no longer existed even among the very poor.*
Without violating the principle of less-eligibility, it was now possible to
give relief to those in "distress" rather than actual destitution. Thus the
destitution and workhouse principles could be abandoned, not only for
the aged poor but for all the poor.[46]

Among the other changes that had occurred since 1834, Marshall
cited the change in economic theory itself. He had earlier criticized the
old political economy for failing to appreciate the human realities of
working-class life; regarding labor as a commodity, it made no allowance
for the passions and habits, the sympathies and antipathies, the class
antagonism and class adhesiveness of the workers.[47] Now he repeated
and expanded upon this charge. The old idea that taxing the rich and
distributing the money to the poor would result in an increase in the
numbers of the poor and a decrease in their wages, thus leaving the poor
no better off than they had been before, may have been true in the early
part of the century, given the state of the economy and the condition of
the working classes at that time. But the present situation called for a new
theory explaining that money could be given to the poor in such a way as
to raise the wages and standard of living of the working classes as well as
increase the earning power of the next generation of workers. Unfortunately, Marshall observed (with obvious reference to some of the leaders
of the Charity Organisation Society), this new view had not yet penetrated all circles. "It seems to me that whenever I read the Poor Law
literature of today I am taken back to the beginning of the century;
everything that is said about economics has the flavour of that old time."[48]

The new times required not only a more "sympathetic" attitude toward poverty, but also a more "democratic" attitude, a willingness to
involve the working classes themselves in the administration of relief.[49]
This too had a historical justification. In 1834 there had not been a
"working class intelligence" capable of administering its own affairs.

---

* Ten years earlier Marshall had made a large point of this improvement in his
lectures on Henry George. Refuting George's claim that the gap between the working
classes and middle classes was growing, Marshall argued that only the "lowest stratum" of the working classes was being pushed downward, and that that class was far
smaller than it had ever been—less than half the size, in proportion to the population,
than earlier in the century. As for the working classes as a whole, their purchasing
power was about three times what it had been.[45]

Since then, and most dramatically in the previous twenty years (a reference to the Education Act of 1870), the working classes had acquired a knowledge and capacity that made the old "oligarchic" administration obsolete. They also had the incentive for more active participation because it was in their interest to promote a discriminating system of relief—one that would help the deserving poor while applying "all needful discipline to the undeserving, the reckless and the profligate."[50]

IN THE COURSE of his testimony before the Royal Commission on the Aged Poor, Marshall uttered one sentence that would have been banal if it had come from a socialist but was most remarkable coming from a "neoclassical" economist. Explaining his reservations about some pension proposals, he said that he was afraid they would perpetuate themselves after the need for them passed. "I should regard all this problem of poverty as a mere passing evil in the progress of man upwards; and I should not like any institution started which did not contain in itself the causes which would make it shrivel up, as the causes of poverty itself shrivelled up."[51]

This was not the only occasion when Marshall entertained the prospect of the elimination of poverty. In the opening pages of the *Principles,* he went so far as to question whether there need be any "so called 'lower classes' "—that is, "whether there need be large numbers of people doomed from their birth to hard work in order to provide for others the requisites of a refined and cultured life; while they themselves are prevented by their poverty and toil from having any share or part in that life." As history had led to a diminution of pauperism, so it would lead to a diminution and eventual elimination of poverty. The rise of wages, the spread of education, the use of the steam engine instead of brute human labor, the increase of skilled work in proportion to unskilled, the advance of communication by means of railways and the printing press—all of this had already altered the nature and relation of the classes. Indeed a great part of the artisan class no longer belonged to the "lower classes" as that term was originally understood; some had attained a more "refined and noble" life than had been the privilege of the majority of the upper classes only a century ago. This progress in the condition of the working classes, accompanied by the growing "earnestness of the age" (a moral earnestness, or social consciousness), made it possible to contemplate a future in which poverty and ignorance would be extinguished and thus the lower classes would cease to exist.[52]

The extinction of the lower classes (or "working classes," as Marshall elsewhere said) did not imply that everyone would be in a state of equality; he had no expectation of that or even inclination for it. It did mean that no one would be in a state of degradation. This required the elimination not only of poverty but of the kind of work that was inherently degrading—"hard corporeal" work, "excessive" work, work that made "producing machines" of workers, leaving them "with bodies exhausted and with minds dull and sluggish." Equally degrading was the supposedly "light work" of needlewomen, who toiled endless hours without respite until their hearts and minds were as benumbed as their hands.[53] The abolition of these kinds of work would mean the abolition of the working classes in the invidious sense of that term. "In so far as the working classes are men who have such excessive work to do, in so far will the working classes have been abolished."[54]

This image of the degraded, dehumanized worker recalls the famous "immiseration" passage, as it has been called, in Smith's *Wealth of Nations*—a passage all the more shocking because it was so at variance with the general tone of the book. Smith described the "stupefying" effects of the division of labor upon the factory worker who spent his entire working life performing a few simple operations requiring no exercise of intelligence or imagination.

> He naturally loses, therefore, the habit of such exertion, and generally becomes as stupid and ignorant as it is possible for a human creature to become. The torpor of his mind renders him, not only incapable of relishing or bearing a part in any rational conversation, but of conceiving any generous, noble, or tender sentiment, and consequently of forming any just judgment concerning many even of the ordinary duties of private life.[55]

Marshall's "immiseration" scene provides an interesting contrast to Smith's. Smith's worker was dehumanized by the simple, mindless, effortless work in a factory. Marshall's worker was dehumanized by long hours of physically arduous labor. For Smith the only remedy was education, an education that would restore the intelligence and humanity that was being destroyed by the division of labor. For Marshall the remedy was the machinery that made possible the division of labor, thus relieving the worker of those long hours of backbreaking, mind-numbing, degrading labor. Marshall did not explicitly refute Smith, but he did so implicitly, when he said that the use of machinery increased the proportion of skilled to unskilled labor and of mental to manual work, and reduced both the expenditure of physical energy and the time spent on monotonous tasks. Thus the modern weaver, managing several looms simultaneously, was engaged in more skilled, less monotonous work than the old-fashioned weaver plying his single loom. Moreover, the social life around the factory was stimulating, so that even those workers who seemed to be engaged in the most monotonous operations displayed "considerable intelligence and mental resource."[56]

It was in this sense, as a result of the progress of skilled industry and the elimination of arduous labor, that Marshall looked forward to the "abolition" of the "working classes." This did not mean that men would cease to be workers; work itself, proper work, was "the healthy exercise of the faculties." But they would become workers who had the opportunity and the motive to stimulate their "higher energies" and "higher nature." This, in turn, would result in a momentous change in the relationship of the classes. "The question is not whether all men will ultimately be equal—that they certainly will not—but whether progress may not go on steadily if slowly, till the official distinction between working man and gentleman has passed away; till, by occupation at least, every man is a gentleman. I hold that it may, and that it will."[57]

One has to remind oneself that this was the economist Marshall, not the novelist Trollope, who spoke of the "working man" as, at least potentially, a "gentleman." Or perhaps it was the economist-cum-moral philosopher. For Marshall went on to say that the distinguishing mark of the working man, as opposed to the gentleman, was not the fact that he worked; the rich man, insofar as he was a "true man," did that. Nor the fact that he worked with his hands; the sculptor did that. Nor the fact that he was paid for his labor and had to obey his superiors; the army officer did that. Nor the fact that he was paid to perform disagreeable duties; the surgeon did that. Nor even the fact that he worked hard for little pay; the governess did that. The distinctive fact was the effect of his work upon him.

> If a man's daily task tends to give culture and refinement to his character, do we not, however coarse the individual man may happen to be, say that his occupation is that of a gentleman? If a man's daily task tends to keep his character rude and coarse, do we not, however truly refined the individual man may happen to be, say that he belongs to the working classes?[58]

IF "GENTLEMAN" was an unfamiliar word in the lexicon of economists, "chivalry" was positively bizarre. Marshall used both words often, and not rhetorically but in all seriousness. In an advanced and enlightened society, he believed, workers would be gentlemen, and gentlemen would be chivalrous. He first broached the idea as early as 1885 and he alluded to it repeatedly in his later lectures and essays.[59] In the final pages of the *Principles,* deploring the "anti-social strategy" of financial speculation and manipulation, he spoke of the "social possibilities of economic chivalry" as a curb on these and other evils of the present system. Economic chivalry, expressing the devotion of the rich to the public welfare, would help turn "the resources of the rich to high account in the service of the poor," thus removing "the worst evils of poverty from the land."[60]

The theme was developed more fully in "The Social Possibilities of Economic Chivalry," a title that must have looked strange in the pages of the *Economic Journal.* * Just as medieval chivalry, Marshall argued, had mitigated the horrors of warfare, so economic chivalry would mitigate the evils of commercial competition. As medieval chivalry had elicited an unselfish loyalty to prince or country, so economic chivalry would cultivate a spirit of public service. And as knightly chivalry put a man's courage and endurance to the test, so economic chivalry would take "delight in doing noble and difficult things because they are noble and difficult." Indeed there was already much "latent chivalry" in business; this was one of the symptoms of evolutionary progress. Unfortunately there was also "much getting of wealth that is not chivalrous, and much expenditure that has no

---

* There were earlier usages of "chivalry" in this sense, although none as elaborate as Marshall's. Thomas Carlyle spoke of the "Chivalry of Labour," that exalted sense of work which gave it a spiritual, indeed a divine, character, and which would ultimately inspire the "Master-Worker" (the employer) to give his employees a "permanent interest" in their joint enterprise. Perhaps inspired by him, the Christian Socialist Gerald Massey wrote a poem entitled "Chivalry of Labour." In a speech on sanitary reform, the Christian Socialist leader Charles Kingsley called on everyone to become a "knight-errant or lady-errant," devoted to the chivalrous work of alleviating the misery of the poor, a work "just as chivalrous as if you lived in any old fairy land, such as Spenser talked of in his 'Faerie Queen.' "[61]

Comte (who shared Carlyle's reverence for the "Captain of Industry") devised an "Order of Chivalry" for those industrialists and propertied men who demonstrated a special concern for the poor and unprivileged. Later still, William Booth quoted the passage from Carlyle, explaining that it had been brought to his attention by a friend who was struck by the similarity to Booth's views. Marshall himself did not cite this passage, but he did praise Carlyle and Ruskin for their "splendid teachings . . . as to the right aims of human endeavour and the right uses of wealth," at the same time deploring their assumption that economics dealt only with the "selfish desire for wealth" or that it "inculcated a policy of sordid selfishness."[62]

touch of nobility." Economists studying the behavior of businessmen would be able to distinguish the chivalrous and noble from the selfish and ignoble. They would then impart that knowledge to the public, and public opinion would take it upon itself to act as an "informal Court of Honour," paying homage to the high-minded, public-spirited businessman and discrediting the vulgar, self-serving one. Wealth acquired by "chicanery" would then no longer be a "passport to social success," and a business enterprise, even if it did not produce great wealth, would be esteemed so long as it was honorable in its aims and methods.[63]

If Marshall's metaphor was in some respects inapt—surely it was not the medieval ethic but the Puritan ethic that believed that the inheritance of great wealth was bad for the character and that a noble spirit was seldom formed without the "pains of some self-compulsion and some self-repression"[64]—it did dramatically express his revulsion against the utilitarianism that he saw exemplified in orthodox economics as well as in socialism. It is interesting that he chose to repeat, in the final paragraph of his last book, the remarks he had made almost four decades earlier:

> The age of chivalry is not over: we are learning how dependent the possibilities of leading a noble life are on physical and moral surroundings. However great may be our distrust of forcible socialism, we are rapidly getting to feel that no one can lay his head on his pillow at peace with himself, who is not giving something of his time and his substance to diminish the number of the outcasts of society; and to increase yet further the number of those who can earn a reasonable income, and thus have the opportunity of living a noble life.[65]

It comes as no surprise to find Marshall aligning himself with the "optimists" in the perennial debate over the effects of industrialism. He was, in fact, more of an optimist than Smith, because he saw not only the progressive effects of the increased wealth of the nation upon the working classes but also the progressive effects of the division of labor itself. He also saw the progressive possibilities in social legislation—measures designed to enhance rather than undermine the system of free enterprise. Thus he advocated maximum hours of work, especially for manual workers; minimum wages (one level for men, another for women, preferably adjusted to the family income); higher taxes on unearned income (such as land) than on earned income; the expenditure by the government of a large sum of money (comparable to that spent on the Boer War) to improve the environment and reduce pollution; old age pensions (for the working classes alone); profit-sharing plans; cooperatives; and above all, the expansion of the system of education. He was less well disposed to trade unions, suspecting some of them of operating against the public interest.[66]

On the subject of education Marshall went well beyond most of the reformers of his time, for he favored not only compulsory education but nonutilitarian, nonvocational education. The children of the working classes, he insisted, as much as the children of the middle classes, had need of a "truly liberal general education." Even the technical part of their education should go beyond the teaching of manual dexterity and a knowledge of machinery, which could be acquired on the job; what might more profitably be taught were "artistic skills and knowledge, and methods of investigation." More important was the kind of liberal education that would develop the children's intellectual faculties, character, and culture—in short, their "higher nature." This kind of education could only be provided by the state, and for this worthy purpose "public money must flow freely."[67]

MUCH HAS BEEN made of Alfred Marshall's sympathy for socialism, especially in his early years.[68] He himself recalled that his favorable view of socialism was "fortified" in 1879 by his reading of Mill's essays on socialism. But even then, the writings of the socialists repelled him almost as much as they attracted him, because they were so "far out of touch with realities."[69] He later came to believe that it was "more important to dwell on the truths in Mill's *On Liberty* than those in his *Essays on Socialism*."[70] (In fact, the two were not as different as this suggests.) He also conceded that by the lax definition of socialism prevalent at the time, he might still be regarded as a socialist. "We are told sometimes that everyone who strenuously endeavours to promote the social amelioration of the people is a Socialist—at all events, if he believes that much of this work can be better performed by the State than by individual effort." In that sense of the word, he said (and only in that sense), nearly every economist of his generation was a socialist; he himself had been one before he knew anything of economics, and he became an ever more convinced one.[71]

In any more rigorous sense, however, Marshall was never a socialist, even in his early years, still less later. By the time the *Principles* appeared, socialism (or "collectivism") seemed to him to be productive of far more evil than good. It was likely to "deaden the energies of mankind, and arrest economic progress," to "destroy much that is most beautiful and joyful in the private and domestic relations of life," and to give rise to all the dangers inherent in any "sudden and violent reorganization of the economic, social and political conditions of life."[72] In an essay written the same year, he repudiated socialism together with orthodox laissez-faireism—the latter because of "the cruelty and waste of irresponsible competition and the licentious use of wealth"; the former because of "the tyranny and the spiritual death of an ironbound socialism."[73] The chief dangers of socialism, he wrote in the *Times,* came not from the desire for a more equal distribution of income—"for I can see no harm in that"—but from "the sterilizing influences on those mental activities which have gradually raised the world from barbarism."[74] Although in later years he professed to admire the socialists for their devotion to "social well-being" and conceded that their efforts might be temporarily beneficial, he was more than ever critical of their practical goals and long-term effects. Nor did he intend "economic chivalry" as a euphemism for "socialism." On the contrary, the essay in which he developed that concept was a critique of socialism. Socialism (or collectivism), he argued, would be as fatal to a "chivalric" economy as to an unremittingly competitive one.

> The pressure of bureaucratic methods would impair not only the springs of material wealth, but also many of those higher qualities of human nature, the strengthening of which should be the chief aim of social endeavour.
>
> The world under free enterprise will fall far short of the finest ideals until economic chivalry is developed. But until it is developed, every great step in the direction of collectivism is a grave menace to the maintenance even of our present moderate rate of progress.[75]

In one respect Marshall retained a lingering sympathy with socialism—not with its policies or theories or practical consequences, but with its vision of human nature. And not with its vision of human perfectibility; this had no historic or scientific warrant and could only encourage actions that were "always insufficient and not seldom pernicious."[76] But buried among the "wild rhapsodies" of the socialists was an appreciation of the "hidden springs of human nature." It was this sense of the depths of human nature that "business-like economists" lacked and that they could profitably learn from the socialists.[77]

LIKE SMITH'S *Wealth of Nations,* Marshall's *Principles of Economics* was immediately hailed as a major intellectual event. The two books had a curiously similar history. Each was long in the making and long awaited, with the expectation that it would become an instant classic. And each, in spite of its formidable subject matter and length, was recognized as an important public event, of interest to laymen as much as to professionals. Marshall's reviewers ranked him with the giants of economic thought, a worthy successor to Smith, Ricardo, Marx, and especially Mill, whose *Principles of Political Economy* had been the reigning classic and which was now thought to be superseded by Marshall's work.

Marshall, the reviewers agreed, gave a new, even a revolutionary, direction to economics. The old "dismal science" had finally been humanized. Political economy, once notorious for its "hard and stony heart," was now "as full of pity as it was formerly believed to be devoid of it."[78] The *Manchester Guardian,* recalling Coleridge's warning that political economy would "dig up the charcoal foundations of the temple of Ephesus to burn as fuel for a steam engine," was relieved to find that the new political economy would do no such thing.[79] Even some of the socialists were impressed by it. Sidney Webb, who said that he read it (all six hundred pages) in a single sitting, pronounced it a "great" book although not radically new. "Economics," he reported to Beatrice Potter, "has still to be remade"; either she would have to help him do it or he would have to help her.[80] After a more careful reading for purposes of a review, he decided that it was an excellent book and that it cut the ground out from under him; he was not sure he had enough left to fill his own book.[81] His review, respectful but not overly enthusiastic, commended Marshall for treating economics as the science of "social life" as well as the science of wealth.[82]

The reviews also agreed that Marshall's great achievement was to humanize economics without sacrificing its scientific character. The *Athenaeum* praised him for retaining his "sharp mathematical accuracy" while "sharing to the full the most enthusiastic reformers' sympathy with distress."[83] The *Times* took the occasion to remind its readers that the ethical aspect of economics was not the whole of it; there was a technical and scientific aspect that was no less important. Marshall's book was a "masterly treatment of human action and motive in their bearing on economic problems," but its purpose and emphasis were purely scientific. "It recognized, in fact, that the 'Laws of Economics' are statements of tendencies expressed in the indicative mood, and not ethical precepts in the imperative."[84] Even the *Pall Mall Gazette,* despising the old political economy (which had begun to "stink in the nostrils of so many earnest men"), warned its readers that there was "a strict limit to the extent to which these trespassing 'ethical forces' are to be allowed on scientific preserves." The reviewer told the story, perhaps apocryphal, of Marshall being asked what he thought of the proposal to construct "a Christian Science of Economics," to which he replied: "I have no objection, if they will first construct a Christian Chemistry, a moral Euclid, or an altruistic algebra."[85]

For those who still adhered to the principles of laissez-faire, this anecdote dramatized the basic flaw in Marshall's work. In trying to make ethics the handmaiden of economics, they protested, he was trying to construct something like a "Christian Science of Economics," which was neither good economics nor good ethics.[86] This was, however, a distinctly minority point of view. It is interesting how little serious criticism there was, either from the "old economists" (as Marshall called them) or from the new socialists.[87] The reception of the *Principles* was overwhelmingly favorable, on the part of professionals as well as laymen. And it was accepted, for the most part, at face value, as an economic theory that was at the same time scientific and ethical.

One historian has argued that Marshall was respected, among economists at any rate, not because of but in spite of his ethical professions. "It is remarkable how consistently his persistent moralizing has been ignored and yet how undeviating has been the attachment of economists to the analytical intricacies of his extraordinary engine of analysis." And they ignored not only his ethical principles but the practical policies that flowed from them. The paradoxical effect was that they used his economic theory to buttress the old laissez-faire policies. "The precision and thoroughness of his formal analysis completely obliterated the insistences of his explicit policy conclusions. All that was remembered was the implicit message: *laissez faire*."[88]

If this does describe some of the later academic literature on Marshall, it hardly does justice to those notable economists who were acutely aware both of Marshall's ethical and social principles and of the extent to which his economic theory itself undermined laissez-faire. Keynes cited approvingly Edgeworth's comment that the "great philosophical importance" of Marshall's theory was his proof that "laissez-faire breaks down in certain conditions *theoretically* and not merely practically, regarded as a principle of maximum social advantage."[89] This judgment was echoed by Schumpeter, who had no high regard for Marshall's ethical concerns (his conception of the "Noble Life," Schumpeter said, was modeled on "the typical life of a Cambridge professor"), but who credited him with being "the first theorist to prove *theoretically* that laissez-faire, even with perfect competition and independently of those evils of inequality, did not assure a maximum of welfare to society as a whole." That theoretical proof, Schumpeter added, was reinforced by some of his practical proposals (regarding taxation, for example) which were a significant "breach" in the old wall of laissez-faire.[90]

Whatever the subsequent reputation of Marshallian economics, there is no doubt that in his own time—in the "Marshallian Age" dating from his accession to the chair of political economy at Cambridge in 1885 and extending well beyond his death in 1924—Marshall dominated economic thought precisely because he seemed to integrate economics and ethics into a single discipline. Perhaps John Maynard Keynes was so appreciative of him (he pronounced him the "first great economist *pur sang*") because his father was one of Marshall's devoted disciples.[91] It was John Neville Keynes who wrote, in 1893, that while in the past a certain school of economists tried to solve practical economic questions "without adequate recognition of their ethical aspects," there was now "no such tendency discernible amongst economists who have any claim to speak with authority."[92] In the same year Goschen, in his presidential address to the British Economic Association, complained that the old theory of "economic man" had given away to the equally unreal theory of "ethical man." He attributed that fallacious idea, however, not to Marshall but to the socialists. "If the economic man is a monster, the ethical man, as pictured by the Socialists, is an angel who will not walk upon this terrestrial globe."[93]

MARSHALL IS REPORTED to have said of his own work: "It's all in Adam Smith."[94] In an important sense, this was Marshall's great contribution—to return political economy to the position it had in Smith's time as an essential part of moral philosophy. For Smith, man was a rational being capable of making rational decisions in his own interest; but he was rational because he was a moral and a social being, incorporating in himself the principle of "sympathy" that made him respect the interests of his fellow men as he respected his own interests. By the same token, society was rational and moral. This was implicit in the idea of the "invisible hand," the assumption that the free marketplace, operating naturally and without the intervention of any external force, made the interests of the individual congruent with the general interest. "By pursuing his own interest he [the individual] frequently promotes that of society more effectually than when he really intends to promote it."[95] The same free and natural process ensured the progressive growth of the economy, and this, in turn, brought about the progressive improvement of the lower classes. Thus the interests of the individual were compatible with those of society and the exigencies of economics with the imperatives of morality.

It was Smith's successors, Malthus and Ricardo, who broke the link between individual interest and the general interest, between the wealth of the nation and the welfare of the lower classes—and thus between moral philosophy and political economy.[96] It was they who transformed "economic man" into amoral man (immoral man, their critics charged), and in the process transformed an "optimistic" political economy into a profoundly "pessimistic" one. Where Smith (like Marshall) saw the growth of the population as the precondition for a "progressive" economy and thus the increasing affluence of the entire population, including the poor, Malthus saw it as the inevitable, even fatal, limitation on progress, with especially baneful consequences for the poor. And where Smith envisaged the general interest emerging from the free play of individual interests, Ricardo depicted an economy in which the interests of the landed class were necessarily antagonistic to those of the other classes. What was left of Smith's system of "natural liberty" was a laissez-faire system devoid of any moral justification. This was the truly "pessimistic" effect of Malthusianism and Ricardianism. The poor were not only pauperized; they were "de-moralized," deprived of their moral status as individuals and as members of society. And political economy was similarly "de-moralized," divorced from moral philosophy. It is no accident that Ricardo, not Smith, was the inspiration for Marxism, which sought to illegitimize capitalism as a prelude to overthrowing it.

Marshall restored that original moral dimension to political economy.[97] "It's all in Adam Smith." In fact there was more in Marshall— by way of moral philosophy as well as social policy—than there had been in Smith. The moral basis of political economy, and with it the legitimacy of capitalism, had been so eroded by Smith's successors that Marshall could restore it only by making explicit what had been implicit in Smith. This was most obvious on the practical level of economic policy. Where Smith had relied upon the Invisible Hand to bring about the general interest, Marshall felt obliged to call upon the government to supplement the workings of the Invisible Hand—to supplement it, however, not to supersede it. It was a minimum of intervention that Marshall sought; the hand of government was to be as light and unobtrusive as possible. But that minimum was greater than anything anticipated by Smith. "Let the State be up and doing," Marshall counseled, and at the same time, "Let everyone work with all his might."[98] The message was clear: individuals should do all that they could do, and the government should do what it alone could do efficiently.

It was not only in the realm of public policy that Marshall went beyond Smith; it was also in the realm of morality. Smith's economic man did not have to be told to be moral. He was that naturally, unconsciously, unwittingly; in acting in his own interests he promoted "an end which was no part of his intention."[99] Marshall's economic man had to be reminded to be moral, enjoined to pursue the good of others and act in accord with his "higher nature." And Marshall had a more elevated view of that "higher nature." All that was expected or required of Smith's economic man was "sympathy"; Marshall's economic man was called upon to exercise the more arduous virtues of "duty" and "chivalry." That higher nature, moreover, intruded into large areas of Marshall's economics. He argued in favor of higher wages, for example, on the ground that they encouraged those of firm character to work harder and to aspire to "higher aims than work for material gain."[100] Similarly he defended shorter hours of labor even if they led to lower wages and a smaller national dividend, provided that the loss of income "could be met exclusively by the abandonment by all classes of the least worthy methods of consumption; and that they could learn to spend leisure well."[101] He was more censorious than Smith of the way both rich and poor spent their time and money. An increase of working-class income, he said, contributed to the "fulness and nobility of human life" so long as it was used primarily for the satisfaction of "real wants," but not if it was expended in the kinds of display and luxury that were all too common among the well-to-do. Conversely, a "wisely ordered magnificence" on the part of the rich was commendable if it was free of personal vanity and used for such "true and worthy" purposes as the public welfare and culture. "The world would go much better if everyone would buy fewer and simpler things, and would take trouble in selecting them for their real beauty."[102] And the country as a whole would be much benefited by "the subordination of the desire for transient luxuries."[103]

Marshall did not propose to enforce these moral strictures by legislation; sumptuary laws, he recognized, were futile. But neither did he intend these judgments, as one historian has suggested, to be mere obiter dicta, personal asides or digressions with no real bearing upon his theory.[104] While he did not seek to legislate morality, he did count upon the "moral sentiment of the community" to achieve that purpose.[105] And he assumed that such a moral, communal sentiment would come in the wake of the ethical progress that was an inevitable concomitant of economic progress. Talcott Parsons, comparing Max Weber to Marshall, praised Weber for being immune from any "surreptitious teleology."[106] This was not meant to imply that Marshall's was a surreptitious teleology; Smith's was that. Marshall's was a deliberate, overt teleology—a teleology only once removed from a theodicy. One is reminded that Marshall came from a family of clerics, and that his father, although not a clergyman himself, was an ardent Evangelical who dearly wanted his son to become an Evangelical minister. Instead the son became an agnostic in religion and an evangelical in economics.[107]

IF MARSHALL was more of a moralist than Smith, he was only a little less of an individualist. Neoclassical economics "moralized" both society and political economy: society by making the public good an end in itself rather than the product of an Invisible Hand; and political economy by recognizing the role of economics as well as law in promoting the public good. But it tried to do both while retaining the moral integrity and primacy of individuals—the responsibility of individuals for their own lives as well as their responsibility for each other.

This was the crucial difference between socialism and the new economics. The socialists "moralized" society at the expense, so to speak, of the individual. Socialism, Marshall said, was "a movement for taking the responsibility for a man's life and work, as far as possible, off his shoulders and putting it on to the State."[108] Socialism made the state responsible for the conduct of social and economic affairs, because it held society to be responsible for poverty, unemployment, bad housing, even drunkenness and immorality. As society was the cause of these evils, it was also (through its instrument, the state) the remedy for these evils. Thus the individual, having been the passive victim of the old system, was to be the passive beneficiary of the new.

To a later generation, Marshall's "new economics" as he called it— "neoclassical economics" as it is now known—is sometimes seen as a *via media,* a bridge between laissez-faireism and socialism, a feeble and finally untenable attempt to reconcile the irreconcilable. To Marshall and a good many of his generation, it was a plausible and rational system in its own right, a recognition of a reality that was an inextricable compound of the economic and the moral, the individual and the social. By affirming the principle of a free, competitive economy and at the same time providing significant exceptions to that principle, by seeing individuals as free and independent moral agents fulfilling their own "higher natures" by promoting the general good, Marshall sought to reaffirm the moral character of the individual as well as the moral nature of society.

From this perspective Marshall's new economics appears as a corollary of Green's positive liberalism—and as a practical alternative to socialism.

Economic Ideology and Economic Reality

A PROVOCATIVE ESSAY by Calvin Woodard provides an alternative explanation for the emergence of neoclassical and, later, welfare economics.[109] On this hypothesis the new economics represented the accommodation of economic ideology to economic reality. The shift from laissez-faire to a welfare state was related to the shift from an economy of scarcity to an economy of abundance. In the early industrial period (the "takeoff" stage, as it has been called), when the economy was incapable of significantly ameliorating poverty, poverty was viewed as an inevitable condition of life, and the only forms of relief available were those grudgingly provided by the parish or by private charity. Since the economy then required a high level of production, political economy gave priority to production over consumption, and society made much of the moral character of the individual and of the virtues conducive to productivity— temperance, diligence, thrift. Later, as industrialism "matured" and the productive capacity increased, a high level of consumption became more important than a high level of production. It then became possible to withdraw people from the labor market by raising the age of child labor and reducing the number of hours worked by adults. It was also feasible to relieve poverty through the instrument of the state and without any moral stigma, and to define poverty in terms of impersonal economic forces rather than the moral failings of the individual.

This is an intriguing and plausible theory, and it may at least in part explain the shift from the old to the new economics. But it does not explain the whole of that shift or take into account important aspects of both the old and the new economics. It makes no mention, for example, of those theories early in the century which put great emphasis on consumption—Say's theory, for example, according to which supply creates its own demand and demand itself is infinitely expandable; or, earlier still, aspects of Smith's theory which anticipated Say's Law, such as the idea that "consumption is the sole end and purpose of all production."[110] Nor does it account for those influential thinkers later in the century—Green, Toynbee, Marshall, Booth, even the Webbs—who were so insistent upon the moral character of individuals, so suspicious of luxury and excessive or undesirable consumption, so appreciative of the virtues of abstinence, temperance, prudence, responsibility. Ideology and reality have, in fact, a more complicated, less deterministic relationship than this theory suggests.[111]

Book Five

"WE ARE ALL
SOCIALISTS NOW"

"We Are All Socialists Now"

"WE ARE ALL socialists now." The remark was reputedly made in 1888 by Sir William Harcourt, a prominent Liberal Member of Parliament.[1] By 1895 that sentiment had become so commonplace that it was echoed, perhaps cynically, by the Prince of Wales.[2]

By the commonly accepted definition of socialism today, and even by that of some socialists at the time, the statement was, of course, not true. Even by the laxer standards of the time it was not literally true. Certainly it did not apply to Herbert Spencer, A. V. Dicey, Helen Bosanquet, W. H. Mallock, G. J. Goschen, Henry Maine, the Duke of Argyll, the members of the Liberty and Property League, and all the others who resisted any suspicion of socialism, any deviation from the old school of political economy. They did so, however, knowing that they were fighting a losing battle. In 1885, after the publication of his testament of individualism, *The Man Versus the State,* Spencer told Andrew Carnegie that he was giving up political writing. "The wave of opinion carrying us toward Socialism and utter subordination of the individual is becoming irresistible."[3]

If socialism was becoming "irresistible," if "we are all socialists now," it was not only because of the emergence, within a few years, of the single-tax and land nationalization movements, the Social Democratic Federation, the Socialist League, the Fabian Society, and assorted religious socialist groups. It was also because the word "socialism" was used in the most latitudinarian sense to connote any social reform, any act of state intervention, any degree of "collectivism" (a word that came into currency in the 1880s and that was a common synonym for socialism)— even any concern with the "social problem."* As early as 1882, before

---

* The first example of "collectivism" in the Oxford English Dictionary is from the

any of the socialist groups had been founded, Alfred Milner, then a young journalist in London, gave a talk in Whitechapel which opened: "Socialism has become a word of everyday use, and, like other words of everyday use, it means almost anything according to the context or the degree of education and the bias of the speaker."[5] The following year, inspired by a lecture by William Morris, the *Oxford Magazine* put the question "Is the new Oxford movement to be a Socialistic one?" The answer was yes, the magazine explained, on the understanding that what was meant by socialism was an interest in social questions.[6] Canon Barnett's definition of "practicable socialism" included such measures as the poor law, the education act, the Irish land acts, the housing act, and the libraries act. This was not very different from Sidney Webb's "unconscious socialism," which also included the poor law, education act, and all the other reforms that had already set England, as Webb saw it, on the path to a full-fledged socialism.[7]

It was not for want of a more rigorous definition that contemporaries spoke of socialism so loosely. Thirty years earlier, in what became the standard text of political economy, John Stuart Mill had defined socialism as "any system which requires that the land and the instruments of production should be the property, not of individuals, but of communities or associations, or of the government."[8]* That definition would have satisfied a later generation of Marxists, as well as some critics of socialism. A. J. Balfour, the leader of the Conservative Party, protested against the confusion of social legislation with socialism. Social reform was not only different from socialism, he insisted; it was "its most direct opposite and its most effective antidote."[9] This was not, however, the prevailing view. More often social reform was seen, by socialists and anti-socialists alike, as in a continuum with socialism.

Saturday Review in 1880, where it was defined as the theory that "everything is to be done and managed by a society." A. V. Dicey explained that he used the word as the "antithesis to individualism," a usage that was "etymologically correct" and justified by the "novelty and vagueness of the term."[4]

* Mill distinguished socialism from communism, which, on the Continent at least, usually meant "the entire abolition of private property." In fact, in Mill's time as later in the century, and in England as on the Continent, the two terms were often used interchangeably. If socialism was more common in late-Victorian England, it was because it lent itself to a laxer meaning, "social reform" being often identified with "socialism."

* * *

IT WAS THIS latitudinarian interpretation that made it possible for some politicians to be accused of being socialists and others to lay claim to that title. In 1883, when Lord Salisbury proposed low-interest government loans to subsidize housing for the poor, Joseph Chamberlain publicly criticized that "socialistic" scheme.[10] Two years later Chamberlain issued his own "Unauthorized Programme" advocating reforms in local government, education, landholding, and taxation. It was not a communistic program, his supporters explained: "Communism means the reduction of everything to a dead level, the destruction of private adventure, the paralysis of private industry, the atrophy of private effort." But it could properly be regarded as socialistic. "This will be called Socialism with a vengeance," for it sounds the "death-knell of the laissez-faire system" and continues the "path of legislative progress in England [that] has been for years, and must continue to be, distinctly Socialistic."[11]

Just as social reform was conflated with socialism, so "Tory democracy" was conflated with Tory socialism. When Randolph Churchill spoke of Tory democracy (which he did less often than has been supposed), he generally meant the democratizing of the Conservative Party rather than the adoption of social reforms. But he was not averse to the latter. One of his opponents in the Conservative Party, objecting to his proposal to convert urban leaseholds into freeholds, said that it was "rank Socialism—a policy of plunder and confiscation."[12] In his biography of Churchill, in 1906, Lord Rosebery described him as very nearly equating "Tory Democracy" with "Tory Collectivism," which Rosebery himself equated with socialism.[13] Winston Churchill, in his biography of his father published shortly before, intimated that Randolph Churchill might well have been a true "Tory socialist" had he survived into the twentieth century.[14] (It is curious to find a very different kind of Conservative, Harold Macmillan, declaring half a century later that "Toryism has always been a form of paternal Socialism."[15])

Even Gladstone, who was not, in any sense, a socialist, who remained a Cobdenite at heart, committed to laissez-faire, free trade, and economic government, was sufficiently responsive to the political realities to lend his support to factory and land reforms. To critics like the Duke of Argyll, who accused him of condoning socialism, he replied that he did in fact "deeply deplore" and "radically disapprove" of socialism, but that it was a decided trend in both parties.[16] He gave much the same assurance to Queen Victoria when she urged him to disavow the Chamberlain wing of his party and explain to the electorate "that *liberalism* is *not Socialism* and that *progress* does *not* mean *Revolution*."[17] To Lord Acton he complained about the "demagogism" of the Tory democrats and the doctrine of "construction" (a euphemism for socialism) that was gaining favor in his own party—a policy of "taking into the hands of the state the business of the individual man."[18] Yet Acton himself told Gladstone's daughter that she should be proud to know that her father was the "most illustrious representative in England" and the "most eminent practical teacher in the world" of the school of "academic Socialists." Acton also said, again in praise, that he agreed with Chamberlain that "there is a latent Socialism in the Gladstonian philosophy."[19] (This "latent" or "academic" socialism was very different from the Marxism that Acton condemned as "the worst of all enemies of freedom."[20])*

"WE ARE ALL socialists now." No, not quite. Yet it would be a mistake to dismiss this remark as a bit of rhetorical hyperbole, or to belittle a "socialism" that was so all-embracing. The word was not used lightly and its usage was significant. That so many serious, thoughtful people were prepared to identify themselves as socialists testifies to the gravity of their social concerns; it also suggests that they sensed that something new and momentous was happening, something that, however diffuse and varied, warranted that provocative label.

Their socialism, then, was serious, even if it did not mean what it might be taken to mean today. The common equation of "socialism" with "collectivism" implied not so much a rejection of capitalism (in most cases, it did not imply that at all) as a rejection of laissez-faire. Laissez-faireists, we are often reminded, were never as laissez-faireist in practice as in theory (and perhaps not as much in theory either). The doctrine had always allowed for some measures of social reform—exceptional measures for specified groups in special circumstances (children, women, or men in hazardous industries). What was novel about the reforms of a later generation, reforms regarded as "collectivist," was that they were not excep-

---

* This view of Gladstone as a "latent" socialist is echoed by one historian who finds that in his last administration Gladstone "went a surprisingly long way down the Socialist road," what with the imposition of death duties on landed estates, the establishment of a Labour Department, the expansion of factory regulation and inspection, the provision of an eight-hour day for railwaymen, and the passage of a workmen's compensation act.[21]

tional measures but normal ones, applying to a large part of the population, adults as well as children, men as well as women, in the regular course of their lives.

Collectivism too (like laissez-faire) was less rigorous than it might have been. It was, one might say, a permissive rather than prescriptive principle; it allowed for government intervention when that seemed desirable, but did not mandate any thoroughgoing or systematic involvement of the government. Nor did it imply any commitment to egalitarianism. Nor was it meant to preclude individualism. On the contrary, the avowed purpose of almost all socialists was to institute such reforms as would enable the poor to become more responsible and independent individuals. It was in this sense that so staunch an individualist as Bernard Bosanquet (who managed to combine Hegelian metaphysics with laissez-faire economics) spoke approvingly of "moral socialism." This form of socialism was salutary, he said, because it exposed the evils of egoism, materialism, and Epicureanism, at the same time that it made the public good part of the "moral essence of the individual."[22]

Late-Victorian socialism meant different things to different people. But it was sufficiently meaningful to be applied, at one time or another, to Gladstonians and Disraelians, new radicals and new liberals, land nationalizers and gas-and-water socialists, Christians and Positivists, Marxists and Fabians, members of the Ethical Societies, and others who often used that label for want of another.

CHAPTER 20

Land Nationalization

THE MAN CREDITED by contemporaries with having the greatest influence on English socialism in the 1880s was an American who denied that he was a socialist, indeed who insisted that he was providing the only feasible and just alternative to socialism.[1] And the book that was the vehicle of this influence, not only among middle-class radicals but among large numbers of industrial workers, was a five-hundred-page work of economics on the subject of land.

Progress and Poverty received little attention when it first appeared in America in 1879. It was reprinted in England shortly afterward in a modest edition of a thousand copies under the imprint of an obscure publisher. After its unexpected success abroad, a sixpenny edition was published in England, and within a few years 100,000 copies of this and other cheap editions had been sold.[2] Interest in the book was stimulated by several much publicized lecture tours by the author throughout Britain. By the end of the decade, Henry George was the most prominent and influential radical in a field crowded with competitors, and his "single tax" scheme was the best known of the many plans for radical reform.

It was a good season for reformers, and land reformers in particular. The Irish Land Act had generated much discussion and sympathy; Green and Toynbee were typical of many who urged similar measures for England. Several organizations were devoted exclusively to the issue of land reform. George delivered his first lectures in England under the auspices of the Land Nationalisation Society; his later lectures were sponsored by the Land Reform Union, which included moderate reformers as well as advocates of nationalization. The most notable proponent of land nationalization was Alfred Russel Wallace, better known as the co-discoverer with Charles Darwin of the theory of natural selection. It is ironic that what differentiated George from Wallace, and accounted for George's greater popularity, was the specific mechanism he proposed for carrying out nationalization—much as the distinction and fame of Darwin (and, to a lesser extent, Wallace) came not from the theory of evolution as such but from the particular mechanism that explained the process of evolution. Just as natural selection transformed evolution from a general, speculative notion into a specific, plausible theory, so the "single tax" transformed land nationalization from a revolutionary or utopian ideal into what seemed to be a legal, practical, reasonable reform, no more extreme or fanciful than any other tax measure.*

Some commentators have made much of the fact that the expression "the single tax" did not appear in *Progress and Poverty*. It has been said that George first used it in lectures delivered in 1885, and that it did not become a conspicuous part of the social vocabulary until later in the decade.[4] "A single tax," however (with the indefinite article), appeared at least twice toward the end of *Progress and Poverty* in the section entitled "The Remedy."[5] George left no doubt that such a tax was a crucial part of his plan, and that its purpose was nothing less than the nationalization of the land: *"We must make land common property."*[6] He was equally emphatic about the means to achieve that end. In a succession of italicized propositions he spelled out the logic of his proposal. *"It is not necessary to confiscate land; it is only necessary to confiscate rent."* To confiscate rent all that was required was to *"appropriate rent by taxation."* Once this was done, the government would be able to *"abolish all taxation save that upon land values."*[7] The implication of this sequence of propositions was a single tax on land, which would have the great virtue of nationalizing the land without violating the institution of property as such. It would also enable the state to become the sole proprietor of the land (the "universal landlord") without having to create any new agencies of government or even to expand the existing machinery of administration.

> In this way, the State may become the universal landlord without calling herself so, and without assuming a single new function. In form, the ownership of land would remain just as now. No owner of land need be dispossessed, and no restriction need be placed upon the

---

* There is a further irony in the fact that both Wallace and George, in subscribing to some form of land nationalization, had to repudiate Social Darwinism, which made competition rather than cooperation the principle of social life. Wallace did this explicitly, George implicitly when he attacked Malthusianism for positing an "analogy . . . between the lower forms of life and man."[3]

amount of land any one could hold. For, rent being taken by the State in taxes, land, no matter in whose name it stood, or in what parcels it was held, would be really common property, and every member of the community would participate in the advantage of its ownership.[8]

This seemingly modest proposal would not only solve the land problem; it would solve the industrial problem as well, first by eliminating the "unearned increment" represented by rent which weighed so heavily on the entire economy, and then by eliminating all taxes on industry itself. This was the novelty of George's proposal. Other reformers, including Mill, had recommended specific taxes on land: a capital-gains tax on the sale of land, or inheritance and estate taxes, or a tax on the income from land that owed nothing to the labor or enterprise of the landowner. What George proposed was not a partial tax on this or that aspect of landownership, but a tax equivalent to the total income from land—in effect, a confiscatory tax. And this tax on land would be the sole tax levied on the population, a single tax that precluded the need for any other taxes. The result would benefit everyone (except, of course, the landlord). The seamstress and factory owner, the farmer and merchant, would all be liberated from the burden of taxation that was a deterrent to productive labor and enterprise. Where the existing system of taxation penalized the producer for adding to the general wealth, the single tax would reward him for being industrious and thrifty. The laborer would receive the full value of his labor, the capitalist the full return of his capital, and society the boon of a free and prosperous economy. With the proceeds of this one tax the state would be able to finance all the social services currently provided and whatever others might be thought desirable.

At this point the case for the single tax turned into an argument against socialism. If it made redundant all other taxes, it also obviated the need for the system of "governmental regulation of industry and accumulation" that George saw as a necessary feature of socialism.[9] Society would thus be spared the undesirable consequences of socialism: the substitution of government action for individual action, the attempt to obtain by restriction what could better be secured by freedom, the increased number of government officials, the corresponding growth in the temptations to corruption, the diminution of the incentive to industry, and the demoralization of the public. Socialism was also impractical because it required what no longer existed: a strong religious faith to sustain it. However "grand and noble" the ideal of socialism might be, it could not be artificially manufactured, and any attempt to impose it in the modern world would inevitably result in a "retrogression that would involve anarchy and perhaps barbarism."[10]

The appeal of George's scheme was obvious. It was bold and radical, yet concrete and, so it seemed, practicable. It was compatible with the reformist and socialist temper of the time, while professing to avoid the difficulties and disadvantages of socialism. It promised to achieve a social revolution without the violence of revolution and without strengthening or expanding the powers of the state—indeed by nothing more than an imaginative reconstruction of the existing system of taxation. It promised, in short, to transform society without any of the painful effects usually accompanying such a transformation.

Above all, it had the virtue of simplicity. Like Mill's "one very simple principle" for the protection of liberty, George's single tax purported to be "at once radical and simple," a "simple yet sovereign remedy" for poverty.[11] To a generation distressed by the complexity and intractability of that problem, the prospect of a simple, single solution was obviously seductive. Even so sophisticated a thinker as Lord Acton commended George for his "plain, vigorous directness" and for his prescience in expressing "the ideas of the age that is to come."[12]

Acton's prediction was not borne out. One of the many paradoxes in the history of this subject is the discrepancy between the enormous success of George's book and lectures and the total failure to implement his ideas, then or later. Even when taxes on land did become an important issue in Lloyd George's budget of 1909 (Henry George had died a dozen years earlier), the single tax, or anything remotely approximating it, was never proposed as a serious legislative measure. Lloyd George's budget called for a tax of 20 percent on unearned increment from the sale of land and a halfpenny in the pound on undeveloped land and minerals—a far cry from Henry George's twenty shillings in the pound on all rents. Although single-taxers hailed the budget as a progressive step toward their ultimate goal, the goal itself continued to elude them. The principle of a single, confiscatory tax, which would at the same time nationalize land and make unnecessary all other taxation, remained as remote as the socialist principle of the nationalization of all property.

IT IS NOT REMARKABLE that the single tax on land failed to be adopted, as Acton had expected, in "the age that is to come," or in any age. What is remarkable is that the idea was so popular in the late-Victorian era, at a time when poverty was increasingly identified as an industrial and urban problem rather than an agricultural and rural one, and when the dominant image of class conflict was that of the factory worker versus the capitalist rather than the laborer versus the landlord.* The most dramatic episode in working-class history in this period was not the organization of the National Agricultural Labourers Union in 1872 (which lost momentum almost immediately as a result of the agricultural depression the following year), but the dockers' strike of 1889 and the rise of the "new unionism." Even the agricultural depression, which one might think would focus attention on the rural economy and thus on land reform, did not have this effect, for the worst sufferers of that depression were the landlords themselves, not the laborers.[13]

George anticipated the objection that it was industry rather than land that was at the heart of the social problem. The subtitle of his book described it as an inquiry into the cause of "industrial depressions"—not agricultural depressions. The tax on land, he claimed, would alleviate industrial depressions because it would benefit industry as much as agriculture. His main argument, however, involved a redefinition of the class struggle. "The real parties pitted against each other" were not "labor and capital" but "laborers on the one side and the owners of land on the other." Between labor and capital the struggle was much more equal, for the power of capital to hold out in a strike was only a little greater than that of labor. The landlord, however, could hold out much longer because land, unlike capital, did not go to waste or cease to reproduce when labor was withdrawn.[14]

This argument did not disarm George's critics, who insisted that the single tax, like any land nationalization scheme, was irrelevant to the most urgent issues of the time: business crises, industrial unemployment, and urban housing. Some socialists suspected that the effect of his proposal, and perhaps its intent, was to deflect attention from the real problems of an industrial economy and from the industrial solutions appropriate to them—indeed, from the true nature of the class struggle. The Social Democrats, after initially welcoming George as a fellow traveler in the cause of nationalization, turned against him when it became clear (as it should have been from the beginning) that he did not intend the nationalization of land as a prelude to the nationalization of all property. They

---

* It is also curious that it should have been even more popular in America, where the Homestead Act had been in effect for almost two decades, providing virtually free land for anyone who wanted it.

then accused him of being "the salaried and befeasted lackey of the plundering capitalist class," and they denounced the single tax as a "burden-shifting trick which . . . would benefit the capitalists without helping the workers in the least."[15]

Many radicals, on the other hand, including some socialists, welcomed the single tax as the first stage on the road to a more comprehensive program of nationalization and even social revolution. The theory of unearned increment, one historian has pointed out, was to the Fabians what the theory of surplus value was to the Marxists.[16] Earlier generations of radicals had been introduced to the idea of unearned increment by the classical economist David Ricardo, but George revived it in a form that was more accessible and more adaptable to a radical program. George Bernard Shaw was one of many Fabians to come to socialism by way of "Georgism." He declared himself a convert to George after hearing him lecture and reading his book, and he promptly brought the good word to a meeting of the Democratic Federation, where he tried to persuade Hyndman and the other socialists of the superiority of George to Marx. The only result of this encounter was to provoke Shaw to read Marx and be converted to socialism (although not Marxism). Extrapolating from his own experience, he credited *Progress and Poverty* with having "more to do with the Socialist revival of that period in England than any other book."[17]

H. G. Wells was a schoolboy of fifteen when he came across a sixpenny edition of the book in 1881. He was later surprised to discover that this was the first time he had ever thought about socialism. His reaction to the book was that of a student of science; it seemed to him to be like a "laboratory demonstration" of a theory, an "extremely simplified and plausible story" of the progressive appropriation of land, the unearned increment of rent, and the single tax that would restore that increment to the community. It was an "easy argument to understand" and he was able to "modify and complicate" it for himself; the process, he later reflected, was "like working kindred mathematical problems of progressive complexity under a common Rule."[18] The book also made converts among trade union leaders, many of whom were Georgists before going on to become full-fledged socialists. Keir Hardie read it after attending one of George's lectures and found that it "unlocked many of the industrial and economic difficulties which beset the mind of the worker trying to take an intelligent interest in his own affairs." It also led him, he wryly commented, "much to George's horror in later life when we met personally, into Communism."[19]

The popularity of this idea—land nationalization as a remedy for industrial poverty—suggests that this movement (like some of the socialist movements of the time) reflected a sympathy with reform in general rather than a commitment to this specific reform. It also reflected a desire to promote reform without exacerbating the class struggle. One need not subscribe to the "capitalist lackey" interpretation to recognize that by singling out landlords as the enemy, George in effect exculpated other classes to which that dubious distinction might have been assigned— manufacturers, merchants, financiers, capitalists, property owners of one form or another. Indeed these groups became allies of the working classes in the common struggle against the landlords.

THE THEORY also had the effect of redefining the "social problem," so that it became not so much an economic or class problem as a moral problem. The moral issue was implied in the title *Progress and Poverty*. The disparity between progress and poverty, wealth and want, "the House of Have and the House of Want," was, on the face of it, unjust and immoral.[20]* This was a familiar enough theme, a staple of radical literature for centuries. What distinguished George's book from most specimens of the genre was the presumption that there was a simple economic explanation for this immoral situation and a simple economic remedy for it. Again, this was not the first such panacea. But it came at an especially propitious time, when social sensibilities were heightened and orthodox political economy was too enervated to resist a determined attack. The 1840s had also been a time of social ferment, but then the economic orthodoxy had been too firmly entrenched to be easily subverted. With the diminished authority of the classical economists, the way was open for heretical theories that invoked a new set of economic and ethical principles.

Economics in the service of morality—this was the potent combination that gave *Progress and Poverty* its appeal. And it was all the more

---

* The impassioned rhetoric of the book (and sometimes its plain language) suggested that the poor were getting poorer while the rich were getting richer. Occasionally, mindful of all the statistics to the contrary, George qualified this argument. At the very end of his chapter on wages, he reminded his readers that he was "using the word wages not in the sense of a quantity, but in the sense of a proportion." When he said that "wages fall as rent rises," he did not mean that "the quantity of wealth obtained by laborers as wages is necessarily less, but that the proportion which it bears to the whole produce is necessarily less."[21]

potent because economics, as George presented it, was itself a surrogate for morality. This is why the economic arguments against the single tax, however valid, were largely irrelevant. Arnold Toynbee might protest that it was a "delusive panacea" based upon mistaken facts and a false theory.[22] Or H. M. Hyndman might characterize George as a "sort of intellectual Anarchist who could not look upon production and still less upon exchange from other than the individual point of view."[23] But these objections were beside the point for those who saw the private ownership of land as the symbol of all social injustice. Not private ownership in general—not industrial property or financial capital—but land. For land represented the basic means of subsistence without which life itself was impossible. This was the "one great principle," the "great fundamental fact," upon which George ultimately based his case.

> For land is the habitation of man, the storehouse upon which he must draw for all his needs, the material to which his labor must be applied for the supply of all his desires; for even the products of the sea cannot be taken, the light of the sun enjoyed, or any of the forces of nature utilized, without the use of land or its products. On the land we are born, from it we live, to it we return again—children of the soil as truly as is the blade of grass or the flower of the field. Take away from man all that belongs to land, and he is but a disembodied spirit.[24]

This was the moral rationale of the single tax and the source of its popular strength. It was the time-honored appeal to natural rights. In George's work one hears echoes of Locke: "The measure of property Nature well set, by the extent of men's labour and the conveniency of life."[25] Or Rousseau: " 'You are undone if you once forget that the fruits of the earth belong to us all, and the earth itself to nobody.' "[26]* So too Henry George: "The Almighty, who created the earth for man and man for the earth, has entailed it upon all the generations of the children of men by a decree written upon the constitution of all things—a decree which no human action can bar and no prescription determine."[28]

Shortly before George's death in 1897, J. A. Hobson tried to account

---

* Mill invoked the theory of utility rather than natural right for the same purpose, but with diminished effect. Unlike "moveable goods," he argued, which were created by labor and which others could acquire by their labor, land was neither made by man nor infinitely available. The private property in land is "wholly a question of general expediency," and when it is not expedient, "it is unjust."[27]

for his extraordinary influence in England. It was not, he wrote, the economic theories about the nature of land that impressed George's readers and attracted disciples. It was rather "the spirit of humanitarian and religious appeal" that had a powerful effect upon a large section of "what I may call typical English moralists." Hobson met these "typical moralists" as he himself traveled about the country lecturing on political economy. In almost every community he found "a certain little knot of men of the lower-middle or upper-working class, men of grit and character, largely self-educated, keen citizens, most nonconformists in religion." For these men, who were mainly "free-trading Radical dissenters," land nationalization, taxation of unearned increment, and other radical land reforms rested upon a "plain moral sanction"; the common ownership of the land and equal access to it was a " 'natural right,' essential to individual freedom."[29] This theory of natural right explained both the enthusiasm of the more liberal-minded socialists, who welcomed George's proposal as the first step toward their kind of socialism, and the hostility of the "organized socialists," who were committed not to free trade and individual freedom, still less to the theory of natural right, but to the nationalization of all capital and the regulation of all industry.

"Thus, in the beginning, all the world was America." So Locke envisioned the state of nature when no one possessed more than was necessary for the "conveniences of life."[30] Henry George brought with him to England something of that free, natural, virtuous spirit that America still symbolized—a mythical, aboriginal America of unlimited wilderness and opportunity, before land had been usurped and justice perverted, and before progress had brought with it the unnatural and immoral corollary of poverty. The single tax was conceived in this spirit, as a "simple measure" that was "easy of application" and a "sufficient remedy" for all evils. "It will substitute equality for inequality, plenty for want, justice for injustice, social strength for social weakness, and will open the way to grander and nobler advances of civilization."[31] In fact it led the way back to that primeval time when land was owned in common and when "all the world was America."

CHAPTER 21

Marxism, English Style

FROM THE CONVENTIONAL socialist view—which is to say, the Marxist view—English socialism in this period hardly deserves the name, consisting as it did of Philosophical Idealists, social reformers, religious missionaries, land (and only land) nationalizers, Positivists, cooperativists, Fabians, and gas-and-water socialists, all parading (sometimes reluctantly) under the banner of socialism. There were, to be sure, a group of professed Marxists among them, but even they hardly fit the conventional model. The founder of the Social Democratic Federation was H. M. Hyndman, a wealthy stockbroker and "venture capitalist" (as he would now be called). His habitual attire, at street-corner meetings as in the City, was a frock coat and top hat, and he displayed some of the affectations and prejudices appropriate to that dress. By his own standards (although not Marx's), he was a Marxist, but that did not preclude him from also being a nationalist and imperialist, or, as the occasion arose, from being antiunionist, anti-feminist, and anti-Semitic. William Morris, the founder of the rival Marxist group, the Socialist League, was no less an "oddity," as he described himself.[1] An avowed Marxist, he loathed industrialism quite as much as capitalism, and for aesthetic and moral, more than economic, reasons. When he was in his most Marxist and revolutionary phase, he was derided by Engels as a "sentimental socialist."[2]

A more serious anomaly (again from a Marxist perspective) was the notable failure of Marxism in the country that should have been, according to Marxist doctrine, most hospitable to Marxism. The first industrial nation should have spawned the first popular Marxist movement— indeed, the first successful Marxist revolution. Yet the Marxists, such as they were, were considerably less numerous than the single-taxers and less influential than the Fabians. Marxism itself was an "oddity" in England, a foreign import that never became completely domesticated—like

Marx himself, who lived in London for almost thirty-five years but was almost unknown outside the circle of German émigrés. His death in 1883 was recorded in exactly two English obituaries, one by Hyndman in the *St. James's Gazette,* the other by the Paris correspondent of the *Times,* who spoke of his reputation on the Continent.

Even the *Communist Manifesto,* published thirty-five years earlier, was virtually unavailable in England at the time of Marx's death. The first English translation had appeared in 1850 in an obscure and short-lived radical journal, and some small, badly translated editions were imported from America in the 1870s. But it did not become generally accessible until 1887 with the publication of a new translation supervised by Engels. It was *Das Kapital,* not the *Manifesto,* that attracted the attention of a few "advanced" Englishmen. Published originally in German in 1867, it appeared in France in installments between 1872 and 1875, and in an English edition only in 1887; it was the French translation that most of the early English commentators on Marx read. There had been two short notices of the German edition in the English press under the heading "German Literature." The *Saturday Review* was respectfully critical of Herr Marx, a "political economist of the most advanced democratic school," whose views were "pernicious," but who impressed the reviewer by "the plausibility of his logic, the vigour of his rhetoric, and the charm with which he invests the driest problems of political economy." The *Contemporary Review* was also of two minds, commending Marx for the "human interest" he brought to political economy, but doubting that Germans had anything to teach the English on this subject.[3]

The first serious article on Marx in England, in 1875, had the author complaining that Marx was only a "shadow of a name" in the country where he had so long resided and that even educated Englishmen knew nothing of his writings or of his considerable influence abroad.[4] Four years later the Positivist-Marxist Ernest Belfort Bax, one of the very few Englishmen to read *Das Kapital* in German, published two appreciative (although not entirely accurate) articles on him in a little-known journal, *Modern Thought,* which were then reprinted as a pamphlet. There were passing references to Marx the following year in two unsigned essays on socialism in the *Pall Mall Gazette* written by George Gissing, better known for his novel *Demos* published several years later, which was a bitter attack on socialism. A few economic historians identified Marx with the German school of "Academic Socialism" (*Kathedersozialismus*); William Cunningham and Arnold Toynbee were among the few actually to read him, and the latter mentioned him casually in his lectures on the industrial revolution, taking issue with him on the dating of the disappearance of the yeomanry.[5] When John Rae published a long, analytic essay on Marx in the *Contemporary Review* in October 1881, he felt called upon to make the familiar observation that his writings might make foreign governments quake, but they were totally unknown in the country where Marx himself thought them to be "preeminently applicable."[6]

MARX MIGHT HAVE been better known had Hyndman chosen to acknowledge him in his book *England for All,* published in 1881 and reissued in a cheap edition only a month before Rae's article appeared. Hyndman had met Marx the previous year about the same time that he decided to stand for Parliament as an independent candidate. His few discussions with Marx and an exchange of letters were not reflected in his campaign, where he expressed such moderate views that he failed to receive the endorsement of the local Radical group. He might have found more favor with the Tories, for he supported household (but not universal) suffrage, land reform (but not nationalization), and a foreign policy that would "maintain the power and dignity of England abroad."[7] Many years later a member of the Marylebone Radical Association (who also belonged to the First International) recalled Hyndman's objection to universal suffrage: "He asked me if I meant to say that a loafer at the East End of London was to be placed on an equality with myself."[8]

Withdrawing his candidacy when he failed to get any support from his constituency, Hyndman embarked on a business trip to America, where he was involved in a silver-mining company. It was then that he read the French edition of *Das Kapital* (lent to him by a friend who was a Conservative MP). "I have learned more from its perusal, I think," he wrote to Marx from America, "than from any other book I ever read."[9] Returning to England, he resumed his acquaintance with Marx and wrote an article warning of the "dawn of a revolutionary epoch" unless radical constitutional reforms were enacted.[10]

At the same time, perhaps because he still felt closer to Tory Radicalism than to Marxism, he sought an interview with the aged and feeble Disraeli, a few weeks, as it happened, before Disraeli's death. According to his own account (written much later and probably overdramatized), Hyndman told Disraeli that "Peace with Comfort" might be a more suitable slogan for the Conservative Party than "Peace with Honour," upon which Disraeli commented that it was not a bad phrase but what did "comfort" mean? "Plenty to eat," Hyndman answered, "enough to drink, good clothes, pleasant homes, thorough education and sufficient leisure for all." "Utopia made to order," Disraeli retorted. "The moment you tried to realize it on our side you would find yourself surrounded by a phalanx of the great families who would thwart you at every turn: they and their women. And you would be no better off on the other side." When Hyndman continued to press his point, the old man summed up the experience of a lifetime. "It is a very difficult country to move, Mr. Hyndman, a very difficult country indeed, and one in which there is more disappointment to be looked for than success."[11*]

Even before this memorable (and unverifiable) interview with Disraeli, Hyndman was engaged in negotiations for the founding of the Democratic Federation and the publication of the book he was to distribute at its inaugural conference in June 1881. *England for All: The Text Book of Democracy* was a thoroughly eclectic work. It drew upon William Cobbett for the image of a pre-Reformation "merrie England" (Hyndman used that phrase, not ironically), when the common laborer enjoyed all the "necessaries and conveniences of life," when even the "poorest sort lived upon beef, pork, veal, and mutton every day," and when every worker was a "well-to-do free man."[13] The chapter on the colonies conjured up a vision of a "great colonial empire" represented in an imperial parliament and designed to ensure the "future expansion of our race"; while that on foreign affairs was thoroughly Disraelian in its opposition to Russia and its contempt for the little-Englandism, pacifism, and non-interventionism of the Liberals.[14] In his discussion of land Hyndman echoed Henry George's theory of unearned increment, without, however, going so far as to recommend the nationalization of the land; this might be the ultimate solution, he granted, but the more immediate remedy was the restriction of property rights and the acquisition by the state of some land to be used for the common interest.[15]

The only chapters clearly indebted to Marx were those on labor and capital, which denounced the "infinite mischiefs of capitalism," the usurpation by the capitalist of the "surplus value" created by labor, the divorce of the working class from the "means of production," and the reduction of that class to the status of an "industrial army of reserve." Even here,

---

* Disraeli's biographer improved upon Hyndman's account by adding some final words and gestures:

"One can make it [England] do this"—and Lord Beaconsfield's hands, at first pressed one against the other, were separated half an inch, very painfully, as if the old Minister, to force them apart, had had to lift a whole world—"and then this"—and he managed one more half inch, "but never this—"

And the fleshless hands of the mummy, after one last vain effort to open further apart, fell back upon his knees.[12]

Hyndman did not propose that the means of production be nationalized but only that they be "controlled."[16] And his program of "reasonable and practicable remedies" included such familiar demands as the eight-hour day, free and compulsory education, municipal housing, cheap transport, manhood or adult suffrage, and annual or triennial parliaments. In a footnote he observed that while he himself might have preferred more stringent reforms, the people who suffered most under the present system were not prepared to alter it radically.[17]

Even that part of the economic analysis which was most evocative of Marxism was not explicitly or consistently so. It was not Marx who was quoted in the chapters on labor and capital but Smith, Ricardo, Mill, and Henry Fawcett. When Hyndman spoke of "surplus value," he did not mean the Marxist theory of labor as the source of value but the classical theory of labor as the measure of value, a measure of exchange. The only allusion to Marx appeared in the preface: "For the ideas and much of the matter contained in Chapters II and III, I am indebted to the work of a great thinker and original writer, which will, I trust, shortly be made accessible to the majority of my countrymen."[18] This anonymous testimonial was hardly pleasing to Marx, who did not suffer rivals (or even disciples) lightly; it was all the more galling, he complained, to have his book "pilfered" by someone who did not even bother to study it properly.[19] Marx broke off relations with Hyndman, refusing to be pacified by Hyndman's later tributes to him. Engels, who had never met Hyndman, spurned his overtures even after Marx's death. (Hyndman blamed Engels for this rupture, accusing him of being jealous and suspicious that Hyndman would replace him as Marx's confidant and financial supporter.)[20]

NOT ONLY did Hyndman's book fail to mention Marx or *Das Kapital*; it never used the word "socialism." Nor did the Democratic Federation, officially inaugurated in June 1881, include that word in its name or program; it went beyond Hyndman's book only in calling for adult rather than manhood suffrage and land nationalization rather than control. Within a few months, the Federation started to show the first signs of a gradual, if erratic, movement from radicalism toward socialism. It lost the support of all except one of the Radical clubs originally affiliated with it when a committee chaired by Hyndman opposed an Irish candidate endorsed by the local Radicals, and when it compounded the injury by attacking the "hollowness and hypocrisy of capitalist Radicalism."[21] The following year the Federation acquired a new contingent of Radicals inspired by Henry George—this in spite of Hyndman's public rebuke of

George for not appreciating the truth of Marx's dictum that "the capitalist class rob the working class by means of the surplus value . . . more than the landlord class do by their monopoly of land."[22] At its annual conference that year the Federation passed its first distinctively socialist resolution (although not a socialist program). In 1883, after the influx of a group of more militant members (William Morris, John Burns, Henry Champion, Belfort Bax), it was emboldened to publish the manifesto "Socialism Made Plain" calling for the nationalization of the means of production and distribution. The old "practicable" remedies now appeared as "stepping stones to a happier period."[23]

The change of name in 1884 to Social Democratic Federation signified a more overt and militant socialist stance—although not as overt or militant as "Socialist Party" might have done.* Even then its socialism was notably eclectic, combining elements of populism, radicalism, land reform, Christian socialism, municipal socialism, "national socialism" (as Hyndman referred to Ferdinand Lassalle's doctrine), and Marxism. Many of the members of the SDF belonged at the same time to the Land Nationalisation Society, the Land Reform Union, the National Secular Society, the Positivist Society, the Fabian Society, or one of the Christian Socialist groups. (One of the publications controlled by the SDF was the *Christian Socialist*.) And some of those who regarded themselves as Marxists were better versed in Ricardo and Mill than in Marx and Engels. Hyndman himself, in his *Historical Basis of Socialism* published in 1883, presented a sympathetic account of Marx's hated rival Lassalle as well as of the conservative state-socialist Johann Rodbertus.

The Social Democratic Federation was barely inaugurated before it experienced the first of many defections. The increasingly militant pos-

---

* The term "social democratic" was generally taken as a euphemism for "socialist." It was most familiar at the time as the name of the German Social Democratic Party, established in 1869 by August Bebel and Wilhelm Liebknecht. In 1877 the party received almost half a million votes and won thirteen seats in the Reichstag. Although Marx and Engels cooperated with the party, they were never entirely happy with it, especially with the Lassallean faction in it. Nor did they approve of the name "Social Democrat," which smacked to them of bourgeois reformism. As early as 1850 in *Class Struggles in France,* Marx spoke of the "social-democratic party" as a temporary and artificial unity of "the social and the democratic party, the party of the workers and that of the petty bourgeois," which gave a deceptively "red" complexion to that amalgam.[24]

In England, the Social Democrats did not even constitute a "Party" but only a "Federation." Not until 1909 did the SDF become the Social Democratic Party. (Morris's group was no better—a "League" rather than a "Party.")

ture of Hyndman himself (he predicted, for example, that a revolution would take place in England on the centenary of the French Revolution, five years thence), the doctrinaire rhetoric of the official journal *Justice,* and, not least, Hyndman's personal arrogance and abrasiveness alienated the more temperate socialists. Helen Taylor, Mill's stepdaughter and a charter member of the Federation, seceded together with a group of working-class followers. A more serious rupture occurred a few months later when Hyndman found himself outflanked on the left by William Morris, Edward Aveling (Marx's son-in-law), and others, who accused him of being opportunistic, jingoistic, and tyrannical; one member charged him with pursuing a policy of *"persönlich Machtpolitik."*[25] In December 1884 more than half of the executive board, including Morris, resigned and founded the Socialist League.

The charge of "opportunism" was revived the following year when it was revealed that two of the SDF's parliamentary candidates had been subsidized by the Tories. It was also rumored that Hyndman had made an offer to Joseph Chamberlain to withdraw these candidates in return for a safe seat for himself.[26] The "Tory Gold" scandal, as it was dubbed, resulted in yet another defection, this time of a group of Fabians. More important was its effect outside the movement. It not only tarnished the moral reputation of the SDF; it made the organization seem politically frivolous and inept, all the more because the two candidates whose place on the ballot had been purchased so dearly received a combined total of fifty-nine votes—at a cost, George Bernard Shaw calculated, of £8 per vote.

WHAT KEPT the SDF alive, in spite of dissension and disrepute, was the state of the economy. One historian has pointed out that whereas trade union and labor movements generally declined during periods of unemployment, the SDF thrived upon them.[27] Although its members were largely drawn from the middle class and upper working class (only a few branches included unskilled workers in the more depressed trades), its principal and most conspicuous public activity was what was called "agitation." Shaw protested at the time that the unemployed were not the natural constituency of a socialist party: they were "as great a nuisance to socialists as to themselves . . . they do not want a revolution: they want a job."[28] But to the SDF, in the absence of a working-class membership that did want a revolution, the unemployed provided an audience and a mission. Perhaps more important, they served as the occasion for a political forum, a visible, dramatic presence on the public scene.

In the winter of 1885–86, when the Tory Gold scandal threatened to devastate the SDF, it was fortuitously rescued by an especially severe depression that left many Londoners unemployed, destitute, and discontent. The SDF did not initiate the mass demonstration that took place in Trafalgar Square on February 8, 1886; indeed it joined as a "counter-demonstration," protesting not only against the fact of unemployment but also against the program of public works and tariffs that the Tory organizers of the demonstration proposed as the remedies for unemployment. Waving a red kerchief, the SDF speakers denounced the "capitalists who had fattened upon the labour of the working men," threatening to hang them as the Parisian revolutionaries had done. When a substantial part of the crowd was led out of the square along Pall Mall toward Hyde Park, the rioting started that earned it the epithet of "Black Monday." No one was seriously hurt, let alone killed, but windows along the route of the march were smashed, shops looted, carriages overturned, and the occupants relieved of their jewelry and money. (As it happened—surely by chance—one of the buildings that had its windows broken was the New University Club, from which Hyndman had been expelled shortly before. Morris's own shop escaped damage and plunder.)

Although the newspapers made much of the event, with headlines and placards about "London in Danger from Socialist Plots," and citing ridiculously inflated estimates of the number of rioters, the affair had a farcical quality. Hyndman himself was amused by the sight of the looters (hooligans, he insisted, not the original demonstrators) stopping in Green Park to try on the garments they had stolen. The mob finally dispersed in the East End with the singing of "Rule, Britannia." Four leaders of the SDF, including Hyndman, were tried for seditious conspiracy. After a much publicized trial, during which they disclaimed any intention of violence but reaffirmed their dedication to socialism, they were acquitted.[29]

This was a high point in the history of militant socialism. Morris saw it as "the first skirmish of the revolution," and Hyndman announced his intention of disappearing for six months and then reappearing in "a much more serious fashion."[30] The previous year, shortly after the founding of the Socialist League, Morris told Engels that the SDF had 400 members in London and no more than 100 in the provinces.[31] And *Justice,* deprived of Morris's subsidy, was finding it hard to compete with *Commonweal,* the organ of the Socialist League. After Black Monday, *Justice* was reported as having a circulation of 3,000 to 4,000, and one newspaper said that the SDF in London alone had as many as 10,000 supporters.[32] ("Supporters," in this context, signified little more than those who might attend its rallies, and at this time, only a week after the riot, even this figure was undoubtedly exaggerated.) Engels estimated the combined membership of the Federation and the League as 2,000 and the circulation of both papers as no more than 5,000, the majority of them "sympathetic bourgeois, parsons, literary men, etc."[33] According to other sources, the League alone was said to have increased its membership from 230 in mid-1885 to 600 or 700 after the riot (but these figures too are said to be inflated). In 1887 the paid membership of the SDF was put at 689; considering the fact that dues were only a penny a week, this was hardly an auspicious number for a movement intent upon social revolution.[34]

There is no doubt, however, that both organizations profited from the publicity generated by the riot. More important was its effect on their own morale. They were confirmed in their revolutionary credentials— and this at no cost of life, limb, or even freedom. The lesson was not lost on Hyndman, whose New York message in 1887 proclaimed "vehement agitation" to be more effective than parliamentary elections in achieving "revolutionary political change."[35]

The lesson was not lost on the government either. The next serious demonstration, in Trafalgar Square on November 13, 1887, became known as "Bloody Sunday," and for good reason. The occasion this time was not unemployment (although it was sometimes represented as such), but rather a demonstration in support of the imprisoned Irish nationalists, especially the notorious William O'Brien, who had refused to wear prisoner's garb in jail and had been punished by being deprived of his trousers—hence the rallying cry "O'Brien's Breeches." To prevent a repetition of Black Monday, the government first prohibited the demonstration and then forcibly dispersed it. The result was scores of injuries (hundreds, according to some accounts), one to three fatalities, and the imprisonment of two of the leaders.[36]* Shaw described the event as a "violent farce," "the most abjectly disgraceful defeat ever suffered by a

---

* Contemporaries were quick to invent such dramatic labels as "Black Monday" and "Bloody Sunday" and as quick to forget them, leaving it to historians to immortalize them. One historian has described "Black Monday" (when no one was seriously injured and when the "agitators" were acquitted) as "something akin to the *grande peur*"[37]—the period after the fall of the Bastille when the insurrection spread to the countryside. "Bloody Sunday" was in fact bloody, but far less so than that other, more famous "Bloody Sunday" in St. Petersburg in January 1905, when a procession of workers tried to present a petition at the Winter Palace and was fired upon by soldiers; the official figures of casualties were 130 killed and 299 seriously injured. Even this was comparatively mild compared to a more bloody "Black Monday" in the American Civil War, when news of the first battle of Bull Run was received—a battle that resulted in over 3,500 casualties, including 1,250 deaths.

band of heroes outnumbering their foes a thousand to one."[38] Although both Annie Besant and Eleanor Marx urged another demonstration the following week—Eleanor Marx thought it would be "*very* useful to the whole movement" if the troops actually opened fire—neither the SDF nor the League (and certainly not the Fabian Society) had the heart for it.[39]

If the earlier riot invigorated the revolutionary organizations, the later one demoralized them. Both the SDF and the Socialist League were torn by internal dissension. The following year the Marxist faction in the League (including Morris) withdrew, leaving the much depleted organization to the anarchists. Shortly afterward three of the most active leaders of the SDF—Henry Champion, Tom Mann, and John Burns—left that organization, after failing to convince Hyndman and his followers that the class war could be better waged by parliamentary and trade union means. Hyndman himself, having achieved this Pyrrhic victory, then reconsidered his strategy. London, he decided, was the heart of England, which meant that the London County Council and School Board were important institutions worthy of his attention and that "municipal socialism" (public provision of gas, water, lighting, education, housing) could be the prelude to the true social revolution.

Even then, however, when Hyndman seemed to be retreating to something like a parliamentary or reformist position, he continued to present himself as a Marxist. Perhaps for this reason the SDF played no part in the most significant radical and working-class movements of the time: the emergence of the "new unionism" and the founding of a parliamentary labor party. While even Engels was acknowledging the importance of the increasingly militant and populist unions, Hyndman remained contemptuous of what he had described to Marx, long before, as the "trade union fetish."[40] The SDF lent nominal support to the striking dockers in 1889, but with far less enthusiasm than was displayed by thousands of middle-class sympathizers. The dockers, in turn, were equally suspicious of the socialists, welcoming their support, as Champion remarked, "not because of their socialism but in spite of it."[41] When the Independent Labour Party was in the process of formation, the best the SDF could do by way of encouragement was to extend to it "an attitude of benevolent neutrality."[42]

THE CENTENARY of the French Revolution came and went, and the English revolution Hyndman had predicted was even more remote than it had been five years earlier. Although by that time Marx was, if not a household name, then familiar enough in radical and socialist circles,

Marxism was as far as ever from being dominant or even influential among those groups, let alone among the working classes as a whole. By the end of the decade the SDF, the only remaining Marxist organization in Britain, was reduced to several hundred members.[43] When the Second International convened in Paris in 1889, the SDF was conspicuously absent; the British contingent consisted of a few individuals with no organizational affiliations.

Like any millenarian confronted with the nonappearance of the millennium, Hyndman revised the date for that apocalyptic event. In January 1891 he predicted that by 1900 England would witness "the full sweep of that great Social Revolution of which we can already see plainly the beginning."[44] That date too came and went uneventfully. Although the dues-paying membership of the SDF grew to almost 2,500 in the last decade of the century, that was largely a by-product of the stimulus given to radicalism in general by the SDF's more successful competitors, the new trade unions and the Independent Labour Party.[45] The SDF itself consistently, and humiliatingly, lost all the elections it contested. In 1892 its two candidates received a combined total of 659 votes. In 1895 all four of its candidates lost, including Hyndman, who came in at the bottom of the poll in spite of the fifty speeches he delivered in his constituency. And in 1900 the three SDF candidates lost although they had the endorsement of the Labour Representation Committee (while two other LRC candidates won).

The failure of the SDF—there is no other way of putting it—cannot be measured only in terms of members or electoral returns. More significant was the fact that it made no significant impact on the political culture, either directly through its own organization or indirectly, as the Fabians did, by permeating other institutions and achieving its end through other means. Some commentators, seeking evidence of the influence of the SDF, find its "offspring" in the new trade unions, the Independent Labour Party (which in turn spawned the Labour Party), and the London County Council.[46] If these were indeed offspring, they were illegitimate, undesired, and unloved. The fact is that the SDF actually opposed each of these movements, or, when opposition became too impolitic, bestowed upon them the dubious blessing of "benevolent neutrality."

It is difficult to write about either the SDF or the Socialist League without referring to the personal idiosyncrasies and animosities, the peculiarities of character and vagaries of will, the petty sectarianism and organizational ineptitude, which play so large a part in their history. Such explanations do not sit well with Marxist historians, for whom, as E. J.

Hobsbawm has said, the SDF has always been a "problem child."[47] An alternative explanation would be ideological: the contradictory, sometimes inchoate doctrine that made the SDF incapable of appealing to the working class and inspiring a revolution. But whatever its doctrinal deficiencies, there is no evidence that a more rigorous, principled Marxism would have been more effectual.[48] On the contrary, the most influential of its members were those who left the organization and abandoned Marxism. It was not Marxism that inspired the leaders of the new unions or of the Labour Party but precisely the reformism that Marxism deplored; if they retained any vestige of Marxism, it was the nostalgia for a militant youth or the ever receding mirage of a revolutionary future.

In 1891, reviewing the history of English socialism and of the SDF in the preceding decade, John Rae commented on the irony that continues to perplex socialists and to intrigue historians: "Every requisite of revolution is there, and yet the people will not rise."[49] Almost a century later the question is still being put: "Why was there no Marxism in Great Britain?"[50] Why, in the first country to meet the conditions for a mass Marxist movement, was there no such movement? Why, in the country that gave birth to the industrial revolution, was there no social revolution? Why, in the first country to produce a proletariat worthy of the name, was the very word "proletariat" alien? Why, in the nation of "two nations," was there no irreconcilable class struggle?

The answer, as Elie Halévy and others have long since demonstrated, lies in the history and social structure of modern Britain: in political processes responsive to change and reform, in an economy conducive to individual improvement and social mobility, in a society open to talent and advancement, in classes that were not homogeneous, in institutions like the family, church, and community which mediated between the individual and the state, in civic traditions encouraging moderation, toleration, compromise, and conciliation. All of this made for alternative ways of coping with social problems, short of revolution: voluntary and private agencies addressed to particular needs and designed to supplement state aid; and ideas designed to reconcile individuality and communality, self-help and the public good. These agencies and ideas did not begin to resolve all problems. But they did go far to discourage a Marxist ideology that gave priority to class over the individual, material interests over moral principles, struggle and revolution over consensus and reform, and state ownership and control over private initiative and competition.

CHAPTER 22

Religious Socialism

"CHRISTIAN SOCIALISM is but the holy water with which the priest consecrates the heart-burnings of the aristocrat."[1] This may be the most famous, certainly the most damning, comment ever made about Christian socialism. It was in the *Communist Manifesto* that Marx delivered this judgment, in the appendix, where Christian socialism (or "clerical socialism") was subsumed under the category of "feudal socialism" and the latter under "reactionary socialism." While that dictum is still quoted (because it is so eminently quotable), it is generally thought to be more revealing about the author than the subject. Even radical historians are no longer so dismissive of a mode of socialism that may have been naive and ineffectual but was not as hypocritical or Machiavellian as Marx suggested—a socialism espoused by the middle class more than the aristocracy and by militant members of the working class as well.

The generic form of Christian socialism was not "feudal" socialism but religious socialism. In this ecumenical form it was present among all the late-Victorian socialist groups, including the most radical of them. The rhetoric of religion that was so pervasive was not "mere" rhetoric, not a casual figure of speech or an emotional effusion. When William Morris declared, in the manifesto of the Socialist League, that the new organization would be devoted to "the religion of Socialism,"[2] or Keir Hardie described socialism as "the embodiment of Christianity in our industrial system,"[3] or Beatrice Webb found in Fabianism a modern version of the Religion of Humanity, they were all testifying to the power of an idea that for them was an essential part of the moral and social reality. However much the devotees of a Religion of Socialism or a Religion of Humanity tried to secularize that religion—to transfer, as Beatrice Webb said, the "impulse of self-subordinating service" from God to man—that transference was rarely complete.[4] What remained, for many socialists, was a spirit that transcended man, a moral idea rooted in religion which provided the ultimate rationale for socialism.

It was not the militant socialist who resisted that idea but the militant materialist and secularist. The most obdurate enemies of religious socialism were rigorous Marxists so committed to a materialistic theory of history that they rejected any suspicion of spirit in man and any taint of spirituality in socialism, and rigorous secularists (like Charles Bradlaugh) determined to rid society of any vestige of religious faith. But there were not many rigorous Marxists in Victorian England; most socialists were not Marxists at all, or were, at best, "incomplete" Marxists, accepting the economics but not the metaphysics of Marx (much as the "incomplete" Positivists accepted the sociology but not the theology of Comte). And secularism went into a rapid decline when socialism appeared on the scene—not only because secularism was identified with Bradlaugh's version of free-trade radicalism but also because it failed to provide the spiritual satisfaction that socialism offered.[5]

As there were "complete" and "incomplete" Positivists and Marxists, so there were "complete" and "incomplete" religious socialists, the "complete" variety being the Christian socialists who were part of an organized church. Although the churches themselves continued to lose members, especially among the working classes, the rise of Christian socialism may have prevented an even more precipitous decline. The professed aim of the Christian socialists was to "Christianize" society, to infuse society with the social and moral ideals they associated with Christianity. But in the process they also "socialized" the churches, making them more responsive to social problems and more sympathetic to socialism itself.

Christian socialism has sometimes been equated with "primitive" Christianity, an ancient, mythical religion that tolerated no poverty, no inequality, no social strife. It is interesting that the Christian socialists of the late-Victorian period rarely invoked this ideal. Their lineage was more recent, going back only a few decades to the founders of the creed: F. D. Maurice, Charles Kingsley, and J. M. Ludlow. There were important differences among the earlier generation, as among the later: Ludlow was more interested in the economics of the cooperative movement than in the niceties of Christian doctrine; Kingsley was more effective as a spokesman for the cause than as a thinker or a political activist; and Maurice, the most sophisticated of them theologically, was also, especially in his later years, the least radical (he even opposed the Reform Act of 1867). It was Maurice's theology, not his politics, that inspired the later generation of Christian socialists. Maurice was Professor of Moral Philosophy at Cambridge from 1864 until his death in 1872. Stewart Headlam attended his lectures as a student, and B. F. Westcott was, for a time, his colleague (although not, apparently, his friend). Many who did not have the privilege of knowing him declared themselves "Mauricians" on the basis of his early and major work, *The Kingdom of Christ*. Kingsley was also at Cambridge as Professor of History; he resigned in 1869, later served as canon of Westminster and chaplain to the Queen, and died in 1875. Ludlow was the only one of the three to survive into the later period of Christian socialism; he died in 1911 at the age of ninety-one.

STEWART HEADLAM, generally credited with the revival of Christian socialism, was an unlikely convert to that cause. Appointed to a parish in Drury Lane shortly after his ordination, he displayed an unseemly liking for actors, chorus girls, and bohemians, which soon earned him a well-deserved reputation as an eccentric—all the more because he adhered to an extreme form of high-church ritualism. Transferred to Bethnal Green, he discovered there his other great passion, the cause of the poor, and became involved in local radical and philanthropic activities. It was not, however, his political views that offended the hierarchy but his defense of secularism. He opposed religious oaths and tests (when Bradlaugh was later denied a seat in Parliament, Headlam was one of his staunch supporters), and he publicly supported a strictly secular system of education. He also alienated conventional churchmen by his belligerent opposition to Sabbatarianism, temperance, and other manifestations of what he regarded as Puritanism. In 1878, after delivering an especially provocative lecture in praise of theaters and music halls, and after appearing at a Hyde Park rally with a Fenian politician where he took the occasion to call for the abolition of the House of Lords, he was deprived of his license to preach and was dismissed from his curacy. He never again held an official position in the church.[6]

The year before his dismissal, in the course of his other ill-assorted activities, Headlam founded the Guild of St. Matthew. At first a parish organization, it soon acquired branches in London, Oxford, and other cities. At its height in the early 1890s, it had no more than four hundred members, but its influence extended far beyond that number. Since a quarter of its members were priests, the message of the Guild was disseminated in sermons and parish gatherings, in meetings addressed by like-minded clerics and socialists, and in the *Church Reformer,* a journal that belonged to Headlam and was the unofficial organ of the Guild.

The principles of the Guild as originally formulated were threefold: to eliminate prejudices against the church, especially on the part of secularists, and thus (in Kingsley's phrase) to "justify God to the people"; to promote sacramental worship; and to study social and political questions "in the light of the Incarnation."[7] These explain Headlam's seemingly contradictory positions on secularism and sacramentalism. The secular and the sacred were equally part of the divine purpose; indeed all of human experience partook of divinity. The Christian church itself was "the great Secular Society," and the Kingdom of Heaven was not a future state but "a Divine Society established in this world."[8] At this point Headlam diverged from Maurice and the earlier Christian socialists. While they interpreted socialism so as to be compatible with Christianity, he interpreted Christianity so as to be compatible with socialism. Thus Jesus appeared to him as the supreme social and political "Emancipator," the church as the instrument of social redemption, and the sacraments as the analogues of social principles (baptism, for example, represented equality). Later, after his quarrels with the hierarchy became more embittered, Headlam decided that the Kingdom of Heaven could be achieved only if the Church of England were disestablished—this in spite of his belief in the divine nature of the state.

If the Christian part of his Christian socialism was somewhat confused, the socialist part was more so. The first plank in the economic program of the Guild was land reform, Headlam being an enthusiastic disciple of Henry George and an active member of the Land Reform Union. He was also one of the founders of the SDF and a long-standing member of the Fabian Society and of its executive committee.[9] Sidney Webb identified him with the "left wing" of the Society—a description that does not quite accord with his proposal on one occasion that the Fabians should try to "organise more drawing-room meetings and to attract the upper middle class by lectures at fashionable centres."[10] He was not, in fact, entirely comfortable with the Fabians, either with their bureaucratic disposition or with their ascetic and moralistic tendencies. (He alienated some Fabians as well as members of his own Guild when he provided bail for Oscar Wilde at the time of his trial and publicly greeted him after his release from jail.)

Headlam's socialism was unorthodox and inconsistent. He was a collectivist in the sense that he favored a large measure of state intervention; in 1892 he wrote a Fabian tract entitled "Christian Socialism" which called upon all good men "to seize the State and to use it for the well-being of the masses instead of the classes."[11] But he also worried that a strong state would encroach upon individual liberty and impose a regimented and puritanical morality. He supported trade unions, a minimum wage and maximum hours, some redistribution of wealth and limitation of competition. But apart from land reform, he had no great interest in economics. He was also (like some Fabians) strenuously opposed to the formation of the Independent Labour Party, and he himself remained a loyal member of the Liberal Party. At his memorial service, a fellow Guild member paid a fitting tribute to him when he called him "a true Liberal, a Conservative and a Socialist."[12]

He was, in fact, not so much a socialist (or a Liberal, or a Conservative, or even, perhaps, a Christian) as an educational reformer. He looked to education to stimulate the "divine discontent" that would make people impatient with social evils and eager to correct them.[13] This was yet another source of friction with the Anglican hierarchy. At a time when the Church of England was struggling to retain control of state education, Headlam was seeking a secularization of the entire system of public education. From 1882, when he was elected to the London School Board, he made education, even more than the Guild of St. Matthew, the focus of his attention. When the Board was dissolved in 1903 he was temporarily bereft, but his election to the London County Council four years later permitted him to resume his educational work. After the dissolution of the Guild in 1909, the education committee of the LCC occupied him until his death in 1924.

Small in numbers, torn by dissension, distracted by Headlam's personal enthusiasms and aversions, the Guild of St. Matthew nevertheless played an important part not only in the revival of Christian socialism but in providing a larger base for socialism in general. One historian credits it with bringing about a reinterpretation of Christian dogma in the light of industrialism, "without which Victorian religion might not have survived."[14] It might be as plausible to credit it with a reinterpretation of socialist dogma in the light of religion, without which Victorian socialism might not have survived—or at least thrived.

THE GUILD of St. Matthew, it has been said, provided the "shock troops" of Christian socialism, while the Christian Social Union was the "army of occupation."[15] The Guild consisted of prophets; the Union, of popularizers.[16] The Guild were the parents; the Union, the children (wayward, juvenile parents, in contrast to their eminently respectable, mature children).[17] One can use other metaphors to differentiate the two groups: dissidents and conformists, missionaries and settlers, heretics and establishmentarians. They all overstate the contrast, which in any event was more characteristic of the founders than of the disciples. Yet there was a significant difference, if not quite so dramatic a one.

The Christian Social Union was founded by Brooke Foss Westcott, Scott Holland, and Charles Gore in 1889, when the Guild of St. Matthew was reaching the peak of its strength but already exhibiting the weaknesses that were to lead to its decline and demise. Westcott, the first president of the Union, was a full generation older than Headlam. Two years after Headlam was graduated from Cambridge, with a low third-class degree, Westcott was appointed Regius Professor of Divinity. While Headlam was making the rounds of the poor in Bethnal Green, drinking with his parishioners in the local pubs, making passionate speeches for unpopular causes, and beginning to organize the Guild of St. Matthew to propagate the idea of a "sacramental socialism," Westcott was delivering recondite and ill-attended lectures on biblical scholarship to undergraduates at Cambridge and serving as chaplain to the Queen.

Westcott's theological views were neither novel nor radical, but they did provide the basis for his later more radical social and political views. The main tenets of his "Incarnational" theology were the consecration by Christ of the material and social world, and the duty of humanity to elicit and elevate the divine purpose in the world. This idea of "Incarnation" converged with Maurice's "Kingdom of Christ" and Headlam's "Kingdom of Heaven." For all of them, the divine kingdom was realizable on earth because divinity was already incarnate or immanent in this world. This theology later became the groundwork for a social gospel.

Westcott traced his concern with the poor to his youth when he witnessed a Chartist demonstration addressed by Feargus O'Connor, and to his college days when he read Disraeli's novel *Sybil*. But he gave little evidence of any interest in or knowledge of social affairs until 1883. It was then, in a climate charged with radicalism and social consciousness, that he began to give his theology a social dimension. Even then there was nothing original about his ideas and nothing memorable in his formulation of them. Religious regeneration, he preached, required social regeneration; individual improvement required social improvement; and social improvement required moral improvement. Holland recalled (not unkindly) that after Westcott had delivered the inaugural address at the founding of the Christian Social Union, no one could remember what he had actually said, but everyone felt "lifted, kindled, transformed."[18]

About one thing Westcott was clear: "Behind every social question there lies not only a moral but also a religious question."[19] These moral and religious issues, rather than any practical social proposals, were the primary concerns of the Christian Social Union. Its professed objectives were the establishment of "Christian law" as the ultimate authority over "social practice"; the application of the "moral truths and principles" of Christianity to the social and economic problems of the time; and the presentation of Christ as "the living master and King, the enemy of wrong and selfishness, the power of righteousness and love."[20] Today these principles seem merely social rather than socialist, but to Westcott and his associates they were socialist in the only acceptable sense of that word. In a speech widely circulated as a pamphlet, Westcott dissociated socialism from the "extravagant and revolutionary schemes" with which it had been unfortunately associated, schemes dependent on "violence, or confiscation, or class selfishness, or financial arrangement." Socialism's real quarrel, as he saw it, was not so much with capitalism, certainly not with private property, as with an immoral, antisocial individualism.

Individualism and Socialism correspond with opposite views of humanity. Individualism regards humanity as made up of disconnected or warring atoms; Socialism regards it as an organic whole, a vital unity formed by the combination of contributory members mutually interdependent.

It follows that Socialism differs from Individualism both in method and in aim. *The method of Socialism is cooperation, the method of Individualism is competition.* The one regards man as working with man for a common end, the other regards man as working against man for private gain. The aim of Socialism is the fulfillment of service, the aim of Individualism is the attainment of some personal advantage, riches, or place, or fame. Socialism seeks such an organization of life as shall secure for everyone the most complete development of his powers; Individualism seeks primarily the satisfaction of the particular wants of each one in the hope that the pursuit of private interest will in the end secure public welfare.[21]

To the extent to which this conception of Christian socialism did constitute an argument against capitalism—against a competitive, acquisitive, materialistic, self-seeking capitalism—it was also an argument against those forms of socialism that were no less competitive, acquisitive, materialistic, and self-seeking. A socialism that substituted class interests for individual interests and the class struggle for individual competition, or that merely sought to redistribute wealth from one group to another, or that aspired to material gain without any larger moral or spiritual purpose, or that was violent, revolutionary, egalitarian, or otherwise destructive of traditional relationships, was no better than an individualism that was equally inimical to a cooperative, moral, organic society.

AS THE PRESIDENT and senior leader of the Christian Social Union, Westcott carried a good deal of weight in the movement. But it was the younger men, Holland and Gore, products of Oxford rather than Cambridge, who took the initiative in founding and organizing it. (Holland, the first secretary of the Union, had earlier helped establish Oxford House, a settlement house modeled on Toynbee Hall.) They were part of a group of high-churchmen who had made a stir in the church and academic community earlier that year with the publication of *Lux Mundi: A Series of Studies in the Religion of the Incarnation*. Edited by Gore and including essays by himself, Holland, and other Oxford colleagues, the volume was widely suspected of the heresy not of socialism but of secularism. The quasi-secularist theology, however, did provide the rationale for the quasi-socialism of the Christian Social Union. Gore and Holland were not only more enterprising than Westcott; they were more radical and more socialistic. Westcott would not have said, as Holland did, "We must have all we can get of State order, of State machinery."[22] Nor would he have been as bold as Gore in calling for the "impeachment" of the present industrial system.[23] (A few years later Gore founded a religious order, the Community of the Resurrection, which had links with radical and socialist movements in the north.) Their differences were submerged, however, in the agreement that the Union would be primarily an association for the study and publicization of social problems and, unlike the Guild, would not propose any specific program of reform. They also agreed (in this respect, like the Guild) that any satisfactory program of reform would have to be moral and religious as well as economic and material.

Although the Union was theologically more coherent and respectable than the Guild, its great achievement was not theological but social—and social not in the sense of propounding an original or systematic social philosophy, but of making Christian socialism socially acceptable in the Church of England. This was, in fact, the most conspicuous difference between the Union and the Guild. Many of the original members of the Union came from the Guild, and some remained members of both. But the Union was not saddled with a leader known as the "dancing priest," who defended Bradlaugh and Wilde, opposed religious oaths and tests, favored secular education, and advocated the disestablishment of the Church of England—all of this while professing high-church creeds and rituals. The Christian socialism of the Guild had the reputation of being eccentric, eclectic, almost raffish. With the Union it became eminently respectable. Westcott's biographer reported, a few years after his death, that many people joined the Christian Social Union because they were confident that under his leadership it would not become "an instrument of Liberals or Radicals, and that though good Conservatives, they were safe in joining it."[24]

The organization they were joining was indeed "safe," institutionally as well as ideologically. Its leaders were the Regius Professor of Divinity at Cambridge, the Canon of St. Paul's, and the Principal of Pusey House. (Later Westcott became the Bishop of Durham, Holland the Regius Professor of Divinity at Oxford, and Gore the Bishop of Worcester.) By the time of the First World War almost a third of the newly appointed bishops in the church came from the Union, which now had about six thousand members. It was, in fact, more influential than these numbers suggest, for it permeated the church establishment, as Fabianism did the political establishment.* Its appeal was almost entirely to the middle and upper classes. For a brief period after one of Westcott's rare interventions in working-class affairs (his successful mediation of the Durham coal miners' strike in 1892), he seemed to be following the example of Cardinal Manning, who had emerged as one of the heroes of the dockers' strike. But Westcott drew back, refusing to participate in demonstrations of the unemployed or to have the Union identified with specifically working-class activities.

If the Christian Social Union was not as socialistic as some socialists would have liked (or even as other Christian socialists would have liked), it did personify and publicize a mode of thought that was significantly different from the older, conventional Anglicanism. In 1888 the Lambeth Conference of the Church of England, reflecting the temper of the time, appointed a committee to inquire into socialism. The Christian Social

---

* There is another curious resemblance between the Webbs and Westcott. At the time of the Boer War they discovered a common enthusiasm for the British Empire. Like the Webbs, Westcott declared that the empire, rather than the nation, was the proper unit for the fulfillment of "the brotherhood of men." "An Empire is the embodiment on a large scale of two ideas characteristic of our generation—association and service"; "a world-wide Empire is a faint earthly image of the Kingdom of God."[25]

Union, established the following year, became, in a sense, a standing committee within the church testifying to its concern with social problems. One of the journals sponsored by the Union was the *Economic Review*. Published at Oxford from 1891 to 1914, the *Review* was academic and scholarly, "barely distinguishable," according to one historian, "except for its 'ethical' overtones," from a normal learned economics journal.[26] That "exception" was a large one; it was no mean accomplishment to have "moralized" respectable, academic economics. (It was in that journal that Alfred Marshall published some of his most provocative essays.) Similarly, it was no mean accomplishment to have made the idea of socialism respectable within the church, even if that idea was barely distinguishable from social reform or the still more innocuous social consciousness.

BOTH THE Guild of St. Matthew and the Christian Social Union (as well as the more radical Church Socialist League, founded in 1906) were exclusively Anglican. Other Christian socialist groups, although nominally interdenominational, were in fact predominantly Nonconformist. The best known of these was the Christian Socialist Society, an offshoot of the *Christian Socialist*. Founded in London in 1886, it lasted only six years (surviving the journal by six months). It was distinguished from the other groups by a more militantly socialist program (calling for "the public control of land, capital and all means of production, distribution and exchange") and by a membership that included mainly "non-sacerdotal Christians"—that is, non-Anglicans. The contemporary historian of socialism, John Rae, sarcastically observed that while the Society professed Marxism, the real Marxists thought little of it.[27] Other Nonconformist groups were no more successful. The Christian Socialist League, founded in 1894 by a Baptist minister who was also a Fabian, was renamed the Christian Social Brotherhood four years later and survived under that title for another four or five years. A Swedenborgian New-Church Socialist Society was established in 1895 and lasted until 1901, but it was directed exclusively to Swedenborgians and was of limited influence even among them. The Socialist Quaker Society was more long-lived; established in 1898, it lasted until 1924, but it too was confined entirely to its own sect.

At first glance, the greater influence and prominence of Anglicans in the Christian socialist movement seems paradoxical. Historians have always credited the Nonconformists with a major role in radical, socialist, and working-class movements. One recalls the familiar quip that Wesley, not Marx, was the father of English socialism, and the common observation that trade unions and Labour Party leaders were born and bred in the chapel. Yet it was precisely for this reason that the Nonconformists had less need of Christian socialism. The Primitive Methodists, for example, had such strong ties to working-class and radical groups that a Christian socialist society would have been redundant; they were Christian and socialist enough without it. Other Nonconformist sects had become so secularized and their religion so attenuated that they too felt no need for any form of Christian socialism; they were perfectly at home in the secular socialist groups—the Fabian Society, most notably. The Congregationalists, on the other hand, tended to be so individualistic (if also radical) that they were disinclined to any kind of organization. Still other Nonconformists, such as the Baptists, were too conservative to entertain even the idea of socialism.*

Anglicans, however, caught up in the social ferment of the time, had an incentive to develop special organizations to express concerns that the established church had traditionally ignored or even opposed. And because they (and especially the high-churchmen among them) were attached to the sacerdotal forms of the church, they found it expedient to express those concerns in a specifically Anglican context. The Roman Catholics might have been expected to follow the same pattern, especially after Cardinal Manning's success in the dockers' strike. Yet Manning remained something of a maverick in the Catholic hierarchy. Throughout the eighties and nineties, the church was hostile to social reform (still more to socialism), which it interpreted as secularist and anti-Catholic. It looked upon public education as a threat to its own parochial schools, resisted laws for the protection of children which might place Catholic children under the care of secular or non-Catholic authorities, and suspected social legislation of shifting moral responsibility from the individual to society and from religious to secular institutions. It was not until

---

* It is interesting that while the other Nonconformist sects were experiencing a decline in membership, the Baptists alone, the most conservative of them, kept up their numbers. In 1909 they formed the Nonconformist Anti-Socialist Union, whose express purpose was to "exterminate socialism from Church and State" and "discountenance politics in the pulpit."[28] Their relative strength suggests an inverse relationship between religion and politics. The Baptists retained their vitality, one might conclude, because they did not dilute their religion with political or social concerns, while the radical sects lost their religious identity in the course of acquiring a political one.

1909 that the Catholic Social Guild was founded as a counterpart to the Christian Social Union.

THE RELIGIOUS socialist movement that had the closest relationship to the labor movement also had the most equivocal relationship to religion, which is why the Labour Church is discussed at some length in the definitive work on the origins of the Labour Party, but not, except in passing, in the principal books on Christian socialism: one consigns it to the history of popular religion or working-class culture; another dismisses it curtly as a "replacement for religion."[29] Yet if the Labour Church subscribed to no specific religious creed and had no ties to any organized religion, it was religious in its own terms and in this respect notably different from the secular socialist groups.

The first Labour Church was founded in 1891 by the Unitarian minister John Trevor. Reacting against the Puritan hell-and-brimstone background of his childhood, Trevor joined the least religious of all the religious denominations, and then, finding even Unitarianism too confining, established his own church in Manchester. Other Labour Churches were soon organized, mainly in Lancashire and Yorkshire, by former Unitarians, Congregationalists, and, less frequently, Anglicans; in some cases the members of the new churches retained membership in their old communions as well. (Services were sometimes scheduled so that members could attend both.) The nature of the movement may be deduced from the speakers invited by Trevor to address his congregants in the early days of his church: the Fabian Robert Blatchford, the labor leaders Ben Tillett and Tom Mann, the Unitarian minister and economist Philip Henry Wicksteed (under whom Trevor had earlier served), and a leader of the London Ethical Society, Stanton Coit. (Coit later criticized those Labour Churches which were so benighted as to persist in using the formula "Fatherhood of God" rather than the secular "ethical god of duty.")[30]

Because the local Labour Churches were often indistinguishable from the local branch of the Independent Labour Party, Trevor tried to give them some unity and identity by establishing a monthly journal, the *Labour Prophet,* and by forming a Labour Church Union. The principles of the Union were notably latitudinarian. The labor movement was said to be a "religious movement," the religion not of a class but of all those who sought the abolition of "commercial slavery"; it was a "free religion," one neither sectarian nor dogmatic; its goal was the emancipation of labor in accord with the "economic and moral laws of God"; and the essential conditions of that emancipation were the development of personal character and the improvement of social conditions.[31] Although socialism was not specifically mentioned among these principles, it was assumed that the Labour Church was a socialist church. Trevor himself favored the nationalization of the means of production, distribution, and exchange. His primary purpose, however, and the distinctive feature of his church was to proclaim the "Brotherhood of Man and the Fatherhood of God," without which, he believed, socialism would be vain and meaningless.

At its peak in the mid-1890s, the Labour Church Union comprised some fifty churches. Apart from weekly church services and the publication of the journal, it was actively involved in the organization of adult education classes, the establishment of Sunday schools, and cooperation with the local branches of the ILP. (Trevor himself was one of the founders of the ILP, as well as a member of the Fabian Society.) By the turn of the century, the Labour Church was in decline, its failure a direct consequence of the success of the ILP. Trevor himself severed his ties with it when it became so closely identified with the ILP that it lost its religious mission. But before then it played an important part in the formative years of the labor and socialist movements in giving expression to a religious impulse that was not satisfied by the more secular organizations. Religion was, to the Labour Church, what Marxism was to the SDF or Positivism to the Fabian Society—not a binding or even clearly definable dogma but a mode of thought and sensibility that inspired and sustained it. However "free" the religion of the Labour Church, it was a religion of sorts. Its rituals were not the orthodox ones, but there was surely something distinctively religious in a church whose recommended order of service was: 1) Hymn, 2) Reading, 3) Prayer, 4) Solo or Music by the Choir, 5) Notices and Collection, 6) Hymn, 7) Address, 8) Hymn, 9) Benediction.[32]

Keir Hardie was a prime example of this religious sensibility. The first Labour candidate for Parliament, the first chairman of the ILP, and one of the founders of the Labour Party, he was also the most popular speaker at the Labour Churches. And his speeches were laden with religious terms and symbols—not for rhetorical effect but to convey his message: that social salvation was as much a moral and spiritual affair as an economic and material one. In 1893, he looked back upon the earlier years of the labor movement when it threatened to "founder," as he said, "on the rocks of materialism." "Bread and butter politics were in the ascendant, and men spoke and wrote as if bread and butter were the end and the means." Fortunately that was only on the surface of the movement. Its teachers and prophets (an ecumenical group, as he described them—Carlyle, Mazzini, Whitman, Ruskin, Tennyson, Morris) had left a far different impress on it. "The great message of their deliverance has been the elevation of the spiritual side of man's being, showing how all material things are but useful in so far as they serve to aid in developing character."[33]

For Hardie, as for Trevor, "character" was the necessary basis of socialism, and religion the necessary basis of character. It was this conjunction of morality and religion that distinguished them from those of their colleagues in the socialist and labor movements who believed that both the economic and ethical imperatives of socialism could be divorced from religion, that a socialist party or even a Religion of Humanity could be truly man-centered rather than God-centered. "The Ethical flag," Trevor wrote, "flies at half mast and signifies death in the upper reaches." Only a "God relationship" could give meaning to the "facts of life" and to "our moral struggles and defeats."[34]

That expression, "God relationship," revealed the weakness, perhaps fatal weakness, of this form of religious socialism. For it alienated not only the secularists who denied the need for any relationship to any God but also the religious for whom a "God relationship" was a feeble substitute for a belief in God. Beatrice Webb was one of the latter. Before she became a Fabian, she visited some distant relatives in Yorkshire and was much taken with the "religious socialism" of their dissenting community, a socialism, she was pleased to report, that pervaded the cooperative and chapel alike. Her worry was that the two might grow apart, that the cooperative would become secularized and the chapel would see it as a rival. "One wonders where all the *feeling* will go, and all the capacity for *moral* self-government."[35] Several years later, after attending a meeting presided over by Trevor, she derided those "pseudo-religionists" who offered up morality in the form of a "would-be religiosity." The Labour Church was nothing more than the "love of man masquerading in the well-worn clothes of love of God—one feels half-inclined to tear them off with contempt, half-inclined to denounce the wearer as a simple thief." Trevor seemed earnest enough and "the moral note rang true." It was the religious note that rang false for her.[36]* (She herself, throughout her

---

* Her animus against the Labour Church may have been provoked as much by its politics as by its pseudo-religion. At a time when the Fabians were resisting the demands for the formation of an Independent Labour Party, the Labour Church was actively involved in its establishment.

years as a Fabian, remained a believing and practicing Christian, regularly praying at home and less regularly, but often enough, attending services and taking communion at St. Paul's.)

Another Fabian, Robert Blatchford, was better disposed to the Labour Church. It was necessary, he said, to widen the definition of socialism, to "draw out all the ethical and spiritual implications of these desires and efforts for a juster social order." The labor movement was but one sign of a new spirit, a new conception of life, "to which it is affectation, if not folly, to refuse the name of Religion."[37] His words may be instructive for a later generation as well, for historians who are inclined to refuse the name of religion to the Labour Church because it was insufficiently religious, or to refuse it the name of socialism because it was insufficiently socialist—or for those who find the very idea of religious socialism "ambiguous" and "enigmatic."[38]

Whatever one may think today of religious socialism either as a political and social movement or as an intellectual and spiritual idea, there is no doubt that in late-Victorian England it was a movement of some importance and an idea of some cogency and respectability. In 1851 the Unitarian minister James Martineau longed for the day when employers would put up "a moral resistance to the full swing of economical laws." In 1886 he deplored the fact that so many people, including nearly the "whole body" of the Anglican clergy, had "in their humanitarian enthusiasm, [been] betrayed ... into vain and disastrous struggles against social and economic laws, which will be found as unyielding as the law of gravitation."[39]

CHAPTER 23

Fabianism

For the right moment you must wait, as Fabius did most patiently, when warring against Hannibal, though many censured his delays; but when the time comes you must strike hard, as Fabius did, or your waiting will be in vain, and fruitless.

THIS MUCH QUOTED TEXT, explaining the name of the Fabian Society, appeared in January 1884 as the epigraph of the first Fabian tract.[1] The motto is not without its ironies. For one thing, it was not the classical text it was originally thought to be. When the source could not be identified, a motion was introduced to remove it, but the vote was tied and the motto was retained, at least through several printings. The episode is telling in view of the Fabians' fetish of facts; among their most popular tracts were *Facts for Socialists, Facts for Londoners, Facts for Bristol, Figures for Londoners*. The motto is also ironic because, as H. G. Wells pointed out, Fabius never did "strike hard."[2] (Nor did Fabius defeat Hannibal; it was Scipio Africanus who did that.) Nor did the Fabians strike hard. Their waiting and delaying tactics were not an expedient to postpone action until the "right moment" came; it was by waiting and delaying that the whole of the Fabian program was to be achieved. There was to be no decisive blow against capitalism, no class struggle or revolution, but only a series of maneuvers to harass and weaken capitalism and thus advance the cause of socialism.

The motto had been proposed by one of the founders of the Society, Frank Podmore, whose intellectual and institutional peregrinations are as revealing as the motto itself. A clergyman's son, Podmore moved, in rapid succession, from Anglicanism to spiritualism (he was one of the founders of the Society for Psychical Research) to radicalism. He joined the Democratic Federation only to find it excessively materialistic, helped establish the Fellowship of the New Life, which soon proved to be excessively ethereal, and on January 4, 1884 (the date commemorated as the "birthday" of Fabianism), was one of the group that seceded from the Fellowship to form the Fabian Society. After serving on the Fabian executive committee for four years, he resigned from the executive (although not from the Society) to resume an active role in the Society for Psychical Research.

This kind of eclecticism, or ecumenicalism, was typical of the early Fabians, many of whom belonged, successively or simultaneously, to the Fellowship of the New Life (which survived, although barely, until 1898), the Social Democratic Federation, the Progressive Association, the Spiritual Society, the Society for Psychical Research, the Theosophical Society, the Land Reform Union, the Land Nationalisation Society, the Positivist Society, the Secular Society, the Guild of St. Matthew, the Labour Church, even the Charity Organisation Society. Edward Pease, the first full-time secretary of the Fabian Society (and, later, its first historian), was a member of the Democratic Federation and the Progressive Association (the latter believing, *contra* the Federation, that moral reformation had to precede social reformation) before helping to found the Society for Psychical Research, the Fellowship of the New Life, and finally the Fabian Society.[3] Frederick Keddell, a part-time secretary of the Society, was at the same time a member of the SDF; he resigned from the Fabians when they denounced the SDF in the "Tory Gold" episode. Annie Besant, a prominent member of the Fabian executive, also belonged to the SDF; she left the Society soon after the publication of *Fabian Essays in Socialism* (to which she contributed) and became an active member of the Theosophical Society. Charlotte Wilson, another member of the executive, remained nominally in the Fabian Society while devoting herself to the English anarchist movement; years later she resumed active membership in the Fabians and was reelected to the executive.

George Bernard Shaw once explained that he joined the Fabians rather than the Democratic Federation because the latter contained too many "cranks."[4] But the Fabians had their own share of cranks, most notably Shaw himself. In addition to being a confirmed vegetarian, he was a fervent "woolener" (or "Jaegerite"), convinced that the wearing of wool, and only wool, would rid the body of noxious vapors and thus restore physical and moral health. (Hence his habitual attire—a reddish-brown woolen suit with knee breeches and woolen stockings.) Another prominent Fabian, Edward Carpenter, combined the apostleship of "spiritual love" (a euphemism for homosexuality) with a belief in the spiritual efficacy of sandal-wearing, the liberation of the feet being a necessary prelude to sexual liberation.*

Fabians characterized their oddly assorted group as *"une nouvelle couche sociale,"* an "intellectual proletariat," a "literary proletariat," a "black-coated" or "professional proletariat."[6] The "new class" image is apt for people who defined themselves by their ideas and beliefs rather than by their economic interests or social status. But "proletariat" hardly does justice to bohemians like Shaw and Carpenter, Annie Besant and Charlotte Wilson, or to the large bulk of the membership ranging from the aspiring lower middle class to the affluent upper middle class. Shaw admitted that his decision to join the Fabians rather than the SDF was "guided by no discoverable difference in program or principles," but solely by an instinctive feeling that the Fabians were more likely to attract men of "my own bias and intellectual habits"—the Fabians being "middle class all through, rank and file as well as leaders," in contrast to the SDF and the Socialist League, who were "quite proletarian."[7]† Joseph Schumpeter called them "bourgeois intellectuals."[9] It was a fitting description for the many writers, teachers, civil servants, and social workers among them, some of whom had small independent incomes to supplement their earnings or were sufficiently wealthy to devote themselves entirely to writing or politics, as Webb eventually did. (The Webb household normally included four or more servants and one or two research assistants. Charlotte Wilson, the wife of a stockbroker, had a grand house in Hampstead; it was there that the Karl Marx Club met.)

IN OCTOBER 1886, a year after he joined the Fabian Society, Sidney Webb wrote what might well stand, together with the motto about Fabius, as the epigraph of the Society. "Nothing in England is done without the consent of a small intellectual yet practical class in London not 2,000 in number."[10] That figure referred not to the number of members the

---

*One is reminded of George Orwell's account of the socialists of a later generation (he surely had the Fabians in mind): "One sometimes gets the impression that the mere words 'Socialism' and 'Communism' draw towards them with magnetic force every fruit-juice drinker, nudist, sandal-wearer, sex-maniac, Quaker, 'Nature Cure' quack, pacifist and feminist in England."[5]

†Elsewhere Shaw gave a generational explanation. The leaders of the SDF and the Socialist League—Hyndman, Morris, Helen Taylor—were "bourgeois," but "they were too old for us; they were between forty and fifty when we were between twenty and thirty."[8]

Fabians hoped to attract but to the number of well-placed people they hoped to influence. He later complained that "it is absurd that a Society of 88 members should not raise more than £30 a year";[11] the absurdity was not that the Society should have only 88 members but that it should raise only £30 a year. Eventually the membership did grow substantially. In 1891 there were about 350 members in the London Fabian Society and by the turn of the century 800. The provincial membership fluctuated more widely; at one time in the early 1890s there were as many as 1,500 members in 72 societies. But many of them were only nominally Fabian, and with the founding of the Independent Labour Party in 1893, both the number of provincial societies and the membership fell precipitously. By 1900 there were only four provincial societies with a total of 153 members, and another four university groups with 61 members.[12]

Membership figures, however, were irrelevant, since this was not primarily a membership organization, still less a mass organization. One of the annual reports curtly declared: "It does not ask the English people to join the Fabian Society."[13] Indeed it sometimes seemed to discourage them from joining. Candidates for membership had to attend at least two meetings as visitors before being formally sponsored and seconded for membership, and then had to be elected unanimously by the executive committee (or council, as it was sometimes called). It was not uncommon, especially in the early years of the Society, to have candidates turned down merely because the seconder did not appear at the meeting in person.[14]

"The Fabians were intelligence officers without an army," the historian G. M. Trevelyan has said, "there was no Fabian party in Parliament—but they influenced the strategy and even the direction of the great hosts moving under other banners."[15] Their mission was to educate and influence people in power rather than to recruit them to their own ranks—to make converts to Fabian policies rather than to the Fabian Society. Sometimes they short-circuited the educational process by a strategy of "permeation," designed to "permeate," "penetrate," and "infiltrate" the institutions of power. The Fabians, said Sidney Webb, were "the 'Society of Jesus' of Socialism," without, he hastened to add, the "mental subjection" or "moral shiftiness" commonly (and erroneously, he thought) associated with the Jesuits.[16]

Although the primary target of the Fabians was that "small intellectual yet practical class," they also took it upon themselves to educate a larger class of less influential but politically conscious people. Almost their first official action was the formation of a publication committee, and the Fabian tract soon became the hallmark of the Society. The first tract,

Why Are the Many Poor?, was a banal four-page pamphlet whose only distinctions were the motto about Fabius and the fact that it was drafted by the sole worker among them (actually a retired worker). Yet it attracted the favorable attention of Shaw and went through many editions (one revised by Shaw himself). By the end of 1891, twenty-seven tracts had been published with a total circulation of 100,000, the shorter ones (five to twenty pages) selling for a penny, the others (up to fifty pages) for sixpence. Together with a host of free leaflets, the total came to 335,000—this at a time when the membership of the London Fabian Society was all of 350. (By the turn of the century, almost a hundred tracts had appeared.)[17] The Fabian lecture program was equally enterprising. In 1888–89, 700 lectures were given by members of the Society to political and workmen's clubs in London as well as to Fabian groups. With the expansion of the provincial societies two years later, over 3,000 such lectures were delivered, most by a handful of members. (And sometimes to a handful of auditors. Shaw recalled one occasion when he chaired a talk by Samuel Butler on one of Butler's favorite themes, the authorship of the *Odyssey,* before an audience of four people, including Shaw himself.)[18]

THE PAMPHLETS and lectures were as varied as the authors. The second tract was a *Manifesto* written by Shaw soon after he was elected to the Society. It called for the nationalization of land, implied that the established government was illegitimate, and boldly declared, "We had rather face a Civil War than such another century of suffering as the present one has been."[19] After officially approving the tract, the members repudiated what seemed to be a threat of civil war. For all its incendiary rhetoric, the *Manifesto* never uttered the word "socialism." That word first appeared in 1885 in a tract entitled *What Socialism Is*. It says a good deal about the amorphous character of the Fabians at this time that they asked Engels to write this crucial document, and after he refused, assigned it to a member of the executive committee, Charlotte Wilson, who was an avowed anarchist and a disciple of Kropotkin. In an effort to be evenhanded, she gave equal space to socialism and anarchism; the result was greeted with derision by the Fabians and press alike. Four years later, Shaw, who had earlier toyed with the anarchist position, wrote another tract under the same title that was unambiguously collectivist.

To the extent to which the Society had any official creed, it was expressed in the "Basis" adopted in 1887, which remained unchanged until 1919 (except for an amendment on women's suffrage in 1907). The Fabian Society was said to "consist of Socialists," and socialism was defined as "the reorganization of Society by the emancipation of Land and Industrial Capital from individual and class ownership, and the vesting of them in the community for the general benefit." The "extinction" of private property in land and the transfer to the community of the "administration" of most industrial capital was to be effected without compensation (though possibly, a parenthetical clause allowed, with such "relief" as might be seen fit). All this was to be achieved by the spread of socialist opinions, the dissemination of knowledge about the proper relations between the individual and society, and "the social and political changes consequent thereon."[20]

Although the "Basis" was not much more satisfactory than the earlier tracts, it survived because the membership could not agree upon any revision. It was a "minimum" commitment, Pease explained, rather than a complete "confession of faith," and was meant only for internal use.[21] For public consumption, a multitude of tracts were available, and it was these that gave Fabianism its distinctive character: a socialism that was pragmatic rather than dogmatic, evolutionary rather than revolutionary, regulatory rather than confiscatory, collectivist rather than "anarchist."

The most influential single publication of the Society was *Fabian Essays in Socialism,* edited by Shaw. Delivered originally as lectures and published in December 1889, the first edition of 1,000 copies priced at six shillings sold out in a month; another 1,000 copies were issued a few months later, and 25,000 copies of a shilling edition the following year. (The book has been reprinted repeatedly, without revision but with new prefaces by Webb and Shaw.) In the original preface, anticipating the criticism that the essays were often inconsistent with each other, Shaw explained that he had deliberately kept his editing to a minimum so as to preserve their individuality. All they had in common was that their authors were prominent Fabians (they were all on the executive committee) and were "Social Democrats" agreed upon a single principle: "the necessity of vesting the organization of industry and the material of production in a State identified with the whole people by complete Democracy."[22]

In the most militant essay in the volume, Hubert Bland insisted that socialism meant not merely "state control" but "the common holding of the means of production and exchange, and *the holding of them for the equal benefit of all.*" This was to be achieved not by a "drizzle of Radicalism" or the "permeation of the Radical Left," but by a "really homogeneous Socialist party" pledged to the "communalization of all the means of production and exchange."[23] Shaw's essay was only a little less militant. He used the term "Social Democracy" rather than "socialism" to describe the system in which the state would be entrusted first with the rent of the country and then with the land, capital, and the organization of industry—"with all the sources of production, in short, which are now abandoned to the cupidity of irresponsible private individuals." This was consistent with a policy of gradualism because the transfer to the state would be effected "not in one lump sum, but by instalments." With typical Shavian cynicism, he explained that "this inevitable, but sordid, slow, reluctant, cowardly path to justice" would be congenial to the British, for it had the "stamp of the vestry" and eschewed such "un-English" ideas as socialism and revolution, the Rights of Man and the guillotine.[24] (It is little wonder that William Morris, then in his most radical phase, praised the essays by Bland and Shaw in an otherwise bitter attack on the book.[25])

The other essayists were more solicitous of the "vestry" mentality of the English. Sidney Webb set the tone by placing socialism in its "historic" context, in which it appeared not only as the inevitable end of the evolutionary process but as inherent at every stage of that process. Indeed England already enjoyed a form of "unconscious socialism." "The Socialist philosophy of today is but the conscious and explicit assertion of principles of social organization which have been already in great part unconsciously adopted."[26] Socialism was the economic analogue of democracy; as democracy had been progressing irresistibly, so had socialism. Introducing a metaphor that was to be much favored by the Fabians, Webb explained that social reforms of one kind or another had already "pared away" the liberty of the owners of property and cut off "slice after slice" from the profits of capital.[27] Fabianism proposed only to continue this paring and slicing process.

In effect Fabianism claimed for itself the great advantage of Marxism, historical inevitability, without the disadvantage of class struggle and violent revolution. Fabianism, the argument went, was no more dangerous and no less practical than any of the reforms that had already been enacted. All it called for was more of the same: more measures like those "two great socialistic institutions," the poor law and public education; more reforms that "converge irresistibly" toward socialism; more "installments" of Social Democracy such as had already improved the condition of most of the people (the Fabians did not hold with the Marxist theory of "immiseration"); more "slices" off the liberty and profits of capitalists and landlords. It was all innocent and unthreatening, a socialism that would bring about the "socialization of land and capital" by the application of "nothing else than Common Sense."[28]

* * *

THIS "UNCONSCIOUS," evolutionary, and inevitable socialism was peculiarly English, not only because it was already under way in English society but also, Pease explained, because it was based on economic science as taught by "accredited British professors" rather than "the speculations of a German philosopher."[29] That "German philosopher" was, of course, Marx, who was mentioned in passing only a few times in *Fabian Essays* but who lurked in the shadows, a ghost at the table of good old English common sense.

Fabianism was not merely non-Marxist; it was consciously anti-Marxist. By the time the Fabian Society came on the scene, *Das Kapital* had become something of a cult book among "advanced" radicals, more of whom knew of it than had actually read it.[30] Shaw was first introduced to it by a member of the SDF, went off to read it (in the French translation) in the British Museum, and instantly, according to his own account, became a "furious Socialist."[31] (This was not his first encounter with socialism; he also claimed to have read George, Morris, Proudhon, and Lassalle.) Even after this Marxist epiphany, however, Shaw was not quite "furious" enough to join the SDF, although he did attend its meetings and contribute to its journals. Instead he became a member of the Fabian Society and, almost immediately, of its executive committee. He also participated in a reading circle (consisting of Fabians, SDFers, assorted radicals, and economists) devoted to the study of *Das Kapital*, where he started by passionately defending Marxism, but soon became very critical of it. Under the influence of Sidney Webb and of the marginal-utility economists P. H. Wicksteed and F. Y. Edgeworth, he discovered the fallacies of the Marxist theory of surplus value, as well as of the scenario of class struggle and revolution.*

Fabians did not have to know anything about economics or the theory of surplus value to reject Marxism. They were offended by a materialistic, deterministic form of socialism that was no better, in their opinion, than a materialistic, individualistic capitalism. When the Fabians dissociated

---

* Shaw's education in Marxism continued the following year when Webb undertook to teach him German through the reading of the second volume of *Das Kapital,* which may well have confirmed both of them in their aversion to Marxism. Webb, who had a high threshold of boredom, warned Shaw that he himself found the book "very dull—in fact, I fear, quite unendurable," but as good a way as any of learning German. Several days later, reporting this bizarre teaching experiment to another Fabian friend, Graham Wallas (who had gone to Germany to learn the language), Webb said that he found it very interesting, but as a linguistic, not an intellectual, exercise.[32]

themselves from the Fellowship of New Life (although some continued to belong to both), it was because they believed that the moral reform of individuals required the economic reform of society, and that selfishness could never be eradicated from human nature until competitiveness was eliminated from society. But their ultimate aim, for the individual as for society, was moral reformation. One of the first resolutions passed by the Fabians reasserted that moral purpose: "The Fabian Society further endeavours to help forward the Regeneration and Evolution of Society by insisting that only a general high sense of duty and subordination of individualistic aims to the general good can bring about true liberty, and assure the true dignity of Man."[33]

THIS PRONOUNCEMENT might have issued from the prospectus not of the Fabian Society but of the Positivist Society. If there was any single dominant strand in the eclectic body of thought that made up Fabianism, it was Positivism, particularly the Comtean form that was most familiar in England at the time. This has been obscured by the later dominance of Marxism—the identification of Marxism with socialism *tout court*— which makes it difficult for historians (although not for contemporaries) to credit Positivism as a serious form of socialism.[34] Comte did not, to be sure, propose to expropriate or nationalize private property; he only—but this was a large "only"—sought to use property for the interests of society as a whole and to bring capitalists under the dominion of the intellectual and moral "priesthoods." John Stuart Mill characterized Comte's view of the relation of capital to society as "essentially that of Socialists," even if his means of effecting change were different from theirs.[35] In 1886 Sidney Webb read a paper to the Fabian Society, "The Economics of a Positivist Community," explaining that he himself was not a Positivist because he was not at all sure that "the capitalist can be moralised," but that "Positivists, so far as they have thought out their economic system, come clearly under the definition of Socialism."[36] Frederic Harrison, the leading English Comtean, described Positivism as socialism in its largest sense: "Positivism is a complete, universal, and religious socialism—not a socialism limited to material products. It is a socialism founded on social science and inspired by religion."[37]

The early Fabians were Positivists (or Positivist "sympathizers") before they had so much as heard of Marxism—or, for that matter, of Fabianism. Beatrice Webb (then Beatrice Potter) had been familiar with Comte from her schoolgirl reading of Mill, Harrison, and George Eliot;

by 1884 her diary contained frequent references to Comte and excerpts from his writings. Long before he met her, Sidney Webb had heard about Comte at the Zetetical Society and later at the London Positivist Society. He and his friends Sydney Olivier, a fellow clerk in the Colonial Office, and Graham Wallas, a young schoolmaster, were so taken with Comte that they embarked upon a systematic reading of all his works. In 1885, "the three Musketeers," as they were known, joined the Fabian Society, where they found themselves in the company of other Positivists— Edward Pease, Annie Besant, William Clarke, and W. L. Philips (the author of the first Fabian tract, *Why Are the Many Poor?*). Of the seven contributors to *Fabian Essays* five were Positivists to one degree or another. (The two who resisted that creed were Shaw and Bland.)

It was their exposure to Positivism that immunized most Fabians to Marxism and gave the movement, at least in the early decades of its history, its distinctive character. Theirs was not the "complete" Positivism of the true believers, which comprised a new theology ("Catholicism without Christianity," as it was dubbed) and a new church militant. (By the 1880s, the English Comteans had not one but two Churches of Humanity, each claiming to be the keeper of the true faith.)[38] The Fabians were "incomplete" Positivists, interested less in the theological and sacerdotal aspects of the philosophy than in the social and political implications of the "Religion of Humanity." After accompanying Harrison to a Positivist meeting in 1889, Beatrice Webb confided to her diary, "Practically we are all positivists; we all make the service of man the leading doctrine of our lives."[39]

To Marxists this moral *qua* religious creed testified to the incorrigibly utopian nature of Fabianism. To the Fabians it was the moral imperative that inspired not only the social objective of the movement, the "regeneration" of society, but also their personal involvement in it. In the incessant lecturing, writing, and meeting that seemed to occupy all their waking hours (save those grudgingly spent in gainful employment), they felt themselves literally fulfilling the Comtean precept: "Live for others."

So far from thinking of themselves as "utopians," they believed that they, not the Marxists, were the only true exponents of "scientific socialism"—not "scientific" in the Marxist sense of a deterministic, materialist theory of history, or in the sociological sense of an empirical, factual account of society. Theirs was the vision of Saint-Simon and Comte, of a society that was scientifically—which is to say, rationally—organized, in which all the parts were arranged, ordered, regulated, planned, so as to make for the most efficient and equitable whole. Such a society could come about only through the conscious effort of intellectuals and "scientists" ("social scientists," we would say) who were prepared to dedicate themselves to the public good and bring their superior reason to bear upon the reorganization of the social order. In Sidney Webb's comment about that "small intellectual yet practical class in London not 2000 in number,"[40] one hears the echo of Saint-Simon declaring that without its "3000 leading scientists, artists, and artisans" France would be a "lifeless corpse";[41] or Comte describing the "Priesthood of Scientists," the "Intellectual Providence" that was to preside over the Positivist society.[42]

It was this Positivist sense of science that distinguished the Fabians from the Charity Organisation Society, which also invoked the name of science. When the COS called for the "scientific organization" of charity, it was to encourage the development of free, responsible individuals in a free, individualistic society. When the Fabians called for the "scientific organization" (or "reorganization") of society, it was not to promote the freedom of individuals but rather to create a more rational, coherent, efficient order. Like the Positivists, the Fabians regarded individualism and laissez-faireism as characteristic of the state of "anarchy," which was to be superseded by a later and higher stage of "organic society." Society, Webb explained (or the community—he used the words interchangeably), so far from being an "aggregate of so many individuals," transcended its components and had an existence independent of them. Although the "social organism" had originally evolved from a union of individuals, by now the individual was itself a creation of the social organism. And the purpose of social evolution was to bring about not the fittest individual but the fittest society. "The French nation was beaten in the last war, not because the average German was an inch and a half taller than the average Frenchman, or because he had read five more books, but because the German social organism was, for the purposes of the time, superior in efficiency to the French." To compete in this process of natural selection, the British would have to learn to subordinate the "self-conceit" of individuality to the "higher end, the Common Weal."[43]*

*   *   *

---

*Years later the Webbs were to find this Comtean ideal embodied in the Soviet Union, where individual interests were subordinated to the general welfare and public policy was determined by administrators whose "professed faith is in science." It might seem paradoxical, they admitted, but they thought it plausible, that something like Comte's Religion of Humanity was "the spirit inspiring the extraordinary experiment of Lenin and Stalin" in creating social institutions that conformed to an "applied science of society."[44]

THE AMALGAM of Positivism and Darwinism made for a powerful argument for collectivism. Positivism, being evolutionary as well as communal, lent itself to a collectivist rather than laissez-faireist version of Social Darwinism, in which the struggle for existence was waged among species (or societies or nations) rather than among individuals. In a nice play on the Comtean "law of three stages" (the theological, metaphysical, and scientific or positive), Sidney Webb said, "Comtism is the metaphysical stage of Collectivism, and Collectivism is the positive stage of Comtism."[45]

"The collectivists alone have the faith to grind out a science of politics."[46] Beatrice Webb made that comment in connection with plans for the establishment of the London School of Economics. But it was more than an academic "science of politics" that she had in mind. It was the realization of that science in society—the "rationalization" (in the Weberian sense) and collectivization of institutions which would result in the "positive" society that Saint-Simon and Comte represented as the final stage of civilization. Only a collectivist society could be "scientific" because only collectivism could curb the "anarchy" of individualism and promote a truly rational, "organic" society.

The Fabians' emphasis on evolution and gradualism may obscure the extent of their commitment to collectivism. If there was to be no revolutionary seizure of power, no dramatic expropriation or nationalization of property, there was nevertheless to be a gradual, incremental, inevitable, and, finally, decisive transfer of power and property from individuals to the state. The litany of precedents for such a transfer—factory acts, mining acts, land acts, trucking acts, regulation acts, education acts, even the poor law—were meant to convince the public that Fabianism, as Shaw put it, was not "catastrophic," because it did not have to be imposed all at once.[47] But this did not mean that it was any the less socialistic or collectivist. Shaw himself provided the philosophical rationale for collectivism by claiming for the democratic state the "boundless" right, in theory at least, to curb the liberty of any individual and to appropriate his property. "As to Property and Liberty then, every man's property is the property of the State, which it can dispose of as it pleases, whether he will or no. And every man's liberty is the liberty of the State, which it can curtail or extend as it pleases, whether he will or no." To be sure, it was generally not expedient for the state to exercise that full measure of power, but so long as it had the right to do so, no individual could claim any counter-right to either liberty or property.[48]

The identification of Fabianism with "municipal socialism" had a similarly reassuring effect. How could one be alarmed by all those tracts with those innocent, indeed soporific titles: *The Municipalisation of the Gas Supply, The Municipalisation of the London Docks, The Municipalisation of Tramways, The Municipalisation of the Milk Supply, Municipal Water, Municipal Drink Traffic, Municipal Pawnshops, Municipal Slaughterhouses, Municipal Bakeries, Municipal Hospitals, Municipal Fire Insurance, Municipal Steamboats.* In a tract with the official-sounding title *Report on Fabian Policy,* Shaw made it clear that municipal ownership or control was only one of several forms available to socialism, that the "organization and conduct" of industry and the "appropriation" of all forms of economic rent by the "nation as a whole" could be achieved by whatever public authorities—"parochial, municipal, provincial, or central"—were suitable for the purpose.[49]

The issue for the Fabians was not municipalization versus nationalization—this was a question of expediency and efficiency—but collectivism versus individualism. And on this matter they were unambiguous. In an essay, "Socialism in England," written at the same time as the *Fabian Essays,* Webb defined socialism as a commitment to collectivism—economic, political, and ethical.

> On the economic side, Socialism implies the collective administration of rent and interest, leaving to the individual only the wages of his labour, of hand or brain. On the political side, it involves the collective control over, and ultimate administration of, all the main instruments of wealth production. On the ethical side, it expresses the real recognition of fraternity, and universal obligation of personal service, and the subordination of individual ends to the common good.[50]

When Beatrice Webb joined the Fabian Society in 1891, she still had some doubts about socialism and a lingering attachment to individualism. Those doubts soon disappeared, but perhaps because of her long friendship with that arch-individualist, Herbert Spencer (who removed her as his literary executor when she married Sidney), she was especially aware of the extent of the Fabian commitment to collectivism. The Fabians, she discovered, were "far more extreme in their opinions and projects than their phrases conveyed to the ordinary citizen." They "translated economics and collectivism into the language of prosaic vestrymen and town councillors." They talked about factory acts and gas and water, but they were actually dedicated to a far-reaching collectivism: "collective ownership where ever practicable; collective regulation everywhere else; collective provision according to need for all the impotent and sufferers; and collective taxation in proportion to wealth, especially surplus wealth."[51]

Their strategy was to achieve these ends not by revolution but by "impregnating all the existing forces of society with Collectivist ideals and Collectivist principles."[52]

FOR ALL THEIR professions of gradualism and inevitability, the Fabians were neither passive nor quietistic. They did not rely upon the evolutionary process to work itself out naturally, without external intervention (as evolution functioned in nature). Because they were not Marxists— because they had no faith in the dialectic of history, no confidence in the mission of the proletariat, no belief in the efficacy of revolution—they were all the more committed to the conscious articulation and advancement of their socialist program. They saw themselves as the effective actors in history, not strutting on the stage but working behind the scenes, writing the lines, directing the production, manipulating the players, and giving shape and meaning to the historical drama.

This was the rationale for their strategy of "permeation."* It was why the Fabians never aspired to become a mass party in their own right and why they resisted for so long the formation or even support of a parliamentary socialist or labor party. "We, like the homeopathists and the old Radicals," Sidney Webb wrote, "shall win without being acknowledged victors, by permeation of the others."[54] In retrospect, the Fabian resistance to an independent party may seem "anomalous" or "aberrant."[55] In fact it was perfectly consistent with their principles. In 1893, when the Liberals failed to adopt a policy of reform, the Fabians supported the independent candidates who stood for Parliament; when the results of that election proved disappointing, they felt confirmed in their distrust of direct political action and relations with the ILP became decidedly cool. Three years later, when Ramsay MacDonald stood as a candidate for the Independent Labour Party, Beatrice Webb asked him, "Do we want to organize the *un*thinking persons into socialist societies, or make the *thinking* persons socialistic?"[56] It was not until the end of the decade that the Fabian executive agreed, with a marked lack of enthusiasm, to become one of the constituent units of the Labour Representation Committee (which later became the Labour Party).

Throughout these early years, the Fabians continued to permeate,

---

* The Fabians were not the first to use the word, still less the strategy. In 1882 Charles Dilke said that the Radicals sought to "permeate" the Liberal party as "a leaven in the liberal lump."[53] But the Fabians were the first socialist group to develop the concept consciously and apply it systematically.

impregnate, and propagate their ideas wherever and however they could—in the London County Council (to which Sidney Webb was elected in 1892), the London School of Economics and Political Science (which the Fabians founded in 1894), parliamentary committees and royal commissions (Sidney Webb drafted the Eight Hour Bill of 1889 and the Minority Report of the Royal Commission of Labour in 1894, and Sidney and Beatrice together wrote the Minority Report of the Poor Law Commission in 1909), the Liberal Party (when the Webbs cultivated the Liberal Imperialists), and the Tory Party (when they supported the Education Act of 1902). In the general election of 1906, thirteen Fabians stood for Parliament; of the seven elected, four were members of the newly formed Labour Party, one stood as a Progressive and Labour candidate, and two, including one member of the Fabian executive, were Liberals.*

The Fabians were permeators because they were not, in the conventional sense, democrats. In 1886, Sidney Webb explained why he opposed the creation of a socialist party: "I don't believe 10% of us are fit for a socialistic state yet."[58] With the outbreak of the Boer War he discovered just how unfit the English people were—unfit not only for a socialist state but for a capitalist one as well. The thousands of volunteers rejected for military service gave the Fabians dramatic confirmation of the need for social reform, and at the same time brought to a head a dispute among themselves about the British Empire.[59] While none of the Fabians defended the conduct of the war, some of them (Webb, Shaw, Pease) favored a victory of the British, and others (Wallas, Olivier, MacDonald) were passionately pro-Boer. The issue was taken to the membership, which rejected a motion to denounce the war and imperialism. Although the vote was not an endorsement of either the war or imperialism, it was generally understood as such—an impression reinforced by the resignation of the anti-war members of the executive committee and by the publication a few months later of the tract *Fabianism and the Empire,* written by Shaw after intensive discussion by the membership.

Those Fabians who supported the war and empire did so not for

---

*A more private mode of permeation was pursued by Beatrice Webb, who boasted, "I could insinuate myself into smoking-rooms, business offices, private and public conferences, without rousing suspicion."[57] Dinner parties, especially her own, were her favored milieu, for her guests were a captive audience (she did not conceal her displeasure when one absented himself to go to the lavatory), and the meal itself only a pretext (a bare pretext, since she skimped on the food and wine) for a discussion carefully orchestrated by herself.

nationalistic or patriotic reasons but precisely because they were socialists.[60] The British Empire was deemed "progressive" because it was in the best interests of Britain as a whole and of the British working class in particular. Imperialism was in effect socialism on a larger scale. As Beatrice Webb explained to Bertrand Russell, the Fabians wanted to make "the Empire the 'Unit of Consideration' rather than the 40 millions in this island."[61] They made common cause with the Liberal Imperialists (the "Limps," as Haldane, Asquith, and Grey were known) because the latter were "at once collectivists and imperialists"—"collectivists" at least to the extent of opposing free trade and favoring social reforms to enhance "national efficiency."[62]

In a famous article published in 1901, "Lord Rosebery's Escape from Houndsditch," Sidney Webb advised Rosebery to transform the Liberal Party into a party of "National Efficiency," which would enact social and educational reforms, restore Britain's industrial and commercial superiority, eliminate inefficiency in the government, and establish a "National Minimum" standard of life, all designed to "insure the rearing of an Imperial race."[63] The following year Webb formed the "Co-Efficients," a dining club made up of Fabians, Liberal Imperialists, and progressive Unionists, dedicated to "the aims, policy and methods of Imperial Efficiency at home and abroad."[64] Modeled upon a shadow cabinet for a Party of National Efficiency, the club consisted of twelve members with portfolios in municipal affairs (Webb), law (Richard Haldane), foreign affairs (Sir Edward Grey), army (L. S. Amery), philosophy and science (Bertrand Russell), literature (H. G. Wells), and so on.*

THE CO-EFFICIENTS had no ministry of "Eugenics," but they could well have had. When Sidney Webb exhorted the Liberal Imperialists to take steps to "insure the rearing of an Imperial race," he literally meant "race," not merely "nation." In this usage he reflected the views of the eugenics movement that became prominent during the Boer War.

The "science" of eugenics started in the early 1880s at the same time

---

* The titles of the cabinet posts were more revealing than the individuals named to them, reflecting the importance the Webbs (like the Positivists) attached to philosophy, science, literature, law, journalism, geography—hardly the usual cabinet components. ("Geography," in this cabinet, was a euphemism for "empire," the occupant of that seat, H. J. Mackinder, being a Reader in geography at Oxford with a "geopolitical" approach.)

that socialism became popular, and for some of the same reasons. The eugenicists wanted to reform not only society but the race, and to do so by controlling the biological nature of human beings as well as their social environment. (A smaller group of eugenicists held to the contrary view: that the survival of the fittest was best promoted by the unimpeded process of natural selection.) The term was coined by Francis Galton, a cousin of Charles Darwin and a friend of Beatrice Webb's family; when she first met him she pronounced him "the ideal man of science."[65] Galton's chief disciple was Karl Pearson, a socialist who regarded the "science" of eugenics as an essential feature of a truly scientific socialism. It was the Boer War, with the clamor about racial degeneration and national efficiency, that converted eugenics from a "science" to a "movement."[66]

Eugenics was especially congenial to the scientific-minded, efficiency-oriented Fabians who, as Beatrice Webb once said of Sidney, had the temperament of the "social engineer."[67]* In *The New Machiavelli,* H. G. Wells remarked that if the Baileys (the fictional counterparts of the Webbs) "had the universe in hand," they would take down all the trees and put up stamped tin green shades and sunlight accumulators in their stead; "Altiora [Beatrice] thought trees hopelessly irregular and sea cliffs a great mistake."[69] He might have added that they also thought the conventional process of human breeding "hopelessly irregular" and would have liked to improve it so as to create a fitter race, a race better adapted to a Positivist, socialist order.

Wells himself, one of the "twelve wise men" in the select company of Co-Efficients and for a few years a leading figure among the Fabians, was an enthusiastic eugenicist who heartily endorsed Pearson's proposal for the "sterilisation of failures."[70] In 1901 the Webbs read Wells's *Antici-pations*; "the most remarkable book of the year," Beatrice pronounced it, "a powerful imagination furnished with the data and methods of physical science working on social problems . . . full of luminous hypotheses and

---

* The Fabians were more receptive to eugenics than the Marxists, who assumed, in theory at least, that the nationalization of the means of production and the resulting change in "social relations" would suffice to correct whatever deficiencies there were in human beings. A later generation of Marxists was more sympathetic to eugenics, perhaps because they no longer had that faith in the redemptive powers of national-ization, perhaps because they saw in the Soviet Union the instrument for a more direct, scientific, biological control over human beings. J. B. S. Haldane in England and H. J. Muller in America were prominent exponents of what was known as "Bolshevik Eugenics."[68]

worth careful study by those who are trying to look forward."[71] This remarkable book was a utopia, a "new republic" governed by a "new ethics," whose purpose was "to favor the procreation of what is fine and efficient and beautiful in humanity—beautiful and strong bodies, clear and powerful minds, and a growing body of knowledge—and to check the procreation of base and servile types, of fear-driven and cowardly souls, of all that is mean and ugly and bestial in the souls, bodies, or habits of men."[72]

It was an ethic worthy of Nietzsche, differing from his only in invoking the authority of "modern science." In that utopia, science would identify, prevent, and eliminate the "base and servile types" who contaminated society—the "feeble, ugly, inefficient, born of unrestrained lusts, and increasing and multiplying through sheer incontinence and stupidity." Unfit couples would exist "on sufferance," on condition that they did not procreate, and would be killed if they violated that condition. The leaders of the new republic need not be "squeamish" about inflicting death because they had "an ideal that will make killing worth the while," the means of performing that killing mercifully ("with an opiate"), and the satisfaction of knowing that such killing was more humane than long-term imprisonment or conventional penal measures. If the latter were called for, they too would be humane—"good, scientifically caused pain, that will leave nothing but a memory." Similar results could be achieved by laws designed to "keep the black, or yellow, or mean-white squatter on the move," and by the eradication of rookeries, which would destroy the breeding ground of the "mean-spirited, under-sized, diseased little man, quite incapable of earning a decent living for himself, married to some under-fed, ignorant, ill-shaped, plain, and diseased little woman, and guilty of the lives of ten or twelve ugly, ailing children." It was with great satisfaction that Wells contemplated his utopia: "Consider what it will mean to have perhaps half the population of the world, in every generation, restrained from or tempted to evade reproduction! This thing, this euthanasia of the weak and sensual is possible."[73]

The following year Beatrice Webb was captivated by another work on this "most important of all questions." After listening to Shaw read aloud his new play, *Man and Superman,* she reflected that only his "audacious genius" could do justice to this issue. "*We* cannot touch the subject of human breeding—it is not ripe for the mere industry of induction, and yet I realize that it is the most important of all questions, this breeding of the right sort of man."[74] The "right sort of man" was "superman," an idea Shaw generously credited to "that German Polish madman" Nietzsche.

But it was his own idea to have the superman produced by a process of "artificial selection." The old socialist dream of "the socialization of the means of production and exchange" was obsolete, Shaw decided; the only form of socialism feasible now was "the socialization of the selective breeding of Man." To further this end a "State Department of Evolution" should be created with a seat in the cabinet and a budget sufficient to defray the cost of experiments and to provide incentives to individuals to engage in selective breeding.[75]

If *Man and Superman* seems satiric, even facetious (an appendage to the play was entitled "The Revolutionist's Handbook and Pocket Companion"), Shaw himself was perfectly serious. And because he was prominent in both the eugenics and Fabian movements, the two tended to become identified. A regular lecturer for the Eugenics Education Society, Shaw advocated the "eugenic religion" as the only salvation for civilization: "We must eliminate the Yahoo or his vote will wreck the commonwealth."[76] Indeed he was so zealous in the cause that Pearson had to urge caution upon him, reminding the editor of *Fabian Essays* that "the doctrines of Eugenics will be best served, like those of socialism, by a slow process of impenetration."[77]

By 1907 the Webbs evidently judged that the process of "impenetration" had gone far enough to permit them to speak out publicly on the subject. In a Fabian tract that year Sidney Webb noted that while the birthrate was declining among the "abler" classes, it was increasing among the "thriftless and irresponsible." This "adverse selection" would inevitably lead to a "degeneration of type" and "race deterioration, if not race suicide"—at the very least to the country "gradually falling to the Irish and the Jews." At this point Fabian caution prevailed, and the only remedy Webb proposed was the "endowment of motherhood": family allowances paid by the government to encourage "the production of healthy, moral and intelligent citizens."[78] Later, in the course of their campaign for the "breakup" of the poor law, the Webbs were somewhat bolder. Disputing the laissez-faire interpretation of eugenics, that the state should not interfere with the natural process of selection, they advanced the true "Eugenist" view that the progress of society depended on an "intelligently purposeful selection" designed to encourage the birth of "well-born" children and "prevent the persistent multiplication of the congenitally feeble-minded." Among the preventive measures they recommended were the abolition of the workhouses, which were breeding grounds for the feeble-minded, and the creation of a special government authority with jurisdiction over all the feeble-minded whether destitute or not: "the feeble-minded mother of illegitimate children, the feeble-minded vagrant wandering along the road, and the feeble-minded parasite of urban soup-kitchens and free shelters." These people were to be "permanently segregate[d], under reasonably comfortable conditions and firm but kindly control." If such a policy was justified in the case of lunatics, the Webbs reasoned, it was surely justified for the feeble-minded, who were more likely to procreate and thus contribute to "our undoing as a nation."[79]

It was this policy of eugenics, as much as imperialism, that alienated the New Liberals from the Fabians. Leonard Hobhouse, who had earlier been sympathetic to the Fabians, was repelled by their talk of "racial" improvement. Social evolution, he insisted, had to do with the "socially fit," not the biologically fit, and in any case was antithetical to any policy of government intervention.[80] J. A. Hobson was at first better disposed to eugenics, but he too became wary of it.[81] Webb himself confirmed the worst suspicions of the New (and old) Liberals when he wrote, "No consistent eugenist can be a 'Laisser Faire' individualist unless he throws up the game in despair. He must interfere, interfere, interfere!"[82]

THE COMMON DENOMINATOR behind such Fabian "aberrances" as their partiality for imperialism and eugenics and their aversion to the Independent Labour Party was their distrust or depreciation of political democracy. They were all in favor of government *for* the people but not necessarily *of* or *by* the people. When they spoke of the need for democracy, it was in terms of the link between economic and political democracy. "Organic change," Sidney Webb explained in the *Fabian Essays,* had to be "democratic," that is, "acceptable to a majority of the people and prepared for in the minds of all"; once the people had political control, they would be able to control "the main instruments of wealth production."[83] In the same volume, Shaw made it the distinctive task of "Social Democracy" to "gather the whole people into the State" so that the state could then be entrusted with "all the sources of production."[84] In both essays, democracy was valued not so much as a means of government as a means of facilitating and legitimating the state's control over the economy. And that control was to be vested not in the people, not even in their parliamentary representatives, but in a class of "experts." Like the Positivists, the Fabians thought of politics in terms of administration rather than parliamentary government: the "administration of things" rather than the "government of persons."* The administration of things required not laymen or politicians but expert administrators, people as expert in matters of "social reconstruction" as engineers were in the building of bridges or lawyers in the interpretation of the law.[87]

The belittling of political democracy in the conventional sense accounts for another Fabian "aberrance"—their conspicuous absence from the women's suffrage movement. They made a few token references to universal suffrage, but when it was suggested that they publish a tract on women's suffrage, they could not agree on an acceptable formulation and the tract was never issued. In 1906, when the suffrage movement was at its height, the executive committee first refused and then grudgingly consented (at "pistol-point," as Margaret Cole put it) to amend the "Basis" so as to include women's suffrage.[88] According to Pease, the Fabians were reluctant to endorse this principle because it was "a question of Democracy rather than Socialism"; one could be a socialist, he said, without being a suffragist, and a suffragist without being a socialist.[89]

Beatrice Webb not only failed to support women's suffrage; in 1889 she signed the manifesto drawn up by Mrs. Humphry Ward opposing it. She recanted only in 1906, and then more for reasons of expediency than of principle. She later attributed her "anti-feminism" to a nature that was "conservative by temperament, and anti-democratic through social environment," to a dislike of the "parliamentary politics" of both parties, and to the fact that she herself never suffered the disabilities associated with her sex. (Indeed she found that being a woman was an asset as a social investigator and spared her the need to earn a living.)[90] When the suffrage was finally granted after the war, this most important domestic event of the year, she later wryly noted, went unmentioned in her diary. She had always assumed political democracy to be a "necessary part of government," but had never "exerted" herself to get it. "It has no glamour for me—I have been, for instance, wholly indifferent to my own political disfranchisement."[91]

---

* This formula was made explicit in the Webbs' constitution for a socialist Britain: "To use an old slogan of the Socialists, the government of men must be distinguished from the administration of things." They proposed to implement it by creating a bicameral system in which a "political parliament" would have jurisdiction over foreign and judicial affairs, and a "social parliament," not burdened by a cabinet or by ministerial responsibility, would control social and economic affairs.[85] (The "old slogan" came from Saint-Simon, who first said that a "governmental" regime would be followed by an "administrative" one, and Comte, who wrote that in a "scientific" political system, "the government of things replaces that of man.")[86]

If one could be a socialist without being a suffragist, one could also, it would seem, be a socialist without having much respect for the ordinary people. The books by Shaw and Wells that the Webbs found so "luminous" were flagrantly undemocratic; both were based on the assumption that the "common people" were inferior, morally and politically as well as physically. The message of *Man and Superman* was brutally expressed in its preface: "We are all now under what Burke called 'the hoofs of the swinish multitude' "; if Paine had triumphed over Burke, it was only in the sense that "the swine are now courted electors." By returning to power the old ruling class, the new electorate, the populace, proved itself incapable not only of governing but of choosing benevolent governors. In spite of all the efforts to feed and educate them, the common people were still "riff-raff." "To hand the country over to riff-raff is national suicide, since riff-raff can neither govern nor will let anyone else govern except the highest bidder of bread and circuses."[92]

In Wells's *Anticipations,* the riffraff were the "people of the abyss," the "great swollen, shapeless, hypertrophied social mass" which dominated present-day democracies and which would be replaced in the new republic by a class of "modern efficients."[93] This new class reappeared in *A Modern Utopia* in the guise of the "Samurai," a natural (not hereditary) nobility charged with the creation of the new, rational order. Dedicated to the public weal, the Samurai observed the highest standards of "moral and bodily health and efficiency." Their "Rule" prescribed strict dietary restrictions (no meat, tobacco, or alcohol); a daily routine of cold baths, exercises, and the like, to ensure not only physical perfection but also the "constant exercise of will"; and sexual chastity (although not celibacy— marriage was permitted, but to avoid the "uxorious inseparableness" that was demeaning for both partners, Samurai had to sleep alone at least four nights out of five). They were also limited to vocations that were socially productive (manufacturing, for example, but not advertising or selling).[94]

When Beatrice Webb congratulated Wells on this book, he told her that the chapters on the Samurai would "pander to all your worst instincts"—an allusion to her own puritanical, almost ascetic inclinations.[95] And when she said that Wells had "no great faith in government by the 'man in the street' and, I think, has hardly realised the function of the representative as a 'foolometer' for the expert," this too applied to the Webbs, who had no faith in government by the "man in the street," but who did think that they could manipulate his representative, the "foolometer" in Parliament, for their own purposes.[96] In *The New Machiavelli,* Wells had Sidney explaining to the Pentagram Circle (the fictional version of the Co-Efficients) that "democracy was really just a dodge for getting assent to the ordinances of the expert official by means of the polling booth."[97] Wells could not have known that Beatrice had used similar expressions in her diary to describe the London County Council: "The Council is a machine for evolving committees, the committee a machine for evolving one man—the chairman. Both alike are machines for dodging the democracy (in a crude sense) by introducing government by a select minority instead of the rule of the majority."[98] (The passage was especially pointed since Sidney was a leading figure in the Council, frequently a chairman, and always an excellent "committee man," as she said.[99]) She herself had no compunctions about "dodging the democracy" in order to make her minority prevail; this was literally what she tried to do on the Poor Law Commission, and when she failed, she threatened to turn over her plan to the Conservatives—"which," she remarked in her diary, "I should prefer in many ways—there would be no nonsense about democracy!"[100]

The Webbs were perfectly conscious that socialism as they understood it had only a tenuous relationship to democracy in the usual sense of the word. Beatrice once described her brother-in-law Leonard Courtney, a Liberal Member of Parliament, as a "democrat at heart" who believed that "the government of the country should be the reflection of the free desires and views of the whole body of the people," unlike the Webbs, who believed in government by experts.

> Possibly he [Courtney] is more of a democrat than we are ourselves, for we have little faith in the "average sensual man"; we do not believe that he can do much more than describe his grievances, we do not think that he can prescribe the remedies. . . . We wish to introduce into politics the professional expert, to extend the sphere of government by adding to its enormous advantages of wholesale and compulsory management, the advantage of the most skilled entrepreneur.[101]

"AVERAGE SENSUAL MAN" was the Webbs' synonym for the ordinary man who was incapable of exercising control not only over political and administrative affairs but even over his own "sensual" nature.[102] The expression was especially poignant for Beatrice Webb, who was engaged in a constant battle with her own nature, fearing that her "sensual side" was growing "at the expense of the intellectual."[103] Her dinner parties were notoriously sparing of food and drink, but they were positively luxurious compared with the regimen she imposed upon herself. She begrudged herself any morsel of food beyond the minimum required for sustenance (she literally weighed every bite she took), she abstained from meat and alcohol, and she made a valiant (not always successful) effort to give up coffee and cigarettes when she found herself enjoying them too much. Believing that overeating was the cause of most physical ills (including pneumonia and cancer), and most moral ills as well, she strove for a diet that combined "the lowest level in abstemiousness and the highest in efficiency."[104]

If Beatrice Webb felt herself to be so vulnerable, she had even less confidence in the ability of the ordinary man to resist his sensual nature. One of the evils of capitalism, as she saw it, was the stimulation of sensuality, and one of the virtues of socialism was the diminution of sensuality. So long as people were driven by sensual, physical, material desires, they would pursue their private interests and passions at the expense of the public interest and a rationally organized society. "Physical appetites," Beatrice Webb confessed, "are to me the devil: they are the signs of the disease that ends in death, the root of the hatred, malice and greed that make the life of man a futility."[105] Social evolution, like socialism itself, was the process by which the individual learned to subordinate "his physical desires and appetites to the intellectual and spiritual side of his nature."[106] Sidney Webb was less eloquent than his wife (and less self-agonizing and self-denying), but he was no less committed to the same ascetic conception of socialism. Soon after joining the Fabians (and before meeting Beatrice), he described socialism as a "call to frugal and earnest living," a system based upon "extreme social asceticism," in which the "perfectly socialised man" was one who "puts constraint on himself in every direction."[107]*

---

*It was this ascetic disposition that drew the Webbs to the Comtean rather than Saint-Simonian school of Positivism. The Saint-Simonians saw the good life in terms of the expansion and gratification of desires—material, physical, psychic, sexual; the Comteans as a limitation and inhibition of desires, an exercise in restraint and abnegation. (In his last years Comte declared celibacy a virtue and predicted that ultimately reproduction would become a function of woman alone, thus precluding any sexuality.) Similarly in economic affairs: the Saint-Simonians had an expansive, venturous, optimistic view of the economy, while the Comteans disapproved of large productive units, frowned on the production of luxuries, and favored sumptuary laws to curb consumption.

It was also this ascetic quality of Comteanism, as well as its scientific creed, that

The aversion to the "average sensual man" was not a private eccentricity of the Webbs. It was reflected in the idea of the "National Minimum" that was the Fabians' distinctive contribution to the welfare state. As originally formulated in 1897, the National Minimum meant minimum standards for wages, health, education, employment, and leisure.[109] Wages became less important to them as their attention turned to the idea of national efficiency and the "housekeeping state."[110] Rather than putting money in the hands of the workers, they preferred to provide them with the services that would improve their physical, mental, and moral condition—and to make certain that these services were utilized. Indeed more money might actually be counterproductive by encouraging workers to indulge their sensual nature, thus contributing to the further degeneration of the race. One of the Webbs' objections to social insurance was that it gave the sick and unemployed money in compensation for the loss of wages—money they could spend "as they choose."[111]*

The same distrust of the "average sensual man" was implicit in the idea of "national efficiency." For the Fabians, the objective was not an increase of production (what we would now call the Gross National Product) or even an increase in the purchasing power of the workers. They had, in fact, as little faith in unregulated consumption as in unregulated production—as little confidence in the will or ability of workers to judge what was good for them as in the will or ability of capitalists to judge what was good for society. Beatrice Webb confided in her diary what she could not say in public.

---

made the Webbs see the hand of Comte in the work of Lenin and Stalin. After her visit to the Soviet Union, Beatrice Webb contrasted the "average sensual man" in the West, whose conception of the good life was materialistic and hedonistic, measured in terms of housing, food, and cars, to the new Soviet man, whose higher values included learning, personal hygiene, and self-control. As a result of the "reformation of manners and morals" in the Soviet Union, she was pleased to report, "there is no spooning in the Parks of Recreation and Rest."[108]

* In the preface to *Major Barbara* Shaw ridiculed this suspicion of money. Poverty, he argued, was a lack of money and could be remedied by giving the poor money. This was what the poor craved and what they deserved. "The crying need of the nation is not for better morals, cheaper bread, temperance, liberty, culture . . . , but simply for enough money." He might have been satirizing the Webbs when he said that the poor did not want an ascetic or aesthetic life; they wanted the same material vulgarities the rich had—or that "the elect souls among the rich turn away with loathing." It is no wonder that Beatrice Webb found the play unconvincing. "There is something lacking in his presentment of the crime of poverty."[112]

The urgent question nowadays is not maximum production or even equality of distribution but the *character of consumption,* the vital problem of whether the use of a particular commodity or service does or does not increase efficiency? Probably we could, with advantage, cut away half the private expenditure of the nation and absolutely increase its happiness and capacity if we were permitted to select which part to cut off. At present we leave this vital problem of character of consumption to be solved by the appetites of each individual, even to the extent of permitting them to poison themselves and their children. It will not be so very long before a whole system of sumptuary laws—at any rate as regards non-adults, will come into force. That was a brilliant suggestion of H. G. Wells that we should divide the world into adults and non-adults. For some purpose we would raise "the age of consent" to say, fifty![113]

Raise "the age of consent" to fifty—it was only a half-facetious suggestion, for it reflected the perfectly serious view that the "average sensual man" was little more than a child, a "non-adult" incapable of controlling his appetites or judging his own best interests. It also exposed the "nanny" mentality evident in so many Fabian pronouncements and policies. If the ordinary people were incapable of governing themselves, a class of experts was ready and able to govern them in their best interests.

THIS FORM of "nannyism"—the word may be more fitting than "paternalism" to describe the "housekeeping state"—revealed itself most dramatically in the debate over the poor law in 1909. Although that subject properly belongs to the Edwardian rather than the Victorian period, it illustrates a mode of thought that was distinctively Fabian from the beginning.

The Fabian position on the poor law is generally identified with the Minority Report of the Poor Law Commission (Beatrice served on the commission and Sidney helped write the report), in contrast to the Majority Report largely drafted by Helen Bosanquet. Where the majority proposed to reform the poor law by expanding the range of services and relief provided under the law, the minority sought to "break up" the poor law by creating separate authorities for specific purposes: an education authority for poor children, a health authority for the sick, an asylum authority for the mentally ill, a national labor exchange for the unemployed, a pension authority for the aged.[114] The more significant contrast, however, is with the National Insurance Act of 1911, which was based upon the principle of a compulsory, contributory system of insurance. Beatrice Webb tried to dissuade Lloyd George and his advisers from adopting any insurance plan. "I tried to impress on them that any grant from the community to the individual beyond what it does for all, ought to be conditional on better conduct and that any insurance scheme had the fatal defect that the state got nothing for its money—that the persons felt they had a right to the allowance whatever their conduct."[115] Although the Fabians felt it impolitic publicly to oppose the National Insurance Bill, some of them privately confessed that they would have preferred to see it defeated.[116] The fundamental flaw of any insurance plan, they argued, whether for sickness, accident, or unemployment, was its "unconditionality." "Indeed, the fact that sick and unemployed persons were entitled to money incomes without any corresponding obligation to get well and keep well, or to seek and keep employment, seemed to us likely to encourage malingering and a disinclination to work for their livelihood."[117] This had been the experience, the Webbs said, of the Workmen's Compensation Act of 1897, which tempted workers to make "the most of every mishap," avoid treatment so as to collect compensation, and then squander the money and become a charge upon the community.[118*]

For the same reason, the minority opposed the recommendation that the sick receive treatment *"without charge and without disfranchisement"* (the words were italicized in the Minority Report, as if to emphasize their absurdity), and the "even more extraordinary" proposal that the patient be given "a free choice of doctors"—a policy that would encourage the patient to choose the doctor "who interferes least with his habits" and who would be most likely to order "medical extras" such as food and alcohol.[120] The Webbs raised the same objection to the National Insurance Act, which provided for "gratuitous" benefits and a free choice of doctors and thus was an invitation to "malingering." The government, they complained, would be "paying the people to be ill!"[121]

Instead of such "gratuitous" and "unconditional" benefits, the minority favored a system of compulsory services which the poor would be

---

* The Fabians supported old age pensions because, unlike other forms of insurance, the money went to those who were beyond working age and thus past the temptation of "malingering." The pensions act excluded those who were known to be of "bad character." Sidney Webb wanted to go further, not only to withhold the pension but to authorize the local authority "compulsorily to remove to an appropriate institution (as now for insane, and infectious disease cases) anyone found incapable of keeping himself decently clean and healthy: in short to prevent a public nuisance."[119]

obliged to utilize and pay for according to their means. Thus a sick person, in return for an affordable fee, would be assigned a doctor and required to undergo whatever treatment was recommended. Similarly, an unemployed person would have to register with the local labor exchange and accept whatever employment was regarded as suitable. Unlike the majority proposal (incorporated in the National Insurance Act) for a system of voluntary exchanges, the minority called for compulsory exchanges to be administered by a Ministry of Labour that would have exclusive control over the hiring of all the unemployed (except for those in "permanent situations" experiencing temporary unemployment). The labor exchanges would be supplemented by a network of Training Establishments for redundant workers and Detention Colonies for recalcitrant workers or idlers—those whose "morbid state of mind" prevented them from being useful members of the industrial order.[122] The same principle was applied to charity and public relief; here too the evils were "indiscriminate" charity and "unconditional" relief.[123] "It is no use," Beatrice Webb wrote to her sister, "letting the poor come and go, as they think fit, be helped or not—helped as the charitable choose. That is really pauperism and encourages persons to be parasites. Destitution must be prevented and where necessary penalised as a public nuisance."[124]

Perhaps only Beatrice Webb could have described the Minority Report—not ironically but proudly—as a "great social drainage scheme."[125] The metaphor evokes echoes of the "residuum," a term commonly used, especially in early-Victorian England, to describe both the refuse of sewage and the "refuse" of the population.[126] It is interesting that the Minority Report, in its concluding paragraph, reverted to this earlier usage and made precisely the same analogy. Arguing that the report was not, as some had said, "utopian," it recalled the time when a solution of the sewage problem seemed to be utopian.

> To combine these festering heaps into a single main drainage system seemed, to the Statesmen and social reformers of 1820 or 1830, beyond the bounds of possibility. We now take for granted that only by such a concentration is it possible to get rid of the festering heaps and scientifically treat the ultimate residuum. . . . What has been effected in the organisation of Public Health and Public Education can be effected, if we wish it, in the Public Organisation of the Labour Market.[127]

* * *

IT IS CURIOUS that the Fabians should have acquired the reputation they have, as the pioneers of the welfare state, in spite of their adamant opposition to one of the basic principles of the welfare state, social insurance.[128] But the reputation is deserved. If they did not furnish the blueprints of the welfare state, they were its architects in a more fundamental sense, for they provided the rationale for a vast expansion in the authority and machinery of the state. They lost the battle over social insurance, but won the war over the welfare state.* Their socialism has been aptly termed "welfare statism"[129]—the assumption by the state of responsibility for an increasing number of services, administered by a growing class of experts, and supported by an expanded apparatus of the state.

If Fabian socialism seems more bureaucratic than socialistic, it is because social engineering left little room for the sentimentality, as the Fabians thought it, of "workers' control." Beatrice Webb described herself and Sidney as belonging to the "B's" of this world, "bourgeois, bureaucratic, and benevolent," in contrast to the "A's," "aristocratic, anarchist, and artistic."[130] She might also have distinguished them from the "M's" of this world, "Marxist, militant, mass-oriented." The rejection of the ideology of class struggle, some historians have said, deprived the Fabians of any influence among the increasingly class-conscious workers, especially in the north.[131] This may be true (although the more Marxist SDF was not notably successful in appealing to those workers). By the same token, however, the Fabians were all the more influential among the "bourgeois, bureaucratic, and benevolent" middle class, who became the bearers of this English-style socialism.

Fabianism was most important, politically, socially, even culturally, in the decades before and after the Second World War. But its distinctive ideology and policy emerged in late-Victorian England. If Fabianism occupies so much more space in this history than the other reformist and socialist groups of the time, it is because its influence has been more enduring and its nature less appreciated. As Fabianism is inexplicable without Positivism, so the welfare state is inexplicable without Fabianism.

---

* They lost the battle, it is generally said, for fiscal rather than ideological reasons: a contributory insurance scheme was less a drain on the treasury than the independent authorities the Webbs favored—even taking into account the Webbs' proposal that the beneficiaries of those services make at least nominal payments for them.

On Fabianism and Webbism

ONE OF THE DIFFICULTIES in assessing the influence of Fabianism is the difficulty in defining its ideology. There was no single authoritative statement of doctrine beyond the nebulous "Basis." The leadership spoke with many voices, some (Shaw's, most notably) deliberately ironic and facetious, others eccentric and inconsistent. And the membership, in the strict dues-paying, meeting-attending sense of that term, provides no measure of its influence. What the Fabians lacked as an organization, they more than made up for as a movement, a movement composed not only of members but of "fellow travelers" and "sympathizers" (terms more often applied to the Communist movement but no less applicable to the Fabians). As Trevelyan said, they were "intelligence officers without an army" but commanding "great hosts moving under other banners."[132] If they had no binding creed, no indisputable articles of faith, they did have a mode of thought, a distinctive approach to social problems—a "disposition" that was perhaps more influential, in the intellectual and political climate of England, than any "ideology" might have been.

A good deal of that influence must be credited to the Webbs. Yet here too there is a problem. For "Webbism," as José Harris has said, is not synonymous with Fabianism.[133] The Webbs were not even synonymous, so to speak, with each other (although in public the "Webb firm" presented a united front), still less with such free spirits in the leadership as Shaw and Annie Besant, or with the amorphous and inconstant membership. Nevertheless, they did occupy a unique position both in the organization and in the movement. They were the reigning couple, combining in themselves the ceremonial and functional roles of both monarch and prime minister. Sidney was a member of the executive for just short of half a century (from 1886 to 1935), always coming in at the head of the poll, and unquestionably (as even Shaw conceded) the dominant figure in the Society. (He was also the de facto representative of the Fabians in the London County Council and, later, in the Labour Party.) Beatrice did not join the executive until 1911 (she too remained until 1935), but she played an active role before then, as writer, lecturer, organizer, and permeator par excellence. An institution in themselves, the Webbs were the driving force behind the creation of those other institutions that later brought Fabianism to a still larger audience: the London School of Economics, the *New Statesman,* the Fabian Summer School, the Fabian Research Department. (The latter was captured by the Guild socialists, who then joined forces with the Fabians.)

Perhaps more important were the products of the Webb partnership—the scholarly tomes on trade unionism, local government, and the poor law which gave historical and theoretical legitimization to Fabian principles, and the mass of tracts, pamphlets, essays, and books which popularized and propagated their policies. (Webb wrote twenty-five of the first sixty Fabian tracts, as well as many of the anonymous ones.) If the historian quotes so extensively from the Webbs, it is not only because they were such prolific and quotable writers but also because their writings were often decisive in formulating Fabian principles and policies. The case of the poor law was typical. The Minority Report was written by the Webbs; the National Committee for the Prevention of Destitution was entirely their (especially her) creation, and the whole issue was defined and dominated by them personally. Yet it became a major commitment of the Fabian Society. Well before the Minority Report was issued, its analysis and recommendations were anticipated in a tract written by the secretary of the Society; the report itself was printed and distributed by the Fabians; the National Committee was staffed and promoted by them; and the "breakup" of the poor law was their official and highly publicized slogan.

So it was with the objectives and methods that were formulated most sharply by the Webbs but that became distinctively Fabian: a socialism to be achieved not by class struggle but by permeation and education, a collectivism that was to come about gradually and inexorably, an economic and social revolution that was to be a fundamental moral revolution, a society that was to be organized, planned, and directed so as to be rational, efficient, and scientific—the very model of a Positive society.

Toward the Welfare State

"THE STRANGE DEATH OF MORAL ENGLAND," the title of the final chapter of a book on L. T. Hobhouse, is a fitting epitaph for the "New Liberalism."[1] (It echoes, of course, the well-known book by George Dangerfield, *The Strange Death of Liberal England*.)[2] Hobhouse, one of the leading exponents of the creed that dominated social thought in the early years of the twentieth century, attributed that death to the First World War, which destroyed his generation's illusions about the inevitability of moral progress and social harmony. In fact, the signs of mortality had appeared earlier, in the heyday of the new liberalism.

The term was first prominently used, in this context, by Richard Haldane in 1896 in an article entitled "The New Liberalism"; but it became popular only after the turn of the century.[3] Apart from Hobhouse and Haldane, the leading theorists of the new liberalism included J. A. Hobson, C. F. G. Masterman, Herbert Samuel, and William Beveridge. If the movement did not attract anything like the public attention enjoyed earlier by the single-taxers or the Fabians, it did represent a significant development in English social and intellectual life, if only because it belied the familiar expectation that, among the "vanguard" at least, socialism would be the wave of the future, the natural evolution of progressive thought.[4]

Socialism did not cease to exist in the 1900s, but it did cease to be the rallying cry of "advanced" thinkers. It may seem paradoxical that talk of socialism subsided at a time when social reforms were being adopted on a far bolder and more comprehensive scale than ever before. Indeed many of the reformers, so far from embracing socialism in any form, consciously dissociated themselves from it. Some, having earlier been attracted to Fabianism, were disaffected by its espousal of imperialism and eugenics and its opposition to social insurance. Others simply felt no need to define themselves as socialists. With laissez-faire no longer an issue, they could be serious reformers without assuming that provocative label.

From the perspective of socialism, the new liberalism was regressive, a return to the older liberalism of Green. That lineage had been clearly established by Haldane in his article, which quoted extensively and approvingly from Green. In its inception and intention, the new liberalism was as much an ethical creed as the older "positive liberalism." Like Green, the new liberals believed in a "best self" that was more than the material interests of the individual, in a "common good" that was larger than the good of the individual, and in a social order in which moral obligations and responsibilities were paramount.[5] They gave the state a significantly larger role in legislation and administration than Green would have countenanced, but not nearly the role the socialists gave it. Unlike the socialists, who were collectivists in principle—the SDF committed to the nationalization of the means of production, and the Fabians to the regulation and organization of all the resources of society—the new liberals were collectivists for limited, pragmatic, expediential purposes, for the sake of particular reforms that required the intervention of the state.

In this pragmatic sense, Lloyd George and Winston Churchill might be regarded as practitioners, if not professed adherents, of the new liberalism, and the social reforms of the Liberal government might be taken as its main accomplishments. While Churchill was still a junior member of the government, he was pleased to announce that the Liberals were about to embark on a novel and adventurous experiment designed to "draw a line below which we will not allow persons to live and labour" and (changing the metaphor) to "spread a net over the abyss."[6] Later, as the head of the Board of Trade, he used other metaphors (sometimes mixed metaphors) to the same effect. "I say," he wrote to Asquith, "thrust a big slice of Bismarckianism over the whole underside of our industrial system, and await the consequences whatever they may be with a good conscience."[7] That "slice of Bismarckianism" was the social insurance plan, which would serve as "a complete ladder, an unbroken bridge or causeway, as it were, along which the whole body of the people may move with a certain measure of security and safety against hazards and misfortunes." While the state could not "carry the toiler on to dry land," it could "strap a lifebelt around him, whose buoyancy, aiding his own strenuous exertions, ought to enable him to reach the shore."[8]

Beatrice Webb, who was a moralist as well as a collectivist—indeed a collectivist in order to ensure a moral order to her liking—objected to the social insurance plan because it did not enforce any principle of morality. The fatal defect of any insurance scheme, she argued, was that it gave people money allowances unconditionally, without any return in the way of better conduct; it gave them unemployment benefits without any obligation to seek and keep work, and sickness benefits without any obligation to seek and accept medical help.[9]

Churchill boldly admitted as much. Social policy, he wrote in a memorandum in 1909, should not be grounded in moral criteria.

> I do not feel convinced that we are entitled to refuse benefit to a qualified man who loses his employment through drunkenness. He has paid his contributions; he has insured himself against the fact of unemployment, and I think it arguable that his foresight should be rewarded irrespective of the cause of his dismissal, whether he lost his situation through his own habits of intemperance or through his employer's habits of intemperance.

He went on to say that insurance did not necessarily entail a "diminution of personal responsibilities" since personal efforts would still be rewarded, and people would be inspired to greater exertions if they were relieved of severe distress. In a single sentence, however, he dramatically broke with the moral constraints of the past: "I do not like mixing up moralities and mathematics."[10]

At the same time that Churchill was proposing to sever individual morality from social policy, William Beveridge was effecting the same separation between individual responsibility and social problems. In 1909 Beveridge published *Unemployment: A Problem of Industry*. The title encapsulated the message: unemployment was a problem of industry, rather than, as was once thought, a problem of the unemployed. The implication for the larger problem of poverty was obvious: poverty too was a problem of society rather than of the poor, and thus a responsibility of society rather than of the individual.

This principle was reflected in the major reforms of this period—old age pensions, labor exchanges, and the National Insurance Act—but only partially and with reservations. Each of them imposed "qualifying conditions" that retained a semblance of the distinction between the "deserving" and "undeserving." The pensions act, for example, excluded paupers and those who "habitually failed to work," while the contributory provision of the National Insurance Act had something of the same effect, since paupers and those who habitually failed to work did not contribute to the plan and therefore did not receive benefits from it.[11]

It was the welfare state that finally brought about the divorce of morality from social policy. The divorce was finalized when the services and benefits provided by the state were made available to everyone regardless of merit or even need. And it was legitimized when it became a moral principle to eschew moral distinctions and judgments. There was an ethical theory implicit in this policy of moral neutrality: it was the theory that society was responsible for social problems and that therefore society (in the form of the state) had the moral responsibility to solve those problems. This was the import of the *Beveridge Report*, as it became known, the document issued in 1942 which heralded the welfare state as the next "British revolution," a revolution that was "a natural development from the past."[12]

THE "DE-MORALIZATION," as it were, of the problem of poverty was accompanied by a "relativization" of the problem. That poverty was a relative concept was hardly a novel idea. Adam Smith had given it its classic formulation in his definition of the "necessaries" of life: "By necessaries I understand, not only the commodities which are indispensably necessary for the support of life, but whatever the custom of the country renders it indecent for creditable people, even of the lowest order, to be without."[13] For evidence of the degree to which the "custom of the country" redefined those "necessaries" in the course of the twentieth century, one need only look at the sequels to the Booth and Rowntree surveys.

The Booth sequel was directed by his chief assistant, Hubert Llewellyn Smith, who made a conscious effort to replicate Booth's standards and poverty line. The research was begun in 1928, the first volume of *The New Survey of London Life and Labour* appeared two years later, and the ninth and final volume in 1935. The study, based upon a detailed street-by-street survey, found that 8.7 percent of the population (or 9.5 percent using a somewhat different base) was in poverty—a "vast diminution," the authors reported, from the 30.7 percent in Booth's time. This was no cause for complacency, they added, since there were still nearly half a million people living below a poverty line fixed at the low standards of a much earlier generation.[14]

The last volume of *The New Survey of London* was barely published before Rowntree embarked upon a new survey of York. In 1941, forty years after the publication of *Poverty*, Rowntree published the sequel, *Poverty and Progress*. The change of title is as significant as his findings. The figures for "primary" poverty declined from 9.9 percent of the population and 15.5 percent of the working classes to 4.2 percent and 6.8 percent, respectively, while those in "secondary" poverty declined from 27.8 percent and 43.4 percent to 17.8 percent and 31.1 percent. The comparison is even more striking than these figures suggest, for 1899, when the first survey was conducted, was a year of relative prosperity, whereas 1936, when the second was begun, was a time of great unemployment and depression. The new study, moreover, redefined the poverty line itself, so that it was no longer a line of "bare subsistence" but of decent "living." Instead of 30s.7d. for a family of five, which would have been the equivalent (adjusted for inflation) of the old line, it was now set at 43s.6d.—an increase in the standard itself of almost 50 percent.

The new poverty line was based not only on higher dietary requirements but also on such newly defined necessities as a daily newspaper, beer, tobacco, the rental of a radio, and an occasional cinema. Although Rowntree himself made a large point of the decline in the hours of work, from 54 hours a week to 44 or 48, and thus the greater leisure time available to workers, this was not reflected in the poverty line or in the poverty statistics. Nor were such other improvements in the standard of living as paid vacations, old age pensions, unemployment and sickness benefits, better sanitation, and an extension of free education. Like the authors of the Booth sequel, Rowntree warned his readers against undue optimism. "The satisfaction which we may rightly feel at this great improvement must be qualified by a serious sense of concern that so large a proportion of the workers are living below a poverty line which few, if any, will regard as having been fixed at too high a level."[15] In fact the main criticism of the book at the time was that it set the poverty line at too low a level. A more suitable line, one study suggested, would have placed almost half of the working classes of York below that line.[16]

Another sequel by Rowntree in 1951 (in collaboration with G. R. Lavers) produced still more striking results. Based on a poverty line of 100s.2d. (which was considerably higher than the 1936 equivalent), it concluded that "primary" poverty had been virtually eliminated, declining from 17.8 percent of the population (31.1 percent of the working classes) in 1936 to 1.7 percent and 2.8 percent fifteen years later. Much of the decline, the authors conjectured, was the result of the benefits provided by the welfare state, but they did not try to prove this statistically.[17]

* * *

WHATEVER OTHER factors were responsible for the decline of poverty after the Second World War—economic growth, social mobility, educational advances, cultural changes—the idea of poverty itself was significantly altered by the very conception of the welfare state. In a literal sense, "poverty" was displaced by "welfare." Instead of being concerned with the poverty of the few, the welfare state assumed responsibility for the welfare of the many. In effect, it turned attention from social *problems* to social *conditions*—the conditions of everyone, problematic or not. This was implied in the welfare system itself, a system of comprehensive, universal, "across-the-board" services and benefits, directed not only to the poor, not even to the working classes, but to all citizens alike.

The humanitarian motive behind the idea of "welfare" was the desire to remove the stigma attached to "relief." By eliminating the means test for family allowances, medical services, and the other benefits provided by the state, the poor would be helped without being stigmatized as the beneficiaries of the public largesse—indeed without being defined as "poor." The ideological motive was egalitarianism, the diminution and eventual extinction of all class differences and advantages. These two motives sometimes worked at cross-purposes. The "across-the-board" policies, it was discovered, often benefited the middle classes more than the working classes, the former being more adept at coping with the bureaucratic requirements and more sophisticated in exploiting the available resources (psychological treatment, for example). On occasion the egalitarian principle dramatically contravened the humanitarian one. In 1949, when the old Housing of the Working Classes Act was being replaced by a new Housing Act (the change of name is itself significant), a Labour Member of Parliament pointed out that the new bill repealed a clause of the old one that was especially beneficial to working-class tenants. He was promptly rebuked by the Labour Minister of Housing for applying "obsolete class distinctions."[18]

The egalitarian spirit emboldened some of the advocates of the welfare state to discard the "minimum standard" that defined the poverty level and replace it with an "optimum standard" that would define a universal welfare level. The Labour Party election manifesto in 1945, "Let Us Face the Future" (which more than most manifestos became the basis of the Labour Party program in office), proclaimed that "the best health services should be available for all" and that free health centers should provide "the best that modern science can offer." When the "best" was clearly unfeasible, the "good" was invoked: "good wages" for all workers and "a good standard of accommodation" for every family. The other operative word was "all": "fair shares for all," "jobs for all," "security for all."[19]

IF IT WAS UTOPIAN to expect the welfare state to achieve equality, it was not utopian to expect it to abolish poverty. Yet it failed to do that as well. "Pockets of poverty" were soon discovered that eluded the ministrations of the welfare state. To reach those pockets Parliament passed a National Assistance Act providing for "supplementary benefits," a euphemism for the old poor law. These benefits helped produce the remarkable decrease in poverty that Rowntree attested to in 1951. But soon a different kind of poverty emerged.

The "rediscovery" of poverty in the 1960s—the word echoed throughout the scholarly and journalistic literature—recalls the "rediscovery" in the 1880s, reflecting not so much a rise in the number of poor as a "raising of consciousness" on the part of publicists. In America the "war on poverty" was launched at a time when, by objective criteria, poverty was less widespread and less onerous than ever before. Only a few years earlier, in 1958, John Kenneth Galbraith had written a best-seller, *The Affluent Society*, denouncing the vulgarity and materialism of the age. Poverty made its appearance belatedly in that book in the twenty-third chapter, as an "afterthought," since it affected only special "cases" (those with mental or physical disorders) and "insular" groups (urban slums or rural backwaters). Four years later Michael Harrington published *The Other America*, and the problem of "affluence" was promptly displaced by the problem of "poverty." The troubled 1960s came to an end with a new edition of Galbraith's book, showing that prices had risen in the course of that decade by 16 percent while median family income had risen by 100 percent. Yet it continued to be widely held, by professionals as well as the public, that the "war on poverty" had failed, that poverty was a major social problem, and that the impoverished "other America" included a good part of the working classes. This belief was given statistical verisimilitude by the simple device of raising the poverty line to keep pace with the rise of median income.

In England the rediscovery of poverty took a more imaginative turn. Instead of merely revising the poverty line, sociologists redefined the very conception of poverty.[20] Poverty was no longer seen as a matter of needs or even "felt needs." Nor was it measured in terms of a standard of "subsistence," however elevated; such a standard was now regarded as a measure of "destitution" rather than "poverty." Instead poverty became a function of "relative deprivation," the degree to which some people fell short of the prevailing, "normal" standard of life—or rather the "quality of life," as it was now put, to emphasize cultural rather than merely material factors.[21] In a bolder version of this theory, relative deprivation was further relativized to reflect not the deprivation actually felt or experienced by the poor themselves, but that which the social inquirer regarded as such. The anthropologist Mary Douglas explained that she saw poverty as "primarily" a matter of the "restriction of choice," because this gave the "most scope to anthropological analysis."[22] And the sociologist Peter Townsend based an elaborate statistical and analytical study of poverty on such "indicators of poverty" as the lack of hot breakfasts, fresh meat fewer than four times a week, infrequent parties and holidays, and the absence of the habit of dining out.[23] (Even a university professor, one suspects, might bear some of these deprivations—hot breakfasts, for example—with equanimity.)

Critics have pointed out that relative deprivation is a measure of inequality rather than of poverty. Yet in this version it is less a question of inequality (defined in the usual terms of income, status, or standard of living) than of heterogeneity—different habits, tastes, judgments, desires, capacities, "lifestyles," as is said. It is ironic to find ostensibly objective and progressive social scientists returning to subjective and even moral criteria, making of poverty once again a matter of manners and morals, of individual character and social ethos.

A still more ironic, and tragic, development is the emergence of a new "underclass," a "culture of poverty" reminiscent of the "Mayhewian" poor a century and a half ago. Although this class is more conspicuous in America than in England, the symptoms are similar: a growing rate of illegitimacy and single-parent families, a "social pathology" of crime, violence, and drugs, and a dependency on welfare that cannot be entirely attributed to unemployment and low wages. In America this class has attained the status of a major social problem; in England it is still regarded as an anomaly, a "pocket of poverty" which will eventually disappear in an expanding economy and which in the meantime can be coped with by fine-tuning the welfare system. Whatever the outcome or resolution of this problem, it reminds us once again that "poverty" is as protean and diverse as the remedies proposed for it.

WE HAVE LEARNED much in the past century about both the "problem" of poverty and its "solution." Above all we have learned how much we still do not know. Sociologists and statisticians have developed sophisticated techniques for calculating the incidence of poverty—the "arithmetic of woe," as Booth so memorably put it—and have become equally sophisticated, and skeptical, about the "objective" meaning of their figures. Economists have been confirmed, from the recent experiences of socialist and "third world" countries, in their theory that a free and prosperous economy does more to raise people above the poverty line than government decrees and regulations—and have been at a loss to understand the emergence of kinds of poverty and classes of the poor which seem to be impervious to economic growth. Reformers and administrators have been ingenious in devising social policies to accommodate all the contingencies and "pockets" of poverty—and are distressed to witness the unintended and often unfortunate effects of these policies. Philosophers and politicians alike are more than ever aware that material progress is precarious unless accompanied by moral progress—and are disconcerted by the frequent disparity between the two. And the poorest of the poor are frustrated by their seeming inability to control their lives, to break the "cycle of poverty" that dooms them and their children to something very like the condition of "misery and vice" that Malthus had so dramatically described two centuries earlier—a condition that the "progress of civilization" was long since supposed to have rendered obsolete.

In the course of "rediscovering" poverty, and discovering what we do not yet know about poverty, we have much to learn from the late Victorians, who were also engaged in a self-conscious process of discovery and rediscovery. Indeed we are now rediscovering one of the things that the late Victorians did not have to discover, only because they knew it almost instinctively. After making the most arduous attempt to objectify the problem of poverty, to divorce poverty from any moral assumptions and conditions, we are learning how inseparable the moral and material dimensions of that problem are. And after trying to devise social policies that are scrupulously neutral and "value-free," we are finding these policies fraught with moral implications that have grave material and social consequences.

The Victorians have no solutions for our problems, if only because their problems are not ours. Today it requires a strenuous exercise of the moral imagination to recover the sensibility that came so naturally to them. To make that effort, to try to understand them as they understood themselves, is to understand ourselves better than we have done of late.

Notes

(The complete bibliographical information for each reference
appears in the first citation of that source in each chapter.)

INTRODUCTION

1. *The Life, Unpublished Letters and Philosophical Regimen of Anthony, Earl of Shaftesbury,* ed. Benjamin Rand (London, 1900), p. 158.

2. Adam Smith, *The Theory of Moral Sentiments* (Oxford, 1976 [1st ed., 1759]), p. 10 (Part I, sect. 1, chap. 1). The modern idea of compassion is generally associated with Rousseau's *Emile.* In England it derives from the English and Scottish moralists of the late seventeenth and eighteenth centuries—the school of Shaftesbury, as it is sometimes described.

3. M. G. Jones, *The Charity School Movement: A Study of Eighteenth Century Puritanism in Action* (Cambridge, 1938), p. 3.

4. Brian Harrison, *Peaceable Kingdom: Stability and Change in Modern Britain* (Oxford, 1982), p. 241.

5. Beatrice Webb, *My Apprenticeship* (Penguin ed., London 1971 [1st ed., 1926]), p. 164.

6. Leslie Stephen, *The Life of Sir James Fitzjames Stephen* (London, 1895), p. 157. (This is a paraphrase by Leslie Stephen of an unidentified article by his brother.)

7. I am indebted to the excellent essay by Clifford Orwin ("Compassion," *American Scholar,* 1980, p. 330) for this quotation from Kant's *Observations on the Feeling of the Beautiful and Sublime* (1760).

8. See below, pp. 102 ff. Subsequent references in this paragraph, to the Charity Organisation Society, Settlement House, etc., are explicated in the relevant chapters.

9. E. P. Hennock denies that the 1880s were a "watershed" in English social history because he sees no essential change in "social theory" or "social thought." He admits, however, that poverty became "more visible and more critically a matter of public concern" in the eighties than in previous decades. ("Poverty and Social Theory in England: The Experience of the Eighteen-Eighties," *Social History,* 1976, pp. 67 ff.) My own view is that the enormous stimulation of interest in social problems in the eighties, manifested, among other things, in the rise of new organizations and insti-

tutions, did amount to a critical change in social attitudes and ideas. Some of the ideas of the eighties were anticipated, as Hennock says, by some people in the sixties. But their widespread acceptance later does suggest a dialectical transformation of quantity into quality. One need not take literally the familiar slogan "We are all socialists now" to see in it a significant change in social thought. This is not to belittle the innovations either of the 1860s or of the late 1890s, or to deny the elements of continuity throughout this period. But it is to place the emphasis where contemporaries did—on the 1880s.

10. Helen Bosanquet, *Social Work in London, 1869–1912* (London, 1914), p. 74.

11. Alexis de Tocqueville, *Democracy in America,* trans. George Lawrence, ed. J. P. Mayer and Max Lerner (New York, 1966 [1st ed., 1835–40]), p. 538 (Part III, chap. 1).

12. Kathleen Woodroofe, *From Charity to Social Work in England and the United States* (London, 1968 [1st ed., 1962]), pp. 31–32. (See below, p. 197.)

13. Beatrice Webb, *My Apprenticeship,* pp. 345 and passim.

14. Gertrude Himmelfarb, "Victorian Values/Jewish Values," *Commentary,* 1989.

15. Stefan Collini, "The Idea of 'Character' in Victorian Political Thought," *Transactions of the Royal Historical Society,* 1985, p. 30. See also Collini, *Liberalism and Sociology: L. T. Hobhouse and Political Argument in England, 1880–1914* (Cambridge, 1979), p. 31.

16. Collini, "The Idea of 'Character,' " p. 31.

17. The word is even appearing in the titles of books, and without the protective shield of quotation marks: F. M. L. Thompson, *The Rise of Respectable Society: A Social History of Victorian Britain, 1830–1900* (Cambridge, Mass., 1988); Thomas Walter Laqueur, *Religion and Respectability: Sunday Schools and Working Class Culture, 1780–1850* (New Haven, 1977); F. M. Leventhal, *Respectable Radical: George Howell and Victorian Working Class Politics* (Cambridge, Mass., 1971).

18. Michael Mason, "Victorian Consumers" (review of F. M. L. Thompson, *The Rise of Respectable Society: A Social History of Victorian Britain, 1830–1900,* and Asa Briggs, *Victorian Things*), *London Review of Books,* Feb. 16, 1989, p. 14.

19. Harrison, p. 158.

20. "The Labour Party and the Books That Helped to Make It," *Review of Reviews,* 1906, pp. 568–82.

21. Harrison, p. 176.

22. See, for example, Melvin Richter, *The Politics of Conscience: T. H. Green and His Age* (Cambridge, Mass., 1964), pp. 292, 297, 329; Harold Perkin, *The Origins of Modern English Society, 1780–1880* (London, 1969), pp. 446 ff; Bentley B. Gilbert, *The Evolution of National Insurance in Great Britain: The Origins of the Welfare State* (London, 1966), p. 40. See also below, pp. 260, 278.

23. E. P. Thompson, "The Political Education of Henry Mayhew," *Victorian Studies,* 1967, p. 43. T. H. Marshall also refers to the "rediscovery" of poverty: "Changing Ideas about Poverty," in *The Right to Welfare and Other Essays* (New York, 1981), p. 39.

24. Thompson, p. 62.

25. For an account of Mayhew's work and this confusion of identity, see Gertrude Himmelfarb, *The Idea of Poverty: England in the Early Industrial Age* (New York, 1984), pp. 307–70.

26. See below, chapter 8.

27. A. V. Dicey, *Lectures on the Relation between Law and Public Opinion in England during the Nineteenth Century* (London, 1962 [1st ed., 1905, based on lectures delivered in 1898]), p. 14 (quoting essay 7 of Hume's *Essays*).

28. Ibid., pp. 10, lxiii (introduction to 2nd ed., 1914).

29. *The Letters of Sidney and Beatrice Webb,* ed. Norman MacKenzie (Cambridge, 1978), I, 101 (Sidney Webb to Edward Pease, Oct. 24, 1886).

30. For a critical account of these views, see John Baker, "Social Conscience and Social Policy," *Journal of Social Policy,* 1979.

31. Harold Perkin, *The Rise of Professional Society: England since 1880* (London, 1989).

32. There is an enormous literature on this subject. For bibliographies of working-class autobiographies and memoirs, see John Burnett, David Vincent, and David Mayall, eds., *The Autobiography of the Working Class: An Annotated Critical Bibliography, 1790–1900* (Brighton, 1984); Nan Hackett, ed., *Nineteenth Century British Working-Class Autobiographies: An Annotated Bibliography* (New York, 1985).

33. Harrison, pp. 159–60.

34. E. P. Thompson, *The Making of the English Working Class* (New York, 1964).

35. Gareth Stedman Jones, "Working-Class Culture and Working-Class Politics in London, 1870–1900: Notes on the Remaking of a Working Class," *Journal of Social History,* 1974, pp. 495–500.

36. Elie Halévy, *England in 1815* (vol. I of *A History of The English People in the Nineteenth Century*), tr. E. I. Watkin and D. A. Barker (London, 1960 [1st ed., 1913]), p. 387.

I. SOCIAL STATISTICS

1. Charles Booth, *Life and Labour of the People in London* (London, 1892), I, 178. The section on East London had been published in 1889 under the title *Life and Labour of the People.* (See below, chapter 7.)

2. Ibid., p. 178.

3. For a discussion of this issue and of the historiographical debate, see Gertrude Himmelfarb, *The Idea of Poverty: England in the Early Industrial Age* (New York, 1984), pp. 135–37, 549–50 n. 5. Most of this debate has focused on the earlier industrial period. For the later period, see David Cannadine, "The Present and the Past in the English Industrial Revolution, 1880–1980," *Past and Present,* 1984.

4. John Foster, *Class Struggle and the Industrial Revolution: Early Industrial Capitalism in Three English Towns* (London, 1974), p. 96.

5. Robert Giffen, *Essays in Finance: Second Series* (New York, 1886), p. 380.

6. Ibid., p. 473.

7. Leone Levi, *Wages and Earnings of the Working Classes* (London, 1885), p. 31.

8. Michael Mulhall, *Fifty Years of National Progress, 1837–1887* (London, 1887), p. 98.

9. A. L. Bowley, *Statistical Studies: Relating to National Progress in Wealth and Trade since 1882: A Plan for Further Enquiry* (London, 1904), p. 33.

10. George H. Wood, "Real Wages and the Standard of Comfort since 1850," *Journal of the Royal Statistical Society,* 1909, pp. 102–3.

11. J. M. Ludlow, review of Henry Mayhew's "Labour and the Poor" in the *Morning Chronicle, Fraser's Magazine,* January 1850, p. 8.

12. J. M. Ludlow and Lloyd Jones, *Progress of the Working Class, 1832–1867* (London, 1867), p. 297.

13. James E. Thorold Rogers, *Eight Chapters in the History of Work and Wages* (London, 1894 [1st ed., 1884]), p. 188.

14. *Transactions of the National Association for the Promotion of Social Science,* 1884, p. 635.

15. Ibid., p. 637.

16. *Journal of the Royal Statistical Society,* 1886, p. 96.

17. Charles H. Feinstein, "Wages and the Paradox of the 1880s," *Explorations in Economic History,* 1989, p. 241; David Greasley, "British Wages and Income, 1856–1913: A Revision," ibid., p. 251; Ian Gazeley, "The Cost of Living for Urban Workers in late Victorian and Edwardian Britain," *Economic History Review,* 1989, pp. 214, 216–17.

18. G. D. H. Cole and Raymond Postgate, *The British Common People 1746–1938* (New York, 1939), p. 394.

19. Helen Merrell Lynd, *England in the Eighteen-Eighties: Toward a Social Basis for Freedom* (New York, 1968 [1st ed., 1945]), p. 48.

20. E. J. Hobsbawm, *Industry and Empire* (vol. III of *The Pelican Economic History of Britain,* London, 1969), pp. 159–60.

21. Booth, *Life and Labour* (1892 ed.), I, 174.

22. Gareth Stedman Jones, *Outcast London: A Study in the Relationship between Classes in Victorian Society* (Oxford, 1971), pp. 30–31.

23. Ibid., p. 216. One historian finds it difficult to reconcile statistics of indoor pauperism with the reputed rise of wages. But it is this group that would be least likely to benefit from such a rise; many were not wage earners at all. Even here, however, in the case of the "very poor," the author's pessimism is somewhat tempered: "For most groups of the very poor, improvements in living standards were at best slight." (Mary MacKinnon, "Poor Law Policy, Unemployment, and Pauperism," *Explorations in Economic History,* 1986, p. 333.)

24. Mss. version of Beatrice Webb's Diaries, May 17, 1886, London School of Economics, Webb Mss. collection, IX, 21–22. (This entry does not appear in the published version.)

25. John Burnett, *Plenty and Want: A Social History of Diet in England from 1815 to the Present Day* (rev. ed., London, 1979), p. 132.

26. W. W. Rostow, *The Stages of Economic Growth: A Non-Communist Manifesto* (Cambridge, 1967 [1st ed., 1960]), p. 73; Sidney Pollard and David W. Crossley, *The Wealth of Britain, 1085–1966* (New York, 1969), pp. 229–30. See also Rostow, *British Economy of the Nineteenth Century* (Oxford, 1966 [1st ed., 1948]), p. 215, for evidence of the rise of consumption from the 1870s on. Although Eric Hobsbawm is generally identified with the "pessimist" position, he makes a point of the variety and quantity of goods available to the poor in the last quarter of the century. (*Industry and Empire*, pp. 161–64.) For more detailed evidence of changes in consumer products, see Hamish Fraser, *The Coming of the Mass Market 1850–1914* (London, 1982).

27. E. J. Hobsbawm, *Workers: Worlds of Labor* (New York, 1984), p. 241. There is a large literature on the consumer economy of the late-Victorian and Edwardian periods. See, for example, Michael Winstanley, *Life in Kent at the Turn of the Century* (Folkestone, 1978); Hamish Fraser, *The Coming of the Mass Market 1850–1914* (London, 1982); Paul Johnson, *Saving and Spending: The Working-Class Economy in Britain, 1870–1939* (Oxford, 1985).

28. E. P. Thompson, *The Making of the English Working Class* (New York, 1964), p. 444.

29. J. L. Garvin, *The Life of Joseph Chamberlain* (London, 1932), I, 202.

30. Elizabeth Roberts, "Working-Class Standards of Living in Three Lancashire Towns, 1890–1914," *International Review of Social History,* 1982 (Part 1), p. 64; John Woodward, "Medicine and the City: The Nineteenth-Century Experience," in Robert Woods and John Woodward, eds., *Urban Disease and Mortality in Nineteenth-Century England* (New York, 1984), p. 77. See also J. M. Winter, "The Decline of Mortality in Britain 1870–1930," in M. Drake and T. Barker, eds., *Population and Society in Britain 1850–1980* (London, 1982); Anthony Wohl, *Endangered Lives: Public Health in Victorian Britain* (London, 1983). (There was, however, Wohl also points out, no decline in the infant mortality rate, which may be due to the lack of medical advance in this area.)

31. Paul Johnson, "Conspicuous Consumption and Working-Class Culture in Late-Victorian and Edwardian Britain," *Transactions of the Royal Historical Society* (London, 1988), p. 38.

2. RISING EXPECTATIONS AND RELATIVE DEPRIVATIONS

1. Thomas Carlyle, "Chartism," in *English and Other Critical Essays* (London, Everyman ed., n.d.), pp. 165–67.

2. John A. Hobson, *Problems of Poverty: An Inquiry into the Industrial Condition of the Poor* (New York, 1971 [1st ed., 1891]), p. 28.

3. E. J. Hobsbawm, "The Standard of Living Debate: A Postscript," in *Labouring Men: Studies in the History of Labour* (London, 1964), p. 124; J. A. Banks, "The Contagion of Numbers," in H. J. Dyos and Michael Wolff, eds., *The Victorian City: Images and Realities* (London, 1973), I, 115.

4. See below, chapter 21.

5. Robert Giffen, *Essays in Finance: Second Series* (New York, 1886), p. 405.

6. Leone Levi, *Wages and Earnings of the Working Classes* (London, 1855), p.

55. These figures have been sharply criticized by Harold Perkin, who estimates a rise in average business profits of 60% between 1850 and 1880 while average wages (allowing for unemployment) rose by only 39%. (Perkin, *The Origins of Modern English Society 1780–1880* [London, 1969], pp. 414–16.) But some of Perkin's own statistics are confusing; at one point (p. 414) he seems to be "allowing for unemployment" twice over.

7. A. L. Bowley, "Changes in Average Wages (Nominal and Real) in the United Kingdom between 1860 and 1891," *Journal of the Royal Statistical Society,* 1895, pp. 225, 250–51; Bowley, *Wages in the United Kingdom in the Nineteenth Century* (London, 1900), p. 126. Harold Perkin makes much of the growing inequality in the class distribution of income, but he takes as his period 1880–1914, not the period of the Great Depression. (*The Rise of Professional Society: England since 1880* [London, 1989], pp. 28 ff.)

8. Hobson, p. 26.

9. L. G. Chiozza Money, *Riches and Poverty* (New York, 1980 [1st ed., 1905]), p. 311.

10. Phyllis Deane and W. A. Cole, *British Economic Growth, 1688–1959: Trends and Structures* (rev. ed., Cambridge, 1967 [1st ed., 1962]), p. 150.

11. Sidney Pollard and David W. Crossley, *The Wealth of Britain, 1085–1966* (New York, 1969), p. 236.

12. Roderick Floud and Donald McCloskey, eds., *The Economic History of Britain since 1700* (Cambridge, 1981), II, 126–27.

13. François Crouzet, *The Victorian Economy,* trans. Anthony Forster (New York, 1982), p. 61.

14. S. G. Checkland, *The Rise of Industrial Society in England 1815–1885* (London, 1964), pp. 56, 226. See also Peter H. Lindert and Jeffrey G. Williamson, "Reinterpreting Britain's Social Tables, 1688–1913," *Explorations in Economic History,* 1983, p. 100; Jeffrey G. Williamson, *Did British Capitalism Breed Inequality?* (Boston, 1985), p. 28.

15. Friedrich Engels, *The Condition of the Working Class in England,* in Marx and Engels, *On Britain* (Moscow, 1962), p. 28.

16. Ibid., p. 29.

17. Ibid., p. 28.

18. Ibid., p. 31.

19. Ibid., p. 32.

20. E. J. Hobsbawm, "The Labour Aristocracy in Nineteenth-Century Britain" (1954), reprinted in *Labouring Men: Studies in the History of Labour* (London, 1964).

21. Ibid., p. 293. Hobsbawm dismisses Alfred Marshall's evidence to the contrary as "exceptionally unreliable" or "wishful." But his own is no less so, consisting of unrelated and not especially trustworthy statistics drawn from various trades, at various times, and various sources. A single paragraph on the size of the labor aristocracy, for example, starts with Dudley Baxter's estimate in 1867 of the number of workers earning 28s. or more, goes on to the Webbs' estimate in 1892 of trade union membership, and concludes with Mayhew's estimate in 1850 of the percent-

age of "society men" in the average London craft. "These estimates," the paragraph closes, "are really based on more or less plausible guesses, and are here given only because they are not inconsistent with the better ones for the subsequent period" (p. 279). Since the issue is precisely the relation between this and the "subsequent period" (the 1890s to 1914), and, indeed, the changes within this very large and volatile period itself (the 1840s to 1890s), this final sentence is almost incomprehensible.

22. E. J. Hobsbawm, *Workers: Worlds of Labor* (New York, 1984), p. 249. See also Hobsbawm, "Lenin and the 'Aristocracy of Labour' " (1966), in *Revolutionaries: Contemporary Essays* (New York, 1973).

23. Gareth Stedman Jones, *Languages of Class: Studies in English Working Class History 1832–1982* (Cambridge, 1983), pp. 14, 63. While this criticism is directed particularly against John Foster's book on the earlier part of the century, Stedman Jones intimates that it applies as well to the later part (p. 74).

24. Henry Pelling, *Popular Politics and Society in Late Victorian Britain* (London, 1968), pp. 37–61. For other views of the concept, see H. F. Moorhouse, "The Marxist Theory of the Labour Aristocracy," *Social History,* 1978; Alastair Reid, "Labour and Society in Modern Britain," *Historical Journal,* 1982.

25. E.g., *Royal Commission Report on the Constabulary* (London, 1839), p. 70; Henry Mayhew, *London Labour and the London Poor,* ed. John D. Rosenberg (New York, 1968 [1st ed., 1861–62]), I, 92. For other examples of the earlier usage, see E. P. Thompson, *The Making of the English Working Class* (New York, 1964), p. 237; Pelling, p. 37; Michael A. Shepherd, "The Origins and Incidence of the Term 'Labour Aristocracy,' " *Bulletin of the Society for the Study of Labor History,* Autumn 1978 (and reply by Joseph L. Melling, ibid., August 1979); Gertrude Himmelfarb, *The Idea of Poverty: England in the Early Industrial Age* (New York, 1984), p. 321.

26. Alfred Marshall, *Principles of Economics* (London, 1982 [reprint of 8th ed., 1920]), p. 596. (See also p. 3.)

27. Bowley, *Wages in the United Kingdom,* p. 70.

28. Bowley, *Statistical Studies: Relating to National Progress in Wealth and Trade since 1882: A Plan for Further Enquiry* (London, 1904), p. 11.

29. This new "lower middle class" was different from that described in 1867 by Dudley Baxter in his statistical survey of the national income. Baxter had distinguished not one but two "lower middle classes," the lower of which earned under £100 a year, which was less than the earnings of a skilled artisan. (G. D. H. Cole and Raymond Postgate, *The British Common People 1746–1938* [New York, 1939], pp. 318–19. See also G. Crossick, *The Lower Middle Class in Britain, 1870–1914* [London, 1977].)

30. See, for example, Jeffrey G. Williamson, "The Structure of Pay in Britain, 1710–1911," *Research in Economic History,* 1982, p. 16; E. J. Feuchtwanger, *Democracy and Empire: Britain 1865–1914* (London, 1985), p. 144; E. H. Hunt, *British Labour History, 1815–1914* (Atlantic Highlands, N.J., 1981), p. 280; Chris Wrigley, ed., *A History of British Industrial Relations* (Boston, 1982), pp. 4–5.

3. UNEMPLOYMENT AND THE CASUAL LABORER

1. E. P. Thompson, "The Political Education of Henry Mayhew," *Victorian Studies,* 1967, p. 43; John A. Garraty, *Unemployment in History: Economic Thought and Public Policy* (New York, 1978), p. 103.

2. E. P. Thompson, *The Making of the English Working Class* (New York, 1964), p. 776 n. Thompson's statement is sometimes taken as the definitive refutation of that "legend." See, for example, Richard T. Vann, "The Rhetoric of Social History," *Journal of Social History,* 1976, p. 227; Raymond Williams, *Keywords* (New York, 1976), pp. 273–74.

3. Beatrice Webb, who made a point of the late usage of "unemployment" (she also said, mistakenly, that "unemployed" originated in the eighties), altered a diary entry dated August 13, 1885, referring to the "Mansion House Enquiry into unemployed," to read in the published version: "Mansion House inquiry into unemployment." (*My Apprenticeship* [Penguin ed., 1971 (1st ed., 1926)], p. 274.)

4. Charles F. Bahmueller, *The National Charity Company: Jeremy Bentham's Silent Revolution* (Berkeley, 1981), p. 132. The plan was published under the title *Pauper Management Improved.* See Gertrude Himmelfarb, "Bentham's Utopia," in *Marriage and Morals among the Victorians* (New York, 1986).

5. T. S. Ashton, "The Relation of Economic History to Economic Theory," *Economica,* 1946, p. 86. Ashton's other example ostensibly of this usage referred to "the unemployed," not "unemployment."

G. M. Young, in an early version of his essay "Portrait of an Age," remarked upon the fact that early-Victorian reformers had no word for unemployment and that he himself had not observed it "earlier than the sixties." (*Early Victorian England: 1830–1865* [London, 1934], II, 436 n.) When he reissued that essay as a book, he omitted the reference to the sixties, noting instead that the word "only becomes common in the eighties." (*Victorian England: Portrait of an Age* [New York, 1954], p. 46.) In fact, it did not become "common" even then.

6. Alfred Marshall, *Official Papers* (London, 1926), p. 93. The index to this volume does not have an entry for "unemployment," but does have "employment," with a subentry for "irregularity of . . . ," and another entry, "irregularity of employment."

7. Alfred Marshall, *Principles of Economics* (9th variorum edition, London, 1961), I, 710–11. The word appeared once in the first volume of Booth's work published in 1889, but not, to my knowledge, in the later volumes.

8. The essays appeared in the *Contemporary Review* of May 1895.

9. José Harris, *Unemployment and Politics: A Study in English Social Policy 1886–1914* (Oxford, 1972), p. 4 n.

10. L. G. Johnson, *The Social Evolution of Industrial Britain: A Study in the Growth of Our Industrial Society* (Liverpool, 1959), p. 132 (quoting James Samuelson, ed., *The Civilization of Our Day* [1896], p. 169).

11. Sidney and Beatrice Webb, *English Poor Law History* (London, 1929), Part 2, II, 633.

12. The "industrial system" was the term commonly used in the socialist literature of the mid-century as the source of most social evils. Toward the end of the century the problem of the "unemployed" was often attributed to the same "industrial system." Michael Freeden cites one such usage in 1893 by J. A. M. Macdonald, a Liberal Member of Parliament identified with the Radical wing of the party. (*The New Liberalism: An Ideology of Social Reform* [Oxford, 1978], p. 207.)

13. Thomas Allan Ingram, "Unemployment," *Encyclopaedia Britannica* (London, 1911), XXVII, 578–80.

14. David Owen, *English Philanthropy 1660–1960* (Cambridge, Mass., 1964), p. 211. See also Jessica Gerard, "Lady Bountiful: Women of the Landed Classes and Rural Philanthropy," *Victorian Studies,* 1987, p. 189.

15. Harris, p. 42.

16. Ashton, p. 86. See also J. H. Clapham, *Economic History of Modern Britain* (London, 1932), II, 455; Henry Pelling, *The Origins of the Labour Party 1880–1900* (Oxford, 1965 [1st ed., 1954]), pp. 7–8.

17. R. A. Church, *The Great Victorian Boom, 1850–1873* (London, 1975), p. 72.

18. Peter Mathias, *The First Industrial Nation: An Economic History of Britain 1700–1914* (London, 1983 [1st ed., 1969]), p. 346. (On p. 364 the figures for the same period are given as 4.6% and 5.4%.) See also W. W. Rostow, *British Economy of the Nineteenth Century* (Oxford, 1966 [1st ed., 1948]), pp. 48–49.

19. B. R. Mitchell and Phyllis Deane, *Abstract of British Historical Statistics* (Cambridge, 1962), p. 64.

20. J. A. Hobson, *Problems of Poverty* (London, 1891), p. 15.

21. See below, p. 118.

22. See below, p. 174.

23. *Report of the Mansion House Committee Appointed March, 1885, to Inquire into the Causes of Permanent Distress in London, and the Best Means of Remedying the Same* (London, 1886), p. 11.

24. *Annual Register,* 1886 (Feb. 3), p. 6.

25. For a fuller account of this and the "Bloody Tuesday" riot the following year, see below, pp. 330–32.

26. Gareth Stedman Jones, *Outcast London: A Study of the Relationship between Classes in Victorian Society* (Oxford, 1971), pp. 292–93; Bentley B. Gilbert, *The Evolution of National Insurance in Great Britain: The Origins of the Welfare State* (London, 1966), p. 32.

27. Webb collection, London School of Economics (VIII, 4–5a). This letter, dated Feb. 28, 1886, was inserted in the manuscript copy of her diaries. It has not been published, so far as I know.

28. Norman MacKenzie, ed., *The Letters of Sidney and Beatrice Webb* (Cambridge, 1978), I, 28.

29. Ibid., pp. 53–54 (early March 1886).

30. Harris, p. 75.

31. Ibid., pp. 76–77.

32. T. W. Hutchison, *A Review of Economic Doctrines 1870–1929* (Westport, Conn., 1975 [1st ed., 1953]), p. 422.

33. Henry Mayhew, *London Labour and the London Poor,* ed. John D. Rosenberg (New York, 1968 [1st ed., 1861–62]), pp. 301–10. (Most of this work had been published in newspapers and pamphlets between 1849 and 1852.)

34. See below, pp. 144–45.

35. These and the other figures cited are from contemporary newspaper accounts excerpted in *The Great Dock Strike 1889,* ed. Terry McCarthy (London, 1988), pp. 101, 117. For other contemporary evidence, see Hubert Llewellyn Smith and Vaughan Nash, *The Story of the Dockers' Strike* (London, 1889); H. H. Champion, *The Great Dock Strike in London, August 1889* (London, 1890).

36. Ibid., pp. 244–45. On socialism in the dock strike and the new unions, see Henry Pelling, *The Origins of the Labour Party 1880–1900* (Oxford, 1965 [1st ed., 1954]), pp. 83–85.

37. McCarthy, pp. 164–65.

38. Norman and Jeanne MacKenzie, *The Fabians* (New York, 1977), p. 107; Pelling, *Labour Party,* p. 83.

39. John Saville, "Trade Unions and Free Labour: The Background to the Taff Vale Decision," in *Essays in Labour History,* ed. A. Briggs and J. Saville (London, 1960), p. 317.

40. *Times,* Sept. 9, 1889, p. 4.

41. McCarthy, p. 238.

42. The last years of the nineteenth century and the first decade of the twentieth were years of decline for most of the unskilled London unions. In the rest of the country, however, conditions were much better, and by 1912 the new unions had recovered their strength (although they still remained a small segment of the total union movement). See Sidney and Beatrice Webb, *The History of Trade Unionism* (New York, 1973 [1st ed., 1894]), p. 406; Henry Pelling, *A History of British Trade Unionism* (London, 1963), pp. 109–14, 123–48; E. J. Hobsbawm, "National Unions on the Waterside," in *Labouring Men: Studies in the History of Labour* (London, 1964), pp. 204, 214–15.

43. T. S. and M. B. Simey, *Charles Booth: Social Scientist* (Oxford, 1960), p. 121 (quoting *Journal of the Royal Statistical Society,* 1892, p. 522).

44. E. J. Hobsbawm, "The 'New Unionism' in Perspective" (1981), in *Workers: Worlds of Labour* (New York, 1984), p. 160.

45. Jones, p. 315. In his preface to the edition of 1984, Jones conceded that this was a "hyperbole" by usual academic standards (p. xxiii).

46. Ibid., pp. 315–16.

47. Jones refers to Booth's class B. See below, pp. 123–24.

48. Jones, pp. 318–19. "Pyrrhic victory" appears in a quotation from the leader of the blacklegs (scabs)—an odd source for Jones to be quoting and endorsing.

49. Ibid., p. 320.

50. Karl Marx and Friedrich Engels, *On Britain* (Moscow, 1962), pp. 566–67 (Aug. 22, 1889). Jones quotes this letter (although not in the chapter on the dock strike) (p. 347).

51. Marx and Engels, p. 568 (Engels to F. A. Sorge, Dec. 7, 1889).

52. P. J. Waller, *Times Literary Supplement,* Feb. 7, 1886 (review of Gordon Phillips and Noel Whiteside, *Casual Labour: The Unemployment Question in the Port Transport Industry 1880–1970* [Oxford, 1985]).

4. THE HOUSING OF "OUTCAST LONDON"

1. Arnold Toynbee, *The Industrial Revolution* (Boston, 1956), p. 116. *Lectures on the Industrial Revolution* (as the title appeared in the first edition) was published posthumously in 1884 on the basis of lectures delivered in 1880–81. (See below, chapter 18.)

2. The most comprehensive study of housing in this period is Anthony S. Wohl, *The Eternal Slum: Housing and Social Policy in Victorian London* (Montreal, 1977). See also Stanley D. Chapman, ed., *The History of Working-Class Housing: A Symposium* (Totowa, N.J., 1971); Enid Gauldie, *Cruel Habitations: A History of Working-Class Housing 1780–1918* (London, 1974); John Nelson Tarn, *Five Per Cent Philanthropy: An Account of Housing in Urban Areas between 1840 and 1914* (Cambridge, 1973); H. J. Dyos, "The Slums of Victorian London," *Victorian Studies,* 1967; H. J. Dyos and Michael Wolff, *The Victorian City: Images and Realities* (2 vols., London, 1973); H. J. Dyos, *Exploring the Urban Past: Essays in Urban History,* ed. David Cannadine and David Reeder (Cambridge, 1982); Donald J. Olsen, *The Growth of Victorian London* (London, 1976).

3. Emile Durkheim, *The Division of Labor in Society,* trans. George Simpson (Glencoe, Ill., 1947), p. 257.

4. Asa Briggs, *Victorian Cities* (New York, 1965), p. 330.

5. Donald J. Olsen, *The City as a Work of Art: London, Paris, Vienna* (New Haven, 1986), p. 180.

6. Anthony Wohl has almost half of the "working classes" paying that proportion on rent. (*Eternal Slum,* p. 40.) One reviewer pointed out that this estimate applied only to the lowest segment of the working classes. (David Rubinstein, *Victorian Studies,* 1979, p. 139.)

7. *Report of the Mansion House Committee Appointed March, 1885, to Inquire into the Causes of Permanent Distress in London, and the Best Means of Remedying the Same* (London, 1886), p. 10.

8. George Rosen, "Disease, Debility, and Death," *Victorian City,* II, 633.

9. *The Royal Commission on the Housing of the Working Classes* (Minutes of Evidence and Appendix), II, 10; *First Report of Her Majesty's Commissioners for Inquiring into the Housing of the Working Classes* (London, 1885), I, 9.

10. Olsen, *City as a Work of Art,* pp. 178–79.

11. On the model buildings movement, see below, chapter 14.

12. *Morning Chronicle,* Dec. 18, 1849. On Mayhew's work and the reception to it, see Gertrude Himmelfarb, *The Idea of Poverty: England in the Early Industrial Age* (New York, 1984), pp. 350 ff.

13. The most extensive account of Sims's articles is in Wohl, *Eternal Slum,* pp.

201–2. For an earlier version of this account, see Wohl, "The Bitter Cry of Outcast London," *International Review of Social History,* 1968.

14. The two series were published by Sims in 1889 under the title *How the Poor Live and Horrible London.*

15. Ibid., p. 3.

16. Ibid., p. 21.

17. Ibid., p. 45.

18. Ibid., p. 44.

19. Ibid., p. 105.

20. Ibid.

21. On the disputed authorship of *The Bitter Cry,* see Wohl, "Bitter Cry," p. 205; Wohl, *Eternal Slum,* p. 207; Peter d'A. Jones, *The Christian Socialist Revival, 1877–1914* (London, 1968); W. H. Chaloner, prefatory note in *Homes of the London Poor and The Bitter Cry of Outcast London* (London, 1970); Chaloner, letter to the editor, *Times Literary Supplement,* March 5, 1971.

22. *The Bitter Cry of Outcast London: An Inquiry into the Condition of the Abject Poor* (London, 1883), p. 5. (This has been reprinted in *Homes of the London Poor and The Bitter Cry of Outcast London* [London, 1970], which is a facsimile of the original editions, retaining the original pagination.)

23. Ibid., pp. 6–8.

24. Ibid., pp. 8–9.

25. Ibid., p. 6.

26. Ibid., p. 10.

27. Ibid., pp. 14–17. Some of these scenes, such as the corpse lying for days in the room occupied by the family, were adapted from newspaper accounts cited by Sims. (*How the Poor Live,* p. 61.)

28. Ibid., p. 18.

29. Ibid., pp. 14–15.

30. Ibid., p. 4.

31. Ibid., pp. 18–19.

32. Ibid., p. 9.

33. See examples of such references in Wohl, "Bitter Cry," p. 208 n. 2.

34. *The Works of Alfred Lord Tennyson* (London, 1894), p. 566. (I am indebted to W. H. Greenleaf, *The British Political Tradition* [London, 1983], p. 287, for this reference.)

35. Beatrice Webb, *My Apprenticeship* (Penguin ed., 1971 [1st ed., 1926]), p. 324.

36. Raymond L. Schults, *Crusader in Babylon: W. T. Stead and the Pall Mall Gazette* (Lincoln, Neb., 1972), p. 29 (quoting Matthew Arnold in *Nineteenth Century,* 1887).

Stead became famous for the series of articles, two years later, against prostitution and "white slavery"—the "Maiden Tribute of Modern Babylon," as he memorably dubbed it. In this case he himself initiated the campaign with a report by the paper's "Secret Commission."

37. Wohl, "Bitter Cry," p. 189.

38. Samuel Barnett, "Sensationalism and Social Reform," *Nineteenth Century,* 1886, p. 280.

39. More surprising is the fact that few historians have expressed much skepticism about the pamphlet. One historian, perhaps impressed by the statement that it was based on evidence derived from "house after house, court after court, street after street," gave *The Bitter Cry* a scientific status that even the author did not claim for it. The pamphlet, Bentley Gilbert said, was "essentially a primitive attempt at house-to-house surveying." (*The Evolution of National Insurance in Great Britain: The Origins of the Welfare State* [London, 1966], p. 28.)

40. Sims, p. 29.

41. Wohl, "Bitter Cry," p. 209 (quoting *Lancet,* Dec. 15, 1883). On the model buildings movement, see below, chapter 14.

42. Robert Salisbury, "Labourers' and Artisans' Dwellings," *National Review,* 1883.

43. Wohl, *Eternal Slum,* p. 228. Unlike these contemporaries, some historians have described Salisbury's position as "ambiguous," "anomalous," and "ambivalent," and his proposals as "mild" and "conservative." (Wohl, *Eternal Slum,* pp. 228, 239, 244; Peter Marsh, *The Discipline of Popular Government: Lord Salisbury's Domestic Statecraft, 1881–1902* [Sussex, 1978], p. 52.) But these characterizations assume that only a more radical reform (of an unspecified nature) would have been a rational and proper response to the problem. In fact Salisbury's proposals were more specific and more radical than those in either *The Bitter Cry* or *How the Poor Live.* A more considered judgment is that of the historian who sees nothing remarkable about the fact that a man of his "evangelical belief" and "Christian persuasion" should react as he did to the evidence of suffering. (Gauldie, p. 150.) See also Gwendolyn Cecil, *Life of Robert Marquis of Salisbury,* III, 77 ff.

44. 3 Hansard 284:1689 (Feb. 22, 1884).

45. *First Report of Her Majesty's Commissioners for Inquiring into the Housing of the Working Classes* (London, 1885), I, 7.

46. Ibid., p. 17.

47. Ibid., p. 13.

48. Ibid.

49. Wohl, *Eternal Slum,* p. 245.

50. Ibid., p. 248. This judgment is all the more noteworthy because it comes from a historian not given to excessive enthusiasm. Only a few pages earlier Wohl took a rather cynical view of the commission report, describing it as "paternalistic" because it did not invite the slum dwellers to "tell their own story," and as "suffused throughout with middle-class notions of comfort and respectability" (p. 242).

51. See also Wohl, "The Housing of the Working Classes in London 1815–1914," in *The History of Working-Class Housing,* pp. 40–42.

52. For an analysis of the Poor Law Report of 1834, see Himmelfarb, chapter 6.

53. Schults, p. 57.

5. THE "GREAT DEPRESSION" AND THE "GREAT DECLINE"

1. C. F. G. Masterman, *The Condition of England* (London, 1909), pp. 211–12.

2. For a review of the historical controversy on this subject, see H. L. Beales, "The Great Depression in Industry and Trade," *Economic History Review,* 1934; Charles Wilson, "Economy and Society in Late Victorian Britain," ibid., 1965; S. B. Saul, *The Myth of the Great Depression* (1969); Harold Perkin, *The Rise of Professional Society: England since 1880* (London, 1989). Perkin has a different interpretation of the effect of falling prices, seeing it as contributing to an increase of class inequality and thus of class hostility (pp. 38 ff).

3. W. H. B. Court, *British Economic History 1870–1914: Commentary and Documents* (Cambridge, 1965), p. 35.

4. Ibid., p. 51.

5. See F. M. L. Thompson, *English Landed Society in the Nineteenth Century* (London, 1963), pp. 309 ff., on the divergent interests of corn farmers and stock and dairy farmers.

6. Alfred Marshall, *Official Papers* (London, 1926), pp. 98–99.

7. Peter Mathias, *The First Industrial Nation: An Economic History of Britain 1700–1914* (London, 1969), p. 398 (rev. ed. [1983], p. 365); Henry Pelling, *The Origins of the Labour Party 1880–1900* (Oxford, 1965 [1st ed., 1954]), pp. 7–8.

8. Mathias, p. 397; rev. ed., p. 364.

9. The *Economist* opened a series of articles in January and February 1851 by announcing that the "Golden Age" was the proper designation not of the past but of the present. Some historians have perpetuated this label. A volume of documents on the mid-Victorian period is entitled *Human Documents of the Victorian Golden Age* (ed. E. Royston Pike, London, 1967); this is a sequel to *Human Documents of the Industrial Revolution in Britain* (London, 1966).

10. W. L. Burn, *The Age of Equipoise: A Study of the Mid-Victorian Generation* (London, 1964); Trygve R. Tholfsen, *Working Class Radicalism in Mid-Victorian England* (New York, 1977), p. 11. (Tholfsen uses the term without quotation marks and without attribution to Burn, as if it were a matter of fact rather than of interpretation.)

11. The argument that these reforms did not actually amount to "adult manhood suffrage" is based on the fact that some categories were excluded in principle (domestic servants resident with employers, sons living with parents, soldiers, lunatics, criminals, aliens, and those receiving poor relief) and that others were temporarily excluded (as they still are) by registration requirements. In 1911, it has been estimated, only 40 percent of adult males were on the register. (Neal Blewett, "The Franchise in the United Kingdom, 1885–1918," *Past and Present,* 1965, pp. 27–56.)

12. See below, pp. 175–76, 365–66.

13. There has been much dispute about the precise timing and details of the climacteric. See, for example, David Greasley, "British Economic Growth: The Paradox of the 1880s and the Timing of the Climacteric," *Explorations in Economic*

History, 1986; E. H. Phelps Brown and S. J. Handfield Jones, "The Climacteric of the 1890s," *Oxford Economic Papers,* 1952; David S. Landes, *The Unbound Prometheus: Technological Change and Industrial Development in Western Europe from 1750 to the Present* (Cambridge, 1969), pp. 235 ff.

14. Correlli Barnett, *The Collapse of British Power* (New York, 1972), p. 23. See also Barnett, *The Pride and the Fall: The Dream and Illusion of Britain as a Great Nation* (New York, 1987), which carries the theme of decline to Britain's performance in the Second World War.

15. Martin J. Wiener, *English Culture and the Decline of the Industrial Spirit, 1850–1980* (Cambridge, 1981).

16. E. J. Hobsbawm, *Industry and Empire* (London, 1968), pp. 187–88.

17. Paul Kennedy, *The Rise and Fall of the Great Powers: Economic Change and Military Conflict from 1500 to 2000* (New York, 1987), pp. 229–30; Bernard Porter, *The Lion's Share: A Short History of British Imperialism 1850–1970* (London, 1976), pp. 353–54.

18. Aaron L. Friedberg, *The Weary Titan: Britain and the Experience of Relative Decline, 1895–1905* (Princeton, 1988).

19. Donald N. McCloskey, "Did Victorian Britain Fail?" *Economic History Review,* 1970. For other views of the decline, see N. F. R. Crofts, "Victorian Britain Did Fail," ibid., 1979; Bernard Elbaum and William Lazonick, *The Decline of the British Economy: An Institutional Perspective* (Oxford, 1986); Sidney Pollard, *Britain's Prime and Britain's Decline: The British Economy 1870–1914* (London, 1989); M. J. Daunton, " 'Gentlemanly Capitalism' and British Industry 1820–1914," *Past and Present,* 1989; James Raven, "British History and the Enterprise Culture," ibid.; Charles Dellheim, "Notes on Industrialism and Culture in Nineteenth-century Britain," in *Notebooks in Cultural Analysis,* ed. Norman F. Cantor and Nathalia King (Durham, N.C., 1985), vol. I.

20. Karl Marx and Friedrich Engels, *On Britain* (Moscow, 1962), pp. 562–63 (Jan. 18, 1884).

6. CHARLES BOOTH: A MAN OF PROPERTY AND CONSCIENCE

1. One historian has Booth resigning from the "managing directorship" of his firm in 1886 when he came to London to begin his inquiry. (A. M. McBriar, *An Edwardian Mixed Doubles: The Bosanquets versus the Webbs: A Study in British Social Policy 1890–1929* ([Oxford, 1987].) In fact, he came to London in 1875 and continued as an active member of the firm throughout the publication of the work, retiring in 1905 at the age of sixty-five.

2. Beatrice Webb, *My Apprenticeship* (Penguin ed., 1971 [1st ed., 1926]), pp. 228–29.

3. The editor of one volume of selections from *Life and Labour* speaks of "the essential conflict and inconsistency between Booth the businessman and Booth the humanitarian." (Harold W. Pfautz, ed., *Charles Booth, On the City: Physical Pattern and Social Structure* [Chicago, 1967], p. 16.) The editors of another volume see the

contradiction as between the businessman and the social scientist: "Clearly, Booth in his role as investigator was a radical, willing to go wherever his pursuit of the truth led him. But as a man of affairs he still remained an implacable conservative. The gap between these two sides of Booth's personality emerged whenever he offered his own judgments and evaluations." (Albert Fried and Richard M. Elman, eds., *Charles Booth's London: A Portrait of the Poor at the Turn of the Century, Drawn from His "Life and Labour of the People in London"* [New York, 1968], p. xxiv; see also pp. xxv, xxix.) The major full-length study of Booth by T. S. Simey and M. B. Simey, *Charles Booth: Social Scientist* (Oxford, 1960), is refreshingly free of this assumption.

4. See A. H. John, *A Liverpool Merchant House: Being the History of Alfred Booth and Co., 1863–1958* (London, 1959), and Harriet Anna Whitting, *Alfred Booth: Some Memories, Letters and Other Family Records* (Liverpool, 1917). The latter, by Alfred Booth's daughter, was privately printed in an edition of 75 copies. (I am grateful to H. T. Turner, formerly of the firm of Alfred Booth and Co., Ltd., for access to this book as well as to manuscripts relating to the history of the company.)

5. The differences between the brothers persist to the present day, amounting, if not to a feud, at least to a perceptible coolness between the two branches of the family. The descendants of Alfred now run the shipping firm of Alfred Booth and Co., Ltd., whose central office is in London, while the descendants of Charles are represented in the leather firm of Booth and Co. International, Ltd., located in Nottingham.

6. Booth Mss., University of London Library, I/1300 (Aug. 2, 1881). Unless otherwise stated, the quotations from manuscripts are from this collection. Another collection at the British Library of Political and Economic Science (the London School of Economics) consists mainly of the source books for *Life and Labour of the People in London.*

7. Simey, p. 29.

8. Mss. II/86/10 (recollections of W. T. D. Ritchie).

9. Simey, p. 28.

10. John, p. 164.

11. Mss. II/26/40 (1873).

12. Mss. II/25/2.

13. The Webbs were also Positivists in this modified, Anglicized sense. See below, pp. 358–60.

14. Mss. I/1232 (Aug. 20, 1879); I/1281 (Dec. 13, 1880).

15. Mss. II/26/15/i–iv (probably written in 1883).

16. The Simeys speak of Booth as having "finally repudiated his tentative support of the Positivist faith," and again of his "final rejection of Comtism," in a context that would seem to locate this in the early 1880s (pp. 60, 66). He had rejected many specifics of the faith from the beginning, but the "final" rejection, if it can be called that, must have come somewhat later, to judge by the manuscripts of 1883. Many years later, commenting on the Simeys' book, Booth's son-in-law, T. W. D. Ritchie, wrote: "He rejected Positivism after careful consideration—as of Darwin's theory of natural selection. This latter fact I know as it was often a subject of conversation between us" (Mss. II/86/9c). But that note gives no date for the rejection of Positivism, and it is not clear whether he is supposed to have rejected the scientific theory

of natural selection or the social theory known as Social Darwinism; the latter he had rejected much earlier—indeed when he first espoused Positivism in opposition to the unrestrained "struggle" for wealth. (See above, p. 16: Mss. II/25/2.) That he also rejected the scientific theory is suggested in the fifth paragraph of his credo. (Mss. II/26/15/vii–x.)

17. Mss. II/26/15/xi. He composed this "prayer" himself, to judge by the lines crossed out and rewritten. It may have been part of an early version of the testament quoted immediately below.

18. Mss. II/26/15/vii–x.

19. Mss. II/26/15/xi–xiv.

20. On the social and philanthropic situation in Liverpool, see M. B. Simey, *Charitable Effort in Liverpool* (Liverpool, 1951); P. J. Waller, *Democracy and Sectarianism: A Political and Social History of Liverpool 1868–1939* (Liverpool, 1981); David Owen, *English Philanthropy 1660–1960* (Cambridge, Mass., 1964), pp. 453 ff.

21. On Mary Macaulay and her background, see Simey, pp. 38 ff, and the book by the Booths' granddaughter, Belinda Norman-Butler, *Victorian Aspirations: The Life and Labour of Charles and Mary Booth* (London, 1972), pp. 17 ff.

22. Mss. I/3284 (MB to CB, Sept. 6, 1880).

23. Ibid., I/3293 (June 28, 1882). On other occasions she described Gladstone as "malignant," "unscrupulous, rough and insolent," a "thriving spirit of evil." (I/3381 [July 7, 1886], I/3377 [June 28, 1886].)

24. Mss. I/3393 (Sept./Oct. 1886); I/3189 (April 19, 1878).

25. Mss. I/1271 (Aug. 31, 1880); I/3287 (Sept. 13, 1880); I/3285 (Sept. 8, 1880).

26. Norman-Butler, p. 41.

27. Mss. I/3179 (March 21[?], 1878).

28. Mss. I/3219 (June 26, 1878).

29. William Rathbone, *Social Duties, considered in Reference to the Organisation of Effort in Works of Benevolence and Public Utility* (London, 1867). The original title of this book was *Method versus Muddle in Charitable Work.*

30. Asa Briggs, *Victorian Cities* (New York, 1965), p. 339. According to Briggs, London became even more important in the 1880s and '90s than it had been earlier in the century because it underwent more dramatic changes than other parts of the country and was more affected by unemployment and sweated labor. Had Dickens been writing *Hard Times* in the 1880s, Briggs says, he would have chosen London, not Lancashire, as the setting for the strike.

31. See below, Books III and V.

32. Noel Annan, "The Intellectual Aristocracy," in *Studies in Social History,* ed. J. H. Plumb (London, 1955), p. 244.

33. On the Booths and Barnetts, see Mary Booth, *Charles Booth: A Memoir* (London, 1918), p. 15. In her biography of her husband, Mrs. Barnett recalled a lecture delivered by Booth at Toynbee Hall in which he had said that "the first impulse of this labour" had come from Barnett. (Henrietta Barnett, *Canon Barnett: His Life and Work* [London, 1918], II, 52.) The lecture is not dated or documented,

and there is no other record of it. If Booth did say something to this effect, it does not necessarily mean, as one historian has said, that Barnett "suggested" to Booth the idea of the survey. (G. Kitson Clark, *Churchmen and the Condition of England, 1832– 1885* [London, 1973], p. 278.) It could as well mean that the "impulse" came from the example of Barnett's dedication or from the frequent visits by the Booths to Whitechapel.

34. Mss. I/3181 (March 26, 1878).

35. Norman-Butler trivializes the issue when she describes Barnett as advising Mrs. Booth to "concentrate for the moment on her family and keep her powder dry" (p. 52). The choice was not between organizational work and family but between organizational work and reflection—and, perhaps, research. In fact Barnett himself, while essentially an activist, was wary of hasty solutions that did more harm than good. In an article aptly called "Sensationalism in Social Reform," he attacked the idea that "things done *for* people are more effective than things done *with* people." The problem was a lack of patience, an unwillingness "to examine, to serve, to wait, and even to fail, so long as what is done shall be well done." (*Nineteenth Century,* Feb. 1886, reprinted in Barnett, *Practicable Socialism: Essays on Social Reform* [London, 1888], pp. 181–82.)

36. Mss. I/3215 (June 21, 1878).

37. See above, p. 88 (I/3219 [June 26, 1878]).

7. THE SCIENCE OF SOCIAL RESEARCH

1. See above, pp. 84, 88.

2. H. M. Hyndman, *The Record of an Adventurous Life* (New York, 1911), p. 303. Hyndman's name seems to present curious difficulties for Booth's biographers and editors. He was commonly known under the initials H.M., for Henry Mayers. The Simeys give the initials as F.D. (evocative of F. D. Maurice, a socialist of another color). (T. S. and M. B. Simey, *Charles Booth: Social Scientist* [Oxford, 1960], p. 69 and index.) His editors Albert Fried and Richard M. Elman, obviously basing themselves on the Simeys, repeat the error. (*Charles Booth's London: A Portrait of the Poor at the Turn of the Century, Drawn from his "Life and Labour of the People in London"* [New York, 1968], p. xvii.) Another editor uses the initials C.S. (as in C. S. Loch, the secretary of the Charity Organisation Society). (Harold W. Pfautz, ed., Charles Booth, *On the City: Physical Pattern and Social Structure* [Chicago, 1967], p. 17.)

3. Booth himself made conflicting and ambiguous remarks about his original expectations. See E. P. Hennock, "Poverty and Social Theory in England: The Experience of the Eighteen-Eighties," *Social History,* 1976, pp. 72 ff.

4. Hyndman, pp. 303–5.

5. Among those who accept Hyndman's version at face value are Simey, pp. 69–70; Fried and Elman, p. xvii; Pfautz, pp. 21–22; Norman and Jeanne Mac-Kenzie, *The Fabians* (New York, 1977), p. 130; Gareth Stedman Jones, *Outcast London: A Study in the Relationship Between Classes in Victorian Society* (Oxford,

1971), p. 306; Belinda Norman-Butler, *Victorian Aspirations: The Life and Labour of Charles and Mary Booth* (London, 1972), p. 70. The first historian to question it seriously was David Rubinstein, "Booth and Hyndman" ("Labour Notes and Queries"), *Bulletin of the Society for the Study of Labour History,* 1968, pp. 22–24. (See also Hennock, who supports Rubinstein's findings [*Social History,* 1976, pp. 70–71].) Rubinstein points out that although the meeting between Hyndman and Booth is generally assigned to the period immediately following the Trafalgar Square riot on February 8, 1886 (e.g., Simey, p. 70 n. 1), a careful reading of Hyndman's memoir suggests that the SDF inquiry would have had to antedate the founding of *Justice* (January 1884) and the changing of the name of the Democratic Federation to the Social Democratic Federation (August 1884). But even in that earlier period there is no evidence of such a survey. Rubinstein suggests one piece of evidence that may tell in favor of Hyndman: the fact that the memoir was published in 1911 while Booth was alive and could have refuted it. But it would have been out of character for Booth to have made an issue of this, even if he happened to read Hyndman's book.

6. *Pall Mall Gazette,* Feb. 24, 1886, p. 1. The title of the introductory article was "The Truth about the Distress."

7. Ibid., March 15, 1886, p. 3.

8. In her diary, on August 22, 1885, Beatrice Webb referred to some earlier "shallow and sensational" accounts in the *Pall Mall Gazette.* (*The Diary of Beatrice Webb,* ed. Norman and Jeanne MacKenzie [Cambridge, Mass., 1982–83], I, 137.) Six months later, on February 18, 1886, Beatrice Potter made her first appearance in print with a letter to the editor of the *Gazette* published under the title "A Lady's View of the Unemployed at [*sic*] the East." The Simeys (pp. 69–70) suggest that this letter was written in "protest" against the SDF study and against the *Gazette,* which "sprang to the Federation's defence." But the letter did not mention either the SDF or the *Gazette* study, which in fact appeared only subsequently. Directed against current proposals for public works, it did not challenge any figures about unemployment, still less about poverty.

9. Bentley Gilbert, introduction to C. F. G. Masterman, ed., *The Heart of the Empire: Discussions of Problems of Modern City Life in England* (Brighton, Eng., 1973 [1st ed., 1901]), p. xv; Gilbert, *The Evolution of National Insurance in Great Britain: The Origins of the Welfare State* (London, 1966), p. 53; Wohl, *Interntional Review of Social History,* p. 228. Wohl, who says that *The Bitter Cry* had a "most direct and indeed most potent influence" upon Booth, and that his study was "inspired directly by the desire to test the astounding facts" in that pamphlet, cites the Simeys' book in support of this statement. But what the Simeys actually wrote was that while some of Booth's later colleagues attributed his work to the reading of *The Bitter Cry,* "no evidence in support of this claim has been discovered" (p. 66). Wohl has since modified this claim, saying that "the agitation over *The Bitter Cry* led indirectly" to Booth's study. (*The Eternal Slum: Housing and Social Policy in Victorian London* [Montreal, 1977], p. 220.)

10. Jones, p. 306. On this and later riots, see below, pp. 330–31.

11. Mss. I/3399 (Nov. 13, 1886).

12. Henrietta Barnett, *Canon Barnett: His Life and Work* (London, 1918), II, 52. See above, p. 89.

13. *The Diary of Beatrice Webb,* ed. Norman and Jeanne MacKenzie (Cambridge, Mass., 1982), I, 137 (Aug. 22, 1885). This entry is reproduced in *My Apprenticeship* with "unemployed" changed to "unemployment." (Penguin ed., 1971 [1st ed., 1926], p. 274.)

14. *Report of the Mansion House Committee Appointed March, 1885, to Inquire into the Causes of Permanent Distress in London, and the Best Means of Remedying the Same* (London, 1886), p. 13. For a discussion of this committee and the report, see above, pp. 44–46.

15. Booth, "Occupations of the People of the United Kingdom, 1801–81," *Journal of the Royal Statistical Society,* 1886, pp. 314–48. (Reprinted in Guy Routh, *Occupations of the People of Great Britain, 1801–1981* [London, 1987], pp. 1–17.) Based on the census returns from the beginning of the century, the paper concluded with a series of recommendations to make the census more useful for analytical and historical purposes. Five years later, Booth, then president of the Royal Statistical Society, was a consultant in designing the census of 1891.

16. *Jubilee Volume of the Statistical Society* (London, 1885), pp. 8–10. Beatrice Potter, who borrowed the journals from Booth, quoted in her diary the sentence defining statistics as the science of the structure of human society. The mss. of the diary bears the date May 6. In *My Apprenticeship,* the date is given as May 4, 1886 (p. 292). The published version of the *Diary* does not include this passage, although it does print part of the entry for that date.

17. Frederic J. Mouat, "History of the Statistical Society," *Jubilee Volume,* p. 54.

18. Robert Giffen, "Further Notes on the Progress of the Working Classes," in *Essays in Finance: Second Series* (London, 1886). His 1883 paper, also reprinted in this volume, was entitled "The Progress of the Working Classes in the Last Half-Century."

19. His wife informed him of the meeting on January 14, 1886 (Mss. I/3367). At the next meeting of the society, Booth delivered his second paper and Giffen commented on it.

20. Mary Booth, *Charles Booth: A Memoir* (London, 1918), pp. 14–15.

21. Webb, *My Apprenticeship,* p. 165.

22. Ibid., p. 186.

23. Ibid., p. 166.

24. Ibid., p. 171 (letter to her father, Nov. 1883).

25. Ibid., p. 284 (diary, July 1886). (This entry is not in the published edition of the *Diary.*)

26. Ibid., p. 291.

27. Ibid.

28. Simey, p. 78; Norman-Butler, p. 86 (Booth to Beatrice Potter, July 27, 1886).

29. Mss. I/1308 (July 31, 1886). In Simey, these two letters are given as one (p. 78). The letter of July 31 is in typescript in the University of London collection. The original of this letter as well as that of July 27 are missing from the Booth Mss.

collection at the University of London and from the Webb collection at the London School of Economics.

30. Ibid.

31. Booth, "Dock and Wharf Labour," *Journal of the Royal Statistical Society,* 1892, p. 521. (See above, pp. 50–51.)

32. Webb, *My Apprenticeship,* p. 341.

33. For a discussion of Mayhew, see Gertrude Himmelfarb, *The Idea of Poverty: England in the Early Industrial Age* (New York, 1984), pp. 307 ff. One of the very few references to Mayhew in Booth's work appears in an excerpt from one of the investigator's notebooks describing a man of seventy. "He knew something of our work, and had known the Mayhews, whom he met when they were preparing their book" (3:III, 65). There is also a single reference to Mayhew in Mary Booth's *Memoir.* Referring to earlier attempts to portray the people, she mentioned Frederick Eden in the eighteenth century and the "brothers Mayhew" in the nineteenth, who "compiled their fascinating records of observation of humble life in London" (p. 103). It was not, of course, the Mayhew brothers who had written that work but Henry Mayhew alone.

34. Other members of his family assumed more traditional philanthropic roles. His sister Emily, for example, made frequent visits to the docks to investigate and relieve cases of hardship. She later served as a Guardian of the Poor in Liverpool. See A. H. John, *A Liverpool Merchant House: Being the History of Alfred Booth and Co., 1863–1958* (London, 1959), p. 162.

35. Simey, p. 27.

36. Webb, *Diary,* I, 165 (April 18, 1886). (This is slightly differently worded in *My Apprenticeship,* p. 292.)

37. I/3507 (MB to CB, Sept. 19, 1893).

38. The confusion of titles has been compounded by the different abbreviated versions appearing on the spines of library-bound copies. The Library of Congress, for example, features vol. I (in the library binding) as *Life and Labour of the People of England,* the rest of the first and the whole of the second series (in the publisher's binding) as *Life and Labour of the People,* and the third series (some in the publisher's and some in the library's binding) as *Life and Labour in London.*

39. Simey, p. 85 (CB to BP, Sept. 10, 1886).

40. *Life and Labour of the People in London* (1892 ed.), 1:I, vi. In the citations to this work, in this and the following chapters, the series are kept distinct, with volume numbers referring to the volume in that particular series. Thus 2:III, 45 would signify the third volume of the second series, page 45. Unless otherwise indicated, citations are to the 1902 edition.

41. Ibid. (1897 ed.), 2:V, iv.

42. This series had been anticipated from the beginning. In the discussion following the presentation of Booth's paper to the Statistical Society in 1887, the suggestion was made that in addition to the classification of the population according to classes and occupations, there should be an inquiry into the "moral division of the community." In reply Booth promised that "the moral questions would form a third set of inquiries." (*Journal,* 1887, p. 401.)

43. On the crowding index, see Michael Cullen, "Charles Booth's Poverty Survey: Some New Approaches," in T. C. Smout, ed., *The Search for Wealth and Stability: Essays in Economic and Social History Presented to M. W. Flinn* (London, 1979), pp. 166–67.

44. *Journal,* 1887, p. 327.

45. 1:IV, 256.

46. Samuel Papers, House of Lords Record Office, A/155 I(10) (Booth to Herbert Samuel, Nov. 10, 1891).

47. *Journal,* 1887, p. 327. The idea of using school board visitors for this purpose may have come to Booth from Joseph Chamberlain, by way of Beatrice Potter. In his testimony before the Royal Commission on Housing in 1885, Chamberlain alluded to the part played by school visitors in an earlier inquiry into slum conditions in Birmingham. (Webb, *My Apprenticeship,* p. 237; Mary Booth, pp. 17–18.)

48. 1:I, 25.

49. Webb, *My Apprenticeship,* pp. 300, 325–27. Both of her essays appeared first in the *Nineteenth Century,* the one on her experiences as a "trouser-hand" ("The Pages of a Workgirl's Diary" in October 1888) giving her a pleasurable degree of notoriety. Less pleasurable was the occasion when she gave evidence before a committee of the House of Lords on the sweating system, and was accused of misrepresenting her experiences. One of the charges, that her identity was known in the shop, was unwarranted. But another, that she had exaggerated the number of weeks she had worked, was true, and she then improperly altered the transcript of her evidence to correct that exaggeration.

50. 1:I, 158; 3:I, 7. This practice once gave rise to the rumor that Booth was planning a study of poverty in Liverpool. (Margaret B. Simey, *Charitable Effort in Liverpool in the Nineteenth Century* [Liverpool, 1951], p. 124 n.) Because the houses and families were described in some detail, the names of the streets were altered so that the people he had lived with would not be identifiable.

51. Norman-Butler, p. 92.

52. 1:I, 11–14.

53. Webb, *My Apprenticeship,* p. 237.

54. Philip Abrams, *The Origins of British Sociology: 1834–1914* (Chicago, 1968), p. 26. Abrams makes the point that "pure" statistics, as typified by this article, was often an exercise in methodology rather than in social research, the statisticians being more interested in displaying their technical skills than in elucidating social conditions or problems. He also argues—and here he may be on less firm ground—that this school, while professing to be hostile to all ideologies, was itself ideological, committed to the "atomistic, optimistic" perspective of political economy, "Adam Smith's blueprint" (pp. 26–27). In fact, "political economy" at this time was not nearly as rigid as this assumes (nor, for that matter, was Adam Smith's "blueprint"). And even those who were committed to it in its more orthodox form (some of the leaders of the COS, for example) were not at all reluctant to examine social conditions and problems; indeed the journal of the COS was full of such studies.

55. 1:I, 6.

8. POVERTY AND THE POOR

1. William Beveridge, *Voluntary Action* (New York, 1948), p. 128.

2. T. S. and M. B. Simey, *Charles Booth: Social Scientist* (Oxford, 1960), p. 88. See also p. 184.

3. In addition to the citations in the following footnotes, see, for example, Sidney and Beatrice Webb, *History of Trade Unionism* (1st ed., London, 1894), p. 367 (2nd ed., p. 381); E. Grebenik and C. A. Moser, "Statistical Surveys," in A. T. Welford et al., eds., *Society: Problems and Methods of Study* (London, 1967 [1st ed., 1962]), p. 6; Derek Fraser, *The Evolution of the British Welfare State: A History of Social Policy since the Industrial Revolution* (London, 1973), pp. 126–27; R. I. McKibbin, "Social Class and Social Observation in Edwardian England," *Transactions of the Royal Historical Society,* 1978, p. 175; Michael Cullen, "Charles Booth's Poverty Survey: Some New Approaches," in T. C. Smout, ed., *The Search for Wealth and Stability: Essays in Economic and Social History Presented to M. W. Flinn* (London, 1979), p. 159; A. M. McBriar, *An Edwardian Mixed Doubles: The Bosanquets versus the Webbs: A Study in British Social Policy 1890–1929* (Oxford, 1987). Harold W. Pfautz is almost alone in referring consistently to "line of poverty." But he quotes the Simeys' remark about Booth's "invention" of the Poverty Line without comment, as if in agreement. (Pfautz, ed., Charles Booth, *On the City: Physical Pattern and Social Structure* [Chicago, 1967], pp. 29, 34.)

4. Albert Fried and Richard M. Elman, eds., *Charles Booth's London: A Portrait of the Poor at the Turn of the Century, Drawn from his "Life and Labour of the People in London"* (New York, 1968), p. xxxv. See also p. xix.

5. John Gross, *New York Review of Books,* Jan. 30, 1969, p. 13.

6. Belinda Norman-Butler, *Victorian Aspirations: The Life and Labour of Charles and Mary Booth* (London, 1972), p. 100.

7. Each footnote reference by the Simeys to "Poverty Line" turns out to be a citation to "line of poverty."

8. "The Inhabitants of Tower Hamlets (School Board Division), their Condition and Occupations," *Journal of the Royal Statistical Society,* 1887, pp. 329, 339, 375.

9. Ibid., p. 394.

10. "Conditions and Occupations of the People of East London and Hackney, 1887," *Journal,* 1888, pp. 278, 283, 289.

11. 1:I, 33, 37, 50, 54, 59, 133; II, 33; IV, 24. (The last is in Beatrice Potter's essay on the dockworkers.) In 1:II, 20, the table of classes corresponds to a similar table in 1:I, 33, except for the omission of "line of poverty," which had appeared in the earlier table. (I may have missed one or two references, but not many, and certainly no prominent ones.)

12. 2:V, 15n., 25, 425, 427.

13. *Daily News,* May 16, 1888. *Century Magazine,* Dec. 1892, referred to the "line of comfort" but not the "line of poverty" (p. 247). According to Norman-Butler, "*The Times* called it 'the grimmest book of our time' because it substantiated the fact

that over 30 per cent of Londoners lived under 'the Poverty Line,' in Charles's expressive phrase" (p. 100). But the *Times* did not use that expressive phrase in its review, or even the less expressive one, "the line of poverty."

The earliest references I have found to "poverty line," before the publication of Rowntree's book, were by the Webbs, in their *History of Trade Unionism* (London, 1894), p. 367; and in the Fabian tract by Sidney Webb, *Facts for Socialists* (7th ed., 1895 [1st ed., 1887]), p. 12. But Sidney Webb could not have been overly impressed by the phrase, because another of his tracts, *Facts for Londoners* (1889), cited Booth's second paper and the first volume of *Life and Labour,* without mentioning either the "line of poverty" or "poverty line."

14. See below, chapter 12.

15. Helen Bosanquet, in an otherwise shrewd analysis of both works, may have started the misattribution. In an article entitled "The 'Poverty Line,'" published in the *Charity Organisation Review* in 1903, she pointed up their different definitions of poverty while attributing to them both the "Poverty Line." (See below, pp. 176–77.)

16. 1:I, 33.

17. 2:V, 426.

18. *Journal,* 1887, pp. 328, 339–40.

19. 1:I, 136–37.

20. 1:II, 208–9.

21. Ibid., p. 40.

22. 2:V, 15.

23. Ibid., p. 25.

24. Ibid., p. 427.

25. *Journal,* 1887, p. 328; 1:I, 33.

26. 1:I, 133.

27. 2:V, 14–15, 427.

28. Ibid., p. 160.

29. Mss. I/1309 (Sept. 5, 1886). "Opinion" was underlined by Booth.

30. *Journal,* 1887, p. 328.

31. 1:I, 136, 24. It is not clear why Booth deliberately refrained from asking the visitors to "obtain information specially for us"; perhaps he thought that that would interfere with their regular duties, or that information explicitly solicited would be less reliable than that which came their way indirectly. In fact, the visitors rarely ventured even an opinion about income, and the notebooks kept by Booth and his researchers only occasionally mentioned income.

32. 2:V, 13; Simey, p. 203.

33. 1:I, 136–37.

34. Michael Cullen, "Charles Booth's Poverty Survey: Some New Approaches," in T. C. Smout, ed., *The Search for Wealth and Stability: Essays in Economic and Social History Presented to M. W. Flinn* (London, 1979), p. 172.

35. 1:I, 33.

36. *Journal,* 1888, p. 293. 1:I, 131 gives this as the "problem of poverty," omitting the word "true."

37. 1:I, 33.

38. Ibid., p. 132. See also p. 33; *Journal,* 1888, pp. 293–94.

39. *Journal,* 1888, p. 339.

40. 1:I, 38. Booth's readers would have recognized this class as the "residuum," although he did not use that expression. Elsewhere he did refer to "the residuum element" (1:III, 208).

41. 1:I, 176.

42. Ibid., p. 43.

43. Ibid., p. 131.

44. Ibid.

45. Ibid., pp. 45–48.

46. Ibid., pp. 48–50.

47. Ibid., p. 51.

48. Ibid., p. 53.

49. It was not until the penultimate volume of the second series that Booth described at some length this not inconsiderable class (2:IV, 207–89).

50. 1:I, 61.

51. Ibid., p. 50.

52. Ibid., pp. 74–75.

53. 2:I, 396.

54. 1:II, 20–21.

55. 1:I, 42.

56. 1:II, 19.

57. Ibid., pp. 18–19.

58. Ibid., p. 19.

59. *Journal,* 1887, p. 328.

60. 1:I, 33.

61. 3:II, 116.

62. 2:V, 5. (Italics in original.)

63. 1:I, 33, 131, 161; 2:V, 431.

64. 2:I, 12.

65. *Journal,* 1887, p. 328. See also 1:I, 33.

66. 1:I, 146.

67. Ibid., p. 147. This is a simplified version of Booth's table. I have included under "Habit" the 4% he itemized separately as "Loafers."

68. Ibid., pp. 151–52. Booth had hoped to clarify this point in the Industry series but a footnote in the 1902 edition explained that he failed to do so (p. 151).

69. One of the rare instances of this usage is 1:I, 151. For a discussion of "unemployment," see above, chapter 3.

70. 2:V, 340–46.

71. John Brown, "Charles Booth and Labour Colonies, 1889–1905," *Economic History Review,* 1968, p. 354.

72. Sidney and Beatrice Webb, *English Poor Law History* (London, 1927), Part 2, II, 636, quoting Booth, 1:I, 152.

73. 1:I, 152–53. The Webbs quoted the rest of this passage in a footnote, omitting the word "but" which linked it to the previous quotation. They also said that

Booth had added the rest of this passage in 1892, suggesting that it was an after-thought. In fact this passage first appeared in the *Journal* paper of 1888 (p. 298) and was reproduced in vol. I and all later editions.

74. Well into the twentieth century, both Beveridge and the Webbs, while em-phasizing "involuntary unemployment," also pointed to bad habits and "work-shyness" to explain why some men rather than others were the victims of unemployment. (W. H. Beveridge, *Unemployment: A Problem of Industry* [New York, 1930 (1st ed., 1909)], p. 3; Webb, *English Poor Law History,* Part 2, I, 633.)

75. 2:V, 332, 337–38.

76. "Dock and Wharf Labour," *Journal,* 1892, p. 554.

77. 2:V, 361.

78. Some of those familiar with Booth's work managed to ignore this part of it. In an essay on the other Booth—"General" William Booth and his "Salvation Army"—written soon after the appearance of Charles Booth's first volume, Charles Loch, secretary of the COS, spoke of drink as a principal cause of distress. (*Criticisms on "General" Booth's Social Scheme* [London, 1891], p. 71.) Some of Booth's later commentators have also misrepresented his views on this question. One of his editors has written: "The problem of lower-class drinking loomed large in the middle class eyes of Booth and his staff" (Pfautz, p. 146). Other historians have ignored both his statistics and his conclusions. (See, for example, J. B. Brown, "The Pig or the Stye: Drink and Poverty in late Victorian England," *International Review of Social History,* 1973.)

79. 1:I, 38, 43, 45.

80. 3:XVII, 59.

81. 1:I, 114.

82. 3:VIII, 64–68, 112.

83. 1:I, 48.

9. "THE CRUX OF THE PROBLEM"

1. Beatrice Webb calculated that there were over three million in that class in the United Kingdom as a whole, but she gave no evidence for that figure. (*My Appren-ticeship* [Penguin ed., 1971 (1st ed., 1926)], p. 261.)

2. 1:I, 43–44, 176. (See above, p. 109.)

3. Ibid., pp. 162–63.

4. Ibid., p. 176.

5. Ibid., p. 167.

6. Ibid., pp. 166, 168.

7. Ibid., p. 166.

8. *Charity Organisation Review,* 1889, p. 398.

9. Ibid.

10. This was a familiar view of the poor law. See, for example, Sidney Webb's account of the evolution toward socialism in England (below, p. 356).

11. 1:I, 166.

12. Ibid., p. 167.

13. On old age pensions, see below, pp. 146–47.

14. "Heroic" was the term applied to it by the *St. James's Gazette,* April 17, 1889, and the *Liverpool Daily Post,* April 19, 1889.

The characterizations of the plan as "retrograde," etc., are from T. S. and M. B. Simey, *Charles Booth: Social Scientist* (Oxford, 1960), p. 195; Albert Fried and Richard M. Elman, eds., *Charles Booth's London: A Portrait of the Poor at the Turn of the Century, Drawn from his "Life and Labour of the People in London"* (New York, 1968), p. xxvi; Gareth Stedman Jones, *Outcast London: A Study in the Relationship between Classes in Victorian Society* (Oxford, 1971), pp. 308 ff. A reviewer of Jones compared it with what he said was a similar plan adopted in the German town of Elberfeld: "From this to the Nazi system of invigilation does not seem very far." (Victor Kiernan, "Victorian London: Unending Purgatory," *New Left Review,* 1972, p. 89.)

On the other hand, one commentator sees Booth's proposal as a "plan for a Welfare State." See Kathleen Woodroofe, *From Charity to Social Work in England and the United States* (London, 1968 [1st ed., 1962]), p. 16; see also p. 14.

15. John Ruskin, preface to *Unto This Last,* in Works, eds. E. T. Cook and A. Wedderburn (London, 1903–12), XVII, 22. (George Watson, *The English Ideology* [London, 1973], p. 231, directed me to this source.)

16. For the Mansion House Committee proposal, see Booth mss., University of London, 801/9B (Loch's Diary, Nov. 1, 1888).

17. For the Salvation Army colony, see below, pp. 221–22. One historian maintains that the popularity of the idea of labor colonies in the decade and a half following the publication of *Life and Labour* was directly attributable to that work. (John Brown, "Charles Booth and Labour Colonies, 1889–1905," *Economic History Review,* 1968, p. 354; Brown, "Social Judgments and Social Policy," ibid., p. 111.) Another denies that claim, pointing to the many similar schemes predating Booth's. (Trevor Lummis, "Charles Booth: Moralist or Social Scientist?" ibid., 1971, p. 104.)

18. *Manchester Guardian,* April 17, 1889.

19. *Saturday Review,* April 20, 1889.

20. Annual Report of the COS, 1889–90, quoted by David Owen, *English Philanthropy 1660–1960* (Cambridge, Mass., 1964), p. 239.

21. *Charity Organisation Review,* 1889, p. 282.

22. Jones, p. 314 (quoting *Today,* June 1889). Jones calls *Today* a Fabian journal. According to Tsuzuki, Hyndman, the leader of the SDF, edited it until May 1889; it is not clear whether it remained an organ of the SDF after that. (Chushichi Tsuzuki, *H. M Hyndman and British Socialism,* ed. Henry Pelling [Oxford, 1961], p. 60.)

23. Sidney Webb, *Facts for Londoners: An Exhaustive Collection of Statistical and Other Facts Relating to the Metropolis; with Suggestions for Reform on Socialistic Principles* (Fabian tract 8, London, 1889), pp. 18–19. Webb also reviewed the first volume of *Life and Labour* for the *Star* and lectured on it to the Fabian Society. (Edward Pease, *The History of the Fabian Society* [New York, 1963 (1st ed., 1918)], p. 80.)

24. John A. Hobson, *The Problem of the Unemployed: An Enquiry and an Economic Policy* (London, 1896), p. 137.

25. 1:I, 177. Booth's recent editors profess to understand better than Booth himself, or his contemporaries, which class the plan would benefit. "In the long run," Fried and Elman say, "it was the middle class that stood to gain most from the Draconian measures Booth recommended," for it was that class that would benefit by a policy designed to "exorcise the threat of 'Socialism and Revolution' [and restore the] 'forces of individualism' " (p. xxvi).

26. 1:I, 154.

27. Ibid., pp. 38, 131.

28. Ibid., p. 175.

29. C. S. Loch, *Charity Organisation* (London, 1892 [1st ed., 1890]), pp. 11–12. (The lecture was originally delivered in 1889 and published in England in 1890.)

30. 1:I, 131.

31. Ibid., p. 154.

32. Ibid., p. 33.

33. *Charity Organisation Review,* 1889, p. 398.

34. 1:I, 176–77.

35. Ibid., p. 178.

36. Ibid., p. 6.

37. While most historians have emphasized Booth's accounts of the poor and the very poor, Henry Pelling has drawn attention to his findings about the working class as a whole. Citing the figure for class E—42.3 percent of the population of East London—Pelling disputes E. J. Hobsbawm's contention that the "labor aristocracy" constituted only 10 percent of the working class. (*Popular Politics and Society in Late Victorian Britain* [London, 1968], p. 54.)

38. 1:I, 161; *Charity Organisation Review,* 1889, p. 398.

39. 1:I, 154, 162.

40. Ibid., p. 169.

41. 1:II, 177–78.

42. 1:I, 160–61.

43. Ibid., p. 99.

44. Webb, *My Apprenticeship,* p. 252.

45. See above, pp. 23–25.

46. 1:I, 172. See also 3:I, 5. Occasionally Booth did provide historical figures, although more often regarding population and trades than wages or poverty (e.g., 1:IV, 4–9).

47. 1:I, 174. Sidney Webb, in a Fabian tract comparing 1837 with 1897, deduced from Booth exactly the opposite conclusion. Quoting Booth's phrase "in a state of chronic want," Webb remarked, "We may be certain that the lot of these classes can, by the nature of things, never have been any worse even in 1837." As for the 32% (as Webb mistakenly put it) who earned no more than a guinea a week, Webb found it "difficult to believe that, even in 1837, the percentage of persons at a corresponding low level can have been greater." (*Labor in the Longest Reign (1837–1897)* [London, 1899 (1st ed., 1897)], p. 5.)

48. 1:I, 155.

49. Alfred Marshall, "Social Possibilities of Economic Chivalry" (1907), *Memorials*, ed. A. C. Pigou (London, 1925), p. 328.

50. Bentley B. Gilbert, introduction to C. F. G. Masterman, ed., *The Heart of the Empire: Discussions of Problems of Modern City Life in England* (London, 1973), p. xv.

51. A. S. Wohl, "Octavia Hill and the Homes of the London Poor," *Journal of British Studies,* 1971, p. 129; Wohl, *The Eternal Slum: Housing and Social Policy in Victorian London* (Montreal, 1977), p. 221. See also T. K. Derry and T. L. Jarman, *The Making of Modern Britain: Life and Work from George III to Elizabeth II* (New York, 1962 [1st ed., 1956]), p. 202.

52. 1:I, 178.

10. "SPECIAL SUBJECTS": WOMEN, CHILDREN, JEWS, THE AGED

1. This is the subtitle of the biography of Booth by T. S. and M. B. Simey, *Charles Booth: Social Scientist* (Oxford, 1960).

2. "Special Subjects" was the title of Part 1 of vol. III in the Poverty series, but it applies to the rest of that volume as well as much of the following one. In the 1889 edition, the chapters "Influx of Population," "The Jewish Community," and "Sweating" appeared in the first volume. In the 1892–93 edition, the first two of these subjects were moved to vol. III and the last to vol. IV.

3. This chapter was not written by Beatrice Potter, although she had previously written journal articles on the subject, one of which was based on her own experiences in a shop. The author of the chapter was Clara Collet, who also wrote the sections on girls' secondary education and on women tailors in the West End.

4. Millinery and dressmaking were treated elsewhere, it was explained, because they were not unique to East London, which was the subject of this volume.

5. 1:IV, 310.

6. Ibid., p. 322.

7. Ibid., p. 323.

8. 1:III, 216.

9. Ibid., p. 204.

10. Ibid., p. 232.

11. 2:V, 398–99.

12. Beatrice Webb, *My Apprenticeship* (Penguin ed., London, 1971 [1st ed., 1926]), p. 260.

13. 1:III, 229; 3:II, 49–50.

14. 1:IV, 330–31. (See also Beatrice Potter's account of the docks, 1:IV, 20.)

15. Ibid., p. 338.

16. Jay M. Pilzer, "The Jews and the Great 'Sweated Labor' Debate: 1888–1892," *Jewish Social Studies,* 1979, pp. 267–68.

17. In his first *Journal* paper of 1887, Booth said that he would not express an opinion on whether the Jews should be "refused settlement" (p. 368). In his sec-

ond paper of 1888, his only reference to the Jews was the comment that drink was a far less common cause of poverty in Whitechapel than anywhere else (4% in Whitechapel compared with 14% in East London), largely because the predominantly Jewish population, "whatever their faults may be, are very sober" (pp. 296–97).

18. For a discussion of this issue, see Yosef Gorni, "Beatrice Webb's Views on Judaism and Zionism," *Jewish Social Studies,* 1978; Deborah Epstein Nord, *The Apprenticeship of Beatrice Webb* (Amherst, 1985), pp. 173–76, 276 n. 53; Gertrude Himmelfarb, "Victorian Values/Jewish Values," *Commentary,* 1989, p. 25.

19. 1:III, 185–86. (This chapter was reprinted in Sidney and Beatrice Webb, *Problems of Modern Industry* [London, 1898].)

20. Ibid., pp. 187–89.

21. Ibid., p. 190.

22. Ibid., pp. 191–92.

23. This was best described—not pejoratively and not, except in passing, with special reference to the Jews—by Max Weber in 1904 in the first of the essays published under the title *The Protestant Ethic and the Spirit of Capitalism.* Werner Sombart applied it to the Jews in *The Jews and Modern Capitalism* (1911). Since then it has become a subject of much scholarly (and not so scholarly) controversy.

24. Karl Marx, "On the Jewish Question" (1844), *Writings of the Young Marx,* ed. Lloyd D. Easton and Kurt H. Gruddat (New York, 1967), pp. 243–46.

25. J. A. Hobson, *Problems of Poverty: An Inquiry into the Industrial Conditions of the Poor* (London, 1913 [1st ed., 1891]), pp. 60–63. The *Newcastle Daily Journal* (Nov. 11, 1887) made much the same point in commenting on Booth's first paper, but concluded only that pauper immigrants should be excluded—which, as Booth pointed out, would not have applied to the Jews.

26. *Times,* April 15, 1889.

27. *Newcastle Daily Chronicle,* April 17, 1889. The *East End News* (April 19, 1889) also compared the Jews favorably with other groups living in the area. The Jewish papers, of course (*Jewish World* and *Jewish Chronicle*), were delighted with this chapter. Llewellyn Smith, one of Booth's associates on *Life and Labour,* used the image of the Jews as economic man, in the favorable sense, in an article in the jubilee issue of the *Jewish Chronicle.* (Lloyd P. Gartner, *The Jewish Immigrant in England, 1870–1914* [London, 1960], p. 64.) Perhaps the greatest tribute to Beatrice Potter came in the form of the wholesale adoption of her facts and judgments, sometimes with little or no acknowledgment. The chapter on the Jews in Walter Besant, *East London* (London, 1901 [1st ed., 1899]), was based in large part on her essay.

28. *Charity Organisation Review,* 1889, p. 327.

29. 1:IV, 23–24, 12.

30. Ibid., p. 24.

31. Ibid., p. 32.

32. It was difficult to assign "proportions" to these groups since they varied so much from day to day, season to season, and dock to dock. On the London and St. Katherine docks, there were 1,070 permanently employed and anywhere from 1,100 to 3,700 irregularly employed, of whom 450 were preference men. On the West and

East India docks there were 818 regularly employed, 600–2,355 irregularly employed, and 700 preference workers.

33. 1:IV, 26.

34. Ibid., p. 33.

35. Ibid., p. 34.

36. 1:I, 147.

37. Ibid., p. 41. This list was repeated later, with "young persons" distinguished by sex and the addition of "infants," but again with no mention of the aged (p. 132).

38. Ibid., pp. 74–93.

39. *Journal of the Royal Statistical Society,* 1891, pp. 600–43.

40. Booth, *The Aged Poor in England and Wales* (London, 1894), pp. 14, 35.

41. On the response of the labor movement, see Henry Pelling, *Popular Politics and Society in Late Victorian Britain* (London, 1968), pp. 10 ff. Pat Thane, on the other hand, speaks of the "labour-based" National Committee. (Thane, "Non-Contributory Versus Insurance Pensions 1878–1908," in *The Origins of British Social Policy,* ed. Pat Thane [London, 1978], p. 94.)

42. Webb, *My Apprenticeship,* p. 218.

43. The final volume would have been an obvious place for an extensive discussion of the subject. It was raised there but occupied only a few pages.

44. Booth, *Aged Poor,* pp. 36, 420.

45. Yet Booth himself confused the issue in his title *The Aged Poor,* where "poor" clearly meant "paupers."

The Simeys suggest a different explanation for the neglect of this subject in *Life and Labour.* Booth, they say, was unwilling to be "diverted from the plan he had originally laid down"—the twofold method of class and occupation (p. 206). But he was diverted from that plan when he introduced the crowding test, which was, in effect, a third method.

11. RELIGION, MORALITY, IDEOLOGY

1. John Brown, "Charles Booth and Labour Colonies, 1889–1905," *Economic History Review,* 1968, pp. 349–60; Trevor Lummis, "Charles Booth: Moralist or Social Scientist?" ibid., 1971, pp. 100–5; Brown, "Social Judgements and Social Policy," ibid., 1971, pp. 106–13.

The charge that Booth was unduly moralistic appears in most modern discussions of him. It is one reason why E. P. Hennock denies that his work represented any "watershed" in social thought, any significant change from earlier Victorian attitudes. ("Poverty and Social Theory in England: The Experience of the Eighteen-Eighties," *Social History* [English journal], I [1976].) See also Michael Cullen, "Charles Booth's Poverty Survey: Some New Approaches," in T. C. Smout, ed., *The Search for Wealth and Stability: Essays in Economic and Social History Presented to M. W. Flinn* (London, 1979), p. 159.

2. Lummis, p. 105.

3. Ibid.

4. As the Simeys put it in what is still the most comprehensive and balanced study of Booth: "The interplay between fact and value, and the interaction of induction and deduction, was of fundamental importance in his system of thought." (T. S. and M. B. Simey, *Charles Booth: Social Scientist* [Oxford, 1960], p. 27.) The Simeys do not deny Booth's "preconceptions," but they see these as affecting his remedies or "interpretations" rather than the facts themselves (p. 193). See also T. S. Simey, *Social Science and Social Purpose* (London, 1968), pp. 26–28.

5. 3:I, 7.

6. Ibid., p. 82.

7. Ibid., p. 149. Booth quoted this passage again in the final volume of the series (3:VII, 424).

8. 3:VII, 401; II, 128; VII, 425.

9. 3:I, 41, 83.

10. 3:III, 81.

11. 3:VII, 342.

12. 1:I, 126. See also 3:VII, 338.

13. 3:I, 82.

14. 3:III, 84.

15. 3:VII, 426.

16. 3:I, 89.

17. Final vol., p. 43.

18. Ibid., pp. 43–44.

19. Ibid., pp. 121–31.

20. Ibid., p. 211.

21. Albert Fried and Richard M. Elman, eds., *Charles Booth's London: A Portrait of the Poor at the Turn of the Century, Drawn from his "Life and Labour of the People in London"* (New York, 1968), pp. xxi–xxv, xxix.

22. Standish Meacham, *A Life Apart: The English Working Class 1890–1914* (Cambridge, Mass., 1977), p. 7; Harold W. Pfautz, ed., Charles Booth, *On the City: Physical Pattern and Social Structure* (Chicago, 1967), pp. 88, 146; Donald Winch, *Economics and Policy* (London, 1969), p. 48.

23. Winch, p. 48.

24. John Brown, " 'Social Control' and the Modernisation of Social Policy, 1890, 1929," in Pat Thane, ed., *The Origins of British Social Policy* (London, 1978), pp. 129–30.

25. Karel Williams, *From Pauperism to Poverty* (London, 1981), pp. 338–39.

26. Gareth Stedman Jones, *Outcast London: A Study in the Relationship between Classes in Victorian Society* (Oxford, 1971), pp. 288, 305–8, 137–38, and passim. In a later essay, Jones was somewhat more appreciative of Booth, as one of the first "middle-class observers" to realize that "the working class was not simply *without* culture or morality, but in fact possessed a 'culture' of its own." ("Working-Class Culture and Working-Class Politics in London, 1870–1900: Notes on the Remaking of a Working Class," in *Languages of Class: Studies in English Working Class History 1832–1982* [Cambridge, 1983], p. 183.)

27. On Positivism and socialism, see below, pp. 358–60.

28. See below, chapter 20.

29. Mss. 797/II/27/13.

30. Mary Booth, *Charles Booth: A Memoir* (London, 1918), p. 15.

31. In September 1884, Mary Booth reported to her husband that Theresa (Beatrice Potter's sister, then married to Alfred Cripps) was "much interested in your Democratic Federation experiences." (Mss. I/ 3320 [Sept. 8, 1884].)

32. Mss. 797/II/27/7. The manuscript is entitled "A Discussion of Socialism." The catalogue of the Booth Mss. dates this as 1879, but internal evidence suggests a much later date. Cripps was married to Theresa Potter in 1881; Hyndman's disavowal of "bureaucratic state socialism" could only have been made in 1883 or 1884. The fall of 1884 is suggested by a letter from Mary Booth to her husband facetiously referring to the time when their children would be grown and she would be entertaining her boring lady friends in the drawing room while he "with a set of intelligent and enlightened unwashed friends discuss positivism and social dynamics in the dining room." (Mss. I/3381 [Nov. 13, 1884].)

33. Mss. 797/II/27/7.

34. Ibid.

35. Simey, *Charles Booth,* p. 58. (This was on the occasion of a seven-month visit to the United States in 1878.)

36. Edward Spencer Beesly (Professor Beesly, as he is often referred to), translator of Comte, acquaintance of Marx, and an important figure in the international socialist movement, was married to Booth's cousin, Emily Crompton. (See above, pp. 82–83 n.) For an account of Beesly's activities and ideas, see the essays by Royden Harrison: "The Positivists: A Study of Labour's Intellectuals," in *Before the Socialists: Studies in Labour and Politics 1861–1881* (London, 1965); "E. S. Beesley and Karl Marx," *International Review of Social History,* 1959; "Prof. Beesly and the English Working-class Movement," in Asa Briggs and John Saville, eds., *Essays in Labour History* (London, 1960).

37. *The Diary of Beatrice Webb,* ed. Norman and Jeanne MacKenzie (Cambridge, Mass., 1982), I, 87 (May 24, 1883).

38. Webb, *Diary,* I, 194 (March 12, 1887).

39. Mss. I/3424 (July 31, 1888). (This passage is incorrectly transcribed in Norman-Butler, p. 97.)

40. Mss. I/3425 (Aug. 2, 1888).

41. Mss. 797/II/29/2 (paper read at a meeting of the Political Economy Club, April 1888).

42. Webb, *Diary,* I, 325–26 (Feb. 15, 1890).

43. 2:V, 165–68. Mrs. Booth was especially pleased with these passages, quoting them at length (although somewhat differently worded) in her memoir. It was on her insistence that this volume was sold singly and therefore went out of print before the rest of the second edition.

Citing the same passages in their *Poor Law History,* the Webbs were reminded of a paragraph in Nassau Senior's *Political Economy* which, according to them, expressed his view of "the positive enjoyment of unemployment by the unemployed!" (Sidney and Beatrice Webb, *English Poor Law History* [London, 1927], Part 2, II, 636.)

44. 2:V, 174. For Booth's view of unions, see also his presidential address to the Statistical Society in 1892, "Dock and Wharf Labour," *Journal of the Royal Statistical Society,* 1892. In her memoir, Mrs. Booth said that he later came to "regret" the tendencies of modern trade unionism—the "exclusiveness, the hostility, the indifference to the claims of others, the clamour for privilege" (p. 34). But since she was much more conservative than he, it is possible that she was projecting her own views upon him.

45. 3:V, 404.

46. Ibid., p. 405.

47. Sidney Webb, *Problems of Modern Industry* (London, 1889), p. 109.

48. 2:V, 296.

49. Booth's collection of reviews is in the Booth Mss. collection in the British Library of Political and Economic Science (the London School of Economics).

50. *Daily News,* April 16, 1889; *Manchester Guardian,* April 17, 1889.

51. *St. James's Gazette,* April 17, 1889.

52. *Spectator,* June 20, 1891.

53. *Athenaeum,* April 27, 1889. Perhaps it was the same reviewer who wrote of the second series that the "extraordinary success" of the first one would have been more justified had it been as good as the second (Sept. 14, 1895).

54. *Life of Octavia Hill as told in her Letters,* ed. C. Edmund Maurice (London, 1913), p. 515 (Hill to S. Cockerell, Nov. 22, 1890). When Booth sent her a complete set of the final edition, Hill thanked him warmly, especially for his appreciative remarks on her own work. (Booth Mss., University of London, I/4912 [Sept. 10, 1903].)

55. *Daily News,* April 16, 1889.

56. *Star,* May 7, 1889.

57. *Progressive Review,* March 1897, p. 568, and May 1897, p. 186; *Westminster Review,* July 1890, p. 621. See also *Graphic,* April 20, 1889.

58. *Pall Mall Gazette,* Oct. 13, 1887, May 8, 1889, July 31, 1892. The comment about the first paper troubled Booth, who alluded to it in introducing his second paper. (*Journal of the Royal Statistical Society,* 1888, p. 278.)

Jones (p. 321) cites the criticism of the first paper from the *Gazette,* but not the later reviews of the volumes from the same journal. He gives the Simeys as the source of the quotation from the *Gazette,* but does not explain, as the Simeys did, that this was the only journal to criticize Booth's paper "with any severity," and that the editor of the *Gazette* may have been annoyed to find Booth taking the limelight from his journal, which had specialized in exposés of this kind. (Simey, *Charles Booth,* pp. 92–93.)

59. San Francisco *Sunday Chronicle,* Oct. 22, 1887.

60. *Journal,* 1887, p. 375.

61. *Journal,* 1888, pp. 288–89.

62. *Speaker,* June 13, 1891. C. S. Loch wrote a similar letter to the *Times* pointing out that William Booth had depicted all of Charles Booth's "poor" as starving and dangerous. (*Times,* Dec. 1, 1890.) Years later Alfred Marshall was to make the same point. (Alfred Marshall, "Social Possibilities of Economic Chivalry" [1907], *Memorials,* ed. A. C. Pigou [London, 1925], p. 328. See above, pp. 133–34.)

63. *Economic Journal,* Sept. 1891; *Journal of the Statistical Society,* 1889, p. 350; *Liverpool Daily Post,* April 19, 1889; *Leeds Mercury,* April 22, 1889; *Bristol Times,* April 22, 1889; *Scotsman,* April 29, 1889.

64. *Saturday Review,* April 20, 1889.

65. *Manchester Guardian,* April 17, 1889.

66. *St. James' Gazette,* May 20, 1887. This reviewer was evidently including class C among the one in five in poverty and D among those with an adequate income.

67. *Spectator,* April 20, 1889; *Leeds Mercury,* April 22, 1889; *East London Advertiser,* April 27, 1889; *Fireside News,* April 26, 1889.

68. *Charity Organisation Review,* 1889, p. 281; 1897, pp. 295–96. The COS became even more hostile after Booth publicized his proposal for old age pensions, and, later still, after the appearance of Seebohm Rowntree's book on York, which seemed to confirm Booth's.

69. *Justice,* July 13, 1891. (The review was signed H. W. Hobart.)

70. George Bernard Shaw, *The Road to Equality: Ten Unpublished Lectures and Essays, 1884–1918,* ed. Louis Crompton (Boston, 1971), p. 99 (Sept. 19, 1890).

71. J. A. Hobson, *Problems of Poverty: An Inquiry into the Industrial Condition of the Poor* (London, 1891), p. 171.

72. Michael Freeden, *The New Liberalism: An Ideology of Social Reform* (Oxford, 1978), p. 8.

73. See, for example, a letter by W. H. Dickinson, Dec. 9, 1900, asking him to serve on the Commission on Hooliganism. (Booth Mss. I/1502.)

74. Llewellyn Smith was Secretary of the Board of Trade in the Liberal government of 1906 and helped establish the state labor exchanges and the unemployment insurance system. (In 1927 he became chairman of the New Survey of London sponsored by London University and intended as a sequel to Booth's study.) Ernest Aves was government commissioner on the Wages Board, and later industrial conciliation and arbitration adviser to the government of New Zealand, and chairman of the Trade Boards. George Duckworth (half brother of Virginia Woolf) was secretary to Austen Chamberlain. Clara Collet, one of the first women graduates of the University of London, later worked at the Board of Trade.

75. José Harris, *Unemployment and Politics: A Study in English Social Policy 1886–1914* (Oxford, 1972), p. 214.

76. Ibid., p. 155.

77. 4 Hansard 147:1116–17 (June 20, 1905).

78. Ibid., 153:1346–47 (March 14, 1906).

79. Ibid., p. 1357.

80. There were some minor, but very minor, reforms of the poor law adopted, and there were a few, but very few, farm colonies established after the passage of the Unemployed Workmen Act, which authorized them.

81. Maurice Bruce, ed., *The Rise of The Welfare State: English Social Policy, 1601–1971* (London, 1973), p. 138 (extract from the *Report of the Royal Commission on the Poor Laws and the Relief of Distress,* appendix vol. VIII, p. 15). See also Harris, pp. 172–73.

82. William Beveridge, *Unemployment: A Problem of Industry* (London, 1909),

pp. 208–9, 229–30. (There are numerous other references to *Life and Labour* in this book.)

83. These provisions were removed only after the war, in 1919.

84. Bruce, p. 142 (extract from the Old Age Pensions Act).

85. Bruce, p. 156 (extract from Churchill's speech to House of Commons, May 19, 1909). Harris, on the other hand, says that the act had little effect on casual laborers and was not designed to solve their employment problems (p. 349).

86. Derek Fraser, *The Evolution of the British Welfare State: A History of Social Policy since the Industrial Revolution* (London, 1973), p. 156 (quoting Lloyd George's notes for a speech delivered in Dec. 1911).

87. Simey, *Charles Booth,* p. 172. See also P. Ford, *Social Theory and Social Practice: An Exploration of Experience* (Shannon, Ireland, 1968), p. 85.

88. *Life and Labour,* final volume, p. 208.

89. See below, the Epilogue.

90. Simey, *Charles Booth,* p. 261.

12. BOOTH AND ROWNTREE

1. Letter dated July 25, 1901, quoted by B. Seebohm Rowntree, *Poverty: A Study of Town Life* (London, 1902 [1st ed., 1901]), pp. 300–1. See also Booth, *Life and Labour,* final volume, pp. 28–30.

2. Rowntree, p. 301.

3. William Ashworth, *An Economic History of England, 1870–1939* (London, 1960), p. 252.

4. Elizabeth Roberts, "Working-Class Standards of Living in Three Lancashire Towns, 1890–1914," *International Review of Social History,* 1982. E. P. Hennock also questions Rowntree's claim that York was "typical," but praises him for shifting the discussion from London to the provincial towns, and concludes that York was probably typical at least of the smaller cities. ("The Measurement of Urban Poverty: From the Metropolis to the Nation, 1880–1920," *Economic History Review,* 1987.)

5. See, for example, Philip Abrams, *The Origins of British Sociology: 1834–1914* (Chicago, 1968), pp. 138–39; John Brown, "Charles Booth and Labour Colonies, 1889–1905," *Economic History Review,* 1968, pp. 352–53; Brown, "Social Judgements and Social Policy," ibid., 1971, p. 107; E. P. Hennock, "Poverty and Social Theory in England: The Experience of the Eighteen-Eighties," *Social History,* 1976, p. 74. It is interesting that Rowntree's principal biographer, Asa Briggs, does not make any invidious comparison between Brown and Rowntree. (*A Study of the Work of Seebohm Rowntree 1871–1954* [London, 1961].)

6. In a variation on this theme, J. H. Veit-Wilson argues that Rowntree had a "relativistic" view of poverty and precisely for this reason was "progressive." ("Paradigms of Poverty: A Rehabilitation of B. S. Rowntree," *Journal of Social Policy,* 1986, pp. 69–99.) See reply by Peter Townsend (ibid., pp. 497–98) and rebuttal by Veit-Wilson (ibid., pp. 503–7). A Foucauldian study by Karel Williams (as he himself describes it) finds Rowntree as "reactionary" as Booth in this respect, since

both were committed to a form of "naive empiricism" that obscured the real nature of poverty. (*From Pauperism to Poverty* [London, 1981], p. 360.)

7. For Rowntree's background, see Briggs, chapter 1; Anne Vernon, *A Quaker Businessman: The Life of Joseph Rowntree, 1836–1925* (London, 1958); Ian Bradley, *Enlightened Entrepreneurs* (London, 1987).

8. Rowntree, pp. 230 ff.

9. Ibid., pp. 31 and 117. On the discrepancy between Rowntree's classes and his poverty statistics, see E. P. Hennock, "Concepts of Poverty in the British Social Surveys, from Charles Booth to Arthur Bowley," to be published in *The Social Survey in Historical Perspective: Britain and the United States 1880–1940,* ed. Martin Bulmer, Devin Bales, and Kathryn Kish Sklar.

10. Rowntree, pp. x, 86–87.

11. Rowntree made it clear that while the sum required for food was based on a minimal nutritional standard, the sum for rent was based on the actual expenditure of each family.

12. Rowntree, p. 143. Oddly enough, these figures appeared in the middle of a chart almost halfway through the book and were rarely cited again.

13. Ibid., pp. 115–16.

14. In his exchange with Helen Bosanquet, Rowntree explained: "The fixing of my 'primary' poverty line depends absolutely upon a money basis, while the fixing of my 'secondary' poverty line depends upon observations regarding the conditions under which the families were living." (Rowntree, *The "Poverty Line": A Reply* [London, 1903], p. 20.)

Here too the statistics were oddly presented. Rowntree did not say that his investigators actually found 17.93% in a condition of secondary poverty—rather that they found a total of 27.84% in a condition of poverty, of whom 9.91% were in primary poverty. Subtracting the latter figure, they deduced that there were 17.93% in secondary poverty. (*Poverty,* pp. 117, 140.)

15. Rowntree, *Poverty,* pp. 60–61.

16. Veit-Wilson does not see this as a problem, because he interprets the concept of primary poverty (or the poverty line) as a "heuristic device" to focus attention on the larger problem of poverty (p. 84). Hennock does see it as a problem and offers an explanation for it. Rowntree, he says, failed to use income rigorously as the standard of poverty for the same reason that he assigned so wide an income range to class C: because his principal aim was to compare Booth's findings about London with his own about York. For this purpose he had to "identify" poverty as Booth had done and to use Booth's class divisions.

It is true that Rowntree needed a category of secondary poverty in order to arrive at anything like the 30% of poverty that Booth had publicized. But in other crucial respects Rowntree ignored or violated Booth's definitions and classifications. He paid little attention to what Booth took to be one of the most important identifying marks of poverty, the irregularity of employment. And his classes were blatantly different from Booth's, in terms of both labels and characteristics. The class to which Booth assigned the range of 21–30s. was class E, which was not poor; in such a class the large margin of income was not surprising or unreasonable. But Rowntree used those figures to define class C, most of whom were presumed to be poor, where a range of 9s. was considerable.

17. Rowntree, *Poverty,* p. 60.

18. Ibid., pp. 140–45. Of these five pages, the first was on primary poverty and the last two were by nature of apologia.

19. Ibid., p. 142.

20. Briggs, p. 34.

21. Rowntree, *Poverty,* pp. 144–45.

22. Ibid., p. 145.

23. See below, pp. 364–65, for a more extensive discussion of this subject.

24. Helen Bosanquet, "The 'Poverty Line,'" *Charity Organisation Review,* 1903, pp. 9–23. Similar objections were voiced, although less cogently, by the secretary of the COS, C. S. Loch, in his book *Charity and Social Life* (London, 1910 [1st ed., 1902]), pp. 386 ff. Some modern historians share the suspicion about the minimum standard of efficiency. Paul Johnson maintains that Rowntree's "minimum expenditure was not a bare subsistence standard, since minimum dietary needs could have been achieved with about half the expenditure on food that Rowntree actually allowed." ("Conspicuous Consumption and Working-Class Culture," *Transactions of the Royal Historical Society,* 1988, pp. 31–32. Johnson also cites a dissertation by Ian Gazeley and Veit-Wilson's "Paradigms of Poverty.")

25. Rowntree, *The "Poverty Line,"* pp. 25, 28–30.

26. Bosanquet, "The 'Poverty Line,'" *Charity Organisation Review* (1903), p. 325.

27. Rowntree, *Poverty,* p. 145. (See above, p. 175.)

BOOK III: THE "TIME-SPIRIT"

1. Beatrice Webb, *My Apprenticeship* (Penguin ed., London, 1971 [1st ed., 1926]), p. 158. At this point Webb spoke of it as the "mid-Victorian Time-Spirit," the spirit of the "middle decades" of the century. A few pages later, however, she described "the influence of the Time-Spirit on the social activities of the last quarter of the nineteenth century" (p. 165). In fact most of her evidence and the bulk of her discussion concern the 1870s and '80s. (See, for example, the references to the "seventies and eighties" in the quotations below.)

2. Ibid., p. 158; *The Diary of Beatrice Webb,* ed. Norman and Jeanne MacKenzie (Cambridge, Mass., 1982–83), I, 126 (Nov. 19, 1884).

3. Webb, *Apprenticeship,* pp. 146–47.

4. Ibid., pp. 158–59.

5. Webb, *Diary,* I, 120 (Sept. 8, 1884); *Apprenticeship,* p. 164.

6. Webb, *Apprenticeship,* p. 147.

7. Frank Prochaska, *The Voluntary Impulse: Philanthropy in Modern Britain* (London, 1988), p. 28.

8. Ibid., pp. 191, 273; *Diary,* Aug. 12, 1885. For a contemporary account of these "governing women," see Henrietta Barnett, "Women as Philanthropists," in T.

Stanton, ed., *The Woman Question in Europe* (New York, 1884). For historical accounts, see F. K. Prochaska, *Women and Philanthropy in Nineteenth-Century England* (Oxford, 1980); Anne Summers, "A Home from Home—Women's Philanthropic Work in the Nineteenth Century," in Sandra Burman, ed., *Fit Work for Women* (New York, 1979). These philanthropic women were very different from the "lady bountifuls" described by Jessica Gerard, "Lady Bountiful: Women of the Landed Classes and Rural Philanthropy," *Victorian Studies,* 1987.

9. Webb, *Apprenticeship,* p. 193.

10. Charles Dickens, *Bleak House* (1st ed., 1853), chapter 4; George Eliot, *Middlemarch* (Penguin ed., London, 1981 [1st ed., 1871–72]), p. 418.

11. For a critique of this "social conscience thesis," see John Baker, "Social Conscience and Social Policy," *Journal of Social Policy,* 1979.

13. THE SCIENCE OF CHARITY

1. Henry James, "An English New Year," in *English Hours* (Boston, 1905), p. 271.

2. The controversy started within five years of the founding of the society when Charles Bosanquet, *The History and Mode of Operation of the Charity Organisation Society* (1874), was challenged by Thomas Hawksley, *Objections to "The History."* This was followed by rebuttals and counter-rebuttals by W. M. Wilkinson, G. M. Hicks, and others. The dispute was revived in the 1890s and again in the 1900s and has by now produced a substantial literature. See Charles Loch Mowat, *The Charity Organisation Society, 1869–1912: Its Ideas and Work* (London, 1961), p. 18; David Owen, *English Philanthropy 1660–1960* (Cambridge, Mass., 1964), pp. 218–19; Kathleen Woodroofe, *From Charity to Social Work in England and the United States* (London, 1968 [1st ed., 1962]), p. 25. (Some of the contemporary literature, in England as well as America—Booth's *Life and Labour,* for example—spelled "Organisation" with a "z.")

3. Ford K. Brown, *Fathers of the Victorians: The Age of Wilberforce* (Cambridge, 1961), p. 317.

4. Ibid.

5. Woodroofe, pp. 26–27; Brian Harrison, "Philanthropy and the Victorians," in *Peaceable Kingdom: Stability and Change in Modern Britain* (Oxford, 1982), p. 216. For varying estimates of the number of societies and expenditures, see Geoffrey Best, *Mid-Victorian Britain 1851–1875* (New York, 1972), p. 138; E. H. Hunt, *British Labour History, 1815–1914* (Atlantic Highlands, N.J., 1981), p. 126; Anthony S. Wohl, *The Eternal Slum: Housing and Social Policy in Victorian London* (Montreal, 1977), p. 141; E. C. P. Lascelles, "Charity," in *Early Victorian England 1830–1865* (London, 1934), II, 322; Derek Fraser, *The Evolution of the British Welfare State: A History of Social Policy since the Industrial Revolution* (London, 1973), pp. 115–16.

6. Rathbone's book published in 1867, *Social Duties, considered in Reference to the Organisation of Effort in Works of Benevolence and Public Utility,* had as its original title *Method versus Muddle in Charitable Work.* For an account of Rathbone, see M. B. Simey, *Charitable Effort in Liverpool* (Liverpool, 1951).

7. Judith Fido, "The Charity Organisation Society and Social Casework in London 1869–1900," in A. P. Donajgrodzki, ed., *Social Control in Nineteenth Century Britain* (London, 1977), pp. 211–12.

8. Ibid., p. 212.

9. C. S. Loch, *Charity Organisation* (London, 1892 [1st ed., 1890]), p. 106.

10. On the relations of the COS with other philanthropies, see Madeline Rooff, *A Hundred Years of Family Welfare: A Study of the Family Welfare Association (Formerly Charity Organisation Society) 1869–1969* (London, 1972); Helen Bosanquet, *Social Work in London, 1869–1912* (London, 1914); Pat Ryan, "Politics and Relief: East London Unions in the Late Nineteenth and Early Twentieth Centuries," in *The Poor and the City: The English Poor Law in its Urban Context, 1834–1914,* ed. Michael E. Rose (New York, 1985); A. M. McBriar, *An Edwardian Mixed Doubles: The Bosanquets versus the Webbs: A Study in British Social Policy 1890–1929* (Oxford, 1987).

11. *Report from His Majesty's Commissioners for Inquiring into the Administration and Practical Operation of the Poor Laws* (London, 1834), p. 147. For a discussion of the report, see Gertrude Himmelfarb, *The Idea of Poverty: England in the Early Industrial Age* (New York, 1984), pp. 155–68.

12. Fido, p. 224 (quoting a COS statement of 1896).

13. R. I. McKibbin, "Social Class and Social Observation in Edwardian England," *Transactions of the Royal Historical Society,* 1978, p. 180.

14. Mowat, p. 37.

15. Beatrice Webb, *My Apprenticeship* (Penguin ed., London, 1971 [1st ed., 1926]), p. 213.

16. Woodroofe, p. 23; Fido, p. 214.

17. W. H. B. Court, *British Economic History 1870–1914: Commentary and Documents* (Cambridge, 1965), p. 374.

18. See, for example, the statement that the COS accepted the "misplaced assumption that distress was only temporary." (Michael J. Moore, "Social Work and Social Welfare: The Organization of Philanthropic Resources in Britain, 1900–1914," *Journal of British Studies,* 1977, p. 89.) For more nuanced and complicated accounts of the COS, see McKibbin, pp. 176–99; Andrew Vincent and Raymond Plant, *Philosophy, Politics and Citizenship: The Life and Thought of the British Idealists* (Oxford, 1984), pp. 94 ff.; C. S. Yeo, introduction to reprint of Helen Bosanquet, *Social Work* (Brighton, Eng., 1973).

19. *Charity Organisation Review,* 1885, pp. 170–71.

20. Helen Bosanquet, *Social Work,* p. 284, and *Rich and Poor* (New York, 1970 [reprint of 2nd ed., 1898]), pp. 221 ff.; Mowat, pp. 97–98.

21. Woodroofe, p. 48. The quotation is from the Reverend Henry Solly, whose ideas are thought to have inspired the founding of the COS. See also C. S. Loch, "Charity and Charities," *Encyclopaedia Britannica* (11th ed., London, 1910), V, 885.

22. The term does not appear in the 1893 edition of the Oxford English Dictionary.

23. *Report . . . [on] the Poor Laws,* p. 148.

24. Himmelfarb, pp. 164–65.

25. Fraser, p. 121.

26. M. A. Crowther, "Family Responsibility and State Responsibility in Britain before the Welfare State," *Historical Journal,* 1982, p. 135 (quoting P. Ford, "Means Tests and Responsibility for Needy Relatives," *Sociological Review,* 1937).

27. Charles Bosanquet, *London: Some Account of Its Growth, Charitable Agencies, and Wants* (London, 1868), pp. 67 ff.; Mowat, p. 10; Brown, pp. 238 ff.; F. K. Prochaska, *Women and Philanthropy in Nineteenth-Century England* (Oxford, 1980), pp. 97 ff.

28. Charles Dickens, *Bleak House* (New York, 1977 [1st ed., 1853]), p. 94.

29. Helen Bosanquet, *Social Work,* p. 64.

30. Brian Harrison, "Miss Butler's Oxford Survey," in *Traditions of Social Policy: Essays in Honour of Violet Butler* (Oxford, 1976), ed. A. H. Halsey, p. 67.

31. Ibid., p. 56.

32. McKibbin, p. 187.

33. Helen Bosanquet, *Rich and Poor,* p. 120.

34. Harrison, p. 39.

35. Loch, *Charity Organisation,* pp. 35, 41.

36. Woodroofe, pp. 31–32.

37. Willard Wolfe, *From Radicalism to Socialism: Men and Ideas in the Formation of Fabian Socialist Doctrines, 1881–1889* (New Haven, 1975), p. 14.

38. Mowat, p. 67.

39. Woodroofe, p. 32.

40. Helen Bosanquet, *Rich and Poor,* pp. 138–39.

41. Beatrice Webb, Mss. of the Diaries, May 18, 1883 (Webb Mss. Collection, London School of Economics). The published version omits an important part of this quotation. (*The Diary of Beatrice Webb,* ed. Norman and Jeanne MacKenzie [Cambridge, Mass., 1982–83], I, 85.)

42. Helen Bosanquet, *Social Work,* p. 53.

43. Mowat, p. 71.

44. Fido, p. 209 (quoting a brochure of 1893).

45. Loch, *Charity Organisation,* pp. 61–62.

46. Woodroofe, p. 49 (quoting a report of 1877).

47. Ibid., p. 23.

48. Mowat, p. 38.

49. Fraser, pp. 117–19.

50. Fido, pp. 224, 228.

51. Ibid., pp. 215–16.

52. Gareth Stedman Jones, *Outcast London: A Study in the Relationship between Classes in Victorian England* (Oxford, 1971), pp. 251–52, 26. More recently, Jones has criticized the social control thesis in general on the grounds that it is too vague to be useful and because it is incompatible with a conflict model of society. ("Class Expression versus Social Control? A Critique of Recent Trends in the Social History of 'Leisure,'" in Jones, *Languages of Class: Studies in English Working Class History 1832–1982* [Cambridge, 1983], pp. 76 ff.)

For other statements of the social control thesis applied to social reforms in general, see A. P. Donajgrodzki, ed., *Social Control in Nineteenth Century Britain* (Totowa, N.J., 1977); J. Higgins, "Social Control Theories of Social Policy," *Journal of Social Policy,* 1980; Roger Davidson, *Whitehall and the Labour Problem in Late-Victorian and Edwardian Britain: A Study in Official Statistics and Social Control* (London, 1985), pp. 11 ff. For critiques of this thesis, see Himmelfarb, pp. 41, 59–60; F. M. L. Thompson, "Social Control in Victorian Britain," *Economic History Review,* 1981; Alan Heesom, "The Coal Mines Act of 1842, Social Reform, and Social Control," *Historical Journal,* 1981; Martin Wiener, "Social Control in Nineteenth Century Britain," *Journal of Social History,* 1978–79. A more equivocal critique is by Thomas L. Haskell, "Capitalism and the Origins of the Humanitarian Sensibility," *American Historical Review,* 1985.

53. For different views of late-Victorian morality and the idea of respectability, see Gertrude Himmelfarb, "Manners into Morals: What the Victorians Knew," *American Scholar,* 1988, pp. 223–32; Paul Johnson, *Saving and Spending: The Working-Class Economy in Britain 1870–1939* (Oxford, 1985), pp. 225 ff.; F. M. L. Thompson, "Social Control," p. 196; Robert Gray, *The Aristocracy of Labour in Nineteenth-Century Britain, c. 1850–1900* (London, 1981), pp. 36 ff.; Standish Meacham, *A Life Apart: The English Working Class 1890–1914* (Cambridge, Mass., 1977), pp. 26 ff.; Patrick Joyce, *Work, Society and Politics: The Culture of the Factory in Later Victorian England* (New Brunswick, N.J., 1980), pp. xvi–xvii, 171 ff., 284 ff.; G. S. Jones, "Working-Class Culture and Working-Class Politics in London, 1870–1900: Notes on the Remaking of a Working Class," *Journal of Social History,* 1974, pp. 460–509; James Walvin, *Victorian Values* (Athens, Ga., 1987).

54. Owen, p. 477.

55. Ross Terrill, *R. H. Tawney and His Times: Socialism as Fellowship* (Cambridge, Mass., 1973), pp. 29–30.

56. Webb, p. 206.

57. Owen, p. 508. Melvin Richter repeatedly uses the word "curious" to describe T. H. Green's view of charity, which was essentially the same as that of the COS. (*The Politics of Conscience: T. H. Green and His Age* [Cambridge, Mass., 1964], pp. 332, 334, 335.)

58. See below, pp. 252–54.

59. Loch, *Charity Organisation,* p. 4.

60. T. H. S. Escott, *Social Transformations of the Victorian Age: A Survey of Court and Country* (London, 1897), p. 67.

61. *Letters of Lord Acton to Mary Gladstone,* ed. Herbert Paul (New York, 1905), p. 99 (March 15, 1880).

62. Bernard Bosanquet, "Charity Organisation and the Majority Report," *International Journal of Ethics,* 1910, p. 399.

14. MODEL DWELLINGS AND MODEL HOMES

1. Benjamin Disraeli, *Lothair* (London, collected ed., 1870 [1st ed., 1870]), p. 16.

2. For the etymology of "rookery" and "slum," see Thomas Beames, *The Rook-*

eries of London: Past, Present, and Prospective (London, 1852), pp. 1–2; H. J. Dyos, "The Slums of Victorian London," *Victorian Studies,* Sept. 1967, pp. 7–8; Anthony S. Wohl, *The Eternal Slum: Housing and Social Policy in Victorian London* (Montreal, 1977), p. 5; Gertrude Himmelfarb, *The Idea of Poverty: England in the Early Industrial Age* (New York, 1984), p. 307.

3. H. M. Hyndman, *The Record of an Adventurous Life* (New York, 1911), p. 48.

4. Brian Harrison, "Philanthropy and the Victorians," *Victorian Studies,* 1966, p. 360.

5. Charles Dickens, *Sketches by Boz; Illustrative of Every-Day Life and Every-Day People* (London, 17-vol. ed., n.d. [1st ed., 1836–37]), p. 229.

6. Wohl, p. 63.

7. Arnold J. Toynbee, *Lectures on the Industrial Revolution* (Boston, 1956 [1st. ed., 1884]), p. 116. (See above, p. 54.)

8. Helen Bosanquet, *Social Work in London, 1869–1912* (London, 1914), pp. 164–77; Wohl, pp. 93–95.

9. The original name of the society, founded in 1832, was the Labourers' Friend Society. The name was changed in 1844.

10. A history of housing has taken this as its title: John Nelson Tarn, *Five Per Cent Philanthropy: An Account of Housing in Urban Areas between 1840 and 1914* (Cambridge, 1973).

11. Wohl, p. 172.

12. *The Letters of Sidney and Beatrice Webb,* ed. Norman MacKenzie (Cambridge, 1978), I, 47 (Nov. 1885); Gareth Stedman Jones, "Working-Class Culture and Working-Class Politics in London, 1870–1900; Notes on the Remaking of a Working Class," *Journal of Social History,* 1974, p. 470.

13. Wohl, p. 175.

14. The main biographical sources are *Life of Octavia Hill as told in her Letters,* ed. C. Edmund Maurice (London, 1913); *Octavia Hill: Early Ideals, from Letters,* ed. Emily S. Maurice (London, 1928); E. Moberly Bell, *Octavia Hill: A Biography* (London, 1942); William Thomson Hill, *Octavia Hill: Pioneer of the National Trust and Housing Reformer* (London, 1956).

15. John Ruskin, *Fors Clavigera: Letters to the Workmen and Labourers of Great Britain,* in *The Works of John Ruskin,* ed. E. T. Cook and Alexander Wedderburn (New York, 1907), XXIX, 356–57.

16. Beatrice Webb, *My Apprenticeship* (Penguin ed., London, 1971 [1st ed., 1926]), p. 273; *The Diary of Beatrice Webb,* ed. Norman and Jeanne MacKenzie (Cambridge, Mass., 1982), I, 136 (Aug. 12, 1885).

17. According to Belinda Norman-Butler, the Booths and Octavia Hill met for the first time at a dinner party in November 1890. (*Victorian Aspirations: The Life and Labour of Charles and Mary Booth* [London, 1972], p. 109.) But in her memoir Mary Booth included Hill among those whose acquaintance Booth had made in the period before he started *Life and Labour.* (Mary Booth, *Charles Booth: A Memoir* [London, 1918], p. 15.) There is no mention of their meeting in Hill's published letters.

18. Webb, *Diary,* I, 169 (May 28, 1886).

19. Booth Mss., University of London, I/3150 (Aug. 1877).

20. Webb, *Diary,* I, 170 (May 28, 1886); *Apprenticeship,* p. 270 n.

21. Webb, *Diary,* I, 136–37 (Aug. 12, 1885). *My Apprenticeship* has a slightly differently worded version (p. 273).

22. Webb, *Letters,* I, 48 (Nov. 1885).

23. Octavia Hill, *Homes of the London Poor* (London, 1883 [1st ed., 1875]), p. 7.

24. Ibid., pp. 17–18, 38.

25. Kathleen Woodroofe, *From Charity to Social Work in England and the United States* (London, 1968 [1st ed., 1962]), pp. 53–54 (quoting Hill in the *Nineteenth Century,* 1893).

26. Wohl, pp. 179–99.

27. Ibid., p. 189 (quoting the *Morning Post,* Aug. 15, 1912).

28. Hill, p. 34. (This essay was first published in 1869.)

29. Ibid., p. 40.

30. Ibid., p. 42.

31. Woodroofe, p. 52 (quoting a speech by Hill in 1869).

32. Hill, p. 37.

33. Ibid., pp. 29–30.

34. Ibid., p. 90.

35. Hill, "Colour, Space and Music for the People" (May 1884), reprinted in *Nineteenth-Century Opinion: An Anthology of Extracts from the First Fifty Volumes of The Nineteenth Century, 1877–1901* (London, 1951).

36. Ibid., pp. 45–46.

37. Hill, *Homes,* pp. 14, 31, 40.

38. Ibid., p. 31.

39. Wohl compares Booth's classes with Hill's (p. 182).

40. In *Eternal Slum,* Wohl points out that some of the model building societies—the Peabody Trust, most notably—did accommodate laborers as well as skilled workers (pp. 155–57). But in an earlier essay, on the basis of the same evidence, Wohl gave the impression that even the Peabody Trust catered almost entirely to the artisan rather than laborer class. (*The History of Working-Class Housing: A Symposium,* ed. Stanley D. Chapman [Totowa, N.J., 1971], p. 39.)

41. David Owen, *English Philanthropy 1660–1960* (Cambridge, Mass., 1964), p. 388.

42. Peter Malpass, "Octavia Hill," *New Society,* Nov. 4, 1982.

43. Gareth Stedman Jones, *Outcast London: A Study in the Relationship between Classes in Victorian Society* (Oxford, 1971), pp. 195–96, 204, 229.

44. Wohl puts the number of inhabitants at 3,000 to 4,000. (*Eternal Slum,* p. 180.) Gauldie speaks of 5,000 to 6,000 *houses* (not people, as Wohl says). (Enid Gauldie, *Cruel Habitations: A History of Working-Class Housing 1780–1918* [London, 1974], p. 218.)

45. Wohl, p. 198.

46. Hill, *Homes,* p. 35.

15. THE SALVATION ARMY AND THE BARNARDO HOMES

1. St. John Ervine, *God's Soldier: General William Booth* (2 vols., London, 1934), I, 407. See also Harold Begbie, *Life of William Booth: The Founder of the Salvation Army* (2 vols., London, 1920), pp. 437–38.

2. For estimates of the strength of the movement, see Victor Bailey, "In Darkest England and the Way Out: The Salvation Army, Social Reform and the Labour Movement, 1885–1910," *International Review of Social History,* 1984, p. 135; Alan D. Gilbert, *Religion and Society in Industrial England: Church, Chapel, and Social Change, 1740–1914* (London, 1976), pp. 42–43. (See also the sources cited by Bailey.) Booth himself gave different figures. In 1890 he claimed 4,506 officers and 1,375 corps in the United Kingdom, and another 4,910 officers and 1,499 corps abroad. (*In Darkest England and the Way Out* [London, 1970 (1st ed., 1890)], appendix and p. 243.)

3. Booth, p. 45.

4. Bailey, p. 139.

5. Ibid., p. 150.

6. Booth, pp. 91–115, 283, and passim.

7. Ibid., p. 45.

8. Ibid., pp. 241, 277.

9. T. H. Huxley, letter to the *Times,* Dec. 9, 1890, in *Evolution and Ethics and Other Essays* (New York, 1898), p. 251.

10. Begbie, II, 85–86.

11. H. G. Wells, *Modern Utopia* (New York, 1905), chapter 9. (See below, p. 371.)

12. Beatrice Webb, *Our Partnership,* ed. Barbara Drake and Margaret I. Cole (London, 1975 [1st ed., 1948]), pp. 400–1 (quoting diary entry, Feb. 2, 1908).

13. Booth, pp. 242–43.

14. Huxley, letter to the *Times* (Dec. 1, 1890), in *Evolution and Ethics* (New York, 1898), p. 239.

15. Booth, p. 245.

16. Begbie, I, 470.

17. Booth, pp. 19–20.

18. Gertrude Himmelfarb, *The Idea of Poverty: England in the Early Industrial Age* (New York, 1984), pp. 323 ff.

19. Booth, pp. 14–15, 36.

20. Jack London, *The People of the Abyss* (New York, 1906 [1st ed., 1903]), pp. vii, 7–8, 17, 35, 38, 43, and passim.

21. George Bernard Shaw, *Major Barbara* (Penguin ed., 1968 [performed 1905, 1st ed., 1907]), p. 77.

22. Bailey, p. 141. According to Charles Booth, many of the recruits were not from the "poor," as he defined them, but from the "better sort of working-class people." This observation, however, applied not to the East End but to a better part of London. (*Life and Labour,* 3:III, 327.)

23. *Life and Labour,* 1:I, 155.

24. William Booth, pp. 49, 63–64. He estimated that there were half a million drunken men. He did not say how many of the three million were men; taking account of the women and children among them, a million men would seem reasonable, which would mean that half of the men in this group were drunken.

25. Ibid., p. 85.

26. Helen Bosanquet, *Social Work in London, 1869–1912* (London, 1914), pp. 343–44.

27. Huxley, letter to the *Times,* Dec. 9, 1890, in *Evolution and Ethics,* p. 248.

28. Bailey, pp. 156–58.

29. Engels to Paul Lafargue, Dec. 29, 1887, quoted in introduction to Engels, *Socialism, Utopian and Scientific* (New York, 1935 [1st ed., 1892]), p. 24.

30. Shaw, p. 98. Beatrice Webb, on the other hand, was pleased with the colony scheme as a means of coping with a troublesome class. (Webb, *Our Partnership,* p. 400.)

31. The best account is Victor Bailey, "Salvation Army Riots, the 'Skeleton Army' and Legal Authority in the Provincial Town," in *Social Control in Nineteenth Century Britain,* ed. A. P. Donajgrodzki (Totowa, N.J., 1977), pp. 231–53. Bailey uses the expression "Skeleton Army" (or "Skeleton Armies") as if this is what they were familiarly called. In other accounts, it is used more rarely. In Begbie it appears only once in the index (referring to I, 482), and in Ervine it does not appear in the index at all and only occasionally in the text (e.g., I, 612).

32. Ervine, I, 513, 537. There were similar attacks on the Salvation Army abroad—in France, Switzerland, the United States, New Zealand—and there too the authorities generally sided with the mobs. (Ervine, II, 619.)

33. On the charges of sweating, see Ervine II, 728–29; Norris Magnuson, *Salvation in the Slums: Evangelical Social Work, 1865–1920* (Metuchen, N.J., 1977), p. 171. So far from sweating their workers, the Salvation Army claimed, its matchbox factory protected them because it was the first in the world to manufacture only "safety" matches, thus eliminating the phosphorus that was responsible for a form of cancer.

34. Bailey, in *Social Control,* pp. 236–40.

35. Ibid., pp. 247–49.

36. Bailey, in *International Review of Social History,* pp. 135, 171.

37. Ibid., p. 171.

38. Ibid., p. 158.

39. The most objective and scholarly account of his complicated life is Gillian Wagner, *Barnardo* (London, 1979). The other biographies, including the much reprinted one by A. E. Williams, *Barnardo of Stepney: The Father of Nobody's Children* (London, 1st ed., 1943; 3rd ed., 1966), are more of the nature of hagiographies, having been written by members of his staff and, in most cases, under the supervision of Mrs. Barnardo. (Wagner herself was chairman of the Barnardo Council and thus sympathetic to the institution, but objective about the man and his times.) The account in the *Dictionary of National Biography* is unreliable and eulogistic.

40. Some of the photographs are reproduced in *The Camera and Dr. Barnardo,*

which includes essays by Gillian Wagner and Valerie Lloyd, published by the Barnardo School of Printing, Hertford, Eng. (n.d.).

41. Wagner, *Barnardo,* p. 84.

42. Wagner, in *The Camera,* p. 8.

16. TOYNBEE HALL

1. Arnold Toynbee, *"Progress and Poverty": A Criticism of Mr. Henry George* (London, 1884), p. 54.

2. See, for example, G. Kitson Clark, *Churchmen and the Condition of England 1832–1885* (London, 1973), p. 287.

3. Toynbee, p. 54.

4. Alon Kadish, *Apostle Arnold: The Life and Death of Arnold Toynbee 1852–1883* (Durham, N.C., 1986), p. 215.

5. For the origins of Toynbee Hall, see Henrietta O. Barnett, "The Beginning of Toynbee Hall," *The Nineteenth Century,* 1903. For its history, see Standish Meacham, *Toynbee Hall and Social Reform 1880–1914: The Search for Community* (New Haven, 1987); Asa Briggs and Anne Macartney, *Toynbee Hall: The First Hundred Years* (London, 1984). Perhaps the best portrait of it, from the point of view of a resident, is a fictional one, the novel by Mrs. Humphry Ward, *Robert Elsmere,* published in 1888.

6. See below, pp. 252–54. On the idea of citizenship as developed in Idealist philosophy and exemplified in the settlement movement, see Andrew Vincent and Raymond Plant, *Philosophy, Politics and Citizenship: The Life and Thought of the British Idealists* (Oxford, 1984), pp. 132 ff.

7. Meacham, p. 25.

8. Briggs and Macartney, p. 22.

9. Between 1884 and 1900 there were 102 residents. Of the 87 that have been traced, 52 came from Oxford (12 from Balliol) and 27 from Cambridge. (See Meacham, p. 44.)

10. Meacham, pp. 46–47.

11. W. Reason, ed., *University and Social Settlements* (London, 1898), pp. 170–73. These were the courses and lectures offered in October 1897 (most within a two-week period); some were held in neighboring halls. Another list may be found in Booth, *Life and Labour of the People in London,* 1:I, 122–24.

12. Meacham, p. 58.

13. Matthew Arnold, *Essays, Letters, and Reviews,* ed. Fraser Neiman (Cambridge, Mass., 1960), pp. 256–57 (from the *Times,* Dec. 1, 1884). An editorial note to this speech makes the common mistake of identifying Toynbee as "the founder of Toynbee Hall" (p. 260 n. 5).

14. William Beveridge, *Voluntary Action* (New York, 1948), p. 130.

15. Ibid., p. 131.

16. Jane Addams, *Twenty Years at Hull-House* (New York, 1910), pp. 90 ff.; Louise W. Knight, "Jane Addams' Views on the Responsibilities of Wealth" (un-

published paper delivered in June 1889), quoting Ellen Starr to her sister Mary Blaisdell, Feb. 2, 1889 (Starr Papers, Sophia Smith collection, Smith College).

17. Meacham, pp. 37–38.

18. George Lansbury, *My Life* (London, 1928), p. 130.

19. Briggs and Macartney, pp. 135–36 (quoting speech by Attlee in March 1947).

20. Meacham, p. 40 and passim.

21. *The Letters of Sidney and Beatrice Webb,* ed. Norman MacKenzie (Cambridge, 1978), I, 352 (Dec. 12[?], 1891).

22. Jane Addams, *Democracy and Social Ethics,* ed. Anne Firor Scott (Cambridge, Mass., 1964 [reprint of 1907 ed.; 1st ed., 1902]), p. xxii.

23. See below, chapter 17.

24. Beveridge, p. 130 n. 1.

17. "POSITIVE" LIBERALISM

1. The three volumes of *The Works of Thomas Hill Green,* edited by R. L. Nettleship (London, 1885–88), do not include the *Prolegomena to Ethics,* which was published separately after his death; but they do include a 150-page memoir by Nettleship. By 1911 six editions of the *Works* had appeared and five editions of the *Prolegomena.*

2. Melvin Richter, *The Politics of Conscience: T. H. Green and His Age* (Cambridge, Mass., 1964), p. 160 n.

3. J. Cotter Morison, *Macaulay* (London, 1902), p. 50 (paraphrase from letter by Macaulay). G. H. Lewes wrote one of the earliest articles on Hegel in 1842, but not until 1865, with the publication of J. H. Sterling's *Secret of Hegel,* was there a serious book on him. Benjamin Jowett, who had long been familiar with Hegelianism but not entirely sympathetic toward it, became something of a convert about this time.

4. Richard Burdon Haldane, *An Autobiography* (New York, 1929), p. 198.

5. W. H. Greenleaf, *The British Political Tradition* (London, 1983), II, 127.

6. Mrs. Humphry Ward, *Robert Elsmere* (Chicago, n.d. [1st ed., 1888]), p. 645.

7. Green, "Essay on Christian Dogma," in *Works,* III, 184. The importance of Green's theology in his own thought (in the concept of the "Christian citizen," for example), and its influence upon his contemporaries, is emphasized by Andrew Vincent and Raymond Plant, *Philosophy, Politics and Citizenship: The Life and Thought of the British Idealists* (Oxford, 1984). See also Bernard M. G. Reardon, "T. H. Green as a Theologian," and Andrew Vincent, "T. H. Green and the Religion of Citizenship," in *The Philosophy of T. H. Green,* ed. Andrew Vincent (Aldershot, Eng., 1986).

8. Beatrice Webb, *My Apprenticeship* (Penguin ed., 1971 [1st ed., 1926]), pp. 114, 122, 204, 345. See above, p. 6.

9. *The Diary of Beatrice Webb,* ed. Norman and Jeanne MacKenzie (Cambridge, Mass., 1982–83), II, 236, 335–36; Beatrice Webb, *Our Partnership* (Cambridge, 1975), p. 120.

10. Green, "Liberal Legislation and Freedom of Contract" (1881), in *The Political Theory of T. H. Green: Selected Writings,* ed. John R. Rodman (New York, 1964), pp. 51–52.

11. The best-known critique of positive freedom is Isaiah Berlin, "Two Concepts of Liberty" (1958), in *Four Essays on Liberty* (Oxford, 1969).

12. Green, "On the Different Senses of 'Freedom' as Applied to Will and to the Moral Progress of Man," in *Works,* II, 315 (#8).

13. Ibid., pp. 322–23 (#17–18).

14. Green, "Liberal Legislation," in *Political Theory,* pp. 52–53.

15. Matthew Arnold, *Culture and Anarchy,* ed. J. Dover Wilson (Cambridge, 1957 [1st ed., 1869]), pp. 6, 95, and passim. The theme is repeated in Arnold's *Essays in Criticism.*

16. Green, *Lectures on the Principles of Political Obligation* (London, 1941 [1st ed., 1882]), p. 129 (#121).

17. Ibid., p. 135 (#141).

18. Ibid., p. viii (introduction by Lord Lindsay).

19. R. L. Nettleship, *Memoir of Thomas Hill Green* (London, 1906 [reprinted from vol. III of *Works*]), pp. 170–71.

20. Green, *Political Obligation,* p. 130 (#122).

21. Green, "Liberal Legislation," in *Political Theory,* p. 52.

22. See the "Postscript" to this chapter.

23. Green, *Political Obligation,* p. 66 (#50).

24. Ibid., p. 206 (#207).

25. Ibid., p. 39 (#17); p. 218 (#219).

26. Immanuel Kant, "What Is Enlightenment?" (1784), in *On History,* ed. Lewis White Beck (Indianapolis, 1963), p. 3. "Tutelage" is a translation from *Unmündigkeit,* literally nonage.

27. Green, "Liberal Legislation," in *Political Theory,* p. 70.

28. Green, *Political Obligation,* pp. 39–40 (#18).

29. Ibid., pp. 218–19 (#219).

30. A. V. Dicey, *Lectures on the Relation between Law and Public Opinion in England during the Nineteenth Century* (London, 1962 [1st ed., 1905, based on lectures delivered in 1898]), p. 409. Dicey's use of these terms has been criticized as simplistic and biased. Recently they have been revived by W. H. Greenleaf and made the dominant theme of his *British Political Tradition.* Greenleaf prefers "libertarianism" in place of "individualism" in order to suggest that some "collectivists" (like Green) were that in the best interests of individuals and of a higher individualism. It is interesting that Greenleaf says that his own analysis of the British political tradition derives in part from the Philosophical Idealists (I, 9).

31. Green, "Liberal Legislation," in *Political Theory,* pp. 51–52.

32. Ibid., pp. 57–58.

33. Nettleship, *Memoir,* p. 45.

34. Green, "Liberal Legislation," in *Political Theory,* p. 69.

35. Ibid., p. 72.

36. See Brian Harrison, *Drink and the Victorians: The Temperance Question in*

England 1815–1872 (Pittsburgh, 1971); Peter P. Nicholson, "T. H. Green and State Action: Liquor Legislation," in *The Philosophy of T. H. Green*.

37. John Stuart Mill, *On Liberty,* ed. Gertrude Himmelfarb (Penguin ed., 1974 [1st ed., 1859]), pp. 148–50, 167.

38. Ibid., p. 68.

39. Nicholson, in *The Philosophy of T. H. Green,* p. 90 (April 12, 1879).

40. Dicey, p. 264.

41. Green, "Liberal Legislation," in *Political Theory,* p. 61.

42. Ibid., p. 54.

43. Ibid., p. 61.

44. Green, *Political Obligation,* p. 217 (#217); pp. 212–14, (#213–14).

45. Ibid., p. 219 (#220).

46. Ibid., p. 221 (#223).

47. Ibid., pp. 228–29 (#230–31).

48. These words are a constant refrain in Richter's book; see, for example, pp. 24, 115, 250, 259, 266, 267, 283, 288, 293, 297, 329, 340. Sometimes they are varied by such words as "tension" and "strain" (p. 201), "vague" and "fuzzy" (p. 291), or "curious" (pp. 332, 334, 335). See also Vincent and Plant, pp. 29, 32, 67, 86; Stefan Collini, "Political Theory and the 'Science of Society' in Victorian Britain," *Historical Journal,* 1980, p. 227; Peter Clarke, *Liberals and Social Democrats* (Cambridge, 1978), pp. 14–15.

49. The charge that Green's social philosophy was fundamentally flawed because it was insufficiently critical of capitalism and excessively individualistic is a prominent theme in much of the literature on Green. Standish Meacham makes the point explicitly: "Logic might have encouraged a move toward socialism beyond the mild interventionism Green and Toynbee preached." (*Toynbee Hall and Social Reform 1880–1914: The Search for Community* [New Haven, 1987], p. 20.) See also Richter (pp. 274, 276, 281, 291); I. M. Greengarten, *Thomas Hill Green and the Development of Liberal-Democratic Thought* (Dissertation, University of Toronto, 1981), pp. 6, 87–89, 108–11, 123–25, 129; Michael Freeden, *The New Liberalism: An Ideology of Social Reform* (Oxford, 1978), pp. 56–59. For a criticism of this interpretation of Green, see the essays by John Morrow: "Property and Personal Development: An Interpretation of T. H. Green's Political Philosophy," *Politics,* 1983; "Liberalism and British Idealist Political Philosophy: A Reassessment," *History of Political Thought,* 1984; "Ancestors, Legacies and Traditions: British Idealism in the History of Political Thought," ibid., 1985. See also Peter P. Nicholson, "A Moral View of Politics: T. H. Green and the British Idealists," *Political Studies,* 1987; Paul Harris, "Moral Progress and Politics: The Theory of T. H. Green," *Polity,* 1989. (Harris finds flaws in Green's philosophy, but not in this respect.)

50. Richter, p. 14.

51. Ibid.

52. James Bryce, *Studies in Contemporary Biography* (New York, 1903), pp. 93, 95, 99. See also R. B. Haldane, "The New Liberalism," *Progressive Review,* 1896, pp. 135 ff.

53. Henry Sidgwick, *Lectures on the Ethics of T. H. Green, H. Spencer, and*

J. Martineau (London, 1902). See also J. B. Schneewind, *Sidgwick's Ethics and Victorian Moral Philosophy* (Oxford, 1977), pp. 22, 384, 392.

54. Some commentators see the New Liberalism as essentially a development or extension of Philosophical Idealism, others as a reversal or repudiation of it. See Richter, pp. 267 ff.; Vincent and Plant, pp. 43 ff.; Stefan Collini, *Liberalism and Sociology: L. T. Hobhouse and Political Argument in England 1880–1914* (Cambridge, 1979), pp. 125 ff.; Collini, "Hobhouse, Bosanquet and the State: Philosophical Idealism and Political Argument in England 1880–1918," *Past and Present,* 1976, pp. 107 ff.; Peter Clarke, *Liberals and Social Democrats* (Cambridge, 1978), pp. 22 ff.; Freeden, pp. 16 ff., 55 ff.; Morrow, *History of Political Thought,* 1984, pp. 91 ff.; Morrow, ibid., 1985, pp. 507 ff.

55. On the relationship between Philosophical Idealism and socialism, see Adam B. Ulam, *Philosophical Foundations of English Socialism* (Cambridge, Mass., 1951), pp. 16 ff.

56. Greenleaf, I, 288.

57. Ibid., II, 127 (Green to H. S. Holland, 1869).

58. Edward Caird, preface to *Essays in Philosophical Criticism,* ed. Andrew Seth and R. B. Haldane (New York, 1971 [1st ed., 1883]), pp. 4–5.

59. Mill, *On Liberty,* pp. 181–82.

60. John Stuart Mill, *Auguste Comte and Positivism* (London, 1865), p. 78.

61. Sidney Webb, in *Fabian Essays in Socialism,* ed. George Bernard Shaw (Dolphin ed., New York, n.d. [1st ed., 1889]), p. 80. In another essay written about the same time, Webb wrote: "The economic influence most potent among the Socialist radicals is still that of John Stuart Mill." (*Socialism in England* [London, 1893 (1st ed, 1889)], p. 185.)

62. J. W. Mackail, *The Life of William Morris* (Oxford, 1950 [1st ed., 1899]), II, 85. Mackail went on to cite an article written by Morris ten years after his conversion where he referred to Mill's essays on socialism as having put the "finishing touch" to his conversion. Mackail himself thought that even this was an "unconscious overstatement," Morris having confused the causes of his conversion with the reasons justifying it.

63. John Stuart Mill, "Land Tenure Reform," in *Essays on Economics and Society,* ed. Lord Robbins (vol. VI of *Collected Works,* Toronto, 1967), II, 690–95.

64. Alfred Marshall, *Industry and Trade* (London, 1919), p. vii. See below, p. 296.

65. See, for example, Willard Wolfe, *From Radicalism to Socialism: Men and Ideas in the Formation of Fabian Socialist Doctrines, 1881–1889* (New Haven, 1975), pp. 23–65, where the discussion of Mill as one of the "precursors" of English socialism occupies an entire chapter. Wolfe concedes that Mill's socialism was based on moral sympathies, not economic principles, that he was not a "collectivist" in the proper sense of that word, and that those collectivist measures that he favored were not socialistic. What remained of his "socialism," and made him a precursor of Fabianism, were his "Socialist values," his idea of a "cooperative commonwealth," his Positivism, and his advocacy of such measures of "Radical collectivism" as reforms of land tenure, education, and labor conditions.

Casual references to Mill's "last, socialist phase," his "reformist socialism," or his "evolutionary socialism" appear in Ulam, p. 78; George Lichtheim, *The Origins of Socialism* (New York, 1969), p. 141; Joseph A. Schumpeter, *History of Economic Analysis,* ed. Elizabeth Boody Schumpeter (New York, 1954), p. 532. According to Leslie Stephen, Mill was "well on the way to state Socialism," adopting "not only Socialism, but even a version of Socialism open to the objections on which he sometimes forcibly insisted." But this judgment was entirely on the basis of the revised *Political Economy,* Stephen having dismissed *Chapters on Socialism* in a footnote as unworthy of publication. (*The English Utilitarians* [London, 1900], pp. 230, 237, 224.)

For more sustained and skeptical discussions of Mill and socialism, see Lord Robbins, *The Theory of Economic Policy in English Classical Political Economy* (Philadelphia, 1978 [1st ed., 1952]), pp. 142–68; Pedro Schwartz, *The New Political Economy of J. S. Mill* (Durham, N.C., 1972), pp. 153–92.

66. John Stuart Mill, *Autobiography* (World's Classics ed., Oxford, 1958 [1st ed., 1873]), pp. 194–98.

67. Ibid., pp. 198–99.

68. Ibid., p. 210. For evidence from his letters, see Gertrude Himmelfarb, *On Liberty and Liberalism: The Case of John Stuart Mill* (New York, 1974), pp. 227–33.

69. Mill, *Principles of Political Economy,* ed. V. W. Bladen and J. M. Robson (*Collected Works,* Toronto, 1965), II, 978.

70. Ibid., I, 209.

71. Ibid.

72. Ibid., p. 207.

73. Ibid.

74. Ibid., p. 213.

75. Ibid., p. 208.

76. Michael St. John Packe, *The Life of John Stuart Mill* (London, 1954), p. 481.

77. Mill, *Chapters on Socialism,* in *Essays on Economics and Society,* II, 728.

78. Ibid., p. 736.

79. Ibid.

80. Ibid., p. 737.

81. Ibid., pp. 739, 747.

82. Ibid., p. 738.

83. Ibid., p. 740.

84. Ibid., p. 746.

85. Ibid., p. 749.

18. THE NEW RADICALISM

1. Alon Kadish, *Apostle Arnold: The Life and Death of Arnold Toynbee 1852–1883* (Durham, N.C., 1986), p. 160.

2. Ibid., p. 218.

3. Alfred Milner, "Reminiscence," introduction to Arnold Toynbee, *Lectures on the Industrial Revolution of the Eighteenth Century in England: Popular Addresses, Notes, and Other Fragments* (London, 1908 [1st ed., 1884]), p. xxi. (Milner's "Reminiscence" was delivered at Toynbee Hall in November 1894 and published as a pamphlet. It was included in the 1908 edition of *Industrial Revolution*.)

4. Ibid.

5. Toynbee, "The Ideal Relation of Church and State" (1879), in *Industrial Revolution*, p. 250.

6. Ibid., p. 257.

7. Ibid., pp. 255–56.

8. Kadish, p. 52.

9. Ibid., p. 72.

10. Ibid., p. 64.

11. Toynbee, "Wages and Natural Law," in *Industrial Revolution*, p. 169.

12. Toynbee, "Ricardo and the Old Political Economy," ibid., p. 163.

13. Ibid., p. 143.

14. Ibid., p. 157.

15. He had delivered much the same address at Newcastle in December 1881 and again at Bradford the following month.

16. Toynbee, "Are Radicals Socialists?" (1882), in *Industrial Revolution*, p. 233.

17. Ibid.

18. Ibid., p. 238.

19. Toynbee, "Wages and Natural Law," in *Industrial Revolution*, p. 190.

20. Toynbee, *"Progress and Poverty": A Criticism of Mr. Henry George* (London, 1884), p. 54. (See above, p. 235.)

21. Kadish, p. 235. Marshall cited Toynbee only once in a footnote in his *Principles of Economics*, and again in an appendix (8th ed., London, 1982 [1st ed., 1890]), pp. 325, 632.

22. Toynbee, *Industrial Revolution*, p. 6. The printed version of these lectures was based on notes taken by his students, including Ashley. Four editions appeared in the first decade and numerous others in the course of the century since his death. At least one edition is still in print.

23. For the history of the term, see G. N. Clark, *The Idea of the Industrial Revolution* (Glasgow, 1953).

24. Toynbee, *Industrial Revolution*, p. 64.

25. Ibid., pp. 122–32. In a later lecture Toynbee somewhat modified this view, suggesting that in the south the conditions of agricultural laborers had deteriorated. (Kadish, p. 200.)

26. Toynbee, *Industrial Revolution*, p. 135.

27. Bernard Shaw, "The New Radicalism," in *The Road to Equality: Ten Unpublished Lectures and Essays, 1884–1918*, ed. Louis Crompton (Boston, 1971), p. 19.

28. Ibid., p. 74; "Are Radicals Socialists?" ibid., p. 236.

29. Toynbee, *Industrial Revolution*, pp. 86, 84.

30. Ibid., pp. 76, 79.

31. Toynbee, *"Progress and Poverty,"* p. 8.

32. Ibid., p. 54.

33. Melvin Richter, *The Politics of Conscience: T. H. Green and His Age* (Cambridge, Mass., 1964), pp. 288–91; Deborah Epstein Nord, review of Alon Kadish, *Apostle Arnold,* in *American Historical Review,* 1987, p. 1212; Standish Meacham, *Toynbee Hall and Social Reform 1880–1914: The Search for Community* (New Haven, 1987), p. 20.

34. Richter, p. 291.

35. Milner, p. xiv. See also F. C. Montague, *Arnold Toynbee* (Baltimore, 1889).

36. Kadish, p. 218.

37. Ibid.

19. THE NEW ECONOMICS

1. John Maynard Keynes, *The General Theory of Employment, Interest and Money* (London, 1936), p. 383.

2. John Stuart Mill, *Principles of Political Economy with Some of Their Applications to Social Philosophy* (Toronto, 1965 [1st ed., 1848]), II, 456 (Book III, chapter 1, par. 1).

3. John Maynard Keynes, "Alfred Marshall," in *Essays in Biography* (London, 1951 [1st ed., 1933]), p. 182. Keynes's memoir of Marshall first appeared in the *Economic Journal* in 1924 and was reprinted in Marshall's *Memorials,* ed. A. C. Pigou (London, 1925). Unless otherwise indicated, references to Keynes in these notes are to the memoir in the *Essays.* This is still the best brief account of Marshall in a literature that by now has grown to vast proportions. (Recent entries include two books by David Reisman, *The Economics of Alfred Marshall* [New York, 1986], and *Alfred Marshall: Progress and Politics* [New York, 1987].)

4. For the account of the dinner and the remarks of the speakers, see W. S. Jevons, "The Future of Political Economy," *Fortnightly Review,* 1876, pp. 619–31; T. W. Hutchison, *A Review of Economic Doctrines 1870–1929* (Westport, Conn., 1975 [1st ed., 1953]), pp. 1–5.

5. Quoted by Beatrice Webb, *My Apprenticeship* (Penguin ed., 1971 [1st ed., 1926]), p. 190.

6. Walter Bagehot, "The Postulates of English Political Economy," in *Economic Studies* (1880), *The Collected Works of Walter Bagehot,* ed. Norman St. John-Stevas (London, 1978), XI, 223.

7. Alfred Milner, "Reminiscence," introduction to Arnold Toynbee, *Lectures on the Industrial Revolution of the Eighteenth Century in England: Popular Addresses, Notes, and Other Fragments* (London, 1937 [1st ed., 1884]), p. xxv.

8. Ibid.

9. Joseph Schumpeter, *History of Economic Analysis,* ed. Elizabeth Boody Schumpeter (New York, 1954), p. 830.

10. Parts of *Economics of Industry* reappeared in Marshall's *Principles of Economics,* without any indication of the sources. Keynes and others thought better of this book than Marshall did (Keynes, p. 178).

11. Keynes, p. 208. The quotation about Marshall's influence is from H. S. Foxwell, "The Economic Movement in England," *Quarterly Journal of Economics,* 1887–88, p. 92.

12. Marshall, *Memorials,* p. 71.

13. Booth Mss., I/1310 (Oct. 18, 1886). This is the first letter from Booth to Marshall of which we have a record. It refers to an earlier letter from Marshall to Booth on the 15th. The Marshalls and Booths soon became good friends and frequent visitors to each other's houses. (See, for example, a letter from Mrs. Booth to her husband dated Oct. 22, 1889 [I/3438].)

14. Charles Booth, "The Inhabitants of Tower Hamlets (School Board Division), Their Condition and Occupations," *Journal of the Royal Statistical Society,* 1887, p. 392.

15. Keynes, p. 138.

16. Benjamin Jowett, the great eminence at Oxford, wrote Marshall that he saw "a considerable element of Hegelianism" in the *Principles.* There are many references to Hegel not only in the *Principles* but in Marshall's other writings as well. (See Stefan Collini, Donald Winch, and John Burrow, *That Noble Science of Politics: A Study in Nineteenth-Century Intellectual History* [Cambridge, 1983], p. 331.)

17. Keynes, p. 138.

18. Marshall, *Memorials,* p. 422 (Marshall to A. L. Bowley, March 3, 1901).

19. Marshall, *Principles of Economics* (9th variorum ed. based upon the 8th, London, 1961 [1st ed., 1890]), pp. 404, 368, 778. (The first volume of this edition is the text, the second the notes. Unless otherwise specified, references to the *Principles* are to the first volume of this edition.)

20. Marshall, *Memorials,* pp. 428–29 (Marshall to Bowley, Oct. 7, 1906). (I have transcribed some of the dashes as commas.)

21. Ibid., pp. 435–37 (Marshall to F. Y. Edgeworth, Aug. 28, 1902).

22. Henry Sidgwick, *The Principles of Political Economy* (London, 1883), p. 12. This was his definition of the "science" of political economy, the subject of the first two books of his work. The "art," or practical application, of political economy occupied the third book, and dealt with some of the ethical concerns that Marshall later featured more prominently. The last chapter, "Political Economy and Private Morality," explained that what the government ought to do by way of affecting economic behavior depended upon what private persons could be expected to do, and this in turn depended upon what they conceived it their duty to do. Even in their ordinary work, which was the subject of the "science" of economics, "men are not influenced merely by the motive of self-interest, as economists have sometimes assumed, but also extensively by moral considerations." This was all the more true in the "art" of political economy (p. 581).

23. Marshall, *Principles,* p. 1.

24. Calvin Woodard, "Reality and Social Reform: The Transition from Laissez-Faire to the Welfare State," *Yale Law Journal,* 1962, p. 315.

25. Ellen Frankel Paul presents Marshall as a "utilitarian" and "instrumentalist." (*Moral Revolution and Economic Science: The Demise of Laissez-Faire in Nineteenth-Century British Political Economy* [Westport, Conn., 1979], pp. 265 ff.) But she uses

these terms in so general a sense that any economic theory seeking any practical results may be said to be utilitarian. Both Talcott Parsons and Schumpeter made much of Marshall's use of the concept of marginal utility, but also of the ethical dimension of his thought, which differentiated him radically from the Benthamite mode of utilitarianism. (Parsons, "Wants and Activities in Marshall," *Quarterly Journal of Economics,* 1931, and "Economics and Sociology: Marshall in Relation to the Thought of His Time," ibid., 1932; Schumpeter, p. 1056.) See also Keynes, p. 136; Collini et al., pp. 316–20; C. J. Dewey, " 'Cambridge Idealism': Utilitarian Revisionists in Late Nineteenth-Century Cambridge," *Historical Journal,* 1974, pp. 75 ff.; Bruce Wearne, "Talcott Parsons's Appraisal and Critique of Alfred Marshall," *Social Research,* 1981.

26. Keynes, p. 136.

27. Marshall, *Principles,* p. 9.

28. Marshall, *Memorials,* p. 285 (1890).

29. Joseph A. Schumpeter, *Ten Great Economists* (New York, 1965), p. 104. This echoes Jacob Viner's judgment that "Marshall's political doctrines carried the hallmark of Victorian complacency and gentility." ("Marshall's Economics, in Relation to the Man and his Times," *American Economic Review,* 1941, p. 227.) Viner's criticism was directed primarily against Marshall's assumption that the problem of poverty could be resolved within "the limits of British parliamentary democracy and of a free enterprise economy." But he also criticized the idea that "good will," "economic understanding," and "sound moral preaching" could contribute to the material and moral progress of the working classes. See also J. K. Whitaker's comment on Marshall's "tendency to moralize and a certain parochialism and narrowness of vision." ("Some Neglected Aspects of Alfred Marshall's Economic and Social Thought," *History of Political Economy,* 1977, p. 196.)

30. Marshall, *Principles,* p. 17 n. 1.

31. Whitaker, p. 187 (quoting a talk by Marshall, "The Aims and Methods of Economic Study," Oct. 9, 1877).

32. Marshall, *Principles,* p. 243.

33. Ibid., p. 680.

34. Ibid., pp. 6, 9. See also p. 680.

35. Marshall, *Official Papers* (London, 1926), p. 205.

36. Keynes, pp. 137–38.

37. Hutchison, p. 33.

38. Ibid., p. 284.

39. Marshall, *Memorials,* p. 83 (lecture in 1883).

40. Marshall, *Principles,* pp. 1–3.

41. The earlier editions of the *Principles* contained several citations from Booth, but some of these were deleted from later editions because the statistics were outdated or the points no longer relevant. For the citations that were retained, see pp. 184 and 573; for those that were deleted, see II, 254, 332, and 617. See also *Memorials,* p. 328.

42. Marshall, *Memorials,* pp. 144–50 ("Where to House the London Poor," 1884). Marshall did not use the word "residuum" in this article, but he did repeatedly

elsewhere: e.g., *Principles,* pp. 2, 714; *Memorials,* p. 373 (letter to Rev. J. Llewellyn Davies, Feb. 1886), p. 387 (letter to Bp. Westcott, Jan. 24, 1900); *Official Papers,* pp. 210, 233 (evidence before the Royal Commission on the Aged Poor, 1893). In his talk to the Industrial Remuneration Conference in 1885, he spoke of "those who have a poor physique and a weak character—those who are limp in body and mind." (Charles Dilke, ed., *Report of Proceedings and Papers of the Industrial Remuneration Conference* [London, 1885], p. 197.) In the *Principles* he recommended "the application of the principles of Eugenics to the replenishment of the race from its higher rather than its lower strains" (p. 248).

In view of his many references to this subject, it is curious to find one commentator stating that Marshall did not share the prevailing views about the deterioration of the urban population. (Eric E. Lampard, "The Urbanizing World," in *The Victorian City: Images and Realities* [London, 1973], I, 30.)

43. Gareth Stedman Jones, *Outcast London: A Study in the Relationship between Classes in Victorian Society* (Oxford, 1971), p. 11.

44. Marshall, *Official Papers,* pp. 199, 244–45.

45. "Alfred Marshall's Lectures on Progress and Poverty," ed. George J. Stigler, *Journal of Law and Economics,* 1969, pp. 188–90. See also Marshall's comments on the misinterpretation of Booth's statistics, in which he pointed out that the condition of the English poor had considerably improved in recent times and that their present condition was far superior to that of the German poor. (*Memorials* ["Economic Chivalry," 1907], p. 328.)

46. Marshall, *Official Papers,* pp. 239, 246–47. Marshall made the same points in a talk to the British Economic Association that same year. (*Economic Journal,* 1893, p. 390.)

47. Marshall, *Memorials,* p. 155 ("The Present Position of Economics," 1885).

48. Marshall, *Official Papers,* p. 225.

49. Ibid., p. 245.

50. Ibid., pp. 203, 211, 233.

51. Ibid., p. 244.

52. Marshall, *Principles,* pp. 3–4.

53. Ibid., pp. 105–7.

54. Marshall, *Memorials,* p. 118 ("Future of the Working Classes," 1873).

55. Adam Smith, *An Inquiry into the Nature and Causes of the Wealth of Nations,* ed. Edwin Cannan (New York, 1937), p. 734. For an analysis of this passage, see Gertrude Himmelfarb, *The Idea of Poverty: England in the Early Industrial Age* (New York, 1984), pp. 55–60.

56. Marshall, *Principles,* pp. 261–63. The account in the early editions (until the major revision of the 5th edition) was more pointedly, if implicitly, directed against Smith. Where Smith had compared the factory worker unfavorably to the agricultural laborer, Marshall reversed that, finding in the factory worker "more intelligence and mental resource than has been shown by the English agricultural labourer whose employment has more variety" (II, 329).

57. Marshall, *Memorials,* pp. 115, 102 ("Future of the Working Classes," 1873).

58. Ibid., p. 103.

59. *Report of . . . Industrial Remuneration Conference,* pp. 182–83; *Memorials* ("Co-operation," 1889), p. 251; ibid. ("Some Aspects of Competition," 1890), pp. 281–82; ibid. ("The Old Generation of Economists and the New," 1897), pp. 307–11.

60. Marshall, *Principles,* p. 719.

61. Thomas Carlyle, *Past and Present* (Everyman ed., London, 1941 [1st ed., 1843]), pp. 271, 266, 285, and passim; Charles Kingsley, quoted by Walter E. Houghton, *The Victorian Frame of Mind, 1830–1870* (New Haven, 1957), pp. 319–20.

62. John Stuart Mill, *Auguste Comte and Positivism* (London, 1865), p. 161; William Booth, *In Darkest England and the Way Out* (London, 1970 [1st ed., 1890]), appendix, pp. xxviii–xxix; Marshall, *Principles,* pp. 22, 780 n.

63. Marshall, *Memorials* ("The Social Possibilities of Economic Chivalry," 1907), pp. 330–43.

64. Ibid., p. 345. Parsons used the concept of the Protestant ethic to describe Marshall's moral philosophy. ("Economics and Sociology," pp. 321 ff.)

65. Marshall, *Money, Credit and Commerce* (London, 1923), p. 263. The wording differs slightly in the *Report of . . . Industrial Remuneration Conference,* p. 183. There are also echoes of this passage in the concluding words of his inaugural lecture at Cambridge. (*Memorials* ["The Present State of Economics," 1885], p. 174.)

66. See Anastasios Petridis, "Alfred Marshall's Attitudes to and Economic Analysis of Trade Unions: A Case of Anomalies in a Competitive System," *History of Political Economy,* 1973.

67. Marshall, *Principles,* pp. 208–9, 718–20.

68. This has been most extensively documented in Rita McWilliam-Tullberg, "Marshall's 'Tendency to Socialism,'" *History of Political Economy,* 1975. Unfortunately some of the quotations are incomplete, omitting crucial qualifications, and the essay is marred by the author's assumption that Marshall's refusal to commit himself to a forthrightly socialist position represents an "ambiguity," "puzzle," or "enigma" (pp. 83, 97, 99).

An essay by E. J. Hobsbawm demonstrates how little attention Marshall paid to Marx. ("Dr. Marx and the Victorian Critics," in *Labouring Men: Studies in the History of Labour* [London, 1964], pp. 248–49.)

69. Marshall, *Industry and Trade,* p. vii.

70. Marshall, *Memorials,* p. 444 (letter to H. Bosanquet, Sept. 28, 1902).

71. Ibid., p. 334 ("Economic Chivalry," 1907).

72. Marshall, *Principles,* p. 713.

73. Marshall, *Memorials,* p. 291 ("Some Aspects of Competition," 1890).

74. *Times,* March 24, 1891.

75. Marshall, *Memorials,* pp. 334, 342 ("Economic Chivalry," 1907).

76. Ibid., p. 109 ("Future of the Working Classes," 1873).

77. Marshall, *Principles,* pp. 763–64. This passage appeared in the earlier editions but was removed to an appendix in the 5th edition, together with the historical discussion of which it was part.

78. *Ladder,* April 1891. I am indebted to an unpublished dissertation by Gail Benick for this and most of the excerpts cited below from the daily and weekly press.

79. *Manchester Guardian,* Aug. 29, 1890.

80. *The Diary of Beatrice Webb,* ed. Norman and Jeanne MacKenzie (Cambridge, Mass., 1982–83), I, 337 (July 27, 1890).

81. Sidney Webb to Beatrice Potter, Aug. 21, 1890 (Passfield Mss., London School of Economics; not printed in MacKenzie ed. of the Webbs' letters).

82. *Star,* July 30, 1890.

83. *Athenaeum,* Oct. 24, 1891.

84. *Times,* July 24, 1890.

85. *Pall Mall Gazette,* July 19, 1890; July 21, 1890.

86. On the laissez-faire school in this period, see John W. Mason, "Political Economy and the Response to Socialism in Britain, 1870–1914," *Historical Journal,* 1980.

87. Marshall himself repeatedly spoke of the "new economists" in contrast to the "old." In 1896 he made this the subject of an address, "The Old Generation of Economists and the New." (*Memorials,* pp. 295–311.)

88. Theodore Levitt, "Alfred Marshall: Victorian Relevance for Modern Economics," *Quarterly Journal of Economics,* 1976, pp. 440–41. In contrast to Levitt, A. W. Coats has argued that Marshall's "sociological assumptions" and "ethical preconceptions" might be "irrelevant to his technical economics and could usually be taken or left according to the reader's individual taste," but they "directly enhanced his effectiveness as the leader of a sociological group." ("Sociological Aspects of British Economic Thought (ca. 1880–1930)," *Journal of Political Economy,* 1967, p. 709.)

89. Keynes, p. 186.

90. Schumpeter, *History of Economic Analysis,* pp. 129 n, 765, 985–86.

91. Keynes, p. 205.

92. Woodard, "Reality and Social Reform," p. 293.

93. J. G. Goschen, "Ethics and Economics" (1893), in *Essays and Addresses on Economic Questions* (London, 1905), p. 340.

94. Schumpeter, *History of Economic Analysis,* p. 835. For an analysis of the actual relationship between Marshall's economics and that of the classical economists, in contrast to Marshall's own statements, see Denis P. O'Brien, "Marshall's Work in Relation to Classical Economics," in *Centenary Essays on Alfred Marshall,* ed. John K. Whitaker (Cambridge, 1990), pp. 127–63.

95. Smith, p. 423.

96. For an analysis of the contrast between Smith and Malthus, see Himmelfarb, *Idea of Poverty,* chapters 2 and 4.

97. Some economists have placed Marshall in a direct line of descent from Ricardo: e.g., G. F. Shove, "The Place of Marshall's *Principles* in the Development of Economic Theory," *Economic Journal,* 1942, p. 295; R. D. Collison Black, introduction to W. Stanley Jevons, *The Theory of Political Economy* (Penguin ed., 1970), p. 34. Others (e.g., Schumpeter, pp. 837–38) have emphasized the differences between Marshall and Ricardo. But whatever elements of Ricardian theory Marshall may have retained, he totally repudiated the "iron law of wages" and the fundamentally "pessimistic" and amoral character of Ricardianism.

98. Marshall, *Memorials* ("Economic Chivalry," 1907), p. 336.

99. Smith, p. 423.

100. Marshall, *Principles,* p. 528. (I am indebted to Levitt, p. 436, for directing me to this and the following two quotations.)

101. Ibid., p. 720.

102. Ibid., pp. 136–37.

103. John Dennis Chasse, "Marshall, the Human Agent and Economic Growth: Wants and Activities Revisited," *History of Political Economy,* 1984, p. 393 (quoting Marshall, *Economics of Industry*).

104. Levitt, p. 443.

105. Marshall, *Principles,* p. 136.

106. Talcott Parsons, "Economics and Sociology: Marshall in Relation to the Thought of His Time," *Quarterly Journal of Economics,* 1932, p. 344.

107. Marshall was a lowercase "evangelical," not an "Evangelical" in the theological and doctrinal sense. On the latter, see Boyd Hilton, *The Age of Atonement: The Influence of Evangelicalism on Social and Economic Thought, 1795–1865* (Oxford, 1988). Hilton is concerned with an earlier period, but some of the mid-Victorian Evangelicals he discusses survived into the late-Victorian period. (Although he lowercases "evangelicalism," he consistently uses that term in a precise theological sense.)

108. Marshall, *Memorials,* p. 462 (letter to Lord Reay, Nov. 12, 1909).

109. Woodard, pp. 286–328.

110. Smith, p. 625. On Say's Law, see Thomas Sowell, *Say's Law: An Historical Analysis* (Princeton, 1972).

111. A further refinement of this point has been made by Boyd Hilton, who has said, in connection with mid-Victorian England, that the shift away from a strict policy of laissez-faire to a greater degree of government intervention came about not so much (or not primarily) in response to new economic theories as in response to religious and theological ideas. (*Age of Atonement,* pp. viii–ix and passim.)

BOOK V: "WE ARE ALL SOCIALISTS NOW"

1. A. G. Gardiner, *Life of Sir William Harcourt* (London, 1923), I, 90. No date or source is given here, but the phrase was attributed to him at least as early as 1889 by Hubert Bland in his contribution to *Fabian Essays in Socialism* (New York, Dolphin ed. [n.d.] [1st ed., 1889]), p. 255. See also J. A. Hobson, *Problems of Poverty* (New York, 1971 [1st ed., 1891]), p. 195.

2. Quoted by Maurice Cranston in *Wall Street Journal,* August 24, 1983, p. 25.

3. Herman Ausubel, *In Hard Times: Reformers among the Late Victorians* (New York, 1960), pp. 144–45. For the opposition to socialism, see John W. Mason, "Political Economy and the Response to Socialism in Britain, 1870–1914," *Historical Journal,* 1980, pp. 565 ff.

4. A. V. Dicey, *Lectures on the Relation between Law and Public Opinion in England during the Nineteenth Century* (London, 1962 [1st ed., 1905]), p. 64 n. 1.

5. Alfred Milner, "A View of Socialism," *National Review,* Jan. 1931, p. 36. (This is the first printed version of the lecture delivered in 1882.)

6. Asa Briggs and Anne Macartney, *Toynbee Hall: The First Hundred Years* (London, 1984), p. 7.

7. Samuel Barnett, "Practicable Socialism," *Nineteenth Century,* April 1883; Sidney Webb, "Historic," in *Fabian Essays,* pp. 47, 70, 77. In 1891 John Morley urged Lord Rosebery to make himself "the exponent and the leader of a practicable socialism" in the Liberal Party. (John Morley, *Recollections* [New York, 1917], I, 313.) In the same year, J. A. Hobson spoke of the "practical socialism" and "unconscious socialism" that expressed itself in the social legislation of the time and in the familiar slogan "We are all socialists today." (Hobson, *Problems of Poverty: An Inquiry into the Industrial Condition of the Poor* [New York, 1971 (1st ed., 1891)], p. 199.)

8. John Stuart Mill, *Principles of Political Economy* (Toronto, 1965 [1st ed., 1848]), p. 203 (Book II, chapter 1, par. 2).

9. Elie Halévy, *Imperialism and the Rise of Labour* (vol. V of *A History of the English People in the Nineteenth Century,* trans. E. I. Watkin (London, 1951 [1st ed., 1926]), p. 231 (quoting speech by Balfour in January 1895).

10. Robert Salisbury, "Labourers' and Artisans' Dwellings," *National Review,* Nov. 1883; Joseph Chamberlain, "Labourers' and Artisans' Dwellings," *Fortnightly Review,* Dec. 1, 1883.

11. *The Radical Programme* (London, 1885), pp. 13, 59. See also Chamberlain's speech "State Socialism and the Moderate Liberals," April 28, 1885, in *Mr. Chamberlain's Speeches,* ed. Charles W. Boyd (Boston, 1914), I, 161–66.

12. R. E. Quinault, "Lord Randolph Churchill and Tory Democracy, 1880–1885," *Historical Journal,* 1979, p. 148. See also R. F. Foster, *Lord Randolph Churchill: A Political Life* (Oxford, 1981), pp. 81, 153 n. 40, 369–70.

13. Lord Rosebery, *Lord Randolph Churchill* (London, 1906), p. 154.

14. Winston Churchill, *Lord Randolph Churchill* (London, 1952 [1st ed., 1906]), p. 762.

15. Samuel H. Beer, *British Politics in the Collectivist Age* (New York, 1966), p. 91.

16. John Morley, *The Life of William Ewart Gladstone* (New York, 1903), III, 221 (letter to the Duke of Argyll, Sept. 30, 1885).

17. Philip Guedalla, *The Queen and Mr. Gladstone* (London, 1958), p. 177.

18. Morley, III, 173 (Feb. 11, 1885).

19. *Letters of Lord Acton to Mary Gladstone,* ed. Herbert Paul (New York, 1905), pp. 287–88 (Feb. 9, 1884), p. 328 (Nov. 11, 1885). "Academic" socialism was Acton's translation of the German *"Katheder"* socialism, which approached political economy from a historical and ethical point of view.

20. Lord Acton, *Essays in Religion, Politics, and Morality,* ed. J. Rufus Fears (Indianapolis, 1988), p. 561. For other expressions of Acton's views on socialism, see Gertrude Himmelfarb, *Lord Acton: A Study in Conscience and Politics* (Chicago, 1952), pp. 172 ff.

21. Ian Bradley, *The Optimists: Themes and Personalities in Victorian Liberalism* (London, 1980), pp. 249–50.

22. Stefan Collini, "Sociology and Idealism in Britain 1880–1920," *Archives européennes de sociologie,* 1978, p. 46.

20. LAND NATIONALIZATION

1. On George's influence on contemporary socialism, see Sidney and Beatrice Webb, *The History of Trade Unionism* (New York, 1973, reprint of 1920 ed. [1st ed., 1894]), pp. 375–76; Edward R. Pease, *The History of the Fabian Society* (London, 1963 [1st ed., 1918]), pp. 16, 19–21, 275; Max Beer, *A History of British Socialism* (New York, 1979 [1st ed., 1920]), II, 242–45; Elwood P. Lawrence, *Henry George in the British Isles* (East Lansing, Mich., 1957), pp. 3, 75 ff.; A. M. McBriar, *Fabian Socialism and English Politics 1884–1918* (Cambridge, 1966), pp. 29–30; Peter d'A. Jones, "Henry George and British Socialism," *American Journal of Economics and Sociology*, 1988, pp. 473–91.

2. The sales figure often cited is 60,000 in England by 1885. See, for example, John Rae, *Contemporary Socialism* (New York, 1901 [1st ed., 1891]), p. 441; Helen Merrell Lynd, *England in the Eighteen-Eighties: Toward a Social Basis for Freedom* (New York, 1968 [1st ed., 1945]), p. 143; Richard D. Altick, *The English Common Reader: A Social History of the Mass Reading Public 1800–1900* (Chicago, 1957), pp. 243, 390. But Altick's only source is Lynd, and Lynd gives no source at all. (It may have been Rae.) A persuasive case for the larger figure is made by Lawrence, p. 34. Willard Wolfe gives 100,000 as the size of the first cheap edition. (*From Radicalism to Socialism: Men and Ideas in the Formation of Fabian Socialist Doctrines, 1881–1889* [New Haven, 1975], p. 85.)

3. Henry George, *Progress and Poverty: An Inquiry into the Cause of Industrial Depressions, and of Increase of Want with Increase of Wealth. The Remedy* (New York, 1879), p. 117.

4. Charles Albro Barker, *Henry George* (Oxford, 1955), p. 444; Lawrence, pp. 53 ff., 88 n. 37.

5. George, pp. 383, 389.

6. Ibid., p. 295.

7. Ibid., pp. 364–65.

8. Ibid.

9. Ibid., p. 287.

10. Ibid., p. 288.

11. Ibid., pp. 269, 364. The word "simple" appears repeatedly in the book.

12. *Letters of Lord Acton to Mary Gladstone,* ed. Herbert Paul (New York, 1905), p. 288 (Feb. 9, 1884).

13. See above, chapter 5.

14. George, p. 282.

15. John Plowright, "Political Economy and Christian Polity: The Influence of Henry George in England Reassessed," *Victorian Studies*, 1987, p. 246.

16. Jones, p. 479.

17. Pease, p. 275. See also George Bernard Shaw, "The New Politics" (Dec. 20, 1889), in *The Road to Equality: Ten Unpublished Lectures and Essays, 1884–1918*, ed. Louis Crompton (Boston, 1971), pp. 83–84.

18. H. G. Wells, *Experiment in Autobiography: Discoveries and Conclusions of a Very Ordinary Brain (Since 1866)* (New York, 1934), pp. 132, 142.

19. Fred Reid, "Keir Hardie's Conversion to Socialism," in *Essays in Labour History, 1886–1923,* ed. Asa Briggs and John Saville (London, 1971), pp. 17–18. See also Jones, pp. 486–87.

20. George, p. 9.

21. Ibid., p. 195.

22. Arnold Toynbee, *Progress and Poverty: A Criticism of Mr. Henry George* (London, 1884), p. 8. (See above, chapter 18.)

23. H. M. Hyndman, *The Record of an Adventurous Life* (New York, 1984 [1st ed., 1911]), p. 290.

24. George, p. 266.

25. John Locke, *An Essay Concerning the True Original Extent and End of Civil Government* (Second Treatise of Civil Government), chapter 5, par. 35.

26. Jean Jacques Rousseau, *Discourse on the Origin and Foundations of Inequality among Men (Second Discourse),* Part 2, par. 1.

27. John Stuart Mill, *Principles of Political Economy: with Some of their Applications to Social Philosophy* (Toronto, 1965 [1st ed., 1848]), I, 230 (Book II, chapter 2, par. 6).

28. George, p. 304.

29. J. A. Hobson, "The Influence of Henry George in England," *Fortnightly Review,* Dec. 1897, p. 841.

30. Locke, chapter 5, par. 49.

31. George, p. 296.

21. MARXISM, ENGLISH STYLE

1. E. P. Thompson, *William Morris: Romantic to Revolutionary* (New York, 1977 [1st ed., 1955]), p. 298.

2. Ibid., p. 471.

3. Kirk Willis, "The Introduction and Critical Reception of Marxist Thought in Britain, 1850–1900," *Historical Journal,* 1977, p. 439.

4. Ibid., p. 428.

5. Arnold Toynbee, *Lectures on the Industrial Revolution in England* (Boston, 1956 [1st ed., 1884]), p. 34.

6. John Rae, *Contemporary Socialism* (London, 1891 [1st ed., 1884]), p. 128. The original article, reproduced in this book, appeared in *Contemporary Review,* Oct. 1881. In spite of the fact that Rae was generally critical of socialism, his analysis was careful, objective, and accurate. He also gave a remarkably perceptive account of the source of Marx's thought in the work of the Young Hegelians, especially Feuerbach.

7. H. M. Hyndman, *England for All: The Text Book of Democracy* (London, 1973 [1st ed., 1881]), p. ix (introduction by Chushichi Tsuzuki).

8. Chushichi Tsuzuki, *H. M. Hyndman and British Socialism,* ed. Henry Pelling (Oxford, 1961), p. 30.

9. Ibid., p. 33 (Oct. 1, 1880).

10. This was the title of Hyndman's article in *Nineteenth Century,* Jan. 1881.

11. Hyndman, *The Record of an Adventurous Life* (London, 1911), pp. 241–45.

12. André Maurois, *Disraeli: A Picture of the Victorian Age,* trans. Hamish Miles (New York, 1928), p. 355. There is no record of this meeting, or any mention of Hyndman, in the classic biography of Disraeli by Monypenny and Buckle. Those of Disraeli's biographers who refer to this meeting seem to accept Hyndman's account at face value. (E.g., Robert Blake, *Disraeli* [New York, 1966], pp. 763–64; Paul Smith, *Disraelian Conservatism and Social Reform* [London, 1967], p. 318.) Given Hyndman's reputation for exaggeration and self-aggrandizement (and the fact that his account was written so long after the event), one may well be suspicious, if not of the fact of the interview, at least of the details—the wording and even the purport of Disraeli's remarks and the inordinate length of the interview. Is it likely that a very feeble Disraeli would spend three hours speaking with, still less listening to, a man he did not know?

13. Hyndman, *England for All,* pp. 9–10. A dozen years later the Fabian Robert Blatchford was to write a best-selling utopia entitled *Merrie England.*

14. Ibid., pp. 167, 152, 169 ff.

15. Ibid., pp. 26 ff.

16. Ibid., pp. 79–86. Earlier, in the chapter on the land, a footnote specified that "nationalisation" (in quotation marks) of the land was the only logical outcome of land reform; "but this, unless accompanied by nationalisation of railways and of capital, would be of little use to the mass of the workers of the country" (p. 30 n. 1).

17. Ibid., pp. 84, 93.

18. Ibid., preface.

19. Marx and Engels, *Selected Correspondence, 1846–1895,* trans. Dona Torr (New York, 1942), pp. 397–98 (Marx to Friedrich Adolph Sorge, Dec. 15, 1881).

20. Out of pique, Hyndman destroyed all except one of Marx's letters to him.

21. Tsuzuki, p. 47.

22. Ibid., p. 46. Unlike Marx, however, George remained friendly with Hyndman, at least until Hyndman's attacks became more vehement. When they met in debate in 1888, Hyndman attacked George as a reactionary playing into the hands of the capitalists.

23. "Socialism Made Plain," in *The Challenge of Socialism,* ed. Henry Pelling (London, 1968 [1st ed., 1954]), p. 132. See also Hyndman and Morris, *Summary of the Principles of Socialism* (London, 1884). For biographical sketches of the new recruits, see Willard Wolfe, *From Radicalism to Socialism: Men and Ideas in the Formation of Fabian Socialist Doctrines, 1881–1889* (New Haven, 1975), appendix A (pp. 301–3).

24. Marx, *The Class Struggles in France,* in Marx and Engels, *Collected Works* (New York, 1978), X, 97. See also "Address of the Central Committee to the Communist League" (March 1850), ibid., p. 279.

25. Tsuzuki, p. 61.

26. Wolfe, p. 100 n. 93. Wolfe has three candidates being subsidized, although

other reports speak of subsidies only for the two London candidates. The nature of the proposal to Chamberlain varies from account to account. According to Tsuzuki, Hyndman suggested to Chamberlain that John Bright be withdrawn from Birmingham so that Hyndman could stand against Randolph Churchill (pp. 70–71). But if Churchill was the Tory candidate, would this be a safe seat for Hyndman? (Both Wolfe and Tsuzuki cite Shaw's letters to Andreas Scheu, the Austrian émigré who was one of the leaders of the opposition to Hyndman on the executive committee; but they give different dates for these letters.) E. P. Thompson has Hyndman threatening Chamberlain with more socialist candidates if Chamberlain did not support the Eight Hours Bill in the next session of Parliament (p. 404). Pelling has Hyndman promising to support Chamberlain in return for a seat in the Birmingham area (p. 40).

27. Paul Thompson, *Socialists, Liberals and Labour: The Struggle for London 1885–1914* (London, 1967), p. 114.

28. Ibid., p. 115 (quoting Shaw, Feb. 11, 1886).

29. Hyndman, pp. 400–3; Tsuzuki, p. 73; T. A. Critchley, *Conquest of Violence* (London, 1970), pp. 148–52.

30. Thompson, p. 407.

31. Ibid., p. 350 (Engels to Bernstein, Dec. 29, 1884).

32. Tsuzuki, p. 77, quoting the *Daily Chronicle*, Feb. 15, 1886.

33. Marx and Engels, *Selected Correspondence*, p. 448 (Engels to Bebel, April 12, 1886).

34. Ibid., p. 414 and n. 2; Henry Pelling, *The Origins of the Labour Party 1880–1900* (Oxford, 1965), p. 44 n. 1; Tsuzuki, p. 81.

35. Tsuzuki, p. 78.

36. The death generally attributed to the demonstration, which was followed by a long funeral procession through the streets, was in fact the result of an injury incurred not during this demonstration but during another a week later. See Tsuzuki, p. 78; Thompson, p. 491; Pelling, p. 43; Critchley, pp. 157–58; Donald C. Richter, *Riotous Victorians* (Athens, Ohio, 1981), pp. 142 ff.; Yvonne Kapp, *Eleanor Marx* (London, 1976), II, 237–41, 277.

37. Gareth Stedman Jones, *Outcast London: A Study in the Relationship between Classes in Victorian Society* (Oxford, 1971), p. 292. Bentley B. Gilbert compared the violence of this decade with "the mob fury of European capitals of 1848." (*The Evolution of National Insurance in Great Britain: The Origins of the Welfare State* [London, 1966], p. 24.)

38. Michael Holroyd, *Bernard Shaw* (New York, 1988), I, 185.

39. Kapp, II, 230.

40. Stanley Pierson, *Marxism and the Origins of British Socialism: The Struggle for a New Consciousness* (Ithaca, N.Y., 1973), p. 67.

41. Tsuzuki, p. 90.

42. Ibid., p. 95.

43. Ibid., p. 81. In the autumn of 1887, Champion (then still a member) said that the membership of the SDF was 689.

44. Ibid., p. 97.

45. In 1896 the SDF reported to the Second International a membership of over 10,000, and in 1900 *Justice* gave the figure as 9,000. But these were probably not the dues-paying membership. See Tsuzuki, pp. 108, 284; Max Beer, *A History of British Socialism* (London, 1921), II, 266.

46. Helen Merrell Lynd, *England in the Eighteen-Eighties: Toward a Social Basis for Freedom* (New York 1968 [1st ed., 1945]), p. 390. In support of this view, Lynd cites R. A. Woods, *English Social Movements* (New York, 1891) and Godfrey Elton, *"England, Arise!" A Study of the Pioneering Days of the Labour Movement* (London, 1931).

47. E. J. Hobsbawm, "Hyndman and the SDF," in *Labouring Men: Studies in the History of Labour* (London, 1964), p. 231. One of the chief virtues Hobsbawm finds in the SDF, and his main rebuttal against its critics, is the fact that it survived (pp. 231 ff.).

48. Another historian faults the SDF for being more rigid and dogmatic than Marx and Engels. (Henry Collins, "The Marxism of the Social Democratic Federation," in *Essays in Labour History, 1886–1923*, eds. Asa Briggs and John Saville [London, 1971], pp. 48 and passim.)

49. Rae, p. 83.

50. This is the title of an article by Ross McKibbin, *English Historical Review*, 1984, reprinted in *The Ideologies of Class: Social Relations in Britain, 1880–1950* (Oxford, 1990).

22. RELIGIOUS SOCIALISM

1. Karl Marx and Friedrich Engels, *The Communist Manifesto*, ed. Harold J. Laski (New York, 1967), p. 165.

2. Stephen Yeo, "A New Life: The Religion of Socialism in Britain, 1883–1896," *History Workshop*, 1977, p. 6.

3. Henry Pelling, *The Origins of the Labour Party 1880–1900* (Oxford, 1965), p. 140.

4. Beatrice Webb, *My Apprenticeship* (Penguin ed., 1971 [1st ed., 1926]), p. 158.

5. On the decline of secularism, see Booth, *Life and Labour,* 3:II, 128; 3:VII, 424. On the relationship between secularism and socialism, see Stanley Pierson, *Marxism and the Origins of British Socialism: The Struggle for a New Consciousness* (Ithaca, N.Y., 1973), pp. 54–55.

6. The standard biography of Headlam is F. G. Bettany, *Stewart Headlam: A Biography* (London, 1926). Shorter accounts of Headlam as well as the other Christian socialists are included in Edward Norman, *The Victorian Christian Socialists* (Cambridge, 1987); and Peter d'A. Jones, *The Christian Socialist Revival 1877–1914: Religion, Class, and Social Conscience in Late-Victorian England* (Princeton, 1968). For a largely Marxist view of Christian socialism, see Gilbert Clive Binyon, "Christian Socialism in England in the Nineteenth and Twentieth Centuries," in *Christianity and the Social Revolution,* ed. John Lewis, Karl Polanyi, and Donald K.

Kitchin (New York, 1935). For religion and the working classes more generally, see Hugh McLeod, *Religion and the Working Class in Nineteenth-Century Britain* (Atlantic Highlands, N.J., 1984).

7. Norman, p. 105.

8. Ibid., p. 107.

9. John Rae, *Contemporary Socialism* (London, 1891 [1st ed., 1884]), p. 84; A. M. McBriar, *Fabian Socialism and English Politics 1884–1918* (Cambridge, 1966), p. 9.

10. Jones, p. 103; *The Letters of Sidney and Beatrice Webb,* ed. Norman MacKenzie (Cambridge, 1978), I, 109.

11. Norman, p. 111.

12. Ibid., p. 117.

13. Ibid., p. 114.

14. Jones, p. 158.

15. Ibid., p. 164.

16. Norman, p. 162.

17. Jones, p. 164.

18. Norman, p. 162.

19. Ibid., p. 169.

20. Standish Meacham, *Toynbee Hall and Social Reform 1880–1914: The Search for Community* (New Haven, 1987), p. 97.

21. Brooke Foss Westcott, *Socialism* (London, 1907), pp. 3–4. This was originally delivered as a speech to a church congress in 1890.

22. Jones, p. 195.

23. John Lewis et al., eds., *Christianity and the Social Revolution,* p. 191.

24. Norman, pp. 162–63.

25. Ibid., p. 180. On the Fabians and the empire, see below, pp. 364–65.

26. Jones, p. 181.

27. Rae, p. 88.

28. Jones, p. 392.

29. Henry Pelling, *The Origins of the Labour Party 1880–1900* (Oxford, 1965), pp. 132–44; Jones, p. 29; Norman, p. 10. See also the account in Pierson, pp. 226–45.

30. I. D. MacKillop, *The British Ethical Societies* (Cambridge, 1986), p. 141.

31. Pelling, pp. 135–36.

32. Yeo, pp. 33–34.

33. Pelling, p. 140.

34. Pierson, p. 233.

35. Webb, *My Apprenticeship,* p. 180; *The Letters of Sidney and Beatrice Webb,* ed. Norman MacKenzie (Cambridge, 1978), I, 61 (Oct. 1886). (Italics in original.)

36. *Letters,* I, 386 (Jan. 25, 1892).

37. Yeo, pp. 5–6.

38. Jones, p. 453. The concluding chapter of Jones's book is called "The Enigma of Christian Socialism."

39. Boyd Hilton, *The Age of Atonement: The Influence of Evangelicalism on Social and Economic Thought, 1795–1865* (Oxford, 1988), p. 268.

23. FABIANISM

1. *Why Are the Many Poor?* quoted by Edward R. Pease, *The History of the Fabian Society* (London, 1963 [1st ed., 1918]), p. 39; Margaret Cole, *The Story of Fabian Socialism* (New York, 1961), p. 1; Norman and Jeanne MacKenzie, *The Fabians* (New York, 1977), pp. 41–42. (The several versions are differently punctuated. I have not been able to locate the first edition of this tract.)

2. Pease, p. 39.

3. In his *History of the Fabian Society* Pease spoke mockingly of his ghost-hunting expedition with Podmore (p. 28).

4. George Bernard Shaw, "The New Politics" (Dec. 20, 1889), in *The Road to Equality: Ten Unpublished Lectures and Essays, 1884–1918*, ed. Louis Crompton (Boston, 1971), p. 87.

5. George Orwell, *The Road to Wigan Pier* (London, 1937), p. 206. On Shaw's Jaegerism, see Michael Holroyd, *Bernard Shaw* (New York, 1988), I, 159–60. On Carpenter, see MacKenzie, *The Fabians,* pp. 180–81.

6. E. J. Hobsbawm, "The Fabians Reconsidered," in *Labouring Men: Studies in the History of Labour* (London, 1964), p. 258.

7. Shaw, *The Early History of the Fabian Society* (London, 1892), p. 4.

8. Pease, p. 62 n. 1.

9. Joseph Schumpeter, *Capitalism, Socialism, and Democracy* (New York, 1950 [1st ed., 1942]), p. 322.

10. *The Letters of Sidney and Beatrice Webb,* ed. Norman MacKenzie (Cambridge, 1978), I, 101 (SW to Pease, Oct. 24, 1886).

11. Ibid., p. 108 (SW to Pease, Nov. 16, 1887). According to the official records, there were 87 members in June 1886, with receipts of £35-19-0 and expenditures of £27-6-6 (Pease, p. 60).

12. MacKenzie, pp. 279, 326; Pease, pp. 99–102; A. M. McBriar, *Fabian Socialism and English Politics, 1884–1918* (Cambridge, 1966 [1st ed., 1962]), pp. 165–67.

13. "Fabian Society Report," 1896, reprinted in *The Challenge of Socialism,* ed. Henry Pelling (London, 1968), p. 171.

14. Cole, p. 336.

15. G. M. Trevelyan, *British History in the Nineteenth Century (1782–1901)* (London, 1922), p. 403.

16. Webb, *Letters,* I, 204 (Sidney Webb to Beatrice Webb, Oct. 9, 1890). (In these notes and in the text, Beatrice Potter is generally referred to, for purposes of simplicity, as Beatrice Webb.)

17. MacKenzie, p. 148. According to the list provided by the Fabian Society, 98 tracts had appeared before 1900. McBriar (p. 352) gives the number as 92 because he attributes some of the later ones to 1900 rather than 1898–99.

18. Pease, p. 105 n. For the number of lectures, see *Fabian Essays in Socialism,* ed. George Bernard Shaw (Dolphin ed., New York, n.d. [1st ed., 1889]), p. 5;

Pease, 102–5. Because these and membership figures derive from the annual report, the year starts and ends in April.

19. *Manifesto,* reprinted in Pease, p. 43.

20. Cole, pp. 337–38; Pease, p. 284.

21. Pease, p. 72.

22. *Fabian Essays,* p. 6.

23. Hubert Bland, "The Outlook," ibid., pp. 262, 265. (Italics in original.)

24. Shaw, "Transition," ibid., pp. 224–25, 245.

25. E. P. Thompson, *William Morris: Romantic to Revolutionary* (New York, 1977 [1st ed., 1955]), p. 548.

26. Webb, "Historic," *Fabian Essays,* p. 47. The phrase "unconscious socialism" was repeated (e.g., pp. 70, 77).

27. Ibid., p. 65. William Clarke also used this "paring" and "slicing" metaphor (p. 102).

28. Sydney Olivier, "Moral," ibid., pp. 158–61; Shaw, "Transition," ibid., p. 234; Graham Wallas, "Property Under Socialism," ibid., p. 175.

29. Pease, pp. 90–91.

30. Pease's own copy of the French edition of *Das Kapital* was dated October 8, 1883; but he doubted that any of the original Fabians, including himself, had read the book or assimilated its ideas at the time the Society was founded. (Pease, pp. 24–25.) On Marxism and Fabianism, see George J. Stigler, "Bernard Shaw, Sidney Webb, and the Theory of Fabian Socialism," in *Essays in the History of Economics* (Chicago, 1965), pp. 268 ff.

31. Shaw, "The New Politics" in *The Road to Equality,* p. 84. Another version is in Shaw, *Sixteen Self-Sketches* (London, 1955), p. 58. Willard Wolfe gives the quote as "furious Marxist." (*From Radicalism to Socialism: Men and Ideas in the Formation of Fabian Socialist Doctrines, 1881–1889* [New Haven, 1975], p. 121.)

32. Webb, *Letters,* I, 91 (Webb to Shaw, Aug. 5, 1885); ibid., p. 93 (Webb to Wallas, Aug. 17, 1885). (Wolfe attributes this second quotation to a letter by Webb to Sydney Olivier dated July 7, 1885, which would antedate the letter to Shaw. (Wolfe, p. 179 n. 78.) There is a letter by Webb to Olivier of that date, but it does not include this passage. (Webb, *Letters,* I, 88.)

33. Wolfe, p. 167. (The resolution was adopted May 30, 1884.)

34. The MacKenzies flatly assert, "The Positivists were not socialists," and describe Webb's attraction to Positivism as a "transitional stage between reformist Liberalism and socialism" (pp. 61–62). This "transitional" theory is echoed, in almost identical words, by T. R. Wright, *The Religion of Humanity: The Impact of Comtean Positivism on Victorian Britain* (Cambridge, 1986), p. 269. See also Noel Annan: "Unlike his predecessors [the Saint-Simonians] Comte was no socialist. He was a notable conservative believing in order as the prerequisite to progress." (*Leslie Stephen: The Godless Victorian* [New York, 1984], p. 193.) Royden Harrison, on the other hand, makes much more of the influence of Positivism on the English socialists of the 1880s. (*Before the Socialists: Studies in Labour and Politics, 1861–1881*) [London, 1965], pp. 333, 340–41.) And Wolfe singles out Comte as "the most powerful intellectual influence on the formation of Fabian theory" (p. 266).

On the controversy among historians about the relation of Positivism and Fabianism, see Wolfe, p. 193 n. 30. On the general question of Positivism in England, see Noel Annan, *The Curious Strength of Positivism in English Political Thought* (London, 1959).

35. John Stuart Mill, *Auguste Comte and Positivism* (London, 1865), p. 162.

36. Royden Harrison, p. 340.

37. Frederic Harrison, "Moral and Religious Socialism" (1891), in *National and Social Problems* (New York, 1908), p. 429.

38. On the two churches, see above, pp. 82–83. On the distinction between "complete" and "incomplete" Positivism, see Wolfe, pp. 194–95. It is because some historians define Positivism exclusively in its "complete" form that they pay almost no attention to its social teachings and vastly underestimate the extent of its influence among Fabians, other socialists, and, indeed, other intellectual and social movements of the time. One such work is Wright, *Religion of Humanity.*

39. Beatrice Webb, *My Apprenticeship* (Penguin ed., 1971 [1st ed., 1926]), p. 164 (March 15, 1889).

40. See above, note 10.

41. Henri de Saint-Simon, *Social Organization, the Science of Man, and Other Writings,* ed. and trans. Felix Markham (New York, 1964), p. 72.

42. Auguste Comte, *Positivist Catechism.*

43. Webb, "Historic," *Fabian Essays,* pp. 77–80.

44. Sidney and Beatrice Webb, *Soviet Communism: A New Civilization?* (London, 1935), p. 1133; S. and B. Webb, *Methods of Social Study* (Cambridge, 1975 [1st ed., 1932]), p. 259 n. 1. See also Beatrice Webb, *Our Partnership,* ed. Barbara Drake and Margaret I. Cole (London, 1948), pp. 255–56 n. 1.

45. Wolfe, p. 183.

46. *The Diary of Beatrice Webb,* ed. Norman and Jeanne MacKenzie (Cambridge, Mass., 1982–83), II, 106 (Jan. 18, 1897); *Our Partnership,* p. 137.

47. Shaw, "The New Radicalism" (October 1887), in *Road to Equality,* p. 29.

48. Shaw, "Freedom and the State," ibid., p. 41. This essay was not published, perhaps because it put the case for collectivism (statism, more precisely) so baldly.

49. Pelling, ed., *The Challenge of Socialism,* p. 174.

50. Quoted by W. H. Greenleaf, *The British Political Tradition* (London, 1983), II, 390–91. This essay was printed originally by the American Economic Association in 1889 and was published separately in England the following year. Parts were incorporated in Webb's chapter in *Fabian Essays,* but this passage was not.

51. Beatrice Webb, *Our Partnership,* p. 107.

52. Sidney and Beatrice Webb, *History of Trade Unionism* (London, 1920 [1st ed., 1894]), p. 414. Wolfe claims that the Fabian rhetoric of collectivism exceeded the reality, that the "consummation" of Fabian socialism was projected into so distant a future that it did not much affect practical policies (p. 261).

53. Wolfe, p. 75.

54. Webb, *Letters,* I, 101 (to Pease, Oct. 24, 1886).

55. "Fabian 'Aberrances'" was the title of the chapter in Margaret Cole's book discussing Fabian policies on the Boer War, education, and tariffs; she also applied the

word to their view of an independent labor party (pp. 95 ff.). E. J. Hobsbawm also speaks of Fabian "anomalies" (pp. 256, 263).

56. Beatrice Webb, *Diary,* II, 94 (April 18, 1896); *Our Partnership,* p. 132. Wolfe argues that the Fabians intended from the beginning to support a labor party as soon as there was an adequately educated (i.e., socialistic) constituency for it. (Appendix C, pp. 309–12.)

57. Beatrice Webb, *Our Partnership,* p. 12.

58. Webb, *Letters,* I, 102 (to Pease, Oct. 24, 1886).

59. See above, pp. 175–76. Jonathan Rose points out that the "national efficiency" movement was not simply a result of the physical deficiencies revealed by the Boer War since it was as strong in America as in England. He relates it to the emergence of a "new class" of professionals who sought to persuade the government and the public that "national efficiency could be maximized by 'experts'—that is, themselves." (*The Edwardian Temperament, 1895–1912* [Athens, Ohio, 1986], p. 119.) See also G. R. Searle, *The Quest for National Efficiency: A Study in British Politics and Political Thought, 1899–1914* (Berkeley, 1971).

60. One historian explains that they were imperialists because they were "utilitarians"; but that term is used almost as a synonym for socialism. (Fred D. Schneider, "Fabians and the Utilitarian Idea of Empire," *Review of Politics,* 1973.) The best account of the relationship between imperialism and socialism, as the Fabians understood it, is Bernard Semmel, *Imperialism and Social Reform: English Social-Imperial Thought, 1895–1914* (London, 1960).

61. Webb, *Letters,* II, 185 (to Russell, [late May?] 1903).

62. Beatrice Webb, *Our Partnership,* p. 104. Much the same argument had been used earlier by the New Liberal Herbert Samuel, who saw a positive relationship between imperialism and social reform (rather than socialism). See *Minutes of the Rainbow Circle, 1894–1924,* ed. Michael Freeden (London, 1989), p. 74 (paper delivered Jan. 17, 1990).

63. Sidney Webb, "Lord Rosebery's Escape from Houndsditch," *Nineteenth Century and After,* Sept. 1901, p. 386.

64. Sidney Webb, *Letters,* II, 170 (SW to Wells, Sept. 12, 1902). In *The New Machiavelli,* written after he had become disaffected with the Fabians, Wells parodied the dining club under the name of the "Pentagram Circle." (Penguin ed., 1966 [1st ed., 1911], pp. 254 ff.)

65. Beatrice Webb, *My Apprenticeship,* pp. 150–51. This Francis Galton (1822–1911) is not to be confused with the Francis (or Frank) W. Galton (1867–1952) who joined the Fabian Society in 1891, became secretary to the Webbs after their marriage, and served as general secretary of the Fabian Society from 1920 to 1939.

66. The movement was also stimulated by the publication of the government *Report on Physical Deterioration* in 1904. In fact the report warned against exaggerating the extent of physical and racial deterioration, but as often happened, the very existence of the commission and the publication of the report had the effect of arousing public anxieties.

67. Beatrice Webb, *Our Partnership,* p. 6.

68. Diane Paul, "Eugenics and the Left," *Journal of the History of Ideas,* 1984.

69. Wells, *The New Machiavelli*, p. 165.

70. Semmel, p. 51. Galton used this phrase in an essay reprinted in *Sociological Papers* (1904).

71. Beatrice Webb, *Diary*, II, 226 (Dec. 1901). See also ibid., p. 240 (Feb. 28, 1902); Webb, *Letters*, II, 144 (Sidney to Beatrice Webb, Dec. 8, 1901).

72. Wells, *Anticipations: Of the Reaction of Mechanical and Scientific Progress upon Human Life and Thought* (New York, 1901), pp. 322–23.

73. Ibid., pp. 323–32.

74. Beatrice Webb, *Diary*, II, 267 (Jan. 16, 1903). "We" is italicized in the extract from the diary published in *Our Partnership* (p. 257), but not in the MacKenzie edition of the diary.

75. Shaw, *Man and Superman*, in *Plays by George Bernard Shaw* (New American Library ed., New York, 1960), pp. 252, 416, 433. The latter passages are from "The Revolutionist's Handbook" appended to the play. They may have been among the sections of the "Handbook" that were read aloud at a performance attended by Shaw during his visit to the Soviet Union in 1931. (Shaw, *Collected Letters, 1926–1950*, ed. Dan H. Laurence [New York, 1988], IV, 255 [Shaw to Charlotte Shaw, July 27, 1931].)

76. Shaw, *Man and Superman*, p. 433.

77. Karl Pearson, *The Life, Letters, and Labours of Francis Galton* (London, 1930), IIIa, 260–61.

78. Semmel, p. 51 (quoting *The Decline in the Birth Rate* [1907]). Another tract the following year by another Fabian eugenicist was called *The Endowment of Motherhood*. See also Sidney Webb, "Eugenics and the Poor Law: The Minority Report," *Eugenics Review*, II (1910–11), 233–41.

79. Sidney and Beatrice Webb, *The Prevention of Destitution* (London, 1912), pp. 46, 52–53, 56, 58–59.

80. Leonard Hobhouse, *Social Evolution and Political Theory* (London, 1911), pp. 40 ff.

81. Hobson's anti-Semitism outlived his eugenicism. See John Allett, "New Liberalism, Old Prejudices: J. A. Hobson and the 'Jewish Question,' " *Jewish Social Studies*, 1987. On eugenics and the New Liberals, see Michael Freeden, *The New Liberalism: An Ideology of Social Reform* (Oxford, 1978), pp. 185 ff.; Stefan Collini, *Liberalism and Sociology: L. T. Hobhouse and Political Argument in England 1880–1914* (Cambridge, 1979), pp. 171 ff.

82. Quoted by Paul, p. 570. See also Christopher Shaw, "Eliminating the Yahoo—Eugenics, Social Darwinism and Five Fabians," *History of Political Thought*, 1987. It is interesting how many books on the Fabians ignore the subject of eugenics, perhaps because it belies the conventional moderate, benign view of Fabianism. Margaret Cole, for example, does not discuss eugenics in her chapter on "Fabian 'Aberrances' " or elsewhere in her book. Nor do other important writers on the Fabians: Pease, Pugh, Pierson, Wolfe, McBriar, and the essayists in *The Webbs and Their Work*, ed. Margaret Cole (London, 1949).

83. *Fabian Essays*, p. 51.

84. Ibid., p. 224.

85. Sidney and Beatrice Webb, *A Constitution for the Socialist Commonwealth of Britain* (Cambridge, 1975 [1st ed., 1920]), p. 111.

86. *The Doctrine of Saint-Simon: An Exposition, First Year, 1828–1829,* trans. and ed. Georg G. Iggers (New York, 1972), p. 29 n. 5.

87. Sidney and Beatrice Webb, *The Prevention of Destitution,* p. 331.

88. Cole, pp. 127–28.

89. Pease, p. 177.

90. Beatrice Webb, *Our Partnership,* p. 361.

91. *Beatrice Webb's Diaries, 1912–1924,* ed. Margaret I. Cole (London, 1952), p. 122 (June 16, 1918).

92. Shaw, *Man and Superman,* p. 436.

93. Wells, *Anticipations,* pp. 172, 284, 298–303, 318, 321.

94. Wells, *A Modern Utopia* (New York, 1905), chapter 9 (pp. 258 ff.).

95. Beatrice Webb, *Our Partnership,* p. 305 (April 17, 1905).

96. Ibid., p. 231 (Feb. 28, 1902).

97. Wells, *The New Machiavelli,* pp. 264–65.

98. Beatrice Webb, *Diary,* II, 34–35 (July 30, 1893).

99. Beatrice Webb, *Our Partnership,* p. 6.

100. Ibid., p. 418 (Nov. 15, 1908).

101. Beatrice Webb, *Diary,* II, 63 (Dec. 28, 1894).

102. Ibid., p. 236 (Feb. 28, 1902); p. 336 (Jan. 21, 1905).

103. Ibid., p. 224 (Dec. 9, 1901).

104. Ibid., p. 333 (Nov. 12, 1904).

105. Beatrice Webb, *Diaries* (Cole ed.), p. 50 (Nov. 14, 1915).

106. Beatrice Webb, *Our Partnership,* p. 366 (diary, Nov. 30, 1906).

107. Wolfe, pp. 211–12, 277.

108. Drake, in *Webbs and Their Work,* p. 226.

109. Beatrice and Sidney Webb, *Industrial Democracy* (London, 1897), p. 787.

110. Beatrice Webb, *Our Partnership,* p. 149.

111. *The Public Organization of the Labour Market: Being Part Two of the Minority Report of the Poor Law Commission* (London, 1909), p. 302.

112. Shaw, *Major Barbara* (Penguin ed., 1968), pp. 21–22; Beatrice Webb, *Our Partnership,* p. 315 (diary, Dec. 2, 1905). In his review of *Our Partnership,* F. R. Leavis took special note of her criticisms of Shaw. (Leavis, ed., *A Selection from Scrutiny* [Cambridge, 1968], II, 217–18.)

113. Beatrice Webb, *Diary,* II, 298 (Oct. 5, 1903). (Italics in the original.)

114. Sidney Webb mocked the Majority for abandoning the principles of 1834 and expanding, rather than limiting, the scope of poor relief. (Webb, "The End of the Poor Law," *Sociological Review,* 1909, pp. 128–30.)

115. Beatrice Webb, *Our Partnership,* p. 417 (Oct. 16, 1908). See also p. 430 (June 18, 1909).

116. Ibid., p. 476 (May 26, 1911).

117. Ibid., pp. 478–79.

118. Sidney and Beatrice Webb, *The Prevention of Destitution,* 181–82.

119. Bentley B. Gilbert, *The Evolution of National Insurance in Great Britain:*

The Origins of the Welfare State (London, 1966), p. 214 (quoting a memorandum by Webb dated Sept. 29, 1907). On old age pensions, see also E. P. Hennock, *British Social Reform and German Precedents: The Case of Social Insurance, 1880–1914* (Oxford, 1987), pp. 117 ff.

120. *The Break-Up of the Poor Law: Being Part One of the Minority Report of the Poor Law Commission* (London, 1909), p. 513.

121. Sidney and Beatrice Webb, *The Prevention of Destitution*, pp. 186–88.

122. *Minority Report,* Part 2, p. 308. The best account of the unemployment provisions of both the Majority and Minority Reports—and of the issue of unemployment in general during this period—is José Harris, *Unemployment and Politics: A Study in English Social Policy, 1886–1914* (Oxford, 1972). For alternative proposals for labor exchanges, see José Harris, *William Beveridge: A Biography* (Oxford, 1977).

123. *Minority Report,* Part 1, pp. 547, 569.

124. Webb, *Letters,* II, 367 (March 1911).

125. Beatrice Webb, *Our Partnership,* p. 431 (quoting her diary, July 22, 1909).

126. It also recalls Jeremy Bentham's characterization of his pauper scheme as a "utopia." See Gertrude Himmelfarb, *The Idea of Poverty: England in the Early Industrial Age* (New York, 1984), pp. 78 ff., 358 ff.

127. *Minority Report,* Part 2, pp. 324–25.

128. See, for example, the conclusion of David Owen's account of the Poor Law reports: "In not a few respects, the Minority draft turned out to be a prospectus for the mid-twentieth century Welfare State." (*English Philanthropy 1660–1960* [Cambridge, Mass., 1964], p. 521.) See also Derek Fraser, *The Evolution of the British Welfare State: A History of Social Policy since the Industrial Revolution* (London, 1973), p. 149.

129. José Harris, "The Partnership of the Webbs," *New Society,* Nov. 25, 1982, p. 340.

130. Cole, p. 69.

131. Stanley Pierson, *Marxism and the Origins of British Socialism: The Struggle for a New Consciousness* (Ithaca, N.Y., 1973), pp. 138–39. For a somewhat different version of this theory, see E. J. Hobsbawm, *Labouring Men,* pp. 250 ff.

132. See note 15 above.

133. José Harris, "Public Life, Private Doubts," *Times Literary Supplement,* Oct. 11, 1985.

EPILOGUE: TOWARD THE WELFARE STATE

1. Stefan Collini, *Liberalism and Sociology: L. T. Hobhouse and Political Argument in England, 1880–1914* (Cambridge, 1979), p. 245.

2. George Dangerfield, *The Strange Death of Liberal England* (London, 1935).

3. R. B. Haldane, "The New Liberalism," *Progressive Review,* 1896, pp. 135–36, 142–43. The previous November, Herbert Samuel read a paper to the Rainbow Circle on the new liberalism, proposing it as an alternative both to the old liberalism of Bentham and Smith and to the socialism of the SDF and the Fabian Society. The

new liberals were prominent in the Rainbow Circle, where many of its ideas were first articulated. See *Minutes of the Rainbow Circle, 1894–1924,* ed. Michael Freeden (London, 1989), pp. 27–28 and passim.

Bentley Gilbert gives the term a later origin, ascribing it to the editor of the *Nation,* H. W. Massingham, in a foreword to a book of speeches by Winston Churchill, *Liberalism and the Social Problem,* published in 1909. (Gilbert, introduction to a new edition of C. F. G. Masterman, ed., *The Heart of the Empire: Discussions of Problems of Modern City Life in England* [Brighton, Eng., 1973], p. xxxv n. 8.)

4. The large literature on the new liberalism in recent years, as well as the many reprints of their works, have been a salutary corrective to the familiar "Whig fallacy." To take this movement seriously, as these authors do, is to resist the temptation to read the social history of England as a steady and inevitable progress toward the welfare state and socialism. See Michael Freeden, *The New Liberalism: An Ideology of Social Reform* (Oxford, 1978); Peter Clarke, *Liberals and Social Democrats* (Cambridge, 1978); Stefan Collini, *Liberalism and Sociology: L. T. Hobhouse and Political Argument in England 1880–1914* (Cambridge, 1979); Peter Weiler, *The New Liberalism: Liberal Social Theory in Great Britain, 1889–1914* (New York, 1982); John Allett, *New Liberalism: The Political Economy of J. A. Hobson* (Toronto, 1981); Andrew Vincent and Raymond Plant, *Philosophy, Politics and Citizenship: The Life and Thought of the British Idealists* (Oxford, 1984).

5. Freeden assigns a smaller role to Green as the founding father of the new liberalism than most commentators, but he does not deny the similarities in their thought.

6. Randolph S. Churchill, *Winston S. Churchill: Young Statesman, 1911–1914* (Boston, 1967), II, 268.

7. Ibid., p. 269; companion vol. II, Part 2, p. 863 (Dec. 29, 1908).

8. Winston S. Churchill, *The People's Rights* (New York, 1970 [1st ed., 1909]), pp. 144, 146.

9. See above, p. 376.

10. Bentley B. Gilbert, *The Evolution of National Insurance in Great Britain: The Origins of the Welfare State* (London, 1966), p. 272 (quoting manuscript by Churchill, "Notes on Malingering," addressed to H. Llewellyn Smith, June 6, 1909).

11. See above, p. 376.

12. William Beveridge, *Social Insurance and Allied Services* (London, 1942), p. 17. Beveridge himself disliked the term "welfare state." See José Harris, *William Beveridge: A Biography* (Oxford, 1977), p. 448.

13. Adam Smith, *An Inquiry into the Nature and Causes of the Wealth of Nations,* ed. Edwin Cannan (New York, 1937 [1st ed., 1776]), p. 821.

14. H. Llewellyn Smith et al., *The New Survey of London Life and Labour* (London, 1930–35), VI, 27.

15. Seebohm Rowntree, *Poverty and Progress: A Second Social Survey of York* (London, 1941), p. 462.

16. Asa Briggs, *A Study of the Work of Seebohm Rowntree 1871–1954* (London, 1961), p. 297.

17. Ibid., pp. 330–31.

18. D. N. Pritt, *The Labour Government 1945–51* (New York, 1963), pp. 305–6.

19. "Let Us Face the Future," in Harry W. Laidler, *British Labor's Rise to Power* (New York, 1945), pp. 20–30.

20. The "rediscovery" of poverty in Britain is often credited to Brian Abel-Smith and Peter Townsend, *The Poor and the Poorest* (London, 1965), which proposed a simple quantitative measure of poverty: 140% of the Supplementary Benefits allowance. Thus no matter how generous the state might be by way of benefits, poverty would always remain more or less constant.

21. The expression "relative deprivation" was first given prominence by W. G. Runciman, *Relative Deprivation and Social Justice* (Berkeley, 1966).

22. Mary Douglas, "Relative Poverty—Relative Communication," in *Traditions of Social Policy: Essays in Honour of Violet Butler,* ed. A. H. Halsey (Oxford, 1976), pp. 197 ff.

23. Peter Townsend, *Poverty in the United Kingdom: A Survey of Household Resources and Standards of Living* (London, 1979).

Index